CERTIFIED PROFESSIONAL SECRETARY®
EXAMINATION REVIEW SERIES

OFFICE SYSTEMS & ADMINISTRATION

Fourth Edition

Betty L. Schroeder, Ph.D., Editor
Northern Illinois University

AUTHORS

Betty L. Schroeder, Ph.D.
Northern Illinois University

Diane Routhier Graf, CPS, Ed.D.
Transformation Dynamics

A joint publication of
International Association of Administrative Professionals™

and PRENTICE HALL
Upper Saddle River, New Jersey 07458

Library of Congress Cataloging-in-Publication Data

Schroeder, Betty L.
   Office systems and administration / Betty L. Schroeder, Diane Routhier Graf..--4th ed.
     p. cm--(Certified professional secretary examination review series)
   Includes bibliographical references.
   ISBN 0-13-084324-5
   1. Office practice--Automation. 2. Office management. I. Routhier Graf, Diane, 1943-
II. Title. III. Series.

  HF5547.5 .S364 2001
  651.3'076--dc21   00-029355

Acquisitions Editor: *Elizabeth Sugg*
Production Editor: *Lori Harvey, Carlisle Publishers Services*
Production Liaison: *Eileen O'Sullivan*
Managing Editor: *Mary Carnis*
Editorial Assistant: *Brian Hyland*
Development Editor: *Judy Casillo*
Manufacturing Manager: *Ed O'Dougherty*
Director of Manufacturing & Production: *Bruce Johnson*
Marketing Manager: *Shannon Simonsen*
Compositor/Interior Design: *Carlisle Communications, Ltd.*
Cover Design: *Joe Sengotta*
Printer/Binder: *Banta Harrisonburg*

The following are registered marks owned by the International Association of Administrative Professionals™:

Trademarks and Registered Service Marks

IAAP™
International Association of Administrative Professionals™ (formerly Professional Secretaries International®)
10502 N.W. Ambassador Drive, Kansas City, MO 64153, 816-891-6600

A.I.S.P. (French equivalent of PSI®)
L'Association Internationale des Secretaries Professionailes

CPS®
Certified Professional Secretary®

CSI^SM
Collegiate Secretaries International^SM
Professional Secretaries Week®
Professional Secretaries Day®
Office PRD®

FSA®
Future Secretaries Association®
International Secretary of the Year®
Secretary Speakout®
Secretary on the Spot®

Printed in the United States of America

10 9 8 7 6 5 4 3 2 1

ISBN 0-13-084324-5

Prentice-Hall International (UK) Limited, *London*
Prentice-Hall of Australia Pty, Limited, *Sydney*
Prentice-Hall Canada, Inc., *Toronto*
Prentice-Hall Hispanoamericana, S.A., *Mexico*
Prentice-Hall of India Private Limited, *New Delhi*
Prentice-Hall of Japan, Inc., *Tokyo*
Pearson Education Asia, Pte. Ltd., *Singapore*
Editora Prentice-Hall do Brasil, Ltda., *Rio de Janeiro*

Contents

CHAPTER 12 *Reprographics Management*   363

Overview   363

Key Terms   363

Preface

The Certified Professional Secretary Examination® (CPS®) Review Series, the three-volume set of review manuals and their corresponding Self-Study Guides for each of the three parts of the Certified Professional Secretary Examination, is a joint publication of Prentice Hall and the International Association of Administrative Professionals™ (IAAP™). The content of each module is based on the current CPS Examination Review Guide published by IAAP.

CPS Examination

The rewards for achieving the Certified Professional Secretary (CPS) rating are numerous, as attested to by the more than 57,000 CPS holders. These include: pride in accomplishment, increased self-esteem, greater respect from employers and peers, and confidence to assume greater responsibilities as well as possible college credit toward a degree, pay increases, bonuses, and opportunities for advancement. In today's workplace, having the CPS credential can be assurance of employability.

The CPS Examination is a one-day, three-part examination based on the premise that a professional secretary should know how to apply the principles of good human relations and have basic knowledge of finance, business law, economics, communication, and management. It is expected that a competent secretary is thoroughly familiar with current techniques in office practice and procedures and is aware of developments in office systems and technology. **To apply for approval to take the CPS Examination, request the "Capstone" from IAAP. The "Capstone" provides detailed information about the examination and an application form.**

**CPS Examination
Review Series**

The CPS Examination Review Series provides valuable assistance to the administrative professional preparing for the CPS Examination, whether it is used for group review sessions or for self-study. The series provides an excellent learning tool that is focused on key topics that are necessary for passing the exam.

The format used for each of the manuals in the series is identical. The CPS Examination Review Series provides as much relevant information as possible to help in preparing for the CPS Examination. **However, this does not imply that all information presented in the series will be included on the examinations.**

Each chapter contains:

- An overview introducing the reader to the chapter and its content

- Text in outline form, with examples highlighted in italics, to enhance the explanation given in the text

- Illustrations to aid understanding of concepts

- Review questions at the end of each chapter, developed in formats *similar* to those found in the CPS Examination

- Solutions to the review questions, with some explanation of correct answers, where needed, and references to portions of the outline that explain the answer more fully. For example:

1. *(b) [A-2]*
The outline reference pertains to: Section A, Point 2 in the chapter.

When a solution seems unclear, it is recommended that the section be reviewed for further clarification.

A complete Glossary of terms and definitions is included at the end of each manual. A reference is made to the chapter where the term may be found in context.

CPS Examination Review Series Self-Study Guides

Each manual has a corresponding Self-Study Guide written as a companion tool rather than a formally structured workbook. These guides enhance material presented in the CPS Examination Review manuals and may be used for independent study and in accelerated, short-term group review courses.

The question arises as to why this series is formatted in this particular way. The response is simple: We want you to have a thorough, efficient review of the content that *may* appear on the CPS Examination. The purpose of the Self-Study Guide is to assist you in researching and building your own information bank.

CPS Examination Review Guide

The current CPS Examination Review Guide should be used to direct any course of study. The Guide includes the examination outline, sample questions, bibliography of recommended study materials, and suggestions for exam review. The CPS Examination Review Guide is available for purchase through the IAAP Distribution Department: 10502 NW Ambassador Drive, PO Box 20404, Kansas City, MO 64195-0404; phone 816-891-6600; fax 816-891-9118; e-mail distribution@iaap-hq.org

Acknowledgments

Through the sincere and dedicated efforts of a number of individuals interested in the certification of professional secretaries, the fourth edition of the *Certified Professional Secretary® Examination Review for Office Systems and Administration* was prepared to complement the current study outline for the Certified Professional Secretary® Examination. Like the other two reviews in the series, *Office Systems and Administration* will be a successful review tool because of the critiques and contributions of the following people.

The International Association of Administrative Professionals, through the Institute for Certification, has provided not only the incentive for the development of the fourth edition of this review but also valuable input during the review process. We are sincerely grateful and thank IAAP and the Institute for their continued support and enthusiasm for the development and revision of the series.

Specifically, we acknowledge the many contributions of Paulette Gladis CSJ, Ph.D., Dean, Institute for Certification; Pamela J. Brown, Asheville-Buncombe Technical Community College, Asheville, North Carolina, member, Institute for Certification; and Kathy L. Schoneboom CPS, Certification Manager, IAAP, for their extremely helpful reviews and critiques of the manuscript.

Another special acknowledgment recognizes the Illinois Division of IAAP and, in particular, those members of the Kishwaukee Chapter, DeKalb, Illinois, who are pursuing or have received their professional certification. These groups have continued to be extremely supportive and positive about this review series; their friendship is very much appreciated.

We also acknowledge the expertise of Dr. Paula C. Williams, Mississippi County Community College, Blytheville, Arkansas, and Dr. Susan A. Timm, Northern Illinois University, DeKalb, Illinois, in drafting and refining records management and communications content for previous editions that became the foundation on which future editions are based.

Lastly, we appreciate the assistance and leadership demonstrated by Elizabeth Sugg and Judy Casillo of Prentice Hall and their continued support of the series. It is a joy to work with individuals so professional in their judgment of what administrative professionals need to prepare appropriately for the CPS Examination.

We hope that all the input provided by professionals throughout the revision process will continue to make this review series the "leader" in preparing professional secretaries everywhere for the CPS Examination in the future.

Betty L. Schroeder, Ph.D.
Diane Routhier Graf, CPS, Ed.D.

CHAPTER 1

Information Processing

OVERVIEW

Information processing involves both data processing and word processing. Business organizations can no longer function without the complete services of an information processing system that is capable of functioning with a variety of software applications. Such a system may utilize a mainframe computer, a minicomputer, or microcomputers at various locations around the organization. The computer has literally revolutionized business in such a way that many decision-making strategies are feasible only if a computer is used. Because of technology advancements and the integration of computer systems in business, many now refer to this function as information processing: data referencing data input and information referencing output. In this chapter we review the processing cycle, from the origination of input into the system to the development and distribution of appropriate output.

Processing technology (hardware and software developments) is outlined so that office professionals will have an opportunity to review the "basics" of the system. Various input/output media and devices are summarized, providing the secretary with the basic terminology used in the field. Often confusing to office personnel are the differences among mainframe, minicomputer, and microcomputer. These systems are also outlined briefly, addressing the multifaceted nature of microcomputers from desktop workstations to the personal computer for home use.

Processing operations are divided into basic operations (e.g., recording or classifying data) and basic operations modes. Naturally, businesses are interested in specific applications of information processing technology. Some specific examples from accounting, marketing, and word processing are highlighted. In Chapter 2 we focus primarily on word processing applications.

Of course, we are all interested, even somewhat apprehensive at times, about what will happen in the future. The chapter ends with a summary of some possible innovations that appear to be present today in some form and will continue to be developed further in the future.

KEY TERMS

Access time
Applications programs
Background printing
Batch processing
Bit
Byte
Central processing unit
   (CPU)
Chip
Data
Database
Data element
Data field
Direct access
Direct entry
Encryption
Field
File
Graphical user interface
   (GUI)
Hard copy
Hardware

Impact printer
Information
Intelligent printers
Interactive operations
Mainframe computer
   system
Microcomputer system
Microprocessor
Minicomputer system
Modem
Multiprocessing
Multiprogramming
Nonimpact printer
Nonvolatile storage
Object program
On-line device
Operating systems
Plotter
Primary storage
Processor unit
Programming

Random access memory
   (RAM)
Read-only memory
   (ROM)
Real-time processing
Record
Secondary storage
Sequential access
Soft copy
Software
Source data automation
Source document
Source program
Stored program
System programs
Transfer rate
Turnaround time
Utilities
Virtual memory
Volatile storage

A. The Processing Cycle

The major function of processing data is to take unorganized facts (data) and produce meaningful business information. Files are established for the retention of the raw data and information for future use. Processing involves manipulation of the raw data through mathematical or logical operations. The basic processing cycle consists of input, process, and output. The six steps of the cycle involve data origination, data input, processing, storage, output, and distribution (see Figure 1–1).

1. *Data Origination:* Data origination readies data for input. During this step of the cycle, original (raw) data are organized for processing.

   a. *Batch processing:* Many business transactions are processed as a group.

      EXAMPLES: *Payroll, inventory control, purchases.*

      This type of processing is referred to as *batch processing.* In batch processing, the raw data are collected for future processing.

   b. *Real-time processing:* Other business transactions are processed immediately.

      EXAMPLE: *Bank withdrawals or deposits.*

      This type of processing is referred to as *real-time processing.* For the immediate processing of a transaction, the peripheral devices must be on-line to the central processing unit.

   c. *Source documents:* Some processing situations require that an original record, called a *source document,* be prepared; at this point, the business transaction is recorded for the first time. A quick analysis of source documents can reveal the type, nature, and origin of the transaction. Source data automation eliminates the

Figure 1–1   The Processing Cycle

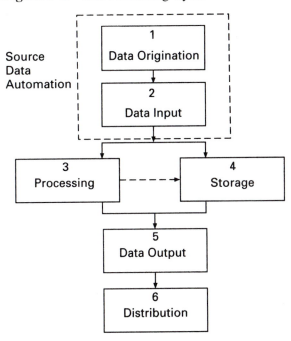

need for a source document. Traditional data entry methods are replaced with machine-readable codes at the time the transaction originates.

EXAMPLE: ABC Company wishes to purchase a new 586 computer from AJAX Corporation. At the time of the sale, a source document (the sales order form) is used to obtain all the pertinent data.

Type of source document: *The source document is the sales order form, with a sequential job (sale) number on it, 17478.*

Nature of source document: *The source document shows that the ABC Company wants to purchase a 586 computer.*

Origin of source document: *When AJAX's sales representative met with ABC Company, the representative completed a multicopy sales order form that has a sales number preprinted on the form. The sales representative presents the form to the sales department; the multicopies are used to activate inventory control, manufacturing, shipping, and billing. Data input to the computer system is obtained from the sales order form (source document).*

2. *Data Input:* Data input can be entered in a batch or as each transaction originates. For batch input, initial data are collected in some convenient format—a source document. This method requires data to be recorded twice. Data recorded on a source document (and any other required data collected) are entered at a later time through a keyboard or terminal connected to the computer. Data are stored onto an input medium such as disks or tapes.

When data are entered as each transaction originates, the need for a source document is eliminated. With source data automation, previously stored data can be retrieved, eliminating repeated input (e.g., item descriptions, prices, and customer addresses).

Data from the transaction are immediately stored in the computer. Source data automation improves the speed and accuracy of data input and lowers cost. Hardware configurations for input can include the following:

- Terminals (a microcomputer with video display [CRT] and keyboard)
- Optical character recognition (OCR) device (optical scanning wands or laser scanners)
- Magnetic ink character recognition (MICR)
- Voice (microphone with voice recognition unit)

EXAMPLES:

Using an on-line point-of-sale terminal in a retail store, all product descriptions and prices are stored in the computer's secondary storage. The product bar codes read by the laser scanner produce the data needed for the sale. In some retail establishments, inventory control is also maintained through data collection at the time of the sale.

ABC Company wishes to purchase a new 586 computer from AJAX Corporation. With source data automation, the sales representative uses a laptop microcomputer and wand to read the computer number codes in the catalog. Other variable data (quantity and customer name) are entered using the microcomputer keyboard. The data are stored on secondary storage of the laptop microcomputer. These data are then read into AJAX Corporation's minicomputer, where product descriptions, prices, and previously stored data are merged with the new sale data to complete the process of the sale.

3. *Processing:* Input data are changed and/or combined with other data to produce information. Information is data processed in a meaningful and usable format.

   a. *Processing time:* The length of time required for processing will depend on the amount of data being processed, the type of information to be obtained as a result, the type of processing (batch or real-time), and the processor unit.

      (1) *Batch processing:* When data are processed in batch, the input data are collected and all input transactions processed at the same time.

      (2) *Real-time processing:* Real-time processing is necessary when one transaction needs to be processed immediately. Real-time processing produces immediate results for the receiver of the information.

      In both batch and real-time processing, *turnaround time* (the time it takes between submission of the data and receipt of the output) is important to the user, the recipient of the results.

   b. *The central processing unit:* The computer (the central processing unit) itself is the part that processes and manipulates the raw data, moving information around and performing any arithmetic or logic operations required.

   The processing step may involve a sequence of basic operations: classifying, sorting, calculating, recording, and summarizing data.

4. *Storage:* Storage is important to both the input and the processing steps. Data input is stored for batch processing. The results of processed data are also stored for future use. Storage is where data and information (processed data) are electronically held for future use. Storage takes place in secondary storage (e.g., disks or tapes). Data are stored as records.

   a. *File:* A *file* is the term given to a unified set of data in storage, for example, a personnel file.

5

b. *Record:* Each file contains a number of related *records*. A record contains the data pertaining to one unit. Figure 1–2 illustrates that one record in the personnel file contains the identification number, name, address, and telephone number for one employee. When a record is used, all data pertaining to that particular unit are available. In batch processing, the central processing unit processes each record sequentially (one after the other). In real-time processing, one individual record is processed, and then the central processing unit can be directed to access any other record within that file (direct access).

(1) *Data fields:* A data field contains descriptive characteristics of a person, place, or thing. A data field is also referred to as a *data element.* Each data field within a file has a different variable name. The data field variable names in the personnel file (Figure 1–2) are IDNUMBER, LASTNAME, FIRST-NAME, HOMEADDRESS, CITY, STATE, ZIPCODE, and TELEPHONE.

(2) *Key fields:* For most processing operations, one of the fields must contain unique data; that is, no other record can contain identical data within that field. Such a field is referred to as a *key field* or a *control field* and can be used to identify that person, place, or thing. In Figure 1–2, the IDNUMBER is the key field. For each employee record, the IDNUMBER will be different.

EXAMPLE: Notice that in the schematic of a personnel file shown in Figure 1–2, the name for each field within one record is unique. However, the field name repeats itself from record to record. The data within each field for each record will be unique to that employee. It may be possible that identical data (names or city names) will appear in different records. Only the identification number (IDNUMBER field) will be unique to each record, and that field could be used as a key field or a control field. Also, users involved in identifying data fields for a file should break down a field to its smallest possible element.

In Figure 1–2, notice that LASTNAME and FIRSTNAME are two separate fields. These two fields could have been identified in a single field under the variable

Figure 1–2   Schematic of a Personnel File

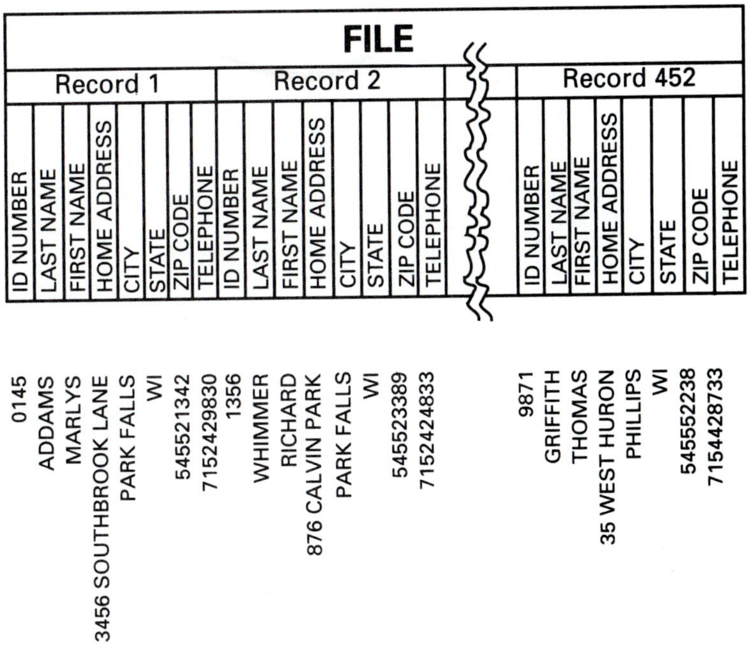

reference NAME. However, if a data processing job required a search of the file for all employees by the LASTNAME of Johnson, this would be difficult to accomplish. When the last name is a field by itself, such a search is easily accomplished.

5. *Data Output:* When all business data have been processed, computations made, and any other manipulations completed, the information must be communicated to others. Information may be presented to users by printing reports and distributing these to interested individuals. Also, executives can access the report at their desk terminals. The printed report is called *hard copy*. The output viewed on the CRT screen is *soft copy*. More than one type of output can be produced. The form of the output information depends on how it will be used by individuals who are internal or external to the company. Figure 1–3 illustrates printed output for internal distribution.

Figure 1–3   Electronic Processing

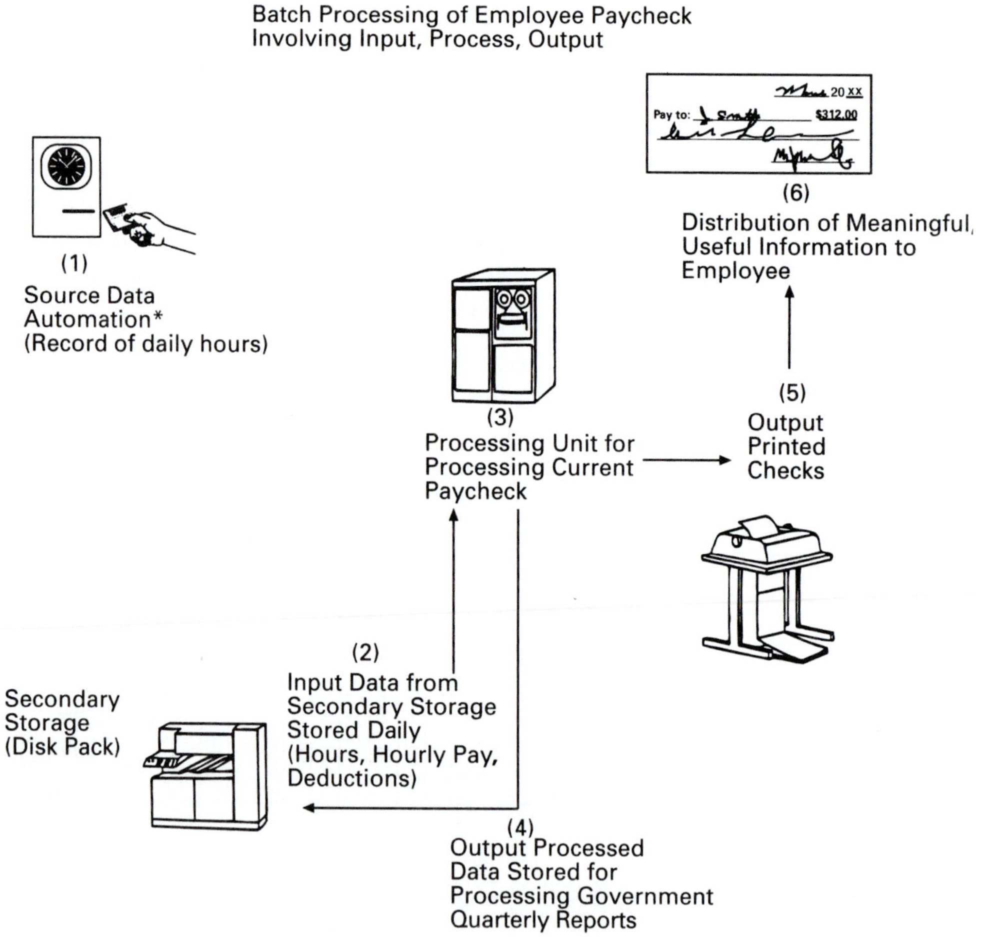

Batch Processing of Employee Paycheck
Involving Input, Process, Output

(6)
Distribution of Meaningful,
Useful Information to
Employee

(1)
Source Data
Automation*
(Record of daily hours)

(3)
Processing Unit for
Processing Current
Paycheck

(5)
Output
Printed
Checks

(2)
Input Data from
Secondary Storage
Stored Daily
(Hours, Hourly Pay,
Deductions)

Secondary
Storage
(Disk Pack)

(4)
Output Processed
Data Stored for
Processing Government
Quarterly Reports

*With source data automation, the need for a source document (time cards) and keyed
data input by an entry operator have been eliminated.

6. *Distribution:* Information in the form of reports can be distributed internally to users either electronically or in printout form or externally to receivers in the outside business world. In business, hard-copy output is often referred to as *report documents.*

B. Processing Technology

Computer technology has changed the business world drastically in the last 30 years. Today, the computer is an important tool in the business office. The technology has gone through five generations of change; a summary is provided of the major developments within each generation. Included in the technology are computer hardware, computer languages, systems software, and application software.

1. *Computer Generations:* "The Father of Computers," Charles Babbage, conceived the analytical engine in 1833. After his death in 1871, the engine was constructed by Babbage's son.

   In 1944, the Mark I was produced as a joint effort by Harvard University, International Business Machines (IBM), and the U.S. Department of War. The automatic calculations in the Mark I were based on Babbage's design.

   John Antanasoff and an assistant, Clifford Berry, produced an electronic device called the Antanasoff-Berry-Computer (ABC). In 1974, a federal court declared Antanasoff the true inventor of the first electronic computer. This court decision was necessary because many considered J. Presper Eckert and John W. Mauchly (University of Pennsylvania) to be the inventors of the first electronic computer. Their computer, the ENIAC (Electronic Numerical Integrator and Calculator), was completed in 1946 and is recognized as the first large-scale electronic digital computer.

   The ENIAC had no internal memory. In the late 1940s, Jon Von Neumann's principle of encoding spurred the development of the first stored-program computer, the EDVAC (Electronic Discrete Variable Automatic Computer). However, the EDSAC (Electronic Delay Storage Automatic Computer) created at Cambridge University, England, was completed several months earlier and is now recognized as the first stored-program computer. The computers were used primarily for scientific applications.

   a. *First-generation computers (1951–1958):*

      (1) *First business computer:* In 1951, the U.S. Census Bureau purchased a UNIVAC 1 from Remington Rand dedicated to data processing rather than military use. In 1954, General Electric Company became the first private firm to use the UNIVAC 1 for commercial business data processing.

      (2) *Characteristics of first-generation computers:*

         (a) The main logic element consisted of vacuum tubes. This caused the computers to be large and to generate much heat.

         (b) Input devices were card oriented.

         (c) Internal storage consisted of a magnetic drum.

         (d) Application software was written in machine-level languages. Later, symbolic languages were developed, making programming easier.

         (e) There was very little in the area of systems software. Application programs were entered one by one and monitored by a computer operator.

         (f) Applications were mainly for payroll, billing, and accounting.

b. *Second-generation computers (1959–1964):*

(1) *Major computers introduced:* The major computers introduced during the second generation were oriented toward scientific uses as well as general business uses. These computers had much faster speeds and larger memory capacities than those of first-generation computers. Higher-level languages (COBOL and FORTRAN) were developed during this period.

(2) *Characteristics of second-generation computers:*

(a) The main logic element was the transistor, which allowed computers to be faster, smaller, and more reliable. The transistor also required less power for operation and increased the internal storage capacity.

(b) Internal storage advanced to magnetic core. This allowed faster storage access speeds.

(c) Internal storage was supplemented with secondary storage through the use of magnetic tape and later the introduction of magnetic disks.

(d) Application software could then be written in high-level languages. This allowed the programs to be application and problem oriented instead of machine oriented.

(e) Although the first real operating system (part of the system software) appeared during the second generation, computer processing was still monitored by computer operators.

(f) Most of the applications were batch processed, relying on magnetic tape and cards for input.

c. *Third-generation computers (1965–1970):*

(1) *First minicomputer:* In 1965, Digital Equipment Corporation (DEC) introduced the first minicomputer, a scaled-down version of the large mainframe computers.

(2) *Characteristics of third-generation computers:*

(a) The main logic element consisted of integrated circuits (ICs), the chip, which enabled computer memories to store up to several million units of information.

(b) Internal storage was moving toward metal-oxide semiconductor memory (MOS).

(c) Secondary storage moved toward greater use of magnetic disks, allowing for more flexible input/output.

(d) More high-level languages were introduced, and associations worked toward standardization of languages. This made application programming easier.

(e) Advancements to the operating system of the system software had a major impact on processing capabilities. An *operating system* is a set of programs that supervise the work of the computer system as well as communicate with peripheral devices (i.e., printer, drives, and terminals). With operating systems controlling the computer operations, there is little need for full-time computer operators.

(f) The advancements in disk storage and operating systems made on-line access, interactive processing, and real-time processing possible for business applications. Remote processing and time-sharing were possible through communication networks.

d. *Fourth-generation computers (1971–1984):*

(1) *First microprocessor:* Ted Hoff of Intel Corporation is usually given credit for the introduction of the microprocessor in 1971. The microprocessor was the control unit and arithmetic/logic unit on a single chip. Today, a *microprocessor* is a single chip on which circuitry of the control unit, arithmetic/logic unit, and internal storage are etched. A microprocessor plus chips for input/output operations form a microcomputer.

(2) *Characteristics of fourth-generation computers:*

(a) The internal components now consist of large-scale integrated circuits (LSI).

(b) Internal storage is mainly semiconductor, where memory is etched onto a small silicon chip.

(c) Secondary storage is now being used along with primary storage (internal storage) in a concept called *virtual memory.* A system that uses virtual memory technology makes it appear to the user that there is more internal storage than actually is available. More complex applications and lengthier files can be processed in a virtual memory environment.

(d) Application software is now becoming more user friendly. Fourth-generation languages (4GLs) are more English-like, making it easier for nontechnical personnel to use the computer.

(e) Systems software has expanded to include database management systems.

(f) Networking is prevalent along with distributed data processing.

e. *Fifth-generation computers (1985–present):*

(1) *Microcomputer and user software:* The boom of the microcomputer; continued improvements in the speed, capacity, and sizes of computer systems; and software designed for user information needs have brought computing power to the desks of business personnel. Each year, the microcomputer continues to get smaller, faster, less expensive, and more powerful. Advancements in expert systems, decision-support systems, and artificial intelligence will expand the use of computer information systems in business.

(2) *Characteristics of fifth-generation computers:*

(a) Very large scale integrated circuits (VLSICs) are chips with small micro-sized transistors placed on silicon chips. This technology allows computers to be faster, more reliable, smaller, and less expensive. The desktop workstation is now popular in offices.

(b) Secondary storage utilizes optical disks, Zip drives, and Jaz cartridges that store vast amounts of data in a relatively small physical space.

(c) Database query languages, decision-support systems, and expert systems are now prevalent in business.

2. *Hardware for Computer Processing Systems:* The equipment used in processing data is called *hardware.* In addition to the computer itself, other equipment that is required includes input, output, and storage devices.

    a. *The electronic computer system:* The *digital* computer is used to organize numbers. Data are represented by strings of numbers that are, in turn, expressed by electrical impulses.

        The digital computer is most often used for processing business data. The other classification of computers is the *analog* computer, which is used as a measuring device. The functional elements that make up the electronic computer system are input devices, secondary storage devices, output devices, and the processor unit (see Figure 1–4).

        (1) *Input devices:* A processing system requires devices that can introduce (enter) the raw data into the system. Typical input devices are optical, disk, or magnetic tape readers; bar-code scanners; and terminals with keyboards, a mouse, or touch screens. The data may be recorded as magnetic spots on the tape or disk, microscopic laser pits on optical disks, or marks on paper. Terminal input devices (keyboards, mouse, or touch screen) provide user input for immediate processing or storage on an input medium (CD-ROM, disk, or tape).

        (2) *Processor unit:* The processor unit consists of primary storage (main memory/internal storage) and the central processing unit (CPU). Primary storage is random access memory (RAM) and is volatile (lost when the electrical power to the computer is turned off). The CPU is the heart of a computer system and consists of the control unit and the arithmetic/logic unit. Figure 1–4 illustrates the three components of the processor unit: primary storage, the control unit, and the arithmetic/logic unit. The CPU processes data transferred to main memory by an input device and, in turn, transfers the results from main memory to an output device (printers or CRT screen) and/or secondary storage.

            (a) *Primary storage:* Primary storage is also called *main memory* or *internal storage.* Data are transferred from the input devices directly to main

Figure 1–4   The Electronic Computer System

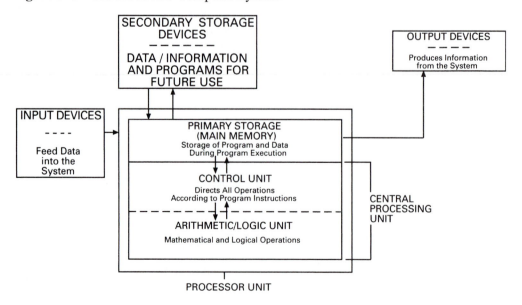

memory and must be in main memory to be sent to the output device or to any peripheral equipment. Main memory stores the following:

- Input data
- Program instructions (both system and application)
- Intermediate processing results
- Processed data (information) ready for output (report)

(b) *Control unit:* Instruction registers and control circuits are included in the control unit. Under stored-program control (system software), the control unit selects one program statement at a time from main memory. This is referred to as *fetching.* The control unit performs the following operations:

- Instruction registers within the control unit are used to select program instructions in the proper sequence.
- The control unit interprets each program instruction as it is selected.
- Control circuits are activated to carry out operations required.
- Results are stored.

The control unit working with main memory makes possible the stored-program concept of computer operation.

(c) *Arithmetic/logic unit:* The arithmetic/logic unit performs all mathematical computations and logical comparisons. The arithmetic circuitry adds, subtracts, multiplies, divides, sets algebraic signs, rounds off, and so on. Logical operations are comparisons for greater than, less than, equal to, and not equal to. Arithmetic operations can be performed only on numeric characters. Logical operations can be performed on numeric, alphabetic, and special characters. Data are transferred as needed from main memory to the arithmetic/logic unit for manipulation and returned to main memory until needed for additional processing or output.

A microprocessor includes the control unit and the arithmetic logic unit mounted on a single silicon chip. Computers containing more than one microprocessor enable the computer to execute more than one instruction, or to process more than one program, at a time.

The microprocessor determines a computer's performance. Microprocessors run at clock speed. One megahertz (1 MHz) equals one million clock ticks per second. Most microcomputers running Windows 98 operating systems and programs require at least 400 MHz. Still newer and faster microprocessor chips are being designed to meet the computing expectations of business users.

(3) *Output devices:* Output, data that have been processed, may be in a form acceptable for another machine (secondary storage for future processing) or in a form usable and understandable by people (information). Typical output devices for information are printers, CRT screens, and voice. When the information is printed, this is called a *hard copy.* When information can be viewed on a screen or heard over a recorder, it is called *soft copy.* Soft information can be stored in secondary storage and a hard copy obtained at a future time.

EXAMPLE: Electronic impulses are used to activate and operate a printer so that a printout can be obtained that is readable in our language, not in machine language.

(4) *Secondary storage devices:* Secondary storage is also called *auxiliary storage.* Data that are to be saved for future processing are stored in secondary storage in a file. These data can be retrieved as needed during processing under the control of the stored systems program. Some processed data (information) and applications programs are also saved for future use in different file names in secondary storage. The most common secondary storage devices are magnetic tape, magnetic disk, optical disk, Zip disk, and Jaz cartridges.

b. *Types of computer systems:* Four categories of computer systems have emerged for use in business: mainframe computer systems, minicomputer systems, microcomputer systems, and supercomputers.

(1) *Mainframe computer systems:* Large organizations have used the mainframe computer, also called the *full-scale computer,* to provide processing services from a centralized location in a computer center. Usually, this type of computer system offers the ultimate in operating speed and storage capacity. The system can support several hundred terminals throughout the organization and hundreds of on-line secondary storage devices. Many different types of input, output, and storage devices can be used to interface with a mainframe system. Information processing personnel, used to interface with a mainframe system, are available within a large organization to assist various departments in determining how the computer can best be used for that department's work.

(2) *Minicomputer systems:* Minicomputers are in between mainframe computers at the high end and microcomputer systems at the low end and do overlap each system in storage capacity and basic system use. Minicomputers tend to use the full range of input/output devices available for mainframe computers. Secondary storage is in the form of fixed disks or disk drives. Within an organization, a minicomputer can be located to provide on-site processing for users located away from the central computer location. This has led to the concept of distributed processing. A minicomputer may also be used as a front-end processor to a large mainframe system.

Most minicomputers can be plugged into standard electrical outlets and do not require special facilities (air conditioning and water cooling) as mainframe computers do. These features, along with the expansion in main memory capacity and speed because of very large scale circuitry, make the minicomputer attractive to many organizations.

EXAMPLE: Through its mainframe computer, a large university can provide computer services to individual departments or faculty all over the university as long as the user has a terminal and an accurate security clearance to use the computer. Within the College of Business (one of the six colleges in the university), there are specific instructional needs not being addressed through the mainframe computer. The College of Business has installed a minicomputer so that 280 microcomputers within a computer lab can be used for classroom instruction in information systems by all business disciplines.

(3) *Microcomputer systems:* The microprocessor is the technology of the microcomputer. Sometimes the microprocessor is referred to as "the CPU on a chip." A more formal definition of a microcomputer is a digital computer, about the size of a typewriter, that uses a microprocessor, an internal storage chip, an input/output chip, and any additional chips required by the system. The basic additional components of the microcomputer system include the following:

- Visual display screen

- Diskette or disk drives

- Printer, if needed

Within a large organization, the microcomputer is quite versatile in handling specific business operations in accounting, word processing, statistical analysis, what-if analysis, and other applications. In most companies the microcomputer and application software (4GL and 5GL) are used to generate information requested by today's business personnel. The information is designed to better meet the user's needs and can be produced in a relatively short period of time.

(a) *Desktop workstation:* The desktop workstation is a powerful microcomputer with graphic, document management, and communications capabilities that can integrate information from diverse perspectives and sources both internal and external to the firm. Either a 486 or a 586 processor (also called a Pentium processor) is typical in desktop workstations. These powerful desktop tools are changing the automated office environment.

(b) *Laptop computer:* Portable computing became popular with the creation of laptop computers (also called a *notebook computer*). Laptop computers are small enough to fit into a briefcase. Weighing as little as 6.5 pounds, laptop computers offer the same processing power and storage capabilities as desktop workstations.

(c) *Personal computer:* The personal computer is a microcomputer that was originally meant to be used for home use. With the software that has been developed, the microcomputer can be used for a variety of applications both at home and at the office. Some microcomputers have keyboards that are labeled for easy operation by people who typically would not have extensive keyboarding skills. Software icons and the use of a mouse or trackball makes it easy for users to point and click software operating commands. The terms *personal computer* and *microcomputer* have become almost interchangeable.

EXAMPLE: Microcomputers operating in a Windows environment use a mouse, which serves as a cursor to move from one part of the screen to another. Another has touch-sensitive controls to aid the operator in activating the system for different operations. Many microcomputers have the control and function keys on the keyboard labeled with very simple language, such as "in" or "out," or use symbols ("file" or "wastebasket") instead of words. These features are meant to provide a more user-friendly system.

From the user's viewpoint, *user friendly* means that the system interacts easily with the business person using the microcomputer. A user-friendly system responds to the user's requests for information with prompts or with signals to indicate that the system is able to interpret the instructions and provide the information.

(4) *Supercomputers:* The supercomputer is the largest, fastest, most powerful, and most expensive computer. Supercomputers are used by the military and large organizations involved in research-and-development activities that are mathematically intensive, such as those found in the aerospace industry, chemical industries, and weather forecasting.

c. *Input devices:* Human beings must be able to communicate with the computer, and they do this by means of input devices. The computer needs both program statements and data for processing, which are entered into a computer system with the aid of an input device (e.g., a disk reader). To facilitate this step, data must be transferred from source documents to an *input medium* that an input device can read. With real-time processing, data are keyed directly into the computer system for immediate processing. Only data required for future processing are recorded on an input medium.

(1) *Input media:* The input medium is the physical material on which data are recorded.

EXAMPLES: Mark-sensed paper, magnetic disk pack, optical disks, magnetic tape, punched card, and punched paper tape.

(a) *Punched card:* The oldest type of input medium is the punched card. Hollerith's 80-column punched card is the one familiar to most people. A smaller 96-column card was introduced by IBM in 1969 to use with business minicomputers.

(b) *Punched paper tape:* Standard paper tape is ¾ of an inch wide. Data bits are represented by punched holes in the tape. Holes are punched along five, seven, or nine channels running parallel to the tape edges. A character is represented by a combination of holes and spaces occurring across the channels at a particular point on the tape.

(c) *Magnetic tape:* Standard magnetic tape for use with computers is usually Mylar tape (½ inch by 2,400 feet) coated on one surface with a magnetizable substance. Bits are recorded in channels running along the length of the tape. Data stored on magnetic tape are sequentially accessed. Today, magnetic tape is used for batch processing and storage backup on large computer systems. *Key-to-tape* systems permit data to be keyed and transferred to the tape in the same operation.

(d) *Magnetic disk packs:* A magnetic disk pack consists of 11 disks sealed in a case to protect the magnetized surface of each disk. Data are recorded as magnetic spots along tracks around the magnetic surface. The disk pack is used by placing it on a drive spindle, which spins it at a high rate of speed.

(e) *Hard disks:* A hard disk is sometimes referred to as a *fixed disk,* as it is a nonremovable magnetic disk assembly. Hard disks may use one or more magnetic disks for secondary storage and are very common in today's microcomputer systems.

(f) *Diskettes:* Magnetic diskettes are used primarily in microcomputers to store data. Many microcomputers now use 3 ½-inch, double-sided, high-density diskettes.

- The 3 ½-inch diskette stores more data than the older 5 ¼-inch, double-sided, double-density diskette.

- Also, the soft jacket on the 5 ¼-inch diskette does not provide as much protection to the programs and data stored.

The amount of information that can be stored on a diskette varies with disk density and quality. Diskettes have a storage capacity ranging from 320 kilobytes (320 K) (320,000 bytes) to approximately 2.8 megabytes (MB) (2,800,000 bytes) for extra-high-density disks. Zip disks can hold more than 125 MB on a single 3 ½-inch cartridge, while Jaz cartridges can hold 2 gigabytes (GB) (approximately 2 billion bytes). Jaz cartridges are common for files utilizing many graphics images.

Care should be taken to protect diskettes so that they are not damaged. Once a disk has a bad sector (section), it cannot be used again. *Key-to-disk* devices permit the data to be keyed and transferred to the disk in the same operation. Key-to-disk systems involve storage on floppy disks used as secondary storage.

(g) *Optical disks:* Optical disk technology uses a laser beam to store and read data instead of magnetic processes. Data are stored by a laser device that burns microscopic pits in tracks on optical disks.

- *CD-ROM:* Large databases that do not change (reference materials), directories, encyclopedias, and multimedia material are typical data stored on CD-ROM (compact disk read-only memory).

- *CD-R:* Compact disk-recordable (CD-R) optical disks provide business users with the ability to store (write once) large volumes of data and information according to their needs. The earlier reference to this technology was WORM (write once–read many).

- *CD-E:* CD-erasable (CD-E) disks now allow the user to store, access, and reuse disks in the same way as diskettes. Some refer to this new technology as CD-RW (compact disk–rewritable). Because of the larger storage capacities of CD-E, magnetic tape will likely become a thing of the past.

- *Magneto-optical disks (MO):* Magneto-optical (MO) disks combine magnetic principles with the new optical technology. Storage capacity for MO disks is measured in gigabytes. The disks are portable as well as durable.

- *Digital video disks (DVD):* The equivalent of up to about eight CD-ROM disks can be stored on a digital video disk (DVD). DVD players can read compact disks (CDs) and CD-ROMs. On a single side, a DVD can hold up to 4.7 GB on a single recording layer. Double-layer disks have capacities of 8.5 GB. DVDs are used to store music, movies, and multimedia packages. Some companies refer to DVDs as *digital versatile disks.*

CD-ROM disks can store up to 650 MB of data on a disk. CD-E disks, allowing users the option to reuse disks, has made an impact on computing storage devices. Optical disks have a 30-year shelf life, are ideal for graphics and audiovisual applications that require large storage capacities, and are revolutionizing the computing storage industry. Magneto-optical disks can be written to nearly a million times without a decline in accuracy. Both magnetic and optical disk technology have made real-time processing possible.

(h) *Magnetic-ink character recognition (MICR):* Introduced in the late 1950s to facilitate check processing in the banking industry, magnetic-ink characters are formed with magnetized particles of iron oxide on the bottom of the check. The magnetic-ink characters can be read by both human beings and machines; therefore, no special data conversion step is needed.

(i) *Optical recognition:* The three basic kinds of optical recognition systems are optical mark recognition (OMR), the bar-code system, and optical character recognition (OCR).

- The simplest optical recognition is *optical mark recognition (OMR),* or *mark sensing.*

EXAMPLE: Many business forms today use OMR requiring the user to code the correct response by darkening the space with a pencil:

Gender: ❏ *Male*   ❏ *Female*
Age: ❏ *21–35*   ❏ *36–45*

- Another type of optical recognition is the *bar code,* where special line codes are read by the computer system. Data are represented in a code by the widths of the bars and the distance between the bars.

EXAMPLE: The most familiar bar code is the Universal Product Code (UPC) found on many grocery products. Many retail establishments now operate point-of-sale systems that read coded data on merchandise tags.

- A third type of optical recognition is *optical character recognition (OCR).* OCR recognizes letters, numbers, and special characters.

The major difference between OCR and OMR is that the data for OCR are represented by the shape of the character, whereas the data for OMR are represented by the position of the mark. Optical recognition is important to the extensive use of source data automation in the business environment.

(j) *Remote input:* By reducing input to one step, source data automation speeds the data flow from input through processing to output. Remote terminals collect data at the point of origination for transmission to a central computer for processing. Typically, data are input through optical recognition devices and transmitted to the central computer via telecommunications equipment (for a discussion of remote terminals for input, see Section [2][e]).

(2) *Input hardware:* Equipment used to prepare the input media and/or transmit the data to the computer is known as *input hardware.* An *on-line* input device is physically connected to the CPU and is under the control of the CPU. An *off-line* device is not physically connected to the CPU.

(a) *The card keypunch:* Punched cards are prepared on a card keypunch. The keyboard is much like a typewriter keyboard with a few variations. The keypunch manipulates and positions the cards automatically and can be set up to repeat certain keypunching procedures. The accuracy of the initial keying in of data is checked by having a second operator key the same data on a *verifier.* Additional hardware used for card input includes the card reader, sorter, and collator. Keypunching has become an obsolete method of data entry. Many computer systems produced today do not accept punched cards as a medium for data input.

(b) *Key-to-tape* and *key-to-disk (diskette):* Key-to-tape and key-to-disk machines were developed to improve the data entry bottleneck. With these devices, data are keyed at a keyboard and stored as magnetized spots on the tape or diskette surface to be used later as input to the computer system. The use of magnetic tape or disk systems significantly increased the efficiency of data processing operations. Today, source data automation is used extensively to improve the speed and accuracy of data input.

(c) *Magnetic-ink character recognition devices:* This input device reads the magnetized-ink characters on bank checks and converts them into machine code. MICR hardware can sort between 700 and 1,500 checks per minute.

(d) *Optical readers:* Various optical input devices are used for different types of input. The marks on an OMR document are sensed by an optical mark reader. The reader converts the mark into machine language. The barcode reader reads the special codes on products, and the optical character reader compares the characters to a font in the reader. A CD-ROM drive is common on most microcomputers today for reading data off CDs. In all cases, data are converted to machine language for the computer. This technology is important to source data automation.

(e) *Direct-entry equipment: Direct entry* takes place whenever a person enters data directly into the computer without intervention from an input medium. Common direct-entry devices are the laptop (portable) computer, the cathode ray tube (CRT) terminal, the intelligent computer, the point-of-sale terminal, touch devices, and voice input.

- *Laptop (portable) computer:* This type of computer, also called a *notebook,* is known for its portability. The busy executive can carry it in a briefcase and use it whenever necessary to access or enter data via the keyboard while connected to the company computer by telephone lines or cable.

- *Cathode ray tube (CRT) terminal:* The CRT terminal is known for its speed of operation, its graphic capabilities, and its ease of operation. Its linkage to the computer is a real asset, permitting the user to view data input through the terminal. With a CRT terminal, the user can *always* see the document or other input that is being created during the input phase.

- *Intelligent computer:* A CRT terminal with a microprocessor (CPU on a chip) to allow programming and to perform special tasks is called a *microcomputer* (intelligent computer). This computer system can lead the user through a sequence of entry operations and can perform many of the data-editing activities normally carried out by the central computer.

- *Point-of-sale (POS) terminal:* Sales data can be collected at their source with point-of-sale (POS) terminals. Some terminals have keyboards for data entry and an optical scanner for reading bar codes as well as other typical cash register features. Some POS terminals have wand readers that can read either the UPC or optical characters imprinted on a price tag.

- *Touch devices:* Popular for issuing computer commands and making selections, touch devices provide an easy-to-use alternative to keyboard input. The more popular touch devices include the mouse or trackball, touch-sensitive screens, and light pens.

  Mouse or trackball: The mouse and trackball are used to move the cursor on the screen and to select options.

  Touch-sensitive screen: Simply pointing to a specific section of the screen activates a particular selection among alternatives presented. Sensors in the screen allow the terminal to become an input device.

  Light pen: Some CRT terminals accept input from the touch of a light pen on the face of the tube. With a light pen, lines can be drawn, creating an object. The light pen is mainly used in engineering and drafting.

- *Voice input:* A human voice may be converted from analog to digital electronic impulses so that the computer can deal with the data or information presented. These systems are currently suitable for low-volume, highly structured input. They are effective in quality control, computer-aided design, and laboratory settings. Applications for voice input are still being researched or are in the developmental stages.

(3) *Interfaces:* A user interface is a combination of hardware and software that makes data input easier. A user interface allows a user to respond to messages presented by the computer, control the computer, and request information from the computer.

  (a) *User interfaces:* User interfaces include function keys, screen prompts, menus, and icons.

  - *Function keys:* Located on the keyboard, function keys are programmed to carry out specific operations. The software directing the function key simplifies a specific operation for the user.

  - *Screen prompts:* These are messages displayed on the screen to help the user while using an application.

  - *Menus:* Menus are special screen prompts providing lists of processing options. The user selects from the menu by pressing a number or letter that corresponds to the option desired. A pull-down menu is one displayed across the top of the screen with submenus pulled down from the top as needed.

  - *Icons:* Icons are pictures that represent text. The icons are displayed on the screen to show the program options available to the user. An interface that uses icons extensively to represent system options graphically is called a *graphical user interface* (GUI).

  (b) *Interface features:* Users should be aware of features that interfaces should include. Being familiar with these features can be helpful in selecting application software and in working with information systems personnel when designing custom in-house systems or reengineering purchased systems.

- All system responses should be meaningful to the user. System responses are the messages displayed and the actions the computer takes when a user enters data. Without system responses, the user does not know if the computer accepted the input or what the computer is doing.

- The simpler the response from the user, the better the interface. Eliminating keystrokes results in faster input and greater accuracy.

- The screen design should be simple, uncluttered, and easily understood. All prompts, menus, and icons within an application should follow a consistent format. Clear screen designs have a significant impact on the usability of the interface.

- When the user makes an error, it should be clear how to correct the error. When an error is made, the user should be notified, the error should be identified as clearly as possible, and it should be clear to the user how to correct the error.

d. *Output devices:* People must be able to use the output from computerized systems. As in the case of input, each output process involves an output medium and an output device.

(1) *Output media:* Output media are the means by which information (processed data) is recorded, printed out, or displayed for human use.

(a) *Paper:* A common output medium is paper. Hard copies of documents are created so that people can use the information readily.

(b) *Display:* Another way to make output available for human use is through visual display of the information on a screen or terminal. Electronic communication has made output to the CRT screen a common medium in business. Information can also be displayed on a screen that is recorded on a microform (microfilm or microfiche) for visual display using special equipment. Display of output on a screen is referred to as *soft copy,* which means that the screen image may not be a permanent record of what is shown. To become a permanent record, the soft copy must be saved on a secondary storage medium. Many business applications utilize the convenience and cost saving of soft copy. Hard copies of the screen display can be printed if the user desires.

(c) *Audio (voice) response:* Prerecorded audio responses are prevalent in computer business applications. The touch telephone often facilitates this type of response, for example, placing orders by following the recorded prompts or time and weather given by dialing a special number. Both GUIs and CD-ROMs have increased the use of audio response in systems.

(2) *Printers and printing devices:* Hardware used to prepare output includes printers and printing devices. The appropriateness of a printer or printing device for information processing output will depend on the print quality desired, the production speed available on the device, the method used for creating images, and the cost of the equipment. The *printer* is the part of the information processing system that transfers images of recorded keystrokes

onto a sheet of paper a character, a line, or a page at a time. The output document produced on paper is called *hard copy.* A printer allows an operator to key in the text for one document while another document is printing out. This process is called *background printing.*

(a) *Impact printing devices:* Images of characters are transferred by a printing device (either a font or a print wheel) as it strikes a piece of paper through the ribbon and leaves an impression. The font or print wheel actually makes contact with the ribbon and paper as the images are being created. The most commonly used impact printing devices that produce solid characters are the *single-element font,* the *daisy print wheel,* and the *thimble.*

 • *Single-element font:* In 1961, IBM introduced the Selectric element and the Selectric typewriter. The element contains all the characters and symbols found on a typewriter keyboard on one circular font. As the operator strikes a character on the keyboard, the element turns and "selects" the character desired. One of the advantages of using the single-element font has always been its interchangeability so that the operator could use several different type styles within the document merely by changing the font.

 • *Daisy print wheel:* The second printing device, the *daisy print wheel,* was developed by Diablo in 1974. The print wheel is a circular device used in a printer, with different characters on each spoke of the wheel. The print wheel rotates until it reaches the character desired. A hammer hits the character against the ribbon and paper, causing the image to print through the ribbon onto the paper.

 • *Thimble:* Another impact device, developed by NEC Information Systems, Inc., is the NEC Spinwriter. This single-element device, known as the *thimble* because of its general appearance, seems to be quite reliable and durable.

(b) *Types of impact printers:* An impact printer forces the typed character against the ribbon and paper, creating an image directly on the paper. Specific types of impact printers include *high-speed printers,* such as *line printers* (commonly used as computer output devices), which print anywhere from 100 to more than 3,000 lines per minute; *chain printers* and *drum printers* (types of line printers); and *dot-matrix printers* (with groups of dots closely spaced into printed patterns that look like the shapes of characters desired). Impact printers can produce letter-quality or non-letter-quality print.

 • *Impact printers with letter-quality print:* Most impact printers that produce letter-quality print are *serial printers* (capable of printing one data character at a time), which range in speed from 15 to 60 characters per second or 175 to 700 words per minute. These character printers may use type bars, a typing element, a print wheel, or a matrix. Advanced technology has made character printers obsolete. This type of printer is not suitable for graphic output.

 • *Impact printers with non-letter-quality print:* Most impact printers that produce non-letter-quality print are serial printers that produce single characters by using a wire-matrix device. The wires are arranged in a boxlike matrix pattern. Images of characters are formed when a hammer pushes from behind the selected wires to form the shape of the desired character. A ribbon inserted between the wires and the paper facilitates image transfer to the paper. Each character or symbol produced resembles a pattern of pinpoint dots, not a solid pattern. One character consists of a height of seven dots and a width of five dots. The more dots used to compose a character, the closer together are the dots, with less likelihood of seeing white space within the character.

(c) *Types of nonimpact printers:* Several types of nonimpact printers are appropriate for information processing output. Because they tend to be quieter than impact printers, these printers can be located anywhere in the office. There is no printing device hitting on the platen of the printer, as is the case with the impact printer. Instead, images are created on the page through the use of ink-jet, laser, xerographic, or electrothermal imaging processes. Their "quiet" features make nonimpact printers desirable output hardware for the office environment. In today's office, the nonimpact printer is more prevalent unless multiple copies prepared on sensitized paper (carbonless paper) are needed. Then, an impact printer, such as a dot-matrix printer, would be necessary. The most commonly used nonimpact printers include *ink-jet printers, laser printers, fiber optics printers,* and *intelligent printers.*

- *Ink-jet printers:* The ink-jet printer is a nonimpact printer that utilizes a fast-drying electronically charged ink to spray ink droplets through an electronic field to form the character images desired onto a sheet of paper. Ink-jet printing has been particularly useful for high-volume form letters because of automatic paper and envelope handling. The print quality is generally excellent, and the printer operates in a speed range of about 1,100 to 2,200 words per minute (92 to 184 characters per second). Today, most ink-jet printers can print up to four colors of ink at one time and produce high-quality graphics output. With graphic and color highlighting common to most computer software, ink-jet printers with color capability are popular in office environments.

- *Laser printers:* The laser printer has become an extremely popular nonimpact printer to use with information processing. An entire page of information can be printed at one time. Laser printing utilizes an intense low-power light beam capable of carrying millions of characters simultaneously. The laser beam merges with a process that uses light to shape character images onto a light-sensitive paper covering a rotating drum. Toner is used to transfer the image to paper. The laser printer is known especially for its very high print quality, very high-speed printing from 8,000 to 18,000 lines per minute (36 to 300 pages per minute), high-quality graphics output, and color printing capability. Laser printers can *duplex* (print on both sides of the paper) and can be used with a variety of type sizes and styles. The speed, letter quality, and quietness of laser printers make them desirable output hardware for the office environment. The cost of color laser printers continues to decrease.

- *Fiber optics printers:* Fiber optics technology utilizes glasslike tubes that send a light source from one location to another. The light source changes machine signals into light pulses that are transmitted through fiber optic tubes. At the end of the tubes, the light pulses are changed into signals that the receiving machine can recognize. Fiber optics technology is reducing information processing costs by creating high-quality documents at faster speeds.

- *Intelligent printers:* High-speed printers that combine computer, laser, and copying technology are called *intelligent printers.* Some of the more automatic features of this technology enable images to be placed on both sides of sheets and automatic collating and stapling functions to occur. The memory enables the printer to utilize stored programs to perform routine functions.

- *Xerographic printers:* These nonimpact printers use a process similar to that found in office photocopiers.

- *Electrothermal printers:* A heat process is used to produce character images with an electrothermal printer. Hard copies are produced on heat-sensitive paper. Although it is a quiet printer, the special paper required is considered a disadvantage.

(d) Special-purpose printers: One type of special-purpose printer (a *plotter*) outlines drawings. *Drum plotters* move the paper past a stylus (pen). The drum moves up and down, and the pen moves left and right, thus allowing diagonal as well as vertical and horizontal output. *Table plotters* spread the paper over the flatbed (table) of the plotter. Again, the paper and pen are bidirectional, producing graphic output. Plotters are used in engineering, drafting, and design of styled products (e.g., automobiles and dresses).

(3) *Visual displays:* Some output devices produce a visual display so that the user can access the stored data and view it as soft copy on a screen. Visual display terminals (VDTs) are used as both input and output devices. As an output device, the VDT can only *display* output; the terminal does not produce hard copy of the output. Output on a VDT is referred to as *soft copy.* VDTs are used extensively in interactive on-line systems (i.e., the person who uses the VDT interacts with the computer in an exchange of questions and responses). VDTs are also used extensively for graphic displays in highly technical fields. Many people refer to a VDT as a cathode ray tube (CRT). A CRT is a visual display terminal that uses the technology of a cathode ray tube for the visual display. Flat-panel displays include liquid crystal display (LCD), electroluminescent (EL) display, and gas-panel display. Because a flat-panel display weighs less and uses less electricity than a CRT, it is used for laptop (notebook) computers.

(4) *Computer-output microfilm:* To reduce the storage space required for output, a process referred to as *computer-output microfilm* (COM) has been used extensively as an output device. Microfilm outputs may be reel film, individual film frames on aperture cards, or microfiche. This medium is less expensive than paper output if the volume warrants it.

(5) *Audio (voice) response units:* Prerecorded messages are used to provide a response that will not require someone to give the message in person or over the telephone. The computer program composes responses to the inquiries in the

form of coded messages. The coded message is sent to the audio response unit, which transmits the message to the person making the inquiry.

EXAMPLES:

In most cities, you can dial a specific telephone number to receive information on time and temperature. You receive a response such as, "At the tone, the time will be 8:35 A.M. The temperature is 56 degrees."

In response to telephone inquiries from subscribers to a quotation service, the New York Stock Exchange uses a computer to quote verbally the latest price and volume information on stocks listed on the Exchange.

(6) *Special output devices:* Other types of typical output devices include a *hard-copy terminal,* which provides a paper copy of both input and output (much like an electronic typewriter), and *portable terminals* (laptop/notebook computers). Most portable terminals include a built-in modem. A *modem* is a device for converting electronic digital impulses representing data in the sending terminal (portable computer) into sound waves for transmission over telephone lines (see Chapter 3, Section C-2-b[1]). Stored data are in digital form and need to be converted to analog form for transmission as sound over telephone lines. An advantage of the portable terminal with a modem is that the executive can carry it and connect it to any telephone in order to transmit information back to the office.

e. *Storage devices: Primary storage* is the internal storage of the processor unit. It is also referred to as *main memory. Secondary storage* is accomplished through the use of peripheral (add-on) storage devices. Secondary storage is also referred to as *auxiliary storage.*

(1) *Primary computer storage:* Primary storage stores input data, both system and application program instructions, intermediate processing results, and processed data ready for output. For all these elements to be manipulated properly, primary storage must be carefully organized. The storage is divided into locations, with each location identified by an *address* (number). Those items in storage can be located through reference to the appropriate address. Each address within the storage unit contains a fixed number of *bytes* (characters).

(a) *Characteristics of primary storage:* Semiconductor memory is the most widely used form of primary memory. Bubble memory, another type of primary storage, is used in a limited number of situations. Storage units are characterized by the length of addresses available for storage, permanence of the storage, memory protection against accidental destruction of programs needed to operate systems, and the use of auxiliary storage with the CPU.

   • *Data representation:* Data within computers are represented in machine code. The electrical components of a digital computer are either off (0) or on (1). This two-state (binary) condition is referred to as *bits.* Each character requires 8 bits and is called a *byte.*

      EXAMPLE: The character "A" = 1010 0001 = 1 byte (8 bits). This is known as the American Standard Code for Information Interchange (ASCII). Another code representation is the Extended Binary Coded Decimal Interchange Code (EBCDIC). EBCDIC was developed by IBM in the 1950s and is the primary mainframe IBM code. ASCII is used for microcomputers and data transmission.

- *Word length:* The CPU moves data around within the computer system in groups of bits. The number of bits the CPU can move at one time affects the speed (performance) of the system. Common word lengths are 16, 32, and 64. A 32-bit CPU can process 32 bits of data (32 bits is equivalent to four characters, i.e., number, letter, or symbol, including blank spaces) in one machine operation (cycle).

- *Permanence of the storage:* Internal memory that is available to the user is *random access memory* (RAM). Internal memory in computers today is semiconductor memory. With semiconductor memory, the content is lost (erased) when the electrical power to the unit is turned off. This type of storage is *volatile* storage. For today's desktop office applications 64 MB of RAM is recommended with many systems having 128 MB of RAM to handle multiprogramming and graphics efficiently.

  Cache memory (pronounced "cash") is an option that can be added to a computer system to make it run faster. Storing frequently used instructions and data in cache memory minimizes the need to access secondary storage. Using cache memory significantly increases the system's speed.

  Nonvolatile storage is not affected by interruptions of power to the unit. Magnetic core memory, popular in the 1950s, and bubble memory, another internal memory technology, are nonvolatile. Research continues in the area of nonvolatile internal memory.

- *Memory protection:* Internal storage for data representation that does not change is installed permanently by the manufacturer. Manufacturer-specific microcodes and portions of the operating system program are typical programs stored permanently in internal storage. This section of internal storage is referred to as *read-only memory (ROM)*. Programs in ROM can only be accessed by the user through the CPU; the user cannot store (write) data or programs in ROM. Programmable read-only memory (PROM) chips provide the flexibility to store permanently the desired data and instructions that are specialized to the organization. Erasable programmable read-only memory (EPROM) can be used where the CPU's data and instructions change infrequently. EPROM allows the memory chip to be removed from the computer, erased, and reprogrammed with new instructions for the CPU. This type of chip is used frequently in robotic systems. The latest in ROM chips is the electrically erasable programmable read-only memory (EEPROM) chip. By using special programs, the EEPROM can be electrically altered without being removed from the computer.

- *Secondary storage:* Tapes, disks, and mass storage usually provide the auxiliary storage needed. This storage is outside the processor unit. Secondary storage is not lost when the power is shut off because the bits of data are stored as magnetic spots on tape or disks or laser spots on optical disks.

- *Virtual memory:* The length of a program and the complexity of the application depend on the amount of primary storage available. To provide more memory space, long application programs can be split between primary storage and auxiliary storage. During execution, the use of both memory areas for the application program is referred to as *virtual memory.* Management of the application program is handled by the operating system, bringing into primary storage only that part (segment or page) of the program that is needed. This makes the user feel like there is more primary storage than what actually is available.

(b) *Primary storage technology:* Storage devices used today for primary storage include magnetic core and semiconductor memory.

- *Magnetic core storage:* In existence since the 1950s, magnetic core storage was considered the standard primary storage device of second- and third-generation computers. Semiconductor memory has replaced most magnetic core storage. Magnetic core is nonvolatile and geared to individually stored bytes of data.

- *Semiconductor memory:* Metal-oxide semiconductor (MOS) memory is like the integrated circuits (chip) used for the main logic element. Today's semiconductor memory consists of microsized circuits placed on a silicon chip (LSI and VLSI). The advantage of semiconductor memory is that it is smaller than the magnetic core and thus allows faster processing. Although semiconductor memory is volatile, it is the most prevalent internal memory in use today.

- *Other technology:* Magnetic bubble memory was researched during the late 1970s and early 1980s. Current primary storage research is in the area of optical circuits. Bubble memory is nonvolatile (permanent) and very reliable. Magnetized spots (bubbles) in a thin film are used to represent binary codes to allow 100 million bits to be stored on a 1-square-inch garnet wafer. Currently, a number of companies are researching the use of light instead of electricity. Advantages of optical processing relate to speed and space requirements. Researchers envision the development of the optical computer in the future.

(2) *Secondary storage:* The computer system requires the primary storage (RAM) of the processor unit when processing data. The storage capacities of numerous peripheral storage devices to store data and information for future use are important because the cost of primary storage (main memory) is too expensive for storage of data retained for future use. Also, primary storage is volatile where storing data in secondary storage does not require continual electrical power. Main memory is important during processing because fetching by the CPU is faster from main memory than from secondary storage (nonvolatile). Secondary storage, also referred to as *auxiliary storage,* is used to store data, system programs, application programs, and information for future use. Today, most data are stored in a database. Databases are needed for integrated information systems. A *database* is a set of two or more interrelated files with at least one common element. In the database approach to information processing, the data are the central focus. All data available to users are collected together in a central base. The user functions exist on the outer edge

of the database, and the user references the information as needed. Data dictionaries are available to users to assist them in accessing information already stored or in adding new information to the database. Using the database approach, duplication of data should be eliminated, and thus data integrity (accuracy) should be enhanced.

(a) *Characteristics of secondary storage:* Secondary storage units must be attached (on-line) to the CPU through channels in order for data to be transmitted (copied) from the secondary storage device into primary storage. In addition, the type of access, the transfer rate, the access time, and the capacity of the secondary storage device are very important characteristics.

- *Channel:* A *channel* is the necessary communication link that controls the flow of data between the primary storage in the processor unit and the peripheral storage devices. Data flow into and out of primary storage through a port. A *port* is the point where the peripheral is connected for communication with the processor unit.

- *Type of access:* Files may be accessed *sequentially* or by *direct access.* Sequential access is a method of retrieving records from a file where each record is read, one after the other in sequence, beginning with the first record. Magnetic tape can be accessed only sequentially. Batch processing processes data sequentially. Direct access relates to the ability to go directly to the record needed without having to read previous records in the same file. Magnetic disks and optical disks may be accessed sequentially or directly. Direct access requires the use of disks. When data are processed in real time (with immediate results), direct access is required.

- *Transfer rate:* The speed with which data can be transferred from secondary storage to main memory is the *transfer rate.* The transfer rate is usually measured in bytes per second.

- *Access time:* When processing data with direct access, a major concern is the amount of time required to locate the data needed from the particular storage location in secondary storage and transfer the data to internal storage. *Access time* is the measurement of the time to find the data location and the time required to transfer the data. Access times range widely. The range of access times is measured in milliseconds (thousandths of a second).

- *Storage capacity:* The capacity of a secondary storage device is usually stated in terms of number of bytes stored per storage device and in the total number of bytes in all storage devices. The modular design of storage devices today allows for a large range of capacity for secondary storage, even on microcomputer systems.

(b) *Secondary storage hardware:* The most common media used for secondary storage are magnetic tape and magnetic disk. In the microcomputer environment, the disk is the most common type of storage. In the mainframe environment, the disk pack is the most common type of disk device in use. Other types of secondary storage devices include magnetic drums and mass storage.

- *Magnetic tapes:* The first form of secondary storage to be widely used was the magnetic tape. These tapes provide sequential access, have a transfer rate of 50,000 to 400,000 bytes per second, and are nonvolatile. The tape drive reads either one record or a group of records at a time. When records are grouped (blocked), the start/stop tape drives stop at the gaps between the blocks. Tapes are relatively inexpensive storage devices and are ideal for backup storage. R-DAT is the latest in taped technology and can store more than 14 GB on a single 90-meter tape. Because of speed, storage capability, and cost, tape continues to be a popular backup medium. For processing operations, tapes are being replaced by direct-access devices (disks).

- *Magnetic disks:* Data are recorded on circles or tracks on metal or plastic magnetic disks. The circles on the disks are concentric circles with the same amount of data stored on the inner track as the outer track. The data on the inner track are more densely packed. Disks provide direct access of data and thus are necessary when data are processed in real time. There are two types of disk storage: fixed disks and removable disks. *Fixed disks* are permanently mounted and usually have a set of read/write heads for each disk surface. Hard disks are rigid metallic platters, permanently mounted secondary storage in microcomputer systems. *Removable disks* include disk packs, disks, and disk cartridges. Data from a disk pack are transferred by read/write heads of a disk drive. *Disk drives* for disk packs can accept from one to eight packs on a single unit. Systems using single-disk technology offer users the advantages of portability and ease of use. Although many microcomputers have hard disks, a 3 ½- or 5 ¼-inch diskette drive is also configured for portable disk usage. However, since the read/write head actually rides on the surface of the 3 ½- and 5 ¼-inch disk, the surface becomes worn over time. With disk packs and fixed disks, the read/write head floats over the surface. Disk packs and fixed disks are subject to disk crashes if the read/write head should ever touch the disk surface. Zip and Jaz disk cartridges offer storage and fast-access features of hard disks and the portability of the single 3 ½- or 5 ¼-inch disk.

- *Optical disk:* Optical disks are made of hard plastic. Laser beams burn microscopic pits onto the surface. A low-power laser reads the disk by reflecting light off the microscopic pits. The reflected light is converted into a series of bits that the computer can process. CD-ROM is the most popular and least expensive type of optical disk (see Section B-2-c[1][g]).

- *Mass storage:* Mass storage provides file space for large files, backup files, and infrequently used files. Mass storage data cartridges are stored in honeycomb-like cells. The retrieval of a file from mass storage is under the control of the system program.

3. *Software for Processing Systems:* The procedures developed to direct the computer hardware to perform special processing functions are called *software* or *programs.* There are two types of programs: system programs (operating systems) and applications programs.

a. *System software:* The primary function of the system software is to provide overall control and supervision of all the hardware and software elements in the performance of individual tasks. The specific system software program that manages the computer resources is referred to as the *operating system.* The purpose of the operating system is to allocate the computer system resources—CPU, primary storage, and input and output devices. All interaction between a user and the computer system is controlled by the operating system. The various types of operating systems include single program, multiprogram, and multiprocessing. Specific operations controlled by multiprogram and multiprocessing system software include job queuing, priority control, resource allocation, data protection, data management, system program library, and language translation.

(1) *Job queuing:* The operating system can control the input of programs and data for jobs coming in from various departments and queue them up for processing or output so that there is a continuous stream of work.

EXAMPLE: "Print queue" means that as print commands are received by the computer, the print jobs are sequenced and waiting times determined.

(2) *Priority control:* Priorities are set for the processing of specific jobs. Jobs are entered into main memory from secondary storage according to the priority assigned to each job. Jobs are queued for both input and output.

(3) *Resource allocation:* When a particular job is to be processed, the hardware and software resources required will be controlled by the operating system. Those hardware resources controlled include all input/output devices, secondary storage, and the CPU. Software resources controlled include language translators, utility programs, and other programs stored in the system program library.

(4) *Data protection:* In on-line interactive systems (real-time systems that process data immediately), privacy of data from the many users must be protected. Ensuring that each user processes only authorized programs and data is a responsibility of the system software.

   (a) *Time-sharing:* Time-sharing allows users to use the computer system on what appears to be a simultaneous basis. This is possible because of the speeds of today's processors and the transfer rates of direct-access storage devices.

   (b) *Foreground and background programs:* In a multiprogramming environment, programs with high priority are in the foreground areas of main memory. Programs with low priority are in the background area. They are referred to as *foreground programs* and *background programs,* respectively. In a multiprogramming environment, two or more independent programs are loaded into primary storage at the same time and the instructions executed concurrently.

(5) *Data management:* A set of programs for management of data files is included in the systems software. An on-line set of interrelated files (a database) is managed by a database management system and becomes an enhancement to systems software. These database management programs assist users in updating, correcting, and modifying integrated data files.

(6) *System program library:* A system program library is a set of routines and programs that can be used by applications programmers. *Utilities* are generalized routines for performing specific processing functions in an efficient way. The major types of utilities include input/output utilities, transfer utilities, sort utilities, and mathematical routines.

(7) *Language translators:* Language translators are the programs in the system program library that translate programs from assembly, or high-level, language to machine language for processing. A program written in machine language is entered into main memory and then read by the CPU to process data to produce the desired output. The high-level language program is called the *source program.* When the source program is translated into machine language through compilation, an *object program* is created. The *object program* is the one read into the main memory for execution by the CPU. Language translators are also called *compilers.*

b. *Application programs:* The program statements that control the processing of the data are called *application programs.* Application programs are stored in secondary storage and copied into main memory at the time the data are processed. These programs perform specific processing tasks to solve business information needs. Software developers may supply programs for common business operations, such as payroll or billing, or programmers may write application programs to meet specific business needs. (For a more detailed discussion of application programs, see Section C-3.)

EXAMPLES:

Billing program, class scheduling program, and mortgage loan processing program.

Packaged programs are application programs provided by software developers for certain standard computer applications (e.g., inventory control and accounts receivable). Computer programmers in some companies have primary responsibility for special applications for various departments (e.g., class scheduling program).

c. *End-user software:* In the 1980s, a special kind of application software evolved to meet the needs of nontechnical end users and professional programmers. General-purpose application programs and fourth-generation languages (4GLs) are two end-user productivity tools (see Sections B-4-d and C-3-f).

EXAMPLES:

    General-purpose application programs
        Word processing and desktop publishing
        Spreadsheet
        Database management for microcomputers
        Multimedia and presentation packages
    4GLs for nontechnical end users
        Query languages
        Report generators
    4GLs for professional programmers
        Application generators
        Very high-level programming languages

4. *Types of Programming Languages: Programming* is the process of logically translating the steps in a problem solution into sequential instructions for execution by the computer. *A computer will do absolutely nothing without instructions to guide and control its operation.* The coding process required to develop the instructions for the computer can be accomplished through the use of different programming *languages.* The levels of programming languages are machine language, low-level language, high-level language, very high-level language, and object-oriented language.

   a. *Machine language:* A machine language consists of instructions that vary with the requirements and design of the machine being used. A machine language instruction includes an *operation code* and an *operand* (the main memory address location of the data on which the operation is to be performed). The programmer must write an instruction to control each machine operation to be performed. Machine-language programs are written in the binary (1 and 0) numbering system.

      (1) The use of machine language can provide a more efficient method of using the storage capacity of the computer.

      (2) The speed of processing is increased since the computer can understand machine language.

   b. *Low-level language:* Low-level language is used to develop *assembler programs,* which perform the task of recording the address of each unit in the program. *Assembler* allows the use of symbolic names, or *mnemonics,* instead of numeric designations, for machine operations. An assembly-language instruction has three elements:

      (1) *Label:* a tag that represents the first storage location of the instruction to which it is attached

      (2) *Operation code:* the identification of the operation to be performed

      (3) *Operand:* the address location relevant to the operation code of the instruction.

   c. *High-level language:* A program written in English or English-like words instead of machine code or mnemonics is a *high-level language.* Such a program is called a *source program.* To be understood by the CPU, the source program must be translated into machine language. The translation can be either interpreted or compiled. If the translation is compiled, an *object program* (machine-language program) is developed. If the translation is interpreted, each source program statement is translated one at a time and placed in main memory. There is no object program. Thus, if the statement is used again, it must be reinterpreted (retranslated). High-level languages are procedural oriented. A procedurally oriented language places emphasis on the logic and computational steps required to solve a problem. Widely used procedural languages are COBOL, FORTRAN, BASIC, and C. Programs written in these languages allow the programmer to ignore the characteristics of the computer on which the program is to be run. Each language has been developed to meet a specific need.

      (1) *FORTRAN:* Released by IBM in 1957, FORTRAN (*FOR*mula *TRAN*slator) was the first complete compiler language developed for use in scientific problem solving. In 1966, FORTRAN was standardized by the American National Standards Institute (ANSI). Several revisions have been made since that time.

(2) *COBOL:* Introduced in 1960, COBOL (*CO*mmon *B*usiness-*O*riented *L*anguage) was developed by a committee with members from government and business. Because COBOL is very good for processing large files and performing simple business computations, it became widely used for business applications. In 1968, ANSI published guidelines for standardizing COBOL. Since that time, several revisions have been made.

(3) *BASIC:* The most popular of the time-sharing languages, BASIC (*B*eginner's *A*ll-Purpose *S*ymbolic *I*nstruction *C*ode) was designed in 1964 to be used by students working at on-line terminals. With the increase in time-sharing systems, BASIC gained acceptance in both scientific and business processing. A BASIC standard was developed in 1978 for only some of the language syntax. BASIC is not considered a standardized language (see Section B-4-e[2]).

(4) *C:* In 1972, Bell Labs developed the C programming language for writing systems software. C is a powerful general-purpose language with the efficiency of an assembly language and is used to develop software on minicomputers and microcomputers (see Section B-4-e[1]).

Other procedural languages in use are PL/1, ALGOL (a more sophisticated mathematical language), and Pascal (designed for structured programming).

d. *Very high-level languages:* Very high-level languages are also referred to as *fourth-generation languages* (4GLs) or *nonprocedural languages.* These languages are special-purpose languages, having been developed for particular business needs. The programming emphasis is on describing what is needed, usually describing the desired output. A database query language, report generators, and graphic languages are 4GLs that make information access easy for the nontechnical end user.

EXAMPLES:

Query language:	*An interactive on-line system supporting end-user requests, such as "List all plant A employees with pay rate less than 12.5 per hour."*
Report generator:	*Facilitates creating customized reports in database systems.*
Graphics languages:	*VP Graphics, Harvard Graphics, SAS.*

e. *Object-oriented languages:* In high-level languages the focus is on the procedure the computer follows to perform an outcome. Object-oriented programming (OOP) focuses on an object. OOPs gained popularity with the proliferation of graphical user interfaces (GUIs) in the windows environment and the Web. OOP languages include C++, Visual Basic, and Java.

(1) *C++:* C++ contains all the elements of C (procedurally oriented high-level language) plus the event-driven features of OOP.

(2) *Visual Basic:* Designed by Microsoft specifically for windows environments, Visual Basic is used for the development of graphical (icon) interfaces for applications. Another goal of Microsoft was to impact the Internet market. VB Script is embedded in Hypertext Markup Language (HTML) Web pages as a tag.

(3) *Java:* Started at Sun Microsystems in 1991 for consumer electronic products, the first commercial release of Java was in 1996 as a Web language.

The software developed to allow users to observe and interact with Java programs is called HotJava.

C. Processing Operations, Concepts, and Applications

In processing data into information, the computer system can do only what it is instructed to do. These instructions come from programs or people using 4GLs or general-purpose application programs. This requires *trained* people to locate or develop specific business applications for computer use that are compatible with the basic operations and operating modes available for the system. It is very important for office personnel to know what information needs to be processed, how it will be processed, and the rationale for using the computer.

1. *Basic Operations:* Business processing requires specific operations to take place so that specific data can be processed.

   a. *Recording:* Source data are captured (or recorded) for further processing, either manually or by the computer.

   EXAMPLE: Payroll data for hourly employees can be manually recorded on a time card. At the end of the week, the time card becomes the source document for inputting the weekly hours. In an on-line system, the time clock can be connected to a secondary storage device for storage of the in or out time. When the employee slides the magnetized strip of an identification badge through the clock, the employee's ID number is recorded from the magnetized strip, and the input time (or output time) is obtained from the clock. The data are recorded on a secondary storage medium (tape or disk) for processing at a later time.

   b. *Duplicating:* Where it is necessary to create more than one record of the transaction, this can be accomplished through the development of multiple-copy forms, or a second set of data can be stored on another form of media.

   EXAMPLE: One set of data can be stored on magnetic tape while the second set of data can be stored on a magnetic disk pack.

   c. *Verifying:* Checking the accuracy of the data is known as *verification* of the data. Sometimes keyboarding or transposition errors are made while entering data into the computer with a terminal. Source data automation improves data accuracy by eliminating the need for input keying of data.

   d. *Classifying:* Data must be identified and grouped according to at least one characteristic that is useful in making management decisions. Classification may be by type, by source, by importance, or by type of response required.

   EXAMPLE: Sales orders may be classified according to sales districts, amount of sales, sales representative, date (year, month, day), and merchandise sold.

   e. *Sorting:* The physical process of arranging data in specific classifications is known as *sorting.*

   EXAMPLE: Stevens is a part-time sales clerk who works 30 hours per week. Each week she fills out her time card and turns it in on Friday morning to her department supervisor. The time cards are separated into two groups (full-time employees and part-time employees).

   f. *Merging:* Often, two sets of data need to be merged (united) so that a single report may be developed.

EXAMPLE: The information from Stevens' time card (total number of hours worked during the week) will need to be merged with number of exemptions, insurance premiums, hourly wage, social security percentage, and so on to arrive at the figures to be computed.

g. *Calculating:* Perhaps the most important part of the process is the manipulation phase, where any mathematical computation is performed.

EXAMPLE: Stevens' take-home pay will be calculated so that the net pay will appear on the appropriate reports as well as her paycheck.

h. *Storage and retrieval:* The results from processing the data (input) must be retained (stored) in some usable form for future reference as long as the results are needed for the operation of the business. *Retrieval* is the process of searching for and gaining access to stored information.

EXAMPLE: Payroll data for one time period are stored and accumulated so that quarterly and annual reports can be prepared later.

i. *Summarizing:* Often large quantities of data are reduced, or summarized, into a more usable form. Details can be accumulated to obtain totals or compute averages.

EXAMPLE: The total sales for the month can be accumulated for all districts or regions within the company, with totals computed for daily, weekly, and monthly sales. This information can be combined with data from previous months to arrive at an accumulated sales total for the year to date.

j. *Report writing:* Facts obtained through the processing of data need to be analyzed and communicated in some type of report form to persons or groups with the responsibility and authority to use the information for decision-making purposes. Facts become information only when they are received, accepted, and used by decision makers.

EXAMPLE: A report of total sales to date, which includes sales districts; amount of sales per marketing representative; and daily, weekly, and monthly totals, may be combined with a report of the goods that have been sold to make decisions on what products need to receive more advertising and promotion dollars during the coming month.

2. *Operation Modes:* Various methods of operation are available with computer systems to facilitate the needs of businesses with specific types of applications. Here is a brief review of some of these operation modes.

a. *Input/output processing:* There are two ways of processing input data: real-time processing and batch processing.

    (1) *Real-time processing:* As each transaction occurs, the data are entered into the computer system and processed and immediate results produced. Direct-access storage devices are required for real-time processing.

    (2) *Batch processing:* The procedure for processing data for similar transactions by holding them for a predetermined period of time so that they can be processed as a group in a single computer run is known as *batch processing.* All the transactions are processed at the same time in sequence.

b. *Remote access:* Sometimes input/output devices (terminals) located at a remote office (branch office) need to be connected to the central computer to enter data as well as receive processing results.

    c. *Multiprocessing:* When two or more instructions need to be executed simultaneously in a single computer system, *multiprocessing* takes place. This requires the computer system to have two or more processor units (CPUs). In a multiprocessing environment, the instructions being executed could be from one user or instructions from multiple users. The operating system software needs to support multiprocessing.

    d. *Multiprogramming:* To decrease the amount of time a computer is "idle," multiprogramming makes possible the concurrent execution of two or more programs. In other words, there is more than one processing job that is being executed at the same time. This means that there can be multiple users or one user with several programs. Multiprogramming operating system software directs the CPU to switch back and forth between multiple programs (requests).

    e. *On-line operations:* When data entry terminals are connected on-line to the computer, data can be entered directly into the computer. The computer controls the operations involved.

    f. *Interactive operations:* When there is frequent interchange between the user at the terminal and the processor unit during execution of a program, an interactive mode is in effect. The user receives prompts from the computer, responds to them, and receives further information or additional prompts from the computer. The result is a flow of information in both directions.

    g. *Time-sharing operations:* More than one user may need to use the computer system at the same time; each user acts independently of any other user on the system. Since each user would be using a terminal and communicating with the computer on an individual basis, it would seem that he or she is the only person using that system at that time, even though in reality many are.

    h. *Teleprocessing:* Teleprocessing is the transmission of data over standard phone lines or special data lines from terminals at remote locations to the mainframe computer. Once the data have been transmitted to the computer, whatever operations are required are controlled by the computer system and the software programs, with the results reported back over the same communication lines to the remote locations.

    i. *Networking:* In this operation mode, computers that are located at various locations are linked together by communication lines. Data can then be transmitted directly from one computer to another. Networking provides a link between departments and the types of data created in each. Many users believe that such integration capabilities are a necessity in an automated office environment. (For a more in-depth discussion on networking, see Section C-5.)

3. *Application Software:* Within a particular business or industry, there are specific processing applications that have been developed that are the main reasons for businesses to use the computer. These applications vary from department to department according to each department's unique needs. If the application is one to be designed for use on a mainframe computer, information systems personnel will assist in developing and implementing the new application. If, however, the application is one to be used with a minicomputer or microcomputer system installed in a particular department, information resource personnel or possibly the vendor will provide the needed support for the implementation of the new application. Cross-industry application software (e.g., payroll, accounts receivable, or inventory) is software designed for generic use by many users. Industry-specific application software (e.g., credit loan programs, legal programs, or insurance programs) is designed for specialized industries.

EXAMPLE: In most large corporations where the information systems department is assisting with the development of new applications to be used with the mainframe computer, there may be a waiting period of two or three years as priorities are set for these applications. However, applications for use with minicomputers or microcomputers usually take only a short while (days or weeks after installation) because of easy-to-use end-user software now available. This is one reason that many companies are installing microcomputers at such a fast rate.

a. *Accounting applications:* Basic accounting data are very important to a business, especially in the ways data are converted to information that management can use in decision making. Five basic accounting systems are used in most companies: accounts receivable, accounts payable, payroll, inventory, and general accounting.

  (1) *Accounts receivable:* Accounts receivable monitors sales accounts for which the customer has a period of time in which to pay the balance. The functions usually included in the accounts receivable system are the following:

   (a) Recording the sales

   (b) Checking the customer's credit

   (c) Invoicing

   (d) Recording cash sales

   (e) updating accounts as payments are made

   (f) Billing

   (g) Analyzing account balances

  (2) *Accounts payable:* Accounts payable is a system for paying obligations of the company. Computer applications have been particularly helpful in being sure that accounts are paid on time so that the company can take advantage of the discounts that are allowable.

  (3) *Payroll:* Computations in handling the payroll are intricate. The computer system provides the tool necessary to keep all the required reporting in order, especially that required by the government.

  (4) *Inventory:* Computerized inventories are *perpetual;* that is, every addition or deletion from inventory stock is recorded, and the quantity on hand is updated on a regular basis. Daily updating is common. With the computer as an analytical tool, essential information can be obtained from an inventory system, such as an analysis of the demand for each product in order to forecast future inventory needs.

  (5) *General accounting:* Companies must keep track of assets, liabilities, capital, income, and expenses. To do this, every company must establish an accounting system that will produce data for information reports, a balance sheet showing assets, liabilities, and capital and an income statement showing income (revenue) and expenses. Computer systems can perform accounting functions more accurately, faster, and inexpensively than can be done manually.

b. *Marketing applications:* Development of products, pricing, promotion, and distribution of those products are primary concerns of the marketing function in business. Information processing systems provide much information required to perform these functions effectively. With the use of the computer, marketing information can be analyzed more thoroughly to provide management with more consistent information on which to base decisions about the product line.

c. *Financial applications:* Firms must identify sources of funds and acquire enough funds to support marketing, manufacturing, and daily operations. These funds must then be controlled effectively. Information provided by the financial system describes money flow and permits business personnel to handle their financial decision-making responsibilities.

d. *Manufacturing applications:* Computer-aided design (CAD) and computer-aided manufacturing (CAM) are software programs that have automated the product design and manufacturing functions of many production firms. Material requirements planning (MRP) is software that helps a firm anticipate future raw material needs. Production, inventory, cost, and quality are all aspects of manufacturing that can now be automated through manufacturing information systems.

e. *Human resource applications:* Today, government reports are required on the recruiting, staffing, and training and development of a firm's human resources. These processes can be effectively managed with the assistance of a human resource information system.

f. *End-user applications:* With the advancement to user-friendly software, 4GLs, and graphical user interfaces (GUIs), nontechnical business personnel have hands-on use of computing power. The computer can now be utilized to make the dissemination and analysis of information easier, enhancing decision making with more accurate, timely, and relevant reports. The handling of the firm's data is becoming more important as computer systems are used more and more for these types of applications.

(1) *Applications for processing words:* Computers are being used to integrate word processing into the organization. Some of the ways in which the computer is most helpful in the processing of words throughout the organization include text processing and electronic mail.

(a) *Text processing:* Input devices such as terminals (keyboards) or telephones can be used to provide either keyed-in information or spoken (verbal) information to be processed through word processing. With the use of the computer, a number of features are now available that lessen the time of the operator in preparing documents:

- *Electronic dictionaries:* Thousands of words typically used in business are included in a "dictionary" so that the operator can access the dictionary and run a spelling check on the document being produced.

- *Movement of information:* Information contained in a document may be moved around within the document, from page to page, or material may be exchanged easily with new material (updating reports).

- *Document templates:* Standard formats for business letters, memoranda, and other types of business forms are already stored in word processing for use by the end user in adapting to the message to be prepared and sent.

(b) *Electronic mail:* With the computer as a transmission device, messages in the form of electronic mail may be transmitted to various locations quickly and easily. The sender indicates to whom the message is to be sent, keys in the message on a terminal, and requests transmission. In a matter of seconds, the message has arrived at its destination, the electronic mailbox of the receiver, ready for access.

(2) *Electronic spreadsheet applications:* A spreadsheet is an electronic worksheet. Any worksheet application is suitable for use on a spreadsheet. Once each data item is entered in its appropriate cell (row and column), calculations are handled automatically. Business managers utilize this tool in their daily decision-making processes (what-if situations).

(3) *Data management applications:* Many departments have the responsibility of recording and filing information. Now business data can be stored electronically with the use of data management software. The data are stored on a secondary storage device where access can be provided as needed. A popular business situation utilizing data management software is mass mailing lists. In large database environments, a 4GL query language is used to access needed information.

(4) *Graphics applications:* Pictorial data are sometimes easier to understand than the written word. Horizontal bar charts, vertical bar charts, pie charts, and histograms are all possible ways to display the information when graphics software is utilized. A plotter or a printer capable of printing graphics must be connected to the computer using graphics software if a hard copy is desired.

(5) *Desktop publishing:* Combining text, graphics, and advanced formatting features allows companies to design their own documents for printing. This can be accomplished with desktop application software or with the more sophisticated versions of word processing software. The steps to prepare a document using desktop publishing are the same as word processing: create or import text and graphics, format, save, and print, with *page layout* as an additional important initial step required for desktop publishing.

(6) *Multimedia and presentation software:* Uniting sound, text, video, and pictures allows businesses to create multimedia presentations. Special hardware (e.g., speakers, soundboard, microphones, CD-ROM drives, and music boards), along with other technology, such as camcorder, videocassette recorder, digital camera, videodiscs, and scanner, are the components of a multimedia system. The use of authoring software enables input from these components to be combined into multimedia presentations.

Presentation packages enable users to create their own artistic drawings or clip art with a variety of colors, patterns, and text options in documents, slides, and transparencies. Speaker presentations are visually enhanced with these computer aids.

4. *Integrated Office Systems:* Managing the information system requires a view of the entire business as the departments function independently as well as interactively.

Typical departments within an organization that must interact with one another are accounting, marketing and sales, manufacturing and inventory, finance, and human resources (personnel).

In meeting the business objectives, each department performs its specific functions. These functions must then be integrated so that the organizational structure of the entire operation effectively works together.

a. *Levels of management:* Integration has different meanings at different levels within the organization. The primary objective of integrating departmental functions is to provide top-level management with a total picture of companywide operations. Integration within organizations is accomplished through the implementation of workstation, department, organizational, and global strategies (see Chapter 6).

(1) *Top-level managerial decision making:* Top-level managers (executives) are involved with *strategic decision making*—activities required to establish organizational long-range goals and policies.

EXAMPLES: Setting of objectives for growth and additions, approval of plans, and adoption of strategies to achieve these objectives.

(2) *Middle-level managerial decision making:* Middle-level managers are involved with *tactical decision making*—activities required to implement the strategies established by top-level managers. These can be referred to as *short-term goals.*

EXAMPLES: Planning working capital, scheduling production, formulating budgets, and administering personnel functions.

(3) *Lower-level managerial decision making:* Lower-level managers are involved with *operational decision making*—activities required to ensure that specific jobs are completed on time. These are usually recognized as day-to-day decisions.

EXAMPLES: Maintaining inventory records, preparing sales invoices and shipping records, and assigning jobs to workers.

b. *Departmental integration:* As departments work independently, they concentrate on specific departmental objectives. Integration of their functions brings together the overlapping of their organizational goals and objectives. Figure 1–5 illustrates the independence and integration of typical departments.

5. *Networking:* A *network* is a system consisting of a number of peripherals that are accessible to one another through communication links. A network enables data to move among the various components (peripheral devices) of the information system. The sharing of a CPU, business data, and software by local or remote locations is possible with network processing. Every distributed processing system must employ some means of transmitting data required by the central headquarters. (Chapter 3 elaborates on networks in use today.)

a. *Software:* Software for operating the network (network operating system) is required for the central (main) computer, front-end processors, distributed processors, and telecommunications equipment. These programs perform the following basic functions: routing of information, integrity of data, system security, and performance statistics of the network.

Figure 1–5   Typical Business Applications

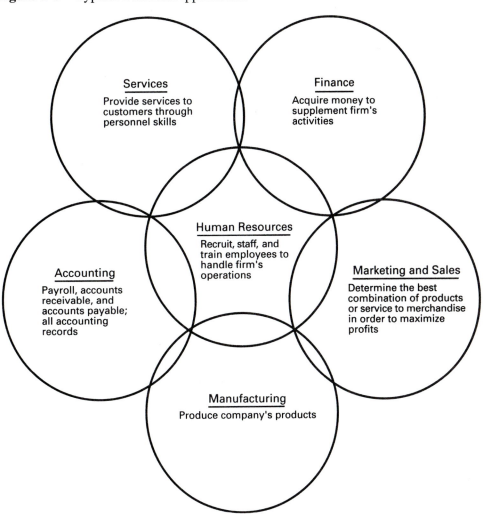

b. *Network configurations:* Network processing may form either local or wide area networks. A *local area network* (LAN) is a system that has peripheral devices connected directly to a CPU within one location. A *wide area network* (WAN) connects the peripheral devices to one (or multiple) CPUs through communication channels over a large geographic area.

(1) *Local area networks:* The sharing of peripheral devices, information, and software is provided through interconnecting computers (including microcomputers) in a single building. Sharing peripheral devices and software reduces the cost of computer services to all departments (see Chapter 3, Section F-2).

EXAMPLE: Each of the three departments within a business (accounting, marketing, and manufacturing/inventory) has its own microcomputer and a dot-matrix printer. For high-speed, letter-quality hard copies, each microcomputer is networked to one central laser printer. Sharing of information is also important in managing the entire information system (the business). Information stored on a central hard disk unit to which each department microcomputer is networked provides greater data integrity. There is less duplication of data. Data can be accessed easily and quickly from any location within the network.

(2) *Network configurations:* Different types of structures can be utilized to implement a network: a bus configuration, a star configuration, and a ring configuration. These configurations are called *network topologies.* For a schematic of the types of network configurations, see Figure 1–6.

(a) *Bus configuration:* In a bus configuration, all peripheral devices are attached by a communications cable. Each device has a communications interface unit that manages the flow of data to and from each device. The bus is a single circuit of limited length where devices can be attached at any point. This configuration, along with the star and the ring, is typical of local area networks. The star and the ring are also topologies for wide area networks (see Figure 1–6).

(b) *Star configuration:* A central computer is required in a star configuration. The central computer is called a *central node, central control, switch,* or *hub.* All transactions are processed through the central CPU before being routed to the appropriate network device. This provides a central decision point. However, if the central CPU is down, all shared processing stops (see Figure 1–6).

Figure 1–6   Types of Network Configurations

BUS CONFIGURATION

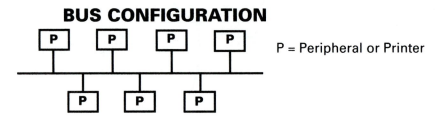

P = Peripheral or Printer

STAR CONFIGURATION

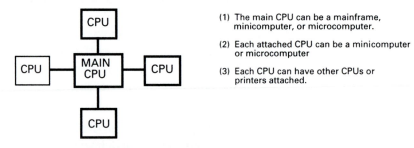

(1) The main CPU can be a mainframe, minicomputer, or microcomputer.

(2) Each attached CPU can be a minicomputer or microcomputer

(3) Each CPU can have other CPUs or printers attached.

RING CONFIGURATION

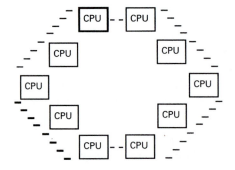

(1) Each CPU can be a mainframe, minicomputer, or microcomputer.

(2) Each CPU can have other CPUs or printers attached.

(c) *Ring configuration:* To eliminate reliance on a central decision point, a ring configuration may be implemented. The CPUs at the remote locations are linked by a unidirectional transmission line forming a closed path. If a CPU or peripheral is down, a "bypass relay" serves as a partial solution to the issue of network reliability (see Figure 1–6).

(3) *Local area network models:* No matter what network configuration is applied, local area networks follow a client/server or peer-to-peer model.

(a) *Client/server model:* The client/server model uses a microcomputer as a server to its clients (users). The server is designed with operating system and application software to specifically meet the client's needs. This model is designed for specific client applications, thus serving the client's needs very efficiently.

(b) *Peer-to-peer model:* The peer-to-peer model is designed so that all computers on the network can access all organizational data, application software, public files, and peripherals connected to the network. This model is recommended for small networks of less than 10 computers, as the network tends to decrease in efficiency with heavy use.

D. Innovations in Information Processing

Processing data is a vital component of any business system. Many organizations would not survive without the supportive services provided by the computer and the many applications for communications, word processing, and records processing. The computer has had a profound effect on the processing of information as well as the social interaction in the office. Here are some of the trends taking place in information processing that affect how businesses function.

1. *Increased Use of Microcomputers, Desktop Workstations, and Laptop Computers:* The advanced technology in processing speed and internal storage size of microcomputers has brought the processing power to the business user while in the office and traveling. This, along with more user-friendly software and lower costs, has made a significant impact on computer processing in business in the 1990s. Computer use for specific accounting, marketing, word processing, and desktop publishing applications, in addition to newer computer operations such as computer-aided graphics and decision support systems, will be felt by business through the 21st century.

2. *Storage Capacity:* Computers will continue to be upgraded with more storage potential. At the present time, such devices as the very large-scale integrated chip (VLSIC) are providing almost unlimited power to computers as far as storage is concerned. VLSICs are packed with as many as 200,000 to 1.2 million circuits per chip. Today, mainframe computers typically have 50 to over 200 MB (1 MB equals 1 million bytes) of random access memory (RAM), with supercomputers having 300 MB or more of RAM to several gigabytes (1 billion bytes equals 1 GB). Minicomputers range between 30 to 125 MB of RAM, desktop workstations (microcomputers) between 64 and 128 MB of RAM, and the standard home microcomputer between 32 and 64 MB of RAM. Continued advancements in internal computer memory and internal processing speeds are being researched through optical processing. These technological advancements make it easier for business to expand computer applications.

3. *Importance of Human Relations:* Contrary to what some might think, human relations in the office is becoming even more important with the utilization of computers

and the rapid processing of information. It is not easy for people to work with high technology, let alone understand exactly how the computer can process information so quickly. It will continue to be important for information systems personnel to be able to work with people in other departments while using the computer as a tool. Electronic mail, intranets, and the Internet will continue to play significant roles in how business personnel, locally and globally, communicate with one another (see Chapter 3). Information is power. To maintain an information edge, it is important for administrative professionals to become familiar with computer technology and how the computer can be better utilized in today's electronic environment.

4. *Ethical and Legal Considerations in Using Computer Systems:* Information systems will continue to see changes in technology, software, and usage in both the home and business. Such changes always challenge existing values and cause society to think about the right and wrong ways to use new innovations. Security measures help prevent unauthorized use of data; intentional damage to hardware, software, and data; and misuse of software.

   a. *Unauthorized use:* When individuals access computer systems without permission, they have access to data that should not be available to them. Unauthorized use of computer data could lead to illegal acts—theft of product plans or illegal transfer of funds. To prevent unauthorized use of data, data storage can be secured through user password, database user directories, and encryption. Through encryption, messages are scrambled before transmission to prevent unauthorized access to the information. Once received, the information must be decripted (unscrambled) in order to be read.

   b. *Intentional damage:* Intentional damage to hardware, software, or data can come from an outsider or a disgruntled employee. Damaged equipment will stop processing, altered system or application software will affect processing results, and altered or deleted records or files will affect data accuracy. A computer virus is one of the most current ways of destroying data and software. A computer virus is a software program written to intentionally destroy stored data or disrupt processing and memory systems. Specific programs called *vaccines* or *antivirus software* have been developed to locate and remove computer viruses. With approximately 175 new viruses created each month, management must continually update their antivirus software to be proactive to this issue.

   c. *Misuse of software:* All computer software is licensed or registered in the name of the owner. A *license* is the right to use the software under certain conditions. Different types of licenses include single-use licenses, site licenses, and network licenses.

      (1) *Single-use licenses:* A single software program is licensed (registered) to be used on a specific computer.

      (2) *Site licenses:* A site license allows multiple computers at one business location to use a copy of the software. In some cases, a site license extends the use of the software to a business employee's home computer for a small additional fee.

      (3) *Network licenses:* A network license allows multiple computers on the network system to have access to the network software.

   Licenses are designed to protect the copyrights held by the developers of software programs.

Review Questions

Directions: Select the best answer from the four alternatives. Write your answer in the blank to the left of the question.

_____ 1. The major function of business processing is

    a. storing data/information for future use.
    b. source data automation.
    c. processing unorganized data into meaningful business information.
    d. preparation of source documents.

_____ 2. XYZ Office Supplies Inc. receives an order for 12 dozen electronic typewriter ribbons from the B&Y law firm. Which of the following is considered the source document for the transaction?

    a. The check issued by B&Y law firm for payment of the invoice
    b. The inventory record of XYZ Office Supplies Inc. showing the quantity of typewriter ribbons available for sale
    c. The invoice issued by XYZ Office Supplies Inc.
    d. The purchase order received from B&Y law firm

_____ 3. Unique data used to identify a person, place, or thing are stored in a

    a. central processing unit (CPU).
    b. key field.
    c. record.
    d. systems program.

_____ 4. The main logic element in today's computers that allows computers to be faster, more reliable, smaller, and less expensive is

    a. magnetic drum.
    b. transistors.
    c. vacuum tubes.
    d. very large-scale integrated circuits (VLSICs).

_____ 5. The main memory of the computer is known as

    a. auxiliary storage.
    b. primary storage.
    c. secondary storage.
    d. virtual memory.

_____ 6. Portable computing became popular with the creation of

    a. desktop workstations.
    b. notebook computers.

c. personal computers.
d. supercomputers.

7. Optical disk technology that allows the user to store, access, and reuse disks is called

    a. CD-E disks.
    b. magnetic disks.
    c. magnetic-ink character recognition (MICR).
    d. WORM disks.

8. Source data automation is made possible through the use of

    a. Jaz cartridges.
    b. magnetic disk pacs.
    c. magnetic-ink character recognition.
    d. optical recognition.

9. The user interface that uses icons to illustrate systems options is called

    a. function keys.
    b. graphical user interface.
    c. menu.
    d. screen prompt.

10. As the executive secretary for the marketing department, Benson uses her desktop workstation to generate sales reports showing daily sales by district. These reports include multicolored graphs that are reviewed by the marketing manager daily. The reports are examples of

    a. character printer output.
    b. computer output microfilm.
    c. ink-jet printer output.
    d. plotter output.

11. A large reprographics department is the most likely location for a/an

    a. character printer.
    b. electrothermal printer.
    c. page printer.
    d. table plotter.

12. With graphics and color common on most hard-copy output, a typical office output device is a/an

    a. impact printer.
    b. ink-jet printer.
    c. plotter.
    d. visual display terminal.

13. A 64-bit CPU means that

    a. the CPU can handle 64 words in one machine cycle.
    b. the CPU can internally move eight characters at one time.

c. the CPU can move 512 characters in one operation.

d. the internal storage capacity is 64,000 characters.

14. An option that can be added to a computer system to make it run faster by mini-mizing the need to access secondary storage is

a. cache memory.

b. random access memory (RAM).

c. secondary memory.

d. virtual memory.

15. Real-time processing requires direct access. Direct access requires

a. magnetic disk storage.

b. magnetic tape storage.

c. mass storage.

d. multiprocessing.

16. In multiprogramming environments where two or more programs are processed at the same time, the operating system makes sure that the jobs do not get intermixed through

a. data management.

b. data protection.

c. job queuing.

d. resource allocation.

17. An example of a 4GL for the nontechnical end user is a/an

a. application generator.

b. inventory control program.

c. query language.

d. spreadsheet.

18. An example of a general-purpose application program for office professionals is a

a. mortgage processing software program.

b. query language.

c. report generator.

d. spreadsheet.

19. A powerful general-purpose language for developing software on minicomputers or microcomputers is

a. BASIC.

b. C.

c. COBOL.

d. Pascal.

20. An object-oriented language designed by Microsoft specifically for windows envi-ronments for the development of graphical user interfaces for applications is

a. C.

b. Hypertext Markup Language (HTML).

       c. Java.
       d. Visual Basic.

21. The computer operation that separates sales orders into cash, credit, and layaway groups is known as

    a. classifying.
    b. merging.
    c. sorting.
    d. verifying.

22. Every two weeks Corporate processes the payroll for hourly employees at all Glory Day offices. The sequential processing of all the hourly payroll at Corporate is known as

    a. batch processing.
    b. direct processing.
    c. multiprocessing.
    d. remote processing.

23. You are being interviewed by the director of the information technology division for an administrative assistant position. In discussing the computer system, it is explained as a multiprogramming environment. You understand this to mean that

    a. the company has a local area network.
    b. the computer has little idle time because the operating system software can direct the CPU to switch between multiple programs during execution.
    c. teleprocessing is a computing option for remote locations.
    d. two or more processor units are in the computer system providing simultaneous program execution.

24. Software that provides information about acquiring and controlling funds to support marketing, manufacturing, and daily operations is

    a. accounting software.
    b. financial software.
    c. manufacturing software.
    d. marketing software.

25. End-user software that best handles what-if decision situations is

    a. graphics.
    b. data management.
    c. spreadsheet.
    d. word processing.

26. To prepare a document using desktop publishing software, the steps are the same as preparing word processing documents with an initial step of

    a. creating text.
    b. formatting the document.

c. importing graphics.

d. designing the page layout.

27. Which one of the following represents the primary objective of integrating the business information system?

a. Departmental independency is eliminated.

b. Departments are allowed to concentrate on the specific departmental objective.

c. Lower-level managers can handle tactical decision making.

d. Top-level management is provided with a total picture of companywide objectives.

28. The sharing of peripheral devices, information, and software through the interconnecting of microcomputers in a single building is known as establishing a

a. local area network.

b. peer-to-peer network.

c. star network.

d. wide area network.

29. Unauthorized use of computer data can lead to illegal acts. To prevent unauthorized use, firms can secure their data by

a. installing a client/server network model.

b. purchasing a site license.

c. purchasing an antivirus program.

d. using passwords or data user directories.

30. Because of company growth, your workload has increased. You would like to work at home but need a copy of the office software. What does the company need to obtain in order to install their software on your home computer?

a. Encryption

b. Network license

c. Site license

d. Software license

Solutions

Answer	Refer to:
1. (c)	[A]
2. (d)	[A-1-c]
3. (b)	[A-4-b(2)]
4. (d)	[B-1-e(2)(a)]
5. (b)	[B-2-a(2)(a)]
6. (b)	[B-2-b(3)(b)]
7. (a)	[B-2-c(1)(g)]
8. (d)	[B-2-c(1)(i)]
9. (b)	[B-2-c(3)(a)]
10. (c)	[B-2-d(2)(c)]
11. (c)	[B-2-d(2)(c)]
12. (b)	[B-2-d(2)(c)]
13. (b)	[B-2-e(1)(a)]
14. (a)	[B-2-e(1)(a)]
15. (a)	[B-2-e(2)(a)]
16. (b)	[B-3-a(4)(b)]
17. (c)	[B-3-c]
18. (d)	[B-3-c]
19. (b)	[B-4-c(4)]
20. (d)	[B-4-e(2)]
21. (c)	[C-1-e]
22. (a)	[C-2-a(2)]

23. (b)   [C-2-d]

24. (b)   [C-3-c]

25. (c)   [C-3-f(2)]

26. (b)   [C-3-f(5)]

27. (d)   [C-4-a]

28. (a)   [C-5-b(1)]

29. (d)   [D-4-a]

30. (c)   [D-4-c(2)]

CHAPTER 2

Word/Information Processing

OVERVIEW

Use of the computer for word processing and other software applications has provided the greatest motivation for change in office systems. Word processing, as an office system, has three primary components, all of which must be present if the system is to be operational: people, technology/environment, and procedures. People are considered the most important component because word processing (or any other business application) cannot be implemented unless there are trained people who are competent to handle the operations.

Word processing, as a part of the total information processing effort within an organization, is the most commonly used software application. The two primary functions included in a word processing system are the word processing support function (the automated preparation of documents in the form of reports, letters, memoranda, newsletters, and other types of publications) and the administrative function (office support, which typically includes those duties requiring telephoning, greeting visitors, filing and records management, or other office procedures). Word processing application software is available in a single program to be used with one computer as well as in integrated suites or packages for networked computers (ranging in number from a few to hundreds) on mainframe, minicomputer, or microcomputer systems.

The microcomputer has become very popular for word processing because of its versatility in supporting other applications software programs (database, spreadsheet, graphics, and desktop publishing) that are integrated with word processing. How technology is used for word processing depends on the particular information processing needs of the organization.

Computer systems with word processing capability are being linked through telecommunications to other office information systems, such as records management and micrographics systems. An extension of word processing, desktop publishing, is providing office professionals with the opportunity to be creative and imaginative in developing professional brochures, newsletters, and other in-house publications. The installation of local area networks (LANs) and other integrated systems is a development that holds much promise for the future.

KEY TERMS

Administrative support	Discrete media	Random access
Analog technology	Disk operating system	Secondary file
Career path	Floppy disk	Shared-resource system
Centralized dictation	Hard copy	Technical support
system	Impact printer	Technology
Computer-aided	Integration	Transcription
transcription	Lateral career path	Transparent
Correspondence	Local area network (LAN)	User
Database	Marketing support	Vertical career path
Default format	Microcomputer	Visual display
Density	Networked system	Windows operating system
Desktop publishing	Partial-page display	Word processing
Digital electronic system	Printer	Word processing support
Digital technology	Procedures	

A. Word Processing

The most commonly used software application in business today is word processing. *Word processing* is the preparation of business documents in correct format by trained personnel using computer hardware and software technology. Whereas information processing is concerned with the entering of numeric text and data for manipulation, word processing is concerned with keying in word text in acceptable format so that business reports, letters, and memoranda can be prepared for business use. Word processing requires the operator to make decisions on what the final document will look like. Primary concern is also focused on how the information is stored for later retrieval.

1. *Document Preparation:* The kinds of business documents typically prepared include correspondence (memoranda and letters) and reports (informational and analytical). Text is keyed into the system with format commands, printed out for review and approval, and stored on magnetic media for later retrieval.

2. *Skills Needed for Document Preparation:* Word processing support specialists need to have a middle to high level of competence with language skills, familiarity with the computer keyboard, the ability to make formatting decisions, and basic computer skills required to perform word processing functions.

    a. *Language skills:* The person who performs word processing functions must have a strong basis in language skills (sentence structure, grammar, punctuation, and spelling). Reading the content of high-quality manuscripts and instructional or operations manuals requires a rather high level of reading skill as well.

    b. *Keyboarding skills:* With the quantity of textual material that needs to be keyed in, the word processing support specialist must be able to key in word text at acceptable rates, perhaps 65 to 95 words per minute. Touch-typing skill is a must! The efficient operator must be able to manipulate the alphanumeric keyboard without looking at the keys. At times the operator will find it necessary to look at the word processing function keys before depressing them since those keys tend to be multifunction keys.

    c. *Formatting skills:* A knowledge of acceptable styles for letters, memoranda, and reports is absolutely essential for the word processing support specialist. In addition, skill will be needed to enter appropriate commands for formatting documents as required in a specific word processing software package. Formatting includes setting margins, headers, footers, page numbers, and any other feature that affects the way the text appears on a page.

d. *Basic computer skills:* Understanding basic computer operations (turning the computer on or off, inserting disks, storing and retrieving documents, and changing defaults) is another essential set of skills. Whereas information processing personnel must be concerned with the inner workings of computers, word processing personnel are more concerned with making accurate decisions about the preparation of documents so that the output (printed copies) will be acceptable for business use and the text stored properly for future retrieval.

e. *Learning skills:* The word processing operator is constantly learning to apply new features or techniques as needed to make documents look more businesslike and professional. The person who spends considerable time working with word processing must have a desire and willingness to continue to learn new skills. The technology will continue to change and become more complex, and the word processing support specialist must be adaptable to such new learning opportunities.

Typically, office professionals enroll for workshops, seminars, or courses in word processing to prepare themselves adequately to use specific software applications on the job. A number of different applications are available, but what a person needs to learn depends on the needs of the organization for whom he or she works. Several word processing software applications programs are available at this time that are proving to be quite popular in business organizations.

**B. Word/
Information
Processing
Personnel**

Word processing requires at least one *user* (author) and support or operational personnel (operators, proofreaders, and supervisors). Considered the most important component of an office system, personnel are becoming highly specialized. Procedures (the way word processing is organized and made available for use) and technology (hardware, software, and environment) are the other components. If people trained in word processing are not present, however, the system cannot become operational.

1. *Document Origination:* The person for whom a document is prepared is known as the *user.* Although *user* is the most common term today, the terms *principal, originator,* or *author* are also appropriate. The user must provide clear instructions and input for documents to be prepared through word processing. When the document is ready, it will be transmitted to the user for final approval or further revision in the form of hard copy (paper) or soft copy (disk copy or electronic mail).

2. *Document Preparation:* Documents prepared through word processing include letters, memoranda, reports, and other kinds of text. Word processing personnel are directly involved in document preparation; they are most often called *word processing support specialists.* Within large firms, there may be different levels of word processing support personnel, from the manager down to the operational level, depending on responsibility and experience. Word processing support can be provided by one or more centralized units. Within a small firm, however, only a few people may be involved directly with document preparation, possibly one to three. Here are some typical job titles within word processing and some of the duties and responsibilities usually assigned to each:

a. *Manager:* Manage all word processing operations and support personnel, research and select new word/information processing technology, evaluate productivity, assess human resource needs, evaluate employee performance, and select and oversee training of new employees.

b. *Supervisor:* Monitor production and scheduling, assist with selection of new technology, conduct employee training or retraining with new systems, and assist word processing support specialists with problems concerning document preparation.

c. *Coordinator:* Maintain productivity records, distribute workload among word processing support specialists, establish and monitor production deadlines, inform supervisor of project status, assist with on-the-job training or retraining as needed, assist personnel with job-related personal situations (vacations, absenteeism, and personal time), and monitor turnaround times for document preparation.

d. *Word processing support specialist:* Use word/information processing technology with computer systems for text processing, prepare a wide variety of documents, submit productivity records (quantity and completion time), and perform document revision and editing functions.

e. *Proofreader:* Proofread documents produced through word processing, understand the style formats to be used throughout the organization, follow standardized proofreading rules based on word usage standards in effect for specific documents, and provide feedback to support specialists for document revisions.

Figure 2–1 shows an example of the structure for levels of word processing support personnel.

3. *Administrative Support:* Those office functions not requiring keyboarding input to the computer for various applications but carried on simultaneously for executives and managers in different locations throughout the firm are known as *administrative support.* Basic responsibilities include telephoning, mailing, receiving visitors, scheduling appointments, and managing records. Administrative support may be

Figure 2–1   Operational-to-Managerial Career Paths in Word/Information Processing

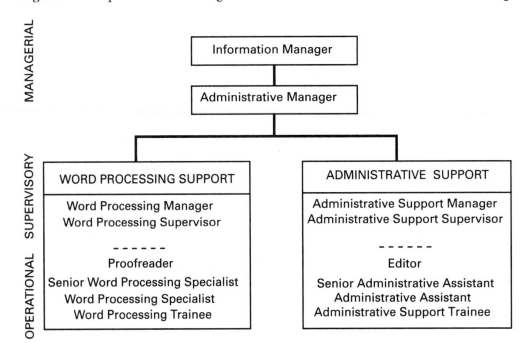

centralized, with services provided through a support center for the organization, or *departmentalized,* with services available within departments or divisions of the firm.

EXAMPLE: Brummell-Standish Inc. specializes in the preparation of procedures manuals to accompany newly developed software programs. A centralized word/information processing center was established several years ago when the volume of documents being prepared began to escalate. However, administrative support has always been maintained within each of the departments to provide adequate assistance with other office operations. The marketing department, for example, must have administrative support (secretaries and administrative assistants) to take care of office responsibilities, especially the communications necessary to handle incoming orders for software programs and manuals each day.

As is true with document preparation, there may be several levels of administrative support personnel within an organization. Here are some job titles and a sample of job responsibilities for each:

a.   *Manager:* Manage all administrative support personnel and operations, establish administrative support procedures to support company policy, assess human resource needs for administrative support, evaluate personnel performance, and recruit and select new administrative support staff.

b.   *Supervisor:* Manage daily administrative support activities within a department, communicate with users about word/information processing requirements, determine turnaround time and quality of document preparation required, distribute work to administrative support coordinator, establish and maintain appropriate records management systems, and make priority decisions.

c.   *Coordinator:* Assign work to administrative support personnel, review specifications for specific assignments, inform supervisor of status of tasks requiring special attention, act as backup person as needed, and assist with the maintenance of the records management system.

d.   *Administrative or executive assistant:* Provide administrative support to principals, prepare documents for review by principals prior to word processing, reproduce or copy documents, assist in research, schedule appointments, and proofread and edit documents.

e.   *Receptionist:* Perform routine reception duties for the firm or office, direct visitors or deliveries to appropriate departments, provide backup telephone support for any office, and perform miscellaneous office tasks as needed.

Figure 2–1 shows an example of the structure for levels of administrative support personnel.

4.   *Career Paths in Word/Information Processing:* Word processing has changed the nature of office careers. In fact, administrative and secretarial positions today include word/information processing as an essential skill. Administrative managers see word processing competence as a possible avenue toward positions of even greater responsibility and challenge. Generally, there are three basic position levels within an organization: operational, supervisory, and managerial. A *career path* is a sequencing of employment positions toward advancement and promotion along professional lines for which one prepares in terms of education, training, and work experience. A *lateral* career path permits people to transfer to positions at a comparable level to the one presently held but located in different departments or work groups. A *vertical*

career path leads upward from the present position to supervisory or managerial levels within the same department or division (see Figure 2–1).

a. *In-house word/information processing careers:* Legal firms, insurance companies, government agencies, and many other types of businesses are identifying word processing as a required rather than a "nice-to-have" function within the business, especially in work that requires the processing of a tremendous amount of information. Career opportunities are emerging for people who enjoy the challenge of implementing new systems or updating systems already in use. Presently, two directions in word processing are receiving much attention: the movement from an operational position to a higher-level supervisory or managerial position in word/information processing and the need for providing in-house training for word/information processing specialists.

(1) *Operational-to-managerial career path:* Within an organization, there is a move toward advancing competent people from within the company.

    (a) *Operational personnel:* In word/information processing, operational personnel are those who actually perform such operations as keyboarding document input, transcription, proofreading, and related operational tasks. Such activities provide the astute person an opportunity to learn more about the company, its organization, its products or services, and basic office operations and functions within the department. The more a person knows about the organization, the better a candidate he or she will be for promotion and advancement.

    (b) *Supervisory personnel:* Supervision of word/information processing specialists takes a keen understanding of word processing as a benefit to the entire organization. A prime concern is how to organize word processing functions to support all users within an organization. Competence in handling interpersonal communication (i.e., discussing assignments with users, delegating, and giving instructions) and supervision strategies needs to be acquired by supervisory personnel. Usually, the word processing supervisor who supervises one or more word/information processing centers is considered a key person to be involved when the purchase or lease of new technology is being considered. It is likely that such a supervisor would be considered a serious candidate for a higher-level position, such as word/information processing manager or administrative manager.

    (c) *Managerial personnel:* Not everyone who works within word/information processing support or administrative support has the opportunity to become a manager, but those with potential will need to demonstrate strong people skills in addition to operational skills. Many organizations prefer to promote from within the organization because persons who have already been involved will have a better grasp of established policies and procedures. Administrative managers, too, may have opportunities to advance into positions that integrate word processing, communications, micrographics, or other office information systems. Familiarity with business information will be an asset in promotional success.

Figure 2–1 indicates possible vertical movements through the various levels of word/information processing toward supervision and management within an organizational structure.

(2) *In-house training programs:* Many companies advertise for office professionals with word processing competence as well as basic language and communication skills. Additional training may be provided so that more advanced, specialized word processing and desktop publishing functions can be mastered. Employers are extremely concerned today about language skills (spelling, punctuation, grammar, and sentence/paragraph structure), keyboarding and formatting, and human relations skills. In-house training programs are available in many organizations to train new employees in word/information processing concepts, operations, and applications that will meet organizational needs. Similar types of programs are popular with secretaries and administrative professionals who may be experienced in secretarial work but need retraining for jobs involving word/information processing. Career opportunities in training are attracting those with word/information processing experience who enjoy teaching and show competence in working with others.

(a) *Trainers:* Organizations hire individuals to teach word/information processing as well as other office skills. Some of the areas in which instruction is available include keyboarding, word processing, office automation, language skills, business communications, transcription, and dictation. Trainers often qualify for certification in teaching specific types of word processing programs (e.g., Microsoft Office or Corel WordPerfect). Such certification programs, administered by specific software vendors, require candidates to complete training and pass examinations before receiving certification as a trainer. Training offered within a particular organization is typically structured to meet specific user or specialist needs.

(b) *Training director:* Usually one person within the company is designated as training director. If the company offers more than one general type of training program, the director might manage all training programs, with a *training supervisor* coordinating aspects of training related to specific skills in word/information processing.

b. *Customer, marketing, and technical support for vendors:* Some people prefer to combine their interest in marketing or sales with their interest in information processing and work in customer, marketing, or technical support for hardware or software vendors. Marketing support representatives are involved with the sale of hardware or software systems (with the actual sale often handled by a sales representative) and training for word/information processing specialists who will be using the newly acquired system. Continuing customer or technical support is provided, usually for a fee, as word/information processing personnel require assistance with more advanced applications or problem solving after the system implementation.

(1) *Demonstrating computer systems and software:* Customer and marketing support representatives participate in the marketing process by demonstrating system operation in performing particular business applications (e.g., word processing, spreadsheet, database, graphics, or desktop publishing) being considered by prospective customers.

(2) *Selling technology and supplies:* Marketing support representatives can be especially helpful to sales representatives since they can research specific applications needed by the organization that is considering the new system. By

discussing possible applications for which the system may be needed with the customer, the marketing support representative is in a position to recommend specific software or procedures to benefit the client's objectives. Recommendations for appropriate supplies and accessories for the system can be helpful, too. In addition to a base salary, the customer, marketing, or technical support representative may earn commissions on the sale of supplies or training support.

(3) *Technical support for vendors:* For the person who is versatile with both the hardware and the software technology, working in technical support for a vendor may be an excellent training ground as well as a career path itself. Whenever a customer purchases hardware or software, the vendor provides a toll-free telephone number to use in case any problem develops that might be answered quickly over the telephone. Typically, technical support specialists are available 24 hours a day to respond to queries about software and specific technical problems. Some software vendors provide such information free of charge to the customer, whereas others charge a fee that depends on the amount of time required in responding to the query. The technical support specialist must be a person who is trained in solving the kinds of hardware or software problems that might be encountered but also has the interpersonal communication skills to be able to explain the solutions over the telephone to the customer.

(4) *Training for operational personnel:* Vendors have developed extensive instructional materials ranging from training disks and videocassettes to tutorials on CD-ROMs. These materials can be adapted by training specialists who will provide the specialized training in word/information processing necessary to operate the new system. Two approaches are generally used:

    (a) *A formal training program:* The vendor may offer a formal training program for one to three days for key individuals who will be the initial operators of the new system. Basic operations and specific applications are usually emphasized in this type of program. Such a formal training program provides the opportunity for the vendor to train the individual designated as the in-house trainer of other operational personnel. This person then trains other office professionals. At any rate, the primary objective of a formal training program is to have the trainee return to the organization ready to implement *basic* word/information processing operations after several hours of intensive training.

    (b) *An informal training session:* The vendor may offer a half- or full-day training session to operators. The training will focus on basic system operation. This training tends to be somewhat informal, with practice in entering text, editing, formatting, integrating with other software programs, and other basic functions. The primary objective is to introduce the operator to the new system, the training materials available, and the basic operations (e.g., turning the system on, opening documents, entering text, editing, and printing). Once the equipment is installed, the operators should have an opportunity to go through the more formal training contained in tutorials or more in-depth instructional programs as directed by their supervisors or trainers within the organization. The informal training program is very helpful to the person who already has previous experience with other word/information processing systems.

With either of these approaches, follow-up training is usually needed for problems developing with either the hardware or the software technology. Another purpose of follow-up is to provide continuing support for more advanced applications, such as graphics and desktop publishing.

EXAMPLE: Edwards has keyed in text for a 20-page report. His initial training in basic word processing skills prepared him well for keying in the text, editing, and running a spelling check. However, he will need to be able to change the format to accommodate headers for each page except the first page, page numbers appearing at the bottom right corner of each page, an unjustified right margin, and scanning graphic images into appropriate places within the report. His manager has indicated that several graphic illustrations and at least one spreadsheet need to be included at designated places within the report.

  c. *Consulting:* A person who learned word processing "through the ranks"—first as a word processing support specialist, then as a supervisor or manager—may want to become a word/information processing consultant either within the organization or privately. Many secretaries and administrative assistants who have become proficient in working with word/information processing software find that they enjoy assisting others in becoming as versatile with the software as they are.

    (1) *In-company consultant/trainer:* User groups have been formed within some organizations to assist individuals or departments as well as clients with the implementation of new office systems. An in-company consultant/trainer may assist employees in strategies that result in the successful implementation of word/information processing strategies or systems analysis. Some firms refer to this assistant as a *coach* (see Chapter 8 in the companion volume *Management*). The aim of the organization is to provide training and assistance for those employees who require it.

    (2) *Private consultant:* A person interested in word/information processing consulting may form, or become a part of, a private consulting firm. Many organizations will hire external consultants to facilitate the development of plans for the installation of new systems or to examine present systems and recommend improvements. Many consultants conduct professional seminars for businesses, professional organizations, and government agencies that focus on specific aspects of word/information processing (e.g., conceptual understanding, basic operations, and advanced applications).

  d. *Systems analysis:* The systems analyst often serves as a link in the information processing function between word processing and the processing of data. The systems analyst conducts feasibility studies and needs assessments, compares new office information software and systems being marketed by competing vendors, and recommends and assists with system installations. In addition, the systems analyst can play an important part in suggesting ways in which present systems can be utilized more effectively.

  e. *Operating office systems services:* Some people are interested in becoming entrepreneurs (business owners) who provide word/information processing services for clients, among other office systems services. Sometimes, executives have not been convinced that they should invest in word processing or feel that their volume of business does not warrant such an expenditure. Instead, a word/information processing service can provide the kind of support needed. Such a business provides more freedom and opportunity for the owner, greater flexibility in hours, and the opportunity to be very creative and to venture into other aspects of office systems such as facsimile (fax), reprographics, records management, or desktop publishing.

EXAMPLE: Whitman decided several years ago to have her own word processing business. Her previous secretarial experience provided her with an outstanding basis from which to work. The kinds of word/information processing tasks that she is able to perform include the preparation of letters, reports, and other types of documents. Her specialty lies in her ability to use word processing in the preparation of theses and dissertations. Besides using the fax machine, Whitman is now on-line with electronic mail. She has several clients who are located several miles away and find it easier to fax or e-mail messages and document copy to her for specific tasks.

f. *Technical writing:* Manufacturers and vendors of word/information processing technology need people who have the ability to write technical materials to support hardware and software development.

EXAMPLES: Systems reference manuals, training manuals for new software applications, audiovisual aids, tutorials, and instructional reference manuals are examples of technical products that are being developed.

Naturally, writing skill and strong language skills are definite "pluses" for this type of work.

g. *Temporary and part-time employment:* Employment agencies are not able to find enough qualified people who are trained in word/information processing to fill the demand for temporary or part-time help. For the person with some word processing knowledge and skill who is not interested in full-time employment at the moment, contact with an agency may provide "leads" toward an excellent temporary placement. Often employment agencies will provide training for those persons who are interested in working with word processing but have not had the opportunity to be properly trained in the software being used.

EXAMPLE: One nationally known employment service has been particularly successful during the past few years training applicants using a generic approach to word/information processing. After initial training conducted by the employment service, applicants are placed with employers who are willing to have the new "temporaries" spend their first few hours on the job learning how to work with the particular word processing applications the company is using.

C. Technology

Advances in computer technology continue to affect the office. *Technology* related to word/information processing consists of computer systems (hardware) available for input, processing, and output and to word/information processing programs and detailed instructions (software) that enable operators to use the hardware for specific applications.

1. *Input Systems:* Manual and automated systems are used to provide word processing input.

a. *Manual input:* Text may be dictated directly to a secretary who writes shorthand at an acceptable rate, or text may be written in longhand, ready for a secretary to type the final drafts. The majority of documents still originate in longhand form, *not typed,* even in rough-draft form. As an alternative, a secretary may be competent in using machine shorthand to record the dictation for later transcription.

b. *Automated dictation input:* Machine dictation is still used to save time in providing input for document preparation. The executive can dictate material without the secretary being present, thus saving valuable support time. Once the dictation has been recorded, the text can be transcribed into final form. Automated dictation is very common in the legal and medical professions.

EXAMPLES:

An ophthalmologist completes an eye examination and immediately dictates correspondence that will be sent to specialists who will provide a second opinion, prescribe lenses to correct the condition, or recommend surgery.

An attorney dictates the directions for preparing a last will and testament for a client, giving all the variable information that will be inserted into standard terminology for the will.

Several types of dictation systems are used to provide automated dictation input. Media that store the dictator's voice for later transcription use *analog technology.* When oral information is converted into digital pulses and then stored on disks rather than cassette tapes, *digital technology* is being used to store the information.

(1) *Portable dictation units:* Handheld units can be carried anywhere and used as the executive travels from one location to another. These portable units store information on microcassettes, minicassettes, or cassettes that are compatible with transcription units back at the office or in the word/information processing center.

(2) *Desktop unit:* A dictation unit, commonly referred to as a *desktop unit,* is placed on a corner of the executive's desk for easy access when dictation needs to be recorded. A microphone with controls is used for dictating information onto a cassette, the most common medium used for recording. Some of the basic features of desktop units include the following:

   (a) Cues indicated by audible beeps and on LCD displays

   (b) Fast-forward review used to monitor a one-hour tape in a matter of minutes

   (c) Rewind/fast-forward feature to rewind or fast-forward a 60-minute tape in one minute or less

   (d) Text insertion option to insert additional recorded information

   (e) Recording and playing text

   (f) Deleting and erasing recorded text

   (g) Last-word and end-of-tape indicators

   (h) Voice activation, which frees both hands while dictating

(3) *Centralized dictation system:* A telephone input system may provide centralized access to users anywhere within the organization or outside the building. Using a touch-tone telephone, a user can access the system and record dictation to be transcribed as needed by word processing personnel. The system is

also equipped to receive dictation from executives who are using cellular or briefcase telephones.

c. *Optical character recognition (OCR) devices:* Documents that are already typed need not be retyped. Through scanning, the keystrokes for the text can be stored on magnetic media. Optical character recognition (OCR) allows revision and updating for documents that have already been keyed.

d. *Storage devices:* Text that has already been stored in the main storage area of the computer system, on a hard disk, or on external storage media (3 ½- and 5 ¼-inch disks, Zip disks, or Jaz cartridges) may serve as input for editing and updating operations. These disks have the advantage of being removable from the system and do provide random access to documents that have been stored. *Random access* is a method of storage through which information is stored in no particular order on the disk but provides for immediate retrieval of any particular document without first having to access the documents preceding it on the disk.

EXAMPLE: The progressive executive may prefer to compose initial drafts of text for reports, speeches, or other writing directly into the computer system and later hand a disk (or send an e-mail message) to a secretary or administrative assistant with directions for revising, editing, and preparing the final draft.

2. *Transcription Systems:* Word processing occurs during the transcription process. *Transcription* takes place when the word processing operator listens to recorded dictation and keys in the text of the material so that the text can be stored and a transcript produced. The advantage of using a word processing system is the ability to store text for later revision or update. Dictation-transcription equipment is available in a variety of models suitable for particular office needs. Equipment presently on the market falls into three categories: *discrete media* systems, *digital electronic* systems, and *computer-aided* transcription.

a. *Discrete media systems:* The recording medium (cassette) is external to the dictating unit and can be removed from the dictating unit as soon as the dictation is completed. The transcription can begin as soon as the secretary inserts the medium (cassette) into a compatible transcription unit and begins to play back the material that has been dictated.

EXAMPLE: McCarthy uses a dictation-transcription unit, with discrete media, to dictate material for Anderson, her administrative assistant, to transcribe. When McCarthy finishes dictating, she removes the cassette from her unit and hands it to Anderson with any additional instructions for preparing the documents according to schedule.

(1) *Advantages of discrete media:* Being able to handle the media separately from the dictation-transcription equipment can be an advantage.

    (a) Dictation can be stored permanently.

    (b) Portable dictation units permit recording to take place anywhere and any time.

    (c) Dictation that is considered confidential or high priority may be stored on separate media.

    (d) Only one person's time is required at a time: the dictator's time when the dictation is recorded and the secretary's time when the dictation is transcribed.

(2) *Disadvantages of discrete media:* As with any kind of recording media, there are some disadvantages that the user needs to know about.

    (a) The cassette must be removed from the dictation unit and handed to the transcriber.

    (b) More than one cassette may be needed to store all the originator's dictation.

    (c) The transcriber cannot begin transcription until the dictator finishes recording the material.

    (d) Discrete media may be misplaced or lost.

b. *Digital electronic systems:* For dictation, a digital electronic system enables the executive to dictate business information, creating digitally recorded electronic files. The dictation is transmitted electronically to the secretary's desktop terminal, which displays complete information on the dictated material—the length of the dictation, the author, and deadlines for each item. The secretary can then sequence the work according to the deadlines indicated.

(1) *Advantages of digital electronic systems:* Some of the advantages of using a digital electronic system include the following:.

    (a) The recording medium is never handled; it remains protected inside the system.

    (b) The recording medium can hold a large volume of dictated items.

    (c) Transcription can take place immediately on transmission to the secretary's terminal.

    (d) Because of the digitally recorded electronic files, a specific item can be located easily for transcription or action. This is especially helpful for high-priority items.

    (e) Other action items can be communicated to the secretary, reducing the need for handwritten notes and reminders.

(2) *Disadvantages of digital electronic systems:* Such a system also has some disadvantages, including the following.

    (a) The transcription is typically handled by one person.

    (b) More than one author may access the system, creating the situation where the secretary must prioritize the tasks carefully to be sure each user's needs are served.

c. *Computer-aided transcription (CAT) systems:* The transcription process for machine shorthand has become more automated. In fact, the tape produced when machine dictation is recorded may be fed into a computer, the codes interpreted by the computer, and a printout of the textual material obtained rather quickly.

EXAMPLE: In the court reporting field, computer-based transcription systems are being utilized to "read" the codes created on the machine shorthand paper tape by the court reporter during the court proceeding. A printout of the transcript can be prepared from the stored information, thus saving the court reporter valuable transcription time. The court reporter will spend considerable time, however, in proofreading and editing.

3. *Components of Computer/Word Processing Systems:* Any computer system with compatible word processing software may be used for word processing. Standard components include visual displays, keyboards, printers, storage media, and support electronics. People who are word processing specialists rely on information processing technicians for expertise in working with the technical components of the computer (the inner workings). These specialists can then devote their efforts to the application of the computer in document preparation utilizing word processing and other software programs. The technology reviewed here relates primarily to word/information processing functions.

a. *Visual displays:* A display system features a screen that shows the document as it is being keyed in or retrieved from storage. There are two primary considerations that affect the type of visual display that is configured within a word/information processing system: the amount of text to be displayed and the type of text to be displayed.

(1) *Displays based on the amount of text:* Basically, visual displays can show a partial page or a full page of text at one time.

(a) *Partial-page display:* A visual display screen that shows only a partial page of text at a time typically displays up to 24 lines. A 24-line display would enable the operator to view one-third of a page of text. A system with a partial-page display will also have a *view document feature* that enables the operator to view a miniaturized version of the entire page of text—too small for proofreading text but very helpful in checking the format or general appearance of the page before it is printed.

(b) *Full-page display:* A full-page display is very helpful to the secretary who is used to working with pages and needs to view the entire page at a glance. Full-page displays usually show the text exactly the way it will print out.

(2) *Displays based on type of text:* The partial- or full-page displays already described are equipped to display paragraphed text in readable form. Sometimes, however, text needs to appear in graphic form or in color. Color displays are equipped to present clear text images in charts, maps, or diagrams in different colors. A specific application is the preparation of visual slides for projecting important points during a lecture or presentation. Hard copies of such visuals can also be produced with a printer that has multicolor capability.

(3) *Flat-panel display:* Over 25 years of research has resulted in a lightweight flat-panel display. This type of display is portable and small enough to fit in a briefcase.

b. *User-interface methods:* Through the use of a keyboard, a mouse or trackball, and power and tool bars, the user is able to interface with the system.

(1) *Keyboards:* Electronic keyboards are similar to typewriter keyboards and usually have the following basic features:

(a) An alphanumeric keyboard with alphabetic, numeric, and special symbol keys.

(b) A 10-key number pad on the right side of the keyboard for math and numeric functions.

(c) Function keys to the left, right, above, or below the alphanumeric keyboard that are activated through the software program, including arrow keys for moving right, left, up, or down within the text.

(d) A template diagramming the use of the function keys, placed above the function keys on the top row of the keyboard or placed over function keys at the side of the keyboard.

(e) Keys lit by light-emitting diodes (LEDs) to indicate special "on-off" conditions (e.g., CAPS LOCK and NUMBER LOCK).

The typical keyboard today is a separate unit attached to the computer by cable. This feature permits the operator to move the keyboard for personal comfort. The vertical slant for some keyboards can be adjusted at the back of the keyboard. Ergonomically designed keyboards also help the operator maintain personal comfort while keying in text.

Some workstations have a sliding platform or shelf under the front of the work surface for the keyboard. When it is not in use, the keyboard can be stored beneath the work surface on this platform.

(2) *Use of the mouse or trackball:* The mouse or trackball provides another way of moving around the screen to manipulate the information. By pointing at the item with the mouse pointer and clicking the mouse button, the user can make selections from the menus. Basic mouse operations include the following:

(a) *Clicking:* pressing the left mouse button to point or drag and pressing the right mouse button to call up a list of options

(b) *Double-clicking:* pressing the left mouse button twice

(c) *Dragging:* pressing and holding down the mouse button to block text, move text, or move icons

With the use of a mouse or trackball, many software packages have migrated to graphical user interfaces (GUIs). A GUI displays icons for the user to click on for manipulating computer operations.

(3) *Power, tool, and menu bars:* Power, tool, and menu bars can be activated at the top of the visual screen. The operator can click on the appropriate icon for the operation desired.

(a) *Power bar:* A row of buttons along the top of a display screen represents features such as point size, type style, justification, line spacing, and zoom, which affect how the text will appear when printed out.

(b) *Tool bar:* A line of icons also appears at the top of the screen to enable the operator to click on the feature desired. The tool bar usually includes features such as bold, italic, underlining, centering, spell check, grammar check, open document, and save document, among others.

(c) *Menu bar:* Changes to be made in a document can be controlled by clicking on features included in the menu bar, such as file, edit, view, insert, format, tools, and help. Each of these has a drop-down menu (list) that appears on the screen so that the operator can click on the appropriate item and make whatever changes are needed in the document.

c. *Printers and printing devices:* The preparation of high-quality documents through word/information processing requires a printer that produces the image quality desired at an appropriate production speed. The cost of the equipment is another important consideration. Printers acceptable for word/information processing applications require higher print quality than those used for data processing applications. Typewriters with printing devices and some types of impact or nonimpact printers are appropriate for word processing output.

(1) *Typewriters with printing devices:* Some typewriters and text editors facilitate both input and output within the same piece of equipment. An electronic typewriter can generally print out at speeds of 150 to 200 words per minute. Typewriters and text editors, however, are becoming obsolete as printing devices.

EXAMPLE: Electronic typewriters are self-contained, and documents are created as keystrokes are being recorded. On those typewriters with document storage capacity, a second copy can be prepared easily by playing back/printing out again.

(2) *Impact printers:* When impact printers are used, character images transferred by a printing device (a font or print wheel) that makes contact with the ribbon and paper as the images are being created. (For a complete review of impact printers and devices, see Chapter 1, Section B-2-c[2][a] and [b].)

(3) *Nonimpact printers:* Some of the nonimpact printers that are appropriate for word processing output include ink-jet printers, laser printers, fiber optics printers, and intelligent printers. Nonimpact printers are quieter than impact printers and thus can be located anywhere in the office. (For a complete review of nonimpact printers, see Chapter 1, Section B-2-c[2][c].)

When selecting a word/information processing system to be installed in the office, a primary concern is the type of printer needed. Of course, this will depend greatly on the types of documents being prepared and the quality of the images desired.

d. *Storage media:* The greatest advantage for word/information processing lies in the ability to save the text that has been created on magnetic storage media for future use and revision. Text that has been electronically stored on magnetic media is called *soft copy.* Historically, storage media have included magnetic tape cartridges, magnetic cards, and cassettes. Today, common types of magnetic storage media include magnetic disks (5 ¼- and 3 ½-inch), Zip disks, Jaz cartridges, hard nonremovable disks, and optical disks.

(1) *Disks:* Magnetic disks, popularly known as *floppy disks,* are thin and very lightweight and are available in two standard sizes—3 ½ and 5 ¼ inches. A 3½-inch disk is enclosed in a square plastic protective jacket coated with a magnetic recording medium. A single disk may be capable of storing 70 to over 1,000 pages of text, or 250,000 to 2,800,000 characters. To accommodate files with extensive graphics, Zip disks and Jaz cartridges can store between 125 million and 2 billion characters on a 3 ½-inch disk. (For a review of input media, see Chapter 1, Section B-2-c[1].)

(2) *Hard nonremovable disks:* A hard disk is a sealed unit within a computer system that contains a number of disks for storage. Nonremovable disks are installed in the system permanently (see Chapter 1, Section B-2-c[1][f]).

(3) *Optical disks:* A laser beam is used to store and read data on optical disks. Optical disks include CD-ROM, CD-R, CD-E, MO, and DVD (see Chapter 1, Section B-2-c[1][g]).

Storage media are capable of storing various amounts of information. The term *density* is used to describe the amount of information that can be stored in a certain area of the media. The normal density of a medium is called *single density.* Density that is twice that of single density is called *double density.* High- and extra-high density disks are capable of storing even greater quantities of text material. The greater the density, the greater the amount of information that can be stored on the medium. The terms *single sided* and *double sided* refer to the capacity to store on one or both sides of the media, respectively.

e. *Support electronics:* The electronic technology that supports the system is located in a separate housing usually placed beneath the visual display screen in a separate disk drive module. The support electronics for the system may include the following:

(1) The microprocessor (the computer on a chip)

(2) An expandable random access memory (RAM)—a temporary storage area where data are read or written for rapid processing

(3) An expandable read-only memory (ROM)—memory that can be read and utilized only by the computer

(4) Hardware slots for application expansions for the system

(5) Serial input/output ports (channels) for external communications

(6) Printer interface

4. *Specialized Word Processing Equipment:* When word processing was first used for document preparation in the 1970s and into the 1980s, specialized word processing systems, known as *dedicated systems* (i.e., not compatible with any other systems), were used to capture keystrokes and commands for preparing text and storing documents. In today's office, it is still common to see electronic typewriters, but few of the dedicated word processing systems are still in use. Computer hardware and software technology has been perfected to such a degree that computers used for word processing are no longer dedicated only to that purpose. Instead, a variety of software applications, including word processing, can be purchased and installed on computer systems. This section reviews some of the main features of intelligent typewriters and text processors that may still be used to a limited extent.

a. *Intelligent (electronic) typewriters:* An intelligent typewriter is an electronic typewriter with a microprocessor (chip) that has some of the less sophisticated characteristics of text editors. Intelligent typewriters are "smart" since they are internally programmed with instructions for performing some of the more routine typing functions.

EXAMPLES: Centering, bold type, underscoring, deleting, indenting, and storing phrases or short documents are typical functions handled automatically on an electronic typewriter.

(1) *Operating ease:* The electronic typewriter operates very much like an electric typewriter, with almost an identical keyboard, except for added control and

special symbol keys. Repetitive typewriting functions are automated, including correction ("lift-off"), paper-up, paper-down, and relocate features.

(2) *Format settings:* Several pitch sizes allow for greater versatility. Left and right margins are set by spacing to the position desired and pressing a margin set key. Tabs can be set anywhere on the line of writing as needed.

(3) *Limited temporary storage:* Temporary storage of phrases or short documents is possible on some models. When the power is turned off, all information stored in the typewriter will be deleted. This means that the electronic typewriter is *volatile.* A battery pack available on some units will hold information stored in the memory for a brief period of time.

(4) *Editing text:* Text is edited within the internal memory of the typewriter since there is no visual display screen. The operator must remember and move backward or forward in memory to locate particular "spots" where changes need to be made.

b. *Text processors:* More sophisticated text editors or text processors have also been in use for a number of years. These are dedicated systems, and many have been replaced recently by microcomputers with word processing software. A text processor is a stand-alone unit with the standard components: a keyboard with standard alphanumeric keys and function keys (codes and actions), a visual display screen, support electronics housing the logic or "brains" of the system, and a separate printer for creating hard copy. The system is usually initialized by inserting a program disk in the appropriate disk drive. Words entered on the keyboard and appearing on the screen may be moved in the revision process. Additional software programs are available for special applications. Some of the basic characteristics of text processors include the following:

(1) *Document storage:* Some text processors temporarily store text in a screen memory as the text is being keyed. Later, the operator commands the system to store the information on disk. Other text processors store text as it is being keyed into the system. Permanent storage is available on floppy disks or hard disks.

(2) *Default format:* When a word processor is initialized for use, a default format (sometimes referred to as a *standard format*) is in effect unless the operator changes it.

EXAMPLE: A typical default format might include the following constraints:

Left margin = 12
Right margin = 90
Standard tabs set every six spaces: 18, 24, 30, 36, 42, 48, 54, 60, and so on
Top margin on each page = 6 lines
Bottom margin on each page = 6 lines
Justification on
Automatic word wrap
Single spacing

The operator can manually change any specific default, depending on the requirements of the document.

(3) *Commands:* With a text processor, the text usually appears on the screen exactly the way it is expected to be printed. Commands to the system are em-

bedded (hidden) in the recorded text (as a communication to the system) but are seemingly transparent to the operator unless specific commands are given to the system to display the commands on the screen, possibly for proofing. (The term *transparent* means that the operator will not need to be overly concerned about the *technical* aspects of the system and can focus on the applications.) Each text processor has its own particular set of system commands.

(4) *Search:* The operator can scan through the document for a particular word or character string either to change the string and replace it with another character string or to eliminate the character string entirely from the text. An automatic procedure called *global search and replace* will replace the character string each time it is encountered in the document if this is what the operator desires.

(5) *Spelling dictionaries:* Proofreading of recorded text may be assisted with the use of spelling software. These dictionaries are meant to locate words that *appear* to be misspelled. The operator still has to know how to spell the given word correctly as it appears in context. The software sometimes enables the operator to choose from alternative spellings. In addition, the operator can add words to the main dictionary or place technical words in a special supplemental dictionary.

(6) *Other software programs:* The text processor has the capability of using other software applications that are available for the system, such as records processing and math packages.

   (a) *Records processing:* Records can be created with specialized records processing programs. Databases of information can be created. File-merge procedures can be initiated to merge data from a database with a document that is *stored.* Select-and-sort procedures assist the operator in using only a part of the database and sequencing data as desired in a particular application.

   (b) *Math packages:* Software applications may include the need for calculating row totals, column totals, percentages, and balances on financial records. Math functions such as these can be handled easily through the use of math software available for the system. The 10-key numeric pad on the keyboard enables the operator to quickly key in the data.

These are only a few of the many options provided on text processors. However, dedicated systems are disappearing in favor of compatible microcomputer systems with a wide variety of software programs available for business applications.

5. *Microcomputers with Word Processing Software:* In most offices today, word processing software is installed on a microcomputer (or personal computer). A *microcomputer* serves as a desktop workstation (stand-alone or networked) with software programs available for a variety of business applications. Its primary purpose is to support business applications (e.g., word processing, database, spreadsheet, graphics, accounting, financial, and productivity). Word processing is the application program used most often on a microcomputer. The compactness of the equipment itself seems to be a very important feature. Because of its small briefcase size, the laptop (notebook) computer serves the office needs while providing the flexibility to "go" with the busy executive. The components of a microcomputer system include visual

display screen, keyboard, processing unit, storage media, and printer. Features of a microcomputer system that most often affect word processing functions include the operating system, storage, other standard system features, and the software program in use.

a. *Operating system:* A set of programs written for a computing system to manage its various functions is called an *operating system (OS)*. These programs tell the computer when to input information from a terminal, print output at a printer, and store and retrieve information located on disk. The operating system manages the loading and execution of application programs written to perform word processing. An application program must be used that is designed for the particular operating system of the microcomputer being used.

(1) *Disk operating system (DOS):* A disk operating system (DOS) is a specific type of operating system first used in the 1980s to help the computer communicate with the application software program. DOS remains relatively transparent to the user as a platform for graphical user interfaces (GUIs) such as Windows 3.1 and Windows for Workgroups. These GUIs operate on top of DOS and enable the user to activate desired operations by pointing to and clicking on icons (pictures) through the use of a mouse, joystick, or touch screen.

(2) *Windows operating systems:* Windows operating systems, such as Windows 95, 98, and NT, were developed in the mid-1990s and continue to be upgraded. Windows NT, introduced in 1993, was designed as an operating system for high-end desktop workstations. Windows operating systems enable more efficient switching back and forth between compatible applications, integrated networking, and interfaces with the Web. In addition, the installation of new hardware is more automated, and start-up and shut-down operations include clearer directions for the operator.

EXAMPLE: When using a microcomputer for word/information processing, the user first loads the operating system and then loads the word processing software. Since the microcomputer is a "temporary" work space, the text being created needs to be saved to a permanent location—either on a portable floppy disk, a hard disk, or the organization's network disk storage (see Section 5-b[1] [a]).

b. *System features:* The microcomputer has some system features that are fairly standard across the industry. Since the major purpose of the microcomputer is to support office professionals with a means to utilize various software programs, the programs available for word processing and other applications have become much more sophisticated than even those designed for dedicated word processors. The person who is involved with high levels of word/information processing needs to continually upgrade his or her knowledge of software capabilities. Upgrades for the software are available from developers and vendors on a periodic basis.

(1) *Document storage:* Temporary and permanent document storage is available with microcomputer systems.

(a) *Temporary storage in screen memory:* When text is keyed in, it is held in the screen memory temporarily until the operator chooses to store it on disk. A suggested procedure is to store every few paragraphs or a page, adding on to the length of the document already stored. The system issues prompts asking whether previously stored text needs to be replaced (if the same document name is used), and the operator can respond with Yes or No. The typical response is Yes since it is an update of material that was previously stored.

(b) *Permanent storage on disk:* Permanent storage is available on disk (3 ½-inch, 5 ¼-inch, hard disk, or network disk space). A microcomputer workstation may be equipped with all four types of disk storage, although the 5 ¼-inch disk is becoming less prevalent. This allows for versatility in transferring documents from disk to disk as well as creating backup copies.

(c) *Timed backup:* Timed backup is also an important storage feature so that the system saves text in a backup file every few minutes. The operator sets the amount of time into the system (e.g., 5 minutes). This means that every 5 minutes the system will prompt the operator that a timed backup has taken place. This is a very helpful feature as the operator continues to key in text but may be concentrating on the content and neglect to save it often enough.

(2) *Directories:* A *directory* is a list of the documents that are stored on a single disk or a path on a hard disk established for storing similar files.

(a) *Floppy disks:* Each disk has a directory that lists the documents that are stored on that disk. Typically, the directory lists the documents alphabetically, along with the length of the document in characters and the date the document was last stored. In addition, the directory shows how much storage (in characters) remains on the disk, which is very helpful as the operator works with longer documents. While a document is being keyed in or edited, a directory can be accessed for reference purposes or to bring in text from another document stored on the same disk.

(b) *Hard disks:* The operator can set up numerous directories on a hard disk because of the massive amount of storage available. These directories enable the operator to group similar files for easier access. The secretary should be cautious in naming directories so that they are descriptive of the files that will be stored within each directory.

(3) *Visual display:* Partial-page 24-line displays have become a standard feature on microcomputer systems.

(4) *"Booting up" the system:* Most microcomputers today "boot up" the system from the computer's hard disk. The word processing software program is also installed in a specific directory on the hard disk. In the Windows operating environment, the user advances from the operating system to word processing by clicking on the appropriate icons. Once in word processing, the user is ready to create a new document or open a stored document.

There are many other system features that distinguish the microcomputer as a useful tool for word processing. Experimentation with a microcomputer system and its accompanying software should lead to the discovery of even more business applications.

c. *The word processing software program:* The software program must be compatible with the operating system of the computer so that business documents can be created and stored on disk. For all practical purposes, only one good word processing software program is really needed. Here is a generic description of the features available on most word processing software programs. Different brands of word processing software (e.g., Microsoft Word® and Corel WordPerfect®) require the operator to learn different sets of commands.

Note: No particular brand of software is used as a frame of reference for the following descriptions; rather, for this review, knowing the feature and what its function or use is will be the best review.

(1) *Default values:* Preset default values are used to create a standard format that the operator may choose to use or change. In other words, margins, tabs, spacing, and placement of text are already in effect once the system is ready for use unless the operator decides to change them. Here are some examples of defaults that may be preset in the system:

- Page size, 8 ½ by 11 inches, standard

- Left and right margins, 1 inch

- Single spacing

- Right justification on

- Standard tabs set every half inch

- Top margin on a page, 1 inch

- Bottom margin on a page, 1 inch

- Spacing between letters, words, and lines

Headers, footers, and page numbers are not a part of the preset default format and need to be set, depending on the format of the document being prepared.

(2) *Screen commands:* Depending on the software program, the visual display screen may show text exactly the way it will print out. The operator may see commands *and* text on the screen or the text highlighted in a specific way. The keyed-in text will appear on the screen along with commands or codes for printing out the text (e.g., bold text, underlined text, or text printed in a different type size or style). *Commands* are coded keystrokes that instruct the computer to perform certain functions. Commands to the printer for special effects, such as bold or underscoring, can appear on the screen or be embedded within the text. The latest versions of word processing software packages use fewer screen symbols and more icons on the top or bottom of the screen for the operator to click on for activation.

EXAMPLE: Here is the way one particular set of commands would be activated when a popular word processing software program is used:

Click on the <u>bold</u> icon
Type in Microcomputer Usage
Click off the <u>bold</u> icon

The icon clicked on either side of the word string is a command to the printer to print these words in bold. On the screen, the operator sees only the text, usually highlighted within the surrounding text, so the operator recognizes that these words will print out in bold.

Sometimes, this particular system feature can be a hindrance. Justified text, for example, may not appear justified on the screen. A printout or a view command will be needed to accurately check the copy. However, as an operator gains experience, the commands do not hinder adequate production.

(3) *Word processing features used in creating a document:* If a new document is to be created, the operator needs to access the word processing program and make sure that the screen is in document mode, ready to accept keyed-in text. Here are the basic steps used in creating a new document, with the specific features highlighted.

(a) *Opening a document:* Some word processing programs require that a new document be opened first. In this case, a name must be assigned to the document immediately, and then the screen is cleared for keying in the text. Other programs bring up a clear screen so that the operator can make format decisions about the document and then begin keying in text. A document (file) name is assigned when the text is ready to be saved to disk.

(b) *Keying in text:* The *word wrap* feature is in effect as text is keyed in. If a word extends beyond the right margin, it will be placed on the next line automatically. Decisions about hyphenation should be made after the document has been keyed in but before it is printed in final format.

(c) *Editing the text:* After the text has been proofread, changes may need to be made. Common editing changes include inserting new text, deleting and undeleting text, and replacing text by keying over it.

- *Blocking sections of text:* A block of text is a word, a group of words, or one or more lines of text. Blocked text may be moved, copied, deleted, or appended to another document.

- *Deleting and undeleting text:* Text may be deleted easily, whether it is one word or one paragraph. Sometimes text is deleted erroneously, and the operator wants to undelete that portion of the text. The computer is usually able to store the last two or three deletions in case an error is made in deleting.

- *Searching for text:* The *search* feature helps locate a specific character string each time it occurs within text. Most search features can search forward or backward through a document to find that character string. When the string has been located, a decision can be made to edit or replace the text.

- *Replacing text:* Incorrect text can be replaced easily by keying in the correct text. The system can make the substitution automatically if the search-and-replace feature is activated.

  EXAMPLE: You want to replace the word computer *with the words* computer system *each time the word appears. You activate the command for the search feature and see the prompt* Search for. *You key in* computer *and enter the appropriate command key. This time you respond to the query* Replace with. *You key in* computer system. *One more thing the computer will ask you is whether you want to confirm each replacement, in other words, check each replacement. You can answer* Yes *if you want to check each one or* No *if you want the system to go ahead and make all substitutions.*

Global search is another feature that locates a character string every time it appears in a document, and *global replace* will replace that string with the new string every time it appears without asking you to confirm each replacement.

(d) *Saving text:* Saving should take place frequently during the keying in of a document. A very short document should be saved immediately after it has been keyed in. A longer document should be saved often during the keying-in process, perhaps after several lines or paragraphs. The operator has two choices in saving text:

- Saving the text but keeping the document open so that more text can be keyed in

- Saving the text but closing the document and either leaving word processing or proceeding to another document

Text can be saved on a floppy disk, a hard disk, or both.

(e) *Running a spell check:* Spelling dictionaries and spell checks are an essential part of word processing software. Text can be run through a spell check by word, page, or document to see whether words in the document appear to be accurate. Words that do not match the words in the spelling dictionary program are highlighted along with a list of possible alternative words. The operator must then make the decision as to whether the word is, in fact, correct or needs editing. The operator can add spelling words to the electronic dictionary. Once corrections in the spelling of words have been made, the document should be saved again.

Note: Cautious proofreading is still necessary to be sure that all spelling errors have been detected and corrected; some words are spelled correctly but used incorrectly in context (e.g., *their* rather than *there).*

(f) *Running a grammar check:* A program that checks the grammar in a document will examine subject-verb usage, punctuation, spacing, and sentence structure to see whether there are any grammatical errors in language usage. The text can be corrected as these grammatical errors are detected. If corrections have been made in the text, the document should be saved again.

(g) *Checking words with the thesaurus:* Sometimes, the same word is used over and over again, and a different word with similar meaning would provide more variety in the writing. As text is being keyed in, the thesaurus feature can be activated to display words that have the same or similar meaning as the one being checked. Words need to be selected carefully that will not change the original meaning. Typical choices available are to look up the word, replace the word, and view the text. If the text for the document is changed in any way, it should be saved again.

(4) *Merging documents:* Information that is *constant* (will not change but will be used on every document produced) can be stored and later merged with *variable* information (will change but will be used on only one document) to be

inserted within the text of the document. With some word processing software, the constant information would be stored in a *primary file* (a document file), and the variable information would be stored in a *secondary file* (a data file).

EXAMPLE: A software package such as Corel WordPerfect®, a well-known word processing program, is used to create a primary file (a letter) and a secondary file (names, addresses, and other variable information for insertion into the letter). Using the text-merge function actually combines the constant information (the letter) with the variable information (name, address, and so on) for each letter that is produced.

(5) *Preparing multiple-page documents:* The format for multiple-page documents such as reports requires the use of additional word processing features, especially headers, footers, page numbers, table of contents, footnotes or endnotes, and bibliography or works cited, among others.

(a) *Headers:* A *header* is a group of words or a short phrase that is to appear within the top margin of each page as an identification of the document. The header is especially helpful if one or more pages of the document become separated from the rest. A header can appear on every page, on every odd-numbered page, on every even-numbered page, or excluded on the first page. A header can be deleted on any page if desired.

(b) *Footers:* A *footer* is a group of words that is to appear within the bottom margin of each page, again identifying the document. The footer functions in exactly the same way as the header. A footer can be deleted on any page if desired.

(c) *Page numbers:* The type of page numbers desired needs to be selected from the choices available in the word processing program. Typically, arabic numbers (1, 2, 3) or roman numerals (i, ii, iii) may be selected. These page numbers may be placed in as many as 10 standard locations. Lowercase roman numerals (i, ii, iii) are typically used on all pages preceding the report itself (title page, transmittal memorandum or letter, table of contents, list of figures or tables). Arabic page numbers are placed consecutively on all pages of the report, the bibliography or works cited, and appendices.

- Top-left corner, every page
- Top-center, every page
- Top-right corner, every page
- Top-left corner, even pages
- Top-right corner, odd pages
- Bottom-left corner, every page
- Bottom-center, every page
- Bottom-right corner, every page
- Bottom-left corner, even pages
- Bottom-right corner, odd pages

The page number can be eliminated on any page if desired.

(d) *Table of contents:* A word processing program can create a table of contents for a document. Several levels of headings can appear within the table of contents. As the text for the document is keyed in, the operator can mark each heading that will be included in the table of contents. When the text for the document is ready for printing, the operator can give instructions for generating the table of contents, complete with leaders and page numbers.

(e) *Footnotes and endnotes:* Many documents include citations to references in the form of footnotes (at the bottom of each page) or endnotes (at the end of a section of the document or chapter). As the text for the document is keyed in, footnotes or endnotes can be keyed in, too. When the complete document is printed out, the pages will include the footnotes or endnotes, whichever style is selected for citations in the document. In case of document revision, footnotes or endnotes are automatically renumbered and placed on the appropriate pages if the text containing the references is moved to another location.

(f) *Bibliography or works cited:* Word processing programs such as Microsoft Word® or Corel WordPerfect® are more sophisticated today and seem to have all the features necessary to develop bibliographies to accompany long documents. Most standard word processing programs include the capability of setting an acceptable format for a bibliography.

(g) *Creating page breaks:* Sometimes in long documents, the operator wants to establish the end of a page. Entering the command for a page break will record the end of the page. A word processing program helps in making automatic decisions about page breaks by eliminating a widow line on the bottom of a page or on the top of a page (one line of a paragraph by itself) if the operator enters the appropriate command into the system.

(h) *Hyphenation mode:* Once a document is keyed and edited, decisions about hyphenation can be made. When the hyphenation feature is activated, the system will do three things:

- Check to see whether the word extends beyond the right margin (the hyphenation zone).

- Check the word with the hyphenation dictionary to see where it might be hyphenated.

- Give a prompt to the operator when a decision needs to be made.

Many other features may be used in working with multiple-page documents, but these are some of the key features that need to be considered.

(6) *Formatting a document:* If the default settings are appropriate for the document being produced, no changes in format will be necessary. The default settings are accepted, and the document is printed.

(a) *Changes in document format:* If the format of the entire document needs to be changed (e.g., the base font used or margins), the text that is affected needs to be blocked and the format change made for the blocked text.

(b) *Changes in format for part of a document:* Sometimes, a section of the document needs a different format (e.g., an indented paragraph that is single spaced or a short table inserted into the text). For format changes such as these, the text for that section of the document needs to be blocked and the format changed.

Other changes in format can be accomplished easily by inserting the appropriate commands at the point where the new format should take effect. Such changes might include the following:

- Changing justification to ragged right rather than having the right margin justified

- Changing a single-spaced document to double spacing

- Inserting commands to bold or underline words or to have words print out in a different type style, such as italics

- Inserting a line to be centered

- Using the indent feature to move an entire paragraph to the right one tab stop or to indent a paragraph an equal amount of space on the left and the right

(7) *Tables:* A table can be designed more easily with word processing than with typewriting. The word processing program enables the operator to set up a tabulation, with or without ruled lines, for the insertion of information. Decisions can be made on the width of each column so that the text will fit within the space desired. If the table includes mathematical computations, the program can perform any required calculations automatically.

(8) *Text in columns:* Text can also be placed in columns on a page. The size of each column can be specified, along with the number of columns. The only restrictions are the space available on a sheet of paper. Usually, text is placed in two or three columns. Illustrations or charts can be inserted within the column text.

A complete summary of all the features available in a particular word processing program is available in the instructional and operations manuals that accompany the software package. The ones presented in this section are those that are applied most often in document preparation.

6. *Software for Other Business Applications:* The microcomputer is especially versatile for a variety of business applications. Some of the preferred applications are desktop publishing, database, spreadsheet, graphics, and communication applications.

a. *Desktop publishing:* A relatively new software application that uses traditional word processing as a base is desktop publishing. The goal of desktop publishing is to combine computer technology with word processing, graphics, page layout, and laser printing to create high-quality documents that incorporate both text and graphics. Text can be created with the desktop publishing program or initially with a compatible word processing program and then converted to desktop publishing. Desktop publishing enables an organization to use in-house services to produce newsletters, manuals, flyers, announcements, brochures, forms, calendars, and similar types of publications. Because the publications being produced require high print quality, attention during the process is on page format, different printing options, artwork used, electronic pasteup, and final printing and finishing.

(1) *Page format:* Margins (left, right, top, and bottom), image area, and size of document pages must be determined. Page format pertains to the number of columns per page, the number of pages in the publication, and any special lines such as banners or headlines. The following format functions are important considerations in establishing an attractive page format:

    (a) *Leading:* the space between the lines

    (b) *Kerning:* the spacing of words and characters on a line to justify copy

    (c) *Track spacing:* adjusting the number of words per line, squeezing or expanding text, and adding or removing space from character combinations on a line

(2) *Print options:* Desktop publishing permits a number of different print options, depending on fonts available, type size, type style, and typefaces.

    (a) *Font:* A *font* is a complete set of the characters of a particular typeface required to print a document. A font includes different *weights,* such as regular, boldface, italic, and bold italic.

    (b) *Type size:* The size of type is measured in points. A *point* is the standard measuring unit for type; 1 point equals $\frac{1}{72}$ of an inch.

    (c) *Type style:* A font includes many type styles, including italic, underlined, bold, shadowed, outlined, or combinations. What prints out depends on the quality of the printer being used.

    (d) *Typeface:* A *typeface* is a family of type with the same basic design for each letter. Typefaces are *serif* and *sans serif.* Serif refers to one of the cross-strokes that project across the ends of an alphabetic letter. Sans serif means "without serif," or without the cross-stroke.

(3) *Graphics and artwork:* Images in the form of graphs, charts, or illustrations enhance the presentation of text. Graphs might be created with spreadsheet or graphics programs and then imported into the desktop publishing program as graphics files. The artwork may also be original drawings or illustrations that can be scanned and digitized for use with desktop publishing.

    (a) *Clip art:* Clip art is a collection of drawings and special borders available in some software packages or by purchase in booklet form or on disk that can be used in documents.

    (b) *Internet images:* Another source of illustrations are pictures, graphs, or other visuals downloaded from Internet sources and inserted within document text. *Downloading* means that the images are first saved as a stored file on the computer and then loaded into the document.

EXAMPLE: People who are involved in creating company publications with desktop publishing should keep in mind that cartoon characters, such as Mickey Mouse and Garfield, are copyrighted. Such illustrations should not be scanned without getting prior permission from the copyright holder. Illustrations or pictures downloaded from the Internet are considered to be used for personal use only.

(4) *Electronic pasteup:* The arrangement of the text and graphics on the page is extremely important. With editing, such features as captions, borders, and

shading for graphic illustrations can be added. The vertical and horizontal placement of illustrations can be adjusted as well. An image can also be rotated (turned or tilted) to give a special effect. One of the most unique effects is to create text that appears over a graphic image.

(5) *Printing:* A laser printer is a necessity in desktop publishing because of the quality desired in the printed document. With the availability of many different fonts, a laser printer is much more versatile. The original printed copy of the document can then be used in a reprographics process to produce high-quality multiple copies.

(6) *Finishing:* The finishing processes used for documents produced through desktop publishing depend on the particular specifications of the document. A newsletter may need to be folded for mailing or distribution. Single sheets may need to be stapled or bound in a booklet. Printed covers (also produced with desktop publishing) may need to be added to the document before binding. The objective is to make the finished product as attractive as possible yet cost effective.

Figure 2–2 is an illustration of a document incorporating text, graphics, and other features into an attractive display.

b. *Database software:* A database software program provides the user with a set of procedures to create a set of records to be stored on disk for later selection and merging with other text. A *database* is a collection of records arranged so that information contained in the records can be manipulated by the user in preparing documents (e.g., reports, letters, or forms).

EXAMPLE: Databases are created for membership records in professional associations. The International Association of Administrative Professionals (IAAP) has a database of all active members. Every time a mailing needs to be prepared for the members, the database provides the basis for the development of mailing labels for the members. Choices can be made as to the arrangement of the labels being produced and exactly what information will be placed on the labels. In addition, the labels can be prepared in a specific ZIP code order to enable the mailing to meet automation standards of the U.S. Postal Service for bulk mailings.

The amount of information that can be included in a database may be somewhat limited by the storage media being used. Single-file databases may be better suited for floppy disk storage. Hard disk storage can accommodate larger sets of files.

EXAMPLE: A typical list of fields of information included in a database may be as follows:

Type of Information	Field Name
Person's title	TITLE
First name	FIRSTNAME
Middle name	MIDNAME
Last name	LASTNAME
Street address	ADDRESS
City	CITY
State	STATE
ZIP code	ZIPCODE
Age	AGE
Gender	GENDER
Birth date	BIRTHDATE

Figure 2–2   Example of Desktop Publishing

Contributed by Sherry Johnson and Donna Peterson, Kishwaukee College.

Figure 2–3 shows an entry in a database with the foregoing kinds of information. Data from this entry can be merged with the text of a letter to create correspondence that is personally addressed to the recipient.

Figure 2–3   Fields of Information in a Database

TITLE~FIRSTNAME~MIDNAME~LASTNAME~ADDRESS~CITY~STATE~ZIPCODE~AGE~
GENDER~BIRTHDATE

Ms.
Suzanne
Marie
Weir
108 Clark Street
Reedsburg
WI
53959–0108
34
F
April 2, 1966

---

c.   *Spreadsheet applications:* The spreadsheet is an electronic version of a spreadsheet or a worksheet written manually on paper. A spreadsheet application can help solve almost any problem that involves numbers and calculations. By using "soft" data (electronic data), the user is able to change the data contained on the spreadsheet, and the spreadsheet is recalculated automatically because of the way the formulas for computation are included within the spreadsheet. Figure 2–4 shows an example of a spreadsheet for a budget and a comparison with actual expenditures for one month.

Figure 2–4   Spreadsheet for Budget and Actual Expenses

MONTHLY BUDGET MARCH 200X

	Estimated Budget	Actual Budget	Difference
Gross income	$2,000	2,000	0
Less 20% tax	400	400	0
Net income	$1,600	1,600	0
Expenses:			
Rent	$350	$450	100
Car payments	150	200	50
Gasoline	30	40	10
Utilities	120	170	50
Entertainment	100	120	20
Food	150	150	0
Clothing	200	180	-20
Total expenses	$1,100	$1,310	-210
Income less expenses	500	290	-210
Less 10% savings	160	160	0
Balance	$340	$130	-$210

d.   *Graphics applications:* Charts and diagrams enhance the presentation of factual data. Data are entered, and decisions can be made as to the type of graphic chart desired: bar charts, pie graphs, histograms, and so on. The information from Figure 2–4 (the spreadsheet) can also be the input for a pie graph (Figure 2–5)

Figure 2–5   Pie Graph of Actual Budget

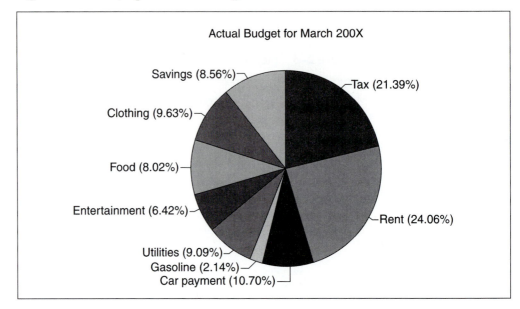

Actual Budget for March 200X

Savings (8.56%)
Tax (21.39%)
Clothing (9.63%)
Food (8.02%)
Entertainment (6.42%)
Rent (24.06%)
Utilities (9.09%)
Gasoline (2.14%)
Car payment (10.70%)

generated by the system. Computer graphics programs can generate charts from stored data and cause these charts to print out in color (with a color printer) so that transparencies and other visual aids can be made directly from the printout.

e. *Presentation software:* The preparation of visual aids to supplement oral presentations has become a very popular business application. Typically, the presentation software in use is part of a compatible suite of software applications so that word processing, graphics, spreadsheet, and presentation software programs can use the same input but in different ways. The result is a very professional set of visuals for presentation as a slide show or transparencies, along with speaker's notes and miniaturized versions of the visuals printed in the form of a handout (see Figure 2–6).

f. *Other business applications:* Microcomputers are also used for accounting, financial, marketing analysis, and many other business applications. Productivity software helps people with time management and document management. The microcomputer may be used in many different ways to automatize tasks that formerly had to be done manually. Only the creativity and imagination of individuals will limit its application.

7. *Configuration of Computer Systems for Word/Information Processing:* Computer systems used primarily for word/information processing, desktop publishing, and other business applications can be categorized according to the way they are configured (arranged) with office processes. Stand-alone systems (completely independent of other systems) or networked systems (shared, interdependent systems) appear to be the most frequent ways in which computer systems are used for these applications.

a. *Stand-alone systems:* A stand-alone system may be used by only one person at a time and is not linked electronically to any other office information system or central computer. This system may be a dedicated word processing system or a microcomputer-based system with word processing software. A keyboard and a mouse or trackball are usually available as input devices. A stand-alone system is self-contained with its own central processing unit (CPU), printer, and software.

Figure 2–6   Sample Handout of Presentation Visuals with Speaker's Notes

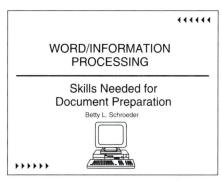

WORD/INFORMATION
PROCESSING

Skills Needed for
Document Preparation

Betty L. Schroeder

Word processing support specialists
need to possess middle- to high-level
competence with language skills, the
computer keyboard, formatting skills,
and basic computer skills.

Language Skills

‣ Sentence Structure
‣ Grammar
‣ Punctuation
‣ Spelling
‣ Reading Skills

Word processing functions require a
strong basis in language skills. In
particular, sentence structure,
grammar, punctuation, and spelling are
very important. Excellent reading
skills help the word processing
specialist understand the content of
high-quality manuscripts as well as
instructional or operations manuals for
word processing programs.

Keyboarding Skills

‣ Touch-Typing Speed and Accuracy
‣ Alphanumeric Keyboard
‣ Multifunction Keys
‣ Ergonomic Keyboard

Typically, large quantities of textual
material must be keyed in by the word
processing support specialist. Typing
rates usually range from 65 to 95
words per minute. Touch-typing skill
enables the operator to manipulate the
keyboard without looking at the keys.
Sometimes it is necessary to look at
the function keys since most of these
keys are multifunction keys.

Formatting Skills

‣ Knowledge of Acceptable Styles
‣ Appropriate Formatting Commands
    ‣ Setting Margins
    ‣ Headers and Footers
    ‣ Page Numbers

Letters, memoranda, and reports
must be prepared in acceptable styles.
Formatting skills require the operator
to enter appropriate commands for
setting margins, inserting headers and
footers into the manuscript, numbering
the pages of the document
appropriately, and handling other
formatting features that affect the
placement of the text on a page.

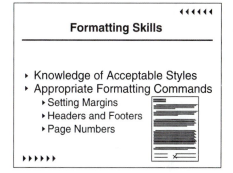

The printer is a separate unit and is activated only by the keyboard unit. Magnetic media used with a stand-alone system may be 3 ½-inch disks, 5 ¼-inch floppy disks, or hard disks.

b. *Networked systems:* A shared or clustered system is a configuration of two or more workstations (terminals) linked to a CPU and/or to one or more printers.

(1) *Shared-resource systems:* In a shared-resource system, each terminal functions independently but shares one or more resources. Each workstation has an intelligent terminal; if one terminal in the cluster is down, the other workstations can still function. *Resource* refers to equipment, storage, or processing power.

If a cluster of three terminals is configured to share one printer, this system can be referred to as a *shared-resource system* since the peripheral equipment (a printer) is shared. Another example of a shared-resource system is a communicating system, with telephone connections to other locations within the organization.

(2) *Networking:* Computers are networked so that business information can be available to all users of the system. Software for word/information processing or other business applications is loaded on the networked system so that all users will be able to select the kind of software application they need. Licensing for software use depends on the configuration and the number of terminals in the network. Local area networks can be established for departments or divisions; wide area networks can be created for organization-wide computer use. (For more information on network configurations, see Chapter 1, Section C-5.)

EXAMPLE: Ferguson is a word processing support specialist in the information processing center for the sales and marketing department. When she is working on lengthy sales reports, she often finds it necessary to use information created in other departments, primarily the financial department. Because her terminal is part of a networked system, she is able to access information that is created within these other departments without having to leave her workstation. Occasionally, she finds that special security clearances are needed to access more confidential information, but for the most part she has ready access to the majority of information she needs.

D. Word/Information Processing Procedures

Another very important component of a word/information processing system is the establishment of procedures for handling word processing functions throughout the organization. These procedures include those used by users (authors) who provide input in the form of a word processing task to be done, those used for processing information with computers and word processing, and those used for evaluating the output of the system.

1. *User Procedures:* Procedures are necessary to assure that work flow from the user to the word processing specialist will be smooth and efficient. Thus, the procedures used at the point of work origination are very important. Here are some major points to consider in assisting the user.

   a. *Methods for originating input:* Input may be in the form of dictation (given in person or recorded on a dictation unit), handwritten material, or documents in rough-draft form.

   (1) *Dictation input:* Some word/information processing centers prefer that the majority of input be recorded dictation, perhaps through a centralized dictation system. This depends on the nature of the business and the type of input technology available to the user. Dictation input is common in legal and medical organizations.

   EXAMPLE: The Republic Life Insurance Company has an information processing center called the InfoCenter. Last year, a centralized dictation system was installed so that the users would have more opportunity to provide dictated input into the system. To use this type of input system effectively, the telephone lines are now open 24 hours a day to receive dictation. The Info-Center is open only from 7:30 A.M. until 6:00 P.M. Dictation received late in the day or the evening will be transcribed the following day.

In this example, working hours are an important consideration in deciding how to provide input into the system. There is a strong need for users within the company to know exactly when they might get their transcribed reports and correspondence from the center—and it will be the job of the center staff to notify users exactly how their work will be processed.

(2) *Handwritten text:* A large percentage of input still comes from handwritten drafts. Although this method is the slowest one for providing input, some people have difficulty dictating material or keying in text themselves.

(3) *Text on disk:* Another way to provide input is to create a draft by keying in the text and then send a hard copy (paper copy) and the soft copy (disk copy) to the word/information processing center for formatting and editing. The hard copy may have changes, revisions, or corrections marked so that the operator can easily make these changes, format the document, and produce a complete final draft.

b. *Training/retraining for users:* The word/information processing manager or supervisor must take responsibility for any training or retraining needed so that users throughout the firm will know the procedures they must use in getting their work processed. Specific training might include some or all of the following:

(1) *Training on dictation equipment:* Specific procedures on how to dictate, what to say, and how to plan dictation should be included in a user training program. Users need to know how to provide input that is acceptable for word processing.

(2) *Word processing demonstrations:* Software and hardware used for applications within the organization may be demonstrated to help users become aware of and understand the capabilities of the system(s) being used. In this way, they may see other ways in which the technology might facilitate their work.

(3) *New applications for word/information processing:* Users need to be thinking about new applications for word processing to facilitate document production within their own work groups. Assistance may be available from other technical specialists in developing these new applications through procedures, working with the software, or both.

(4) *Procedures for submitting work:* Specific procedures to be followed in submitting work for word/information processing must be provided to users. These include job request forms to be filled out as well as ways of evaluating the quality of work being processed through word/information processing. Users need to know, too, how to submit job requests for confidential or rush work.

2. *Production Procedures:* As input for word processing is received from users, the supervisor must be prepared to review each job, determine the priority, and schedule the work to be done. The path the document will follow through the production phase should be the result of developing appropriate production procedures. Perhaps the user (author) will want to check periodically to see how the job is progressing. A logging procedure, computerized if possible, will permit a quick check. Control forms and schedules are needed to guide document preparation.

a. *Initiating job requests:* A specific job request is initiated by a user who brings (sends) the job to the word/information processing center.

    (1) *Job request form:* A work order form, sometimes called the *job request form,* is filled out, specifying all instructions for the particular task. Figure 2–7 shows a typical job request form.

        (a) The user completes the top half of the form, indicating name, department, type of paper to be used, and other general directions. In addition, an area is included for special instructions.

        (b) The lower half of the form will be used by the supervisor in making scheduling decisions about the job and in summarizing the production time required for the job.

    Usually, multiple copies of the form are prepared: one for the user, one attached to the job, and the supervisor's copy.

    (2) *Job ticket log:* The supervisor logs in all job requests on a *job ticket log* so that there will be a listing of all jobs received by word processing. The log is updated as each job is placed in process, completed, or delivered. A summary log can be developed for each working day if desired.

    EXAMPLE: If possible, the supervisor should log each word processing job directly into a computer or word processing file. To determine the status of any job, all the supervisor will have to do is open the file and key in a code or command, and a status line will appear on the visual display, giving a progress report on the work in process. Using such an automated process makes it possible to use printouts of the priority listing for a given day to help the word/information processing specialists stay on target in meeting job deadlines.

b. *Document preparation:* Once the work has been accepted and an operator assigned to the job, the actual document preparation can proceed according to schedule. In some organizations, decisions have been made ahead of time as to what documents will be accepted for word processing (e.g., documents of at least five pages in length, statistical reports, or proposals). In others, there may be a decision that all work requiring word processing is forwarded to word/information processing, with little word processing being done within departments. As the work is processed and documents prepared, however, established procedures need to be followed.

Many firms find that the writing of standard procedures for document production, eventually appearing in a word/information processing manual, has been particularly helpful to users as well as word processing specialists. Standards that are already established are easier to communicate to others in the organization and are useful in training new personnel.

    (1) *Formatting:* The formatting to be used for each document—margins, spacing, tabs, and special displays of text—must be determined *before* processing begins and should coincide with standard practices within the organization.

    (2) *Keyboarding:* Procedures for keyboarding and storing documents on magnetic media (floppy disks, hard disks, or magnetic tape) lead to more efficient and productive work.

Figure 2–7 Job Request Form

WORD PROCESSING JOB REQUEST

DATE _____
JOB NO. _____

SECTION I

ORIGINATOR	ROOM	BLDG	EXT.

DEPARTMENT/UNIT	SUBJECT OR REPORT TITLE

PAPER ☐ INTEROFFICE ☐ CO LETTERHEAD_____ ☐ BOND ☐ OTHER
NAME

☐ RETURN IN SEALED ENVELOPE   SPACING ☐ SINGLE ☐ DOUBLE   ☐ ONE AND ONE HALF

ORIGINAL AND _____ COPIES   ☐ WILL BE REPRODUCED   WHEN NEEDED

NOTE TEXT WILL BE RETAINED ON TAPE FOR THREE WORKDAYS UNLESS REQUESTED OTHERWISE

SPECIAL INSTRUCTIONS

☐ SPECIAL RETENTION ___/___/___
DATE

ATTACHED IS YOUR JOB TYPED IN ACCORDANCE WITH THE ABOVE INSTRUCTIONS. PLEASE RETAIN THIS PART OF THE JOB REQUEST AND ATTACH IT TO THE WORK IF REVISION OR CORRECTION IS NECESSARY.

SECTION II

ASSIGNED TO	INPUT DEPT_____	CATEGORY	
GENERATION ☐ ORIGINAL ☐ REVISION	☐ MACHINE DICTATION TAPE NO._____ ☐ LONGHAND ☐ HARD COPY ☐ EDITED COPY	☐ CORRESPONDENCE ☐ TEXT ☐ FORMS ☐ STATISTICAL	☐ PRE-RECORDED ☐ OTHER _____ _____

PRODUCTION DATA   LINE COUNT _____   PAGE COUNT _____

TYPING		ERRORS		
MEDIA NO.	MACHINE NO.	FIRST PROOF	SECOND PROOF	THIRD PROOF

QUALITY CONTROL   _____|_____   _____|_____   _____|_____

REMARKS

PRODUCTION TIME

HARD COPY	DATE	TIME	MACHINE DICTATION	DATE	TIME
JOB ARRIVED			JOB ARRIVED		
PROOFING COMPLETED			PROOFING COMPLETED		
JOB DELIVERED			JOB DELIVERED		
TURN AROUND TIME			TURN AROUND TIME		

COPY 1 ORIGINATOR'S COPY   COPY 2 SUPERVISOR'S COPY   COPY 3 PRODUCTION COPY

Source: Marly Bergerud and Jean Gonzalez, *Word/Information Processing Concepts: Careers, Technology and Applications,* John Wiley & Sons, Inc., 1981, p. 248.

EXAMPLE: As text is keyed in, the operator has two choices: to key the text as accurately as possible to decrease the number of revisions that will need to be made (speed of keyboarding not being so important) or to key the text as fast as possible, with little regard for errors, and then proofread carefully and make necessary revisions.

(3) *Naming files:* Standard procedures need to be followed in naming document files. The organization should have a companywide procedure in place so that files can be located easily.

(4) *Proofreading:* Recorded documents should be run through spelling and grammar checks before being proofread by the operator and a second time by a proofreader. With formal document preparation, it is important that more than one person has proofed the work. Once the text has been proofread, it is ready for the necessary revisions.

EXAMPLE: With a networked system, it is possible for one person to proofread on one terminal while another operator continues keying in or revising the text.

(5) *User approval:* A draft of the processed document should be submitted to the user for approval or editing before any final drafts are prepared. This is especially helpful in cases where a large number of repetitive documents will be prepared. If the user wants to change any of the text, one last chance is provided before final production of the multiple copies.

(6) *Measuring production:* The quantity of text produced (number of pages or number of documents) may be computed to develop more precise word/information processing production data. In addition, time spent in production of documents sometimes is recorded as well as time spent in tasks such as proofreading and checking that do not require keyboarding.

3. *Evaluation Procedures:* No word/information processing system can function effectively without continual evaluation of the procedures used for document preparation, equipment operation, and the functions performed by word/information processing support specialists.

a. *Work measurement:* Individual production can be measured in terms of words, lines, pages, or documents produced within a particular time frame. The amount of work produced correlates with the effective use of established procedures. Attention needs to be given, however, to analyzing carefully the time spent in word processing.

EXAMPLE: Time can be divided into two categories: productive time *and* nonproductive time. *This does not mean that the operator is idle during nonproductive time. In one particular company, productive time is defined as keyboarding time, or time actually spent keying in the text for a document using word processing. Nonproductive time is defined as "other" time spent in preplanning and organizing before the keying begins or in proofreading and checking after the text has been entered. Amounts for both categories of time are recorded for each job assigned to an individual.*

b. *Predetermined work standards:* Many companies have developed work standards for word processing. Individual performance may vary from the standards established; this will then give the supervisor an estimation of the work level to expect from each employee. These predetermined standards also give the employee a level of expectation and aspiration. Adjustments need to be made, however, for individual differences. A very productive worker may not be the speediest at keying in text for documents but may be extremely accurate so that little revision is ever needed.

4. *Administrative Procedures:* Word/information processing is a service provided to users in departments as well as throughout the firm. Thus, certain administrative procedures may be desirable so that appropriate cost controls can be established within departments.

    a. *Chargeback procedures:* Each department utilizing word/information processing services should be prepared to accept responsibility for any costs involved. A typical procedure used in any office support center is a chargeback system that will charge costs back to the department for whom the services were rendered. In this way, each department utilizing word/information processing services, even if only occasionally, will be charged for that usage.

    b. *Operating costs:* To charge costs back to departments, the administrative manager needs to determine current production costs for document preparation. Many departments will request cost estimates before beginning a large job, and information that is readily available from the word/information processing center will assist in making these types of decisions.

    c. *Equipment investment:* Before additional capital outlays for hardware and software technology can be approved, the manager needs to examine the present utilization of equipment and technology, the production levels possible using the present equipment/technology, proposed future needs of departments for word/information processing services, and projected production levels using both present systems and proposed new systems.

    d. *Employment procedures:* Other administrative procedures relating to the employment of competent word processing specialists are also important. Some companies have initiated procedures for administering employment tests for word processing personnel since this is one area in which *qualified,* experienced people are badly needed.

E. Information Processing Integration with Other Systems

Word processing is integrated with other office information systems. *Integration* means the linkage of two or more technologies to achieve a new set of goals. The integration of office technologies implies the use of communications as the link between technologies if more than one workstation is involved or through software on the same workstation. The primary office technologies that have the most chance of being integrated are voice processing, word processing, data processing, records management, reprographics, and communications.

1. *Integrating the Processing of Words and Data:* Word/information processing systems used in the office today are computers with integrated components and capabilities. The processing of words and data is performed on the same equipment with integrated technology.

    a. *Workstation applications:* Document preparation often calls for some word processing and some data processing; integrated technology (hardware and software) is the answer. In other words, one person at one workstation may need to combine the processing of words and data to obtain and process needed information.

b. *Work group or departmental applications:* Sometimes, the processing of words and data is combined through the use of an intelligent printer or a communication device that serves as the link between the two technologies. A common method used to integrate these two technologies is through the use of a network—a local area network (LAN) or a wide area network (WAN). The network can connect various input/output devices with a host computer, forming an integrated office system. These types of applications integrate work-group or departmental functions.

EXAMPLE: The marketing department utilizes a local area network (LAN) that provides each marketing representative, through an individual terminal, access to the same computerized information about products being sold. The network consists of several terminals connected to a central processing unit (CPU)—the host computer in this case.

2. *Integrating Word Processing and Desktop Publishing:* One of the basic concepts of office automation is to key in information only once, then use it for a variety of applications. The integration of word processing and desktop publishing is very likely since keying in information with word processing software can be input for desktop publishing applications. The difference is that special codes and commands for desktop publishing must be inserted into the text being composed. Input may be provided in various ways.

a. *Communication:* Text can be communicated from word processing to desktop publishing through a communications link.

b. *Optical character recognition (OCR):* Information can be keyed in using a typewriter, then an OCR reader is used to scan the document and store it on magnetic media for later use with word processing or desktop publishing. OCR is also valuable in transferring document storage from one medium to another.

c. *"Black box" interface:* Word processing technology is used to key in and store information on media. Whenever the same information is required for use with another technology, a "black box" interface is needed to convert the signals created with word processing and interpreted by other technologies.

d. *Internet access:* Text and images can be obtained from Internet sources, stored on magnetic media (disks), and downloaded into specific documents that are being prepared.

3. *Integration of Word Processing and Micrographics:* One of the primary concerns with word processing is the ability to find and retrieve information that has been stored in document form. Even with documents (records) stored on magnetic media (disks), this may be a very expensive method to use in arriving at a solution for records storage problems. Micrographics may be an answer for the storage problem.

a. *Use of microforms for document storage:* Documents (records) originally created through word processing can be stored permanently on microforms. When costs are compared for storing on a floppy disk or a microfiche, the microfiche will be found to be very inexpensive. As many as 70 to 80 pages of copy can be stored on one 4- by 6-inch microfiche. Computer output microfilm (COM) is another micrographics method used to store large volumes of records on microforms.

b. *Retrieval of documents from microform storage:* Computer-assisted retrieval (CAR) systems are designed to help users locate specific records that have been stored on microforms. CAR systems combine word processing, data processing, and micrographics technologies to provide a more useful method of retrieving and using stored information.

These are merely a few of the ways in which word/information processing technology is being integrated with the technologies of other office information systems. The communications link provided for such integration will be the primary factor in achieving even more integration in the future.

F. Word/Information Processing for the Future

Just as we used to say that "the typewriter is here to stay," we are now saying that "the computer is here to stay." In the office, we have had to learn to "live" with word processing and to learn how to use it more effectively. The next few years, especially the early years of the 21st century, should be extremely exciting for office information systems. We do know that people who are skilled in word/information processing will continue to be a critical component of the workforce. The human element will require skillful consideration within organizations from the small entrepreneurial home office to medium- or large-sized companies. Here are some possible predictions for word/information processing for the next few years.

1. *Modularity in Word/Information Processing Systems:* Computer systems are modular (keyboard, visual display screen, electronic components [disk drives], and printer). The equipment systems are becoming extremely portable (laptop and notebook computers), with some fitting neatly into a briefcase. The technology is making software and information more portable, too. The prediction can be made that computer systems (with business application software) will continue to be so modular, portable, and versatile that application and upgrading will be greatly simplified for users.

2. *Movement toward Software Sophistication:* There seems to be a strong movement toward increasing the power of microcomputers through more sophisticated software. The software available today far surpasses the software used in the dedicated systems of the past. More sophistication in the software, however, provides a WYSIWYG ("what you see is what you get") result. The compatibility and integration of word/information processing with spreadsheet, graphics, database, desktop publishing, and communications software will continue to be extremely important program features. The Windows operating system has been frequently upgraded during the past few years, and office professionals need to be able to adapt to each upgrade as it occurs. E-mail communications through the Web are producing more informal documents.

3. *Increased Systems Integration and Networking:* The emphasis is currently on systems integration with local area, wide area, and global networks. Networks are transparent to users. It is not necessary for users to know the location or structural details of information they need to access. Information needs to be available to users as needed. Initially, when word/information processing was introduced into the office, the approach was on a workstation basis—one secretary with one word processor. Today, networking of work groups (departmental or division) within local area networks and networking of organizational groups within wide area networks are essential to business success. Global systems integration for word/information processing and other purposes is being applied by numerous organizations seeking communications with firms in other countries. Satellite communications provide the necessary link.

4. *Increased Attention to User Applications:* The key to providing excellent user service is to understand exactly the kinds of applications the user needs. The user will need to be more creative in adapting applications and other software programs best suited for the organization's needs. Systems that are now being designed will be easy to learn and use because of graphical user interfaces, application consistency and simplicity, and effective training programs.

5. *User Input to the System:* Today's technology enables users to provide keyboard input from anywhere by telephone. By connecting a small, portable computer in a briefcase with a telephone network, the busy executive will be able to receive information in correct format ready to use within a matter of minutes. Word/information processing technology is already at the point where executives can access the system, create documents, and receive them back in hard or soft form.

6. *Voice Processing:* Another form of input processing, voice processing, is being used to record dictation, but there are still intermediate steps necessary to be able to use the text that has been dictated. In the future, word/information processing programs may allow voice input in analog format to be processed automatically without having to go through an intermediary. Research and development in voice processing technology continues with attempts to use technology to automate the processing of thoughts and ideas into printed text.

7. *Telecommuting and Home-Office Computing:* A number of companies began conducting work-at-home experiments in word processing several years ago to see how feasible it is to employ office professionals who telecommute to their jobs each day or a few days each week from their home offices. There is no conclusive evidence as to the effectiveness of these procedures, but many organizations are becoming more flexible in accommodating home-office functions. The "office" is no longer a place but rather a function. Word/information processing is one of those operational areas that does not have to be location dependent as long as communications networks are available to connect the sender and the receiver of processed information.

8. *Training for Word/Information Processing Professionals:* One of the most vital (and often overlooked) areas within word/information processing is training. It will continue to be important to train people to "think before acting" as far as word/information processing is concerned. Knowing what one wants to do with word processing is extremely important, and knowing *why* word processing should be used for a particular application in a certain way is even more important. We must teach people to be able to develop more creative and imaginative ways to use word/information processing in the office. Vendors are still providing training, most often for a fee rather than included as a service to the customer. Many organizations are developing their own in-house training staff to work with people who are learning how to use new hardware operations and software programs.

9. *Word/Information Processing for All Office Professionals:* Word/information processing is needed for *all* office professionals (executives, managers, secretaries, general clerks, and word processing specialists) to be knowledgeable and proficient. Basic awareness and skill in adapting to changes in operating systems are already required competencies for many entry-level office positions. New job titles and job descriptions will reflect increased word processing needs.

   EXAMPLE: Look at the classified advertisements in any metropolitan newspaper, and you will find numerous office positions that require word processing skills, such as secretaries and administrative assistants. Also, there is a special section just for word/information processing positions.

10. *Creative Opportunities for People:* There will continue to be a need for creative minds to learn and use word/information processing software being marketed. Software specialists are needed to be sure that word/information processing programs truly meet user needs and expectations. Certification programs are available through some of the developers of word/information processing software for instructors and technical support specialists who become very knowledgeable about the application of that software. Word/information processing is indeed a technological area that will continue to need people with special skills.

Review Questions

Directions: Select the best answer from the four alternatives. Write the letter of your answer in the blank to the left of the number.

_____

1. Word processing is concerned with keying in word text in acceptable format, whereas information processing is most concerned with the

    a. automated preparation of letters, memoranda, and other publications.
    b. entering and analysis of numeric data and text.
    c. preparation of reports and other documents.
    d. application of language skills and formatting text.

_____

2. Word processing support specialists need to have a middle to high level of competence with

    a. decision-making and managerial skills.
    b. skills in processing data.
    c. grammar, sentence structure, and other language skills.
    d. filing and records management skills.

_____

3. The person who provides input for a document to be prepared and for whom a document is then prepared is called a/an

    a. word processing support specialist.
    b. user.
    c. administrative support specialist.
    d. consultant/trainer.

_____

4. The Crystal Corporation has a word/information processing center that serves users from the entire organization. The decision has been made to replace the technology presently in use with a networked computer system and integrated software. Who should have the responsibility for researching and recommending the new system to be purchased?

    a. The word processing support specialist, who will become one of the operators of the new system
    b. The administrative support manager, who has the responsibility for establishing procedures to support company policy
    c. The word processing supervisor, who will conduct training on the new system
    d. The word processing manager, who manages word/information processing operations for the organization

_____

5. Maintaining word processing productivity records and monitoring production deadlines are duties typically performed by the

    a. word processing coordinator.
    b. administrative assistant.

c. word processing support specialist.

d. proofreader.

6. Telephoning, receiving visitors, handling mail, and managing records are referred to as

a. administrative support.

b. centralized services.

c. document management.

d. work flow.

7. A path that permits a person to move to a position in another department at a comparable level to the one presently held is called a/an

a. managerial career path.

b. vertical career path.

c. lateral career path.

d. operational career path.

8. Anderson has been a word processing support specialist for three years, spending the majority of her productive time preparing documents (reports and correspondence). She has been considering the possibility of advancement to a supervisory position and perhaps taking courses in a community college program. Which one of the following avenues would be the most helpful for her to follow at this time?

a. A psychology course that would help Anderson understand her own needs and potential

b. A business communications course that focuses on developing interpersonal skills

c. An advanced word/information processing course that would help her develop operational skills with integrated programs

d. An information processing course to provide her with a background in computer systems

9. Conducting feasibility studies, needs assessments, and analyses of information processing software and hardware systems is typically the responsibility of the

a. private consultant.

b. technical support specialist.

c. word/information processing support specialist.

d. systems analyst.

10. The majority of executive input for word/information processing is provided through

a. face-to-face dictation to a secretary.

b. recorded dictation on a cassette tape.

c. handwritten drafts of documents.

d. typewritten or printed rough drafts of text for documents.

_____   **11.** Immediate retrieval of a specific document that is stored, along with several other
documents, on a disk is possible because of

a. random access storage.
b. use of discrete media.
c. storage on a hard disk.
d. optical character recognition (OCR).

_____   **12.** Recording media that can be removed from the dictation unit as soon as the dictation is completed and then transcribed are called

a. computer-aided transcription.
b. digital electronic media.
c. discrete media.
d. portable dictation units.

_____   **13.** Which one of the following is an advantage of a digital electronic dictation system?

a. The dictation equipment is portable.
b. High-priority dictation is easy to locate on the media.
c. Dictation is stored on discrete media.
d. A telephone located anywhere in the organization can be used to access the system.

_____   **14.** The visual display screen

a. shows the format set for the document.
b. is activated by pressing a special key after the text has been keyed in.
c. shows only one page of text at a time.
d. shows the document in temporary storage until the document is saved.

_____   **15.** The mouse is an interface device that enables the user to

a. control the function keys on the keyboard.
b. key in text for documents of varying lengths.
c. move around the screen and manipulate information.
d. produce hard copy with a laser printer.

_____   **16.** Text for a document that is stored in electronic form on a disk is referred to as

a. double density.
b. hard copy.
c. magnetic storage.
d. soft copy.

_____   **17.** Intelligent typewriters, often referred to as "smart" typewriters, are

a. programmed to handle complex text editing.
b. equipped with permanent storage for documents.
c. programmed with instructions for performing routine typewriting functions.
d. able to communicate with other word processors.

_____ **18.** The primary purpose of a microcomputer is to

     a. provide permanent storage on floppy disks.
     b. enable office professionals to use a variety of business application programs.
     c. check the accuracy of keyed-in text with electronic spell checks.
     d. integrate with other office information systems.

_____ **19.** Programs that tell a computer when to input information from a terminal or to store and retrieve information are contained in the

     a. operating system.
     b. word processing program.
     c. applications software.
     d. document format.

_____ **20.** Using a microcomputer, you key in the text for a 10-page report. If you are using a floppy disk as the storage medium, the text will be stored

     a. on the disk as soon as you key it in.
     b. in the screen memory and on your disk as you key it into the system.
     c. in the screen memory temporarily until you command the system to save the document.
     d. permanently on the hard disk as well as on a floppy disk as you key in the text.

_____ **21.** Which one of the following is typically considered a preset default?

     a. Double line spacing
     b. Envelope size
     c. Right justification on
     d. Standard tabs set at 1-inch intervals

_____ **22.** The feature that allows the operator to look through the recorded document and locate a particular word for replacement is called

     a. merging text.
     b. searching for a character string.
     c. undeleting text.
     d. blocking text.

_____ **23.** The word processing feature that compares the meaning of one word with other words with similar meanings is called the

     a. grammar check.
     b. electronic spelling dictionary.
     c. database.
     d. thesaurus.

24. The margins for a document that has already been keyed in need to be changed from 1 inch to 1 ¼ inches. Which one of the following procedures would be needed to make this format change?

a. Commands for changing the margins need to be inserted at the beginning of the document.
b. Commands for changing the margins need to be placed anywhere in the text for the first page of the document.
c. The text that requires the new margins needs to be blocked before the format can be changed.
d. Commands for changing the margins need to be inserted within the document but before the last page.

25. As an extension of word processing, desktop publishing is a software application that

a. permits electronic computation.
b. stores fields of information for merging with other text.
c. establishes the page layout for a word-processed page.
d. combines text and graphics into a high-quality document.

26. O'Brian finds an image at an Internet source that she wants to insert within a document that she is preparing. First she stores the image on a disk and then transfers the stored image to the spot in the document where she wants the image to appear. This process is called

a. clip art.
b. downloading.
c. kerning.
d. leading.

27. You want to use a database software program to prepare a file of client information. The first step you should follow in setting up the database is to

a. create the fields of information to be included in the database.
b. create a new document called DATABASE.
c. insert the variable information in appropriate fields.
d. key in the text for a primary file.

28. Sawyer has been invited to give a seminar on "Ergonomics for Today's Professionals" for a statewide leadership conference. To highlight the important points she wishes to stress, she is preparing a set of visuals and handouts using

a. desktop publishing software.
b. word processing software.
c. presentation software.
d. database software.

29. Training should be provided so that users within an organization know the procedures they are expected to employ in sending their work to word/information processing. Which one of the following would be the highest priority?

    a. Explanation of specific formats to be used in document preparation
    b. Instruction on how to use the digital electronic dictation system
    c. Demonstration of a spreadsheet application
    d. Evaluation of word/information processing procedures to be used in document preparation

30. When initiating a job request, the user will

    a. assign a word processing support specialist to the job.
    b. complete a job request form.
    c. provide specific information relating to deadlines and job priority desired.
    d. make the scheduling decision about the job.

31. Formatting used in document preparation includes

    a. keying in the information and recording it on disk.
    b. accessing the operating system.
    c. determining the vertical placement and margins for the document.
    d. checking each completed document to be sure that all editing has been done.

32. Which one of the following methods is used to measure word processing production?

    a. Number of documents produced
    b. Chargeback procedures
    c. Number of proofreading errors found
    d. Number of people involved in the production

33. An integrated office system is illustrated in which one of the following situations?

    a. A word/information processing system used at a secretarial workstation primarily for the manipulation of text and data
    b. A local area network linking a secretarial workstation with other nearby workstations
    c. Document transmission to the New York office through a telecommunications channel
    d. Integrated software utilized by the secretary to perform multifunctions

34. When integrating word processing with other office information technologies, an office automation concept to keep in mind is

    a. information needs to be communicated as quickly as possible.
    b. keyed-in information can be checked electronically for possible spelling and grammatical errors, thus reducing the amount of proofreading time required.
    c. information is keyed into the automated system only once so that the recorded text may be applied to a variety of operations.
    d. all information that is keyed in is stored for use in future applications.

Solutions

Answer	Refer to:
1. (b)	[A]
2. (c)	[A-2, A-2-a]
3. (b)	[B-1]
4. (d)	[B-2-a]
5. (a)	[B-2-c]
6. (a)	[B-3]
7. (c)	[B-4]
8. (b)	[B-4-a(1)(b)]
9. (d)	[B-4-d]
10. (c)	[C-1-a]
11. (a)	[C-1-d]
12. (c)	[C-2-a]
13. (b)	[C-2-b(1)(d)]
14. (d)	[C-3-a, C-5-b(1)(a)]
15. (c)	[C-3-b(2)]
16. (d)	[C-3-d]
17. (c)	[C-4-a]
18. (b)	[C-5]
19. (a)	[C-5-a]
20. (c)	[C-5-b(1)(a)]
21. (c)	[C-5-c(1)]
22. (b)	[C-5-c(3)(c)]

23. (d)   [C-5-c(3)(g)]

24. (c)   [C-5-c(6)(a)]

25. (d)   [C-6-a]

26. (b)   [C-6-a(3)(b), E-2-d]

27. (a)   [C-6-b]

28. (c)   [C-6-e]

29. (b)   [D-1-b(1)]

30. (b)   [D-2-a]

31. (c)   [D-2-b(1)]

32. (a)   [D-2-b(6)]

33. (b)   [E-1-b]

34. (c)   [E-2]

CHAPTER 3

Communication Technology

OVERVIEW

In today's dynamic business environment, greater emphasis has been placed on the communications process and the role that communication technology plays to enhance the productivity of the office. *Communications* is defined as the exchange of internal and external messages (both written and verbal) that forms the basis for all office interaction. For more information on communication processes, see the companion volume, *Management,* Chapter 4, and Chapters 16 and 20 of the present volume.

The communications technology that is currently affecting *internal* (interoffice) communication and *external* (intraoffice) communication includes the integration of the telephone and the computer to provide telephone services, data communications, teleconferencing, and electronic means to speed the communications process in the office.

Communications systems for business have been the beneficiaries of the technological developments in the use of the telephone itself, satellites for speeding the communication process, and the integration of computer systems with communications systems to enhance decision-making processes in the office.

KEY TERMS

*69
911
Audio conferencing
Call director
Call forwarding
Call waiting
Caller ID
Cellular call
CENTREX system
Chat rooms
Collect call
Computer conference
Computerized branch
  exchange (CBX)
Conference call
Courier services
Credit-card call
Demand reports

Direct-distance dialing
  (DDD)
Electronic mail (e-mail)
Facsimile transmission
  (Fax)
Fiber optics
Freeze-frame video
Internet
Inward wide area
  telephone service
  (INWATS)
Local area network (LAN)
Marine call
Message unit
Modem
Overseas call
Pager

Paging system
Person-to-person call
Private automatic branch
  exchange (PABX)
Private branch exchange
  (PBX)
Protocol
Reverberation
Scheduled reports
Speed calling
Telecommunication
  systems
Video conferencing
Wide area network (WAN)
Wide area telephone
  service (WATS)
World Wide Web (WWW)

A. Telephone Communications

Since its invention, the telephone has played an important role in American life and in American business. In recent years, the computer has greatly influenced the types of telephone services available to the customer, switching systems for telephone equipment, and features available on telephone equipment.

1. *Telephone Services:* Available telephone services range from basic to special services.

    a. *Basic services:* Business organizations pay a flat rate for telephone service plus a charge for telephone extensions in use throughout the organization. In addition, charges for long-distance calls result from calls made to locations outside the local area. In metropolitan areas, calls between distant points within the local area may be measured in *message units.* Charges for these calls will depend on how many message units were used.

        (1) *Local call:* A local call is one that is placed within a local calling area.

        (2) *Direct-distance dialing (DDD):* Direct-distance dialing is a procedure used to place a long-distance call to another telephone number without the intervention of an operator. An area code plus the number of the party with whom you wish to speak needs to be dialed. (The United States and Canada are divided into approximately 150 calling areas, each one represented by a three-digit *area code.*)

            EXAMPLE: Dial 1 + area code + phone number to place a station-to-station call (a "number-to-number" call). You will speak to anyone who answers the phone. Even if the long-distance call is in the same area from which the call is being placed, the area code is dialed.

        (3) *Person-to-person call:* An operator-assisted call charged to the caller is a *person-to-person call.* The charge is made only if the person being called is able to come to the phone.

        (4) *Collect call:* An operator-assisted call that will be paid by the person or company receiving the call is known as a *collect call.*

        (5) *Credit-card call:* A long-distance call that allows the caller to charge the service to a specific account number is called a *credit-card call.* Personal identification numbers (PINs) are assigned by the credit-card company so that the account number can be verified before the credit-card call is completed and the account charged. Credit-card calls from rotary-dialed phones require operator assistance. Touch-tone systems are programmed to accept the number being called, the credit-card number to which the bill should be charged, and the PIN.

            EXAMPLE: Dial 0 + area code + telephone number if the call is operator assisted (e.g., person-to-person or collect calls). For credit-card calls from a touch-tone telephone, the credit-card calling number plus the PIN must be entered before the telephone number being called.

        (6) *Message unit calls:* Calls between widely separated locations within the same metropolitan area are measured in *message units,* a standard base rate used to determine the cost of the call.

    b. *Special services:* Many businesses are finding the special services provided by telephone companies especially helpful in conducting their business both nationally and internationally.

(1) *Types of special calls:* Conference calls, emergency calls, cellular calls, marine calls, and overseas calls are some of the special types of telephone calls that are available to business today.

(a) *Audio conference:* A telephone call for three or more people to talk with one another is called an *audio conference.* The conference call was the first form of audio conference. Three-way calling features allow the caller to set up the audio conference call. A conference call for larger numbers of participants may require operator assistance to make all the conference connections. With private, high-quality audio communications circuits between conference sites, the audio conference can be established with the flip of a switch.

(b) *Emergency calls to 911:* In addition to providing emergency service when individuals call 911, additional safety features are being added so that the 911 operators will be able to pinpoint the location of the call without the caller even having to give this information to the operator.

(c) *Cellular call:* Cellular telephones, commonly called *cell phones,* enable callers to make or receive calls at any time and in any place. Telephones carried in vehicles can be powered by batteries or the electrical system of the vehicle. Cell phones should be used only when you must place or receive a call. Using the cell phone should not interrupt other conversations, whether in person or on another line. With increased cell phone use, cell phone etiquette, such as the following simple rules, has become extremely important:

- Switch off the cell phone when attending public events or use the silent mode to be notified of calls. The cell phone displays a light or produces a sensation; some cell phones are capable of displaying a short message (SMS service).

- Activate the silent mode or switch off the cell phone when its use can cause an annoyance in public places.

- When in an enclosed space, such as busses or elevators, be discreet with your conversation and speak in low tones.

- When the cell phone ring is active, set the ring on a low setting and answer promptly to avoid disturbing others.

- For safety protection when driving, use a hands-free telephone kit in your vehicle. By doing so, you should avoid annoying other drivers.

- Whenever possible, forward calls to office mail so that you can handle each call personally and in the privacy of your office.

(d) *Marine call:* A call may be made to or from a ship at sea by contacting the marine operator.

(e) *Overseas call:* A call may be placed to an overseas company or individual either by dialing direct or through operator assistance. If direct dialing is used, the overseas area code and phone number are required.

(2) *Answering services:* You may wish to make a special arrangement for your business or home telephone to be answered in your absence by the following:

(a) An independent answering service whereby an operator actually answers calls and records messages

(b) An automated means through a recording device, such as an answering machine used to record the caller's message

(c) A voice mail service, perhaps available through the local telephone company or the Internet as an extra feature for a monthly charge (see Section A-3-f)

(3) *Special telephone features:* During the past few years, telephone companies have been continually adding special features to telephones to make telephone communication easier and more efficient. Some of the more commonly used features are included here as a review. Subscribers will pay a separate cost for each feature, which is added to the monthly cost for telephone service.

(a) *Call waiting:* When the phone line is in use and a second call is incoming, the person being called is interrupted with a soft beep. The first caller can be placed on hold while the second call is being answered.

(b) *Call forwarding:* When you know that you will be at a different phone location, the new phone number can be recorded into the telephone system. Any incoming calls can be forwarded to the new phone location.

(c) *Speed calling:* The telephone can be programmed with a special number code assigned to frequently dialed numbers. Instead of dialing the entire telephone number, you need only dial the special code.

(d) *Caller ID:* A telephone system equipped with the caller ID feature displays information on who is calling before the receiver is picked up. The person being called can decide whether to answer the telephone or to have a message recorded. You can also block the system from displaying your telephone number on someone else's telephone.

(e) *Repeat dialing:* Many telephones have a special button for redialing the previous number called or redialing a busy number. This service is also available on a pay-per-use basis.

(f) **69 feature:* By depressing *69, the phone number of the last incoming call can be obtained with the option to call back. This feature is typically available on a pay-per-use basis.

EXAMPLE: A series of recent television commercials have advertised this relatively new feature. In very fine print at the bottom of the screen, the advertiser indicates that each call to *69 costs 75 cents.

(g) *Taped announcements:* Recorded information can be automatically played over the telephone when incoming calls are received.

EXAMPLES: Movie schedules at a local theater, the time and temperature from a local bank, and daily prayers from a local church.

(4) *Wide area telephone service (WATS):* A firm may want to subscribe to WATS service if numerous telephone calls are made to a national, regional, or state area. The cost of WATS service depends on the time the service is in operation, not on the number of calls made. A fixed monthly fee is paid for the WATS hours. If the company uses more than the allotted hours, an additional

charge is made to the company. The firm can have a full business-day package or a measured time package.

(a) *Full business-day package:* This WATS service provides a fixed number of calling hours per month.

(b) *Measured-time package:* This WATS service provides a smaller number of fixed hours per month allotted to the company.

EXAMPLE: The XYZ Corporation has a regional office serving the state of Wisconsin. The regional office makes most of its customer contacts and follow-ups over the telephone. Therefore, full business-day intrastate WATS was purchased. During the month of June, the total number of hours charged for long-distance calls for the XYZ Corporation's Wisconsin Regional Office was less than the fixed monthly fee for the month of June. Therefore, no additional charge was required.

(5) *Inward wide area telephone service (INWATS):* A firm may want to subscribe to an INWATS service if numerous telephone calls are expected from customers and the firm wishes to pay for these calls. (For the customer, the call is a toll-free call. This means that the firm, not the customer, pays for the call.)

EXAMPLE: Rodriguez wants to order a blouse from the CB Store. By calling the toll-free number (1-800-755-3300), she can order the merchandise by phone, and the company will pay for the long-distance call.

(6) *Leased lines:* Some long-distance telephone connections link business telephones in two locations. Companies pay a fixed monthly charge for the use of a leased line. These private lines care also called *tie lines.*

(7) *Foreign exchange:* A special service called *foreign exchange* provides customers a local number when calling a business located in another city. The toll charge for the call is billed to the listed number.

EXAMPLE: The ABC Company, located in Rockford, Illinois, services equipment installed in a number of offices in Bloomington, Illinois (about 95 miles away). ABC subscribes to a special service that lists a Bloomington number in the Bloomington telephone directory, a local call for Bloomington residents. ABC will be charged for the toll charges on all calls received in the Rockford office on this line.

2. *Telephone Systems:* Telephone calls are routed to and from the public lines of the telephone company to the private lines within a business organization by means of switching and access systems. The organization installs a telephone system to provide the internal and external communication service desired. Some options include private branch exchanges (PBX or PABX), computerized branch exchanges (CBX), and central exchange systems (CENTREX).

a. *Private branch exchange (PBX and PABX):* A PBX switching system accepts and transmits analog (voice) signals and requires that all incoming calls be answered by an attendant who then transfers the calls to appropriate extensions within the firm. Access to outside lines for outgoing calls is also controlled by the attendant. Internal extension-to-extension service, called *direct inward dialing,* may be available within the company just by dialing the desired extension number. The

PABX system is similar to the PBX system, but its features are automatic. PABXs will distribute calls automatically to extensions in the order in which they are received without the intervention of an attendant. Both direct inward dialing (DID) and direct outward dialing (DOD) are accomplished without an attendant's assistance. The increased need for integrated voice and data transmission has made the digital PBX a major component in local area networks.

b. *Computerized branch exchange (CBX):* The CBX is a computer-based telephone communication system that is designed to provide a computerized management system with additional features available, such as the following:

Directory services	*Employees' individual phone extensions are available by entering the name by voice or keying in part or all of the name.*
Records management	*Records are kept of all calls made from telephone extensions and costs incurred for telephone usage.*
Voice mail services	*If the call is not answered within a designated number of rings, the voice mail system will be activated to receive messages.*
Automatic callback	*When a number called is busy, the number is called again as soon as the extension becomes free.*
Call forwarding	*Any incoming calls are directed to ring at another location.*
Call pickup	*Any incoming call can be answered by another person in the pickup group.*
Call waiting	*A second incoming call will interrupt the first with a soft tone.*

c. *Central exchange system (CENTREX):* In a CENTREX system, each extension is assigned a seven-digit number for outside access. Part of that number, the last four digits, represents the extension number for internal calls. A general seven-digit number is assigned as a general company number if the caller does not know which extension is desired. Direct inward dialing and direct outward dialing are available at each extension phone.

EXAMPLE:

Telephone number for company:	*765-2000*
Extension #1	*765-2001*
Internal Calls	*2001*
Extension #65	*765-2065*
Internal Calls	*2065*

Additional features, such as voice mail services, automatic call distribution, speed calling, and other telephone features, are available to enhance the system. A CENTREX system is leased from the regional telephone company, eliminating the need for large capital expenditures for telecommunications equipment.

Such telecommunications companies as Lucent Technologies are developing multiservice platforms that support basic telephone services as well as applications for high-speed analog and digital data transmission for domestic and international markets.

3. *Telephone Equipment:* Secretaries need to take advantage of the telephone system's special features. The following list identifies telephone equipment that has become standard equipment for the office.

   a. *Telephones:* Some of the more commonly used telephones include the key (or button) telephone, the touch-tone telephone, and the speakerphone.

   (1) *Key (or button) telephone:* Connected to several telephone lines, each line is represented by a button on the phone. The button illuminates as the line is used for a call.

   (2) *Touch-tone telephone:* A touch-tone telephone is a telephone with a 12-button keyboard (10 buttons for numbers 0 to 9 plus two buttons for special purposes). Touch-tone telephones are required for computerized systems.

   (3) *Speakerphone:* The speakerphone is equipped with a microphone and a speaker chip that can be activated for ease in projecting the conversation. The speakerphone frees the user's hands in order to work with resource information necessary for the conversation. When there are two or three individuals in one office, a speakerphone allows all to participate in the discussion. Also, a separate speakerphone can be attached to the telephone. The separate speakerphone can provide higher-quality reception and is typically used with larger groups. If the service is desired at both locations of the conversation, two speakerphones will be required, one at each end.

   (4) *Headsets:* When office personnel need to place (or answer) a large volume of calls, a headset equipped with listening and speaking components provides a more ergonomically designed setting for the user. The user wears the headset, keeping hands free and not requiring the use of the telephone handpiece, which many times produces "telephone ear" after extended use.

   b. *Call director:* The call director is a desktop unit that can handle as many as 100 lines at one location and can be connected to a switchboard or an intercom system.

   c. *Pager:* A device called a *pager* can be carried so that an individual can be signaled by use of a tone or buzz that a call to the home office needs to be returned. The number to be called is projected on the pager.

   d. *Paging system:* An in-house communication system (a paging system) signals people who are away from their desks that they need to contact their office.

   e. *Answering machines, answering services, or voice mail:* Businesses or individuals who must frequently leave their telephones unattended often use an answering machine, an answering service, or a voice mail system to receive messages.

   (1) *Answering machine:* An answering machine is a recording device that is activated when the telephone rings. A prerecorded message informs the caller that a message can be recorded. A "tone" lets the caller know when to begin speaking. Some recording devices also "tone" the caller when the allotted recording time is complete. Others record messages of any length up to a maximum amount of recording time, no matter how many messages are recorded.

   (2) *Answering service:* An answering service is maintained by individuals who answer calls personally and take messages. Arrangements are required for the recipient of messages to retrieve them at a later time.

(3) *Voice mail system:* A business computerized system is referred to as a *voice mail system.* A prerecorded message requests the caller to leave a complete message, with date and time. After a "beep" or "tone," the caller can leave a message. Some voice mail systems are designed to save messages for a certain number of days (e.g., six days) or a maximum amount of recording time.

B. Interoffice and Intraoffice Systems

Between 50 and 80 percent of all communications created within an office is interoffice (internal) in nature. The communications network or system used in the office is the central nervous system, providing information paths throughout the organization. Intraoffice networks such as courier and mail service providers help to deliver messages to other organizations. Here are some of the primary ways in which office communications are managed.

1. *Automated Systems:* Because of the tremendous amount of communication from office to office, automated systems not requiring operators are continuing to be of importance in transmitting interoffice communication.

    a. *Conveyor system:* For distributing large quantities of paper to fixed locations within a company, office conveyor systems may be used. Systems such as these minimize the physical movement of office personnel to deliver materials. *Horizontal* conveyors assist in transporting papers between workstations on the same floor or level. *Vertical* conveyors transport papers up and down between floors of a high-rise office building.

    b. *Electronic mail (e-mail) network:* With a computer-based message system (CBMS), an office professional (executive, secretary, or administrative assistant) whose terminal is on the network can "send" communication to anyone in the firm linked to the CBMS with a terminal who can, in turn, "receive" the communication and respond to it. A computer terminal is used by the sender to key in and display the message. The message can be delivered to one or many receivers. The message is held on a direct-access storage device (secondary storage) in the receiver's electronic mailbox. When the receiver signs on the computer system, a message is displayed, indicating that there is mail in the mailbox. The e-mail network identifies previously read messages (opened) from new messages (unopened). The receiver can then display the message on the visual screen (soft copy), or a hard copy can be printed. Accessing the message can be done at a time that is convenient to the user. A reply can be sent easily to the sender's mailbox. All users have electronic mailboxes assigned by the database management system (see Section E).

    EXAMPLE: Kingston, the office manager, wishes to notify the support services supervisors of the agenda for the staff meeting next Monday at 10 A.M. (a meeting already on their electronic calendars). She keys in the agenda on her terminal and sends it to the supervisors' electronic mailboxes. When each supervisor signs on the computer system, a message appears, indicating that e-mail has been received in his or her electronic mailbox. The new message is easily located at the end of the in-box mail and flagged as "unopened." Each supervisor can view the agenda before the meeting and has the opportunity to respond if necessary.

    c. *Pneumatic tubes:* Documents are placed in special carriers that move from one department to another via a network of pneumatic tubes throughout the building. The operator must dial the code for the destination and insert the carrier into the tube.

    d. *Programmed mail cart:* Instead of employing people to deliver incoming mail to departments and pick up outgoing mail, an organization can use a programmed mail cart. The vehicle is battery driven and follows an invisible path created by spraying a chemical on the floor or carpeting. The cart stops for preprogrammed pickup and delivery of documents to individual departments. Office personnel can collect incoming mail from the mail cart and place any outgoing mail on the cart. This mail cart is effective only on one floor of a building.

2. *Intercom Systems:* Intercommunications systems typically used in the office include dial, manual, and paging systems.

    a. *Dial intercom system:* An intercom line connecting two or more telephones makes it possible for individuals to call one another by dialing the intercom number. The appropriate one- or two-digit intercom number is dialed on the intercom line. The receiving party's telephone buzzes, indicating that someone is calling on the intercom line. (For a discussion of the use of telephone extensions for making internal calls, see Section A-2-c).

    b. *Manual intercom system:* A telephone connection only between the executive and the secretary allows communication with each other without dialing a number. The manual intercom is strictly a local line with a tone activated by pressing the intercom buzzer.

    c. *Paging system:* Individuals can be paged through an in-house intercom system or an individual paging system, referred to as a *pager.*

        (1) *In-house intercom system:* With an in-house system, intercom speakers are wired throughout the building. Typically, individuals who need to be contacted frequently are assigned a code (one tone, two tones, three tones, and so on). When a person needs to be contacted, the code is sounded over the intercom system. The person either returns to the office immediately or calls a contact person (usually the company switchboard operator, receptionist, or the person's secretary) to receive the message.

        EXAMPLE: At Douglas Middle School, the principal and the assistant principal make it a practice to be in the halls and visiting classrooms throughout the day. In case of an emergency, the administrators are alerted immediately. The principal's paging code is one tone (ding); the assistant principal's paging code is two tones (ding-dong). The administrative office secretary activates the signal when either one is being paged; the sound carries throughout the school. There are in-house telephones in all the classrooms. If paged, the principal or assistant principal can call the administrative secretary immediately.

        (2) *Pager (individual paging system):* A pager is an individual paging system that consists of a cellular radio that can be worn by the person who needs to be paged. The radio box is attached to a belt or similar article of clothing. The receiver of the page can call back by telephone or receive information given over the pager.

3. *Courier Services:* Shipments of correspondence and parcels can be made through privately operated services as well as the U.S. Postal Service. Interstate shipping is handled by common carriers under the jurisdiction of the Interstate Commerce Commission (ICC). These services are available to the general public on a regularly scheduled basis.

    a. *Express delivery:* Private firms offer express delivery services with next-day or two-day delivery. Automatic daily pickup of parcels is available, or someone may call for pickup of an envelope or parcel. The routing is monitored electronically so that the exact location of the parcel can be tracked.

EXAMPLE: A common carrier that provides express delivery service to all 48 contiguous states is United Parcel Service (UPS). UPS services large metropolitan areas, towns and villages of all sizes, and rural areas. Federal Express is another courier service that provides express delivery service.

b. *Air express:* Commercial airlines as well as air freight companies offer overnight delivery of packages weighing from 1 to a maximum of 150 pounds. Some offer same-day delivery to airports in large cities. Most air express companies offer door-to-door delivery. Airborne, Burlington Air Express, Emery, Federal, Purolator, UPS, and the U.S. Postal Service are some of the organizations currently offering parcel delivery services. In addition, major airlines also offer air cargo services.

c. *Bus express:* Shipments that must be delivered quickly to small communities or in areas where air or rail express is not available can be sent by bus express. Most bus companies offer round-the-clock service, including Sundays and holidays. Frequently, same-day delivery is possible. Delivery is made to a local bus terminal where the receiver must pick up the parcel.

d. *Express mail:* The fastest service provided by the U.S. Postal Service is express mail. The service is available only at selected post offices across the nation. Express mail provides same-day or next-day service as well as Sunday deliveries to most locations.

(1) *Next-day service:* When a letter or package is brought to the post office by 5 P.M., it will usually be delivered to the recipient by noon the next day.

(2) *Same-day service:* Items brought to a designated airport mail facility (*not* a post office) will be delivered to another airport facility on the next flight. A postal driver picks the mail up for same-day delivery.

(3) *International express mail:* Overseas mail can be delivered within two to three days to many foreign cities.

4. *Mail Services:* The U.S. Postal Service provides mail services six days a week, excluding holidays. In an effort to speed mail handling and improve mail service, the U.S. Postal Service initiated the Zone Improvement Plan (ZIP) code in 1963. These five-digit ZIP codes enable machines to sort mail through the use of optical character recognition (OCR). In 1983, ZIP codes were expanded to nine digits for even more precise delivery.

a. *The ZIP code:* The standard ZIP code with its five digits (12345) has been changed to the ZIP + 4 code (see Section B-3-b). Starting from the left, the five-digit ZIP code represents postal codes for sorting the mail with OCR devices. The first digit designates a region. The United States and its provinces are divided into ten geographic areas: 0, 1, 2, 3, 4, 5, 6, 7, 8, and 9. The next two digits narrow the code down to a sectional center within the region. The last two digits represent the local post office for delivery.

EXAMPLE: The ZIP code 12345 would be explained this way:

1 = Region of the United States and its provinces

23 = A sectional center within the region

45 = Local post office

b. *ZIP + 4 code:* ZIP + 4 is the coding system implemented by the U.S. Postal Service in 1983. The ZIP + 4 code should be used for all mail. The new code adds a hyphen and four digits to the five-digit ZIP code. The additional four digits permit sorting by carrier route, city block, lockbox, or firm.

c. *Automatic sorting:* Optical scanning equipment reads the ZIP code (either the five- or the nine-digit codes) and sorts the mail automatically. Sorting automatically is faster; therefore, mail addressed with the nine-digit ZIP code moves the mail faster than mail addressed with the five-digit code. Mail without a ZIP code is placed in a bin for hand sorting, which will take additional time. Some optical equipment reads bar codes on envelopes, which is a translation of the ZIP code. The address is read from bottom to top and right to left. If mail is delivered to a post office box, the address line (PO BOX 123) must appear immediately above the city, state, and ZIP code line. Mail is delayed when the post office box number is separated from the city, state, and ZIP code by a street address. Also, it is important *not* to have any mail notations, such as "Certified" or "Registered," after the bottom two lines of the address in either the lower-left or the lower-right corners of the envelope.

EXAMPLE:

```
MR KARL JACKSON
KETTLESON TOOL & DIE COMPANY
1721 MARION AVENUE
PO BOX 1434
ROCKFORD IL 61101-1434
```

Note: The U.S. Postal Service recommends that single spacing, all capital letters, and no punctuation be used in addresses appearing on envelopes or labels.

5. *Personal Messenger Systems:* Office messenger services are still maintained in some businesses as a matter of convenience to executives. Primary concerns in maintaining messenger service include the limited time required for delivery of material, the size and weight of the material to be delivered, and the number of delivery locations. Labor costs for such a messenger system are relatively more expensive than automated means of interoffice communication. Commercial services are becoming more popular for fast delivery of inter- and intraorganizational information transmitted to other parts of the country and the world.

C. Telecommunications

Telecommunications is the electronic network for the transmission of oral and written communications in the form of text, voice, data, and image (or combinations). Telecommunication encompasses all means of electronic information transfer both internally and externally. Satellites are speeding the telecommunication process by facilitating quick transmission from one location to another. Satellite use is also decreasing communications costs.

1. *Transmission Channels:* Analog transmission signals (voice transmission) or digital transmission signals (data transmission) travel through transmission channels consisting of the following:

a. *Telephone lines:* The conventional twisted wire installed for analog communication.

b. *Coaxial cable:* Thickly insulated copper wire for faster, more interference-free transmission of data than is possible with conventional copper twisted wire. This cable does *not* support analog telephone conversation.

    c. *Fiber optic cable:* Fine glass fibers used to transmit light beams (laser technology) that are faster, lighter, and more durable than wire media.

    d. *Microwaves:* High-frequency radio signals for high-speed transmission of communications in a straight line. Microwave stations send and receive these transmissions. Microwave signals cannot bend to the earth's curvature but can be bounced off satellites for longer-distance transmission.

    e. *Satellite:* Communication systems placed in orbit approximately 23,000 miles above the earth to accept (uplink) and retransmit (downlink) transmission signals from earth stations. Because the satellite rotates with the earth, the earth station remains fixed on the satellite. Satellite transmission has contributed to the advancements in telecommunications.

2. *Types of Transmission:* The major types of transmission found within telecommunications are voice, data, and document. Typically, both data and document communications are enhanced with images and/or graphics.

    a. *Voice transmission:* Voice transmission in a real-time environment requires only the telephone. When several people are gathered together at one location to converse with one or more people at other location(s), speakerphones (microphone and speaker chips) may be required. Voice transmission can also be stored. This system combines two types of communication equipment:

        (1) The telephone

        (2) The storage medium

    One-way voice messages can be recorded when the person called is not present to receive the call. These voice recordings can be stored on tape or transmitted to a computerized voice mailbox. In this way, the receiver can listen to the message(s) at a later time.

    b. *Data transmission:* The transmission of data over telephone lines can be accomplished through the use of an input device (terminal), a device that converts data codes into analog signals for transmission, a communication link that carries data from one location to another, and a receiver capable of receiving the transmitted data. For an illustration of this concept, see Figure 3–1.

        (1) *Modem:* Two modems are required in the transmission of digital data over analog communication channels (telephone lines). A modem is required at the sending location and at the receiving location. The modem at the sending location *MO*dulates the digital data (discrete binary bits) into a continuous stream (analog/voice pitch). When the data reaches the receiving location, it must be *DEM*odulated into discrete binary bits by the receiving location modem for storage in the computer system.

        (2) *Communication link:* The communication link is the channel used for transmission (see Section C-1).

    c. *Document transmission:* Information contained in written documents may be transmitted on the World Wide Web (WWW), through teletransmission, or through facsimile transmission. In all these cases, the result is an actual document or a copy of a document being created at the receiving location.

        (1) *World Wide Web:* With advancements in the World Wide Web, businesses can quickly exchange documents and images over the global network (the Internet).

Figure 3–1 Communications Links

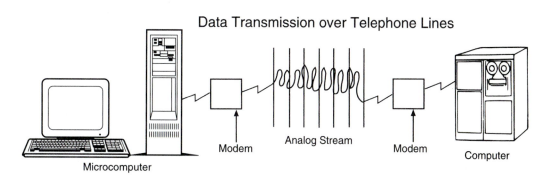

Data Transmission over Telephone Lines

Microcomputer · Modem · Analog Stream · Modem · Computer

The World Wide Web is typically referred to as the Web. Users navigate (move through) the Web through a Web browser, a program coded in a language called Hypertext Markup Language (HTML). The Web browser program translates the HTML document into a Web page. Two popular Web browsers are Netscape Navigator and Microsoft Explorer.

To place a Web page on the Internet, a unique address called a Uniform Resource Locator (URL) is required. The URL requires a unique name, which must be registered in a domain. The seven domains of the Internet are the following:

COM Commercial organization
EDU Educational institution
GOV Government organization (excluding the military)
INT International organization
MIL Military organization
NET Network or service provider
ORG General organization other than the above

For more information on the Internet, see Section E-1.

(2) *Teletransmission:* Telegraph, teletypewriting, telecopying, and videotex services continue to be used in business today to reach customers who may not have computer services at their home or business.

(a) *Telegraph service:* Telegrams may be sent at any time of the day or night, any day of the week. Minimum charges are for a 15-word message. A night letter is an overnight telegram. International telegrams may be full-rate or letter telegrams.

(b) *Mailgrams:* A mailgram is a telegraph service in which messages are transmitted at the speed of light over Western Union's communications network to the U.S. Post Office nearest the addressee. The mailgram will be delivered in the next day's mail. Minimum charges are for a 100-word message.

(c) *Cablegrams:* A cablegram is an international telegram transmitted via underwater cable, radio, or satellite.

(d) *Teletypewriting and teleprinting:* Transmission occurs between two locations, each with a teletypewriter that can be used to send and receive messages. TWX is Western Union's domestic teletype network, whereas Telex is both a domestic and an international network. Messages can be sent from Telex and TWX subscribers to remote locations where computer linkages are available for creating hard copies of the information.

(e) *Telecopying:* Transmission of text and images (graphics) is possible with telecopying. Facsimile transmission is a form of telecopying. Laser beams are used to make copies in color.

(f) *Videotex:* With videotex systems, textual material (newspapers and stock price quotations) are displayed on the CRT screen. Videotex subscription services provide access to their information for a fee.

EXAMPLE: Popular services today include Dow Jones News/Retrieval Service, Lotus One CD/Corporate, and DIALOG.

(3) *Facsimile transmission (fax):* A facsimile unit is like a copier. A picture or duplicate of the original document (handwritten, graphics, or typewritten information) can be transmitted electronically between two points over telephone lines, private transmission lines, or microwave relay systems. Wirefax utilizes telephone lines. Fax is especially useful when rapid transmission is required. Many computer systems are enhanced with facsimile transmission features. The speed of transmission varies from six minutes to less than three seconds, depending on the system (for additional information about fax, see Section E-1).

d. *Private branch exchanges for information transmission:* Telephone communications is the basis for any type of integrated system linking networks that require voice, data, text, and image transmission. Components of telephone communications systems (the station or terminal, transmission facilities, and switching) make both public and private networks available to users.

(1) *Public and private networks:* Public telephone networks cover entire countries, continents, and the world. Private telephone networks connect terminals equipped for voice, data, text, and image processing within an office building, a plant or factory, or even a geographic area. A user at one station can communicate with other private users by using public or private facilities. The World Wide Web operates in this environment.

(2) *PBX interface:* An interface (the private branch exchange) is needed to *connect* a private network to the public or private carrier. The computer-based PBX provides the technology to enable an office professional to utilize telephone, interphone, facsimile, teleprinter, Telex, data terminals, word processors, and other specialized terminals, all through the same network. Because of the need to be able to communicate information through different technologies, an integrated system must be maintained.

(3) *System capabilities:* A specially designed computer-based PBX, consisting of a micro- or minicomputer-supported switch, has the capability of handling these types of functions:

(a) Line control functions

(b) Voice/message input for store-and-forward messages

(c) Voice/message delivery

      (d) Dialog communication (person-to-person, person-to-machine, and machine-to-machine)

      (e) Implementation of Telex and Teletex functions

      (f) Information processing functions

      (g) Facsimile exchanges of information or documents

      (h) Private viewdata functions

      (i) Multifunction workstations

      With PBX systems, added telecommunication features (e.g., automatic route selection, queuing, speed calling, integrated voice-data switching) are available that reduce the need for additional wiring and modems.

With the computer-based PBX, more sophisticated approaches can be utilized to better manage office functions. Here are two examples that illustrate how data measurement may enhance office productivity or project management.

EXAMPLES:

PBX information can be used to assist office personnel (managers as well as support personnel) in managing their time, for example, the quantity of time spent on particular assignments compared with the complexity of the task to determine the individual level of productivity.

PBX information can be used to establish a chargeback system. This is particularly helpful in word processing and information processing environments where support services are provided for various departments. Employees' time spent on specific projects can be electronically recorded; then an individual department can be charged only for time spent on that department's projects.

3. *Telecommunications Applications:* As businesses grow and become more dependent on information both internally and externally, the need to gather data and disseminate information over a wider area is imperative. The computer is able to move data quickly from one point to another by means of the channels of a telecommunications network. All computer-based information systems depend on the communications link in order to gather data and disseminate information. Prevalent computer-based information systems in operation today that rely on the telecommunications network include accounting information systems, financial information systems, manufacturing information systems, marketing information systems, human resource information systems, decision support systems, expert systems, office automation, and end-user information systems. Business personnel interact with these information systems in a number of ways to obtain problem-solving information to make decisions. Typical output from these information systems include scheduled reports, demand reports, informal communication, simulation results, and advice.

    a. *Scheduled reports:* These reports are printed and/or displayed on a regular basis. Typical reports are income statements, monthly sales summaries, and government employment quotas. Reports that are processed automatically on a regular basis can be in either detailed or summary form, depending on the needs of the receiver of the information.

b. *Demand reports:* Demand reports are made available on an ad hoc basis. Databases with an on-line query allow business personnel to display or print the desired information in a format suited to the specific occasion.

c. *Informal communication:* The automated office allows both internal and external business personnel to communicate in written, visual, or oral form. These lines of communication have greatly enhanced the dissemination of informal as well as formal communication throughout the organization.

d. *Simulations:* Decision support systems address business needs through mathematical models for specialized problem areas. The simulation results provide alternatives to consider when making decisions. These support systems can be designed through the use of spreadsheets all the way to the use of programs designed for a specific decision support system.

e. *Advice:* An expert system functions as a consultant, advising the user how to solve a problem. The reasoning followed in reaching a particular solution can also be displayed by an expert system.

Shared information from these computer-based information systems within the organization has a dramatic impact on problem solving and decision making.

D. Teleconferencing and Telecommuting

The technology being used in offices today that enables people to meet face to face while actually being located in different places is *teleconferencing*. Since approximately 60 percent of all communications in the office do not require actual face-to-face meetings, teleconferencing is a viable option. It brings together three or more people through audio, video, or computer technology. *Telecommuting* incorporates the concept of "the electronic cottage"—the view that an office is not necessarily one physical location but rather a person's total workspace. This concept involves the *extended* office, that is, all the places in which a person does work involving business information. Both teleconferencing and telecommuting involve conferencing technologies necessary for the electronic communication of information.

1. *Audio Conferencing:* Audio conferencing is the *audio* (sound) linkage of three or more people at two or more separate locations by means of telephone lines so that each may converse freely with the other participants. When a meeting does not require face-to-face interaction or visual contact between the participants, audio conferencing can be very advantageous. The main advantage of audio conferencing is its cost; it is the least expensive of the teleconferencing alternatives.

a. *Telephone conference call:* The typical audio conference is the telephone conference call linking several people into one conversation. A telephone conference call can connect numerous two-way interactive sites as well.

b. *Audio conference media:* The basic media required when there is more than one person in a room at one location are telephone speakerphones.

2. *Conducting an Audio Conference:* Five guidelines can easily enhance the success of an audio conference.

a. *Distribution of conference agenda:* A copy of the conference agenda should be sent to each participant at least one day in advance. Fax or e-mail is an excellent way to transmit the written agenda.

b. *Moderating the conference:* Whoever organizes the conference should serve as the moderator. The moderator makes sure that all individuals participate and that the conference objectives are accomplished.

c. *Maximum conference participation:* To keep the conference manageable, no more than eight persons should participate in an audio conference. With audio conference monitoring equipment, it is possible for more persons to participate in the conference.

d. *Speaker identification during conference:* Participants should always identify themselves before speaking so that each speaker is identified by all individuals involved in the conference.

e. *Recording the conference:* If required, a recording of the conference can be taped for future reference. Participants need to be notified at the start of the conference that the conference is being taped.

3. *Enhanced Audio Conferencing:* In today's telecommunications environment, audio conferencing can be enhanced with graphics, documents, and still images. Some organizations bypass the cost of real-time enhancement and still benefit from visual images being available to all participants by sending the visuals in advance. When interaction and changes to the visuals are required during the conference, businesses have several options available.

a. *Facsimile transmission (fax):* An exact copy of hard-copy material is transmitted over telephone lines during the audio conference. Output can be in the form of transparencies, documents, or slides. If multiple copies are needed at the receiving location, they can be prepared at a photocopy machine. (For more information on fax, see Sections C-2-c[2] and E-1.)

b. *Electronic blackboard:* Material drawn on a touch-sensitive surface is transmitted electronically to the conference locations, where viewing takes place on a monitor. Two communication links are required: one for the image and one for the voice. This requires two telephone calls.

c. *Slow-scan video:* A video camera scans the object to be viewed. It takes 60 seconds to construct a full picture with three-dimensional effects at the receiving location. The image is displayed on a television monitor.

d. *Freeze-frame video:* A single frame of a moving object is "frozen" and then transmitted. Sometimes, images of the participants are transmitted this way. Freeze-frame transmission is like watching a slide show.

e. *Computer transmission:* Using the electronic mailbox, participants in an audio conference who also have the computer mail link can transmit documents, graphics, or spreadsheets from their computer applications to the mailbox of the recipient. Through the Internet, communicating via the computer in a real-time environment has dramatically changed the conference setting.

4. *Video Conferencing:* Where participants' actions as well as audio contact are important for appropriate interaction, video conferencing is the alternative to consider. Video conferencing is the state of the art in teleconferencing.

a. *One-way video conferencing:* This teleconference allows information transmission of the participant(s) from one location to another but not vice versa. This form of video conference is used for educational lectures, training, and product promotion where seeing the presenter is important to the audience. The audio communication is usually two-way, whereas the video communication is one-way. However, the audio communication may also be one-way.

b. *Full-motion video conferencing:* Two-way conferencing where all participants can see one another in motion and hear one another is video conferencing at its optimum. This is also called an *interactive video conference.* The teleconferencing center must be fully equipped with cameras, overhead microphones, and acoustically treated rooms so that the audio and video transmission is of the highest quality. The participants sit at a conference table as they would at a face-to-face meeting and confer with the other participants as they are viewed on video screens. This is the most complex and the most expensive form of teleconferencing.

EXAMPLE: Some hotels specializing in conferences and conventions are creating conference theaters as available meeting rooms so that teleconferencing can be included as part of the meeting programs. These theaters include the latest in teleconferencing technology to accommodate the needs of a wide variety of business and professional organizations.

5. *Implications for Secretaries:* The successful teleconference depends on many criteria. The most important criterion in selecting the location for teleconferencing facilities is convenience to potential users. However, the room must possess certain characteristics that will accommodate an audio, enhanced audio, or video conference. Location of the room, acoustics, and room design are important factors to consider. In addition, the need to plan for and organize the conference activities is essential. The administrative professional with organizational talent will be of great value to any executive in planning a teleconference.

a. *Location:* Selecting the location that will be established as a teleconferencing center involves compromise among a number of factors: accessibility to primary users, availability of floor space, and environmental conditions. Ideally, the conference room should be a quiet, interior room convenient to all potential users.

EXAMPLE: As the administrative assistant to the vice president of operations, McCae was given the responsibility of securing the room location for the new teleconferencing center. In talking with Bradford, the vice president, she found that four of the five top executives had indicated expanding the executive office area to add a conference room with directional microphones and speakers. However, McCae's research indicated that the main users would be the marketing department for product promotion. One of her recommendations was to establish the teleconference room in a more central location that is close to the marketing department.

b. *Acoustics:* Good conference performance depends on acoustical properties providing low reverberation. Echoes in the room can be determined by clapping the hands sharply. If a pronounced echo is heard, the room will require acoustical treatment. Reverberation in a room is referred to as the *rain-barrel effect,* which characterizes the sound picked up by a microphone.

Several other acoustical factors need to be considered as well: room size; room shape; inside room; ceiling height; wall, ceiling, floor, and furniture coverings; furniture arrangement; mechanical equipment; and participant movement. Some of these acoustical factors require technical assistance. Here are some procedures an administrative assistant can monitor:

(1) Make sure that the microphone(s) is close to the speaker(s).

(2) Inform participants of the conference starting time so that they can plan to arrive on time (unless later attendance for a participant is scheduled).

(3) Do not allow internal motors to run (air conditioning, fans, and heaters).

(4) Do not allow interruptions from noise created by telephones ringing (including cell phones carried by participants), late arrivals, early departures, pagers, copiers, typewriters, or computers.

c. *Room design:* Planning the room design and arrangement for the teleconference is a very important consideration. Here are some ideas that will help facilitate the success of the teleconference:

(1) In a conference room designed for audio conferencing where easy chairs are used, arrangement of chairs within an appropriate distance from the microphone is important.

(2) If the teleconference will be held in a room around a conference table, seating should be arranged so that all participants are seated around the table and near microphones if needed.

(3) Consideration needs to also be given to intraroom conversation. Of the four table arrangements (rectangular, crescent, octagonal, and trapezoidal), the octagonal table offers the best compromise. Such a seating arrangement offers good intraroom eye contact and positions the participants in good viewing range of the television monitor for enhanced audio or video teleconferences.

d. *Conference planning:* A conference is a planned and organized business activity with a clear purpose. Today's teleconference provides a means of closing the geographic dispersion of persons who should be included in the meeting. The success of any type of conference depends greatly on how well it is organized: appointment of a chairperson, room scheduling, preparation of a well-structured agenda, and preparation of printed materials to be distributed during the conference, among other things.

(1) *Appointment of conference chairperson:* The chairperson is responsible for preplanning the meeting and must possess good communication skills. Sometimes, appointing a chairperson at each location is important when various meeting rooms are being utilized.

(2) *Scheduling the conference room:* Arrangements must be made so that the conference room is reserved for the time the meeting is to be scheduled. Conference room assignments are usually handled by one person, and many times a conference room request form must be completed and approved in advance.

(3) *Preparation of a well-structured agenda:* The agenda should be distributed to all participants prior to the meeting and should identify overall goals, objectives, and expected outcomes of the conference. Each participant should receive notification in advance about information that needs to be shared with the entire group, such as formal presentations or handout materials.

(4) *Determination of reports and handout materials:* If the participants need to gather facts or react to a report or other information presented, copies of these materials should be disseminated prior to the meeting so that participants are ready to contribute their ideas and expertise to the discussion.

(5) *Preparation of visuals for the conference:* The means of transmission must be kept in mind when preparing visuals. If the medium does not allow participants at other locations to see where the speaker is pointing on the visual, clues will be helpful. To overcome this pitfall, visuals can be color coded, key words underlined or highlighted, or the visuals superimposed. Handouts of the visuals for the participants will always be helpful in conveying this type of information.

(6) *Responsibilities of participants:* When plans are being made for a teleconference, participants need to know why they are being invited and know what their responsibilities are. A participant may be required to attend only part of the meeting. The entrance/exit should be done as quietly as possible and announced at an appropriate time. Filling the conference room with too many people makes it difficult to conduct the conference.

(7) *Conference protocol:* The protocol should be familiar to all members so that they are aware of specific rules and guidelines in effect for the conference. Adhering to a conference protocol will help ensure that the structure of the agenda is maintained. Teleconferencing dramatizes any deviations from a well-planned, organized format.

A successful teleconference depends on many human as well as technical factors. Once the participants become familiar with the requirements of the new medium, the success of the teleconference hinges on good leadership. A secretary who is well versed in the aspects of successful teleconferencing will affect the executive's leadership techniques.

6. *Computer Conference:* Often, it is difficult for conference participants to gather for a meeting at the same time. This is more evident in today's attempts at global communication in business. The computer conference allows persons to exchange information on a special-topic bulletin board. The computer bulletin board is available only to the participants designated to exchange information on the selected topic. They access the topic bulletin board, read the new information, and add their input for other participants to view and offer comments.

EXAMPLE: The new product research team consists of representation from New York, Seattle, and France. Twice a day, the researchers activate the new product bulletin board (early in the morning and just before leaving at the end of the day). Through this interchange, the input from the researchers is available daily at their convenience.

7. *Chat Rooms:* Through the use of the Internet, two or more people can have a live, interactive, written conference in a chat room. Internet Relay Chat (IRC) is a general chat program for the Internet.

8. *Telecommuting:* With the integration of communication systems with data processing and word processing, some organizations have benefited from employing office support professionals who work from their homes. This can be beneficial to the employee as well, especially in terms of employing mothers with small children at home or per-

sons with disabilities who have the intellectual talent but difficulty traveling from home to office. Through the use of their own microcomputers or by logging onto the company's computer system for the required number of hours each day, the office professional can access work to be done and instructions for completing the work assignment through a computer-conferencing strategy. In some cases, telecommuting consists of a portion of the workweek spent at home, with one or two days spent at the office. Savings occur in some office costs and space. This type of work is sometimes referred to as *cottage industry* or *electronic cottage.*

E. Electronic Mail

Mail sent electronically within a local area network or thousands of miles away is referred to as *electronic mail* or *e-mail.* E-mail is the simplest use of the Internet. Long-distance communication is sent electronically over telephone lines or relayed via satellite networks. A full page can be transmitted in less than 30 seconds. Through the attachment option, additional documents can be quickly transmitted. For the receiver to view the document, however, both sender and receiver need compatible software.

EXAMPLE: Travis and Benson are doing market research for their firm. As Benson collects the data in the field, she enters it into a spreadsheet model, providing direction for continued data collection. At the end of each day, Benson uses her notebook computer and e-mails Travis a message with the spreadsheet attached. The next morning, Travis opens his e-mail and is able to open the spreadsheet document for research analysis at the home office. Both Benson and Travis use the same spreadsheet software.

1. *Computer-Based Message System:* An e-mail network is a computer-based message system that enables the executive to send e-mail messages to others in the firm or externally linked individuals who can receive and respond to these messages. With a computer system, the message is keyed in and displayed on the terminal (CRT). Here are some features of the e-mail system that are particularly useful:

    a. *Speed of transmission:* The sender (whether an executive or an administrative assistant) can key in the message, thus eliminating the need for an intermediary to perform that particular responsibility. The transmission is almost instantaneous. As soon as the command is given, the message is transmitted to a direct-access storage device and will remain in the storage mailbox until accessed by the receiver.

    b. *Store-and-forward capacity:* The message can be stored in the computer and forwarded at a particular time. When the transmission takes place, the computer will forward the notification that there is a message in the receiver's electronic mailbox. The message will remain in secondary storage, however, until the receiver accesses it.

    c. *Record keeping:* The sender can receive notification back from the computer system, indicating whether the receiver has indeed accessed the message and, if so, the exact date and time the message was viewed.

    d. *Electronic mailboxes:* Each user has an individual *mailbox* in which senders will deposit messages. The messages remain in the mailbox until the receiver takes some action on them.

    e. *Communication dialog:* The sender and the receiver create a communication dialogue that can continue until the problem is resolved or the communication process is complete. Responses to each message sent result in a continuing dialogue between the parties.

2. *Facsimile Transmission (fax):* As a primary type of teletransmission, facsimile transmission is a relatively stable part of the communications network in many businesses.

   a. *The fax process:* Fax permits an image of a document (whether it is handwritten, graphic, or typewritten information) to be transmitted electronically over telephone lines, private transmission lines, or a microwave relay system to a receiver. When speedy transmission of only a few originals is needed, fax is an excellent choice.

   b. *Time required for transmission:* Each copy takes from three seconds to six minutes of transmission time, depending on the system. Therefore, lengthy documents sometimes require too much time. If additional copies are needed at the receiving location, they may be made with a copying process.

   Today, many computer systems are enhanced with fax transmission features, or fax mailboxes can provide a central location for receipt of fax transmissions. The recipient can access the mailbox from another fax location and have the documents rerouted.

3. *Networked Electronic Mail Systems:* Once a document is keyed in, it is held in secondary storage prior to transmission to another location. Documents can be created in one location and be available for "sending" over telephone lines to another location. There the document can be printed out if hard copy is needed. Such a system is entirely computer based; therefore, either location has direct access to the text of the document. It is possible that the document would be stored in both locations so that it would have to be transmitted only once.

F. Networks

A network connects a number of terminals and peripherals in a computerized environment through a series of communications links. The data within the information system can be shared and easily communicated to the users of the network. Also, the sharing of resources (computer processing, peripherals, software, and transmission services) is made possible through networks. (See Chapter 1 for information on network topologies.)

1. *Internet:* The Internet is a global network of thousands of computers linked together around the world. The Internet began as a U.S. Department of Defense network to link scientists and university professors around the world. Today, Internet activity includes e-mail, discussion lists, newsgroups, Web browsing, and, most recently, electronic commerce (e-commerce). The Internet is not owned by anyone, and information available on the Internet is widespread. E-mail is the most popular use of the Internet. Web-browsing activities have become more prevalent over the past year. Most recently, e-commerce is opening the door for business to be conducted over the Internet in cyberspace.

   a. *Electronic mail:* The simplest use of the Internet is for e-mail (see Section E).

   b. *Discussion lists:* Mailing lists known as *discussion lists* enable participants to add their names to the lists so as to receive and post mail about topics of interest. To participate in a discussion, an Internet connection and an e-mail program are needed. To request lists, a participant must first define a topic of interest. To participate in the lists provided or in other lists, a person must be familiar with the subscription and posting process. A participant can unsubscribe when he or she no longer wishes to participate.

c. *Newsgroups:* An older use of the Internet involves the newsgroup feature. A participant must identify the newsgroups that he or she might be interested in, depending on the newsreader being used. Win VN, a public domain Windows-based newsreader, or Netscape, a Web browser, are two newsreaders available to participants.

d. *World Wide Web:* An on-line hypertext system designed in Switzerland for sharing information among teams of researchers at remote sites, the World Wide Web is now a system with universally accepted standards for storing, retrieving, formatting, and displaying information (see Section C-2-c[1]).

e. *Electronic commerce (e-commerce):* The global availability of the Internet has created opportunities for the electronic process of buying and selling of goods and services. This new channel for business transactions is referred to as *electronic commerce* (e-commerce). Through this new venture, the purchase and distribution of goods and services is accelerated while reducing traditional business operating costs. E-commerce affects how businesses plan strategically for marketing, delivery, payment, and customer service.

2. *Wide Area Network (WAN):* A *wide area network* (WAN) is a combination of public or private lines, microwave, or satellite transmission for long-distance communications. Common carriers licensed by the federal government provide a network for both interorganizational or intraorganizational communication. With technology in telecommunication rapidly advancing, organizations take advantage of this transcontinental communication link. Wide area networks are shrinking the distances between users who need to exchange business information.

3. *Local Area Network (LAN):* A *local area network* (LAN) is a private network that supports communications within an office, building, or firm. Electronic equipment that is even a few miles away can be connected to a LAN. The LAN links electronic devices so that data can be shared easily and at greater speeds than otherwise provided. Also, the sharing of hardware and software on the network can lower computer costs for a company. A LAN may be connected to other local as well as external networks. This is possible through dial-up and leased lines, microwave, and satellite transmission.

4. *Bulletin Board Service:* A message service known as a *bulletin board service* is available for computer users. By subscribing or connecting into a bulletin board service, users can leave announcements and messages for other users. The bulletin board opens another means of business information sharing to a general audience.

EXAMPLE: Sky Limited has a communication system on its mainframe computer that allows all business personnel with desktop workstations the ability to share corporate data and communicate with one another. The bulletin board service is where all general announcements within the organization are posted. This eliminates having to send messages to all employees or require employees to walk to a central bulletin board location. With the electronic bulletin board service, employees can read announcements at their desktop workstations.

5. *Value-Added Network (VAN):* *Value-added networks* (VANs) are private multimedia, multipath, third-party managed networks. The third party provides an economical communication link for multiple organizations. Subscribers pay a subscription fee plus a fee for the amount of data they transmit. VANs communicate with other VANs to provide communication between firms who are members of different VANs. Infonet, Telenet, and Tymnet are three widely used international VANs.

G. Innovations and Trends in Business Communications Systems

Fast and reliable electronic communication technology will continue to be necessary to manage the vast amount of data and information created and utilized in business organizations. Here are some of the innovations and trends that will affect office communications systems greatly in the next few years.

1. *Satellite Communication:* Most major business organizations will probably own their own satellites or share a satellite with other organizations. The speed of communication when satellites are used is phenomenal, and operating costs are decreasing.

2. *Telemarketing:* Rather than sending marketing representatives "out on the road," many organizations use enhanced audio transmission to communicate on a regular basis with customers.

3. *Integrated Information Systems:* The interrelationships that are developing in telecommunications, information processing, and office automation are indicating a need for managing integrated information systems. Management information systems (MIS) professionals serve the end user in promoting and supporting end-user computing needs.

4. *Mobile Communications Networks:* Through the use of lower-power transmissions from towers located throughout an area, the same frequencies can be used in different parts of town, as long as they do not overlap. Computers keep track of frequency assignments as mobile (cellular) calls are being transmitted. As an automobile travels, the computer will switch the call to different channels automatically. This network enhances mobile communications and the use of cell phones around the world.

5. *Networks:* The integration of information systems within a business will require support for the merging of voice, data, image, text, and video communication. Networking provides the capability to link otherwise separate components of office technology (word processing, information processing, and communications systems) into a single network for integrated business activities. A "paperless office" concept utilizes computerized networks to handle the internal processing of information throughout the business system.

6. *Electronic Data Interchange (EDI):* The direct computer-to-computer exchange between two organizations of standard business transactions, such as orders, billing, and payments, is referred to as *electronic data interchange (EDI).*

7. *Teleworking:* In the next few years, the concept of teleworking will no doubt be explored even further to see how the boundaries of the office can be expanded to make information independent of time and space. Teleworking will involve every person who uses a telephone outside the office building to perform required office tasks, sometimes with the help of a personal computer. The telephone communication could be from home to the office, from other business locations to the office, or from traveling locations to clients or customers. The two technologies that may be the most influential in developing the teleworking environment are the telephone and the microcomputer.

8. *E-Commerce:* The Internet has created the means for conducting business electronically. The electronic market links buyer and seller in order to exchange products, services, and payments. The Web page becomes one of the firm's marketing tools. In the future, manual and paper-based procedures will continue to be replaced with electronic alternatives.

These are only a few of the innovations that are or will be seen in the area of business communication technology. Needless to say, business communications will increase in importance as the office becomes more involved with communicating business information through office automation networks.

Review Questions

Directions: Select the best answer from the four alternatives. Write your answer in the blank to the left of the number.

_____ 1. A long-distance call that allows the caller to charge the service to a specific account number is a/an

      a. collect call.
      b. credit-card call.
      c. inward wide area telephone service.
      d. message unit call.

_____ 2. A service that pinpoints the exact location of a call without requiring the caller to verbally provide the information is

      a. caller ID.
      b. emergency 911.
      c. speed calling.
      d. *69.

_____ 3. To provide quality customer service, Maki selects one day each week to visit clients. To maintain contact with anyone calling the office on the day she is out, she keys her cell phone number into her office phone so that all incoming calls are routed to her cell phone. This service is called

      a. call forwarding.
      b. cellular calling.
      c. repeat dialing.
      d. speed calling.

_____ 4. A toll-free call made by a customer through an INWATS line is a service

      a. available to firms with leased lines.
      b. paid for by the business organization.
      c. provided by the telephone company for businesses with large accounts.
      d. provided through the private automatic branch exchange.

_____ 5. Companies may find it necessary to have special telephone service between headquarters and a particular branch office. Which one of the following would be the best choice if there are a large number of calls per day between these offices?

      a. INWATS
      b. Leased line
      c. Toll-free service
      d. WATS

_____   **6.** In order for a company to have direct inward dialing where each employee's extension is assigned to the seven-digit phone number, the firm needs to install a

a. CENTREX system.
b. private branch exchange (PBX).
c. private automatic branch exchange (PABX).
d. wide area telephone service (WATS).

_____   **7.** An in-house communications system that signals people according to their assigned code is a

a. call director.
b. conveyor system.
c. paging system.
d. speakerphone.

_____   **8.** The majority of all communication created within an office is

a. distributed through conveyor systems.
b. handled through courier services.
c. interoffice correspondence (internal in nature).
d. responses to external inquiries.

_____   **9.** A computer-based system that permits employees to "send" communications to others in the organization who are linked to the CBMS so that the message can be displayed on a terminal is called

a. CBX.
b. electronic mail.
c. a programmed cart.
d. a voice mail system.

_____   **10.** An automated system that provides preprogrammed mail pickup and delivery service for documents is the

a. conveyor system.
b. electronic mail network.
c. pneumatic tube system.
d. programmed mail cart.

_____   **11.** When overnight express delivery to a small, rural community is required, the best service would be

a. air express.
b. bus express.
c. express mail.
d. U.S. Postal Service ZIP + 4 code.

_____   **12.** Southgate, a new employee with the firm, is involved with a mailing to select customers. There are several addresses in the file without ZIP codes, and there is no ZIP code directory in the office. Her best decision would be which one of the following?

   a. Since mail without the ZIP code is not sorted and delivered as quickly as other mail, Southgate should obtain the ZIP code from a government source on the Internet.

   b. Since the bottom two lines of the address are optically scanned/read by OCR equipment, the ZIP code is no longer necessary.

   c. Southgate should copy the nine-digit ZIP code from another envelope that is going to the same metropolitan area.

   d. Southgate can rely on the new bar code added to the address by the post office.

13. The most efficient way to set up mail for automatic sorting is to

   a. key the address in all capital letters with no punctuation.

   b. place all mail notations in the lower-left corner of the envelope.

   c. use the five-digit ZIP code and bar code.

   d. use the ZIP + 4 code.

14. A device that converts digital data into analog signals for transmission over an analog communication channel is a/an

   a. fiber optic cable.

   b. modem.

   c. pneumatic tube.

   d. satellite.

15. To compete in today's electronic market, Long decided to establish a Web page for his business. He has been distributing his agricultural product to the Midwest region for five years with long-range expansion to the east and west coasts. He should register his URL under which one of the following domains?

   a. COM

   b. EDU

   c. INT

   d. NET

16. An international telegram transmitted via underwater cable, radio, or satellite is a/an

   a. cablegram.

   b. facsimile.

   c. mailgram.

   d. videotex.

17. Reports that are automatically sent to employees on a regular basis are referred to as

   a. demand reports.

   b. detailed reports.

   c. scheduled reports.

   d. summary reports.

18. A computer-based system that supports the user as a consultant by providing advice on a problem is a/an

   a. database management system.
   b. decision support system.
   c. expert system.
   d. on-line query system.

19. The new work environment is the employee's total work space that allows employees to work at home or while traveling. Modern technology electronically links the employee with the office and the firm's computer system. This work situation is referred to as

   a. audio conferencing.
   b. home office.
   c. telecommuting.
   d. video conferencing.

20. When both visual contact and audio contact are important for participant interaction, the best conference strategy to use is

   a. computer conferencing.
   b. enhanced audio conferencing.
   c. full-motion video conferencing.
   d. telecommuting.

21. Seating arrangements are important in a teleconference being conducted around a conference table. Of the four table arrangements, which one offers the best intra-room eye contact and viewing of monitors?

   a. Crescent
   b. Octagonal
   c. Rectangular
   d. Trapezoidal

22. The vice president of finance needs to attend a one-way video conference for the last 10 minutes to present a financial projection. She should

   a. arrange for her presentation to be audio so that she can make her presentation from her office without interrupting the teleconference.
   b. attend for the last 15 minutes of the conference with an introduction just prior to her presentation.
   c. attend the entire teleconference, as late arrivals cause interruptions.
   d. call the conference moderator approximately five minutes before the financial presentation to make sure that they are ready for her.

23. When conference participants have difficulty meeting because of time zones, a conference arrangement that allows participants to communicate on a specific topic at their convenience is the

    a. audio conference.
    b. chat room.
    c. computer conference.
    d. interactive video conference.

24. An Internet service providing an electronic process for buying and selling goods and services is referred to as

    a. discussion lists.
    b. e-commerce.
    c. e-mail.
    d. World Wide Web.

25. A private network that supports communications between electronic equipment within an office, building, or firm even a few miles away is a/an

    a. Internet.
    b. local area network (LAN).
    c. value-added network (VAN).
    d. wide area network (WAN).

Solutions

Answer   *Refer to:*

1. (b)   [A-1-a(5)]

2. (b)   [A-1-b(1)(b)]

3. (a)   [A-1-b(3)(b)]

4. (b)   [A-1-b(5)]

5. (b)   [A-1-b(6)]

6. (a)   [A-2-c]

7. (c)   [A-3-d, B-4-c(1)]

8. (c)   [B]

9. (b)   [B-1-b]

10. (d)   [B-1-d]

11. (b)   [B-3-c]

12. (a)   [B-4]

13. (d)   [B-4-c]

14. (b)   [C-2-b(1)]

15. (a)   [C-2-c(1)]

16. (a)   [C-2-c(2)(c)]

17. (c)   [C-3-a]

18. (c)   [C-3-e]

19. (c)   [D, D-8]

20. (c)   [D-4-b]

21. (b)   [D-5-c(2), D-5-c(3)]

22. (b)   [D-5-d(6)]

23. (c)   [D-6]

24. (b)   [F-1-e]

25. (b)   [F-3]

CHAPTER 4

Records Management Technology

OVERVIEW

The primary purpose of automated record systems is to provide users with efficient access to records stored electronically. Two problems associated with manual paper-oriented records management systems have been the inability to retrieve stored information speedily and efficiently and to maintain accurate data when stored at multiple locations. Automated record systems are designed to provide almost instantaneous access to stored information as needed and to improve data integrity through shared databases.

This chapter focuses on characteristics of automated record systems, both computer-assisted and non-computer-assisted systems, and highlights automated search-and-retrieval procedures. Records are currently stored in three different forms: paper, image, and digital impulses. A fourth form of storage, voice storage, is still in research-and-development stages. Records equipment typically used with each form of storage is also described, and examples are provided.

The use of optical disk technology is becoming more prevalent in records management. This type of technology uses lasers to record digitized or image information on high-capacity disks, resulting in quicker processing time, random access to stored images, and simultaneous disk usage by two or more persons. Micrographics, the process whereby documents are reduced in size and stored on microforms, is also a records management technology. Microimages of documents that an organization must retain for a period of time are stored on microforms.

Computer-based records management systems consist of data files and record-tracking systems. Data files are collections of specific records needed for business functions. A data management system utilizes computers to store records and files throughout the life cycle of the records. Computer-based records management systems are an important component of information processing systems.

Records management is only one type of office information systems technology. Records management functions must be integrated with word processing, information processing, and communications technology to provide electronic means of storing active and inactive records for future use.

KEY TERMS

Aperture card
Automated indexing
Automated record system
Closed system
Computer-assisted
  retrieval system (CARS)
Computer-based records
  management system
  (CBRM)
Computer input microfilm
  (CIM)
Computer output
  microfilm (COM)
Database

Descriptor
Digital storage
Document management
Document retrieval
Electronic filing
Electronic mail
Fiche
Identifier
Image storage
Index
Information retrieval
Intelligent retrieval
Jacket
Keyword

Microfiche
Microfiche reader
Microfilm
Microfilm reader
Microform
Microform reader-printer
Micrographics
Optical character
  recognition (OCR)
Optical disk technology
Paper storage
Ultrafiche
Voice storage

A. Automated Record Systems

An automated record system permits the user to store records in image, digital, or voice form for accurate and efficient retrieval at a later time. Record systems are being automated not only to eliminate the large quantity of paper that has been flooding offices but also to replace paper with more effective means for storing and retrieving documents or selected information contained within documents. Information is stored in various locations on electronic storage media (optical disks, diskettes, and magnetic tapes) in coded form. Automated devices and electronic media are providing the means for accomplishing quick, accurate retrieval. Figure 4–1 identifies the basic steps involved in search-and-retrieve procedures with automated systems.

1. *Characteristics of Automated Record Systems:* Automated record systems are non-paper-oriented, electronic systems. As such, practices used with an automated system differ from a more traditional system the moment a potential record is to be created. An initial decision must be made as to whether a document or information contained in a document has the potential of becoming a record that needs to be saved for future use. A *record* contains all data pertaining to one particular unit. The term *file* refers to a unified set of data in storage (e.g., a personnel file). Each file contains a number of related records.

   a. *Identification of documents:* Before the text for a potential record is keyed into the system, the document must be assigned a name or page label. Various terms are used to represent the name of the record, depending on terms used by equipment vendors; *file name, document name,* and *page label* are three of the more common terms used.

   b. *Record indexes:* In addition to assigning file or document names, record indexes can be created that identify keywords or titles to describe the contents of a record. The record is stored in such a way that it can be located by using the keyword in the request. Each document is also assigned a code number that assists in prompt record retrieval.

   c. *Types of retrieval:* Two types of retrieval are used with automated record systems: document retrieval and data (record) retrieval.

      (1) *Document retrieval:* Sometimes, the entire physical file is needed. In this case, the entire file is retrieved. If desired, a hard copy (paper copy) of the file can be printed.

Figure 4–1   Automated Search-and-Retrieval Procedures

Basic Steps in Process	Automation Involved in Each Step
1. Data appearing on a stored record are requested by a user.	1. The file name (document name) is entered on the terminal.
2. The computer begins searching for the requested data.	2. The system compares the file name that was keyed in with directory information in files.
3. Access to the data is given to the user.	3. The system asks for user identification and grants access to the file/record.
4. The requested record containing needed data is retrieved and available for the following: a. Viewing on the visual display screen b. Printing hard copies c. Revising/updating by the user	4. The requested record/data is displayed on the visual display screen. Both the hard copy and soft copy are available to the user.
5. Data management control procedures are in effect at all times during the process. a. The user may choose to revise/update the record. b. The user may decide to transmit a copy of the record to another location. c. The user may purge the record.	5. Controls designed into the system determine how the user will be able to use the files/records/data. a. The system permits users with appropriate security logins to revise the record. b. The system assists in electronic distribution of the information contained in the record. c. The system permits the user with appropriate security logins to purge data, records, or files.

(2) *Record (data/field) retrieval:* With this type of retrieval, it may not be necessary to see the entire file or physical record but only selected portions of the data contained on a record. The data needed are located within the electronic file and can be transmitted electronically to a specific terminal for access.

  d. *Speed of access:* Storage of records within an automated system is extremely precise, with each file, record, and field coded and named for future reference. Keywords (descriptors and identifiers) are used to enable users to locate the desired data or documents. Files, records, and fields will be accessed faster and easier through automated means and will be available when needed.

  e. *Expense involved:* An automated record system tends to be more expensive to develop initially in terms of equipment investment and time required to establish the system. Cost savings occur later as the system begins to function because of decreased salary costs and/or equipment investment and increased efficiency in accessing accurate data. The maintenance of a sophisticated automated record system will depend on the office professionals in charge and their knowledge and skill in working with such systems.

  f. *Automated devices:* Once an automated record system is operational, there will be a continuing need to update the system with even more high-powered automated devices. These devices typically take up less room than more traditional forms of records equipment. However, automated devices will tend to be more expensive to purchase and operate. The kind of supervision required will be more technical in nature; people who are highly skilled in records management and computer technology will be highly sought in this environment. Ongoing research will be necessary to continue to update the automated record system with newer devices for even more efficient storage and retrieval strategies.

 2. *Non-Computer-Assisted Storage/Retrieval Systems:* Not all automated systems require the use of the computer. Non-computer-assisted storage and retrieval systems refer to those equipment systems that are used to store and retrieve paper documents or data stored on microforms without the need for computerized retrieval.

    a. *Paper storage/retrieval systems:* Systems consisting of banks of metal file containers for holding paper documents of any acceptable size (usually in file folders) are used to automate the storage of paper documents. The system is a *closed system;* this means that the system is controlled from a keyboard either at an operator workstation or near the files.

        (1) *Advantages of paper storage/retrieval systems:* Records in paper form are advantageous to many business operations. Here are a few selected advantages of this type of system:

            (a) *File security:* The security and file integrity make these retrieval systems very popular. The files should contain the documents requested if the files have been maintained properly.

            (b) *Space-saving systems:* These types of systems tend to take up less floor space because they fit either into wall storage areas or within cabinets that permit access from both sides. The files will move toward the operator workstation or rotate within the walls or cabinets until the file requested can be removed from the storage area for a particular bank of files.

            (c) *Automatic charge-out features:* Some systems have automatic charge-out features so that an accurate record is kept of the authorized person removing the record or file and the date it is due. If the file is requested by another person before it is returned, the system will indicate that the file is not available. This eliminates much unnecessary time searching for missing files.

            (d) *Standardized filing procedures:* A specific set of filing procedures to be followed is established, with each person within the organization responsible for following these procedures. Color-coded labels based on an alphabetic or numeric system enhance the possibility of keeping the files in a usable and organized fashion.

    b. *Microform storage/retrieval units:* Any record that contains reduced images on film is known as a *microform.* Microforms include microfilm, microfiche, ultrafiche, aperture cards, and jackets. The equipment needed for microform storage includes the following:

        (1) A reader-printer for scanning, reading, and producing hard copies of microform images

        (2) A microfilm camera for filming documents and creating the microform images

        (3) An indexing system for microforms that will allow for quick retrieval of information contained on microforms

3. *Computer-Assisted Storage/Retrieval Systems:* The computer is especially useful in applying effective file management systems to accommodate the vast amount of information to be stored and to assist in accessing, updating, or retrieving data or documents. Here are some descriptions of computer-assisted storage and retrieval procedures that are now being used:

    a. *Automated indexing:* Whenever an office information system is used to create a file, an indexing system is required to name, code, number, or classify the file so that it will be retrievable through electronic means.

      (1) *File inventory:* The index for a computer-assisted system identifies every file and record in the system. The complete inventory of all files and records should include the following:

        (a) The retention period designated for each file or record

        (b) The date by which the file or record must be examined for retention

        (c) Code numbers for retrieval

        (d) Keywords (descriptors and identifiers) for the file or record that describe the stored document and assist in the retrieval of the file or record

      (2) *Records usage:* With the help of a computer, a complete record can be available specifying the exact use of records:

        (a) The number of times and by whom files or records have been retrieved and/or viewed

        (b) The number of times and by whom files or records have been revised and/or updated

      (3) *File management:* A set of file management techniques are needed with computer-assisted storage and retrieval systems for the files to be maintained for efficient and effective use. User needs must also be kept in mind when developing a file management system.

        (a) *Computerized record indexes:* All stored records must be included in computerized indexes that can be updated as new files or records are added or existing files or records are purged.

        (b) *Access to documents:* Individuals should be able to access records in many different ways: by name of correspondent, by type of record, by date, by topic or subject, or by descriptors or identifiers.

      (4) *Bar code indexes:* Bar codes can be used on file folders as file identification measures. These bar codes label the files much as other types of bar codes are used on products in a grocery store. This file identification information can be read by a computer or optical character recognition (OCR) equipment, creating a tracking and managing procedure that will be helpful.

b. *Electronic filing:* Documents may be stored, using digital electronic document storage, without any rekeying of the original information. Electronic filing systems may require combinations of word processing, information processing, and micrographics technologies.

      (1) *Storage of incoming documents:* Documents that have been received in paper form are scanned by OCR devices in order to store the contents electronically on computer storage media. In other words, all incoming records are converted to digital form, without any intermediate rekeying of the information, and stored in the computer.

      (2) *Storage of in-house documents:* Documents prepared within the office may be stored electronically as they are being created. Terminals used for keying in the original information become part of the automated network in the office, and immediate electronic storage takes place directly on disks or in the computer.

(3) *Document imaging:* Signatures, photographs, and other types of images can also be stored with electronic filing systems. Security of electronically stored information is enhanced through precautionary measures like these.

(4) *Database management:* The existence of a database management system facilitates the creation of electronically filed records as well as verification, retrieval, updating, and printing of those records. Records need to be retrievable, whether they are paper documents converted to microform or electronically produced. In the retrieval process, specific records stored in a database often need to be selected and sorted into particular sequences. The database management system serves as a directory, telling the user the location of the document that is stored within the computer memory. The user, however, would still have to be able to retrieve the stored document, with appropriate security clearance, to access the needed information.

c. *Electronic mail:* Any messages that are transmitted by electronic mail to other locations are electronically stored in the receiver's and sender's mailboxes. These electronic documents need to be managed by purging (deleting) from the In and Sent files when no longer needed or moved to electronic file folders for long-term storage. The Trash (discarded) file must periodically be emptied by the user to maintain efficient use of the electronic storage space.

EXAMPLE: Figure 4–2 shows an example of a computer-assisted storage/retrieval system. Input to the automated data management system would consist of both internal and external messages. The internal messages could be created electronically, with users keying information into the data management system. External messages would need to be converted into digital form for storage within available electronic storage. Two storage areas are needed in the system: active storage (to house those electronic files and records that would be accessed often) and remote storage (to house those electronic files that would be accessed occasionally). The user would access files or records only through active storage; this would mean that if a record stored in remote storage is needed, the user might have to wait until that record had been transferred into active storage. With appropriate security clearances, the user would have direct access to electronic data to obtain information for research purposes or to update and revise the stored data when necessary.

Electronically stored information may be transmitted a number of different ways: telecommunications, microwave or satellite transmission, cable television network, data communication network, facsimile transmission, or through electronic message centers. (For more information on electronic mail systems, see Chapter 3.)

B. Forms of Storage and Their Utilization

Files, records, and data are currently stored in three different forms: paper storage, microform storage (images), and digital storage. One other form of storage, voice storage, is still being researched and is receiving more attention as a potential form of storage.

1. *Paper Storage:* Traditionally, data have been stored on paper, and filing systems have traditionally been paper oriented. Paperwork problems have developed as a result of too much paper storage being utilized.

a. *Causes of paper storage problems:* Improper paperwork controls have led to an increase in the amount of paper being processed through the office. Some of the more common problems occurring from paperwork overflow include the following:

Figure 4–2 Communication of Information/Documents through an Automated Data Management System

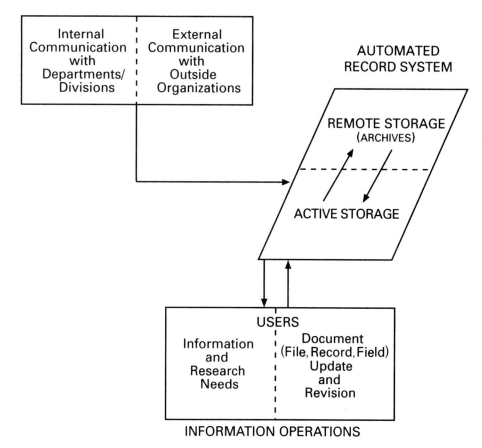

(1) Large quantities of unnecessary copies of records are being made on office copiers.

(2) Many managers are demanding more documentation, resulting in paper "just in case we need it."

(3) Not enough attention is being given to costs involved in creating, using, and storing files or records.

(4) State and federal laws demand the creation and retention of more files and records than ever before ("for tax purposes" is a common everyday phrase being used).

b. *Paper storage solutions:* With the increased need for data management functions, office professionals are turning to better management techniques and cost-consciousness to solve the paper crisis. Here are some of the basic concepts affecting the changing emphasis on data management:

(1) Records are considered *units of information,* either numeric data or text (alphabetic) information. A record contains all data pertaining to one unit in a group.

(2) Value is placed on various kinds of information. Managers are more aware today of the *costs* and *benefits* of information.

(3) A systems approach must be used for solving information problems. Consideration must be given to the effect on the entire organization when information is being stored electronically rather than in some other form.

(4) The use of paper as a form of storage is being deemphasized.

Data stored in paper form consume costly space. Paper storage is measured in terms of linear inches and feet. Paper files vary in size and in handling efficiency. Some paper records stored in files consist of single pages and are relatively easy to store and retrieve. Other multiple-page records can be very cumbersome to store and retrieve. Nonstandard paper forms require special handling and storage equipment.

2. *Image Storage:* The storage of documents or other data that include text, graphics, tables, and pictures is called *image storage*. Optical disk technology and micrographics are the storage and retrieval technologies that comprise image storage.

   a. *Optical disk technology:* The optical disk is fast becoming the most popular image-based form of storage. The compact disk read-only memory (CD-ROM) is the most popular and least expensive type of optical disk. Today's microcomputer typically has a CD-ROM drive as well as disk drives for 3 ½- or 5 ¼-inch diskettes.

   (1) *Types of optical disks:* Optical disks are recordlike devices used to write and read data through the use of laser beams. The types of optical disks presently in use are CD-ROM, WORM (write only–read many), erasable (rewritable) optical disks, and magneto-optical disks (MO). These disks are space saving when compared to paper and microfilm. Special equipment (disk drives, software, scanners, and storage devices) is needed to convert paper, microfilm, and digital information to optical disks.

   (a) *Compact disk read-only memory (CD-ROM):* A CD-ROM optical disk is capable of storing audio, video, digital, and digitized data. The disk fits into a special laser disk drive that is the size of a standard floppy disk drive. CD-ROM disks cannot be changed or altered and are best used when multiple copies of unchangeable information are needed.

   EXAMPLE: An entire set of volumes for an encyclopedia can be put on CD-ROM, thus eliminating the need for storage of the bound volumes. Individual articles or illustrations can be accessed and printed if desired.

   (b) *Compact disk–recordable (CD-R):* A CD-R disk is an optical disk on which data are written once and may be read many times. CD-R disks are created during the normal course of business by a laser that actually burns microscopic pits into the surface of the disk. Documents may be updated by adding the new version to the disk; however, all versions of the document stay on the disk. Older versions of a document are either ignored, or the index is purged from the database. Documents cannot be erased. CD-R disks are good for applications that require single copies of material. CD-R disks have also been referred to as WORM (write only–read many) disks.

   (c) *Erasable (rewritable) optical disks:* An erasable optical disk allows recording, rewriting, and reading of data in the same way that floppy disks are used but with greater storage capacity.

(d) *Magneto-optical (MO) disks:* In addition to erasable features, the magnetic principles of tape and disks are combined with optical technologies. MO disk storage capacities are measured in gigabytes.

(2) *Advantages of optical disk storage:* The primary advantages of optical disk storage involve random access, life span, duplication, disk distribution, and immediate viewing of reduced images.

(a) *Storage space required:* Optical disks can store 1 million documents of 1,000 characters each on 1 gigabyte. In image format, approximately 20,000 documents can be stored on a 1-gigabyte disk.

EXAMPLE: The contents of a standard 26-inch file drawer filled to capacity with about 5,000 sheets of paper, including guides and folders, could be stored on a portion of one CD-ROM disk.

(b) *Preservation of documents:* Optical disks have a life span of approximately 10 to 20 years, a longer life than current magnetic media. This type of image storage is considered excellent for preserving vital records against catastrophic loss.

(c) *Duplication of records:* With the advent of WORM-CD and erasable CDs, some microcomputers have compact disk drives that read and write. These CD-recordable drives, referred to as *CD-R drives,* make it easy to record information and duplicate optical disks. The average roll of microfilm costs about $20 with processing and contains 10,000 images (about 0.2 cents per image). An optical disk costs $15 and contains 50,000 images (0.03 cents per image) and costs as little as $1 per disk to duplicate in mass quantities.

EXAMPLE: Carrying a pricing manual and/or equipment catalog can be cumbersome for the marketing representative who travels around the country selling a product line. Instead, many marketing representatives carry a notebook computer and CD-ROM disks for the entire manual. Erasable optical disks can be updated with catalog and price changes.

(d) *Distribution costs:* Optical disk mailing is comparable in cost to sending diskettes or microforms through the U.S. Postal Service. The cost to mail a CD-ROM is about the same as to mail a letter with one or two enclosures.

(e) *Indexing and coding of records:* Optical disk scanned images are available immediately to users. Retrieval of files or records that are stored on optical disks requires less time and effort than with information stored on paper. Each document is indexed and coded when stored. Whenever a particular record must be accessed, its index number is keyed into the retrieval system and the image located automatically. CD-ROM retrieval takes seconds, with the speed of the drive and the sophistication of the graphics stored on the CD-ROM affecting access time.

(f) *Multiple sets of records:* With optical disks, it is possible to have more than one set of vital and important records available in case of emergency or need. Organizations must be extremely cautious about the effect of catastrophes or disasters on the ability of the organization to maintain its records and continue its business.

(g) *Use of technology:* When documents stored on optical disk are available on a network, several people can use a single disk simultaneously. Scanned images can be used immediately. Therefore, retrieval time is reduced drastically.

(h) *Updating optical disks:* CD-E and MO optical disks can be updated according to the specific technology used.

(3) *Disadvantages of optical disks:* The primary disadvantages of optical disk technology relate to initial investment, need for trained personnel, use of equipment, equipment maintenance, user resistance, and updating content.

(a) *Initial investment:* The initial investment is the most significant disadvantage of optical disk technology. Automated equipment for records management can require a substantial investment. An optical disk system consisting of many components may cost several thousand dollars, while a smaller unit linked to a personal computer can be purchased for much less. However, the cost savings over time that will result from the application of optical disk technology should be considered in determining the feasibility of such an investment.

(b) *Need for trained personnel:* Optical disk technology adds a very technical dimension to records management, and the personnel who will be working with this technology need to be trained to handle all the procedures and equipment involved. The processes of recording documents, searching and locating records, and preparing hard copies as needed involve people who become specialists in handling records in this way.

(c) *Equipment maintenance:* As with other types of office automation equipment, the availability of repair service for the technology will be a primary concern. If organizational records are on optical disk and the equipment is not functioning, the need for service is immediate. Maintenance contracts are available with vendors of automated equipment so that immediate service (or acceptable service within 24 hours) would be available.

(d) *User resistance:* There may be some resistance by users of any new system. Some people may feel that it is much more inconvenient to search for an optical image than to find a paper document. However, research shows that images are quicker and easier to find because of the automatic indexing and coding. User resistance may really be toward the amount of time and effort involved in setting up the system in the first place.

(e) *Updating optical images:* Some images will be easier to update than others. New techniques are being developed for updating optical images more easily.

b. *Micrographics technology:* Micrographics is the process whereby documents (or pages of documents) are reduced through photographic processes and stored on microfilm or fiche. Special equipment systems (cameras, readers, and reader-printers) are needed to photograph records, display those records on viewing screens, and print hard copies of microimages.

(1) *Types of microforms:* Any record that contains reduced images on film is known as a *microform.* No doubt the need for less physical space to store mi-

croform records seems to be the greatest advantage of their use. Microforms also appear to be advantageous for preserving records over time.

(a) *Microfilm:* The oldest type of microform is *microfilm,* which stores images of document pages side by side on 16-, 35-, 70- or 105-millimeter film. Each reel of film has a standard size of 100 feet and can hold up to 2,500 letter-size images or up to 30,000 smaller-size images. When a document that is stored on microfilm needs to be read, the film images are enlarged and projected on a visual display screen.

- *Computer output microfilm:* In the past few years, computer output microfilm (COM) has become an efficient method of working with data stored on electronic storage media. Ordinarily, data are electronically stored in a computer and printed out on continuous-form paper. With COM, only the data needed are obtained in printout form rather than all of the data in a particular file. The greatest advantage of using COM is the saving of space that occurs since only those images needed are printed out. Other advantages include the following:

  - More standardized formats for large volumes of information

  - Time saved in printing out paper copies

  - Economics of producing large office manuals that need to be updated frequently

  - Use of indexing system to locate images

- *Computer input microfilm (CIM):* A relatively recent development, computer input microfilm (CIM), is considered a low-cost method for automatically reading files of information contained on microfilm into the computer for storage. With CIM, there is no need to convert the information first into a form that the computer can understand. A general procedure is illustrated in Figure 4–3.

(b) *Aperture card:* An aperture card is a punched card that contains a slot into which at least one microform can be inserted. Usually, text is punched into the card and/or interpreted on the face of the card. A set of aperture cards can be easily duplicated. There is an added advantage in having an explanation on the card with the microforms.

(c) *Fiche:* A fiche is a sheet of film containing microimages arranged in rows and columns on a card. The number of images that can be arranged on one fiche depends on the reduction ratio being used. The standard size of a fiche is 6 by 4 inches, with the fiche coded for retrieval purposes.

- *Microfiche:* A standard 6- by 4-inch fiche can hold up to 98 page images in 7 rows, with 14 images in each row, when the standard 24× reduction ratio is applied. Each sheet of microfiche is coded to identify its contents.

- *Ultrafiche:* An ultrafiche is like a microfiche except that the page images are reduced more than 90 times. On a standard 6- by 4-inch fiche, hundreds of images can be stored in a similar pattern to that used on a microfiche, from left to right in rows and from top to bottom of the sheet. Ultrafiche stores the largest number of microimages of any microform.

Figure 4–3 Conversion
Procedure for Microfilming
Documents

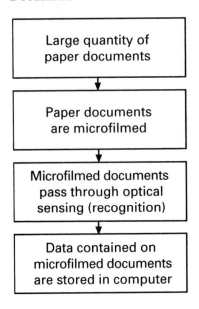

(d) *Microform packaging:* Microforms are packaged in cartridges, cassettes, and jackets.

- *Cartridge:* A roll of microfilm may be housed inside a cartridge. Cartridges are convenient to handle, and the microfilm is protected from fingerprints and possible damage. A cartridge must be rewound before it can be removed from a microfilm reader.

- *Cassette:* A cassette contains two reels: a feed reel and a take-up reel. The microfilm is protected from possible damage by being encased in the cassette. A cassette does not have to be rewound before it can be removed from a microfilm reader.

- *Jacket:* A jacket is a plastic unitized record the same size as a microfiche. Strips of film can be inserted in single or multiple channels on the jackets. As many as 60 images (5 strips with 12 images each) can be inserted into a 6- by 4-inch jacket. Its primary advantage is the ease with which microfilm can be updated. A strip of film can be removed and quickly replaced with a new one. Each jacket is coded for storage and retrieval purposes.

(2) *Advantages of microform storage:* The primary advantage of storing data/information on microforms is the reduction in size from the original document, usually a standard 8 ½- by 11-inch size, thus saving costly storage space.

(a) *Storage space required:* Less space is needed to store and maintain records on microforms. As much as 95 to 98 percent less space is required to store and maintain these records when compared with space required for storage of paper records.

EXAMPLE: A standard 26-inch file drawer can hold about 5,000 sheets of paper (including guides and folders) when filled to capacity. The same documents could be stored on approximately 70 6- by 4-inch microfiche (70 pages per fiche).

(b) *Preservation of documents:* Paper documents deteriorate very rapidly over time, but microforms may be preserved for an indefinite period of time. Microforms are judged to be excellent especially for preserving vital records against catastrophic loss.

EXAMPLE: Microfilmed documents can easily be used in the course of everyday business operations. The routine procedure is to bring the carrier (with microfilm cartridges on it) to the work area in the morning and return it to the vault for overnight storage.

(c) *Duplication of records:* Duplicating microform documents is relatively easy and inexpensive. More than one set of specific records can be available, sometimes each one in a different location for security reasons. Microforms take up little space, are easily transportable, and can be accessed with a microform reader.

(d) *Distribution costs:* Microforms are very economical to mail if external distribution is necessary. The cost to mail three or four fiche is about the same as to mail a letter with one or two enclosures.

(e) *Indexing and coding of records:* Retrieval of documents or pages that are stored on microforms requires less time and effort than with the same material stored on paper because each document must be indexed and coded when the filming takes place. Whenever a particular record must be accessed, its index number is keyed into the retrieval system and the image automatically located.

(f) *Multiple sets of records:* Records security and integrity are very important for organizations today. With microforms, more than one set of vital and important records can be prepared in case of emergency or need. One complete set of records may be located in the headquarters building, while additional sets may be stored in other locations, perhaps even in underground storage in another part of the country. Organizations must be extremely cautious about the effect of catastrophes or disasters on the ability of the organization to continue its business.

(3) *Disadvantages of microforms:* Micrographics technology has many of the same disadvantages as optical disk technology. The initial investment is relatively high because the technology used is very specialized. Office professionals need to be trained to perform micrographics functions, but the result is the development of a system that maintains those important files and records of an organization. (For a review of the disadvantages of optical disk technology, see Section B-2-a[3].)

c. *Legal use of microforms or optical disk technology:* Congress passed the Uniform Photographic Copies of Business Records Act in 1951, which permitted microforms of business documents to be admitted as evidence in courts of law. However, certain conditions must be met:

(1) The filming of any files or records must be done in the normal course of business.

(2) The records must be photographed in their entirety.

(3) The microforms must be legible.

(4) A certificate of authenticity must be included with the microforms.

Legislation tends to specify the length of time a record must be retained, but not the form of storage. The optical disk industry does not have industrywide standards in terms of disk size and format, disk life span, and security. In some cases, courts may accept optical disks as legal documents if the same rules as those outlined previously have been followed, especially the certificate of authenticity. Some vendors are integrating optical disk with COM backup to deal with the legality issue.

3. *Digital Storage:* The third form of storage is within a digital computer, which processes all information in binary code (a special two-number code representing "0" and "1" in different combinations). The system stores information internally within the computer and externally on peripheral or connected storage equipment. The computer also has the capability of locating any record that has been stored. The term that is currently being applied to digital storage is *document management.* Document management refers to computer-based methodology for storage and retrieval of documents that have been stored in a digital format.

   a. *Types of digital storage:* There are several different types of digital storage; magnetic tape and magnetic disk are two of the most common.

      (1) *Magnetic disk:* Records are stored on magnetized spots located on circular tracks in a round format in random order for easier retrieval. Magnetic disk storage tends to be more expensive than magnetic tape storage.

      (2) *Magnetic tape:* Records are magnetized and stored on magnetic tape in rolls of film ½ inch wide and 2,400 feet long. The low cost of storing a large number of records in a relatively small space is an advantage.

   b. *Retrieval of electronically stored information:* To retrieve digital information, a computer terminal must be used to "extract" the information from storage. However, the information remains on the disk until the operator chooses to update or delete it.

   c. *Advantages of digital storage:* In addition to decreasing the chances of misfiling information, several key advantages of digital storage should be noted.

      (1) *Faster information access:* Information that is electronically stored should be accessible within seconds of the initial request. The amount of time required for access seems almost negligible to the user.

      (2) *Less physical space needed:* Because magnetic tapes and disks are the peripheral storage technology in use, the physical floor space needed is much less than with traditional types of filing systems.

      (3) *Use of electronic filing procedures:* Once the system for filing the information is established, there is limited dependence on human knowledge of the actual filing procedures unless something goes wrong with the system.

      (4) *Changing or revising records:* Documents that are already stored electronically can be updated or revised easily by inserting or deleting the needed changes.

   d. *Disadvantages of digital storage:* There are some disadvantages of digital storage that need to be considered as well.

    (1) *Accessing information:* The user must have access to a computer terminal to request needed information.

    (2) *On-line procedures:* The user must be on-line to the server where data are stored. A few seconds are typically required to log on the computer system and access the desired information. It is possible that priorities are established with users; there may be some waiting time to use the needed information.

    (3) *Security controls:* Specific controls are needed to ensure that only users who have security clearances will gain access to stored records or be able to change stored information. A procedure is necessary to authenticate the records to protect the integrity of the information. A related question concerns the need for the organization to make a capital expenditure for a sophisticated data management system.

    (4) *Purging information:* Even though a record or document has been purged (deleted), usually only the address indicator (pointer) has been deleted. The information remains stored and can be retrieved until other information has been stored in the address location.

4. *Voice Storage:* Voice is used with dictating systems and answering devices to provide records created through the use of technology. Additional voice storage systems are coming into use, but current and future research in voice processing will open new avenues for its use.

C. Equipment

Records management equipment includes several different types, depending on the form of storage—paper, microform, digital, or voice. The important thing to remember is that the equipment used will depend on the specific applications for the automated record system within the organization. What is included here is only an outline of some of the basic equipment needed for the forms of storage cited in the preceding section.

1. *Equipment for Paper Storage:* Conventional storage systems are used in many offices where paper is still a form of storage. As other forms of storage increase in use, the file units used for paper storage will diminish in their usefulness. File cabinets, usually three- or four-drawer models, are generally the most conventional filing equipment used.

   a. *Vertical file cabinet:* Paper documents are stored in vertical files on end in a vertical fashion. Each filing unit may contain anywhere from two to six drawers, and each drawer may be 24, 26, or 28 inches in length. A standard 26-inch drawer can hold up to 5,000 sheets of paper plus guides and folders. Generally, file cabinets such as these are easy to set up and use.

   b. *Lateral file cabinet:* Lateral files are available in two-drawer (usually placed by the side of a desk) up to five-drawer capacity. Folders can be stored in two ways: facing the front of the file or facing the side of the cabinet. Each drawer pulls out from the wall to a maximum of 16 inches. Less aisle space is needed to accommodate the lateral file. The lateral file is flush with the wall, and most materials can be filed sideways rather than frontwise, as is true of vertical files.

c. *Stationary shelving unit:* Stationary open-shelf units are a form of lateral files characterized by the "open" view of all the files in the system. The equipment may be completely open shelf, without door enclosures, or there may be doors that pull down over each shelf for overnight security. Some units have closed backs to keep files or books from slipping behind the shelving units. Others allow "through" shelving to accommodate the storage of larger materials. Up to 50 percent savings of floor space usage results from using this system. Typically, labor costs are reduced because of the increased efficiency of the records personnel in working with this type of storage unit. Numeric filing with color coding is the most common classification system used with open-shelf files.

EXAMPLE: Prairie View Animal Hospital has a large open-shelving unit that contains color-coded files for each client (pet owner). Each time a client brings in a pet, the veterinarian is given the appropriate folder so that the pet's medical history is immediately available. These file folders are coordinated with records that are stored on the computer. With approximately 5,000 clients, a four-digit color code, representing the client number, is assigned to each file folder to help in refiling the folder. The office staff are currently revising all records on the computer system so that initial access by client name at the terminal will give the code number of the file folder. (For more information on color-coded filing systems, see Chapter 9, Section C-2-d).

d. *High-density mobile storage:* Mobile storage systems utilize sets of file shelves that slide, either manually or power driven, on tracks embedded in the floor. The sets of shelves can be moved together when not in use or can be moved apart to create aisle space when a person needs to locate a file. Some of the types of mobile storage systems available include programmable systems, power-driven systems, and manual systems.

(1) *Programmable systems:* The aisles of storage in a programmable system can be opened at the touch of a button. LCD displays on each shelving unit indicate the status of the system (e.g., whether portions of the system are in use and certain sections of the mobile storage cannot be moved). Programmable features of the system allow accessibility to stored files and records by moving sections of the mobile system and opening aisle space where desired.

(2) *Power-driven systems:* Aisles in the power-driven system can be opened with levers located on the sides of the individual units. Similar safety features as those on programmable systems are used in power-driven systems. The power allows the storage units to be moved along their tracks more easily. Aisles may be entered as soon as the mobile units are moved to save time.

(3) *Manual systems:* On manual storage systems, a pull handle is used to open aisles between the storage units. The units are easy to move along the tracks regardless of the weight of the contents.

e. *Carousel or rotary file:* The greatest advantage of the carousel file is that the operator can bring the file to the point of use by turning or rotating the file horizontally. The entire file rotates like a Lazy-Susan around a central hub. Large rotary files may be power driven, permitting the operator to control the movement of the file with a push button.

EXAMPLE: The Direct Line rotary file from Spacesaver Corporation may be used to store computer disks, microforms, compact disks, video- and audiocassettes, and other standard filing applications.

f. *Automated conveyor system:* With an automated conveyor system, the operator must dial a code number to let the system know which file is desired. The conveyor revolves around its track and stops automatically at the desired code. A system such as this may use carriers (Lektriever) or actually bring the file folders to the point of use (White's "No-Walk" Mechanized File System). The time involved is relatively short (within a minute or two) if only one file must be located. If numerous files need to be located at one time, time can be saved by locating files with similar codes at the same time.

g. *Filing equipment for card storage:* The size of the cards used for storage will help determine the type of filing equipment that can be used. The most common types of equipment are vertical, visible, wheel, and rotary card file equipment.

(1) *Vertical card files:* Vertical card files, like vertical correspondence files, allow the cards to stand upright and to be compressed tightly within the file drawer. These files may be individual card file drawers or special card file drawers that are part of a vertical correspondence file. The size of the drawer will determine the size of the cards to be used with that drawer.

EXAMPLE: *The most common sizes for cards are 3 by 5 inches or 4 by 6 inches. File drawers that are meant for cards of those sizes should be used.*

(2) *Visible card files:* With visible files, cards are positioned so that one line of information appears in the *visible margin* that overlaps at the front edge of the file. Visible files are stored in flat drawers and trays or suspended on panels so that the operator has ready access to the card records at any time. Color coding may be used so that the cards may correspond to different groups of records. The biggest advantage is that the visible card files may be updated at any time simply by removing the "old" card or adding "new" cards.

(3) *Wheel card files:* Information that needs to be accessible for quick reference may be kept on cards inserted into a wheel card file. The wheel card file looks like a miniature Ferris wheel with the cards inserted in a particular alphabetic or numeric order. Usually, these files use cards up to 5 by 8 inches that take up very little space on a work surface.

(4) *Rotary card files:* Rotary files that move horizontally around a central hub may be used for correspondence, cards, or both, depending on specific office needs.

h. *Filing equipment for noncorrespondence storage:* In addition to business documents recorded on paper and electronic media, numerous other types of noncorrespondence items need to be stored in the office. Each item needs to be examined to see what kind of storage system would provide the protection and durability needed. Typical noncorrespondence items might include plans, drawings, blueprints, maps, photographs, audiotapes, videotapes, compact disks, slides, and computer printouts. Here are some types of storage equipment that might be used for some of these applications:

(1) *File drawers with horizontal drawers:* Flat storage must be provided for maps, blueprints, and photographs.

(2) *Suspension open-shelf files:* Computer printouts require a suspension (or "hanging") type of storage area because of the bulkiness of the printouts and the necessity to keep these files close at hand for easy reference.

(3) *Rolled files:* Maps, plats, blueprints, or posters may be encased in rolls for easier filing.

2. *Equipment for Microforms Preparation and Storage:* Special equipment is needed to prepare microforms for the micrographics system and to view these microforms once they have been developed.

   a. *Microform cameras:* A microform camera records a miniaturized image of each full page of a document onto film. The most commonly used microform cameras are the rotary microfilm camera, the planetary camera, and the step-and-repeat camera.

      (1) *Rotary microfilm camera:* This camera films documents as they pass through an open area within the camera. This is the least expensive method of filming records.

      (2) *Planetary camera:* The planetary camera is an overhead flatbed camera used to photograph flat stationary objects. Filming is more expensive with a planetary camera than with a rotary camera, but a better-quality image results.

      (3) *Step-and-repeat camera:* The purpose of the step-and-repeat camera is to film microfiche. This camera films images onto a 4-inch-wide film that can be cut to the standard-size master microfiche of 6 by 4 inches.

   b. *Processor:* The film used to record images for microforms must be developed in a darkroom on a processor.

   c. *Microfilm reader:* A microfilm reader displays the image of a microform on a viewing screen (much the same as a visual display screen on a computer terminal). Readers are either front projection or rear projection, which refers to the location of the viewing screen.

   d. *Microfiche reader:* Because a microfiche has multiple images, the reader is designed to help the operator locate particular images needed through the use of reader pads and pointers. A "zoom" lens also assists the operator in enlarging or reducing the size of the image reproduced on the screen.

   e. *Microform reader-printer:* Many times it is important not only to be able to view the image on the viewing screen but also to obtain a printed copy of that image. With a reader-printer, the operator may obtain a hard copy whenever needed merely by locating the image, displaying the image on the screen, and pushing a control button that activates the printing mechanism.

   f. *Microform storage equipment:* Microforms are stored in special containers (boxes, cases, binders, and cabinets). Equipment should be selected primarily because it enables the user to retrieve stored microforms more easily.

   g. *Automated retrieval equipment:* Two types of automated retrieval equipment are used to store and retrieve microforms: self-contained equipment and remote-controlled equipment.

      (1) *Self-contained equipment:* Documents in the form of microform storage can be housed within self-contained equipment that will allow electronic scanning in attempting to retrieve a needed record. Retrieval begins when an operator keys in a request on the keyboard of the retrieval equipment. The computer program directs the system to scan the stored microforms, responding with the image of the document showing on the visual display screen or a request for additional information.

(2) *Remote-controlled equipment:* Another type of automated retrieval equipment searches for microforms that are stored external to the retrieval equipment. The request for a needed microform is keyed into a terminal equipped with a visual display screen and then transmitted to a central microform file located elsewhere within the organization. When the record is found in the central file, the image is displayed on the visual display screen. If a hard copy of the image is needed, an automated central filing system can provide this service as well.

Equipment is also available for updating microimages in case an image contained on a microfilm reel or a microfiche becomes obsolete or is inaccurate. One of the techniques used is similar to the splicing process used with other types of film.

3. *Equipment for Optical Disk Preparation and Storage:* Special equipment is needed to transfer images and computer-generated information to optical disk storage.

   a. *Optical character recognition (OCR) scanners:* Documents that are not in digital form (computer generated) can be scanned with OCR scanners and converted to digital images.

   b. *Disks:* Two types of optical disks are glass and polymer, with the glass disk weighing more. Glass disks cost more and do not spin as fast as polymer, reducing data access speed. Polymer disks have the same life span as glass disks.

   c. *Storage equipment:* Most optical disks are stored in devices called "jukeboxes," which can hold 5 to 200 disks.

   d. *Computer:* Information stored on optical disk is accessed through special software housed on a personal computer or within a network. In such a document management system, documents can be full-text indexed. Content words are used to build the index so that more efficient searching is possible. This process is also called *intelligent retrieval.*

4. *Equipment for Digital Storage:* The major types of equipment used in storing information in digital form are the computer, word processing systems, optical character recognition (OCR) equipment, and equipment based on optical disk technology.

   a. *Computers:* Most automated data management systems need computer assistance in order to be effective storage systems. The executive workstation of the future (and the present in many cases) includes a small business computer or microcomputer available for the executive or manager to access any stored data or document available through databases developed for the organization. The vital link between users and the information contained in files and records is the computer.

      (1) *Computer tape storage:* Reel-to-reel computer tapes are stored in round metal containers that can be labeled on the side and stored on open shelves or in lateral files. Today, tapes are mainly used as backup for the data files.

      (2) *Disk storage:* Floppy disks used in microcomputer systems for document storage must be treated with care so that unnecessary damage will not occur. Plastic desktop cases are available in 3½- and 5¼-inch sizes so that disks can be protected when not in use. In some computing systems, backup for documents stored on hard disks is provided with floppy disk storage or Zip and Jaz cartridge storage.

(3) *Information management software:* Custom software packages are now available to accommodate specific requirements for the storage of critical information for the organization. Some of the basic software features include multilevel tracking of files and records within a relational hierarchy and reporting of material movement activity. Work-flow components include features that permit the integration of electronic mail, the intranet within the organization, the Internet, and imaging systems.

EXAMPLE: Infolinx™ is an example of a custom software package designed specifically for information and materials storage management. Spacesaver Systems, Inc., has designed this program so that it can be adapted to specific client requirements and provide organizational information as needed to perform daily tasks.

Note: Chapter 1 contains more complete information on the storage of information on electronic storage media.

b. *Word processors:* Records prepared with word processing systems are stored on electronic storage media, primarily disk storage (floppy disk, Zip or Jaz cartridge, or hard disk) or computer network storage. File management is a crucial issue in word/information processing because of the need to purge the electronic storage of any unneeded documents.

(1) *Disk storage:* Disks used for word processing may be stored in boxes, trays, tubs, suspension files, binders, or rotary files. Desktop box files, a common storage method, allow disks to be locked and stored in safe, secure vaults overnight. Each disk has a protective envelope to help prevent damage to the disk. The software program used for word processing requires the operator to follow certain procedures in storing documents and files on disks.

(a) *Assignment of file or document names:* In storing documents on electronic storage media, a file or document name must be assigned when creating a new document. The parameters are established for these file names (the number of characters permitted or the characters or symbols that can be used may be limited). The operator is reminded by the system to indicate file or document names when a document is opened or each time saving (storing) a document occurs.

(b) *File directory:* The disk directory (sometimes called the *index*) contains a list of all document files stored on that particular disk. Typically, this list is in alphabetical order, with any documents that begin with numbers sequenced first. A hard drive may contain a number of different directories in which documents pertaining to specific subjects or topics may be stored. In the Windows environment, directories are called *folders.*

(c) *Disk capacity:* The system can tell the operator the amount of storage space remaining on the disk. Typically, an indication of percentage of space and/or character storage remaining are two common methods. Most often, this information appears on the disk directory. In this way, the operator can gauge the volume of word processing or data entry to be done and be sure that as disks near full capacity they are "filed" and the work continued on new disks. Some operators use 80 percent full as the cutoff point.

(2) *Magnetic tape cassettes or cartridges:* Any storage of documents on magnetic tape cassettes or cartridges would require special drawers or drawer partitions

for standard filing equipment or desktop rotary equipment. Cassettes used in recording dictation, conference proceedings, and business meetings are often kept on file for a period of time in case any questions or concerns develop.

These are only a few of the ways in which computers with word processing programs influence the way in which documents recorded on electronic storage are managed and stored.

Note: See Chapter 2 for more information on electronic storage media used in word/information processing.

c. *Optical character recognition (OCR):* With optical character recognition (OCR), a document is scanned, and the data are converted to digital form for processing by the computer. The transmission rate is very fast, approximately 300 to 400 characters per second. The OCR system can read typewritten, printed, or handwritten information that is prepared in acceptable formats.

d. *Optical disk technology:* One of the most recent technologies to come under records management scrutiny is the optical disk or optical disk memory. Optical disk development is a major step in digital storage technology. The optical disk has the advantage of having high-density storage and rapid random access. Another positive aspect of the technology is the capability of providing graphics, color video, and stereo sound. In the development process, pictures and sound tracks are recorded in digital form on the optical disk with a laser beam. Optical disks may be utilized to store the following kinds of documents:

(1) *Source documents:* These records represent the original information for business transactions or ventures.

(2) *Computer printout pages:* Technology that takes up much less room than computer printouts will be utilized more in storing data in the future.

(3) *Handwritten documents:* In addition to typewritten or printed documents, handwritten documents can be scanned, copied, and stored on optical disks.

(4) *Photographs or other graphics:* Optical disk technology is an excellent method to use for storing color graphics, photographs, or other illustrated records that need special attention.

D. Computer-Based Records Management Systems

Computer-based records management systems consist of data files and records tracking systems. *Data files* are collections of specific records needed for business functions. A data management system utilizes computers to store records and files throughout the life cycle of the records. Computer-based records management systems are an important component of information processing systems.

1. *Collection of Data Files:* A *database* is a collection of data files containing all records and data fields available. In a computer database, data stored in separate files can be integrated and managed. The number of data files from which information can be drawn varies. Unique field names are needed for information integration and retrieval. It may not be feasible to gather all organization data into one database. Basic considerations in developing a computer database consisting of a number of data files include the following items:

a. *Data entry:* Once a data item is entered correctly, it will not have to be entered again to be ready for users.

b. *Volume of information:* The storage capacity within each database is a prime consideration. The storage media used will have to be able to handle the volume of information stored. A database management system is the software that governs files, records, and data/field storage and retrieval and the way users will be permitted to work with the information.

2. *Databases for a Variety of Topics:* A database holds information in the form of data files on different topics. The advantage of having a database system is that it eliminates the duplication of data fields that would exist from one set of files to another.

3. *Quick Access to Data:* Data can be accessed quickly by users (subscribers) as they need the information to supplement their own knowledge. For public databases, people or organizations pay an annual subscription fee for access to the information on a regular basis. One important feature of a database management system is that information from multiple databases can be merged with information from other sources.

4. *Records Tracking Systems:* These systems track records automatically by tracking in-and-out filing activity. By using bar codes and automated equipment, an organization can keep accurate records of the location of all files. As a result, activity reports for better cost efficiency can be prepared and inactive records, retention periods, and disposal of records managed more effectively.

   a. *Types of systems:* Three types of computer-based records management (CBRM) systems are available: database management software, commercial CBRM systems, and in-house developed software.

      (1) Database management software such as Microsoft Access®, dBASE V®, R:BASE®, and Paradox® can be adapted to specific company needs.

      (2) Commercial CBRM systems that handle one or more aspects of records management are available. Active records management may be the only function needed, or integrated systems that handle several functions are also available. Some examples are Inform Software® and Frolic®.

      (3) In-house developed software is highly specialized and written to suit a company's specific needs. This alternative is more time consuming and expensive.

   b. *Considerations in CBRM system selection:* A thorough needs assessment must be done to determine the volume of active and inactive records and the specific procedures being considered for automation. Basic considerations in system selection include the following:

      • Ease of learning

      • Vendor reputation

      • Other installations in the area

      • Simple, easy-to-understand instructional and operational manuals

      • Training needed and availability of training

      • Free or inexpensive assistance with problem solutions

      • Data security

      • Cost and/or add-on cost

      • Maintenance of the system

E. Integration with Other Systems

Computer technology and records management technology team up in several different types of computer-assisted storage and retrieval systems. Optical disk technology and micrographics technology, in particular, provide an excellent opportunity for the integration of office information systems. In computer-assisted retrieval systems (CARS), documents are stored on microforms and are accessible through the computer system. Four primary types of CARS are in operation at the present time.

1. *CAR System with Off-Line Indexes and Off-Line Reader:* An off-line index is one that is maintained by a computer but printed out on paper or COM-generated microfiche for use by the operator of a stand-alone reader-printer.

2. *CAR System with On-Line Index and Off-Line Reader:* The index is maintained on-line by the computer system, but the microform retrieval device is a stand-alone reader-printer.

3. *CAR System with On-Line Index and On-Line Reader:* An on-line index is maintained on the computer system, and the microform reader is electronically attached to the computer terminal. Information is usually document based and retrieved primarily for reference purposes. The reader will be directed by the computer to find the correct microform image and display it on the visual display screen.

4. *CAR System with On-Line Reader and Minicomputer:* This method is like the one in item 3 except that a minicomputer is used rather than a host computer. The minicomputer may be dedicated to index retrieval for a microfilming operation. The integration of records management technology with word processing and computer technologies is occurring as a result of the procedures used in creating and filing documents electronically, developing information banks for access by researchers, and the need for people to be given access to such stored information.

5. *Integration with Management and Office Information Systems:* Records management technology is an integral part of management information systems (MIS) and office information systems (OIS). The ways in which documents are created, stored, retrieved, and purged are vital aspects of information systems that have been developed. As new technologies are developed, the systems used for document and records management will be refined as well.

F. Future Trends in Records Management Technology

A discussion of present records management technology would not be complete without a brief look at some of the future trends. Records management will no doubt be influenced by the ways in which future technology will be developed and implemented.

1. *Reduction in Paper Storage:* Rather than an increase in paper documents, there will tend to be less. This prediction is based on the way in which office functions are being electronified. The quantity of paper produced and stored must decrease, and office information systems of the future must provide the opportunity for information to be readily available through a computer system.

   EXAMPLE: The electronic mail network in an office information system is being used to eliminate the need for paper and to communicate in a timely fashion. Some executives and managers are using the strategy of transmitting internal communication only on e-mail, which requires employees to access the system to receive internal messages. In other words, if an employee wants to know what is going on, he or she must receive and read e-mail or information posted on the intranet. In the past, the information was available on paper, too, but that option is becoming less prevalent in offices.

2. *Voice Storage:* A popular form of storage is voice storage. One of the ways that voice processing is being used is in message store-and-forward systems. The voice message is stored in the computer in digital form until the receiver accesses an electronic mailbox and asks for messages. In addition, voice recognition (as well as handprint and eye recognition) will become even more common in connection with security systems. Voice regeneration systems will enhance communication for people with disabilities who have difficulty in being understood when speaking. There will certainly be more voice storage in the future; not all information needs to be in the form of the typed or printed word.

   EXAMPLE: Voice mail systems are presently being used to capture incoming communication. With individuals away from their desks for periods of time, the voice mail system is an option that provides valuable and often time-saving information without playing "telephone tag" with other people or organizations. On arriving back at their desks, office professionals need to access both voice mail and e-mail to be sure that all messages are received and handled in a timely manner.

3. *Databases:* Business managers will learn how to use information banks more effectively in the future. To make data retrieval more efficient, many firms are considering object-oriented data management systems. Office information systems technology can be so overwhelming that managers will need to become more aware of those information services available to assist them with decision-making responsibilities.

4. *More Integration with Office Information Systems:* Records management technology, by its very nature, must be seen as an integral part of the entire process of handling information—from document or record creation to final purging. A very close relationship is necessary among information processing, word processing, records management, and communications technologies. People known as *integrated systems managers* or *information managers* are needed to manage planned systems integrations within organizations.

5. *Optical Technology:* Optical disk technology is beginning to replace both paper and microforms and will become the vehicle for electronic filing in the integrated office of the future. The integration of optical technology and micrographics continues to be supported for three reasons:

   a. Optical technology provides quicker processing time, random access to stored images, and the ability for simultaneous disk usage.

   b. The cost of optical technology has dramatically decreased and is fast becoming a more affordable technology for records management.

   c. CD-ROM drives are becoming standard components in the system configuration of microcomputer systems today.

6. *Information Protection:* Concerns for privacy of information will continue to loom over the electronic office. With computer technology being much more available today, information access by unauthorized persons is posing a grave threat to business functions. Another concern for the future is the threat that electronic communications poses—what records need to be purged and which need to be kept.

7. *Copyright Controls:* Developers of software technology are becoming more flexible in how copyrighted software programs are licensed. While initially the majority of software programs were licensed to specific equipment systems, vendors now sell site licenses for specified numbers of users. Wider usage of local area networks and software costs have been the impetus for these changes. (For more information on the types of licenses issued by software developers, see Chapter 1, Section D-4-c; for more information on the Copyright Act of 1976, see Chapter 5, Section E.)

Review Questions

Directions: Select the best answer from the four alternatives. Write your answer in the blank to the left of the number.

_____ 1. In an automated record system, a specific record is requested by keying in the document name. The computer system then

    a. prints out a copy of the requested record.
    b. compares the keyed-in document name with those listed in the files directory.
    c. displays the image of the requested record on the visual display screen.
    d. permits updating or revising of the record.

_____ 2. Document retrieval refers to

    a. messages that are transmitted rapidly to other locations within an organization.
    b. the selection of only certain portions of the information contained in a record.
    c. the use of directory information within an automated records system.
    d. the storage of documents in digital form.

_____ 3. Jamison wishes to retrieve a particular research report that he knows is stored in the computer. He remembers a table showing a set of test comparisons for a new product line. Jamison appears to be most interested in

    a. instantaneous retrieval.
    b. document retrieval.
    c. information retrieval.
    d. using keywords for easier retrieval.

_____ 4. A descriptor or identifier of a stored document is called a/an

    a. data bank.
    b. index.
    c. keyword.
    d. microform.

_____ 5. A closed storage/retrieval system

    a. does not require the keeping of charge-out records because only a limited number of people can access the files.
    b. tends to require valuable floor space because of its size.
    c. maintains file integrity.
    d. allows each department to maintain its own set of filing procedures.

_____   **6.** In an automated record system, written communication received from a customer that is converted to digital form would be immediately stored in which type of storage?

   a. Remote storage
   b. Active storage
   c. Inactive storage
   d. Archives

_____   **7.** A document stored within an automated record system can be retrieved through a/an

   a. file management system.
   b. security system.
   c. file inventory.
   d. an electronic indexing system.

_____   **8.** A document in paper form

   a. can be converted to digital storage through an optical scanning procedure.
   b. will remain in paper form until that information is no longer needed.
   c. can be converted to digital storage only by keying in the information on a terminal.
   d. will become part of the organizational database.

_____   **9.** The deletion of an electronic mail message by a user

   a. removes the pointer that indicates the message's location on the hard disk.
   b. removes the message from the entire computer system.
   c. automatically shreds (destroys) the message.
   d. transmits the message before purging occurs.

_____   **10.** Storing records on paper has resulted in

   a. less demand for the creation of records by government agencies.
   b. more documentation demanded by managers.
   c. preparation of hard copies only as needed.
   d. more attention focused on costs of creating and using records.

_____   **11.** When information is stored electronically, consideration must be given to the

   a. effect on the entire organization.
   b. maintenance of paper as a primary form of record or file storage.
   c. electronic mail messages transmitted throughout the organization.
   d. demand for more paper documentation.

_____   **12.** Use of optical disk technology for storing records and files is advantageous because

   a. no special equipment is needed to convert paper or microfilmed records to optical disk.
   b. CD-ROM disks can be changed or altered easily.
   c. optical disks have a life span of five to eight years.
   d. an optical disk stores about five times the number of images that can be stored on a roll of microfilm.

13. Images stored on optical disk are easier and quicker to locate than a paper copy because of the

   a. automatic indexing and coding.
   b. few components in the optical disk technology being used.
   c. updating of the images.
   d. low equipment investment that is required.

14. The process of reducing the size of documents and storing these images on microforms is known as

   a. document management.
   b. electronic filing.
   c. micrographics.
   d. image processing.

15. Images placed side by side on a reel of film are referred to as a/an

   a. microfilm.
   b. optical disk.
   c. microfiche.
   d. cartridge.

16. Which one of the following is an advantage of using microforms for document storage?

   a. Individual records can be accessed with or without an indexing number.
   b. Microforms deteriorate over time and can be preserved for only a limited period of time.
   c. The cost of equipment for viewing microforms is high.
   d. The cost of duplicating microforms is low.

17. The use of microform technology requires an organization to

   a. convert all documents presently in paper form to microform storage.
   b. establish clusters of workstations with shared terminals.
   c. make a minimal investment in automated equipment.
   d. employ technical specialists who are trained in specific record procedures.

18. Current legislation in effect most influences an organization's decision to

   a. create duplicate copies of records.
   b. maintain paper storage of records.
   c. develop and follow a records retention schedule.
   d. convert records to digital form.

19. Which one of the following represents an advantage of optical disk technology?

   a. An optical disk is the least expensive technology to use.
   b. Several people can use a single disk simultaneously when available on a network.
   c. Scanned images can be used as soon as a conversion process is complete.
   d. The life span of an optical disk is equal to that of magnetic media.

20. Which one of the following is an advantage of digital document storage?

  a. The amount of time required for access is almost negligible for the user.
  b. A computer terminal is required to access documents.
  c. Voice storage is typically a form of digital storage.
  d. The user must be on-line to the computer to access stored information.

21. Mathers is conducting an analysis of the floor space required for the conventional files presently being used in her office. The greatest savings in floor space would result from using which one of the following types of files?

  a. Open-shelf units
  b. Lateral file cabinets
  c. Automated conveyor system
  d. Vertical file cabinets

22. Microform technology enables retrieved documents to be viewed

  a. without any special micrographics equipment.
  b. if a reader-printer is available.
  c. if the microform is housed in self-contained equipment.
  d. if the microform is stored in an internal system.

23. Information that is stored on optical disk can be full-text indexed and accessed through

  a. files directories.
  b. archival retrieval.
  c. intelligent retrieval.
  d. keywords.

24. The vital link between information contained in automated records storage and users is

  a. document management.
  b. micrographics technology.
  c. the computer system.
  d. trained records management personnel.

25. In word processing applications, a crucial need exists for

  a. software programs that assign file names to documents as these documents are being created.
  b. all documents prepared to be stored on electronic storage media.
  c. a disk storage system with unlimited document storage.
  d. file management to maintain electronic storage of only those documents that are needed.

26. An alphabetized list of the names of all documents stored on a disk is called a

    a. directory.
    b. listing.
    c. filing system.
    d. keyword.

27. A database is a

    a. single field of information on a specific topic.
    b. directory of document files stored electronically in the system.
    c. collection of data files, all relating to the same type of information available.
    d. cross-reference for items included in a set of data files.

28. Micrographics technology and computer technology link together in a/an

    a. optical disk system.
    b. optical character recognition system.
    c. electronic mail system.
    d. computer-assisted retrieval system.

Solutions

23. (c)   [C-3-d]

24. (c)   [C-4-a]

25. (d)   [C-4-b]

26. (a)   [C-4-b(1)(b)]

27. (c)   [D-1]

28. (d)   [E]

CHAPTER
5
Reprographics Technology

OVERVIEW

As a part of image processing, reprographics technology has been and continues to be in a constant state of change. Much of the technology that was used a decade ago has become outdated and obsolete because of the speed and quality characterized by newer reprographic processes for producing copies of documents. The term *reprographics* is defined as the preparation of multiple copies of images.

Copy processes are combined with duplicating, printing, and imaging processes to create multiple copies of original documents. When documents need to look professional, such as company brochures, informational bulletins, and notices, a composition or desktop publishing system can be used to create the original camera-ready copy to be used as masters or originals for producing multiple copies.

Imaging processes may be xerographic, electrostatic, or laser in nature. Depending on the type of imaging desired and the quality preferred, these processes help create images that can be reproduced in quantity with a duplicating or printing process. No product is complete until it has gone through some type of finishing process: collating, stapling, binding, and folding.

In this chapter, we provide a brief explanation of the major reprographics processes (copying, duplicating, composition, and imaging, among others) that are involved in office administration functions.

KEY TERMS

Collating
Composition process
Convenience copier
Copying process
Desktop publishing system
Diazo
Digital duplicating
Direct electrostatic
 copying
Duplexing
Duplicating

Electronic master
Electrostatic imaging
Facsimile transmission
Fiber optics process
Finishing processes
Imaging process
Indirect copying
Intelligent copier
Job recovery
Laser process
Offset duplicating

Original
Photocomposition
Phototypesetter
Pica
Plain-paper copier
Point
Reprographics
Spirit duplicating
Stencil duplicating
Xerographic process

A. Copying and Duplicating Systems

Copying, often referred to as *photocopying,* involves the creation of exact images directly from original copies of text material through xerographic, fiber optic, or laser processes. Duplicating is concerned with the creation of *multiple* copies of originals as required for business meetings, internal distribution to employees, and other routine functions. Copying processes tend to be used to produce limited numbers of copies, whereas duplicating processes are used when hundreds and thousands of copies of the same document are needed.

1. *The Copying Process:* Copying involves the creation of exact images directly from one or more originals. An *original* is the actual typewritten, printed, typeset, or graphic copy from which copies can be prepared. Basically, copiers fall into categories based on volume, imaging process, and specialized features. Imaging processes applied in copying technology are based on electrostatic, fiber optic, laser, or digital principles.

   a. *Copiers classified by output volume:* Office copiers can be classified according to the number of copies produced during a given period of time. The following descriptions are divided into low-volume, medium-volume, and high-volume output.

      (1) *Low-volume copiers:* Copiers used for low-volume output are typically located near the users and are often called *convenience copiers.* A particular department may have its own copier, or one or two departments may share a copier. Convenience copiers are affordable for the small business or department, easy to operate, and used most profitably when fewer than 25 copies of a relatively short document are needed. The per-copy cost tends to be higher than with other copying processes.

         (a) *Volume output:* The number of copies produced each month typically is no more than 20,000 copies. Copies are produced at speeds of up to 20 copies per minute. Toner probably needs to be changed every 2,500 to 3,000 copies, while a drum may yield 30,000 to 50,000 copies before replacement is necessary.

         (b) *Basic features:* Here are some of the basic features of low-volume copiers:

            • Copies may be produced on plain or colored paper (17 to 32 pound), company letterhead, or business forms.

            • A 10- to 20-bin collator can be attached to collate pages for a relatively short document.

            • The images on the original copies can be reduced 50 to 99 percent or enlarged from 101 to 400 percent.

            • Manual two-sided color copying is possible.

         (c) *Office use:* Low-volume copiers can produce any type of copying from typewritten or printed pages to artwork. Even address labels can be copied in order to make multiple copies of mailing lists. Overhead transparencies can also be prepared by feeding acetate sheets through the copier.

         (d) *Skills needed:* No special skills are needed to operate a low-volume copier. Clearing paper jams and replacing toner cartridges are among the operations that office workers need to be able to handle.

      (2) *Medium-volume copiers:* Copiers used for medium-volume output are generally operated by a small number of trained operators in the office. In a large

organization, a given department may have its own medium-volume copier, or there may be a more centralized copy center offering 24-hour service to all departments. The per-copy cost is less than copies made with a low-volume copier.

(a) *Volume output:* The monthly copy volume for this category is usually in the range of 20,000 to 125,000 copies. Medium-volume copiers produce 30 to 60 copies per minute, and special features can be added easily to the equipment. Paper (17 to 110 pound) can be used in the equipment.

(b) *Basic features:* Here are some of the basic features of medium-volume copiers:

- The images on the original copies can be reduced to 50 percent or enlarged to as much as 400 percent.

- Automatic sizing of page images permits the use of different paper sizes.

- Black-and-white images on plain or colored paper, company letterhead, or business forms are the most common.

- Automatic duplexing (copying on both sides of paper) is a standard operation.

(c) *Office use:* Medium-volume copiers can produce a wide range of copying, from typewritten or printed documents to those that incorporate illustrations and artwork. Medium-volume copiers have a lower per-copy cost than low-volume copiers and are used for longer documents and reports and larger quantities.

(d) *Skills needed:* Operators of medium-volume copiers need to be trained to operate the equipment, which is typically housed in a centralized in-house copy service. Simple equipment maintenance as well as toner and drum replacement are among the operator's responsibilities.

(3) *High-volume copiers:* Only trained operators would run high-volume copying processes. Jobs would be forwarded to a centralized copy or printing service located within the organization, and finished copies would be delivered within a 24- to 48-hour time period, depending on the schedule and job priorities.

(a) *Volume output:* The monthly copy volume for high-volume copiers ranges from 200,000 to 750,000 copies. Such equipment produces copies at rates from 85 to 120 copies per minute.

(b) *Basic features:* Here are some of the basic features of high-volume copiers:

- Automatic duplexing is a standard feature.

- Stapler-sorters attached to the copier can collate and staple up to 50 pages.

- Reductions from 99 to 64 percent and enlargements to 200 percent are common.

- An automatic feed feature sets the copier to feed in a stack of originals, one at a time.

(c) *Office use:* Copying jobs that entail longer documents needed in quantity are handled very well with high-volume copiers. Once the first copy is produced (the most expensive copy to produce), subsequent copies are produced at a lower cost. When an operator is interrupted while making copies, the copier will "remember" the point where the original job has been stopped and continue the process from that point. This feature, called *job recovery,* makes it possible to do a "rush" job for someone and then continue the previous job. Transparencies can also be made on high-volume copiers.

(d) *Skills needed:* High-volume copiers usually require trained technicians who are equipped to handle troubleshooting, maintenance and replacement of parts, and replacement of toner and drums. These technicians also have to be able to follow directions and establish schedules to complete jobs to meet the deadlines of users in other departments.

b. *Imaging processes:* Although copiers appear to be simple and easy to operate, the imaging processes involved are quite complicated. The most common imaging processes are xerographic, fiber optic, and laser processes.

(1) *Xerographic process:* Plain-paper copiers use a xerographic process to produce images. A camera projects an image of the original onto a positively charged drum. When a sheet of plain paper, which is negatively charged, passes over the drum, the image adheres to the paper and is permanently fixed with heat. A powdered or liquid toner is used to develop the image on the exposed paper.

(2) *Fiber optic process:* With fiber optics, an electrographic process exposes the electrically charged drum to the original document that is being copied. Tiny glass strands replace the lenses and mirrors of more traditional xerographic copiers. These tiny strands transmit information in the form of pulsating laser light from the original document to a drum. Each glass fiber carries a small portion of the image. Toner is fused to the paper instead of the drums, providing a copy of the original document. The light source must remain fixed while the paper moves past the light source on a moving platen. The fiber optics copier has few parts, so the copier tends to be smaller and less expensive than conventional types of copiers. Perhaps the only disadvantage of the fiber optics copier is that it is slower than other low-volume, convenience copiers.

(3) *Laser process:* Desktop laser printers now interface with microcomputers to produce high-quality, high-speed multiple copies for the user. The quality of laser print is comparable to typesetting jobs. Laser technology utilizes a beam of light that reflects off a series of mirrors. The final mirror diverts the image to a drum, which transfers the image to paper.

c. *Specialized copiers:* In recent years, copiers have become even more specialized in preparing custom work in the office. Color copying has become very popular as an enhancement for documents long produced in only black-and-white images. Large and oversized documents can be reduced in size for easier dissemination. Computer technology is revolutionizing copying processes to meet a range of office needs.

(1) *Color copiers:* Copiers that can reproduce color are essential in the office for preparing illustrations and graphics to complement documents and reports. The cost per copy can be relatively high ($1.75 to $2 per page), but the high quality of the color copies produced enables them to be color copied in turn.

   (a) The original copy may be in color, and it may be necessary to be able to reproduce copies (in black and white as well as in color) from that colored original. This can be accomplished on most copiers today.

   (b) Color copiers are used to make color reproductions of the original document. More than one color may be used on a particular original. Although the cost of producing color reproductions is high, the extra cost can be justified easily if the business requires that these types of color reproductions be used.

   (c) Interchangeable color toner cartridges make it possible to have more than one color available when the copier can handle only one color at a time. Some color copiers have the capacity for more than one toner color at a time.

(2) *Intelligent copier-printer:* The intelligent copier-printer integrates the copying technology with digital printing functions. The intelligent copier uses a low-powered laser beam to transfer the electronic code to the paper in a dot pattern. The resolution factor of the dot pattern can be as high as 300 by 300, or 90,000 dots per inch. These copier-printers, often referred to as *page printers,* are relatively expensive because of the integration of copying and printing functions.

   (a) *The process:* An intelligent copier-printer needs to have a significant amount of memory. Its microprocessor technology allows the copier to accept input from one or more machines—a computer, an optical character reader, or other intelligent copier-printers—and to provide hard-copy output at local or distant sites. Intelligent copier-printers are sometimes referred to as *information distributors.*

   (b) *Basic features:* The ability to print hard copy from electronic signals makes the intelligent copier-printer a versatile system for office use. Here are some of the unique features that are particularly helpful:

   • Intelligent copier-printers can print up to 135 pages a minute with a resolution of 600 dots per inch, which is considered high quality.

   • A worthwhile feature is the system's capability to communicate as part of an electronic mail network.

   • Input from a variety of electronic workstations can be integrated to produce the desired output on this high-speed printer.

   (c) *Office use:* Some of the major uses for the copier-printer are in phototypesetting, producing microfilm from electronic records stored in its memory, and receiving and transmitting information from telecommunication lines. This process is efficient and effective for forms design where the form is printed at the same time as the variable data, all electronically generated. With intelligent copiers, data can easily be distributed throughout the business network.

(3) *Multifunction units:* Office technology has now advanced to the point where multifunction units are now being used in many small business offices or home offices. Such units as a copier-printer, a copier-printer-fax, or a copier-printer-fax-scanner provide a combination of functions for the office that has a limited number of copies and faxes to prepare and send or some scanning to be done. One caution that office professionals might heed is that, though the price may be fairly reasonable for this array of technology, any repairs may be a bit more complicated because of the technologies present.

(4) *Large-document reproduction:* Some documents are difficult to copy because of their size. Documents such as computer printouts, large drawings, and oversize sheets (larger than 8½ by 11 inches) often must be reduced to a size that coincides with the size of storage available for these documents.

(5) *Diazo:* Copies of engineering and architectural drawings are often made through the diazo process, which requires that the original document be in a translucent state. Because of this, only documents with printing on one side of the page can be reproduced with the diazo process. A diazo copy will accept ink or pencil additions, and deletions or erasures can be made with special correction devices.

2. *The Duplicating Process:* Whereas a copier prepares copies directly from an original document, a duplicator requires an intermediate step—the preparation of a master to use in reproducing copies. A different type of master is required for each duplicating process. Once the master is prepared, copies may be produced directly from the master. Basic duplicating processes include spirit duplicating (the direct or fluid process), stencil duplicating (mimeographing), and offset duplicating. After many years of use, the spirit and stencil duplicating processes have been replaced with more high-tech, high-volume copying and duplicating processes.

   a. *Spirit duplicating:* Copies are produced directly from the spirit master in this process; that is why the process is sometimes referred to as the *direct process.* Spirit duplicating is the most economical duplicating method available. No more than 300 copies may be produced from a single spirit master. Colors are available—purple (the most common), red, green, blue, and black. Materials reproduced with a spirit duplicating process are usually limited to interoffice distribution. In fact, most companies have now turned to copying or offset duplicating processes for their duplicating needs.

   b. *Stencil duplicating:* Another duplicating process that can produce several thousand copies from one master (or stencil) is stencil duplicating (mimeographing). The equipment that is used for the duplicating is called a *mimeograph* or a *stencil duplicator.* The master (a stencil) is a very fine porous sheet of paper coated with a waxy substance that does not absorb ink. The stencil is "cut" by pushing aside or removing the waxy coating either by writing or drawing with a sharp tool called a *stylus* or by using a typewriter with the ribbon disengaged so that the type can strike onto the stencil. An impression or image is created in the stencil for each character typed or line drawn. Mimeograph paper has a rough finish in order to absorb the ink duplicated on the surface of the paper. A stencil may be stored for reuse at a later time. Additional runs will eventually cause the stencil to lose clarity; it will have to be retyped. Office use is usually limited to interoffice distribution because the quality of the copies produced is not as high as with offset duplicating or with the copying process.

c. *Offset duplicating:* Offset duplicating is based on the principle that grease and water do not mix. The image area is receptive to ink (grease), and the nonimage area is receptive to water.

(1) *Offset masters:* The material to be duplicated is prepared on an offset paper master, an electrostatic master, or a metal plate.

(a) *Offset paper master:* The direct-image master, as this type of master is commonly called, is a smooth paper material that is prepared by typing or writing directly on it. It is necessary to have a typewriter ribbon that is suited to offset duplication (usually marked on ribbon container) or special writing implements (reproducing pens or pencils). One paper master can produce up to 2,500 copies.

(b) *Electrostatic master:* The original material is typed or drawn (usually with black ink) onto a sheet of bond paper. Then it is copied onto a sensitized offset master by inserting the original along with the master into an electrostatic copier. The image is transferred from the original to the offset master during this copying process. Electrostatic masters can be used to duplicate as many as 5,000 copies.

(c) *Metal plate:* Metal plates are especially useful in duplicating forms or other documents that will be rerun from time to time. The plates can be saved and used a number of times before a new plate needs to be made. A camera is used to produce a picture of the original material that is being transferred to the metal plate. This plate is the most expensive of the three types of masters, but it will produce the largest number of copies. Some metal plates can produce as many as 50,000 copies.

(2) *The process:* The offset duplicator may be a tabletop model, a more sophisticated floor model, or a fully automated system with such features as automatic document feeding or master making. The duplicator has three cylinders that work together to produce the duplicated copy.

(a) *Master cylinder:* The master or plate is attached to the master cylinder and inked.

(b) *Blanket cylinder:* The ink on the master creates a reverse image of the material on an intermediate blanket cylinder.

(c) *Impression cylinder:* This image is offset (duplicated) from the blanket cylinder onto a piece of paper moving through the duplicator that is then forced against it by the impression cylinder.

(3) *Office use:* The offset duplicator can quickly produce a large number of copies at an economical cost. The per-copy costs are low, but the initial equipment costs tend to be high. Trained operators are essential. Offset duplicating offers the best possible duplicating quality of the three duplicating processes. Depending on the master, between 2,500 and 50,000 copies can be produced from a single master. Color duplicating (of very good quality) is possible as well as printing on both sides of the paper.

d. *Digital duplicating:* The digital duplicator combines convenience copying with the economy of offset printing. Medium- to high-volume printing requirements can most often be met with digital duplicating systems. Compatibility with personal computers allows digital duplicators to function with a computer interface that requires no additional hardware.

(1) *Basic features:* Low copy cost, color printing, and large image sizes are some of the key features of such a digital system.

- All models incorporate PC or Macintosh compatibility.

- Color cylinders are available in standard colors (up to as many as 15) and unlimited custom colors for effective color copying.

- Up to 120 copies per minute may be produced.

- Typically, print modes include photo, text, and both photo and text.

- Zooming capability from 50 to 499 percent provides a range of reduction and enlargement possibilities.

- A built-in touch-screen editing system allows operators to manipulate documents through the various production phases.

(2) *Office use:* An additional computer interface to a digital duplicating system can create a desktop publishing system to handle the preparation of office publications. With the range of color capabilities, documents and reports could be prepared with a very professional look.

B. Photo-typesetting and Composition Processes

Textual material for professional-looking publications such as newspapers, magazines, newsletters, company brochures, or pamphlets must be prepared through a typesetting process that produces a master copy in the type style and size of type desired. The composition process complements the typesetting process by formatting the text into appropriate page and document layout. Desktop publishing programs are among the latest software developments to enable office professionals to create small publications in the automated office.

1. *Measurements Used in Typesetting and Composition:* Type styles and sizes may vary within the same document. Here are some terms that are used by printers to indicate type size, line length, and type style.

a. *Points:* Character size is measured in points, from 6 points to 72 points. Common point sizes for text are 10 or 12 points. One inch equals 72 points.

b. *Picas:* The pica is the measurement used for the width and length of a line. There are 6 picas to the inch.

c. *Typefaces:* In addition to regular typefaces, such as pica or elite type, a typeface may be light, italic, or bold.

d. *Type font:* A group of letters, numbers, and symbols with a common typeface is called a *type font.* The word *font* refers to the appearance of characters on a printed page. A font consists of three elements: typeface, appearance, and point size.

Example: Times Roman, italic, 10 point

2. *The Typesetting Process:* Phototypesetting (sometimes called *cold type*) uses photographic principles to produce typeset copy by electronically converting typewritten words into professional-looking type. Once text has been keyboarded and stored in the typesetter CPU, it will not have to be keyboarded again before the camera-ready copy is produced. Usually, phototypeset pages will contain approximately 40 percent more copy than an ordinary typewritten page.

a. *Copy input:* Equipment for copy input may be of two types: direct entry or peripheral entry.

    (1) *Direct entry:* The operator keys in the characters to be typeset, along with machine instructions and codes, via the machine's keyboard. These characters appear on a display screen as they are being keyboarded. Proofreading and revision of text may take place *before* the copy is finally typeset.

    (2) *Peripheral entry:* A device other than the phototypesetter is used for copy input, either a typewriter or a text editor. The copy is keyboarded, and the keystrokes are recorded on paper or a magnetic medium. An interface device (black box) is used to translate the material recorded on the input medium for the phototypesetter CPU. This black box enables the text editor to communicate with the phototypesetter.

b. *Copy output:* The exposed photosensitive material (paper or film) is taken from the typesetter and put into a processing unit. The material, once it is processed, is then ready to become part of the original copy. The camera-ready copy (copy that is ready for printing) can then be used to make the plates necessary for printing.

3. *The Composition Process:* The types of composition equipment available to use in actually composing articles, columns, or even pages for a publication include photocomposers and computer-assisted composition processes, including desktop publishing.

a. *Photocomposition:* Often referred to as *direct entry* composition, photocomposition is the process whereby the composer automatically sets the type as the text is being keyed from the keyboard. The typed characters and symbols appear on a cathode ray tube (CRT), and the images on the CRT are photographed in order to create the black-and-white text needed for printing. Here are some of the more outstanding features of photocomposition:

    (1) Both paragraph text and headlines can be produced using the photocomposer.

    (2) A complete page of text material can be composed without the need to prepare text in strips or pieces that need to be pasted up for later printing.

b. *Desktop publishing:* The automated office now includes the ability to produce camera-ready copy for printing at one's desk. This is possible through the use of a microcomputer and desktop publishing software. A desktop publishing environment makes possible many different type sizes and styles; the ability to merge graphs, pictures, and illustrations with text; and special border and background effects.

    (1) *Hardware:* Desktop publishing systems require a microcomputer with graphic capabilities, a high-resolution CRT screen, and a laser printer. The graphic capability is required to project graphs, pictures, borders, and different-size letters. The high-resolution screen allows soft copy to be displayed almost as clear as the printed copy. WYSIWYG (pronounced whizie-wig) is an acronym for "what you see is what you get." The laser printer produces a high-quality image very quickly. Sometimes a scanner is used to digitize pictures and store them on an auxiliary storage unit. These stored images (files) are later merged with desktop publishing text (files).

(2) *Software:* The ability to select different type sizes and styles, to merge illustrations with text, and to incorporate special effects is possible through the use of desktop publishing software. There are several popular desktop publishing software programs available, including PageMaker®.

(3) *Interface with word/information processing:* The features for creating text in most desktop publishing software is typically not as complete as working with a word processing package. For this reason, many create the text with a word processing program and later transfer the text into a desktop publishing file for adding special effects and images. Enhancements to both word processing software and desktop publishing software are overcoming the differences between the two programs. A number of word processing packages now offer desktop publishing features, and word processing features are being added to desktop publishing systems. However, word processing and desktop publishing programs are designed to complement rather than to substitute for each other.

c. *Computer-aided composition:* Original text that has been keyed in with word processing programs such as Corel WordPerfect® or Microsoft Word® can be converted with composition software programs so that master pages for printing and publishing can be created. Codes must be inserted into the recorded text with instructions for headings, type styles, spacing, and other format features. The master (original) pages that are created are then used to print the copies of the document, report, or booklet.

(1) *Illustrations and artwork:* Pictures or original artwork can be scanned or redrawn using such software programs as Adobe Illustrator® or Adobe PhotoShop®. These illustrations can then be imported into the master text at the appropriate locations.

(2) *Master text:* The master pages created for the manuscript must then be proofed and edited by the user (author) to locate any errors in word text, page layout, spacing, or document content.

Whereas desktop publishing programs may be geared toward the preparation of smaller documents, more sophisticated computer-aided composition processes are typically applied to multiple-page manuscripts and books that will be aimed at high-volume reproduction.

C. Imaging Processes

The traditional way to produce a master (original) was to type it. However, computer technology provides the opportunity to key in text for original copies of documents or to prepare originals electronically through various imaging processes such as facsimile and electrostatic imaging.

1. *Facsimile Imaging:* Facsimile (fax) technology is used in two ways in office automation: imaging from one location to another (facsimile transmission) and imaging from an original copy to a duplicating master (electronic scanning).

a. *Facsimile transmission (fax):* Many times, documents (text, drawings, charts, maps, and so on) need to be transmitted from one location to another. This can be accomplished through the use of facsimile transmission over telephone lines or microwaves. This type of communication is machine to machine—from the sending unit to the receiving unit. The time lapse can be from three seconds to six minutes for one page, depending on the technology being used (see Chapter 3, Section C-2-c[2]).

EXAMPLE: Jensen has been directed to send a copy of a five-page document as fast as possible. Her alternatives include facsimile transmission or the U.S. Postal Service. If she decides to send it by fax, it will take approximately 5 minutes (1 minute × 5 pages) to send the entire document. Since the document is short, she may want to send it by fax rather than by express mail, with the cost being less than express mail would be and the copies arriving within a few minutes.

b. *Electronic scanning:* Electronic scanning processes are used for scanning text from a printed page and transferring it to a computer disk or to a master for printing. Different electronic scanners are used for each process.

(1) *Converting text to word processing:* An electronic scanner (a full-page scanner or a partial-page scanner) can be used to convert printed text to word processing.

EXAMPLE: With a typical scanner for the business office costing $200, scanning a page may cost from $3 to $5 per page.

Although it can be relatively expensive, it is an excellent alternative to rekeying text. It is extremely important to proof the stored text to be sure that all scanning errors in text or word processing commands are corrected. Format commands may not be read properly during the scanning process and may need to be reinserted into the text.

(2) *Converting text to master:* Any time a duplicating master can be prepared without having to retype or redraw the document, valuable time is saved in the office. An original copy of a page can be electronically scanned to produce an electronic master to use in reproducing individual copies on a duplicator or printer. This process will produce masters for duplicating processes in approximately four to six minutes.

2. *Electrostatic Imaging:* An offset master or overhead transparencies can be produced from an original that is placed in a copy machine through a process called *electrostatic imaging.*

a. *Creation of master:* Instead of copy paper, a sensitized master is used; the master is immediately ready for use in the offset duplicating process. Sometimes the electrostatic copier is a modular attachment to the offset duplicator.

b. *Production of overhead transparencies:* For overhead transparencies, the blank transparency is used in place of copy paper. The image from the original is transferred to the transparency sheet. Only transparency sheets designated for use in a copier may be used.

D. Finishing Processes

After copies are duplicated or printed, finishing processes such as collating, stapling or stitching, binding, and folding help complete the job and give it that "professional look."

1. *Sorting and Collating:* The process of sorting each page into a set of pages is called *collating.* A stand-alone collator may be used that can collate up to eight pages at one time, or a collator may be attached to a copier or a duplicator that can handle up to 50 pages at one time. On-line sorters allow copies to move directly from the copier or duplicator to the sorter without any intervention by the operator.

2. *Stapling or Stitching:* Some automatic collators will staple or stitch the copies as soon as they are collated. Stitching is particularly useful when the packet of collated pages exceeds the size of ordinary staples. Small electric staplers are helpful in fastening relatively small packets in the office. An assembling unit may be attached to a copier or a duplicator to provide on-line finishing: receiving the copies, jogging the copies into a stack, stapling, and depositing the set in a tray for pickup.

3. *Binding:* In addition to stapling, binding is used to fasten thicker documents together in a booklet format. *Spiral-comb binding* and *flat-comb binding* are the most common forms of spiral binding. Once these bindings are placed along the edge of the document, it is more difficult to remove or add pages to the document. A loose-leaf notebook, with two- or three-hole punched paper inserts, is best when the project requires pages to be added or removed frequently. Other types of binding include hot-melt-glue binding or thermal tape strips along the spine of the document.

4. *Folding:* Often, duplicating material needs to be folded into booklet or pamphlet form. Automatic folding machines can be set to fold single folds, letter folds, accordion folds, French folds, and other types. One top-of-the-line folder can fold at speeds of up to 30,000 sheets per hour. Attractive folding techniques save paper cost because documents can be produced in reduced sizes, ready for mailing and distribution. Some large folding systems fold, insert, seal, and stamp bulk mailings.

E. The Legal Aspects of Reprographics

Given the widespread use of reprographics today, users should be made aware of its legal aspects. Some documents are illegal to reproduce: classified government documents, automobile registrations, passports and citizenship papers, and amateur radio operator licenses. The U.S. Copyright Statute of 1909 was revised in 1976 to provide more stringent guidelines for the reproduction of copyrighted material.

1. *Copyrighted Materials:* Copyrighted materials are defined as "original works of authorship fixed in any tangible medium of expression." Such works are considered copyrighted from the moment of creation whether they are published or not. Textual material prepared for an employer is considered copyrighted by that employer unless an agreement exists between the employer and the employee.

2. *The Copyright Law of 1976:* To help institutions in the promotion of reading and advanced study, a fair-use clause was written into the 1976 copyright legislation. The fair-use clause specified certain circumstances where the reproduction of copyrighted material is appropriate as long as the reproduction is used for the following:

   a. Comment
   b. Criticism
   c. News reporting
   d. Scholarship or research
   e. Teaching, including multiple classroom copies for one-time use
   f. Other circumstances

3. *Reproducing Materials from Copyrighted Sources:* Permission to reproduce copyrighted material can be obtained by writing to the copyright owner, asking to repro-

duce the material. The reasons for reproduction should be stated in the request. In some cases, a fee will be charged to use the material. Credit must always be given to the original author. An information source found on the Internet needs to be checked carefully to see whether the information is copyrighted. If so, permission must be obtained before that information can be reproduced, unless the fair-use clause is in effect. The phrase "Reprinted with Permission" (along with the name of the copyright holder) indicates that permission has been granted.

Review Questions

Directions: Select the best answer from the four alternatives. Write your answer in the blank to the left of the number.

——————————
1. Which one of the following is used most profitably when fewer than 25 copies of a document are needed?

   a. A multifunction unit
   b. A high-volume copier
   c. A digital duplicator
   d. A low-volume copier

——————————
2. One important feature of copiers is duplexing, which means that

   a. a copy job can be interrupted to do a rush job and then return to the first job to complete the process.
   b. copies can be enlarged up to 130 percent.
   c. the copier can copy on both sides of a sheet of paper at the same time.
   d. the copier can feed in two originals at a time for easy feed.

——————————
3. Morgan is sending an announcement to 350 people within the firm, describing an office automation seminar to be held on May 15 and inviting them to participate. She needs quality but economical output. What is the best process?

   a. Multifunction copier-printer-fax unit
   b. Low-volume convenience copying
   c. Medium-volume centralized copying
   d. Digital duplicating

——————————
4. Mason needs to make 20 copies of the agenda for next Monday's ad hoc committee meeting. He also needs to fax the details (location, time) to each member. Mason should use which one of the following types of equipment to complete this task?

   a. Low-volume copier
   b. Fax machine
   c. Multifunction copying unit
   d. Diazo copier

——————————
5. An engineering drawing may be reproduced using a/an

   a. high-volume copier.
   b. diazo copier.
   c. fiber optic copier.
   d. intelligent copier-printer.

6. Offset duplicating requires a _____ for making multiple copies of a business form that will be duplicated whenever the office supply needs to be replenished.

   a. medium-volume copier
   b. metal plate (master)
   c. spirit master
   d. type font

7. A style of type, such as 12-point Courier bold, that indicates the appearance of characters on a printed page is called a

   a. point.
   b. typeface.
   c. type font.
   d. type set.

8. Phototypesetting results in camera-ready copy that is used to

   a. create the plates (masters) needed for printing copies of the document.
   b. reproduce the number of copies needed for the document.
   c. compose the text using desktop publishing software.
   d. create an illustration to accompany the textual material.

9. A two-page newsletter is being prepared to distribute to all employees next Monday. Camera-ready copy of the newsletter can be created with

   a. electronic scanning.
   b. desktop publishing.
   c. phototypesetting.
   d. facsimile imaging.

10. In the few months that Jackson has worked for Flowers Beautiful, she has spent most of her time developing marketing brochures, flyers, and catalog copy. This requires various type styles, graphics, pictures, and special border effects. To develop high-quality camera-ready copy at the office, Jackson should have this equipment:

   a. Microcomputer, laser printer, and graphics software
   b. Microcomputer with color monitor, dot-matrix printer, word processing software, and convenience copier
   c. Microcomputer, laser printer, and scanner
   d. Microcomputer, high-resolution CRT, scanner, laser printer, and desktop publishing software

11. If Benson keys in and records the original text for a manuscript using Microsoft Word®, master pages will be created after

   a. the text is proofread and edited by Benson.
   b. codes are inserted into the recorded text for headings, type styles, and other special effects.
   c. the text has been electronically scanned.
   d. final copies of the manuscript have been printed.

12. Converting a printed page of text to word processing without keying in the text and storing the text on disk is possible through

    a. electronic scanning.
    b. electrostatic imaging.
    c. photocomposition.
    d. facsimile transmission.

13. Grayson is giving a formal presentation on the Certified Professional Secretary® program at the October meeting of the local IAAP™ chapter. She decides that overhead transparencies would complement her 20-minute program. Making the transparencies on a copier is

    a. facsimile transmission.
    b. electronic scanning.
    c. electrostatic imaging.
    d. composition.

14. McDougald is an administrative assistant in the marketing division. One of his responsibilities is selecting the best finishing process for various marketing publications. His current project is training material for the sales representatives that requires monthly updates. The best binding for this project would be a

    a. loose-leaf, hole-punched binder.
    b. spiral-comb binding.
    c. stitching.
    d. thermal tape.

15. The fair-use clause in the Copyright Law of 1976 specifies that reproduction of copyrighted material is legal as long as it is copied for

    a. advertising.
    b. handout materials for training sessions.
    c. publication.
    d. research.

Solutions

Answer	Refer to:
1. (d)	[A-1-a(1)]
2. (c)	[A-1-a(2)(b)]
3. (c)	[A-1-a(2)(c)]
4. (c)	[A-1-c(3)]
5. (b)	[A-1-c(5)]
6. (b)	[A-2-c(1)(c)]
7. (c)	[B-1-d]
8. (a)	[B-2-b]
9. (b)	[B-3-b]
10. (d)	[B-3-b(1)]
11. (b)	[B-3-c]
12. (a)	[C-1-b(1)]
13. (c)	[C-2-b]
14. (a)	[D-3]
15. (d)	[E-2-d]

CHAPTER 6

Software and Hardware Integration

OVERVIEW

Office technologies once considered as separate technologies can now blend together into integrated office automation systems as a result of careful design. The primary objective of office automation systems is to assist office professionals at all levels to become more productive in their work. The vital components of an office automation system are (1) technology, (2) personnel, and (3) organization and procedures. All three components are essential to the system; however, the personnel component is considered the most important. It is possible to have the technology available and procedures established, but trained professionals are essential in putting an office system into operation.

Office automation most frequently occurs in stages: the introduction of automated devices on a one-to-one basis and then the use of multifunctional devices, the introduction of integrated computer-based systems, the introduction of integrated information systems, and finally the completely automated organization. Some organizations have utilized all or most of these steps in implementing office automation; others have gone directly to the total office system concept.

Organizations may implement office automation at different levels using these strategies: the workstation strategy, the department or work-group strategy, the organization strategy, and the global strategy. An understanding of the characteristics of office automation at each of these levels helps the office professional understand how organizations develop and implement fully automated systems.

To develop office automation systems, organizations need to be concerned about the ability to interconnect equipment into an integrated system of technologies. Telecommunications technology enables such interfaces to take place. Integrated software makes possible a variety of business applications for users so that more office functions can be automated.

A quick look at implications for the future indicates the emerging need for people who will be information managers, increased emphasis on telecommuting and teleworking, and greater compatibilities among technologies.

KEY TERMS

Applications software	Integrated software	Office automation
Data integrity	Integrated system	Office information
Department (work-group)	Integration	system
strategy	Interface	Organizational strategy
Electronic calendaring	Local area network (LAN)	System software
Electronic filing	Management information	Technology
Electronic mail	system (MIS)	Workstation strategy
Global strategy		

A. Concepts and Applications

Office automation is the process of integrating separate technologies (text, data, voice, and image processing) into a single system that is capable of managing the information flow for a variety of office applications. The primary objective of office automation is to provide administrative professionals—secretaries and managers—with the opportunity to become more productive and to enhance the communication flow, both internal and external. The automated office complements the organization's objectives and is made possible through electronic technology.

1. *Integration of Office Systems:* A total office information system, far surpassing the original word processing technology that was the forerunner of office systems, involves three vital components: technology, personnel, and organization/procedures. Each of these components must be present for an office system to exist. Figure 6–1 depicts the interrelationship of the three components to form an integrated office system.

   a. *Technology:* The technology of an office system includes hardware and software that accommodate communications, word processing, records management, and information processing systems. In addition, provision must be made for adequate administrative support and any auxiliary support services that are required in terms of technological needs.

   b. *Personnel:* Specialized personnel are needed to perform needed operations within the office system. An important aspect of this dimension is the training and/or retraining for office professionals that may be needed to upgrade system skills. Here are some of the primary factors managers must consider in building the personnel component of the system:

      (1) Selection of office professionals who are knowledgeable in office procedures and systems

      (2) Orientation of new or retrained office professionals to the new office information systems being implemented

      (3) Evaluation of the effectiveness of all office professionals involved in specific job processes

      (4) Appropriate supervision and management of office professionals as office systems are developed, implemented, and revised

      (5) Performance evaluation of new or retrained personnel as well as experienced personnel

   c. *Organization and procedures:* Within an integrated office information system, it is important for procedures and organizational structure to be documented. Every office professional needs to know how he or she fits in with the functional organization of the office. The primary focus of this component is on the office envi-

Figure 6–1   Components of the Integrated Office System

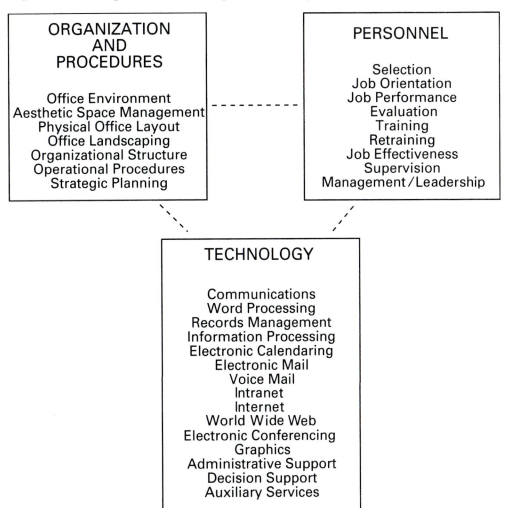

ronment and how it is designed and managed, the formal structure of the organization, the establishment of operational procedures, and strategic planning.

(1) *The office environment:* The office is usually considered to be the physical location in which office professionals perform necessary business support functions. The environment needs to be ergonomically designed, with the individual workstation complementing the worker's comfort needs as well as the organization's work needs (see Chapter 7). The openness of the office arrangement, the use of landscaping techniques, and the aesthetic and physical space arrangements are important elements in creating an office environment that leads to greater productivity for secretaries and managers alike.

(2) *The formal organizational structure:* Everyone within the organization needs to be aware of the formal organizational structure, including a knowledge of span of control and basic management principles affecting business functions within the organization. The development and implementation of office information systems to support the ongoing business functions require that departments share resources and support personnel, that communication takes place within departments as well as among departments within the organization, and

that office professionals understand not only their own positions but also how their particular work fits into a total picture.

(3) *Establishment of operational procedures:* When the office was managed primarily by an executive secretary, it was customary for that secretary to know and remember all of the procedures; others needing the information had to ask for it. The focus is now on the development of an operational office information system that each person in the office—from clerk to secretary to manager—understands and is able to use in the regular business routine. This means that a number of people within the office need to know the procedures associated with the system. Office procedures for the integrated office information system must be documented so that everyone understands what is the "right thing to do" and becomes a contributor to the goals and objectives of the organization.

(4) *Strategic planning:* Strategic planning deals with recognizing the impact that decisions have on the entire organization in the long term. Decisions to expand computer-based information systems to incorporate office automation definitely affect long-term organizational communication. Office automation includes all the formal and informal electronic systems concerned with the communication of information to and from persons, both internal and external to the organization. Office automation enhances the communication flow for all levels of office professionals: operational, tactical (middle), and strategic (upper). Office automation becomes a tool for increasing office productivity as well as enhancing the decision-making processes dealing with product, competition, government, community, production, finance, sales, and service. Improved communications enhance decision making, which in turn affects the growth and profits of the organization. Strategically, electronic calendaring, electronic mail, voice mail, the intranet, the Internet, and teleconferencing all play a role in disseminating information within the automated office.

2. *Phases of Office Automation Implementation:* The automation of the office typically occurs in stages—from initial efforts in automation of the office workstation with word processing to the integration of intercorporate processes. A summary of five key implementation phases of office automation is presented in Figure 6–2. Here is a brief explanation of these five phases:

a. *Phase 1: Introduction of automated devices:* Office automation, at the lowest level of implementation, emphasizes the use of electronic devices on an individual basis to support the more routine, repetitive office functions. The primary objectives are to reduce clerical costs and improve secretarial productivity.

b. *Phase 2: Use of multifunctional devices:* Once an organization has implemented some automated devices successfully during phase 1, attempts can be made to expand the automation effort to improve *office* productivity. More advanced electronic office systems (word processors and microcomputers) are implemented on a *situation* basis as needed. At this point in time, a concerted effort to organize an office's automation efforts might begin.

c. *Phase 3: Use of integrated computer-based systems:* To improve *managerial* productivity, techniques must be used to speed up the movement of information throughout the organization. Electronic calendaring, electronic mail, local area networks, and other ways of enhancing communication efforts are used more effectively to manage the information flow.

Figure 6–2   Implementation Phases of Office Automation

Stage	Objective	Type of Implementation
1 Introduction	Reduce clerical costs Improve secretarial productivity	Use of electronic and electromechanical devices on a one-to-one basis as support for routine, repetitive tasks
2 Use of multifunctional devices	Improve office productivity Increase emphasis on work-group functions	Use of more advanced electronic devices (word processors) on a situation basis
3 Use of integrated computer-based systems	Improve managerial productivity Apply technology to a variety of office applications	Development of techniques for speeding information flow and information management (electronic mail, networking)
4 Introduction of integrated information systems	Improve the decision-making process Provide support for strategic planning	Implementation of integrated information systems throughout the organization
5 Automated organization	Reduce the need for personnel mobility Improve the functioning of intercorporate processes and others	Permit the performance of office functions from many locations (the concept of telecommuting, teleconferencing, notebook computers, Internet, and others)

d. *Phase 4: Introduction of integrated information systems:* As more efforts are used to implement organization-wide information systems, the primary objectives will shift toward improving the decision-making process and providing support for strategic planning. The implementation of integrated information systems permeates the entire organization during this phase of implementation.

e. *Phase 5: The automated organization:* The office of today and the future is linked globally through the World Wide Web. Notebook computers, the intranet within the organization, and Internet connectivity allow office functions to be carried on any time and anywhere. Office functions are not restricted to a particular place called "the office." Telecommuting to the office has become more commonplace for the progressive executive. Business meetings are making greater use of video-conferencing, teleconferencing, and cyberspace (Web) strategies. Improvements can be expected in terms of the functioning of completely integrated information systems within the organization as well as those that must be used to improve intercorporate processes. Within the last several years, improvements in integrated information systems have made a significant impact on the marketing of goods and services and consequently the office of the future.

3. *Office Automation Strategies within an Organization:* Initial efforts at office automation focused primarily on secretarial work and how routine, repetitive tasks could be better processed with electronic devices. The *greatest potential* for utilization of office automation within an organization, however, lies in the work performed by executives, managers, and professional "knowledge" workers. Current emphasis on teamwork among office professionals and the need for managerial support of total office automation efforts are having a positive effect on elevating the role of the secretary.

EXAMPLE: Early research on the role of the secretary focused primarily on the tasks performed by the secretary as a person working in an office (i.e., taking dictation, transcribing, filing, and answering the phone). A more recent focus is on the type of administrative support needed by executives or managers to improve the quality of the "team's" work performance within the organization.

With potential changes in job responsibility and organization of office professionals resulting from automation, the role of the executive or manager must be examined more closely to determine the type of administrative support that is needed to get the job done. Office automation can take place at four strategy levels affecting the organization: the workstation, the department or work group, the organization, and globally.

a. *The workstation strategy:* Initial efforts at office automation aim at making workers more productive and able to achieve greater individual output. The electronic workstation enables one person to utilize computer technology to enhance specific work functions at this level of strategy.

  (1) *The secretarial workstation:* The secretary has a major responsibility for providing administrative support, often for more than one person. Providing such support for as many as nine or ten people is not unusual for the secretary. Keying in information, producing usable documents, and establishing filing or record systems are part of the secretary's routine duties as an office professional, in addition to handling general office responsibilities.

    (a) *Electronic technology:* Stand-alone technology is the central focus of the automation used at the secretarial workstation. A word processing system or a microcomputer with word processing software would be the norm. The telephone is also an integral part of the workstation. Computer-based telephone systems provide voice mail, call forwarding, and other electronic services. Many corporate telephone exchanges incorporate the use of telephone lines as a communications link for information flow to other workstations or to the central computer.

    (b) *Individual control of information:* The secretary who utilizes electronic technology in creating stored information controls the communication of any part or all of that information. The flow of paper documents to other work groups as well as information communicated in an upward direction to management can be controlled by the secretary.

    (c) *Concentration on specific job tasks:* Typically, only those tasks will be automated that the secretary knows how to do (or has been trained to do). As the secretary becomes more proficient, some time begins to be devoted to creating new applications, depending on the purchase or implementation of new software programs. Often only one particular task requiring automation is performed at one time.

    (d) *Isolated job activity:* Any and all tasks are performed in isolation from the rest of the organization. Yet the results of these efforts are expected to be integrated within the entire organization, possibly in a rather manual fashion.

  (2) *The managerial workstation:* The type of work that a manager routinely performs in gathering information, setting up and attending meetings, and supervising administrative professionals within a department or division leads to the development of the electronic workstation concept. The manager's aim

should be to improve his or her own ability to use information in making wise recommendations and decisions, with automation as a very important tool. The power and speed of the desktop workstation allows more sophisticated business applications to be processed at one's desk instead of relying on a mainframe or minicomputer.

(a) *Electronic technology:* The manager may have at least three options as far as computer technology is concerned:

- A microcomputer networked to the mainframe computer

- A microcomputer networked to a departmental minicomputer

- A desktop microcomputer with various types of software applications available at the workstation

Sometimes, a manager will have access to two or three of these options. If word/information processing support personnel use stand-alone systems, the secretarial and managerial workstations will probably function independently of each other. If a work-group strategy (see Section A-3-b) or an organization strategy (see Section A-3-c) are followed, the integrated secretarial and managerial workstations are compatible, and data and information are easily shared through electronic communication channels.

(b) *Control of information:* Controls will be established centrally by the organization (department or division) for access to organizational information or by the individual manager in regard to information generated from a workstation. When managers and secretaries use isolated systems, there is more likely to be a sharing of information between the secretarial workstation and the managerial workstation through face-to-face interaction rather than through technology. Today, sharing of information is usually provided through compatible systems and an electronic communication channel. The integrated office throughout the entire organization is quite prevalent with today's modern automated office technology and the advancements in intranet connectivity.

- *Centralized control:* The individual user will need to supply required password or security code information to access information that is stored in the central computer or departmental minicomputer. Passwords tend to be software specific whereas security codes are company specific. Users need to follow procedures developed by the organization to establish appropriate passwords and security codes appropriate for the computer system being used. Communication within the organization improves as office professionals have access to data and information that have a bearing on their work responsibilities.

- *Individual control:* Information stored at the individual workstation will be controlled by the individual user until it is communicated to someone else in the organization. Paper documents can be transmitted as needed, and other information can be stored on diskette, hard disk, or in central storage until needed. The user has control over any information that he or she generates.

(c) *Concentration on specific job tasks:* A number of specific administrative tasks can more easily be operationalized with an electronic workstation.

In fact, the use of such a concept may allow a manager to "take back" responsibilities formerly assigned to a secretary.

- *Electronic calendaring:* One of the most basic office management activities relates to keeping up-to-date calendars. An electronic calendaring procedure will enable the manager to keep a stored record of appointments, meetings, and other commitments. In an integrated setting, the calendar can be viewed (and sometimes changed) by superiors or assistants. Usually, however, changing the calendar is better managed by only one person: the manager and/or the secretary.

- *Inputting information:* With a terminal or computer, one can input messages and other information whenever necessary. Sometimes, initial drafts of information can be prepared by a manager and then revised by a secretary or administrative assistant as refinements are necessary.

Tasks specific to the manager's position are a primary focus at this strategy level. The manager typically will perform singular tasks because of the nature of the technology available; however, multifunctional integrated software programs for the manager to use are now available.

(d) *Isolated job activity:* Some managers isolate their activities from other managers throughout the organization. This is changing, however, because of the advanced technology in communication networks, both internal and external to the firm (see Sections A-3-b and A-3-c).

(3) *Specific applications:* At the workstation strategy level, a number of specific office applications can be used to improve the secretary's and/or the manager's productivity.

EXAMPLES:

Word processing (increase typing and editing productivity)

Desktop publishing (prepare newsletters, brochures, and other publications)

Electronic spreadsheets (provide decision support and what-if analysis)

Database (improve information access and provide support for decision making)

Presentation graphics (prepare visuals to support formal presentations)

Personal productivity tools (electronic calendar, calculator, clock, alarm, tickler file, and telephone directory)

Decision support systems (simulation model results dealing with specialized issues)

(4) *Electronic workstation technology:* The individual workstation may be equipped in various ways to assist the end user with problem solving through automation. Typical workstation technology for the office professional might include one or more of the following:

(a) *Dedicated word processing systems:* If the type of work involved at the workstation is highly secretarial in nature and demands only high-quality production of correspondence and other documents, a dedicated word processing system may provide the best type of support for the secretary.

The primary purpose of the word processor is to support document preparation functions. Most of this is now provided through word processing software for compatible microcomputers.

(b) *Microcomputers and personal computers:* If the applications required at the workstation involve a variety of business operations, the microcomputer may be the answer. The personal computer, or PC as it is commonly called, is designed for a variety of business applications, including word processing, spreadsheet (worksheet) analysis, database (records) management, graphics, and desktop publishing.

(c) *Microcomputer workstations:* The job tasks may involve direct communication with a mainframe computer or other centralized software applications. Most microcomputers today provide the user with both centralized and individual processing power. Sometimes, these workstations are shared among two or more people since each person does not require continual use of the workstation.

(d) *Desktop workstations:* These workstations are designed to meet specific professional requirements for high-quality, integrated applications. The speed and power of today's top-end microcomputer make the desktop workstation possible.

b. *The department or work-group strategy:* Once the workstation strategy has been implemented, the organization should consider the next office automation strategy: the department or work-group strategy. With the workstation strategy, the user can enter text, compute problems, and draw graphs with automated means. In addition, the user must be able to communicate information, the very information that was developed on an individual basis, to others in the organization in a less cumbersome way than in person. Implementation of the information-sharing concept is an integral part of this strategy level.

(1) *Electronic technology:* A different range of hardware and software applications needs to be available at the department or work-group strategy level. Since the major need is for communication within the work group or department, the compatibility of automated systems being used plays an important role. The ability to share electronically within the work group is also dependent on a communication channel to network the hardware. At this level, users require the ability to share information as well as technologies.

EXAMPLE: At the workstation strategy level, the secretary may be using a dedicated word processor and the manager a personal computer. As long as there is no need for them to share information, the incompatibility will not be an issue. The moment the manager wants to create some textual information for the secretary to refine, a problem of hardware and software compatibility exists.

(2) *Control of information:* As a person inputs information into the system, that information is being controlled. Once the parameters have been determined for the use of that information, any person who is a member of the work group or department can access and use that information. The person who keyed in the original information no longer controls the information; that responsibility is shared by all within the work group.

(3) *Concentration on specific job tasks:* One advantage of office information systems for a department or work group is understanding that together members of the group constitute the entire work process. The members work together to accomplish a common goal. Rather than having several individual jobs, seemingly unrelated to one another, a "mini-networking" atmosphere develops with each person's work clearly contributing to a common goal, completion of an entire work process, or a specific segment of a work process. Such techniques as *job sharing* or *job rotation* become more commonplace in this type of work environment.

(4) *Emphasis on group activity:* When the workstation strategy was implemented, the emphasis was on isolated work activities. When the department or work-group strategy is implemented, the emphasis must be on group activity—the group must cooperate in providing information and communicating this information to others in the organization who need it.

(5) *Office information system technology:* In moving from the workstation strategy to the department or work-group strategy, office information system technology must be introduced to accomplish the quality of information communication desired. Each of these system alternatives poses its own set of controversies. Before one of these alternatives is introduced, however, much research must be conducted to determine its merits for use in that particular department or work group.

   (a) *Local area networks:* The immediate need is for members of the department or work group to communicate and share information. The local area network (LAN) provides for the physical connection of workstations to one another by cable. The LAN also connects other peripherals, such as printers and resources, that must be shared. For most organizations, the specific applications to be shared will determine which type of network should be installed. As an organization enhances its networking operations, networks meeting specific work-group needs are referred to as *distributed environments.* One form of distributed processing is the client/server model (see Chapter 1, Section C-5-b[3][a]).

   (b) *Multiuser (clustered) systems:* A person's existing electronic workstation can be expanded to provide additional support for other workstations or connections to a minicomputer or a mainframe computer. Sometimes another type of centralized computer will be installed to provide shared applications.

   (c) *PBX systems:* Voice communications or a combination of voice/data communications can be provided among electronic workstations. Sometimes, a digital PBX system acts as the hub that provides compatibility among different LANs throughout the organization.

   (d) *Shared resources:* Within the office information system, laser printers, plotters, specialized computers, and common disk storage are some of the peripherals that are shared within local area networks.

(6) *Office information system applications:* The progression from a workstation strategy to a department or work-group strategy makes a number of system applications possible because of the presence of networking and integrated software.

(a) *Electronic filing:* Documents are stored electronically in active and inactive digital storage for access by users within the department or work group. In addition, software programs are available for access by authorized users. Centralized electronic filing provides the same services but on a larger departmentwide scale. One of the noteworthy advantages of centralized electronic filing is the reduction in duplicate files and data and thus an improvement in data integrity.

(b) *Electronic mail:* Information may be transmitted among users using electronic mail (e-mail), sometimes referred to as *electronic messaging*. E-mail may be as simple as transferring information from one user to another or as broad as handling communication among users within one corporate building or across the country. Any user on the network is able to exchange brief typed messages with another user. E-mail is typically informal communication. Computerized records are created of electronic mail so that the sender knows whether the message has been received, the time of access, and any response. If the communication needs to be saved for future reference, office professionals (CEOs, managers, and secretaries) using e-mail need to establish procedures for electronic file folders so that e-mail communications are more easily managed.

(c) *Other applications:* Specific departmental applications focus on access to department-specific information by users. Storage, software, and printing technologies provide the basis for resource sharing to reduce the overall cost of implementing advanced technologies.

c. *The organizational strategy:* The concept of management information systems (MIS) becomes extremely important when an entire organization moves from the department or work-group strategy to the organizational strategy. What this means is that the structure of the organization may change to adhere to an organization-wide plan for office automation. Both top-down and bottom-up strategies are needed in order to implement office automation systems at all levels. The office information systems implemented as a result of the department or work-group strategy become part of the total management information systems effort of the organization.

(1) *Electronic technology:* At this strategy level, all types of technologies will need to be utilized. Such concerns as standardized document formats, compatibility of technology, interconnections among technologies, and the use of software programs for various applications will come into focus.

(2) *Control of information:* At the organizational level, there is even more concern about the issue of information security. With more users gaining access to stored information, the procedures will change to include computer security clearances through passwords, voice recognition, and other means. Another concern focuses on the ability to update and change information that has already been stored. At this level, too, it becomes even more important for the organization to employ an information manager, with possibly a staff of information specialists to assist in planning, implementing, and controlling the organization information system at all levels.

(3) *Concentration on specific job tasks:* Care should be taken at this level not to diminish the importance of the individual. In fact, the work of individuals and

departments within the system is a linkage of skills and knowledges to develop products or services. If one of the links is weak, then the system may not succeed. One should remember that *people* will make or break a system more easily than lack of technology or less-than-perfect procedures.

(4) *Emphasis on group activity:* The higher the strategy level used, implementation focuses on the integration of group activities. The organizational goals and the development of a management information system to assist people in meeting these goals will be paramount. Communication up and down the organizational structure will be vital to the success of various group projects. The networks that develop will be extremely important to the achievement of organizational goals. There will tend to be less involvement in business travel and more attention given to teleconferencing techniques that will bring people together for meetings. Another focus at this strategy level is the client or customer—an attempt to provide the best possible product or service as a response to the needs of the customer. Many businesses today employ in-house consultants who actually help design the business applications that clients or customers will put into practice.

(5) *Management information systems applications:* The word *networking* has special meaning for this particular strategy level. It is at this level that networks are linked together. What began as a local area network within one particular work group has now been expanded to include numerous local area networks throughout the organization that are now parts of one giant network. Networks can communicate with other networks; this makes technological compatibility a very important issue.

    (a) *Wide area networking:* Specific office applications for a large national organization may span several smaller organizations (branch offices) located in different geographic regions of the country. Such issues as access, use of common standards for data compatibility, and the effect of increasing office traffic must be faced at this strategy level.

    (b) *Electronic conferencing:* A technology that has the ability to link departments within an organization with external sources (branch offices, suppliers, customers, and clients) is electronic conferencing. Although video- and teleconferencing are rather expensive technologies, that cost may still be less than what organizations are paying for business travel. The World Wide Web is providing alternate electronic conferencing options for business. Electronic conferencing will grow in its usefulness in presenting information electronically through an office automation system. To be feasible, however, conferencing must be considered part of the organizational strategy.

d. *The global strategy:* With the extensive use of satellite communications and the World Wide Web (global networking), it has become evident that information can be communicated quickly all over the world. In today's quickly expanding global market, all organizations recognize the importance of developing a global strategy. This is the strategy about which there is presently much talk and growth. Although the global network (Web) has had a significant impact with communications, the compatibility of data interchange (codes) among countries will play a vital role in the future of global commerce. Many internationally based organizations are already involved with implementation at this level with specific international organizations.

(1) *Electronic technology:* The global strategy requires networking among organizations in different locations all over the world. The interconnection for networking to take place is satellite communication. The World Wide Web has opened the doors for global communications with electronic mail delivered as quickly around the globe as it is internally within an organization. Electronic commerce (e-commerce) is the next phase for organizations to venture into. Today, networking spans from local area network to wide area network to global network. Communications technology and the regulation within the telecommunication industry will play a major role in the future of growth in this area.

(2) *Control of information:* Because communication channels are carrying information between and among countries around the world, there is a high degree of concern for the security of information generated in one location and communicated via satellites to other countries. Encryption procedures can be used to camouflage or scramble messages during transmission. At this strategy level, the concern is for security of organizational information. In the future, when information leaves a manager's workstation and enters a local area network, that network may be a part of a much larger network, depending on the international aspects of the business. National and international regulation of information is an important issue that companies must address.

(3) *Concentration on specific job tasks:* One of the more interesting aspects of this particular strategy focuses on the employment of people in other countries to operate terminals, entering text and data at less expensive rates than labor costs in the United States. The manufacturing industry has been involved in this type of activity for some time. Employing personnel with an international perspective is becoming important to many American firms. Telecommuting has expanded to involve people in other countries. Technology allows organizations to utilize people's expertise, no matter where they may be located, to solve business application problems.

(4) *Emphasis on group activity:* Conferencing techniques make it possible to consult with work groups from other organizations all over the world. Joint projects by international organizations could become the norm. Managers used to monitoring the activities of departments or work groups within one organization need to learn about facilitating the integration of functions with other organizations. Leadership of group activities requires collaborative skills and techniques. The electronic nature of communication among international participants and language and interpretation issues need to be recognized and properly handled.

Current research dealing with leadership, collaboration, and the ethical and effective use of technology address the future success of global strategies. The greatest advantage is the opportunity to draw on expertise in other countries through the World Wide Web, telecommuting, and teleconferencing techniques.

B. Interfacing Equipment

Integration in office automation is defined as an *interface* among two or more office information technologies: word processing, information processing, communication networks, teleconferencing, and others. For two technologies to interface, they must have the capability of communicating with each other. An *interface* is a connection between two parts of a larger system.

1. *Reasons for Interfacing Equipment:* The basic rationale for interfacing equipment focuses on the need for faster and more accurate communication among work groups that may not be located near one another, decreasing the capital investment needed for equipment, and unifying the work tasks that various work groups are performing.

   a. *Electronic communication:* The most important reason for interfacing equipment is to enhance the use of information through a compatible communication system. Prior to the creation of an interface, the various pieces of equipment could not "speak" with one another. Therefore, information created with one technology was unusable with another, resulting in much duplication of work effort and information. Electronic communication enables work groups that are not necessarily located near one another to share data and information more easily.

   b. *Decreasing equipment investment but increasing capability:* The full capability of equipment technology is rarely used or known. Interfacing equipment will allow the same technology to be used in expanded ways. The capital investment in the equipment will be less because of the expanded use of the equipment. The ways in which the technology is used should be increased to include more applications. Operational costs may increase, however, because of the added communication costs and increased workload of the computer systems.

   c. *Unification of work tasks:* The focus on the entire work process, no matter where that work process is going on, will be enhanced by interfacing equipment. Work groups will be able to communicate through networks. There will be little need for replicating tasks already performed by other work groups if stored information is already available.

2. *Creation of an Interface:* The purpose of an interface is to integrate the equipment and technologies throughout all aspects of an organization. This is no easy task since departments or divisions within an organization may be hesitant to accept the inevitable—one large information systems network for the organization. When an organization begins to develop interfaces among technologies, an information manager is needed.

   a. *Responsibility of the information manager:* The information manager must be able to see the total integrated picture in terms of short- and long-term goals. Selecting equipment and technologies that will automate office functions is one consideration; making sure that each part of the office automation system will integrate with all other technologies is another consideration. Organizations also address the integrated information issue through information steering committees.

   b. *Interfaced technologies:* In the basic office automation system technologies, word processing and information processing will be interfaced. As the organization advances to more sophisticated office functions, electronic mail, electronic filing, teleconferencing, and voice store-and-forward systems should be interfaced to address today's information processing needs. Such an interface requires compatible technology.

(1) *Compatibility of equipment:* When equipment has been purchased for one particular office function, it may not be compatible with other equipment being used. Creating interfaces means that all equipment will be compatible with all other equipment. This is not an easy task because various brands, models, or types of equipment may already have been purchased. The interface is handled through an interface unit (a "black box") that serves as a translator between two or more pieces of formerly incompatible equipment, resulting in the creation of a local area network with presently owned technology.

(2) *Local area networks (LANs):* A local area network (LAN) consists of cable-linking workstations and equipment into a network. Workstations can have either "smart" or "dumb" terminals. LANs provide greater electronic communication capability among peripherals in the network. There is much more computing power available through the LAN than through stand-alone equipment. The primary objective of creating LANs is to increase the free exchange of information among users. Installing a newly acquired LAN is relatively easy because the information manager can ensure the compatibility of equipment.

(3) *Telecommunications technology:* The technology that makes it possible to interface incompatible equipment and technologies is telecommunications. The needed link is provided that enables electronic mail, intranets, the Internet, teleconferencing, and other computer-assisted functions to be utilized in the office. With technological advances being made daily, office technologies quickly become obsolete. Interfacing equipment will continue to mean that information managers and top-level managers will need to select systems that are compatible, capable of expansion, and flexible in meeting organizational needs.

C. Integrated Software

Software is the set of instructions that direct a computer to process data. *Integrated software* consists of programs that provide a variety of software applications to the user at any one time.

1. *Integration of System Software and Application Software:* System software is a set of programs that controls and supervises the operations of the various hardware components of the system and the software elements in the performance of specific tasks. *Application software* is a set of programs that directs the computer to solve specific business problems or perform particular applications. The broad category of application software for microcomputers can be divided into such applications as word processing, electronic spreadsheets, desktop publishing, presentation graphics, and database management. Since system software controls and supervises software elements, all system software must be integrated with the application software of a computer system. A fully *integrated system* provides the exchange of data among different application programs, such as word processing, spreadsheet, graphics, database, and electronic mail.

2. *Benefits of Integrated Software:* Integration of application software and communication among system users provides many benefits for the dynamic business organization. Such integration provides the following benefits:

   a. *Elimination of data duplication:* Throughout the organization, the data that have been stored once can be reused by different users for different applications. In fact, a needs assessment can be completed to determine how many ways within a particular organization the same data can be reapplied.

Figure 6–3   Attendance Report

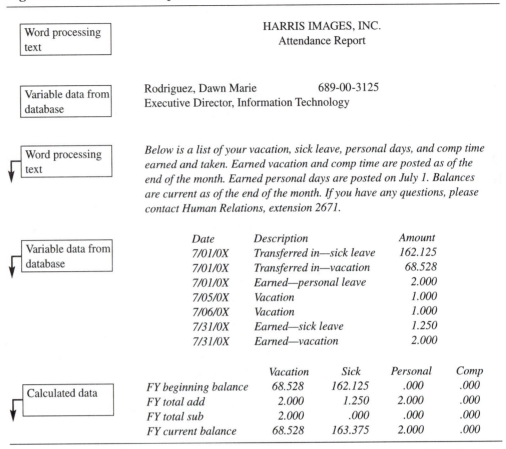

| Word processing text | HARRIS IMAGES, INC. |
| Variable data from database | Rodriguez, Dawn Marie   689-00-3125
Executive Director, Information Technology |

HARRIS IMAGES, INC.
Attendance Report

Rodriguez, Dawn Marie   689-00-3125
Executive Director, Information Technology

Below is a list of your vacation, sick leave, personal days, and comp time earned and taken. Earned vacation and comp time are posted as of the end of the month. Earned personal days are posted on July 1. Balances are current as of the end of the month. If you have any questions, please contact Human Relations, extension 2671.

Date	Description	Amount
7/01/0X	*Transferred in—sick leave*	*162.125*
7/01/0X	*Transferred in—vacation*	*68.528*
7/01/0X	*Earned—personal leave*	*2.000*
7/05/0X	*Vacation*	*1.000*
7/06/0X	*Vacation*	*1.000*
7/31/0X	*Earned—sick leave*	*1.250*
7/31/0X	*Earned—vacation*	*2.000*

	Vacation	*Sick*	*Personal*	*Comp*
FY beginning balance	*68.528*	*162.125*	*.000*	*.000*
FY total add	*2.000*	*1.250*	*2.000*	*.000*
FY total sub	*2.000*	*.000*	*.000*	*.000*
FY current balance	*68.528*	*163.375*	*2.000*	*.000*

b. *Data integrity:* As information changes, the fewer locations where the actual change needs to be made, the more reliable and accurate the data available to the users. Errors may occur in rekeying data; it is more accurate to use data that have already been keyed and verified.

c. *Greater work efficiency:* The integration of data from an electronic spreadsheet with a letter created through word processing saves the time of having to rekey the data.

d. *Electronic communications:* Establishing software standards makes it possible for employees to communicate with one another, electronically sharing files for increased efficiency and effectiveness. This can be done through sharing of diskettes, sharing network files, or sending files electronically through e-mail.

e. *Functional relationships:* The integration of software serves as a facilitator of functional relationships among divisions or departments for the overall benefit of the company.

EXAMPLE: Preparing and distributing an employee status change with an integrated system could take place as follows:

- *The current status is retrieved by the human relations division from the database.*

- *The database is updated to reflect the employee status change. The correct data are now available to all users who have access to the database.*

- *Standard word processing text is keyed into the system and stored for specific communication needs (forms or letters) at a later time.*

- *Variable data (employee data) are merged with standard word processing text for creation of messages transmitted to appropriate electronic mailboxes automatically.*

At the beginning of each month, variable data (employee data) are merged with standard word processing text to send an attendance report electronically to all full-time employees. For an example of such an attendance report, see Figure 6–3.

D. Implications for the Future

Integration of office functions is a very complex and sophisticated matter. The growth of the World Wide Web and telecommunications within the past several years has been the impetus that finally has made it possible for various integrations to take place. With the dynamic growth in this area, the full effect of what integration means in terms of the organization and its interrelationships with other organizations all over the world is still unknown. The emerging need for information managers, telecommuting, global ethics, team leadership, greater compatibility of technologies, and tools for higher-level decision making are among the implications for the future.

1. *Emergence of the Chief Information Officer (CIO) and the Information Manager:* Authority and responsibility for office automation efforts should rest with an information manager, a person whose primary goal should be to make sure that each part of the office automation effort can be integrated with all other parts. The information manager must possess skills that will help him or her see the possibilities of total systems integration. It may be that the information manager's expertise will be in more general areas of business administration rather than specialized within only one of the technology areas. However, expertise in both areas continues to be important. To carry out the integration of information on a global as well as an organization-wide basis, the need for a strategic information systems officer to work with the other strategic officers in the organization is becoming more important. This person usually carries the title of chief information officer (CIO). The CIO has a broad view of organization goals and objectives and addresses information systems from an internal and an external perspective.

2. *Telecommuting:* The office will be viewed more as a business support function than as a place where people go to work. With electronic communication, notebook computers, and Web connectivity available, it will not matter *where* people work (at home, on the road, or at a business location). What will matter is that the necessary communication takes place so that the information will be available *when* needed and in the *form* desired. Integration of technologies makes telecommuting a reality.

3. *Greater Compatibility of Technologies:* For business functions to integrate further, technologies (both equipment and software) are moving toward greater compatibility. The problem has been that many different brands, models, and styles have been available from many different vendors, all vying for business. As new technologies emerge, more products appear on the scene. Managers must make appropriate decisions on what technology to purchase or lease. More standardization of equipment technologies is needed, with increased development in integrated software available for the equipment systems. The focus in the future needs to be on specific applications in the office that need to be automated.

4. *Decision-Making Tools:* In the future people in the office—secretaries, managers, and top-level executives—will all be involved in various levels of decision making.

Integrated technologies can be very powerful decision-making tools for office professionals to use in making decisions about equipment to purchase or lease, determining the usefulness of different software packages, making product comparisons when developing office systems, and in many other useful ways. Helpful information is now available through information services that will ease the amount of time that secretaries and managers need to spend gathering research data in order to make more appropriate business decisions. The knowledge level of office professionals has increased to also include advanced technologies and decision-making skills.

5. *Hypermedia:* A hypermedia system combines text, graphics, sound, and video. The data are stored in files with indexes for links among documents. The user is able to view information by selecting a word or phrase and providing the appropriate system command. The information is displayed as text, graphics, sound, animation, and/or video for a more dynamic presentation of the information. The development of hypermedia systems will continue to be an important aspect of integrated technologies.

6. *Network Revolution:* The impact of the Internet and the capabilities of electronic commerce will enable companies to exchange information and conduct business beyond the traditional organizational boundaries and across great distances.

7. *Electronic Commerce:* Businesses today are establishing Web pages to assist with the marketing of products and services. Many new businesses are being conducted only on the Web, whereas other businesses use the Web as a way of providing additional information about products or services to consumers and other organizations.

Office automation and the integration of technologies to enhance office operations and management will continue to improve and change to meet the information needs of business organizations. The next few years should be particularly exciting for the professional secretary who adapts to the times and is willing to accept the fact that change will continue to occur in the way that offices function and in the way office professionals learn how to work. The secretary will play a very important role ensuring that, as office functions change, integrated applications will enhance, not overpower, the performance of needed tasks.

Review Questions

Directions: Select the best answer from the four alternatives. Write your answer in the blank to the left of the number.

_____ 1. The primary objective of office automation is to

   a. create a working environment that will meet individual needs.
   b. integrate word processing with other information technologies.
   c. enhance internal and external communication flow and provide a more productive work environment.
   d. ensure that training/retraining is provided for office personnel.

_____ 2. The vital components of an office system are

   a. hardware, software, and standards.
   b. strategic planning, organization structure, and operating procedures.
   c. technology, personnel, and organization procedures.
   d. technology, training, and strategic planning.

_____ 3. A new office staff position has been approved for the finance department. Robbins is responsible for all office operations and is concerned that the new employee is able to use the local area network and follow organizational guidelines in completing her tasks. To ensure the quality of the new employee's work, Robbins has decided to develop an operations manual. Which office systems component is Robbins addressing?

   a. Organization
   b. Personnel
   c. Procedures
   d. Technology

_____ 4. Sommers operates a word processing system at his workstation. The primary objective for this type of office automation is to improve his

   a. communication skills.
   b. decision-making ability.
   c. secretarial productivity.
   d. telecommuting opportunities.

_____ 5. To improve office productivity, techniques to move information more quickly throughout the organization (electronic mail and LANs) are important. This describes

   a. the automated organization.
   b. individual office automation.
   c. integrated computer-based systems.
   d. integrated information systems.

6. Today, sharing of information between a secretary and a manager in an integrated environment is usually accomplished by

   a. compatible systems and an electronic communication channel.
   b. desktop workstations.
   c. face-to-face interaction.
   d. stand-alone workstations.

7. Which automated technology best supports the decision-making process with what-if analysis output?

   a. Electronic spreadsheet
   b. Database
   c. Desktop publishing
   d. Word processing

8. At the workstation strategy level, personal productivity tools include

   a. decision support systems.
   b. dedicated word processing systems.
   c. electronic calendar, alarm, and telephone directory.
   d. presentation graphics and desktop publishing.

9. Which office automation strategy began the focus on information sharing?

   a. Global strategy
   b. Organizational strategy
   c. Work-group strategy
   d. Workstation strategy

10. Lawrence's department consists of ten people, including one secretary. The department is responsible for a special project that requires the storing and sharing of information on the computer. A local area network (LAN) with a microcomputer has been installed at each of the ten workstations. Lawrence then assigned each person different responsibilities for parts of the project. This is an example of

    a. automating individual workstations.
    b. a network strategy through satellite communication.
    c. a management information system.
    d. a work-group strategy for office automation.

11. The concept of management information systems (MIS) becomes extremely important when an organization implements the

    a. global strategy.
    b. organizational strategy.
    c. work-group strategy.
    d. workstation strategy.

_____ **12.** The higher the office automation strategy level (workstation, work group, organizational, and global)

    a. the more communication throughout the organization is diminished.
    b. the greater the concern for information security.
    c. the less important the individual becomes.
    d. the less a management information system (MIS) is needed.

_____ **13.** When a national organization links numerous networks located in different geographic regions into one organizational network, this concept is inherent to

    a. management information systems (MIS).
    b. multiuser (clustered) systems.
    c. telecommunications.
    d. wide area networking (WAN).

_____ **14.** A linkage for distant interorganizational and intraorganizational communication is a/an

    a. global network.
    b. management information system (MIS).
    c. office interface.
    d. wide area network (WAN).

_____ **15.** E-commerce using the World Wide Web falls within the

    a. global strategy.
    b. organizational strategy.
    c. work-group strategy.
    d. workstation strategy.

_____ **16.** A basic rationale for interfacing two or more office automation technologies is to

    a. decrease operational costs of the information system.
    b. decrease personnel by eliminating the need for an information manager.
    c. decentralize work tasks.
    d. provide faster and more accurate communication among work groups.

_____ **17.** The person whose primary responsibility is short- and long-term goals for an integrated information system is the

    a. chief executive officer (CEO).
    b. information manager.
    c. systems analyst.
    d. vice president for operations.

_____ **18.** Integrated software enables the user to

    a. communicate with other users in a local area network.
    b. control and supervise the operations of various hardware components.
    c. exchange data among two or more application programs.
    d. perform a specialized business application.

_____   **19.** Ensuring reliable, accurate data for office operations is called

        a. database management.
        b. data integrity.
        c. office automation.
        d. proofreading.

_____   **20.** In recent years and projected for the future, office integration has seen dynamic changes because of the

        a. enhancements of hypermedia.
        b. growth of the World Wide Web and telecommunications.
        c. strategic vision and direction provided by chief information officers (CIOs).
        d. Web page marketing opportunities.

Solutions

Answers   *Refer to:*

1. (c)   [A]

2. (c)   [A-1]

3. (c)   [A-1-c(3)]

4. (c)   [A-2-a]

5. (c)   [A-2-c]

6. (a)   [A-3-a(2)(b)]

7. (a)   [A-3-a(3)]

8. (c)   [A-3-a(3)]

9. (c)   [A-3-b]

10. (d)   [A-3-b]

11. (b)   [A-3-c]

12. (b)   [A-3-c(2), A-3-d(2)]

13. (d)   [A-3-c(5)(a)]

14. (a)   [A-3-d]

15. (a)   [A-3-d]

16. (d)   [B-1]

17. (b)   [B-2-a, D-1]

18. (c)   [C-1]

19. (b)   [C-2-b]

20. (b)   [D]

CHAPTER

7

Ergonomics

OVERVIEW

With the proliferation of computer usage in offices by all office professionals, the importance of designing office environments for comfort, efficiency, and convenience has become very evident. Since the greatest cost of a workstation to the employer is the employee's salary, that person's comfort and productivity are very important to the success of the office. *Ergonomics* is the scientific study of the relationship of workers to their physical environment, including the work space and the automated systems being used. One of the basic goals of office automation is increased productivity for the office. An ergonomic environment is an essential element in promoting and enhancing office productivity. The psychological, physiological, sociological, and interpersonal communication bases for ergonomics are presented to give secretaries and other office professionals a more thorough understanding of the basic theory of ergonomics in the workplace.

While working with office technology, office professionals have sometimes experienced repetitive-stress, visual, musculoskeletal, emotional, and psychosocial problems. Researchers and medical experts have been concerned for a number of years about the presence of possible work and health hazards in the office. It is hoped that environmental and work area designs are enabling managers to address these concerns and provide working conditions that lead to increased productivity while possible hazardous conditions are diminished.

As the result of consideration for specific ergonomic factors, designers of office furniture and equipment are applying new approaches to office design and layout. Workers are responding to the technological environment in the office both positively and negatively, depending on management's willingness to create a conducive environment.

The creation of office layouts and designs necessitates careful office systems analysis that may result in more functional office environments. The private-office arrangement is the traditional approach to office layout, with executives housed in offices separated from general office areas. The open-office arrangement, including landscaped or modular approaches, offers functional work space with modular furniture and aisle space to control the flow of communication through the office. The open-office arrangement has been the trend in office space design since the late 1980s.

More attention is being focused on the design of a person's work area so that workers have quicker and easier access to equipment, work in process, and facilities. Supplies, reference materials, or other accessories should be within reach. Securing new office furniture and equipment requires analytical judgment and participation on the part of office professionals to assist in making selections that will improve the entire office environment.

KEY TERMS

Absorption	Foot-lambert	Peripheral equipment
Ambient lighting	Hardware	Private-office arrangement
Biomechanics	Hot-desking	Procedures analysis
Chat room	Hotelling	Psychosocial disturbance
Cybernetics	Isolation	Reflection
Decibel	Job analysis	Software
Early adapter	Late adapter	Sound control
Emotional disturbance	Lease	Task analysis
Ergonomics	Masking	Task lighting
Euthenics	Modular approach	Time plan
Feasibility study	Musculoskeletal problems	Visual dysfunction
Flowchart	Office landscaping	Work flow
Flow diagram	Office layout	Work logs
Foot-candle	Open-office arrangement	Workstation

A. Rationale for Ergonomics

The scientific study of the relationship of workers to their physical environment, including the work space and the technology being used, is called *ergonomics*. Special attention is given to the worker-technology interface so that the work or working conditions are adapted to give the worker the best possible work environment. The office workers' levels of productivity and morale are extremely important in being able to perform specific job tasks. Any element, whether psychological, physiological, sociological, or analytical in nature, that affects individual attitudes and performance is a part of ergonomics. User needs must be clearly defined in order for automated functions to result in greater productivity, increased efficiency, and improved employee morale.

1. *Psychological Basis for Ergonomics:* People react more favorably toward their work when they realize that changes made in the physical environment will contribute to their own personal comfort and benefit. Psychological factors, in turn, affect individual worker behaviors and attitudes.

   a. *Rationale for automation:* People need to understand the reasons for automating specific office processes. It is very important that open lines of communication flow in all directions—from the top down, from the bottom up, and laterally.

   b. *Functionality for users:* The methods used to implement office systems in a useful, functional manner will affect the users' feelings about automation. Users need to perceive that workstations are designed for the effective performance of office tasks, yet the social needs of the individual need to be met and causes of stress minimized.

   c. *Personnel development:* There continues to be an increasing need for training and/or retraining in the application of automated systems using word processing, spreadsheets, desktop publishing, the Internet, and other applications. Office professionals need to know that technical or systems training or retraining will be available as particular software applications are applied in the daily work routine.

   d. *Challenge:* In an automated environment, the office professional who enjoys trying innovative systems and procedures will indeed face the challenge of adapting automation to tasks formerly completed through more manual means.

EXAMPLE: Using a word processing application program is a learning experience every day. Initially, most secretaries learn enough about the program to perform relatively routine functions. Then, as specific job needs demand, they can learn more advanced applications. Training seminars also assist them in learning new facets of the program.

   e. *Morale booster:* Improvement of employee morale occurs when office professionals have some voice in establishing new processes, revising procedures, or selecting new office equipment. Change within the organization can be viewed in a positive way as a morale booster.

   f. *Employee attitude toward environment:* Sometimes office workers openly express positive or negative attitudes toward their work and their workplace to co-workers or others around them. These attitudes may also be a reflection of the workers' individual work ethics.

   g. *Employee reaction to change:* Office professionals typically exhibit different reactions to change. Employees may be willing to change, wait for others to change first, or resist any possible change.

   (1) *Early adapter:* A person who is quick to change, study a new system, and try to implement it is sometimes known as an *early adapter.* Such a person is seen as a pioneer, one of the first to become familiar with the new system and to demonstrate to others its usefulness. This person is frequently seen as a trainer, one who keeps up to date with the technology and is anxious to show and help others.

   (2) *Late adapter:* A person who waits for others to implement a new system, then tries to "catch up" with the technology, is referred to as a *late adapter.* This person wants to be shown the success of the system before trying it but does see some value to change. The late adapter has a difficult time keeping up to date with technology and is often considered "behind the times."

   (3) *Nonadapter:* The person who prefers the status quo and does not typically accept change very easily may resist change and also encourage others to resist change. Typically, nonadapters begin to feel job-related stress.

   h. *Motivation:* Managers need to create a motivating environment, one that will motivate office professionals to perform their assigned functions. Some people find changes in office systems and procedures to be challenging experiences, the challenge being one of the motivators. Others feel more secure when maintaining systems as they have existed for some time. The self-motivated person is often better able to face change than one who hesitates to try anything new or different.

2. *Physiological Basis for Ergonomics:* The physical structures within the office must be geared to the physical needs of the human anatomy.

   a. *Environmental factors:* Factors such as furniture, lighting, atmospheric conditions, sound, and space design constitute primary environmental factors.

   (1) *Workstation furniture and accessories:* Work areas with work surfaces and chairs sized and shaped to accommodate the individual user are very important in minimizing employee fatigue and maximizing functionality and comfort. The basic premise is that office workers who use ergonomically designed

furniture personalized for their use will be able to produce work of higher quality than those who use more traditionally designed office furniture.

EXAMPLES:

Posture chairs (with adjustments for back rest and height of seat) are contoured to the human anatomy to provide better support for the human body.

Work surfaces that provide a work arc permit the person to work easily from the left to the right, or in the center of the workstation.

Proper positioning of visual display screens and input materials for comfortable viewing can lessen possible eyestrain, physical strain, and head or neck problems.

(2) *Lighting:* Types of lighting as well as placement of lighting contribute to employee comfort (see Section D-1).

EXAMPLE: A medical secretary transcribing from recorded dictation needs to have lighting that will permit easy viewing of visual or hard copy as it is being produced. Ceiling fixtures may not provide adequate task lighting.

(3) *Atmospheric conditions:* Controlled temperature, ventilation, and humidity make the office pleasant and comfortable for employees. Enforcement of non-smoking regulations has become essential in the business environment.

EXAMPLE: Smoking at one's workstation is typically not permitted because of irritation to other employees and air pollution. Instead, designated smoking areas are usually provided in employee lounges or eating areas. Eating or smoking while working with magnetic media (disks and cartridges) may cause damage to the media.

(4) *Office noise:* People react to noise or sound favorably or unfavorably, depending on the intensity of the sound.

EXAMPLES:

Piped-in music may be relaxing and soothing, whereas noise caused by talking may be extremely distracting to someone who is concentrating on writing a detailed report.

Some firms have created quiet work spaces, sometimes called "think tanks," where employees have uninterrupted time for creating and developing their ideas into special projects.

Still other firms permit employees to work at home to ensure uninterrupted, productive time while working on project assignments.

(5) *Work space preferred by employees:* Office workers are affected by the *amount* and *type* of work space provided for them.

EXAMPLES:

Some people prefer a larger office to a smaller office, sometimes for claustrophobic reasons.

The open-office arrangement is preferred by some people, whereas others continue to prefer private offices that help eliminate distractions.

    b. *Physiology of the worker:* Physiological factors are also important to meet the comfort needs of the worker.

       (1) *The worker's body structure:* Physical dimensions, such as height or weight, must be considered in selecting appropriate furniture for workstations. *Anthropometry* is the study of human body measurements in order to design furniture (sizes, heights, and shapes) accurately scaled to the dimensions of workers' bodies.

       EXAMPLE: Office desks are now being designed so that the worker can adjust various work surfaces easily. Most modular work surfaces have continuous adjustments for tilting, raising, and lowering work surfaces.

       (2) *Physical movement demanded of workers:* Work areas are being designed to minimize the strain of performing physical work, reduce worker error, and increase efficiency. The study of the musculoskeletal effort of human beings is known as *biomechanics.*

       EXAMPLES:

       Placement of the telephone in the workstation within easy reach to the left or right ensures functionality.

       Some keyboards now have palm or wrist rests at the front of the keyboard so that operators are able to position hands near the keyboard but not anchor the hand or wrist directly on the keyboard.

       Visual display monitors have swivel bases so that the monitor can be rotated easily from one person to another.

3. *Sociological Basis for Ergonomics:* Sociology is the study of human cultures, social relationships, and underlying principles of human functioning in society. In the office environment, teams are becoming extremely important to the smooth functioning of the office. As people work, they also are part of a social group. Work-group clusters, teamwork among group members, the facilitation of social communication, and the need for worker specialization are affected by the ergonomic nature of the office environment.

    a. *Establishment of work-group clusters:* Office systems require "clusters" of people to function cooperatively and effectively.

    EXAMPLES:

    A computer center's operation requires the joint efforts of the supervisor/manager and all operations personnel. In addition, systems analysts and programmers have the responsibility to assist members of other departments within the firm to utilize computer capability and develop new automated applications.

    The word/information processing center in a large corporation faces similar requirements. To prepare documents for users from various departments, the word processing "cluster" must be ready and able to give prompt and accurate service for users in order to meet their deadlines.

    b. *Emphasis on teamwork:* The success of automating office processes depends on a team effort, with each member of the team willing to take the lead in certain phases of the project and to assist with routine office tasks as needed.

EXAMPLE: The BIG Corporation is using the computer as much as possible to facilitate telephone communications within the firm. Smythe, the communications director, recognizes that the computer is a very important tool in enhancing internal as well as external communication. Callers are greeted with a recorded message that gives them directions on reaching specific extensions. Randall handles any incoming telephone communication that comes through the central switchboard. Each department secretary must in turn be responsible for the many telephone calls received each day in that particular office. One of the many new features that makes telephone communications more versatile at the BIG Corporation is call forwarding. A secretary who needs to be away from the desk temporarily can forward incoming calls automatically to another telephone location.

c. *Worker specialization:* Involvement in office automation requires that some workers become more specialized in applications such as word/information processing, Web page designing, or desktop publishing and that other departmental and supervisory personnel function in a more general capacity.

d. *Individual need for territoriality:* In the office environment, an office worker typically functions within boundaries established as a personal work space. A secretary may choose either privacy (isolation) or involvement with other office professionals, depending on the confidential nature of the work to be performed. To perform effectively on the job, a secretary needs "ownership" of a particular work space.

e. *Qualified applicants:* Men and women who apply for office positions must possess specific entry-level skills to function effectively in these positions.

EXAMPLE: Keyboarding, language, human relations, and computer skills are competencies that are considered essential information processing skills for secretarial positions. Tests as well as interviews are now being used by firms to measure these skills prior to employment. Training programs have been established in many companies to allow employees with potential to further develop essential skills for their present or future positions.

f. *Career development:* People need to know that there are opportunities for advancement through promotion or lateral transfer. The clustering (or leveling) of work groups gives the impression of a hierarchy of positions to which workers may aspire.

4. *Communication Theory as a Basis for Ergonomics:* The office environment must be conducive to the type of communication required (written, oral, nonverbal, face-to-face, or electronic) to perform office tasks quickly, accurately, and efficiently. The physical structure of the office will either facilitate or hinder communication.

a. *Types of communications:* Many office procedures still depend on written and face-to-face communication. More sophisticated telephone communication systems are emphasizing the importance of effective interpersonal communication. Information is also processed and transmitted electronically through networks using word processing disks, electronic mail, intranets, the Internet, and computer storage. The type of communication system utilized depends on availability, speed of transmission, the procedures used, and the value placed on the information.

b. *Use of automated systems:* In the future, communication processes utilizing a variety of storage and transmission media will continue to be an essential component of office systems. People situated anywhere in the world receive and transmit information through computer networks with magnetic storage while linked to satellite communication systems. Decision making continues to be extremely important in transmitting information internally within the firm or externally to other organizations.

EXAMPLE: Instead of requiring a sales executive to travel to each of four branch offices four times a year, a company will create a chat room through their Internet service provider where two or more people can conduct a typed conference in a private manner.

If visual conferencing is essential, a teleconferencing network could be created between the four branch offices. A special conference room equipped with the conferencing technology would be required to conduct the teleconference.

Because it is still important for an executive to visit on site at least twice a year, the other two quarterly meetings will be scheduled at the corporate headquarters.

5. *Other Ergonomic Concerns:* Specific work functions and work-flow processes are affected by the ergonomics of the workplace.

   a. *Work functions:* An analysis of the steps and procedures in each office task, as well as clusters of related tasks, will reveal the people-technology interface required during the work process.

      (1) *Individual office tasks:* Ergonomically, a specific office task must be analyzed to see whether there are ways to better relate the task to the technology used so that the individual employee will be able to work more comfortably and effectively. Ergonomics focuses on the comfort and convenience of the physical arrangement of the office and the appropriateness of hardware, software, and other technology used to perform a particular task.

         (a) *Hardware:* Technology required for a particular type of work, such as a computer system or a telephone system, is called *hardware.*

         (b) *Software:* Application programs and programming support necessary to automate a specific office function, such as a computer program for word processing applications, is referred to as *software.*

      EXAMPLE: Answering every incoming telephone call is very important for The Rug Place, for a large number of potential customers call every day for information. The difficulty that McCoy, the owner, has is making sure that every call gets answered promptly and courteously. A voice mail network solved the problem. If any call is not answered by the third ring, the caller hears a recorded message and is asked to record a detailed message for a callback or may choose to be transferred to someone else for immediate help.

      (2) *Clusters of related office tasks:* Sometimes, groups of related tasks need to be analyzed to determine the best ergonomic arrangement of office space and to ensure proper utilization of office furniture and automated systems to enhance work performance. Within many organizations, data and word/information processing, reprographics, and communications centers have been established for the performance of specific clusters of related tasks.

      EXAMPLE: Johnson, a communications specialist, supervises the communications system for Satellite Systems, Inc. For her and three other members of the staff to function more effectively, a communications center was established recently to house Johnson and her work group. In addition, the local network for shared data/information and communication (e-mail) was enhanced with an intranet where bulletin boards, procedures, and upcoming activities are communicated throughout the firm. The local network replaces four separate communications systems that were in operation for several years. Less physical space will be needed for the new equipment.

(3) *Work logs:* Logging actual time spent in performing office tasks can provide insight into time requirements (in hours and minutes) as well as work allocation each day.

EXAMPLE: If Harrison keeps a log of the time required to key source data each day for one week, he should be able to give his supervisor a more accurate estimate of the continuous time periods that he must sit at the terminal. Personal comfort at the workstation may necessitate a short rest period every two to three hours, or the firm may decide to go to a source data automation environment and retrain Harrison for new responsibilities. Harrison should be involved in the analysis focusing on the use of automated equipment for any of the tasks and for better acceptance of any changes.

b. *Work flow:* Following the path of a business document through the office helps ensure that there is no delay in transmitting the document or the information it contains from one location to another. Accurate preparation of the documents and speedy distribution are vital. In addition, the physical effort exerted by people in moving documents to different work areas is another important consideration (e.g., electronic transmission). Electronic networks require compatibility of hardware and software throughout the firm (see Chapter 3).

B. Understanding Health Hazards

It is estimated that today more than 125 million Americans work at least part of the day at a computer keyboard with a visual display terminal as part of their daily routine. The almost constant use of visual display terminals and keyboards by executives, managers, and secretaries is a concern to manufacturers, vendors, professional associations, and even government agencies conducting research to validate employee concerns and complaints. Employees have been concerned about the possibility of health problems as well as personal discomfort from prolonged user interface with keyboard, display, and input (source) material.

1. *Employee Health Concerns and Complaints:* These complaints tend to focus on these areas: repetitive-strain injuries, visual dysfunction, musculoskeletal problems, emotional disturbances, and psychosocial disturbances. Research efforts have centered on possible causes of employee complaint and discomfort and whether the visual display terminal may be a cause or an influential factor.

a. *Repetitive-strain (repetitive-motion) injury or illness:* The U.S. Department of Labor reports that repetitive-strain or repetitive-motion injuries or illnesses are the fastest growing health danger in the workplace and perhaps the greatest single cause of occupational illness. Repetitive-strain injuries result from tasks that require continuous repetitive motion. Symptoms include stiff or sore wrists, loss of strength in arms or hands, or finger cramps while working.

b. *Visual dysfunction:* Employees who have experienced computer vision syndrome or temporary visual distress (eye irritation, visual fatigue, blurred vision, headaches, and chronic disorders) raise the question as to whether the use of the visual display terminal is causing the visual dysfunction to occur. Discomfort resulting from visual distress appears to be caused by the following:

(1) Poor design of visual display terminals

(2) Poor design of the physical environment of the office

(3) Long intensive work intervals without adequate rest periods

Current research evidence indicates that use of the visual display terminal *does not* in and of itself cause chronic visual disorders or cause the vision of operators to deteriorate faster than the vision of workers in other jobs. A German study found that users of visual display terminals (VDTs) perform up to 33,000 head or eye movements a day.

c. *Musculoskeletal problems:* Some employees complain about pain or discomfort occurring in various body parts (neck, back, shoulders, arms, and fingers) as they work. Positioning of a keyboard at an appropriate height is essential to avoid carpal tunnel syndrome and tendinitis. *Carpal tunnel syndrome* is the compression of a nerve leading into the wrist that results in debilitating pain and muscle weakness. *Tendinitis* is the inflammation of muscles at the points where they insert into the bones of the shoulders, arms, and wrists. Ergonomically designed visual display terminals, furniture, and other workstation components enable the operator to assume proper posture while keying in information at the terminal. Such features as a keyboard detached from the screen, a screen that is tiltable, a variable-height terminal stand, and an adjustable posture chair seem to relieve the musculoskeletal problems that operators may experience.

d. *Emotional disturbances:* Two types of emotional disturbances, mood disturbances and psychosomatic disorders, may affect employees' abilities to perform screen functions.

(1) *Mood disturbances:* Anger, frustration, irritability, anxiety, and depression are some of the typical mood disturbances that employees experience. Executives and administrative assistants should be cognizant to minimize these disturbances so that they do not disrupt others in the workplace.

(2) *Psychosomatic disorders:* Some operators have been afflicted with gastrointestinal disturbances, muscle tension, psychic tension, heart palpitations, and frequent perspiration.

e. *Psychosocial disturbances:* Another area of employee concern focuses on specific problems related to the work environment. Stress related to the job, the workload, the pace of work in the office, and poor or inadequate supervision has been linked to some chronic ailments. Although job-related stress has been linked to some chronic ailments, these problems also arise from organizational, social, and job design changes related to office automation. Such disturbances can be minimized through training prior to implementation of new office systems.

2. *Environmental and Workstation Design:* Research into environmental design and workstation design is influencing ergonomic office systems.

a. *Environmental design:* Screen glare, possible radiation emission, temperature, and humidity are environmental factors being researched continually.

(1) *Screen glare:* The question of glare on the screen is under constant surveillance by systems manufacturers. Vision complaints appear to be well founded if glare and contrast problems are not controlled. Some research indicates that there is a correlation between the measured intensity of glare reflections and annoyance experienced by operators, resulting in possible visual problems. However, research has not as yet established definite relationships between the luminance of reflections and visual impairment.

EXAMPLES:

Some modifications can be made to a screen if glare is a problem. One of the most effective ways to deal with glare is to install a filter over the screen to absorb incoming light rays and reduce the amount of reflection from the screen's surface.

Another method of glare control is to install a hood over the screen to block the screen from reflections.

(2) *Radiation emission:* The National Institute for Occupational Safety and Health (NIOSH) has focused recent research on potential radiation emission hazards. These studies, as well as those of the Food and Drug Administration (FDA), investigated the amount of radiation emitting from visual display terminals. Researchers report that the equipment emitted little or no harmful radiation under normal operating conditions. The emissions that were detected were well below any national and international standards. However, there remain questions of linkage with cancer and other illnesses. Office workers are often cautioned by their doctors to avoid extensive use of visual display terminals during pregnancies because of the *possibility* of a miscarriage or harm to a fetus.

b. *Workstation design:* The type and nature of workstation adjustments will enable proper physical positioning of the person in relation to the keyboard, screen, and input (source) materials. Figure 7–1 shows the primary factors and distances to be considered in designing a workstation to meet physical comfort requirements. Distances in the VDT triangle (eyes to screen to source materials) need to be as short as possible.

3. *Business Research into Productivity:* National surveys sponsored by Steelcase, Inc., indicate that employee comfort in the office directly affects office productivity. Proper humidity and temperature, comfortable chairs, adequate lighting, and worker privacy were identified as having the most impact. Office productivity also increases when training is provided for using new hardware and software.

C. Ergonomic Factors

At the outset of planning, consideration of several key ergonomic factors should result in well-designed offices that will enhance office productivity. Ergonomic standards, workstations, technology (hardware and software), and human physiology envelop many of the factors that should be considered.

1. *Ergonomic Standards:* Developed as a result of research by ergonomic specialists, ergonomic standards are being used in the design of office products for use throughout the world. These standards serve as guides for organizations contemplating the application of ergonomic factors to increase office productivity.

Figure 7–1 Ergonomic Workstation Layout

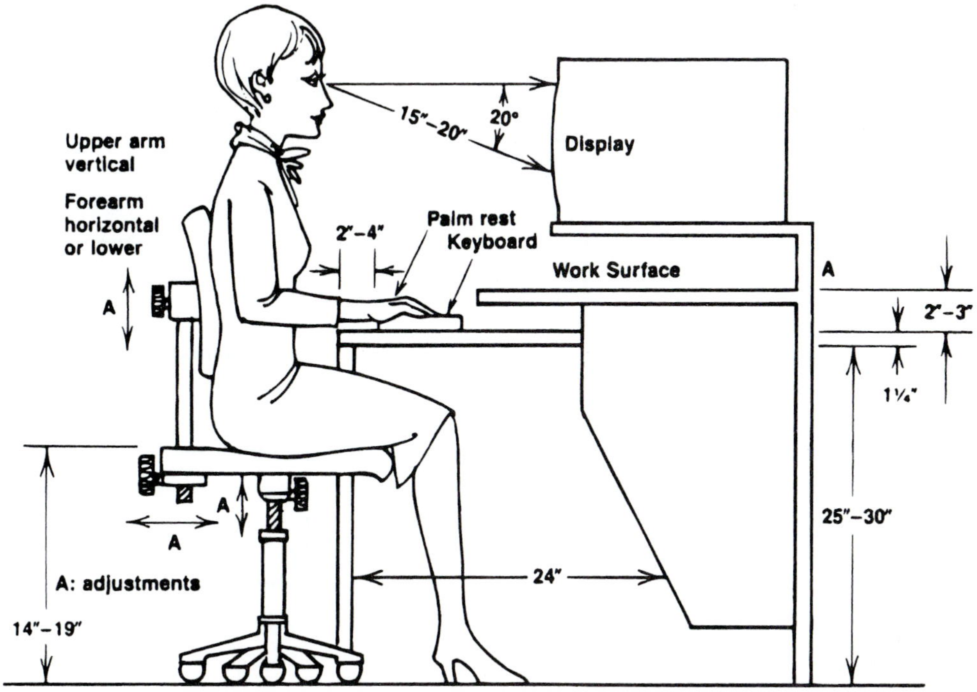

EXAMPLE: The 30 standards developed by the German Institute for Standardization and the Trade Cooperative Association include the following types of items:

- *Keyboards should be detachable and ergonomically designed.*

- *Screens need to be adjustable.*

- *The slope of the keyboard should be no more than 15 degrees.*

- *Visual display screens should display dark characters on a light background.*

- *Workstations and VDTs should meet specific height, depth, viewing angle, and other specifications.*

With a large number of workstation designers and manufacturers expected to introduce new ergonomic products during the 1990s, the Occupational Safety and Health Administration (OSHA) initiated a proposal to issue a set of ergonomic standards for workstations that would have required employers to reengineer the work process to limit the amount of time workers could spend at five repetitive tasks considered risk factors related to repetitive-strain injuries (RSI). These factors included doing the same motion or motion pattern, use of vibrating or impact tools, forceful hand exertions, unassisted frequent or heavy lifting, and working in fixed or awkward postures. Congress continues to be reluctant to permit OSHA to promulgate its set of ergonomic standards and issue ergonomic guidelines to employers until further scientific study of repetitive-stress injuries is conducted.

In 1991, California was the first state to enact standards that required all workers to have seating adjustable for height, support, and backward angle and backrests to provide for lumbar support. Other standards pertain to screens, keyboards, and arm, wrist, and foot rests. Some other states have followed suit and enacted similar standards, especially in terms of allowing workers who work at VDTs constantly to have frequent rest periods.

Figure 7–2   Work Area Arrangements

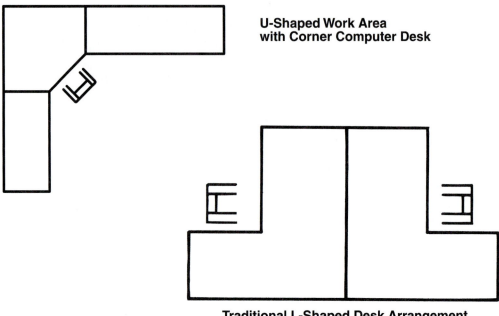

**U-Shaped Work Area
with Corner Computer Desk**

Traditional L-Shaped Desk Arrangement

2. *Ergonomic Workstations:* A well-designed workstation enables a secretary to be both productive and efficient. Professional designers focus on providing a simple, responsive, cost-effective workstation environment. Of utmost concern are the types of activities to be performed at a particular workstation.

   a. *Private work tasks:* Private work requires the office worker to think, read, analyze, or evaluate in a quiet atmosphere. The workstation design can provide protection from many outside distractions.

      EXAMPLE: Work surfaces attached to five-foot panels to form a U-shaped work area can provide a much more private work area than more traditional arrangements (see Figure 7–2).

   b. *Public work tasks:* Some work necessitates face-to-face interaction in a more social setting. Even in this environment, the workstation design should maintain an atmosphere that is free from annoying distractions.

      EXAMPLE: Within the modular work area, a round, freestanding table provides adequate work space needed for two- or three-person conferences. The round table is indicative of open communication.

   c. *Electronic work tasks:* Office professionals, whether secretaries or managers, may use electronic office systems (computers, telephones, and fax machines) in their work. An appropriate interface between people and the systems is essential. Electronic networking with other departments is enhanced by systems integration.

      EXAMPLE: Stevenson uses a computer located within her work area. The equipment is placed so that she need only swivel her chair to the left to use it. The printer is located to the immediate left of the computer, providing her with quick access. Not only is she near the equipment, but because her work area is U-shaped, she can readily communicate with other people who approach her workstation.

The workstation design must provide a work area conducive to the integration of people and the information with which they are working.

3. *Selection of User-Friendly Hardware and Software:* Keyboard arrangement, function keys, user interfaces (the mouse or trackball), printer location, and type of screen must be considered in the ergonomic arrangement of the hardware at the workstation. With more software available that is system compatible, users will continue to have more choices in selecting the most user-friendly software to meet their needs.

4. *Human Physiology:* Perhaps the most important factor is the human element—the worker—and the physical anatomy of the worker. How that individual adapts to the physical office environment is of prime importance.

D. Environmental Factors

Office design involves lighting, color, sound, air, surfaces, static electricity, power, security, and energy conservation as some of the external environmental factors that affect the office professional physically and psychologically.

1. *Lighting:* Primary considerations in analyzing lighting systems include the quantity of light present (foot-candles), brightness (foot-lamberts), contrast light reflectance, absence of glare, and uniformity. A *foot-candle* is the amount of light produced by a standard candle at a distance of 1 foot. A *foot-lambert* is a measure of brightness; it is a unit of measure approximating 1 foot-candle of light transmitted or reflected.

    a. *Task lighting: Task lighting* is direct light that illuminates the work surface.

    b. *Ambient lighting:* Indirect light that illuminates the area surrounding the work surface is called *ambient lighting.*

    c. *Natural daylight:* Even though natural daylight is an efficient lighting source, alternative lighting systems must still be available.

    d. *Fluorescent lighting:* The most commonly used light source in office buildings is *fluorescent lighting;* its illumination resembles natural light.

    e. *Incandescent lighting:* Although incandescent lighting with filament bulbs tends to be less expensive, this type of lighting can produce more glare and shadowing on work surfaces.

    Many offices are installing automatic light control systems as part of their energy conservation programs. These systems turn lights on in areas that will be in use and also turn lights off in areas no longer in use.

2. *Color Conditioning:* The effect of color on the performance of people has been studied extensively. Specific colors cause people to react emotionally to the physical office environment.

    EXAMPLES:

Color	Observed Effect
Red	*Heat, action, excitement*
Orange and yellow	*Warmth, cheerfulness*
Blue, green, and violet	*Coolness, calmness*
Purple	*Dignity*

Color and light are used together to produce varying effects. Dark colors used for wall coverings absorb most of the light falling on them, making the room appear to be dimly lit. Walls or panels of a dark or bright color can make a room or work area seem smaller than it really is. Pale colors on walls or panels will reflect light, making the work area appear brighter and larger than it really is. People often feel more relaxed in rooms that have some variation in color and light.

3. *Sound Control:* Another environmental consideration is the noise level in an office. Concern for sound control influences managers to make use of materials that will absorb, reflect, or isolate sounds.

   a. *Absorption:* The engulfing of sound waves by environmental materials is called *absorption.*

   b. *Reflection:* The bouncing of sound waves off a material and back into space is known as *reflection.*

   c. *Isolation:* The prevention of sound waves from passing through environmental materials is referred to as *isolation.*

   The *decibel* is the unit measure of the intensity of sound. One decibel is the faintest sound that can be detected by the human ear.

   EXAMPLE: Office noises range in intensity from 20 to 90 decibels, with 50 decibels being average for an office. Masking, also called white noise *or* white sound, *refers to the use of a low-level, nondisturbing background noise to blend in with regular office noise, eliminating the "silent" sound (or total lack of sound) or covering distracting noise.*

4. *Condition of Air:* An office professional's productivity is directly affected by the physical atmosphere of the office. Air temperature, air conditioning, humidity control, heating, and ventilation all affect employees' comfort in the office. Among possible office hazards, indoor air pollution may be the most disturbing. Most pollutants can be detected and measured, and office workers may be affected immediately but often only after a period of time.

5. *Surface Textures, Shapes, and Arrangements:* The versatility of office arrangement depends on the use of modular walls and furniture systems with textures, shapes, and arrangements that enable workstations to be comfortable and versatile.

   a. *Movable partitions:* Available in a variety of shapes and sizes, movable partitions can be matched to suit a variety of needs. These panels can be assembled, disassembled, and rearranged easily with a minimum of effort and cost. Additional partitions can be added to existing arrangements. Acoustical control (sound control) provided by the panels depends on the degree to which the material substance of the panels is able to absorb sound.

   b. *Work surfaces:* Shapes and arrangements of work surfaces affect the ability of the office worker to produce good-quality work. Rather than seeing a desk surface of only one level (probably 30 by 60 inches), modular adjustable work surfaces are becoming much more common in workstation design. They may contain one level for keyboard, another for screen, and a third level for copy.

   c. *Seating:* Comfort seating, with adjustments for raising or lowering the seat cushion and raising, lowering, or tilting the backrest, satisfies employee needs. Figure 7–1 shows the various dimensions that affect seating in the office workstation. As a result of the efforts of the Business and Institutional Furniture Manufacturers' Association (BIFMA), the American National Standards Institute (ANSI) has established a standard for evaluating the safety, durability and structural adequacy of general office chairs.

6. *Control of Static Electricity:* Stored data or text can be erased if someone walks by and transmits static electricity. Static electricity occurs when two materials that have been in physical contact are separated. The amount of static charge generated depends on the surface nature of the materials, the amount of contact, the amount of rubbing, and the humidity.

   EXAMPLE: Carpeting, clothing, or furniture are common sources of static electricity. Contact between shoes and a floor covering creates static electricity.

   a. *Static on a person's body:* Static can be dissipated by touching a static dissipative table mat or printer cushion before touching the equipment.

   b. *Static created from walking across a floor:*

      (1) A floor covering of antistatic material will limit the amount of floor-generated static.

      (2) A film treatment applied to carpet or tile floors generates only a very low static charge.

      (3) Antistatic mats (carpet or plastic) in areas immediately surrounding the sensitive equipment prevents the creation of static.

7. *Power Sources:* An extremely important environmental factor is the power source(s) available for the electronic work to be performed in a given work area. Of course, it is essential that there be adequate power for whatever electronic operations are to be carried on in the office so that circuits will not be overloaded. Electrical power outages are seen as a hazard to the electronic workstation. If information has already been stored on a secondary storage medium (diskette or hard disk), there is no problem. However, if an outage occurs as information is being keyed in, the information will be lost from the main memory of the computer system (processor unit). It is recommended that the Save command be used frequently while creating or revising a document.

8. *Security Control:* The employment of security personnel, the use of key cards and auditrons, and television monitoring devices are some security control measures used to secure the physical environment of the office. Additional security measures, such as passwords, affect the person's right to access information from an electronic workstation.

9. *Energy Conservation:* Many offices are establishing energy conservation programs monitored by computers and technicians in an attempt to conserve the amount of energy available for electricity, air conditioning, humidity control, and heating needed in specific areas of the entire office structure.

   EXAMPLE: If a seminar is being held in an auditorium at 10:00 A.M., it will probably be necessary to turn on the air conditioning at 9:00 A.M. and the lights at 9:45 A.M. Immediately after the room is cleared at the conclusion of the seminar, both lights and air conditioning can be turned off automatically. Energy costs will be decreased because of the existence of such an energy conservation program.

10. *Worker Response to Environment:* Office workers may exhibit positive or negative feelings toward the physical office environment as specific ergonomic factors affect

their comfort and efficiency. The U.S. National Institute of Occupational Safety and Health (NIOSH) and the Labour Canada Task Force on Micro-Electronics and Employment recommend that business policies and procedures be modified in the following ways to accommodate the needs of employees who work for extended periods of time at terminals.

  a. *Daily time limit for VDT operation:* The maximum amount of time for VDT operation by a single person should not exceed five hours per day.

  b. *Rest periods:* Hourly rest periods should be provided.

  EXAMPLES:

  One Chicago firm separates information processing work into two types: productive work (work requiring use of a computer for business applications) and nonproductive work (proofreading and other tasks not requiring the immediate use of a computer). A worker's daily routine typically includes both types of work to avoid discomfort resulting from computer operation for long periods of time.

  Several state legislatures have enacted labor laws that mandate frequent rest periods for VDT operators.

  c. *Reassignment to other positions:* Pregnant women should have the option to be reassigned to other positions because of *potential* radiation exposure or physical considerations. Research has not proved thus far that radiation from VDTs does in fact cause miscarriage or birth defects, but pregnant women are being cautious about decreasing time spent operating VDTs. Temporary reassignments should occur without loss of pay, seniority, or benefits.

E. Systems Analysis

When office systems function inefficiently, better ways must be developed to improve the interaction of people with the process and the environment. Traditionally, systems analysis involves major departmental activity (production, accounting, sales, and human resources). However, systems analysis is now being applied to a variety of activities within administrative systems, such as human resource planning, staff development, office layout and design, and planning for technology. As an ergonomic factor, systems analysis is gaining in prominence as an absolute necessity in facilitating work processes.

  1. *Basic Requirements:* Such a step-by-step investigation of office systems leads to a definition of the work process(es) being accomplished and may suggest improvements to be made to perform these operations more effectively. The primary focus is on objectives, organization, and detailed procedures involved in the system.

  a. *Analyzing operations:* An analysis is needed to determine current user objectives, operations, and information flow.

  b. *Identifying existing problems:* Any problems that exist within the present system should be identified and documented.

  c. *Defining user objectives:* Primary user objectives and user operations must be identified.

  d. *Determining documentation needed:* Any new documentation in terms of user requirements, functions, and work flows must be developed.

  e. *Identifying technical support needed:* Hardware, software, database management support, control programs, communications, and other technical support must be identified.

2. *Feasibility Study:* A feasibility study may be conducted to assess the present and future needs of the organization and to serve as a basis for the selection of alternative solutions to best meet user needs. Specific aspects of such a study might include the following:

   a. A summary of the organization's growth during the preceding five to ten years

   b. A summary of the organization's expected growth during the upcoming five to ten years

   c. A summary of the present labor force: number of employees, classifications, present job descriptions, and present job responsibilities

   d. An analysis of present and future space requirements as indicated by departmental plans and user requirements

   e. The organizational structure and pattern of the firm: departmentalization, centralization of support services, decentralization of office services, or combinations of these patterns

   f. Analyses of automated systems and procedures presently in use

   g. A study of the flow of information through the organization, with special emphasis on interpersonal and/or group communication of information and the media used

3. *Tools of Systems Analysis:* A number of different types of analytical tools are used in designing office systems. As these tools are utilized in planning more effective environment/people/process interaction, decisions made by managers will utilize application of specific ergonomic principles. The more prominent systems tools are for task, procedure, motion, and time analyses.

   a. *Task and job analysis:* Task analyses are conducted to find out what skills, knowledge, and behaviors are required for specific tasks required of a secretary, desktop publishing specialist, or other office professional. The task analysis involves all office tasks performed by an office professional, in a specific assignment, over a specified period of time. Job analyses are the accumulation of all tasks required within a particular office position, examined within the framework of entire office functions.

   b. *Procedures analysis:* The study of specific office processes, the number of steps, the time for each step, the distance in each step (if applicable), and the departments involved in the procedure is called *procedures analysis.* The most widely used tools of procedures analysis are the flow process chart, the procedure flowchart, the flow diagram, and the work distribution chart.

   c. *Motion study:* When analysts study office procedures, they may want to study motion to compare the efficiency of the manual operations required in certain types of office activities as compared to more automated operations. Suggestions can then be made to improve the person-task and person-equipment interfaces that exist in many office procedures.

   d. *Time study:* A vital element is time in relation to specific tasks that need to be performed. The person who uses a time plan to chart the progress of a given project over time will probably feel more committed to meeting specified deadlines than will one who does not. Two of the newer techniques are Program Evaluation and Review Technique (PERT) and Critical Path Method (CPM). The Gantt chart, developed by Henry L. Gantt in the early 1900s, depicts work in progress over a period of time, such as a day or a week.

F. Office Layout and Design

The work environment affects office professionals psychologically, sociologically, and physically—whether a traditional or modern office design is applied. The traditional (conventional) arrangement is sometimes referred to as a *private-office design.* Executives and managers are housed in offices separated from general office areas, which contain desks and office equipment for support personnel. The *open-office arrangement* is sometimes referred to as the *modern approach* to office design and includes the planning of office space without permanent walls and with modular furniture and aisle space to accommodate the communication flow through the office. The design of home offices typically tends to reflect the open-office arrangement since a portion of the living space may be remodeled or rearranged into office space.

1. *Planning an Office:* An office environment needs to be planned so that the people who work in that environment will be able to function effectively and productively. These areas should be considered before any long-range decisions about the office environment are made.

   a. *Strategic planning for the business:* The alignment of the physical facilities with the strategic plans for the business over the next few years is essential, resulting in fewer unexpected changes in the direction of the business as well as enhancing the communication flow necessary for office operations.

   b. *Cost of office design:* Costs refer to equipment, furniture, remodeling, renovation, and replacement. Workstations that are more cost effective will be more useful to the business over time.

   c. *Job functions:* The job functions of the office workforce have been changing over the past few years. Computer usage has increased to the point where almost every office worker has a computer at the workstation. The arrangement of the workstation, with appropriate seating and lighting, is very important for those who must have task lighting or special seating requirements. Job functions must be analyzed to determine the allocation of resources to these functions.

   d. *Computer requirements:* Recent studies by Louis Harris and Associates indicate that computer use has intensified in the office. On the average, computers are used more than four hours per day. The number of people who use a computer more than five hours a day has increased to more than 50 percent of all office workers. Additional considerations are the required wiring and cabling, space, and employee comfort.

   e. *Employee expectations:* Employees today are concerned about the work environment and their own health and comfort. Noise control, proper lighting, and VDT-related health issues are of prime importance to employees and should receive serious consideration as new office environments are planned.

2. *Designing Appropriate Office Layouts:* Although the primary responsibility for designing office layouts is usually assigned to an administrative office manager, many professional secretaries do have the opportunity to provide input and suggestions for change.

   a. *Goals of office layout:* The effective arrangement of furniture, equipment, and other physical components will accommodate assigned work tasks and facilitate efficient work flow within available floor space.

      (1) *Analyzing information and work-flow patterns:* Information being processed through the office should flow in a forward direction and in a straight line

whenever possible. The transmission of information, as related to a specific process, through either face-to-face or electronic communication is called the *work flow. Cybernetics* refers to the information flow resulting from the communications systems being used.

(a) *Flowchart or process chart:* Existing office procedures are studied, especially distances and delays involved in the process. The speed of each procedure is examined in relation to the entire process. In addition, overall productivity associated with each step of the process is ascertained and monitored. A *flowchart* is an illustration of existing office procedures, showing the distances and delays involved in the entire process or procedure from start to finish.

(b) *Flow diagram or office layout chart:* The movement of a document is charted using the actual floor plan of the office to develop the resulting work-flow pattern.

These are still useful tools for documenting electronic work flow. Total quality management advocates that a document (process step) should be included only if the individual receiving, reviewing, or sending the document adds value to the final document.

(2) *Allocating space for office functions:* Departments having frequent contact with each other need to be located physically near each other. Central services, such as an in-plant printing center or a word/information processing center, should be located near departments requiring the service. Within a specific department, space should be allocated according to job and employee needs.

EXAMPLES:

Here are suggested space allocations for specific office professionals:

Office Position	Space Allocation (square feet)
Office employees	70–100
Supervisor	100–150
Junior/first-level executive	150–200
Middle-level executive	300–350
Top-level executive	350–500

Office furniture also requires certain space allocations. Here are estimates of the amount of space required:

Furniture	Space Allocation
Secretarial desk (L-shaped)	55 square feet
File cabinet (letter-size)	5–7 square feet
Primary aisles	6–8 feet wide
Secondary aisles	4–5 feet wide

(3) *Providing appropriate office environmental needs:* Proper lighting, sound control, and interior decorating are important in providing an office environment

that meets the comfort and satisfaction needs of employees. *Euthenics* is the science of bettering employee conditions by improving the work environment.

(4) *Eliminating structural barriers:* To provide for handicapped or disabled office professionals, structural barriers must be eliminated. The open-office concept has been very useful in this regard. The Vocational Rehabilitation Act of 1973 requires all new federal buildings and private companies receiving more than $2,500 in federal funds to provide accessibility to handicapped employees. The Americans with Disabilities Act was another federal legislative act that provides for the accommodation of qualified disabled persons in the workplace.

b. *Flexibility in office layout:* Office planners need to be concerned with future expansion, shifting of departmental functions, and increasing personnel. Flexible office layouts can result in improved communication networks as well. As office arrangements are changed, telephone and computer networks must be adaptable, too. An annual space analysis or review may be helpful in maintaining a flexible plan.

3. *Types of Office Design:* There are two basic types of office designs: the private-office (traditional) arrangement and the open-office (modern) arrangement. Depending on the needs of the organization, these two basic designs may be modified to suit specific work needs and preferences.

a. *The private-office arrangement:* The private-office arrangement is known as the traditional *closed plan* or *bull-pen* approach. Executives and managers are typically housed in offices separated from general office areas where office support personnel are located. Here are some of the reasons often given for the popularity of the private-office arrangement:

(1) *Prestige:* The private office often conveys more prestige and status for the manager or executive.

(2) *Nature of the work:* The confidential and private nature of the work can better be accomplished with more secure surroundings.

(3) *Level of concentration required:* Some office work requires a high level of concentration. The private office furnishes a quieter environment within which to work.

The private-office arrangement is not considered an efficient arrangement, however, in terms of space utilization. Some authorities state that only 50 percent of the space devoted to private offices is used efficiently.

b. *The open-office arrangement:* Since 1960, the use of the open-office arrangement has increased, especially in the United States. The open-office approach arranges office professionals and functions in relatively open areas to accommodate the work flow and communication required. The open-office arrangement is characterized by these features: large open areas of office space, with only a minimum of permanent walls; use of modular furniture systems; clustering of workstations; and the use of accent colors to enhance the office decor. Two popular approaches used for open-office arrangements are office landscaping and the modular approach.

(1) *Office landscaping:* The concept of office landscaping was first introduced by the Quickboner Team, a group of German consultants who were commissioned by the University of Hamburg to study offices. The purpose was to develop methods to increase the overall efficiency of office functions through the application of scientific approaches. The team found that the ability to communicate was an important aspect of efficient office operation.

   (a) *Primary focus:* Office landscaping places primary emphasis on analyzing office procedures and controlling work flow.

   (b) *Special features of office landscaping:*

   • A minimum number of permanent walls

   • Workstations located to result in more efficient work flow

   • Utilization of acoustical devices and noise control

   • Uniform air conditioning and humidity control

   • Use of partitions, modular furniture, and planters to provide privacy and beauty

   • Use of well-designed workstations to complement work functions

(2) *The modular approach:* In this type of open-office design, office furniture is used creatively in designing individual work areas to meet the specific needs of employees.

   (a) *Primary focus:* The modular approach focuses on planning and arranging the individual workstation to allow for a variety of interchangeable components to meet individual needs and to serve as a basis for expandable office systems.

   (b) *Special features of the modular approach:*

   • Basic units of furniture: desk surfaces, end supports, filing units, shelves, and drawers

   • Wall panels or partitions on which furniture units can be attached or suspended

   • Electrical outlets for use with electronic equipment and "slots" for electrical cords

   • Built-in lighting fixtures for task lighting

   • Use of color and texture to complement the office design

A relatively new application of the open-office arrangement is called *hotelling,* which features an open office with unassigned desks. Instead of having an assigned personal work space, an office professional would reserve a desk for specific time periods. The term *hot-desking* refers to a desk or work area that is still warm from a previous worker.

EXAMPLE: Some of the Big Six accounting firms have found the practice of hotelling especially economical in making office space available for employees who are on the road most of the time.

   c. *Home office:* Ergonomics is also important to the home office. Although the open-office environment is the most typical arrangement, the following factors should be taken into consideration when establishing an office at home.

     (1) Workstation furniture must minimize employee fatigue and maximize functionality and comfort.

     (2) The amount of storage space will most likely need to be increased by 25 to 50 percent to allow for growth and to accommodate long-range plans. Sufficient work space must also be maintained.

     (3) Proper lighting is required for the entire office area as well as for task lighting.

     (4) All equipment needs to be functional including sufficient outlet connections and safety features such as surge protectors.

     (5) Atmospheric conditions must be a priority consideration.

     (6) Acoustics must be considered to provide privacy when needed.

     (7) An analysis of work and traffic flow supports plans for accessing the office area and making it available to clients.

     (8) The finishing touches of the home office (pictures and personal items) complete the aesthetic appeal of the office.

4. *Space Design:* The allocation of office space depends primarily on the way it will be used. Office professionals who use equipment to perform job functions will need more space than employees who perform primarily desk work (writing, planning, and communicating). Minimum space allocations can be identified that correlate with the task and job requirements (see F-2-a[2]). Office space planning should be a continuous activity because of the need for improving communication and productivity.

    a. *Factors affecting space design:* A number of physical factors such as the following need to be considered in the allocation and utilization of space within the office area.

     (1) Nature and type of furniture

     (2) Structural barriers (posts, pillars, columns, and walls)

     (3) Windows and doors

     (4) Nature of work to be performed

     (5) Horizontal and vertical space required for each job function

     (6) Storage and filing needs at the individual workstation

     (7) Communication requirements for each work area

    b. *Steps in planning office space:* When considering office space requirements, these basic steps should be kept in mind:

     (1) *Defining goals:* The work to be performed must be identified and appropriate goals established.

     (2) *Establishing space requirements:* Information about each work activity must be collected to determine whether the assigned space helps or hinders those functions. Communication and work-flow processes are vital considerations.

Space requirements for individual office workers must be determined on the basis of this analysis.

(3) *Developing new office space plans:* Alternative office layouts need to be developed to facilitate different patterns of information flow.

(4) *Selecting and implementing the best alternative:* Finally, the most feasible alternative needs to be selected for testing and eventual implementation. Flexibility should be a key in planning office space that will permit a variety of office activities to be performed.

5. *Computer Software for Office Design:* Software designed to assist with office layout is now on the market. The features and characteristics of the office structure, including spatial dimensions, can be manipulated so that proposed layouts and designs can be viewed on the computer screen before a final decision is reached. Physical structures in the office as well as workstation arrangements can be studied thoroughly before decisions are made about resource allocations needed for such renovation.

G. Design of Work Areas

The workstation is a work area planned and designed for use by an individual office professional (executive, manager, or secretary). With office functions becoming more automated, increased attention is being focused on ways to lessen fatigue, boredom, mental exhaustion, and stress. A National Institute of Occupational Safety and Health study indicated that office workers who worked with VDTs tended to experience more stress than other types of office workers. Workstation design depends on organizational needs, task performance needs, and behavioral considerations.

1. *Organizational Needs:* Initially, workstations are designed so that the organizational objectives can be met. The workstation must support communication (interpersonal and electronic), flow of information through the organization, and access to record systems with common information files.

   a. *Face-to-face communication:* Within any organization, there is a need for face-to-face interaction with other people for planning and carrying out a particular work assignment.

   b. *Electronic communication:* In addition to interpersonal communication, provision must be made in workstation design for electronic communication (use of computer, telephone, fax, and other electronic devices).

   c. *Information flow:* For business transactions and processes to take place, information must flow easily from task to task, from department to department, and externally to other organizations.

   d. *Record systems:* People need to be able to access information, whether that information has been filed in the form of paper or within an electronic system. Records should be accessible *when* the information is needed and *in the form* required by the user.

2. *Task Performance Needs:* A workstation must be designed and equipped so that specific work tasks can be performed efficiently and accurately according to required time schedules.

a. *Arranging the work center:* One of the "rules of thumb" that secretaries are often required to follow is that the top of the work surface (or desk) and drawers within the work area should be neatly arranged so that working from the desk will be efficient and productive.

(1) *Placement of office equipment:* Deciding where to place specific office equipment (computer, telephone, or label maker) depends on the need for ready access to the equipment.

(a) *Computer system:* The computer should be placed directly in front of the operator to allow for working either to the left or right, whichever is a more comfortable arrangement.

- The keyboard must be easily accessible directly in front of the operator. Many work stations feature a shelf for the keyboard that slides back under the control work area when not in use.

- Any console or desk module that is part of the system should be appropriately placed under the work surface, toward the back of the desk, or beneath the visual display screen so that placement will not interfere with routine computer operations.

- The printer is located on a separate work surface near the computer. If the printer is not a laser or an ink-jet printer, an acoustical sound cover should be placed over the printer so that printer noises will not disturb the entire office area. (If the printer is shared by more than one workstation, it should be placed in close proximity to all terminals sharing the printer.)

- The modular workstation may feature a raised platform for the visual display screen that enables the screen to be viewed more easily.

- Disk drives may be located next to the screen or keyboard for easy access or within the microprocessor positioned immediately under or next to the screen.

- Computer towers typically fit under the desk in an out-of-the-way location.

(b) *Telephone:* The telephone should be placed on the work surface in an easy-to-reach location, with message pad, notepad, and pens within arm's reach. Secretaries who are on the phone for extended periods of time may use headsets for speaking and listening instead of using the telephone handset. Besides improving listening comfort, the headset relieves the secretary's hands for note taking and paperwork required for the conversation.

(c) *Dictation-transcription unit:* For ease of listening and transcribing, this unit should be placed next to the computer. The latest technology provides for dictation and transcription through the local area network. The earphones and foot pedal that connect to the microprocessor are the only additional equipment required by the secretary.

(d) *Peripheral equipment:* Other office equipment used occasionally (copier, postage meter, fax, folding machine, and collator) should be placed in an area where they may be shared with other office workers. Sometimes, work areas with these types of peripherals are available for use by several departments.

(2) *Arranging desk accessories:* A calendar, in/out trays or baskets, small organizer, and other types of desk accessories should be arranged neatly within reach on top of the desk or on a desk extension or work area to the side.

(3) *Arranging office supplies:* In addition to locked storage for supplies purchased in large quantities, small office supplies in limited quantities may be stored systematically in desk drawers: stationery, envelopes, labels, papers, forms, pens/pencils, clips, and diskettes.

(4) *Arranging reference materials:* General office references that should be accessible on, in, or near the secretary's desk may include the following:

(a) An unabridged dictionary

(b) A word finder

(c) A thesaurus

(d) An office procedures manual or handbook

(e) The current ZIP code directory

(f) Directories (internal extension directory and local and/or long-distance telephone directories)

(g) Company policies and procedures manuals

(h) Index file of people and companies with whom the executive has frequent contact

Enhancements in software packages include dictionaries, thesauri, word finders, and general office procedures manuals. Directories of frequent contacts can be set up in electronic address books. Intranets provide electronic internal directories, standard operating procedures, and frequent-contact directories.

Electronic references remove the clutter from the work surface and provide the most dynamic, accurate information when properly updated and maintained.

b. *Utilizing devices for personal comfort:* Mental exhaustion, fatigue, boredom, and stress affect the productivity of the person who works with computers and other automated equipment in the office environment. Here are some ways in which the workstation design and the types of office equipment selected may alleviate the discomfort of the office professional.

(1) *Chair adjustments:* Office furniture manufacturers have created chairs that are adjustable in terms of changing the chair height, tilting the seat, and placing the backrests in the most comfortable position. The contour of the chair can be matched to the physical requirements of a person's body in a custom design.

(2) *Use of modular design:* Individual employees can arrange their own work areas to suit left- or right-handed preferences. Private work areas can be created through the use of privacy panels. Recent research shows that those employees who have the opportunity to help design their own work areas tend to be well satisfied with the office environment.

(3) *Work surface adjustments:* The height of work surfaces can be raised or lowered. Some of the latest designs in modular work areas for computers and word processors have work surfaces in four different positions that can be raised, tilted, or lowered: a center work surface, one to the right of center, one to the left of center, and one to the back of center that can be raised to hold a visual display screen (see Figure 7–1).

(4) *VDT placement:* Placing the screen on a small, raised platform helps bring it to eye level. The screen can also be tilted for ease of viewing and reading, and screen brightness, color, and contrast can be adjusted.

(5) *Keyboard platforms:* Moveable keyboards, attached by cable to screens, can be placed directly on the work surface or on a shelf that may pull out from under the center work surface. Mouse pads typically are to the left or right of the keyboard. When not in use, this shelf can be pushed back under the work surface until needed again.

c. *Maintaining security of information:* Information needs to be kept secure and in many cases private. Only people with security clearances should be permitted access to it. The workstation design can influence the worker's ability to control access to information.

(1) *Placement of partitions and wall panels:* Separate work areas created with panels and partitions help maintain privacy for the person who is working on a particular project. If another person interrupts, the arrangement of work surfaces as opposed to conversation areas will keep the information concealed.

(2) *Positioning VDTs for limited access:* Data and text easily viewed over an operator's shoulder can compromise information security. Better placement of the terminal so that people can be seen entering the work area may be a better idea.

(3) *Screen savers:* In Windows environments, a screen saver automatically appears on the screen in place of the data or text if the operator ceases to work with the text for a designated number of seconds or minutes. This screen saver helps maintain privacy of information that is on the screen.

(4) *Clustering workstations for work groups:* Planning work areas so that access is available only through an intermediary (a receptionist or a locked door) may reduce the tendency of other personnel to gain access to the work area unnecessarily.

3. *Behavioral Considerations:* How the office professional adapts behaviorally to workstation design is very important. Here are some aspects of workstation design that affect such acceptance.

a. *Need for territoriality:* Each worker wants to feel that a particular space or work boundary is available. The individual workstation provides a sense of the person's work space, and clustering of workstations provides a sense of belonging to a work group.

EXAMPLE: Nameplates on modular partitions or a display case, with names of department members listed, give employees a sense of belonging to the organization or work group.

    b. *Personalizing the workstation:* Allowances need to be made for employees to personalize their individual workstations with such items as family pictures, plants, or artwork.

    c. *Social needs:* Facilities adjacent or near the workstations—lounges, cafeterias, recreation areas, and fitness or workout rooms—provide for the social needs of office employees.

4. *Network Requirements:* Any special requirements necessitated by a computer network need to be considered in the design of individual work spaces. Cabling is an important factor since computer terminals need to be able to communicate with each other as well as peripheral equipment (printers). The objective of such planning is to make the presence of the computer at the individual workstation an efficient, easy-to-use tool and the presence of the network almost transparent to each user.

H. Office Furniture and Equipment Procurement

Analytical judgment is necessary in securing office furniture, equipment, and supplies to meet organizational needs. Often, furniture and equipment procurement is centralized for the entire organization, not just for a single office. This can be a complex decision-making responsibility, even for the office professional.

1. *Office Furniture:* Decisions must be made to maintain a private-office arrangement, with conventional workstations (L-shaped secretarial desk with pedestals, computer, and posture chair) or open-office arrangement (modular furniture arranged in clusters with movable privacy partitions). Useful modular furniture designs derive from the careful arrangement of a variety of component parts: one or more work surfaces, shelves, and cabinetry attached to partitions and storage space (drawers and file space). The selection process is affected by the following factors.

    a. *Analysis of present and future use:* The basic purpose for using the furniture must be kept in mind, especially since furniture is usually purchased with long-range objectives in mind. The cost involved necessitates a serious look at the ways in which the furniture will be used now and in the next several years.

    b. *Adaptability to office decor:* Types and sizes of the furniture components must be suitable for the office area. Wood surfaces should blend in with other office decor or match furniture purchased previously. Adaptability for present and future use is very important.

    c. *Suitability of furniture:* Individuals with different physical characteristics will be working in the same office area; the furniture selected must be suitable for each need.

    EXAMPLE: Both tall and short people will find adjustable posture chairs more suitable for their needs. With adjustable work surfaces available in new workstation designs, people will find it possible to fit the furniture to their particular height requirements.

    d. *Versatility to meet work needs:* To select office furniture that will correlate with the work to be done, a thorough analysis of the work being performed at each workstation must be conducted. The workstation must be versatile enough to meet the different work needs that develop.

    e. *Durability:* The purchase of office furniture is an investment not to be taken lightly. The costs need to be compared with the durability of the furniture so that the best quality for the resources available should be purchased.

f. *Prestige value:* The furniture purchased may reflect the hierarchical level of the person who will be using it. An executive may select a mahogany desk and credenza; the secretary who shares the office should have a comparable secretarial desk to complement the office area.

g. *Safety features:* The furniture should have a fire-retardant finish, have blunt-edged corners, and be able to withstand routine wear and tear.

h. *Portability:* The design of the furniture should be such that it will be easy to transport in case the office or work area is redesigned.

EXAMPLE: The human resources department has been located on the 11th floor of the 25-story corporate office building since 1990. At that time, a modular furniture system was installed, with the idea that it could be disassembled and moved if the department's location ever changed. An analysis of the present work flow through the department and the traffic from outside (applicants coming in to apply for jobs) showed that if the department were moved to the third floor, easier access would be available to applicants coming in and people visiting the company. Therefore, the decision was made to move the department entirely to the third floor. Because the furniture was modular, the movers were able to disassemble all the furniture and reassemble it on the third floor within just a few days. Even the telephone system was adaptable to the move because of the outlets built into the furniture components.

2. *Office Equipment:* Basic considerations for choosing office equipment (computers, telephones, dictation-transcription units, fax machines, and copiers) range from an analysis of the equipment operation to planned use of the equipment within the company. A very important consideration in this computer age is the availability of software (programmed procedures) for the specific applications for which the equipment is intended. Here are some basic concerns the alert office professional should keep in mind when involved in selecting equipment for purchase or lease:

a. *The immediate need for equipment:* The primary purpose or need for the equipment must be in the forefront in considering either a purchase or a lease. How the equipment will be used and by whom are serious considerations.

b. *Analysis of specific applications:* Equipment systems must be examined carefully to see whether their component specifications are suited to the specific applications for which the equipment will be used. Vendors should be asked to provide demonstrations on the equipment, showing how sample applications might be processed using particular systems.

c. *Basic operation of the system:* The speed and ease of operation are important from both training and utilization viewpoints. Software available for the system will be important in terms of its applicability for the work to be done. From a training standpoint, the basic operation of the system should be able to be learned within a few days. However, a person will probably need from three to six months to become a productive and innovative system operator.

d. *Cost of the equipment:* The cost of the equipment will depend on whether the equipment is being purchased, rented, or leased.

   (1) *Purchase:* The equipment may be purchased outright, with the title of ownership passing immediately from the vendor to the buyer. Equipment purchase

requires a large outlay of money at one time, although some payment plans can be extended over a two- to three-year period.

(2) *Rental:* Sometimes, equipment may be needed only for a short time, or the company may wish to continue to use up-to-date equipment rather than take the chance of purchasing equipment that might be obsolete as newer technology becomes available. When equipment is rented, the ownership stays with the person or company providing the equipment for rental.

(3) *Leasing:* A *lease* is a contract permitting a user (the lessee) to use equipment by making payments to the vendor (the lessor) over a specified period of time. When the lease terminates, the lessee can renew the lease, return the equipment to the lessor, purchase the equipment, or lease new equipment. Sometimes, the lessee is able to accumulate equity (investment) in the equipment, which can be applied toward its purchase price. Usually, a maintenance contract for the equipment is included in the cost of the lease.

e. *Cost of supplies and/or software:* Another very important consideration in selecting office equipment is the cost that will be incurred for supplies and/or software for specific operations. This is why it is important to know what types of applications and operations will be performed on the new equipment.

f. *Training time needed:* Vendors will indicate that within two to three days, an operator will be proficient with a new system. This may be true for computers, copiers, fax, and telephone systems used for basic business applications. For a person to become productive with automated equipment, several weeks or months may be necessary to learn to handle more complex applications. Training provided by vendors will vary from one hour to one day to several days. A check should be made to see what kind of training is available *before* the system is ordered and whether there are any special costs for the training. Some vendors offer training programs sequenced over a period of time to help the user learn more sophisticated applications.

g. *The availability of training materials:* Most vendors of computer, telephone, and copier equipment have developed instructional and training materials that can be extremely helpful in training operators. People who will most likely become involved in learning the new system should be asked to examine the training materials available to see whether the contents are clear and useful. Especially with computer software, training tutorials and "coaching" lessons may be included with the software program. As the operator works on a specific work assignment and needs assistance, these lessons can be accessed and adapted to the particular task at hand.

h. *Cost of training provided:* Some vendors offer training as part of the regular installation of the system, whereas others charge a fee for extra training. The costs of training and instructional manuals should be investigated and, if needed, included in the purchase or lease agreement.

i. *Estimated delivery time:* There may be a waiting period from the time the order is received and approved by the vendor to the time the equipment is delivered and installed. An estimated delivery time will permit the development of accurate training and implementation plans.

j. *Maintenance and service contracts:* The availability of service is usually a very high priority for the purchaser since downtime for the equipment should be kept at a minimum. Any service or maintenance contract should be scrutinized very carefully to see how quickly service would be provided (24-hour service is usually promised), the basic cost (per month or per year) for maintenance, and exactly what service is provided as part of the agreement.

k. *Maintenance of fixed asset inventory:* All equipment purchased must be recorded as part of the fixed asset inventory for the organization. Appropriate inventory tags should be affixed to the equipment so that an immediate record is created. Because of concern for equipment security, the portability of equipment should be examined to see whether the equipment should be permanently affixed to the workstation so that there is less chance of loss through theft.

3. *Office Supplies:* Selecting and purchasing appropriate office supplies is another administrative function that most secretaries supervise. A procedure for stockpiling enough supplies for a given period of time, such as six months or a year, will keep the office functioning smoothly. Some of the more important considerations in handling office supplies include the following:

a. *Quantity estimates:* The quantity of supplies needed for a designated period of time needs to be estimated.

b. *Cost comparisons:* Quantity prices from several suppliers (local suppliers as well as Internet suppliers) should be compared to take advantage of discounts and competitive pricing.

c. *General office inventory:* The issuance of supplies from a general office inventory will necessitate locked storage and centralized allocation of supplies. Storage space within work areas should be kept at a minimum.

d. *Petty cash fund:* A petty cash fund can be utilized to purchase supplies of relatively low cost and in small quantity that are purchased infrequently. Sometimes, a small quantity can be purchased to replenish the office supply until a larger quantity can be ordered.

A perpetual inventory will provide an accurate record of the quantity of supplies in stock. At specific times, the office professional in charge will need to check the inventory so that replenishment can take place before the supply runs out. To facilitate the quick purchase of small office supplies, an open account can be maintained with a local office supplies firm. Often, commercial discounts are available when this type of open account is maintained with a local firm.

4. *Outsourcing for Equipment or Supplies:* Sometimes, an organization will contract with a third party to perform specific jobs for the company. The third party is a subcontractor, providing the equipment and supplies that are needed for the job. The payment for services rendered typically includes consulting, equipment, and supply expenses. For many companies, this is more beneficial than purchasing equipment and supplies and hiring additional employees.

I. Future Trends in Ergonomics

Ergonomics has received much attention during recent years in business environments as well as industrial settings. The impact that interior design and pollution control have on the quality of work life will require continuous attention from employers, the government, and environmental specialists to ensure that the workplace complements the work to be done and the people who are responsible for performing the work.

1. *Business and Office Designs:* Employers will need to involve their employees—the professionals who are doing the actual work tasks—in redesigning and restructuring offices and other work areas. Interior designers who specialize in business and industrial settings can be helpful, but the majority of the input must come from those professionals who are responsible for the output. These people need to be able to work at the computer for long periods of time or move around the office easily to accomplish their tasks. The comfort level of employees will continue to be an extremely important issue as employers attempt to create environments that are conducive to health, safety, and productivity for all employees.

2. *Emphasis on Quality of Work Life:* A recent study reported that many employees today are angry with the quality of work life that exists in the workplace today. Spending long workdays, often into the evening hours, to meet deadlines keeps employees from handling family responsibilities or enjoying leisure-time activities. Productivity in work settings will depend on the business environment and how conducive it is to the accomplishment of specific work tasks. The more pleasant the work setting (with clean air, sound control, and color complements), the more productive office professionals will want to be.

3. *Privacy Issues:* Ergonomics involves a concern for maintaining personal privacy as well as privacy of information within the office. People cannot be productive if their personal privacy is invaded by the encroachment of others within specific work areas. The invasion caused by noise or physical movement can be very irritating to the office professional who is trying to concentrate on completing a task to meet a fast-approaching deadline. Privacy of information may be in danger as well. Not all people within an office will have security clearance to access the same information. Therefore, office managers will need to continue to develop ways in which privacy of information as well as personal privacy can be maintained.

4. *Government Involvement in Development of Standards:* For the past several years, the Occupational Safety and Health Administration (OSHA) has been attempting to gain permission from Congress to research and develop ergonomic standards for workstations that would lead to the reengineering of specific work processes. Congress has been slow to permit OSHA to pursue research that could verify that specific repetitive tasks are injurious to the physical health of employees. Research-and-development efforts in the future must be focused on the employee and any possible health hazards that are imposed by the technology or the work processes to be performed.

Ergonomics involves research into all aspects of the work process, from repetitive motions to be performed to the comfort and ease with which the employee can perform required work tasks. Instead of the user adapting to the work environment, the work environment must be designed and adapted to the user.

Review Questions

Directions: Select the best answer from the four alternatives. Write your answers to the left of the number.

1. Bradley, a marketing representative, left a new CT system at DynaMatics for a one-week trial period. She conducted a two-hour training session for those people who would be testing the system. When Bradley returned the following week, the office manager indicated that he really liked the system and would like to have one in the office, but the selection committee raised several issues that need to be resolved before a decision is made. Which of the following terms best characterizes the selection committee?

    a. Early adapter
    b. Decision maker
    c. Late adapter
    d. Nonadapter

2. As the training on the new CT system began, one secretary remarked, "This appears to be an easy system to learn; I can see the benefits to office efficiency already." Which one of the following terms best characterizes the secretary?

    a. Early adapter
    b. Decision maker
    c. Late adapter
    d. Nonadapter

3. Attention to the physiological aspects of the person-equipment interface is shown by which one of the following administrative actions?

    a. An ad hoc committee will report at the next office staff meeting on the rationale for purchasing a new computer system.
    b. Task lighting has been installed at each workstation to accommodate detailed work.
    c. A team has been established to develop ideas for increasing office productivity.
    d. Two executive assistants have been selected as information processing training specialists.

4. Biomechanics, the study of the musculoskeletal effort of office workers, addresses which one of the following ergonomic concerns?

    a. Interpersonal factors
    b. Physiological factors
    c. Psychological factors
    d. Sociological factors

5. Work-group clusters, teamwork among group members, and the need for territorial space have become more important and prevalent in the office environment. These factors are addressed by the

   a. communication theories impacting ergonomics.
   b. physiological basis of ergonomics.
   c. psychological basis of ergonomics.
   d. sociological basis of ergonomics.

6. In an automated office environment

   a. chat rooms provide space where employees can take required breaks and meet informally.
   b. face-to-face interaction between managers and office support personnel is required for document processing.
   c. information from electronically stored documents can be transmitted to other locations in a matter of seconds.
   d. written communication results most often in paper documents.

7. A newly designed electronic sales order form is being created by a Web master. The path of the sales form in transmitting information related to the processing of the sales order is called

   a. form design.
   b. job analysis.
   c. procedures analysis.
   d. work flow.

8. Jordan works in the human resources department of a large corporation. He needs to inform the employees with details on the annual company picnic. The best distribution method would be

   a. an audio conference.
   b. e-mail.
   c. fax.
   d. the intranet.

9. Jacobs uses a microcomputer system for three to four hours a day. For the past two weeks, she has been experiencing frequent headaches and blurred vision. During an eye examination, Jacobs remarked, "I've never had this before. The visual display screen I'm using must be causing the trouble." If the doctor who examines Jacobs' eyes is aware of the latest research on the use of VDTs, an appropriate response would be:

   a. "Besides looking at the design of the terminal, you need to also evaluate other physical factors."
   b. "You're right. You really should transfer to a job that doesn't require you to use a VDT."
   c. "You're really suffering from psychosocial problems from overuse of a visual display screen."
   d. "You're right! In your work, you should limit the use of the visual display screen to no more than two hours at a time to keep this from recurring."

_____ 10 One of the managers whom Jacobs works for is in the habit of presenting "crisis work," such as agendas to be sent to 25 committee members that need to be ready for this afternoon's mail. The usual comment is "With your computer system, this job shouldn't take long." Jacobs experiences stress along with frequent headaches and nervousness. Typically, these are symptoms of

a. musculoskeletal problems.
b. psychosocial disturbances.
c. psychosomatic disorders.
d. visual dysfunction.

_____ **11.** Which one of the following is an example of an ergonomic factor important to consider in designing the office environment?

a. Classical music is piped in from 2 to 4 P.M. each afternoon.
b. Incandescent lighting illuminates the area surrounding the work surface.
c. The office walls have been painted a pale blue.
d. Visual display screens should be adjustable and show characters on a light background.

_____ **12.** Ambient lighting

a. illuminates the entire work area.
b. illuminates the task surface.
c. produces glare and shadowing on work surfaces.
d. resembles natural light in its illumination.

_____ **13.** Low-level, nondisturbing background noise is called

a. absorption.
b. isolation.
c. reflection.
d. white sound.

_____ **14.** An electrical power outage is a potential hazard to the electronic workstation because

a. information that is being keyed in when the power outage occurs may be lost.
b. information stored in secondary storage may be lost.
c. the secretary may not be able to reset the system.
d. static electricity is created that may erase stored data.

_____ **15.** Organizations rely on such agencies as the U.S. National Institute of Occupational Safety and Health (NIOSH) to recommend business practices for information workers who use office technology in their daily routines. Research findings also lead to legislation to protect workers from possible hazardous conditions. Recent studies conducted by NIOSH support which one of the following statements?

a. The minimum amount of time for VDT operation should be at least two hours.
b. An office worker who works with a visual display screen more than five hours per day should be allowed rest periods every hour.

    c. Two rest periods (10 minutes in length) need to be scheduled each morning and afternoon.

    d. A worker who experiences some discomfort should be reassigned to another position.

16. An analysis of present and future space requirements is accomplished with a

    a. feasibility study.
    b. motion study.
    c. task analysis.
    d. time study.

17. Total quality management advocates that

    a. ergonomically designed computer systems should be provided to all office employees.
    b. a document process step should be included whenever the individual receiving, reviewing, or sending the document adds value to the final document.
    c. job functions should change.
    d. the responsibility for designing office layouts should be assigned to the tech worker.

18. Proper lighting and sound control are components of the science of bettering employee conditions by improving the work environment. This field is known as

    a. hotelling.
    b. biomechanics.
    c. cybernetics.
    d. euthenics.

19. Which one of the following descriptions characterizes the trend for both office and home-office design?

    a. Clustered workstations using modular furniture systems and wall panels
    b. Ergonomically designed furniture that maximizes fatigue and minimizes functionality
    c. Private offices to increase overall efficiency of office functions through the application of scientific approaches
    d. Walls that provide areas of privacy and work concentration

20. Which one of the following is a characteristic of the landscaped office?

    a. Centralized services for information processing
    b. Plants placed throughout the office and serviced by a firm that ensures proper care for plant growth and aesthetics
    c. Private offices with windows for top management
    d. Use of well-designed workstations to complement work functions

21. An enhancement to the telephone system for speaking and listening that relieves the secretary's hands for note taking and paperwork required for the conversation is a

    a. computer transcription peripheral.
    b. console.
    c. handset.
    d. headset.

22. Electronic references provide the most dynamic and accurate versions of internal directories and standard operating procedures. These electronic references can be found on the

    a. application software packages.
    b. intranet.
    c. Internet.
    d. operating system.

23. Which one of the following would be a primary consideration in the selection process for a new computer system?

    a. Need for equipment: how it will be used and by whom
    b. The prestige value of the system to the particular office or department
    c. The purchase price of the system
    d. Time needed to train users

24. The computer selection committee consists of one member from each department. The committee has selected a computer system that appears to be very well suited for the company's applications. Which one of the following strategies will be most helpful to the selection committee in being sure that the equipment fits the specific needs of the company?

    a. A complete training program by the vendor is included as part of the purchase agreement.
    b. Office personnel need to be assured that within a week's time they will become proficient with the new system.
    c. The selection committee should find out what other companies have installed a similar system and how it is used in each company.
    d. The vendor is requested to provide demonstrations showing actual applications used in the company.

25. The selection committee needs to recommend whether the equipment should be purchased, rented, or leased. The committee anticipates that there may be modifications to the equipment by the manufacturer within the next year. The best route for the company to take at this time would be to

    a. lease the equipment provided that amounts paid can apply to the purchase price later.
    b. purchase the computer system.
    c. rent the equipment from the vendor.
    d. select a system that is not expected to change.

Solutions

	Answer	Refer to:
1.	(c)	[A-1-g(1)]
2.	(a)	[A-1-g(2)]
3.	(b)	[A-2-a(2), D-1-a]
4.	(b)	[A-2-b(2)]
5.	(d)	[A-3]
6.	(c)	[A-4-b]
7.	(d)	[A-5-b]
8.	(d)	[A-5-a(2)]
9.	(a)	[B-1-b]
10.	(b)	[B-1-e]
11.	(d)	[C-1]
12.	(a)	[D-1-b]
13.	(d)	[D-3]
14.	(a)	[D-7]
15.	(b)	[D-10]
16.	(a)	[E-2]
17.	(b)	[F-2-a]
18.	(d)	[F-2-a(3)]
19.	(a)	[F-3-b, F-3-c]
20.	(d)	[F-3-b(1)(b)]
21.	(d)	[G-2-a(1)(b)]
22.	(b)	[G-2-a(4)]

23. (a)   [H-2-a]

24. (d)   [H-2-b]

25. (a)   [H-2-d(3)]

CHAPTER

Business Travel

OVERVIEW

A very important business procedure that office professionals are often required to arrange is business travel. Organizational policy will dictate how travel should be arranged. Some companies with large travel budgets make special agreements with travel agencies, hotels, or transportation companies. The administrative assistant or secretary needs to be aware of procedures to use when (1) the organization has its own travel department, (2) the services of a local travel agency are preferred, or (3) all arrangements for business travel need to be handled within the department or division.

The person who assists the executive in making business travel arrangements must be familiar with various types of services, travel facilities that may be available, and personal preferences of the traveler with regard to dates, times, and types of travel. After the trip, the traveler's satisfaction with the arrangements made for the trip needs to be checked.

Office professionals need to be able to recognize and be familiar with terms associated with business travel as well as procedures for preparing an itinerary, using source books and services of agencies, making reservations, and assembling trip folders for the business traveler.

KEY TERMS

Commercial travel agency
Confirmed reservation
Debit card
Domestic travel
In-house transportation
   department
International travel

Internet travel site
Itinerary
Letter of credit
Official Airline Guide
  (OAG®)
On-line reservation
  system

Passport
Source book
Travel advance
Travelers' checks
Trip file
Visa

A. Organizational Policies and Procedures for Travel

Before any travel arrangements can be made, the administrative assistant or secretary needs to be familiar with organizational policies and procedures concerning approved business travel. The individual traveler must be aware of and follow travel policies and procedures. Coverage for work duties usually performed needs to be reassigned within the office. Eligibility for business insurance coverage during the trip is a major concern.

Business travelers need to follow specific procedures established by the organization in arranging authorized travel.

1. *Approval for Business Travel:* Any employee—executive, manager, or other office professional—must receive supervisory approval for business travel. Typically, a form requesting authorization to travel must be completed, signed by the traveler, and approved by the immediate supervisor. Sometimes an estimate of business expenses to be incurred on the trip will be required on the form. Typical procedures such as these must be followed:

   a. *Travel advances:* Funds advanced to the traveler by the organization must be requested, approved, and acquired prior to the trip.

   b. *Company travel policies:* The company may have specific policies regarding reservations for lodging and transportation that business travelers need to follow.

   c. *Use of credit cards:* Expenses may be charged directly to the organization by using business credit cards issued to the traveler. In other cases, personal credit cards may be used with receipts submitted to the organization for reimbursement.

   d. *Business expense forms:* When the business trip is over, the traveler must report all business-related expenses with original receipts so that a travel record is on file and approved expenses may be reimbursed to the traveler.

2. *Approval for Transportation:* If company-owned vehicles or airplanes are being used for business travel, the traveler will need to complete an appropriate form requesting permission to schedule these forms of transportation. In addition to the traveler's name and driver's license number, other types of information requested on the form may include the following:

   • Date(s) of the business travel

   • Time of departure

   • Date and estimated time of return

   • Destination city or cities

   • Purpose of the trip

   • Approximate number of miles driven or flown

   • Names of other passengers, if any

   Once approval has been granted, the traveler is able to make appropriate arrangements with the transportation department for pickup of the vehicle or boarding the airplane. Many organizations issue credit cards to be used only for gasoline and other transportation expenses during such business travel.

Appropriate approval for business travel and/or the use of company-owned vehicles and carriers is very important for the business traveler. There should be no question that the traveler is on organizational business so that business insurance policies will cover the individual in case of accident or emergency.

B. Preparations for Business Travel

In assisting with arrangements needed for business travel, the administrative assistant or secretary must be prepared to determine what the exact travel needs will be. These needs range from organizational requirements to personal preferences of the business traveler. Before the itinerary (business travel plan) can be finalized with accurate and complete travel information, source books and/or travel services need to be consulted to determine the types of transportation services available, the costs, and the types of travel documents and currency needed.

1. *Organizational Requirements for Travel:* The business traveler represents the organization in conducting business for the organization in various parts of the country and the world. Some of the requirements placed on the traveler by the organization include the following:

    a. *Business meetings:* Specific meetings to attend in destination city(ies), with names and positions of business contacts, addresses, and telephone numbers of companies or organizations involved, must be entered on the calendar.

    b. *Time line:* Dates and times scheduled for certain cities, with appropriate travel information, must be determined.

    c. *Business associates:* Customers, clients, or associates with whom the business traveler must meet need to be identified.

2. *Personal Preferences of Traveler:* The business traveler may have certain preferences for the way in which the travel is arranged. The administrative assistant or secretary must be aware of preferences that the traveler may have, such as the following:

    a. Modes of transportation (e.g., automobile, airplane, bus)

    b. Class of service

    c. Lodging accommodations

    d. Scheduling of appointments during the trip

3. *Need for Office Services:* Business travelers often need various kinds of office services that may range from having an appropriate work area or desk space to utilizing copy or printing services.

    a. *Work space:* Desk space can be leased from firms specializing in providing office services. With the desk space comes telephone service, a receptionist, computer system access, and answering services.

    b. *Business services:* Local business services can be contacted in regard to the preparation of copies, visuals, and photographs. Some services include personal delivery, sending fax messages, or shipping and mailing small parcels. Some large supermarket centers have small copy centers as peripheral services.

    c. *Hotel services:* Many hotels and motels now have business suites complete with desk space, telephone, and on-line computer connection or business centers with computers, copiers, and fax service.

4. *Source Books:* In assisting with travel arrangements, the office professional needs to know how to use source books for specific types of travel information. Guides and indexes commonly called *source books* assist the secretary in making appropriate travel arrangements. Those source books used most often are transportation guides, hotel and motel indexes, timetables, and atlases.

    a. *Transportation guides:* Detailed information on travel accommodations, airline schedules, railway schedules, and bus schedules is included in various types of transportation guides. Here are brief descriptions of some of the most commonly used guides:

(1) *The Official Airline Guides:* Travel agencies and transportation departments subscribe to these guides to have up-to-date information on airline schedules and fares. The *Official Airline Guides* (*OAG*®) are available through a variety of media: portable pocket guides, desk references in print and electronic format, and a customized travel information system for use on a company's intranet or local area network. These publications from Official Airline Guide, Oak Brook, Illinois, are particularly useful in finalizing all types of travel plans:

   (a) *The Official Airline Guide (North American Edition):* This guide, in print and electronic forms, gives detailed information on airline schedules and fares for the North American area (flights, flight times, carriers, classes of service, connecting flights, fares).

   (b) *The Official Airline Guide (Worldwide Edition):* This edition of the OAG gives detailed information on flights outside North America in both print and electronic forms.

   (c) *The OAG Pocket Flight Guide:* This guide is a condensed version of the OAG and is a pocket-size book of information on airline travel (flight schedules, flight numbers, classes of service, meal service). Several editions are available, including the North American, Pacific-Asia, Latin American, Worldwide, and European editions.

   (d) *The OAG Desktop Flight Guide:* North American and Worldwide editions of this electronic flight guide are available.

   (e) *The OAG*® *Travel Information System*™: This interactive system allows an organization's personnel access to travel information. Its network capability enables everyone within an organization to log on and access schedule information. Business travelers who are traveling with a laptop computer can access all flight, destination, and lodging information that is stored within the system.

   All the OAG flight guides are available on computer disk. OAG also publishes *Frequent Flyer* magazine, which is available by subscription.

(2) *World Cruise and Shipline Guide:* This guide, published by OAG, shows all cruise and ferry schedules worldwide.

(3) *Official Railway Guide:* This guide includes detailed information on all railway schedules and fares within the United States and in foreign countries.

(4) *Russell's Official National Motor Coach Guide:* Complete bus schedules and fares are included in this guide for motor coach transportation.

b. *Lodging indexes:* Information on lodging accommodations available throughout the United States and foreign countries is available in a variety of lodging indexes. Some of the more commonly used hotel and motel indexes are the following:

(1) *The Hotel & Motel Red Book:* This source book is the official lodging directory published by the American Hotel & Motel Association.

(2) *Business Travel Planner (North American and Worldwide Editions):* This is another OAG publication that includes hotel and motel rates, maps, and dining and sightseeing information about destination cities.

(3) *Hotel and Travel Index:* This source book, published quarterly by the Reed Travel Group, 500 Plaza Drive, Secaucus, NJ 07096, includes hotel and motel rates, maps, and sightseeing information for the traveler.

c. *Timetables:* Information on railway and bus schedules for all scheduled runs is included in the most commonly used timetables:

(1) *Official Railway Guide* (see Section B-2-a[3])

(2) Bus schedules for Greyhound, Trailways, and other private bus companies

d. *Atlases:* Road maps for the United States as well as other locations within the North American continent or foreign countries are included in many published atlases, such as *Rand McNally Road Atlas for United States, Canada, and Mexico,* published by Rand McNally & Company, Chicago, Illinois. In addition, specific Internet sources can now be accessed by travelers to obtain maps of local areas as well as travel directions to and from specific sites.

5. *Travel Agencies, Transportation Departments, and Internet Services:* The services offered through travel agencies, transportation departments, and Internet travel services are extremely important in planning business travel and making the desired travel arrangements. The preparation of travel schedules and reservations for accommodations represent primary purposes of travel agencies, in-house transportation departments, and Internet travel services. These organizational units assist office professionals in making appropriate plans for business travelers.

a. *Commercial travel agency:* A business firm specializing in making travel arrangements for individuals, companies, and other organizations requesting their services functions as a *commercial travel agency.* In addition to handling commercial accounts, such travel agencies serve the public, scheduling leisure travel as well.

(1) *Services provided:* Services provided by the travel agency include lodging and transportation reservations (air, car rentals, railroad, bus, ground transportation) and other types of travel information. When agencies are helping members of professional associations with travel arrangements pertaining to a conference or convention, a toll-free telephone number is usually available to the member for immediate assistance. Planning more complex travel arrangements, such as those required for a cruise, may require an expert travel agent's advice.

(2) *Cost of services:* The agency receives a commission (percentage) normally based on ticket sales or room rates from those hotels, airlines, and other transportation companies that indicate their willingness to pay the agency a commission on bookings. Typically, the traveler who uses the services of an agency pays no additional surcharge for such service. With certain transportation reservations, however, the agency charges a flat service fee.

EXAMPLE: Morrison is the chief executive officer for Morrison Plastics, a firm with plants in Germany and Japan. Johnson, her administrative assistant, must be sure that appropriate travel arrangements are made for Morrison's bimonthly flights to these locations. Johnson works closely with the Royale Travel Agency whenever tickets and reservations are needed. Any additional information, such as the luggage allowed on a flight, can be requested in a quick phone call to the agency.

Sometimes an agency is not eligible to receive a commission from a particular hotel, airline, or transportation company. In these situations, reservations would need to be made directly with companies for preferred transportation and lodging.

b. *In-house transportation department or agency:* Travel services provided by an in-house transportation department or agency are similar to those of a commercial travel agency, with the exception that these services are provided only to personnel and departments within the company.

   (1) *Services provided:* The transportation department or in-house agency makes all necessary transportation arrangements and reservations directly with carriers. Some in-house departments may be large enough to warrant on-line computer networking directly with the airlines.

   (2) *Cost of services:* Operational costs may be charged to individual departments using in-house transportation services.

c. *Internet travel sites:* Especially if the travel needs are fairly simple, office professionals may prefer to visit on-line sites to research airline fares and to obtain other travel information and costs.

EXAMPLE: A recent study by NPD Online Research (Port Washington, New York) showed that about 30 percent of those people visiting Web sites actually make their reservations through those sites.

Fares should be compared with quotes obtained through local travel agencies to see whether there are any substantial cost savings by using Internet sources to make reservations. Most of the larger travel sites request the customer to furnish itinerary information (dates, times, departure and arrival cities). The site will display a list of possible airline itineraries, fares, lodging quotes, and car rental prices. Customers type in credit-card information, and the purchase is confirmed by electronic mail.

6. *On-Line Reservation Systems:* Commercial travel agencies, transportation departments, and individual office professionals can access on-line reservation systems to provide quick, efficient service to clients and associates. Up-to-date travel information is available through a computer network or on the Internet rather than looking through books, guides, and other publications.

a. *Airline schedules:* On-line systems permit the viewer to access all airline schedules and make appropriate flight reservations. The air fares shown on an on-line system are generally the same as those quoted by the airlines' reservation systems. Most major carriers encourage on-line sales because the airlines pay lower commissions to on-line agents than to off-line travel agencies. Special deals with specific carriers are often offered at on-line sites.

EXAMPLE: A Best Fare Finder feature may be offered at specific travel sites to allow the traveler to locate the least expensive ticket for any specific air route.

b. *Lodging and ground transportation reservations:* On-line systems may be used to make hotel, motel, or other ground transportation reservations directly with the provider.

An on-line network will sometimes permit the operator to pull up an airport map on the screen or access additional information about luggage requirements, ground transportation available, or actual distances involved in traveling from city to city.

7. *Travel Reservations:* As indicated previously, one of the administrative assistant's responsibilities may be to make appropriate travel reservations for transportation, lodging, or conference facilities. The business traveler learns to rely on the assistant's judgment in handling these types of arrangements.

   a. *Transportation reservations:* Whether made directly with the airlines or other transportation companies, reservations should be confirmed and complete information included on the travel itinerary:

      • Flight numbers or schedule numbers

      • Departure and arrival times and dates

      • Type of service reserved

      • Name of carrier

      • Meals furnished (breakfast, lunch, snacks, dinner)

   b. *Lodging reservations:* Business information about needed lodging arrangements needs to be compared with what is available for the business traveler. The following information needs to be considered in making appropriate reservations:

      (1) *Information supplied by the administrative assistant:* To make appropriate lodging reservations, the following kinds of information needs to be considered:

         • A brief description of the room or suite to be reserved, with information about computer network connections required

         • The traveler's preference for specific accommodations (bed, shower, whirlpool bath)

         • The number of persons for whom the room(s) need to be reserved

         • Arrival date/time (guaranteed, if after 6:00 P.M.)
           [*Note:* The term *late arrival* refers to arrival after 6:00 P.M.]

         • An estimate of the length of stay

      (2) *Information supplied by lodging company:* The following information needs to be obtained from the lodging company:

         • Availability of rooms (including computer on-line access)

         • The rate to be charged (room and computer/telephone time)

         • Check-in and check-out times

         • Official confirmation of the reservation

      Once the information supplied on behalf of the business traveler and that supplied by the lodging company have been compared, appropriate reservations can be made. Normally, reservations are held for check-in by 6 P.M. unless the hotel is notified prior to that time and the reservation is guaranteed for late arrival with payment on a credit-card account.

   c. *Reservations for special facilities:* Sometimes reservations must be made for meeting rooms or conference facilities. Special information needed to reserve these types of facilities includes the following:

      (1) The number of meeting rooms that will be needed, based on an estimate of the number of people attending

(2) The contracted rates for the use of these rooms

(3) Specifications of rooms needed for special functions, such as convention exhibits, meals, or banquet, based on an estimate of the number of people attending

(4) Audiovisual or computer equipment rented for meeting rooms

(5) Telecommunications equipment needed for meeting rooms

(6) Special room arrangements: lectern, tables, chairs, projection system

(7) Availability of electrical outlets and/or special conditions required for computer equipment and communications networks

(8) Special arrangements for local tours or transportation to other local sites

8. *Organization of Materials for Trip:* The business traveler will need specific materials organized for the trip. Before the trip takes place, the administrative assistant must make sure that these materials are organized in a trip file.

a. *Trip file:* Setting up a trip file is essential in tracking all information and procedures involved in business travel. Maintenance of a folder in which all notes on errands to run, materials to collect, and other arrangements needed prior to the trip is essential. Other folders, to be carried by the traveler, might contain the following:

(1) Background information pertaining to the purpose of the trip, (e.g., a file containing records of previous transactions with a company)

(2) Confirmations of all travel reservations

(3) Confirmations for lodging accommodations reserved, including the confirmation numbers quoted over the telephone and notations about early or late arrival

(4) Copies of computer disks with needed information stored on them, properly marked and placed in travel carriers so that airport security personnel will handle them accordingly

b. *Confirmed reservations:* Confirmations should be received for all reservations made for travel and lodging accommodations, if time permits.

(1) *Competitive fares/rates:* In making appropriate decisions concerning transportation and lodging accommodations, attention needs to be paid to competitive fares or rates as well as professional or corporate discounts. Fares or rates need to be compared with travel budget allowances if organization policy dictates.

(2) *Receipt of tickets:* To ensure that the traveler has the desired travel accommodations and is able to conduct business efficiently, tickets should be purchased and obtained in advance of the traveler's scheduled departure. In this way, possible errors can be detected more easily and corrections made prior to the departure date.

(3) *Check-in times:* The traveler needs to be aware of times for check-in with the airlines to be sure to get a preferred seat assignment or with the hotel or motel for early or late arrival.

c. *Travel funds:* For business purposes, traveler's checks, letters of credit, and debit cards are convenient and safe ways of carrying funds.

(1) *Traveler's checks:* A safer way to carry funds in a form other than cash is through sequentially numbered traveler's checks available in denomina-

tions of $10, $20, $50, and $100. Traveler's checks are available for a small fee from local banks, credit unions, savings and loan associations, and the American Automobile Association for a small fee or free. The traveler must purchase these in person and must sign each traveler's check at the time of acquisition. When the traveler's check is cashed, it must be signed by the same person in a second place on the check in the presence of the sales agent.

(2) *Letter of credit:* A letter of credit allows a traveler to draw funds on a specific bank or financial institution up to a predetermined amount while on trips.

(3) *Debit card:* Many business travelers prefer to use debit cards to obtain cash through local automatic teller machines (ATMs) while traveling. In some cases, the executive may be provided with a company debit card, or the executive may use his or her own card and be reimbursed later for expenses incurred. A debit card issued by a bank is used to withdraw specified amounts of cash from an existing bank account. The balance in the cardholder's account is immediately decreased by the amount of the withdrawal. A debit card may also be used for the purchase of merchandise and services. As soon as the transaction is completed, a deduction is made from the cardholder's bank account.

Additional funds may be transferred to individuals who are traveling in foreign countries through international services such as American Express, international telegraph services, or local bank services.

d. *Travel advances:* For authorized travel, an individual may request a travel advance from the organization to be applied to the business expenses to be reimbursed. A travel advance enables the traveler to use company funds rather than personal funds for business expenses incurred during the trip (taxi fares, meal expenses).

e. *Credit cards:* Sometimes business travelers are expected to pay for travel expenses out of personal funds and receive reimbursement from the organization after an expense report has been filed. A record of expenses incurred must be kept by the traveler for accounting, reimbursement, or income tax purposes. Out-of-pocket expenses may best be handled through the use of business or personal credit cards. Here are some of the benefits derived from using credit cards for keeping accurate records of travel expenses for business purposes:

(1) *Immediate purchase of goods and services:* Use of credit cards enables the traveler to purchase goods and services from businesses that accept credit cards up to a predetermined credit limit.

(2) *Receipts for purchases:* Credit-card receipts verify business expenditures for tax purposes and for preparing company expense reports.

(3) *Monthly expense statement:* The monthly billing for charges itemizes all charges and services and can serve as a cumulative record of all business-related charges incurred during the month. When credit cards are used overseas, the rate of exchange cannot be determined until the traveler returns home. The rate of exchange used is that of the date of posting and not the date of purchase. Therefore, one must wait until receipt of the invoice from the credit-card company to find out the rate of exchange that was used.

f. *Itinerary:* Once all arrangements for the trip have been approved, final copies of the itinerary need to be prepared (see Figure 8–1 for a sample itinerary.) The itinerary

Figure 8–1   Sample Itinerary

ITINERARY FOR MARLENE BAILEY

January 10–12, 200-

MONDAY, JANUARY 10 (Chicago to New York City)

8:20 A.M. (CST)	Leave Chicago O'Hare Airport on United Airlines Flight 208; 747; breakfast served.
9:33 A.M. (EST)	Arrive at New York LaGuardia Airport. Take limousine to Waldorf Hotel, 2021 Second Avenue, New York (212-542-6000); guaranteed hotel reservation; confirmation in trip file.
1:00 P.M.	Meeting with Roger C. Harper, Jr., President, ACF Corporation, 994 Third Avenue, New York (212-776-1420).
7:00 P.M.	Dinner-Meeting at Stewart's Restaurant, 727 Avenue of the Americas, New York, with Joyce L. Rohrson, Consultant, American Business Systems (212-325-4692).

TUESDAY, JANUARY 11 (New York City)

9:30 A.M.	The National Office Systems Conference, City Conference Center, 1004 Central Parkway, New York (212-554-4200).
9:45 A.M.	Presentation: "The Office Environment—Networking and Today's Automated Office."
1:00 P.M.	Luncheon with Rosalyn L. Bernard, Vice President and General Manager, Wilson Automation, Inc., at the Oakdale City Club, 9250 Fifth Avenue, New York (212-347-3300).
3:00 P.M.	Tour of Advanced Business Systems, Inc., 125 Seventh Avenue, New York. Contact Person: Helen Adams, Office Automation Consultant (212-774-1550).

WEDNESDAY, JANUARY 12 (New York City to Chicago)

9:45 A.M.	Leave Waldorf Hotel by limousine for John F. Kennedy Airport.
11:55 A.M. (EST)	Leave Kennedy Airport on United Airlines Flight 648, business class; lunch served.
2:10 P.M. (CST)	Arrive at Chicago O'Hare Airport. Company limousine will meet you at baggage claim.

is a business travel plan, usually prepared in typewritten or printed form, that typically includes the following types of information:

- Departure date, time, and place

- Type of transportation, including the type of commercial airliner (e.g., Concorde, Boeing 747) or corporate aircraft

- Arrival date, time, and place
- Meals provided by transportation company (breakfast, lunch, snacks, and/or dinner)
- Lodging reservation(s) for each date or segment of the trip (confirmation numbers, addresses, and telephone numbers included)
- Scheduled appointments and meetings (including dinner meetings or other functions, with addresses and telephone numbers, if known)
- Complete travel information for return trip

Copies of the itinerary need to be prepared for the traveler, the traveler's supervisor, the office, and the traveler's family.

g. *Traveler's quick reference form:* Sometimes a synopsis of the information contained in a complete itinerary can be prepared as a quick reference for the traveler to carry in a wallet, purse, or briefcase. Figure 8–2 shows what such a quick reference might look like. More complete information would be contained in the itinerary.

C. Types of Travel

In preplanning the arrangements necessary for business travel, the administrative professional must know the types of transportation services available, the classes of service available for the type of transportation preferred, baggage allowances, and ground transportation available to and from airports. In addition, alternative modes of travel may have

Figure 8–2 Quick Reference Form

Quick Reference

Name	Company	Number
Roger Harper	ACF Corp.	(212) 776-1420
Joyce Rohrson	Am. Bus.	(212) 325-4692
NOS Conference	City Center	(212) 554-4200
* R.L. Bernard	Wilson Auto	(212) 347-3300
Helen Adams	Adv. Bus. Sys.	(212) 774-1550

Notes:

* Luncheon 1/11 at 1:00 p.m. at Oakdale City Club

** Company limo pickup

Frequent Flier Information

Airline/Club	Account Number
United	101-45-1984-B

Itinerary

Date 01/10/200X		Seat 6E
Airline	Flight	Departure Time
United	208	8:20 am (CST)
From	To	Arrival time
Chicago O Hara	NYC	9:33 am (EST)

Date 01/12/200X		Seat 4C
Airline	Flight	Departure Time
United	648	11:55 am (EST)
From	To	Arrival time
NYC **	Chicago O Hara	2:10 pm (CST)

		Seat
Airline	Flight	Departure Time
From	To	Arrival time

		Seat
Airline	Flight	Departure Time
From	To	Arrival time

		Seat
Airline	Flight	Departure Time
From	To	Arrival time

Travel Arrangements

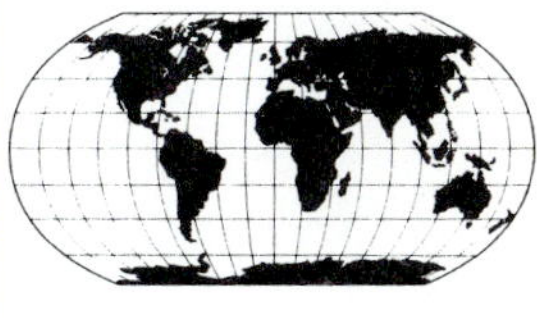

Marlene Bailey

Prepared by	Date	Trip
BLS	01/02/200X	

to be considered in case of bad weather. Depending on the nature of the business travel, combination modes of travel (air-ship, automobile-air) may even have to be considered.

1. *Domestic Travel:* Domestic transportation services (air, railroad, bus, and automobile) provide a variety of options for travel within a country. Selection of those services to be utilized depends on time allotted for travel, cost, and destination.

   a. *Air travel:* Accommodations include first-class, business-class, coach-class, and economy seating. Fares depend on the class of seating selected and special plans established by the airline, (e.g., excursion rates). Air shuttle service is also available between some of the larger U.S. cities within short distances of each other.

   b. *Railway travel:* Amtrak and Conrail are national railway systems that connect metropolitan areas throughout the country. Commuter railway services are available between large cities and suburban areas. Passenger accommodations include first class or coach class, sleeper cars, or auto-train facilities.

   c. *Bus travel:* For some business trips, bus travel may be preferred, especially for short distances. Interstate highways and toll roads make this type of travel acceptable for brief trips.

2. *International Travel:* Travel in and to other countries may necessitate the utilization of various modes of travel.

   a. *Air transportation:* The fastest way to travel, of course, is to fly. The 24-hour clock is used in the timetables for foreign transportation. Scheduling information is included in the *Official Airline Guide (Worldwide Edition)* (see Section B-2-a[1][b]).

   b. *Ship transportation:* Transatlantic liners do provide the option of more leisurely travel, perhaps to combine a business trip with relaxation. Time may be an important factor inasmuch as there may be appointments already scheduled in one of the countries to be visited. A combination air-ship plan might be used.

   c. *Foreign railway service:* Schedules for first-class and second-class train service need to be examined when railway service is required in foreign countries.

   d. *Automobile travel:* Automobile rentals are available through airlines, travel agencies, or car rental firms. A U.S. driver's license is accepted in most countries, but an international traveler may wish to obtain an American International Driving Permit, available through the American Automobile Association, prior to the trip. Also, insurance coverage, shown as a rider on a personal policy or a company policy, must be confirmed for a person who drives a vehicle in a foreign country.

   e. *Lodging accommodations:* Local travel agencies can be very helpful in making lodging reservations. The travel agent will need a complete description of the kind of accommodations preferred (hotel, motel, bed-and-breakfast). It is important to receive from the travel agent a complete description of the reservations actually made and written confirmations if time permits. Following the trip, a list of the most appropriate accommodations should be kept for future reference.

3. *Ground Transportation:* When travel is by air, ground transportation (auto rental or limousine service) may need to be reserved to reach local destinations. Taxi or bus service is generally available at every airport. A check should be made in the *Official Airline Guide* for available ground transportation. This information should also be entered on the traveler's itinerary.

4. *Company Transportation and Lodging:* Company-owned airplanes, ships, automobiles, and lodging may be available for use during business travel. Appropriate reservations for use of these carriers and facilities must be made within a reasonable period of time prior to the planned travel to ensure availability.

D. Documents and Credentials

When traveling to a foreign country, a business traveler must have appropriate documents and credentials to be allowed to leave any country and also to enter a specific foreign country. A traveler needs to provide proof of citizenship to enter Mexico or one of the Caribbean countries. Such proof would be a passport or a notarized copy of a birth certificate.

1. *Passport:* A *passport* is a formal document issued by the citizen's government granting permission to the citizen to travel in certain foreign countries. A passport also certifies citizenship and protection for the traveler. A U.S. passport is valid for 10 years and may be obtained by doing the following:

   a. Completing an application and paying a fee for the passport

   b. Including two identical, recent, signed photographs with the application

   c. Showing a valid driver's license that contains the applicant's signature

   d. Presenting proof of citizenship, such as an original birth certificate, baptismal certificate, or naturalization papers

   Other countries have similar regulations that must be followed by citizens who want to obtain passports.

2. *Visa:* A *visa* is an endorsement stamped or written on a passport, showing examination by the proper officials of a country and granting the bearer entry into that country. A visa is in effect for a specified period of time. Sometimes, a visa is issued as a separate document that must be surrendered on departure from the country.

   EXAMPLE: McDonald is taking a three-week business trip to China. She applies for a business visa, which is usually valid for six months. The visa will be in effect only for that period of time unless she makes application to have it renewed.

   In many foreign countries, a visa is not required. A list of countries requiring a visa should be kept in the office.

   EXAMPLE: France does not require a visa from a person with U.S. citizenship.

3. *Special Requirements:* A check should be made to determine if any inoculations are required to travel in the foreign countries to be visited. In some cases, this requires a series of inoculations or medication that must be completed before the commencement of a trip. Travelers may be required to carry official International Certificates of Vaccination verifying immunization against specified diseases that could be threatening to the United States and other countries (see *Health Information for International Travelers,* a government document published by the Superintendent of Documents, Washington, D.C.).

E. The Administrative Assistant's Role in Executive's Absence

The administrative assistant must be able to function so as to minimize the executive's absence. Many tasks may be handled without the executive being present, but there may be others that require the executive's attention. The administrative assistant must be prepared to work within the limits of authority, to communicate with the executive as needed during the travel period, and to prepare materials that can be handled on the executive's return.

1. *Understanding Limits of Authority:* Decision making in the absence of the executive requires the exercise of careful judgment and clear understanding of the consequences of any action taken. The limits of the administrative assistant's authority in handling business matters should be clearly understood before the executive leaves the office. The question "What can I approve while you are gone?" is typical of queries the alert administrative assistant would make prior to the executive's departure.

   a. *Decisions:* Usually, decisions can be made about office procedures for which there is a precedent, that is, a similar decision made in the past.

   b. *Judgments:* In cases where an exception to the standard procedure has not occurred before, the administrative assistant will need to be more cautious in making an appropriate judgment. If the situation parallels one that has been handled previously, the past situation can be used as an example to determine how to handle the present one. If, in fact, the situation has not occurred before, the administrative assistant should perhaps either inform the executive immediately and ask for a judgment (in the case of a high priority), confer with a colleague of the executive, or hold the item until the executive returns.

   At any rate, the administrative assistant or secretary must be careful to work within the limits of authority already imposed on the position. Any time that decisions or judgments are required, the person making those decisions or judgments must be prepared to face the consequences (positive or negative) of action taken.

2. *Communicating with Traveler:* An administrative assistant must maintain continual communication with the executive prior to business travel as well as during the trip. In this way the office will continue to function effectively during the executive's absence.

   a. *Communicating before the trip:* Certain decisions must be made prior to a business trip, and some of these can be taken care of only by the executive. The administrative assistant or secretary can assist with some of these decisions and also in making preparations for the planned absence from the office. Here are some of the questions that will need to be answered:

      (1) Who will make major decisions while the business traveler is away from the office?

      (2) Should any additional materials or mail be forwarded during the trip? If so, where are these materials located? When should they be forwarded, and by what means?

      (3) Will parcels or packages of materials need to be shipped ahead of time? When do they need to arrive at the destination? How should they be shipped?

      (4) Are all appointments on the itinerary confirmed?

      (5) Is there any correspondence to be sent to firms being visited or to individuals with whom the traveler plans to meet during the upcoming trip?

      (6) Should a time be arranged for communicating by telephone, for example, each morning at 8:30 A.M.? (Remember to keep in mind time zones when setting the time.)

   b. *Communicating during the trip:* Equally important is communication with the traveler as needed during the trip. Additional materials may need to be sent, or important business may need attention.

(1) Electronic mail has become an effective communication channel for the traveler to use in keeping in daily contact with the office. The traveler who carries his or her own computer (or has one available for use) can easily connect by telephone and send frequent messages or respond to messages received.

(2) If necessary during extended trips, copies of mail or other information needed must be forwarded during the trip. (Express mail, fax, or other fast-delivery services will be particularly helpful in this regard.)

(3) If there are changes in the itinerary, such as reservations or flight departure times, the traveler must be notified immediately.

(4) A log of correspondence, folders, or other business matters to be handled on the executive's return must be kept. Prioritizing these items is important.

(5) A log of correspondence that has been handled by the administrative assistant may be kept as an update for the executive.

(6) Dictation may be received from the traveler either through the mail or via the telephone system to a central recorder. Transcription of this dictation should be completed as soon as possible; some items may be urgent.

(7) If regular communication between the traveler and the office will take place through the computer network, the administrative assistant will need to monitor incoming communication to be sure that additional information is transmitted as needed.

3. *Preparing Materials to be Handled on the Traveler's Return:* When the traveler returns from a business trip, the administrative assistant or secretary needs to review any business that has transpired during the absence. Two types of files will be extremely helpful:

a. *For-your-information file:* This file should contain all matters that have already been taken care of but which need to be reviewed for informational purposes (copies of letters mailed).

b. *For-your-attention file:* This file should contain correspondence and other business materials related to those matters that had to wait to be handled until the traveler's return.

A complete report of office events or business activities that have taken place that are of significance to the activities of the business or office needs to be available.

F. Follow-Up Activities

Customarily, follow-up activities are handled as soon as possible. Business expenses incurred during the travel need to be itemized and appropriate reports completed and approved. Any special reports and correspondence need to be prepared while the factual information is readily available. Sometimes the administrative assistant or secretary needs to remind the traveler of deadlines for completing any of these follow-up activities.

1. *Expense Reports:* Appropriate business expense reports must be prepared and submitted to obtain reimbursement if indicated.

a. *Receipts:* All the traveler's receipts must be accumulated and itemized on the expense report.

b. *Travel advances:* If a travel advance was received prior to the trip, the amount must be deducted from the expenses incurred during the trip. Appropriate entries can be made on the expense report.

Once all receipts and travel advances have been accounted for, the business expense report can be prepared. Many organizations have simplified procedures so that this report can be prepared easily on the computer. First, the report form must be accessed and brought up on the screen. The dates, times, and amounts of expenses can be inserted in the appropriate places on the form. The program will calculate the totals and print out a copy for signature. This report is then signed by the traveler and submitted to a supervisor for approval before submission for reimbursement. Usually the original receipts and canceled checks, if any, must be attached to the form.

2. *Special Reports:* One of the administrative assistant's most important follow-up activities will be to assist in the writing of any special reports that need to be submitted to superiors concerning the trip and business transacted during the trip. The preparation of these types of reports should take place within a short time while the information is still readily available.

3. *Correspondence:* Follow-up letters to people with whom the traveler met during the business trip represent a courtesy that is expected. Thank-you letters or confirmation letters are perhaps the most typical. The secretary should reserve adequate time to take dictation, transcribe, and write follow-up letters as soon as possible.

EXAMPLES: Ellenberg just returned from a business trip to New York. On the return trip, his luggage was lost by the airline. Fehrly, his secretary, needs to contact the airlines to see whether the luggage has been located and, if not, to make the appropriate claim.

While in New York, Ellenberg met with Thompson, the president of one of the leading advertising agencies. He contracted with Thompson for the development of a new advertising campaign that Ellenberg plans to present to his superiors for approval. Ellenberg dictates a letter to Thompson, confirming some of the provisions of the new contract.

4. *File Materials:* All business files taken on the trip need to be refiled as soon as possible in case others in the organization must refer to the material. Also, any information collected during the trip needs to be filed as well.

5. *Travel Notes:* Because there will be future business travel to arrange, comments regarding lodging or transportation preferences should be noted for the next trip. Sometimes, meeting notes need to be typed and filed for future reference.

Review Questions

Directions: Select the best answer from the four alternatives. Write your answer in the blank to the left of the number.

_____ 1. Before any business travel arrangements are made, the administrative assistant or secretary needs to

    a. acquire a travel advance for the business traveler.
    b. be aware of the business traveler's travel preferences.
    c. know the organization's policies governing approved business travel.
    d. complete the forms required for authorization to travel.

_____ 2. A business traveler is eligible for coverage under business insurance policies

    a. only in case of unexpected emergency.
    b. as long as the traveler is authorized and approved to travel on company business.
    c. only when using company-owned transportation.
    d. for a specified period of time.

_____ 3. Approved business travel entitles the traveling executive to

    a. secure a travel advance prior to the departure date.
    b. travel only with company-owned vehicles.
    c. use a personal credit card to charge business expenses.
    d. prepare a detailed itinerary for the business trip.

_____ 4. Which one of the following would be considered a source book for making appropriate domestic transportation arrangements within the United States?

    a. *The Official Airline Guide, Worldwide Edition*
    b. *Hotel & Motel Red Book*
    c. *The Official Airline Guide, North American Edition*
    d. *Frequent Flyer* magazine

_____ 5. A commercial travel agency

    a. specializes in making only business travel arrangements.
    b. may charge a surcharge to the traveler for some reservation services rendered.
    c. provides travel services for business travel only within an organization.
    d. charges operational costs to a department of the organization for whom the business travel was arranged.

6. As the administrative assistant for Carlton, executive vice president for Motor Wheels, Inc., you have the option of obtaining all travel reservations through transportation companies and hotels yourself or using the services of a commercial travel agency. You decide to use the services of the Acme Travel Agency, a commercial agency, that will

    a. bill Motor Wheels, Inc., directly for the commission for providing travel services.
    b. affix (add) a commission to the total cost of travel reservations.
    c. receive a commission based only on transportation costs.
    d. receive a commission directly from hotels, airlines, and other transportation companies based on ticket sales and/or room rates.

7. An in-house transportation department assists in planning travel services for

    a. individual employees in any of the firm's departments who are approved for business travel.
    b. clients of the firm.
    c. any employee who requests assistance in making travel reservations.
    d. individual employees who seek assistance with personal travel plans.

8. Arrangements for an executive's travel when the requirements are fairly simple (e.g., one destination for a short stay) might *best* be made through a/an

    a. local travel agency.
    b. airline carrier.
    c. Internet travel site.
    d. corporate travel department.

9. Most major carriers encourage on-line sales of airline tickets because

    a. special prices are often offered at on-line sites.
    b. the airlines pay lower commissions to on-line agents than off-line travel agencies.
    c. the airfares will generally be higher than at an off-line agency.
    d. the on-line fares that can be viewed are from only one carrier.

10. A complete flight reservation includes the following types of information:

    a. flight number, departure time, and fare.
    b. flight number, name of carrier, and departure time.
    c. name of carrier, flight number, departure and arrival times, fare, and class of service.
    d. name of carrier, flight number, fare, class of service, and arrival time.

_____ **11.** Bradford, vice president of Steeps, Inc., has a hotel reservation but finds that she will not be able to arrive at the Blackstone Hotel in Washington, D.C., until 8 P.M. The hotel will

   a. hold the reservation since the reservation had been made two weeks ahead of time.
   b. cancel the room reservation.
   c. hold the reservation if Bradford telephones the hotel prior to 6 P.M. and guarantees payment for the room with a credit card.
   d. arrange for Bradford to stay at another hotel if there is no room left when she arrives.

_____ **12.** Snyder, vice president of operations, needs to travel to New York next week. She asks Williams, an executive assistant, to help with the final preparations. Before the itinerary can be prepared, Williams needs to consult with Snyder to determine

   a. the hotel accommodations preferred.
   b. who will be accompanying her on the trip.
   c. ground transportation available from the airport to the hotel.
   d. her willingness to travel to New York next week.

_____ **13.** Wellington is the program chair for a two-day conference to be held next March in Des Moines, Iowa. The theme of the conference is "Office Technology Systems for the Twenty-First Century." Which of the following facts will she need to make a decision about what hotel facilities to reserve for this meeting?

   a. Confirmed round-trip airfares
   b. Estimated number of people attending who will need hotel reservations
   c. Ground transportation available from the airport
   d. Guest speakers involved in the conference

_____ **14.** A confirmed travel reservation means that

   a. the business travel has been approved.
   b. the transportation carrier has notified the business traveler in writing of the arrangements made.
   c. the business traveler will have to pick up the reservation tickets on the day of departure.
   d. the reservation cannot be canceled or changed.

_____ **15.** Which one of the following is considered a safe way to carry travel funds?

   a. Cash (in U.S. dollars or foreign currency)
   b. Letter of credit
   c. Travel advance
   d. International credit card

_____   **16.** Which one of the following will permit the traveler to withdraw funds from a bank
                    account?

                    a. Credit card
                    b. Travel advance
                    c. Traveler's checks
                    d. Debit card

_____   **17.** Business travelers may prefer to receive a travel advance from the company so that

                    a. all expenses incurred for hotel, meals, and miscellaneous items are prepaid by
                       the company.
                    b. sufficient funds are available for out-of-pocket expenses, thus avoiding the use
                       of personal funds.
                    c. all transportation costs will be prepaid by the company.
                    d. rental of ground transportation can be secured more easily.

_____   **18.** When the amount of a given purchase is paid for from a line of credit established
                    with a financial organization, the travel funds are in the form of

                    a. traveler's checks.
                    b. a credit card.
                    c. a travel advance.
                    d. a debit card.

_____   **19.** One benefit of using a business or personal credit card for out-of-pocket expenses
                    is that it

                    a. enables the traveler to purchase goods and services no matter what the cost.
                    b. provides a complete expense report for the entire trip.
                    c. substitutes readily for cash.
                    d. provides a receipt for each transaction.

_____   **20.** A travel plan prepared with a list of all reservations, scheduled appointments, and
                    meetings is called a/an

                    a. itinerary.
                    b. confirmed reservation.
                    c. agenda.
                    d. visa.

_____   **21.** The selection of the mode of transportation to be used for domestic business travel
                    will depend most on

                    a. how many individuals from the organization will be traveling at one time.
                    b. the availability of ground transportation at the destination city.
                    c. the distance to be traveled in relation to the transportation cost and time allotment.
                    d. the primary purpose of the business trip.

22. A government document issued by the U.S. Department of State that grants permission to a U.S. citizen to travel in certain foreign countries is called a/an

   a. visa.
   b. travel permit.
   c. passport.
   d. itinerary.

23. An endorsement that grants a U.S. citizen entry into a foreign country for a specified period of time is known as a/an

   a. visa.
   b. passport.
   c. itinerary.
   d. travel permit.

24. Before the business traveler leaves on a business trip, the secretary needs to

   a. set up a "for-your-information" file for trip information.
   b. prepare a detailed expense report for the trip.
   c. respond to incoming correspondence on behalf of the executive who is on a business trip.
   d. find out who is designated to make major decisions while the business traveler is away from the office.

25. A technique often used to update the business traveler on office events that occurred during an absence is to

   a. keep a log of hard copies of correspondence and other items that were handled by the secretary during the absence.
   b. write reminders on the traveler's desk calendar.
   c. keep a journal with a detailed day-to-day account.
   d. reserve at least two hours on the traveler's first day back in the office to discuss office operations during the absence.

26. A "for-your-attention" file contains items that

   a. must wait to be handled until the business traveler returns.
   b. have already been taken care of by the secretary prior to the traveler's return.
   c. give a complete report of office events during the absence.
   d. pertain to the detailed expense report to be prepared.

27. Follow-up activities to business travel include

   a. writing summary reports to be submitted to management.
   b. obtaining a travel advance.
   c. writing correspondence to people with whom the business traveler wants to set up appointments.
   d. receiving confirmations for travel arrangements.

_____

28. A typical follow-up letter to a business associate with whom the traveler met during the business trip is a letter

    a. confirming a business appointment.
    b. informing the associate of the trip.
    c. thanking the associate for the opportunity to meet and discuss a business transaction.
    d. summarizing the accomplishments of the entire trip.

Solutions

Answer		Refer to:
1.	(c)	[A]
2.	(b)	[A-1]
3.	(a)	[A-1-a]
4.	(c)	[B-4-a(1)(a)]
5.	(b)	[B-5-a]
6.	(d)	[B-5-a(2)]
7.	(a)	[B-5-b]
8.	(c)	[B-5-c]
9.	(b)	[B-6-a]
10.	(c)	[B-7-a]
11.	(c)	[B-7-b]
12.	(a)	[B-7-b(1)]
13.	(b)	[B-7-c]
14.	(b)	[B-8-b]
15.	(b)	[B-8-c(2)]
16.	(d)	[B-8-c(3)]
17.	(b)	[B-8-d]
18.	(b)	[B-8-e(1)]
19.	(d)	[B-8-e(2)]
20.	(a)	[B-8-f]
21.	(c)	[C-1]
22.	(c)	[D-1]

23. (a)   [D-2]

24. (d)   [E-1]

25. (a)   [E-3-a]

26. (a)   [E-3-b]

27. (a)   [F-2]

28. (c)   [F-3]

CHAPTER
9
Records Management Principles

OVERVIEW

The management of information, an extremely important office support function, enables paper, image, and digital information to continue to serve their purposes effectively within an organization. Records are the products of office work, and they serve as the "memory" of the organization. The average cost of each misfiled record or filing error is approximately $100.

Records management is the systematic control of information from the moment of creation through the use, storage, transfer, and disposal phases of the records cycle. Records management and control is necessary for the continued operation of the entire organization. Managing records within an organization requires a planned approach to records retention as well as easy use and access to stored records by authorized personnel.

Any successful records management program must have top-management support and a knowledgeable and trained staff to direct and control records systems within the organization. A working knowledge of both manual and electronic records management systems is essential for today's office professionals.

KEY TERMS

Active records
Administrative value
Alphabetic classification
  system
Alphanumeric
  classification system
Appraisal of records
Archives
Block codes
Business form
Business report
Chronological system
Classification system
Coded numeric system
Coding
Color coding
Constant information

Conventional format
Correspondence
Cross-referencing
Data
Database
Decimal-numeric system
Direct-access procedures
Dispersal
Duplex-numeric system
Evidence value
Field
File
File folder
Filing segment
Filing unit
Fiscal value
Forms management

Geographic filing
Guide
Important records
Inactive records
Index record
Indexing
Indirect-access
  procedures
Information value
Inspecting
Legal value
Microform
Middle-digit system
Mnemonic code
Nonconventional format
Nonessential records
Nonrecords

279

Numeric classification system	Purging	Secondary guide
Out folder	Record(s)	Straight-numeric system
Out guide	Records cycle	Subject filing
Periodic transfer	Records management	Tab
Perpetual transfer	Records transfer	Terminal-digit system
Posted record	Relative index	Useful records
Primary guide	Research value	Variable information
	Retention schedule	Vital records

A. Analyzing Records and Records Systems

Information in the form of documents in any business organization can be categorized as *records* and *nonrecords*. *Records* refer to official documents of the company or organization valuable enough to be retained, using a format for storing information to be used and distributed later. *Nonrecords* refer to documents prepared for the organization's convenience or temporary use in an operation but normally disposed of after use. Records need to be analyzed to determine what the nature of the present records system is in the business. The two primary aspects of records analysis include examining the types of records in use and the records cycle.

1. *Classifying Records:* Individual records are classified according to either the record activity (use) or the importance of particular records used within the business or both.

   a. *Record activity or use:* Records are either active records or inactive records.

      (1) *Active records:* Those records that are accessed and utilized in the current administration of business functions are known as *active records.* They are often used to generate more business, to follow up on current transactions of the organization, and to develop more information on the organization and its activities.

      (2) *Inactive records:* Those records no longer referred to on a regular basis but still of limited importance are called *inactive records.* They do not relate to current business activities of the organization and are usually transferred to inactive status in a central records storage facility. Such a storage facility could have computer storage as well as physical storage space for files, boxes, and other media.

   b. *Importance of records:* Typically, records are classified as vital, important, useful, or nonessential records.

      (1) *Vital records:* Records classified as vital records are those records *essential* for the effective, continuous operation of the firm. Vital records are irreplaceable records.

         EXAMPLES:

         Insurance policies

         Property deeds

         Copyrights

         Leases

         Accounts payable

         Accounts receivable

         Legal documents

(2) *Important records:* Records classified as *important* records contribute to the continued smooth operation of an organization and can be replaced or duplicated (with considerable expenditure of time and money) if lost or destroyed in a disaster. Copies of important records are usually available, but extra time may be involved in requesting and locating them, causing a delay in their use. Many of these records are available on microforms, magnetic tapes, compact disks, or computer disks.

EXAMPLES:

Tax records for last year

Financial records

Case files

(3) *Useful records:* Records used in the operation of the organization that can be easily replaced are called *useful* records. In case of a disaster, the loss of useful records would not prevent any routine operation of the business, only temporary delay or inconvenience in trying to locate pertinent documents and information.

EXAMPLES:

Copies of complaint letters

Business reports

Customer requests for product information

(4) *Nonessential records:* Records that are not necessary for the restoration of the business, have no predictable value, and probably should be destroyed once their usefulness is over are known as *nonessential* records.

EXAMPLES:

Telephone messages

Surveys

Subscriptions for external publications

2. *The Records Cycle:* A record's life cycle extends from the moment the record is created until its final disposition. An initial decision is made when a record is created as to its life, that is, how long the record must be retained either in active or inactive storage. Decisions are made at various times during the records cycle as to the continued use of the record, the procedure to be used in filing the record, and its retention or disposal. Figure 9–1 highlights the key steps in the records cycle: creation of the record, utilization of the record, retention of the record, transfer of the record, and disposal of the record. Manual filing *and* electronic filing form the basis for a total records cycle since both manual and electronic procedures must be applied to the information and documents involved.

a. *Creation of records:* Only people having the authority to create records within an organization should be permitted to do so. Central control of records stems from careful monitoring of the creation of all records. Basic considerations in the creation of new records should include the following:

(1) The format of the new record

Figure 9–1   The Records Cycle

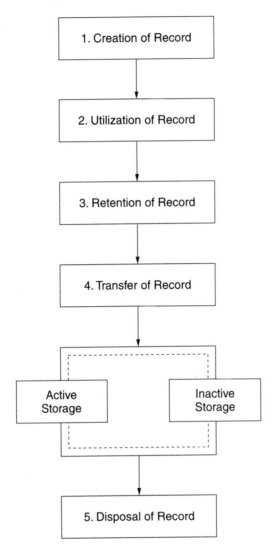

    (2) Procedures established for creating the record

    (3) Justification (rationale) for the new record

    (4) The purpose of the new record

    (5) The cost of producing the record

    (6) The increased office productivity likely to result

    (7) The estimated life of the record

  b. *Utilization of records:* Efficient procedures must be developed so that the record that has been created may be used, stored, and retrieved for the purpose(s) intended. A records inventory will help determine the actual use to which the record will be put as well as the cost of using and retaining the record.

  c. *Retention of records:* The life of a particular record is determined on the basis of the record's administrative, legal, fiscal, or research value (see Section C-4-a). In this phase of the records cycle, retention schedules are developed and the value of records is determined.

(1) *Development of retention schedules:* A records retention schedule estimates the period of time each type of record is to be held in active storage for day-to-day reference, the period of time records should be kept in inactive storage, and if and when records may be purged or destroyed. A retention schedule approved for use within the organization helps to ensure that federal, state, and local regulations are considered in deciding how important specific records are and how long to keep records on file.

(2) *Appraisal of records:* In the process of establishing retention schedules, records are evaluated in terms of their administrative, legal, fiscal, or research value. Once their value has been determined, a set number of years for retention of those records can be established.

d. *Transfer of records:* During its life, a record may be transferred from active to inactive storage or from inactive to active storage, depending on the record activity. A record may be physically removed from the premises and transmitted to remote storage in a computer facility or an off-site records facility.

e. *Disposal of records:* When the record is no longer needed, it may be purged or destroyed.

(1) *Purging of records: Purging* is the process of automatically deleting the contents of a record that has been electronically stored on a magnetic medium. As purging takes place, each record is examined to determine whether it still has value or can be eliminated.

EXAMPLE: Each week, Grayson stores on disk correspondence prepared with word processing. After a one-week period, she reviews the contents of each disk to see whether any of the records can be purged (deleted) from the disk. She labels each disk carefully and keeps all correspondence relating to a particular project on the same disk.

(2) *Destruction of records:* The method of destruction is very important since many records, even though ready to be destroyed, contain confidential information. Special equipment may be used in the destruction of documents, such as shredders, incinerators, and pulverizers.

B. Records Creation, Design, and Control

Business records must be controlled throughout the records cycle to ensure efficient handling. The design of the record enhances the ability of the records manager to control the use of that record within the organization. Once the record has been designed for either manual or electronic use, appropriate steps must be taken to ensure that the record will be used as intended.

1. *Records Creation and Design:* Any record created for organizational use should be planned carefully before actual creation. Control in the creation and design function results in increased quality, improved productivity, reduced costs, and more effective storage and retrieval. The process involves both conventional and nonconventional formats.

a. *Conventional formats:* Correspondence, business forms, and business reports typically appear in conventional formats that result in paper copies (hard copies) or disk copies (soft copies). Appropriate formatting of these types of records makes control of these records within the business an easier task.

(1) *Correspondence:* Written messages in the form of business letters created primarily as external communication and memoranda created as internal communication are referred to as *correspondence.*

    (a) *Letter design:* Many companies use logos, standardized formats, and letter styles to create a positive image as well as to reduce letter-writing costs. Merging form paragraphs and form letters with addresses from mailing lists reduces the average cost of correspondence but still permits the letters to be personalized with individual addresses and salutations.

        EXAMPLE: Since 1930, when the cost of a business letter was estimated at 30 cents, the Dartnell Corporation's Institute of Business Research has continued its annual research into the cost of producing a business letter. By 1960, this cost had increased to $1.83.

        In 1983, the average cost of producing a business letter was estimated at well over $7 per letter. This figure included all labor costs (executive and secretary), overhead costs, and indirect costs.

        Dartnell's 1991 estimate ranged from $12 to $18 because of dictation equipment, personal computers, or typewriters that may have been used to produce the letter. For a one-page, 185-word letter, the cost of producing a letter that was machine dictated and transcribed on a personal computer was $11.77. The same letter transcribed on an electric typewriter cost $17.71.

        The most recent study (1993) indicated that the cost of a business letter can range from $12.28 to $18.54, depending on the technology used to produce the letter. The use of technology (dictation equipment, personal computer, and word processing software) can reduce the cost of producing a letter by approximately one-third, or an average $6.26 per letter, when used properly.

    (b) *Memorandum design:* Standardized formats are also used for memorandum designs that speed up production and cut costs. Decisions are made within departments on whether memos, the telephone, or electronic mail will be used for internal communication. Electronic mail has become a very popular means of transmitting information among departments. With e-mail, keeping a record of e-memos sent and received is a relatively easy task. The sender knows whether the message was received and viewed. The receiver can respond immediately to the e-memo if desired.

    (c) *Maintaining document flow:* Control of the movement of written correspondence through the organization is very important. In large firms, a central distribution area (a mail center) controls all incoming and outgoing correspondence.

    (d) *Development of correspondence manuals:* With so much more information being communicated through various means, many firms develop manuals to outline recommended procedures for the preparation and handling of written and electronic correspondence. This enables a more concerted effort to standardize procedures throughout the organization.

(2) *Business forms:* Forms used in business procedures need to be analyzed on a regular basis to determine whether they are still in use, need to be revised, or can be eliminated. A *business form* is a record that contains *constant* infor-

mation appearing on it (printed or electronically imaged on a computer screen) and space provided for *variable* information to be inserted.

EXAMPLE: Sets of forms are provided within software programs (word processing, graphics, and other types of business software) so that templates for specific forms can be brought up on the computer screen to be filled in with variable information. Completed forms can then be stored under an appropriate file name.

Before a form is redesigned, any problems resulting from either its design or its use should be analyzed.

(a) *Classifications of forms:* Business forms may be classified in two ways: according to specific business functions for which they are intended (external or internal) and the physical way in which they are constructed (single copy, multiple copy, or view copy).

   EXAMPLES: Business forms designed for specific business functions include personnel forms (application for employment, interview evaluation form), accounting forms (purchase requisition, purchase order, invoice, check), and sales or customer service forms (customer order form, repair requisition).

   The physical construction of a business form includes such things as its physical size (8 1/2 by 5 inches), paper stock used, and type styles used for constant information.

(b) *Types of business forms:* Forms may be referred to by the type of form, either a flat form (a single sheet of paper that may be interleaved with other forms to produce multiple copies) or a specialty form (one that requires special equipment to produce or use).

(c) *Forms design:* The process of designing a business form depends on what information needs to appear on the form and the sequence of that information. Sound forms design should be based on the actual use of the form and the standardization of the form in relation to others used in the business. Forms may be designed for manual or automated completion.

   EXAMPLES OF MANUAL FORMS:

   Snap-out or unit-set forms: *A multiple-copy form is used when more than one copy of the same form is needed; carbon paper is interleaved between the copies.*

   Spot-carbon forms: *Only certain areas on each copy of the form are carbonized so that only that information to be transferred to other copies will be copied.*

   Carbonless (NCR) forms: *Specially treated (coated) paper permits the pressure of a pen or pencil on the original to create the same images on the copies.*

   EXAMPLES OF AUTOMATED FORMS:

   Continuous forms: *Forms used with automated printers produce multiple numbers of forms that will have to be separated on the perforations between forms after printing.*

Unit-record forms: *Forms, either in continuous form or in tab-card sets, are used as input and output records in automated systems.*

Magnetic-ink character recognition (MICR) form: *Coded information on the form, such as MICR numbers on checks, can be read by automated equipment and transmitted to a computer for processing.*

Optical character recognition (OCR) forms: *Data typed, written, or mark sensed on the form can be interpreted by OCR readers and scanners for automatic processing.*

View forms or templates: *Forms or templates, created with word processing, spreadsheet, or graphics software, that have been stored (hard disk, floppy disk, or compact disk) can be retrieved as needed for fill in and processing.*

(3) *Business reports:* A business report is the final outcome of a specific information-gathering activity within the organization, summarizing the problem, background, procedures, and results of a business project or research. A business report conveys information to top-level management for decision-making purposes or to external sources who need the information to further their own work. The report tends to be the most expensive type of record created within most organizations because of its originality and time and other costs involved in doing the research.

(a) *Content of reports:* Reports may be either formal or informal. A formal report usually follows a standard format or structure for content, and the style of writing is more formal in nature. Such a report would most likely include the following sections:

Abstract

Introduction to the Problem

Rationale for the Study

Body of the Report

    Methods and Procedures

    Statistical Analysis of Data

Findings

Conclusions

Recommendations and/or Implications

Summary

An informal report is used primarily for internal communication and is prepared for a single purpose within the organization—to provide additional information on a specific topic. The informal report is rather short, perhaps only three to five pages, and may be prepared in a memorandum format.

(b) *Reports design:* As with correspondence, standardized formats are very important in the preparation of business reports. Most reports will be generated through the use of computer systems and word processing software. Particularly in these cases, the more standardized the format, the easier it is to control the actual preparation of the report. Only information absolutely needed should be included in the report.

EXAMPLE: Format features affect the way the final document will look. Some format decisions can be made before the text is keyed in, such as margins (top, bottom, left, right), vertical spacing (single or double spacing), and left justification of text. Other format decisions are best made immediately prior to printing the document. These decisions include the placement of headers, footers, and page numbers.

(c) *Preparation costs:* Costs incurred as a result of preparing a business report include the research involved in gathering the information and data for the report, the salary of the writer, the time involved in researching and writing the report, the length and involvement of the report, fixed costs, and office support and word/information processing costs.

(4) *Card systems:* In records management, cards (3 by 5 inches, 4 by 6 inches, 5 by 8 inches) are used as a means of filing information or referencing information filed elsewhere. Card systems are used for two primary purposes: to create index records and to create posted records.

(a) *Index records:* Cards may be used as a *relative index* for files using a numeric or alphanumeric classification system. As an index record, the card contains only *reference* information. An individual would examine the index record to find out where the original file or document is located.

EXAMPLES OF INDEX RECORDS:

Names and addresses of clients or customers

employee lists

price lists

membership lists

stockroom item locations

telephone numbers frequently used

subscription lists

EXAMPLE: Burton & Smith, a local law firm, uses a numeric system for filing. Each client or case is assigned a separate file number. A relative index is kept on cards in a special card drawer, in alphabetical order, so that if a file needs to be located, the first step is to look in the index under the client's name or the case name to see what number has been assigned to the file. Once the number is located, the file can be located easily in the file.

Such a system may also be computerized by creating a database to organize or manage files electronically. A database may be accessed by keying in the name of the file desired or conducting a search for the individual name or file number. Electronic lists have the advantage of storing data in one location, making data available to more than one user, and improving data integrity when properly maintained (see Section B-1-b[3]).

(b) *Posted records:* Card records may be used to record (post) information (update, change, delete, add to) to bring the record up to date. New information posted on the card form may be entered manually or by computer. Since a source document, the original record, is used to obtain the information to be posted, the posted record is sometimes called a *secondary record.*

EXAMPLES OF POSTED RECORDS:

Stock control cards

payroll cards

repair and maintenance cards for office equipment

auto service records

hospital records

student permanent record cards

dental and medical cards

EXAMPLE: Prairie View Animal Hospital kept all of its animal records on individual owner cards before the system was computerized. Whenever a pet received some type of treatment, medication, or examination, an entry was posted on the card form, indicating what treatment or medication was prescribed, the charge, the date, and any other relevant information. In this way, a perpetual record was kept of the medical history of the pet.

Recently, the records were converted to a computer system. Now, when a pet owner enters the office, the name is keyed into the system to obtain a file number; the appropriate file folder can then be pulled from an open-shelving unit for reference during the examination. The complete medical history of the pet is helpful in making appropriate decisions on medication or treatment. The billing is immediate, too, with the pet owner presented with a statement for payment before leaving the office.

(c) *Design of card forms:* Many card forms are preprinted with descriptors (keywords), horizontal and vertical rulings, and directions for completion. Preprinted card forms are designed so that the user will be able to locate information easily. The descriptors, keywords, or phrases preprinted on the form are called *constant information* since those words appear the same on all copies of a particular form. *Variable information* consists of the words or text inserted on the card form by a user that will change for each user. Card forms must be created on card stock that will be durable, compact, and easy to handle.

(5) *Other conventional records:* In addition to correspondence, business forms, reports, and cards, other types of conventional records include engineering documents, maps, charts, drawings, technical catalogs, and manuals (policies, procedures, operations). The design and use of any of these types of records need to be controlled as well.

b. *Nonconventional formats:* In recent years, with more automation being utilized in offices, a greater variety of unconventional formats have been used for business records. Microforms, audiovisual media, videotapes, and information and image processing media are becoming more versatile in substituting for paper documents.

(1) *Microforms:* Any record that contains reduced images on film is known as a *microform.* The saving of space in the storage of microform records seems to be the greatest advantage of their use. Microforms also appear to be advantageous in preserving records over time. The most commonly used microforms are microfilm, microfiche, ultrafiche, aperture cards, and jackets. (For more information on each of these types of microforms, see Chapter 4, Section B-2-b.)

(2) *Audiovisual media:* Another category of nonconventional records is audiovisual media. Photographs, 35-millimeter slides, electronic slides, compact disks, cassette tape recordings, videodiscs, videotapes, and transparencies are included in this group. Special attention must be given to the indexing, coding, and storing of these types of records since many times special filing cabinets are required for adequate protection. Special equipment is also needed to view or listen to the information contained in these kinds of records.

EXAMPLES:

Compact disks: a compact disk player (for listening to recorded text or music) or a compact disk drive on the computer (for accessing recorded text or music stored on compact disks)

Electronic slides: a computer, a screen, or a projection system

Videotapes: a videocassette recorder-player (VCR) with a television screen

Transparencies: an overhead projector

Videodiscs: a videodisc player with a television screen

(3) *Electronic media:* Information processing media are receiving more attention from records managers. Information recorded on magnetic disks and tapes (soft copies) is extremely sensitive and must be handled with extreme care. Appropriate techniques must be used to protect these types of records from excessive handling and damage. Backup copies are routinely prepared for important documents or for the most recent business transactions (for a specified period of time, e.g., a day or a week) in case the original records are lost, damaged, or destroyed. Electronic media are especially helpful in planning and creating databases of information for application throughout the organization. A *database* is an electronic method of organizing facts and data in one or more computer data files.

(a) *Preliminary planning:* The following types of questions will be helpful in deciding what types of information will be essential or useful as the creation of a database is being planned.

- What types of information will be included in the database?

- Who will be the database users?

- How often will specific types of data and information be accessed?

- Will the information be used to process transactions such as sales?

- Will the information be used as part of a decision support system?

(b) *Database creation:* The creation of an electronic database expedites the efficient use of information and data. Typically, a database consists of two or more related computer data files. To design an electronic database, a database management system (DBMS) is required. Typical microcomputer database systems are Microsoft Access® and dBase®. The following terms are used in the development of databases:

- *Data:* Information items that describe a person, place, event, or object.

  EXAMPLES:

  Employee name   *home address*

  Social Security number   *home telephone number*

- *Field:* Each field of data has a specific type of information (character, data, numeric, logical, memo).

  EXAMPLES:

  Last Name   *First Name*   *Initial*

  Area Code   *Telephone Number*

- *Record:* A document that contains information about a set of related data items.

  EXAMPLES:

  An application form with employee data written on it.

  An index card with employee data recorded on it.

  A database record with related information about a person, place, event, or object:

- *File:* A set of related records that are stored together or under the same file name. In a database environment, a file is referred to as a *table.*

(c) *Database procedures:* A set of logical, step-by-step procedures is necessary in creating and maintaining a database.

- Plan a database structure.

- Create a database file (table).

- Add records to the database file. Identify a key field (unique) for each record.

- Delete records from the database file.

- Combine (join) database files.

- Combine (join) fields within the database file.

- Produce a complete printout of the database structure (data dictionary).

- Produce reports (scheduled report or ad hoc report) arranged in a planned format that consists of selected information (query) obtained from the database.

- Back up a database file (create a duplicate copy).

The use of database files should be related to the overall efficiency of systems used within the entire organization. People throughout the organization should be aware of the availability of information through the use of computer databases.

2. *Forms Management and Control:* Because gathering and processing information is critical in every organization, a forms management and control program yields important benefits. When procedures are established for ordering, designing, procuring, storing, distributing, reviewing, and disposing of each type of form used within the organization, costs for administrative processing can be controlled. An office form consists of a format with constant information (information that remains the same on each document) and variable information (information that changes on each document). Forms may be paper copies (in typewritten or printed copy) or displayed on a computer screen in the form of a template (electronic copy) stored on disk.

   a. *Key factors in forms management:* In some organizations, forms management is controlled through one person, the records manager or administrator, or one work unit. These units control the organization's forms—analysis, design, production, and use. Some organizations contract with firms offering commercial services in forms management. Other companies, however, have not viewed forms as a vital element in the records management process and have not initiated any kind of forms management program. As an organization grows, forms management becomes more important. Some key factors in developing a forms management program include the following:

      (1) *Top-management support:* Any office support service must have the support of top management in actively promoting the program.

      (2) *Forms control:* To be effective, a forms control program must go into effect as soon as possible. Time must be devoted to the proper administration and design of forms.

      (3) *Training for employees:* Office professionals must be trained so they can assist with updating procedures for the organization's forms management program. A training plan must be developed and implemented as part of the program.

   b. *Forms management program:* Forms management is one of the most important elements of a total records management program. Here are some of the primary components of a successful program:

      (1) *Forms management policy:* Policies for managing forms must be developed and supported by top management. Procedures for creating, reviewing, and producing forms must be identified as well as personnel who will be responsible for forms management.

      (2) *Forms analysis:* Forms used within the company and their design need to be analyzed to determine their importance. Those forms that receive high usage need to be analyzed first, hopefully resulting in improvements that will decrease the costs of producing and using the form.

      (3) *Forms specifications:* Decisions must be made on how the forms are to be produced: the type of paper stock to use, the treatment of these materials, automation required to produce the form, and the method used to produce copies or templates of the form.

      (4) *Forms design:* The layout of the form is another very important forms management function. Forms may be designed by professional forms designers or people within the organization who have expertise in forms design. The use of forms design software enables the creation of forms on a computer. Laser

printing permits the creation of a form with a variety of type styles and design features.

(5) *Forms production:* Forms may be produced and printed in an in-house reprographics center or by an outside commercial printer. The decision can also be made about using forms that are stored on disk or on a network and accessed for fill-in and completion purposes.

(6) *Forms recording and filing:* As forms are created for use within the organization, sets of these forms should be maintained, recorded, and filed by the forms manager. For each form, printing specifications, information as to its use within the firm, and the department for whom it is produced should be recorded. When the form is created, a decision also needs to be made relative to its retention, that is, how long this type of record will be kept on file.

(7) *Forms storage and distribution:* Storage and distribution of forms are also very important. Because of high storage costs, estimating the quantities of forms to have on hand is very important. Users must be provided with forms as needed, where needed, and in sufficient quantity. Storage may be as hard copy (paper) or soft copy (disk).

(8) *Forms control:* Forms control procedures ensure that the objectives of the forms management program are being achieved. No system is effective without some types of controls in effect.

C. Filing Procedures for Manual and Automated Systems

If records that have been stored in the records system cannot be found, then the records system in use, whether it is a manual or an automated system, is probably inadequate to handle the organization's records. Records must be stored so that they can be located easily and quickly as needed. Records that have been stored according to a basic set of procedures and a classification system should be retrievable at any time.

1. *Designing Basic Procedures for Records Storage:* Before records can be retrieved, they must be stored (filed) according to a prescribed set of procedures and rules. An organization will adopt a set of procedures and filing rules to be used in storing manual records as well as procedures to be followed for electronic filing. Each person coming into direct contact with records is expected to use the same filing procedures and rules as those used elsewhere in the organization.

EXAMPLE: A set of filing rules necessary for proper records management procedures to be used is similar in nature to a set of golfing rules prescribed for playing a good game of golf. If you know how to index and code a name alphabetically, you can proceed from one name to another. In the game of golf, you move from hole to hole in a systematic manner as you follow the rules of the game.

a. *Accessing files:* Records may be accessed through either direct- or indirect-access procedures.

(1) *Direct-access procedures:* A direct-access file permits a person to go directly to the storage system (file cabinet or computer storage) and locate the file.

EXAMPLE: An alphabetic filing system is a direct-access system. Without referring to any other information, you can go directly to the storage unit and locate the file. If a file folder is labeled Smith, John, all you need to do is to look under "S" in order to find the file.

(2) *Indirect-access procedures:* An indirect-access filing system requires a person to consult a *relative index* to locate the name, subject, or number under which the file is stored.

    (a) *Manual procedures:* A relative index serves as a backup for numeric and alphanumeric systems. The index consists of cards filed alphabetically, providing a complete list of names or subjects already included in the filing system.

    EXAMPLE: In a numeric filing system, you would consult the relative index first to see what number has been assigned to the file you are looking for. If you are looking for a file under Smith, John, you would look in the relative index under "S" to locate the card for Smith, John (filed alphabetically). This card will indicate something like this:

        ⌐ *Smith, John*   *1028* ⌐

    This means that the file for John Smith is File No. 1028. You can proceed to the storage unit containing File No. 1028, and the file should be there in sequential order.

    (b) *Automated procedures:* Electronic systems permit quick storage of records as well as retrieval. As a record is being created or saved in the system, the operator is prompted to provide a file name for the document. Later access to the document requires the operator to view an index or a directory listing first to select the correct record, or, if the file name is known, that name can be keyed into the computer and the document should appear on the screen in a matter of seconds. Random access allows direct access to the document without having to view all other documents stored on the disk or tape.

b. *Inspecting, indexing, and coding records:* Before a record can be filed, it must be *inspected* to ensure that it has been released for filing by an appropriate authority within the firm. Usually, an inspection mark or initials are written on the document to indicate that inspection has taken place. *Indexing* is the term used to indicate the decision making that is necessary in deciding what names or numbers to use in filing. *Coding* refers to making notations on the record itself as to exactly how the record will be stored (under what names or numbers).

EXAMPLE: Summerfield has the responsibility of examining each record to be sure that it has been released for filing and is ready to be indexed and coded. Once he has decided the name under which a record will be filed, he codes the name as it appears on the document in this way:

          2   *3*   *1*   *4*
        James   *G.*   *Blair,*   *Jr.*

The first filing unit should be underlined and the number 1 written above it. Then the numbers 2, 3, and 4 (in this case) can be written above the subsequent filing units.

c. *Color coding:* Many organizations find that color coding the files improves office efficiency and effectiveness in locating and refiling records. A color-coded system requires identifying the topic areas within the organization and/or division. All folders pertaining to one particular topic are of the same color. Pendaflex is a common color-coded filing system used by many organizations.

EXAMPLE: At Waubonsee College, the Business Division color coded the major academic programs like this:

Accounting—green

Management (Human Resources)—purple

Management Information Systems—yellow

Marketing—red

Operations and Logistics—orange

General—gray

d. *Cross-referencing records:* Whenever a record could be filed in more than one place in the files, a cross-reference is needed. The cross-reference indicates where the original document or complete file can be located. In a card file, the cross-reference is another card coded as a cross-reference card. The cross-reference in a document file is indicated on a cross-reference sheet or folder.

EXAMPLE: Sarah Lou Masterson is married to John L. Masterson. In an alphabetic file, the caption for her file would read

MASTERSON, SARAH LOU (Mrs.)

A cross-reference will appear under

MASTERSON, JOHN L. (Mrs.)
  See MASTERSON, SARAH LOU (Mrs.)

to let file users know where the original file can be found. If Sarah prefers to keep her maiden name as part of her married name, she may want her name to appear as

HUGHES-MASTERSON, SARAH LOU (Mrs.)

In this case, there could be a cross-reference under Masterson, Sarah Lou (Mrs.) and under her husband's name. The cross-reference under her husband's name would appear as

MASTERSON, JOHN L. (Mrs.)
  See HUGHES-MASTERSON, SARAH LOU (Mrs.)

In this way, if someone knew only her husband's name, her file could still be located.

e. *Charging out records:* A tracking system must be in place for any records that have been borrowed from hard-copy files. While these records are temporarily removed from the files, a record must be kept identifying the following types of information:

• The name of the person or department borrowing the record or file

• The date the record or file was borrowed

• The probable return date of the record or file

A set of charge-out forms should be maintained for use with the files. Whenever someone needs to charge out a particular record, a *charge-out request form* should be completed and presented to the records clerk in charge. Whenever an individual record is removed from a file, an *out guide* should take its place in the file. If an entire file folder is borrowed, an *out folder* should be substituted in the file for that particular folder.

Files that are filed electronically can be accessed only by those who have authorization to do so. The database management system (DBMS) establishes the creation, use, and maintenance of all information in the database. Security procedures that are established include the use of log-in numbers and passwords to gain access to specific files.

2. *Designing Filing Classification Systems:* The three primary classification systems for filing are alphabetic, numeric, and alphanumeric. Alphabetic systems use the 26 letters of the alphabet as the primary divisions within the system, whereas numeric systems vary combinations of numeric codes. Alphanumeric systems are combination alphabetic and numeric systems. Sets of rules are contained in all standard office procedures or records management references. No attempt is made here to explain all the specific rules that might be used with these classification systems. Some examples are used for clarity and basic understanding.

   a. *Alphabetic classification systems:* The alphabetic system is the oldest form of classification and is the basis for all other types of classification systems. Even a numeric system must have a relative index that is in alphabetic order.

      (1) *Alphabetic rules:* The Association of Records Managers and Administrators (ARMA), the professional organization for the records management field, recommends the following Simplified Filing Standard Rules as the first step toward automated filing and retrieval.

         (a) Files need to be arranged alphabetically in unit-by-unit order and letter by letter within each unit.

            • A *filing unit,* as defined by ARMA, may be a number, a letter, a word, or any combination of those.

            • A *filing segment* consists of one or more filing units (the total name, a number, a subject) used for filing purposes.

         (b) Each filing unit in a filing segment is to be considered, except for *A, an, the, any prepositions, &,* and *any conjunctions.* These words are placed in parentheses to indicate that they need not be used in filing if they are understood. When the word *the* is the first word in a business or organization name, *the* is placed in parentheses at the end of the name. Symbols like $ and # are spelled out and filed alphabetically.

         (c) When filing, "nothing comes before something." Single-unit filing segments are filed before multiple-unit filing segments.

         (d) All punctuation is ignored when alphabetizing. This includes periods, commas, dashes, hyphens, apostrophes, and any other punctuation mark. Hyphenated words are considered one unit.

         (e) Arabic numbers and roman numerals are filed sequentially in numeric order (not spelled out) before alphabetic characters. All arabic numerals precede all roman numerals.

         (f) Acronyms, abbreviations, and radio and television station call letters are filed as one unit.

         (g) The most commonly used name or title is the one that should be used when filing. Cross-reference under other names or titles that might be used in an information request.

(2) *Application of the rules:* Some specific applications will show how the rules for alphabetic filing are used in filing personal, organization, and governmental names.

(a) *Filing personal names:* Personal names are filed with surname considered as the first indexing unit, followed by first name and middle name.

EXAMPLES:

Name	Indexed as
	1 2 3
JoAnn Smith Robinson	*Robinson, JoAnn Smith* *(3 indexing units)*
	1 2 3
Carter L. MacGregor	*MacGregor, Carter L.* *(3 indexing units)*

(b) *Filing organization names:* Company names are filed using each word in the name as an indexing unit but not the words *a, an, &, and, the,* and prepositions. If the word *The* appears as the first word, it is transposed and placed in parentheses to indicate that the word need not be used as an indexing unit.

EXAMPLES:

Name	Indexed as
	1 2
The Royale Corporation	*Royale Corporation (The)* *(2 indexing units)*
	1 2
Center of the World Restaurant	*Center (of the) World* *3* *Restaurant* *(3 indexing units)*
	1 2
Blake & Sons	*Blake (and) Sons* *(2 indexing units)*

(c) *Filing names of governmental and political organizations:* Governmental organizations are filed first under the name of the government, then the name of the department or agency, in sequential order of authority. Words such as *and, the,* and *of* are placed in parentheses and are not regarded as indexing units.

EXAMPLES:

Name	Indexed as
	1 2 3
Internal Revenue Service *U.S. Treasury Department*	*United States Government* *4 5* *Treasury Department* *6 7 8* *Internal Revenue Service* *(8 indexing units)*

Name	Indexed as
	1 2 3
Federal Trade Commission	<u>United</u> States Government
	4 5 6
	Federal Trade Commission
	(6 indexing units)
	1 2
United Kingdom of Great	<u>United</u> Kingdom (of)
Britain and Northern Ireland	*3 4*
	Great Britain (and)
	5 6
	Northern Ireland
	(6 indexing units)

For a complete reference to alphabetic filing rules, consult the most recent edition of *Alphabetic Filing Rules* published by ARMA International, Prairie Village, Kansas.

(3) *Subject filing:* Another classification system that uses the alphabetic system as a base is subject filing. Instead of arranging records by names of individuals or business names, records are arranged in alphabetical order according to topics or categories.

EXAMPLES:

Administration	*costs—administrative*	*human resources*
budgets	*costs—operating*	*research*
business travel		

(4) *Geographic filing:* In a geographic system, records are arranged alphabetically according to geographic locations. Filing by geographic locations may be particularly useful in a company or organization with branch offices or divisions in different parts of the country or the world.

EXAMPLES:

United States	*Northwestern region*
Central region	*Southeastern region*
North-Central region	*Southwestern region*
Northeastern region	*Western region*

b. *Numeric classification systems:* A numeric filing system is an indirect-access system consisting of numeric codes assigned to names of individuals, businesses, or subjects. An *accession record* (an official log listing the names to which numbers have been assigned) and a *relative index* (cards or listing of all names to which numbers have been assigned in alphabetic order) are necessary elements of the system. Typically, a key field in computerized systems tends to be numeric (e.g., employee number, part number, product code). When numeric files are used within a business, correspondents are usually encouraged to put the numeric code (file number) on each piece of correspondence relating to a business transaction.

There are many different types of numeric systems. Those presented here are examples of some of the more commonly used numeric systems.

(1) *Straight numeric:* Files are arranged in consecutive order, from the lowest number to the highest number. *Sequential* or *serial files* are other terms used for this type of system. Color coding can be used to tab folders in a straight-numeric system for quick access when folders are stored in open shelving. The following colors are used in one color-coding system:

0 = red	5 = blue
1 = pink	6 = lavender
2 = yellow	7 = brown
3 = orange	8 = silver
4 = green	9 = gold

EXAMPLE: An administrative assistant who codes the four-digit customer number, 1249, on a file folder would place the following tabs on the folder:

1 = pink
2 = yellow
4 = green
9 = gold

A folder for customer number 1250 would have the following tabs:

1 = pink
2 = yellow
5 = blue
0 = red

One of the primary advantages of color coding is that misfiled folders can be spotted easily because of the arrangement of the color tabs. A color-coded system for paper files can be coordinated with customer databases stored on the computer.

(2) *Duplex numeric:* File numbers have two or more sets of code numbers separated by a dash, comma, period, or space. A relative index is needed so that a complete list of the primary numbers assigned to the major categories within the system can be maintained.

EXAMPLES:

Administration	*20*
Budgets	*20-10*
Business Travel	*20-11*
Costs	*20-12*
Administrative	*20-12-01*
Operating	*20-12-02*
Personnel	*20-13*
Research	*20-14*

(3) *Block codes:* Blocks of numbers are reserved for records that have a common feature or characteristic.

EXAMPLES:

Administration	*201-299*
Production	*301-399*
Sales and Marketing	*401-499*

(4) *Middle digit:* Records are filed numerically by the *middle digits,* not necessarily according to the number as it appears on the record. The file numbers in the accession record are still listed in straight-numeric sequence.

EXAMPLE:

File No. 482311

Indexing Units:

48	23	11
Secondary	Primary	Tertiary
(2)	(1)	(3)

The record will be filed under 23 first, then 48 within the 23 section, and finally in folder 11.

Drawer:	*23*
Guide:	*48*
Folder:	*11*

The middle-digit system is very effective if file numbers have six or fewer digits. When file numbers are more than six digits, other numeric systems would probably be more effective.

(5) *Terminal digit:* Records are filed by the *last digits* (the terminal digits) in the terminal-digit system, which tends to be a more efficient system than middle-digit. The code number is divided into sets of two or three digits as a general rule. File numbers are listed consecutively in the accession record so that a record of the file numbers already assigned in the system is kept. A primary advantage of the terminal-digit system is security in the handling of confidential files or information.

EXAMPLE:

File No. 482311

Indexing Units:

48	23	11
Tertiary	Secondary	Primary
(3)	(2)	(1)

The record will be filed under 11 first, then 23 within the 11 section, and finally in folder 48.

Drawer:	*11*
Guide:	*23*
Folder	*48*

If the same number is grouped in sets of three digits, the coding would be like this:

482   311
Secondary Primary

EXAMPLE: The catalog stores for a prominent retailer use a very simple terminal-digit system to file the orders waiting for customer pickup. When a customer orders merchandise at the catalog store, the customer's telephone number is entered on the order form along with other information such as name, address, account number, and items ordered. When the customer returns to pick up the merchandise, the clerk asks for the customer's telephone number. The last two digits (the terminal digits) are used to locate the order in the storage area.

(6) *Decimal numeric:* A decimal-numeric system permits a filing system to subdivide subjects (topics), thus expanding beyond a simple numeric arrangement. Major divisions of a subject (topic) are assigned a number. A decimal point followed by one digit is placed after the number of the first subdivision, a second digit after the second subdivision, and so on.

EXAMPLE:

350   *Motor vehicles*
350.1   *Minivans*
350.12   *Minivans (7-passenger)*

The Dewey decimal system is perhaps the most widely known decimal-numeric filing system. Developed in 1873 primarily for cataloging library books, the system includes 10 general categories:

000   General Works
100   Philosophy
200   Religion
300   Social Science
400   Philology
500   Pure Science
600   Applied Science or Useful Arts
700   Arts and Recreation
800   Literature
900   History

Each of these 10 categories is then divided into 10 parts, with a further subdivision into 10 more subdivisions. A typical decimal used in cataloging a book would look like this:

650.231 (a book within the Applied Science or Useful Arts category)

(7) *Coded numeric:* Sometimes, records are given numeric codes where the codes are really numbers telling something about the person or item. When the codes used take on additional meaning about the item, we say that a *mnemonic code* is being used.

(a) *ZIP codes:* The ZIP codes used by the U.S. Postal Service for mail delivery are an example of a coded numeric system. The ZIP + 4 codes (9-digit numbers), the expanded code established in 1981, are an extension of the original system.

EXAMPLE:

60115-2623
 6 = area within United States
 01 = sectional center
 15 = local delivery area
 26 = geographic portion of a zone or a portion of a rural route, part of a box section, or official designation
 23 = a specific block face, apartment house, bank of boxes, firm, building, or other specific delivery locations

(b) *Area codes:* Telephone networks across the country are divided into geographic zones called *area codes.* The area code serves as a prefix so that a telephone number can be dialed directly (without intervention by an operator) anywhere in the United States.

EXAMPLE:

(312) 445-2189
312 = an area code within the city of Chicago
445-2189 = telephone number

(c) *Catalog numbers:* Product numbers included in catalogs and on bar codes for merchandise represent information about the items.

EXAMPLE:

 110 22 1260-8

 110 item category

 22 catalog

 1260 item style

 8 color

(8) *Chronological system:* Often, records need to be filed according to *date.* A filing system that utilizes calendar dates as the significant divisions of the system is known as a *chronological* system.

EXAMPLES:

A tickler file is arranged according to dates, with the most recent date first. Reminder notes are recorded/entered on cards or files for particular dates.

A business calendar is arranged by chronological dates (and times). If appointments are entered onto a small handheld computerized calendar system called a personal digital assistant (PDA), *the calendar can be accessed by entering an appropriate code. The appointments will appear on a small screen in chronological order according to times.*

c. *Alphanumeric classification systems:* Whenever a combination of alphabetic characters and numbers are used in a code, the code is *alphanumeric.* In a system like this, it is possible to have the alphanumeric designations on primary guides as well as individual folders. A relative index lists the codes assigned to each letter of the alphabet and any subdivisions.

EXAMPLES:

The Soundex code is an alphanumeric code that includes an alphabetic letter (the first letter of the name being coded) and numbers representing the consonant sounds in the name. Vowel sounds and silent letters are omitted. This code is commonly used for drivers' license numbers.

S636 = S - r - d - r Schrader
The letters c-h-a-e are omitted in the rules for the code.

The Library of Congress system for cataloging library books uses an alphanumeric code that includes one or two alphabetic letters and series of numbers that designate subdivisions (see Chapter 10, Section B-1-a[2]).

3. *Storing Records:* In addition to procedures for filing records for future use, records storage equipment and supplies must be used to guarantee safety of records during their useful life. The costs of maintaining adequate floor space for paper records is encouraging businesses to investigate other methods of records storage such as micrographics and computer storage. The actual cost of records storage equipment and supplies is approximately 20 percent of the overall cost of maintaining a records storage and retrieval system.

   a. *Selecting records storage equipment:* First and foremost, care should be exercised in selecting records storage equipment that will be appropriate for the kinds of records to be stored and for the time period the records will be stored. Here are some of the main concerns to be considered in selecting equipment:

      (1) *Protection of records:* The value of records to the ongoing operation of the business is important to consider in deciding exactly how records should be protected. Records need to be adequately protected against fire, theft, or other disasters.

      (2) *Frequency of record use:* The type of equipment purchased for use with records storage will depend on the frequency with which records will be used and accessed by users.

      (3) *Space requirements:* The volume of records currently housed in records storage as well as the anticipated future volume of records will influence the storage space required.

      (4) *Cost of records storage:* The costs per square foot of office space, compared with the costs incurred in maintaining records storage facilities, are important when deciding where records will be stored—within the office or at a remote location. Sometimes remote storage can be found at a lower cost in low-rent city districts.

      (5) *Efficient use of the system:* Records storage equipment should alleviate the amount of time spent filing or searching for documents. Easy access to records and accuracy in finding them should be strong considerations in deciding what equipment is needed.

b. *Storing correspondence:* Correspondence may be stored on paper, magnetic media, or computer disks. Correspondence may be filed alphabetically, numerically, or alphanumerically, depending on the filing system preferred.

(1) *Filing equipment for paper storage:* Conventional storage systems are used in many offices where paper is the primary medium for storage. File cabinets, usually three- or four-drawer models, are generally the most common filing equipment used.

    (a) *Vertical file cabinet:* Paper documents are stored in vertical files on end in a vertical fashion. These file cabinets may hold letter-size documents or legal-size documents. (For more information, see Chapter 4, Section C-1-a.)

    (b) *Lateral file cabinet:* Lateral files are available from two-drawer (usually placed by the side of a desk) to five-drawer capacity. Folders can be stored in two ways: facing the front of the file or facing the side of the cabinet. (For more information, see Chapter 4, Section C-1-b.)

    (c) *Stationary shelving unit:* Stationary open-shelf units are a form of lateral file characterized by the "open" view of all the files in the system. The equipment may be completely open shelf, without door enclosures, or doors may pull down over each shelf and lock for overnight security. Open shelves allow "through" shelving for the storage of larger materials. (For more information, see Chapter 4, Section C-1-c.)

    (d) *High-density mobile storage:* Mobile storage systems (programmable, power driven, or manual) include sets of file shelves that slide on tracks installed in the floor. These systems are commonly used in business today. (For more information, see Chapter 4, Section C-1-d.)

    (e) *Carousel or rotary file:* The greatest advantage of the carousel file is that the operator can bring the file to the point of use by turning or rotating the file horizontally. The entire file rotates like a Lazy-Susan around a central hub. (For more information, see Chapter 4, Section C-1-e.)

    (f) *Automated conveyor system:* With an automated conveyor system, the operator must dial a code number to let the system know which file is desired. The conveyor revolves around its track and automatically stops at the desired code. (For more information, see Chapter 4, Section C-1-f.)

    (g) *Identification aids and supplies:* Proper techniques must be used to index, code, and store documents so that they can be retrieved easily. Otherwise, the storage system, whether manual or automated, will be ineffective. Correspondence filed in conventional file cabinets requires an identification system consisting of guides and folders prearranged in a sequential manner, depending on the classification system used. Here is a quick review of some of the identification aids that are needed for storage systems for paper documents:

        • *Guides:* These key components of the system form an outline of the classification system used. Guides indicate the sections of the file and serve as dividers for groups of records.

- *Primary guides:* These guides highlight the major divisions and subdivisions of records stored in a file drawer or on a shelf.

- *Secondary guides:* These special guides are used to highlight frequently referenced sections of records, such as "Applications for Employment."

- *Out guide:* This special guide substitutes for a folder or a record that has been temporarily removed from the file.

- *File folder:* An individual folder is used to store the documents pertaining to one correspondent, case, or account. Each file folder has a projection (*tab*) on which is placed a *label* with a typed *caption*.

- *Color coding:* Colored tabs are placed on the sides of file folders to represent numeric or alphanumeric codes. This identification system is of particular value in an open-shelf filing system.

  See Figure 9–2 for an example of the arrangement of guides and folders in a correspondence file.

(2) *Filing equipment for card storage:* The size of the cards used for storage will help determine the type of filing equipment that can be used. The most common types of equipment are vertical, visible, wheel, and rotary card file equipment. (For more information on these types of equipment, see Chapter 4, Section C-1-g[1], [2], [3], and [4].)

c. *Storing noncorrespondence records:* In addition to business documents recorded on paper and magnetic media, other types of noncorrespondence items also need to be stored in the office. Each item needs to be examined to see what kind of storage system would provide the protection and durability needed. Some typical kinds of noncorrespondence items might include catalogs, brochures, schedules, plans, drawings, blueprints, maps, photographs, cassette tapes, videotapes, compact disks, 35-millimeter slides, and computer printouts. Here are some types of storage equipment that might be used for some of these applications:

(1) *File cabinets with horizontal drawers:* Flat storage must be provided for blueprints, maps, and photographs.

(2) *Suspension open-shelf files:* Computer printouts are inserted into plastic binders for suspension in a "hanging" storage area until needed.

(3) *Rolled files:* Maps, blueprints, or posters may be encased in rolls for easier filing and storage.

(4) *Tape drawers:* Videotapes and cassette tapes can be stored in filing order within special drawers designed just for tapes. The drawers are sectioned with small ridges so that individual tapes can fit vertically inside each drawer. Labels with appropriate filing designations need to be attached to each tape and its container.

(5) *Compact disk storage:* Small open-shelf units are available to store compact disks vertically. Labels with appropriate filing codes can be attached to each disk cover.

(6) *Slides:* Acetate sheets with 12 to 15 small pockets on each page are often used to store 35-millimeter slides. These sheets are three-hole punched and ready to put in a three-hole binder for easy storage on an open shelf.

Figure 9–2   The Arrangement of Guides and Folders in a Correspondence System

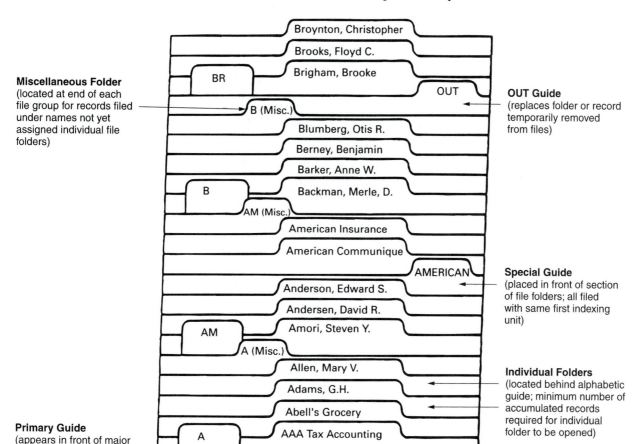

Miscellaneous Folder (located at end of each file group for records filed under names not yet assigned individual file folders)

OUT Guide (replaces folder or record temporarily removed from files)

Special Guide (placed in front of section of file folders; all filed with same first indexing unit)

Individual Folders (located behind alphabetic guide; minimum number of accumulated records required for individual folder to be opened)

Primary Guide (appears in front of major group of folders and special guides; designates major division of file)

4. *Retaining and Disposing of Records:* Decisions must be made on a predetermined basis as to the retention (keeping), protection, and disposal of a company's *vital* records. A records retention schedule identifies the records of the organization that are being kept in active, semiactive, and inactive storage; the period of time they will be retained in storage; and the value of the record to the organization. A *retention schedule* is an agreement between the department creating the record, the user (if not the department of creation), and the records manager. The schedules specifies how long each active record is to be held in active storage, semiactive storage, or inactive storage and when the record may be purged or destroyed, if ever.

a. *Appraisal of records:* For an accurate retention schedule to be developed, the organization's records must be appraised to determine the value of the records. *Value* of records depends on the utilization of the records in ongoing operations. *Primary value* refers to the value of records in active storage, and *secondary value* refers to those records held in semiactive or inactive storage.

(1) *Primary value:* Records that are of primary value are active in nature and are needed for current operations. Primary value may mean administrative, legal, fiscal, or research value.

(a) *Administrative value:* Records that have administrative value are needed for a business to conduct current operations.

EXAMPLES: Policies and procedures, executive directives, purchase requisitions, inventory records, personnel records

(b) *Legal value:* Those documents that have legal value contain provisions or agreements that relate to the legal rights and obligations of the business.

EXAMPLES: Contracts, agreements to purchase new property or equipment, leases for business property

(c) *Fiscal value:* Records of fiscal value usually refer to those documents that relate to the financial transactions of the organization.

EXAMPLES: Budgets, vouchers, tax returns, sales reports

(d) *Research value:* Records consisting of technical information that results from primary or secondary research will have research value to the organization.

EXAMPLES: Records of procedures used in conducting a research project, records of step-by-step procedures in analyzing the historical development in information-processing equipment over the past 10 years

(2) *Secondary value:* Records that are in relatively inactive storage may have historical or archival importance.

(a) *Information value:* Over a period of years, any organization will accumulate records that contain information relating to people, places, events, and other phenomena.

EXAMPLES: Copyrights, patents, blueprints, photographs, maps

(b) *Evidence value:* Records that trace the development of an organization from its beginning to the present may have evidentiary value in providing proof of policies, procedures, and practices during the organization's lifetime.

EXAMPLES: Organizational charts, policies and procedures manuals, articles of incorporation, minutes books

b. *Records transfer:* The physical movement of records from active status within a particular department or office to a centralized records center is known as *records transfer.* Two methods of records transfer are the *perpetual* and *periodic* transfer methods.

(1) *Perpetual transfer method:* Using the perpetual method, records can be transferred at any time that the event has been completed or the case closed and future referral to the records will be infrequent and limited.

EXAMPLE: A perpetual method of records transfer is used in the Lawrence & Brown law firm. Once a court case has been closed, the file is moved immediately to inactive storage. With this method, a case sometimes remains open for two to three years before it can be closed and becomes inactive.

(2) *Periodic transfer method:* Records are transferred as of a specific date each year. All files for a specific period of time are transferred at that time.

EXAMPLE: The Powell Seed Company uses a periodic transfer method because this particular type of business lends itself to a periodic rather than a perpetual method. On July 1 and December 31 of each year, the files are transferred from active to inactive storage. Of course, on those particular dates, all records are perused to see whether they are needed for future reference or can be destroyed.

c. *Records purging and destruction:* Before any records are purged or destroyed at the end of a specified retention period, the department that created and/or used the records is contacted to determine whether the records indeed can be deleted or destroyed. The records retention schedule specifies the period of time a given record should be retained before disposal.

(1) *Destruction of paper records:* Common ways of destroying paper records include shredding, pulverizing, and incinerating.

(2) *Destruction of microform and magnetic records:* Common ways of destroying microform or magnetic records include incinerating, shredding, and pulverizing.

(3) *Purging of electronic records:* Periodically, records that are stored electronically on computer disks should be examined to see whether they can be purged (deleted) from computer storage. Depending on the particular records in question, purging can take place on a weekly, monthly, or annual basis.

Most organizations are now recycling paper, cardboard, and shredded or pulverized paper.

5. *Maintaining Records Centers:* The records center is the depository for the organization's vital, inactive, and/or active records. Vital records may be classified as active or inactive, depending on the current use. Many times, sets of duplicate records exist in the form of electronic tapes, hard copies (paper copies), or microforms. *Dispersal* is the term used to indicate the duplication of hard copies and their storage in other locations.

a. *On-site storage:* In-house records centers, file rooms, or vaults provide records storage on the company's premises. Vital records are sometimes stored in highly protected vaults or in underground storage for even greater security.

b. *Off-site storage:* Records storage in off-premises locations may be space owned by the organization or rented from other commercial firms. Usually, off-site storage is in a lower-rent area and, therefore, will result in a lower records storage cost. A higher degree of security exists in off-site facilities primarily because these locations are not publicized by the organization.

6. *Maintaining Archives:* A *business archive* is a facility that houses records being retained for research or historical value. Archives may be *public* (may be accessed by the general public) or *private* (may be used only by members of the organization). An *accession register* identifies the records in the archive and controls access to documents and retrieval of documents from the archive. Here are some of the basic reasons for the maintenance of archives by organizations:

a. The organization's history can be preserved for posterity.

b. The public image of an organization may be enhanced by permitting the public to use its archives.

c. Relevant administrative, fiscal, or legal information may be maintained for later research and reference.

Documents maintained in an archive are preserved in special storage containers to deter further deterioration. Access to an archive is limited to those individuals whose reasons for using the archive are approved by appropriate officials of the organization.

Review Questions

Directions: Select the best answer from the four alternatives. Write your answer in the blank to the left of the number.

—————————— 1. The systematic control of business information from its creation to its disposal is called

    a. word processing.
    b. communications.
    c. information processing.
    d. records management.

—————————— 2 Individual business records are classified according to the

    a. steps in the record cycle.
    b. form of the record.
    c. method used for creating the record.
    d. use of the record.

—————————— 3. Which one of the following types of records would be classified as a vital record?

    a. A report stored on a computer disk
    b. Copyright for a software program
    c. Tax records for last year
    d. Customer request for product information

—————————— 4. Records needed for the smooth operation of an organization that can be replaced if lost or destroyed in a disaster, usually at considerable expense, are referred to as

    a. vital records.
    b. important records.
    c. useful records.
    d. nonessential records.

—————————— 5. A telephone message would be classified as a/an

    a. vital record.
    b. important record.
    c. useful record.
    d. nonessential record.

—————————— 6. The series of steps from the time the record is created until final disposition is called the

    a. document preparation.
    b. utilization of records in business activities.
    c. record cycle.
    d. records transfer from active to inactive storage.

_____ **7.** A decision is made about the life of a record during this step of the record cycle:

    a. Records creation
    b. Records utilization
    c. Records retention
    d. Records transfer

_____ **8.** Moving a record from active storage to remote storage is accomplished during this step of the record cycle:

    a. Records disposal
    b. Records transfer
    c. Records retention
    d. Records creation

_____ **9.** Which one of the following records is typically designed in a conventional format?

    a. An invoice
    b. One sheet of microfiche
    c. A 35-millimeter slide
    d. A computer disk

_____ **10.** One of the cards in the card catalog of a library is an example of a/an

    a. relative index.
    b. index record.
    c. posted record.
    d. microform.

_____ **11.** Which one of the following records is designed in a nonconventional format?

    a. A business letter
    b. A 3- by 5-inch card for equipment repair
    c. A set of electronic slides
    d. A three-page business report

_____ **12.** Reduced images captured on film are stored on a/an

    a. magnetic disk.
    b. videotape.
    c. OCR process.
    d. microform.

_____ **13.** Before a business record can be retrieved from active files, the record must be

    a. indexed with the exact location of the record.
    b. stored according to a prescribed set of rules.
    c. approved for retrieval by the supervisor.
    d. inspected prior to accession.

_____ **14.** Which one of the following classification systems assumes that direct-access procedures will be used to retrieve records?

    a. An alphabetic system
    b. A numeric system
    c. A color-coded system
    d. A subject system

_____ **15.** An indirect-access filing system requires the use of a relative index to locate the

    a. order in which the files are stored.
    b. directory showing where a file is stored.
    c. color coding used for the files.
    d. subject under which a file is stored.

_____ **16.** Making notations on the record itself indicating exactly how the record will be stored is referred to as

    a. inspecting.
    b. indexing.
    c. coding.
    d. classifying.

_____ **17.** Whenever a record can be filed in more than one place in the files,

    a. a duplicate copy of the record should be filed in each place.
    b. a cross-reference to the original record should be prepared.
    c. a cross-reference should be noted on the original record.
    d. the record should be filed in a special location within the file.

_____ **18.** Hoffman uses an alphabetic classification system based on the ARMA rules in which correspondence is filed alphabetically by name of client. Which one of the following names would be filed *first?*

    a. Roberta L. Bernard
    b. Bernarde Robot Company
    c. Robert Louis Bernard
    d. The Bernard Recreation Association

_____ **19.** When an alphabetic classification system is used, which one of the following names would be filed *last?*

    a. U.S. Department of Labor
    b. United Airlines
    c. U.S. Dept. of Education
    d. United States of America

20. Bromley files correspondence alphabetically, with all correspondence for a particular client filed chronologically with the most recent date first. Which one of the following pieces of correspondence will be filed *first* in the file?

    a. A letter from George R. Johnson dated February 4, 2000.
    b. A letter from G. R. Johnson dated January 3, 2000.
    c. A letter to George R. Johnson dated March 14, 2000.
    d. A letter to G. R. Johnson dated December 28, 1999.

21. The primary purpose for using a relative index with a numeric classification system is so that

    a. cross-references can be located easily.
    b. the record can be retrieved using a direct-access procedure.
    c. a particular record or file can be located quickly.
    d. blocks of numbers can be reserved for certain record categories.

22. If you were filing the following numbered records using a middle-digit filing system that divides the numbers into two-digit groups, which of the following numbers would be filed *first?*

    a. 204573
    b. 134591
    c. 105424
    d. 115429

23. The following numbered records are filed using a terminal-digit system, using two-digit groupings of numbers. Which record would be filed *second?*

    a. 115119
    b. 154517
    c. 225891
    d. 334717

24. In each file drawer Jacobsen arranges guides and folders for correspondence filing. Which one of the following guides and folders would be *last?*

    a. Primary guide for J
    b. Special guide for Johnson
    c. Miscellaneous folder for J
    d. Individual folder for Johnson

25. The value of each active record and the length of time it is to be held in active or inactive storage is specified in the

    a. records appraisal.
    b. relative index.
    c. retention schedule.
    d. records transfer method.

26. Which one of the following types of records would be appraised as having fiscal value?

    a. Company policy on business travel
    b. The administrative budget for the year
    c. Contract for lease of off-site records storage space
    d. Perpetual inventory records

27. Policies and procedures manuals that have been developed for an organization are deemed to have

    a. research value.
    b. fiscal value.
    c. evidence value.
    d. legal value.

28. Electronically stored records need to be examined at frequent intervals to determine whether they should be

    a. dispersed.
    b. purged.
    c. indexed.
    d. documented.

29. Hard-copy storage of a duplicate set of records at a different location is referred to as

    a. retention.
    b. transfer.
    c. dispersal.
    d. destruction.

30. A facility that houses records retained for their research or historical value is called a/an

    a. historical center.
    b. archive.
    c. records center.
    d. micrographics center.

Solutions

18. (d)   [C-2-a (1) and (2)] The names would be filed correctly in this order:
Bernard <u>R</u>ecreation Association (The)
Bernard, Robert Louis
Bernard, Robert<u>a</u> Louise
Bernard<u>e</u> Robot Company

19. (d)   [C-2-a(1), C-2-a(2)(b) and (c)] The names would be filed correctly in this order:

United Airlines
United States (of) America
United States Government
  Education Department
United States Government
  Labor Department

20. (b)   [C-2-a(1), C-2-b(8)] The correspondence would be filed correctly in this order:

Johnson, G. R.—January 3, 2000
Johnson, G. R.—December 28, 1999
Johnson, George R.—March 14, 2000
Johnson, George R.—February 4, 2000

21. (c)   [C-2-b]

22. (b)   [C-2-b(4)] In a middle-digit system, the numbers given in the choices would be filed in the following order: 134591, 204573, 105424, and 115429.

23. (d)   [C-2-b(5)] In a terminal-digit system, the numbers given in the choices would be filed in the following order: 154517, 334717, 115119, and 225891.

24. (d)   [C-3-b(1)(g)] The guides and folders shown in the choices would be sequenced in this way:

Primary Guide—J
Special Guide—Johnson
Individual Folder—Johnson
Miscellaneous Folder—J

25. (c)   [C-4]

26. (b)   [C-4-a(1)(c)]

27. (c)   [C-4-a(3)(b)]

28. (b)   [C-4-c(3)]

29. (c)   [C-5]

30. (b)   [C-6]

CHAPTER 10

Reference Materials

OVERVIEW

As more administrative responsibilities are assigned to the administrative assistant or secretary, the process of researching informational references is becoming more important. Researching information requires a degree of knowledge about the subject or topic, organizational skills, and time to search through libraries, computer files, or the Internet. Sometimes it is difficult to know exactly where to go to find adequate and accurate information for a research report or speech. The secretary must be prepared to spend considerable time "digging" for sources of information.

Research procedures that have proved helpful include discussing the purpose of the research with the person for whom the work is being done *before* actually beginning to search for information. This is one way to determine the basic objectives of the research before embarking on the project. Sometimes, interviews with experts will be necessary to obtain primary data; at other times, book and periodical references will be sufficient. No matter what procedures are used, detailed records of all persons interviewed, references read and consulted, and other useful reference materials need to be kept to develop a complete bibliography of works consulted and cited.

Research facilities such as libraries, in-house research services, and computer search and information services should be utilized in conducting research. In addition, business and professional associations as well as community organizations can also be very helpful.

The list of reference materials included in this chapter is meant to serve as a starting point for researching information under particular headings and becoming familiar with various kinds of references. As new publications relating to the categories included in this chapter are discovered, these might be added to the list so that an up-to-date reference list can be maintained.

KEY TERMS

Almanac	Dewey decimal	Micrographics center
Archive	classification system	Parliamentary procedure
Bibliography	Interlibrary loan	Thesaurus
Biographical directory	Library of Congress	Vertical file service
Computer data bank	classification system	

A. Research Procedures

The secretary's role is changing to include more administrative responsibility in assisting the busy executive with the challenging task of researching and locating information. Such a task demands a high level of organizational skill and ingenuity in gathering

317

accurate information for reports, speeches, and other types of written materials. The kinds of procedures used in collecting the information needed will, of course, directly reflect on the quality of the report or speech produced. Here are some handy guidelines for developing a set of procedures for researching business information.

1. *Understanding Purposes of Research:* Before you can embark on any type of research, you must know the purpose of the research. Know exactly what the outcome will be, and who will make use of the results of the research. Here are some questions that need to be answered before proceeding with the research.

   • How will the information be presented—as a speech? As a report?

   • Who will be the primary audience?

   • Is there a secondary audience?

   • What kind of information is needed—results of research studies? Periodical articles?

2. *Listing Possible Sources of Information:* Your investigation should begin by listing all the possible sources of information you might use.

   a. *Facilities:* Identify facilities, such as libraries, business associations, or community organizations, where you might find the kinds of information you seek.

   b. *Types of references:* Identify specific books, documents, or other types of information that are desired.

   c. *Personal contacts:* List the names of people you need to interview, with their addresses and telephone numbers, so that it will be easier for you to contact them by letter and phone as you proceed with the research.

   d. *Computer searches:* Investigate the possibility of an on-line computer search for some of the types of information you need. Such a search may take place in a library or research center that has access to data base(s) or other libraries you may need to access.

   e. *Internet search:* An Internet search may yield specific information about a particular company or organization, its products or services, or a specific industry. In addition, the Internet permits you to access articles that have appeared in daily newspapers, magazines, or journals, either in abstract or complete form.

3. *Determining Special Research Costs:* It is very important to estimate the cost of doing the background research. Costs include travel to and from research facilities, telephone service, on-line computer searches, copying and printing, and additional office support.

4. *Making Appointments for Research:* A time-saver in performing research functions is to make appointments ahead of time with individuals (inside or outside the organization) who are in a position to help you obtain the kinds of information you seek. Other people (librarians, business executives, research specialists, community leaders) may be busy on their jobs, just as you are, and a formal appointment will ensure you of an hour or two of their undivided attention in responding to your queries.

5. *Keeping Complete Records of Research Information:* As you proceed with the research, you need to keep a written record of everything you do: sources of information, complete sets of notes, interview schedule, and transcribed interview tapes. You

will need this information later when you are ready to develop the information you gathered into the final draft of the speech or report.

   a. *Preparing a bibliography:* Keep a record of each reference you use, manually on a 3- by 5-inch card or electronically in a computer database. Include the following kinds of information:

- Author's name (if any)
- Title of book, article, or other reference
- Name of publishing company or agency
- Place of publication
- Date of publication
- Exact page reference(s)
- Library classification number
- ISBN number for ordering copies

File these bibliography cards in a card file according to a specific filing system. You might consider alphabetical order by author name or subject (topic), unless your speech or report lends itself to an alternative filing system.

If you key entries (with the preceding categories of information) into a database, you must be sure to set up the fields of information with the same reference name for the entire database. *Fields* of information are the labels you use in the creation of a database to identify the different kinds of information to be included in the database.

EXAMPLE: In planning the bibliographic entries, you would establish fields such as the following:

    Author's last name

    Author's first name

    Title of article or book

    Title of publication

    Place of publication

    Date of publication

    Publisher

The software will prompt you to identify the fields of information *before* you begin to key in the variable information for each bibliographic entry. Abbreviated names are usually required in setting up fields, such as *authorLN* for *author's last name.* Once you have told the system you are using these fields, the system will prompt you each time you need to enter a particular kind of information.

   b. *Taking appropriate reading notes:* Reading notes should be complete so that you will not have to return to the original reference later as you begin your writing.

     (1) *Manual procedures for taking notes:* Here are some specific procedures to follow in taking accurate notes as you read various references.

- Use only one side of a note card (preferably a 4- by 6-inch or 5- by 8-inch card so that you have more writing room).

- If one particular reference refers to more than one subject, place the notes pertaining to each subject on a separate card. Identify the source of the material on each card (a code number or author's last name). Complete bibliographic information is in your bibliography file.

- File your note cards in a card file alphabetically by author name or subject (topic) so that they will not become lost.

(2) *Electronic procedures for taking notes:* You may be using word processing or database software to record your notes. Follow the procedures given in the operating instructions for the software you are using so that you know the correct procedures to use. Word processing software permits you to key in your notes and also store these notes on disk for later access. As you work with these notes later, you can insert bookmarks or other notations to help you locate specific facts or data easily.

c. *Duplicating materials for later reference:* You may be using microfilm or microfiche to locate needed materials. It is sometimes an advantage to print copies of those pages with data that you may need to refer to later. Be careful to observe copyright laws carefully when copyrighted articles, theses, and other research information are used.

d. *Recording interview information:* If you find it necessary to conduct an interview with people within or outside your organization, follow these steps so that the interview will be conducted in a concise yet complete and consistent manner.

(1) Develop an interview guide with the questions you wish to ask during the interview. In some cases, it is an excellent idea to send a copy of this guide to the person you are interviewing ahead of time so that he or she will have an opportunity to think about them and prepare some of the responses before you arrive.

(2) During the interview, take notes in a manner that will not be distracting for the interviewee. If you use a written form of shorthand or have a form where responses can be checked (yes/no) or circled (1000–2000, 500–999, 1–499), you should be able to take the notes quickly as the interviewee responds to specific questions while still maintaining eye contact and interjecting additional questions.

(3) If you wish to record an interview for later replay, transcription, and analysis, be sure to ask the interviewee for permission before you begin. Sometimes people do not wish their responses to be recorded, especially if the topic tends to be sensitive.

(4) A typed transcript of the interview (questions and responses) prepared from a recorded tape or notes taken during the interview should be submitted to the interviewee for review to ensure accuracy of the information that has been transcribed.

B. Research Facilities

One of the first items on your list is to identify the types of facilities that may have information relevant to your topic. Libraries, local chamber-of-commerce organizations, business and professional associations, and local businesses may be helpful to you. In addition, various U.S. government departments have excellent libraries, with qualified professional librarians in charge. Some agencies have law libraries as well. Many of these organizations now have Internet sites that enable you to access information from their holdings.

1. *Libraries:* Library services are available primarily through public, company, government, and university libraries. If you are looking for rather general information, a public library may be an excellent source. Many companies, however, have established their own libraries so that library references specific to their own industry may be collected and used more easily. Of course, a university library may be one of the most extensive libraries in your vicinity. Private collections housed in a university library may provide valuable information for your research. Today, many public and university libraries are part of library consortiums with on-line services available that link one library with many others in the network. References that are part of one library's holdings may be borrowed by someone at another library in the consortium.

a. *Classification systems:* Libraries use two standardized classification systems: the Dewey Decimal classification system and the Library of Congress classification system.

   (1) *Dewey Decimal classification system:* This system is based on the premise that all knowledge can be classified into ten primary groupings:

000	General Works
100	Philosophy
200	Religion
300	Social Science
400	Philology
500	Pure Science
600	Applied Science or Useful Arts
700	Arts Recreation
800	Literature
900	History

   Main subjects are identified by the hundreds 000 to 900. Subgroups are assigned numbers 00 to 99 or 0 to 9 if there are two subgroups.

   EXAMPLE:

   347.97 Courts (within 300, Social Science)

   (2) *Library of Congress classification system:* This system, developed in the early 1900s, provides for 21 major areas of knowledge:

A	General Works
B	Philosophy, Psychology, and Religion
C–F	History
G	Geography, Anthropology, and Recreation
H	Social Sciences

J	Political Science
K	Law
L	Education
M	Music
N	Fine Arts
P	Language and Literature
Q	Science
R	Medicine
S	Agriculture
T	Technology
U	Military Science
V	Naval Science
Z	Bibliography and Library Science

The number assigned consists of an alphanumeric code, with the first two letters representing the major classification group and the numbers representing subdivisions.

EXAMPLE:

KF889.3   History, Law

Each year, the Library of Congress adds or modifies more than 7,000 classification numbers to account for new knowledge or current events.

b. *Vertical file service:* A valuable library reference is the list of pamphlets, booklets, and leaflets that are available in vertical files within the library but are not indexed in the card catalog. The list of references, however, may be computerized for easy access by the user.

c. *Reference collections:* Libraries house special collections, either publicly or privately owned. Information contained in such collections may be accessed, but often all research work must be done on the premises. All books and documents in the collection are kept in the library at all times and must be signed out by the researcher. Collections such as these give the researcher an opportunity to view manuscripts, reports, and other materials that might not otherwise be available for public viewing. With special permission, it may be possible for the researcher to make photocopies of some of the materials.

d. *Interlibrary networks:* Interlibrary communication networks or consortiums have been established in many areas to enable people to access information stored in more than one library. With a computer system, it is possible to inquire on a terminal in one library about specific books or references that are available in other libraries cooperating in the library consortium. Within two to four days, if the reference is available, any books not available in the local library can be received as a loan from another library.

e. *Computer information banks or databases:* Many organizations subscribe to computerized information databases available within a particular profession or field.

In the company library, a terminal is available to access the database to obtain abstracts of research studies, court cases, or other materials available through the database (see Chapters 1 and 4).

EXAMPLE: The Information Bank is the actual name of one such data bank that is one of the most comprehensive current affairs data banks in the world. The system's database includes several million items accumulated from more than 80 publications.

f. *Library micrographics centers:* Libraries have research studies, dissertations, and other references stored on microfiche and microfilm that may be accessed on the premises only. If copies are needed of particular pages or charts, a reader-printer may be used to produce copies needed. Other types of audiovisual materials may be available on cassettes and videotapes, too, such as a copy of a speech made by the president of a university.

2. *In-House Research Services:* Within the organization, several in-house research services may be maintained. Each of these research operations would provide personal as well as telephone service in locating factual information.

   a. *Research department:* Organizations that are heavily involved in researching information find it valuable to form a research department to assist office professionals in finding needed information.

   b. *Computer information banks:* As mentioned in Section B-1-e, many organizations subscribe to information services within a particular profession or field. Terminals connect the company to the source of the information so that individuals can access abstracts of information needed or copies of entire documents.

   c. *Business archives:* An *archive* is a collection of business documents of historical value. Businesses, governments, and universities have established archives so that researchers will be able to access information that is protected through a high level of security. The research would need to be done on premises since the research materials are so valuable.

3. *Business and Professional Associations:* Specific information relating to a particular profession may be available through a recognized professional organization. Many of these associations have Web sites on the Internet. These sites typically contain information such as the history of the association, membership, publications available, and general information about the profession. Contacting the association by e-mailing, telephoning, or writing can yield additional information to help with your research. By examining the publications of the professional group, you may update your knowledge of current happenings in the field. Such sources are particularly helpful if you are researching technological developments in the field.

4. *Community Organizations:* Business information may be obtained from organizations such as the local chamber of commerce or the city government. Service clubs, such as Rotary, Kiwanis, or Lions, may also be able to help, depending on the subject of the research. In preparing a speech to be given before a community organization, the executive may ask the secretary to research the group to find out more about the audience. Many community organizations are developing Web sites that are helpful in providing general information about the organization, community, or geographic area. Often, links to Web sites of other organizations within the area are provided.

C. Reference Materials

Depending on the topic being researched, many different types of reference materials are available for researching various types of business information. The following list represents samples of reference materials now available. However, the sources that are included are considered major ones that the professional secretary should be aware of and be able to use in conducting needed research.

1. *Almanacs:* An almanac is a book or publication, usually published on an annual basis, that includes factual information about international and national events of the year.

   Almanac of American Politics (Macmillan Publishing Company)

   The Guinness Book of World Records, published annually (Bantam Books)

   The Guinness World Records 2000, Millennium Edition, (Guinness World Records, Publisher)

   Information Please Almanac, Atlas and Yearbook, published annually (Simon & Schuster, Inc., New York)

   The Official Associated Press Almanac (Hammond Almanac, Inc.)

   Reader's Digest Almanac and Yearbook (W.W. Norton & Company, Inc.)

   Time Almanac 1999 (Information Please LLC, Boston, Massachusetts)

   The World Almanac and Book of Facts, published annually (Newspaper Enterprise Association, Inc., New York)

2. *Biographical Indexes and Directories:* These publications highlight the achievements of noted individuals who contributed to their professions, to government, or the country.

   Biography Index, published annually (The H.W. Wilson Company, New York)

   Webster's Biographical Dictionary (G.&C. Merriam Company, Springfield, Massachusetts)

   Who Was Who in America, published annually (Marquis Who's Who, Inc., Chicago)

   Who's Who, published annually (St. Martin's Press, Inc., New York)

   Who's Who in America, published biennially (Marquis Who's Who, Inc., Chicago)

3. *Book and Periodical Directories:* Directories provide listings of companies, associations, organizations, individuals, or products in a systematic way—alphabetically, geographically, or in subject arrangements.

   N.W. Ayer and Son's Directory of Newspapers and Publications, published annually (N.W. Ayer & Son, Inc., Philadelphia): *Ayer's* lists over 22,000 newspapers and periodicals published in the United States. The listing includes name, place of publication, frequency of publication, circulation, price, and editor's name. There is both a geographic and an alphabetical listing.

   Business Periodicals Index, published annually (The H.W. Wilson Company, New York): This index has a subject index to over 200 periodicals in finance, insurance, banking, accounting, marketing, data processing, and other business-related subjects.

   Cumulative Book Index, published monthly (The H.W. Wilson Company, New York): This index lists most of the books published in the United States from 1928

to date. The books are arranged by author, title, and subject under one alphabetical listing.

Index to Legal Periodicals, published annually (The H.W. Wilson Company, New York): This index includes references to articles on various topics of law and law-related matters. Both subject and specific case name indexes to articles are given.

Reader's Guide to Periodical Literature, published semimonthly (The H.W. Wilson Company, New York): The *Reader's Guide* is a subject and author index to several hundred popular, nontechnical magazines. That is accumulated into annual volumes.

Other book and periodical directories include the following:

Book Review Digest, published monthly (The H.W. Wilson Company, New York)

Books in Print, published annually (R.R. Bowker Company, New York)

McRae's Blue Book, a buying guide published annually (McRae's Blue Book Company)

4. *Business, Governmental, and Professional Directories and Publications:* In addition to book and periodical directories, listings of members of professional associations, governmental directories and records, and business directories and publications are extremely helpful in locating appropriate sources of information.

   a. *Professional associations:*

   American Dental Directory, published annually (American Dental Association, Chicago)

   American Medical Directory, published annually (American Medical Association, Chicago)

   b. *Governmental directories and records:*

   The Congressional Information Service Index to Publications (Congressional Information Service, Washington, D.C.): This monthly index to congressional publications is indexed by subject, witness names, popular law names, report numbers, document numbers, and bill and public law numbers.

   The Congressional Record (U.S. Government Printing Office, Washington, D.C.): *The Congressional Record* is a daily report of the Senate and the House activity and debates. In this publication, the bill debate transcripts are published.

   Congressional Index (Commerce Clearing House): This index is published weekly and presents all the legislation covered by Congress during that week.

   The Federal Register, published daily, Monday–Friday (U.S. Government Printing Office, Washington, D.C.): All regulations and notices issued by federal agencies are published in the *Federal Register.* This includes Presidential Proclamations and Executive Orders.

   United States Government Manual, published annually (Office of the Federal Register, General Services Administration, Washington, D.C.): This manual is a directory of governmental agencies and key personnel with addresses and telephone numbers.

c. *Business directories and publications:*

Directory of Directories (Gale Research Company, Detroit)

Standard & Poor's Register of Corporations, Directors, and Executives, United States and Canada (Standard and Poor's, New York): Directors and executives of nearly 35,000 corporations are listed in the S&P Register. Full biographical information is given for all corporations and their executives. The index is arranged alphabetically by corporate name and executive's name.

Thomas' Register of American Manufacturers, 12 volumes (Thomas Publication Company, New York): The *Thomas' Register* features a listing of over 100,000 manufacturers, giving product lines and addresses. Information is listed by manufacturer's name and product(s) and serves as a buyer's guide.

5. *Business Newspapers and Periodicals:* Current business information is available in numerous newspapers and periodicals published in the United States. Here is an annotated list of some of the more important ones.

Barron's, published weekly (Dow Jones & Company, Inc., New York): National business and financial news is presented in articles on investments, industries, trends, and other business topics; stock and bond prices are included.

Business Week, published weekly (McGraw-Hill Book Company, New York): Articles on specialized business topics present the important business indicators, the investment outlook, and current business developments.

ComputerWorld, published weekly (ComputerWorld, Inc.): The publication includes business-focused technology news and analyses for information technology leaders.

Dun's Review and Modern Industry, published monthly (Dun and Bradstreet, Inc., New York): This publication presents reports on industrial development statistics.

Forbes, published semimonthly (Forbes, Inc., New York): The first issue each year contains the "Annual Report on American Industry." The publication includes articles on business administration, new developments in business, and business outlooks.

Fortune, published monthly (Time, Inc., New York): This publication is known for the famous *Fortune* lists of the largest corporations (the Fortune 500, the Fortune 100). Recently, *Fortune* has included special sections on business automation, communications, and computer technology two or three times per year.

Harvard Business Review, published bimonthly (Graduate School of Business Administration, Harvard University, Boston): This periodical is one of the outstanding business administration journals published today. The articles are written primarily for the practitioner in the field.

InfoWorld, published weekly (InfoWorld Media Group, Inc.): The publication includes articles about current developments in information management and technology to help the business user function with personal computers and other information processing technology.

The New York Times, published daily (The New York Times Company, Inc., New York): This newspaper is very well known for its current business news and coverage of daily business events.

Wall Street Journal, published daily, Monday–Friday (Dow Jones & Company, Inc., New York): This newspaper features business and financial news, articles on corporate strategies and events, and stock and bond prices on the various exchanges.

6. *Dictionaries:* As reference books, dictionaries serve a very important function. Secretaries find dictionaries helpful in finding the correct spelling of a term, the correct meaning and usage of a word or expression, and the correct syllabication of the word. Unabridged dictionaries can be especially helpful since they are the most complete dictionaries and not based on a larger work. Some professional dictionaries include the terminology most pertinent to that profession. Here are some of the more commonly used dictionaries:

The American Heritage Dictionary of the English Language (Houghton-Mifflin Publishing Co., Inc., Boston)

Black's Law Dictionary (Charles Scribner's Sons, New York)

The Dictionary of Occupational Titles (U.S. Government Printing Office, Washington, D.C.)

Encyclopedic Dictionary of English Usage (Prentice Hall, Upper Saddle River, New Jersey)

Funk & Wagnalls (Funk & Wagnalls, New York)

Oxford English Dictionary (Oxford University Press, Oxford, England)

The Random House College Dictionary (Random House, New York)

Merriam-Webster's Collegiate Dictionary (Merriam Webster, Springfield, Massachusetts)

Webster's New Geographical Dictionary (Merriam Webster, Springfield, Massachusetts)

Webster's New International Dictionary, Unabridged (Merriam Webster, Springfield, Massachusetts)

Webster's New World Dictionary of the American Language (Simon & Schuster, New York)

Other professional dictionaries include the following:

The Dictionary of Finance and Investment Terms (Barron's, Dow Jones & Company, Inc., New York)

The Dictionary of Computers (McGraw-Hill, New York)

Foreign-language dictionaries are particularly helpful to the administrative assistant or secretary who must translate correspondence and reports or look up foreign words and phrases. Such dictionaries list words or phrases in two ways, for example, French to English in one section and English to French in another section.

7. *Encyclopedias:* As a general rule, encyclopedias are designed as general reference books on a wide variety of topics. Some encyclopedias are designed to provide very detailed information, while others may be directed toward children's use or people within a particular profession. Many encyclopedias have annual supplements available that describe key highlights and events of the past year. Here is a sample list of some encyclopedias available today:

The Encyclopedia Americana (Grolier, Danbury, Connecticut)

Encyclopedia of Associations (Gale Research Company, Detroit)

Encyclopaedia Brittanica (Encyclopaedia Brittanica, Brittanica Centre, Chicago)

Funk & Wagnalls New Encyclopedia (Funk & Wagnalls, New York)

Random House Encyclopedia (Random House, New York)

The World Book Encyclopedia (World Book, Chicago)

8. *Etiquette References:* Current references on etiquette focus on conventional requirements of social behavior and conduct as established for specific occasions. Some of the more well-known references are the following:

Post, Peggy, *Emily Post's Etiquette,* 16th ed., HarperCollins Publishers, New York, 1997.

Post, Peggy, *Everyday Etiquette,* Harper Paperbacks, New York, 1999.

Tuckerman, Nancy, and Nancy Dunnan, *The Amy Vanderbilt Complete Book of Etiquette,* Doubleday, New York, 1995.

9. *Financial Services:* Subscription services are available to the financial community that will give the latest information on stock prices, industry developments, legislative changes affecting organizations, and other pertinent business and financial information.

Babson's Reports, Inc.: *Investment and Barometer Letter, Washington Forecast Letter*

The Conference Board, Inc.: *Business Scoreboard, Road Maps of Industry Focus, Conference Board Record*

Moody's Investors Service, New York:

Moody's Bank and Finance Manual: Biweekly news reports for banking institutions, insurance, investment, mortgage, real estate, and finance companies.

Moody's Bond Record: Monthly publication that covers over 15,000 bond issues and gives the user information on market position and statistical background.

Moody's Bond Survey: Weekly publication that reports on the bond market and comments on individual issues.

Moody's Dividend Record: A biweekly publication that covers 9,500 issues; each January the *Annual Dividend Record* is also published.

Moody's Handbook of Widely Held Common Stocks: Quarterly publication of summary reports on selected common stocks, including dividends and earnings.

Moody's Industrial Manual: A biweekly report that provides background and financial information on industrial firms in the United States and abroad which are listed on the New York and American Stock Exchanges.

Other manuals or surveys published by Moody's include the following:

Moody's Municipal and Government Manual

Moody's Public Utility Manual

Moody's OTC Industrial Manual

Moody's Stock Survey

Moody's Transportation Manual

Standard & Poor's Corporation, New York:

Standard and Poor's Fixed Income Investor: This quarterly publication presents a basic analysis of 69 major domestic companies.

Standard and Poor's Industry Surveys: This quarterly publication presents a basic analysis of 69 major domestic companies.

Standard and Poor's Stock Reports, American Stock Exchange: This publication is a quarterly service that reports on over 1,200 companies listed on the American Stock Exchange. Income statements and balance sheets are included with an analysis of earnings reports.

Standard and Poor's Stock Reports, New York Stock Exchange: This is a quarterly publication that reports on over 1,400 companies listed on the New York Stock Exchange. Information on sales, earnings, and potential dividends is included, as well as projections on the overall long-term outlook.

Standard and Poor's Stock Reports, Over the Counter: This quarterly service reports on companies' over-the-counter transactions and those listed on regional stock exchanges. The report includes income statement, balance sheet items, earnings reports and information on dividends, price ranges, and capitalization.

10. *Mailing and Shipping Publications:* Changes in postage rates, directions for using ZIP codes, and shipping information will be applied more easily if some of the following references are used:

Address Abbreviations, U.S. Postal Service Publication No. 59 (or more recent edition), U.S. Government Printing Office, Washington, D.C.

Bullinger's Postal and Shippers Guide for the United States and Canada, Bullinger's Guides, Inc., Westwood, New Jersey (published annually).

Directory of International Mail, U.S. Government Printing Office, Washington, D.C. (latest edition).

Dun & Bradstreet Exporters' Encyclopedia, Dun & Bradstreet, Inc., New York (latest edition).

National ZIP Code and Post Office Directory, U.S. Government Printing Office, Washington, D.C. (current edition)

Postal Service Manual, U.S. Government Printing Office, Washington, D.C. (current edition)

11. *Newsletters and Reports:* Some organizations publish weekly or monthly newsletters or reports that present relevant, up-to-date information on new developments in particular business-related areas. Professional organizations often publish newsletters for members.

Kiplinger Washington Letter, published weekly (Kiplinger Washington Editors, Inc., Washington, D.C.): A letter service that covers developments and trends in business and government.

John Naisbitt's Trend Letter, published twice monthly (John Naisbitt's Trend Letter, Inc., Washington, D.C.): An authoritative report on forces transforming the economy, business, technology, society, and the world from 1982 to present.

12. *Newspaper Indexes:* To make it easier for people to research particular topics or subjects that appear in the daily newspapers, some of the larger newspapers in the country have established a printed index to the newspaper issues.

The New York Times Index, published semimonthly (New York Times, New York): This index provides a subject index valuable to researchers in many fields of study.

Included in the index are brief abstracts of articles found in the *New York Times* newspaper, along with date, column number, and page where the entire article may be found.

Wall Street Journal Index (Dow Jones & Company, Inc., New York): This published index includes reference to every news item published in the *Wall Street Journal.*

13. *Office Administration Reference Books:* The professional secretary will find a wide variety of reference books dealing with office administration extremely helpful. Here is a representative list of some of the reference books available:

Branchaw, Bernadine P., and Joel P. Bowman, *Delmar Reference Manual,* Delmar Publishers Inc., Albany, 1994.

Clark, James L., and Lyn Clark, *How 8: A Handbook for Office Workers,* 8th ed., South-Western College Publishing, Cincinnati, 1998.

House, Clifford R., and Kathie S. Sigler, *Multimedia Reference for Writers,* South-Western Publishing Company, Cincinnati (latest edition).

House, Clifford R., and Kathie S. Sigler, *Reference Manual for the Office,* South-Western Publishing Company, Cincinnati (latest edition).

Jaderstrom, Susan, Leonard Kruk, and Joanne Miller, *Professional Secretaries International® Complete Office Handbook,* Random House, Inc., New York (latest edition).

Sabin, William A., *The Gregg Reference Manual,* McGraw-Hill Book Company, Inc., New York (latest edition).

Visaggi, John, ed., *Office Reference Guide,* Dictation Disc Company, New York (latest edition).

14. *Parliamentary Procedures:* The appropriate conduct of business meetings will depend on the application of parliamentary procedures by the people involved. Here are two references that serve as excellent guides:

Jones, O. Garfield, *Parliamentary Procedure at a Glance,* Hawthorn Books, Inc., New York (latest edition).

Robert's Rules of Order Newly Revised, Scott, Foresman and Company, Chicago (latest edition).

15. *Quotations:* The professional secretary who assists the executive in preparing speeches or other presentations may find these books of quotations helpful:

Bartlett, John, and Justin Kaplan, ed. *Bartlett's Familiar Quotations,* 16th ed., Little-Brown, New York, 1992.

Knowles, Elizabeth, ed. *The Oxford Dictionary of Quotations,* Oxford University Press, Oxford, England, 1999.

The Princeton Language Institute, *21st Century Dictionary of Quotations,* The Philip Leif Group, Inc., New York, 1993.

16. *Thesauri:* A *thesaurus* is a lexicon (dictionary) of similar words or information that focuses on synonyms and antonyms. Here are some thesauri that are used frequently:

Roget's International Thesaurus, Thomas Y. Crowell Co., New York.

Roget's Thesaurus in Dictionary Form, Putnam Berkley Publishing Company, New York.

Roget's II: The New Thesaurus, Houghton-Mifflin, Boston.

Webster's Collegiate Thesaurus, Merriam Webster, Springfield, Massachusetts.

Webster's New World Thesaurus, Simon & Schuster, New York.

17. *Travel and Transportation Guides:* Current editions of travel and transportation guides, atlases, and road maps are available through bookstores, automobile associations or motor clubs, and oil companies. Here are some of the most commonly used travel and transportation guides:

Business Traveler's Road Atlas and Guide to Major Cities, Rand McNally, Chicago (latest edition).

Commercial Atlas & Marketing Guide, Rand McNally & Company, Chicago.

Hotel & Motel Red Book, American Hotel and Motel Association, New York (published annually).

The New York Times Atlas of the World, The New York Times Company, Inc., New York.

The Official Airline Guide Electronic Edition Travel Service, Official Airline Guides, Oak Brook, Illinois.

The Official Airline Guide, North American, Worldwide, and International Editions, Official Airline Guides, Oak Brook, Illinois.

The Official Airline Guide Travel Planner Hotel & Motel Red Books, North America, Europe, Pacific Asia, Official Airline Guides, Oak Brook, Illinois (published quarterly).

The Official Airline Guide Worldwide Cruise and Shipline Guide, Official Airline Guides, Oak Brook, Illinois (published six times per year).

Rand McNally Easy-to-Read Travel Atlas 2000, Rand McNally & Company, Chicago.

In addition, road maps are available from various automobile associations, motor clubs, and oil companies. Internet travel sites may also be accessed for road maps and travel information.

18. *Word Books:* The availability of at least one word book is very important to the secretary who operates a typewriter, a computer with word processing software, or dictation-transcription equipment. A word book presents an alphabetical list of the most frequently used words and indicates the spelling, syllabication, and recommended hyphenation.

Perry, Devern J., *Word Division and Spelling Manual,* South-Western Publishing Company, Cincinnati, 1995.

Zoubek, Charles E., and G. A. Condon, *20,000 Words,* McGraw-Hill Book Company, New York (latest edition).

D. Evaluating Information References

In researching specific topics or subjects, the office professional needs to evaluate the content as well as the source for that information in judging whether its use will be beneficial to the work in progress. Of particular concern is information found on the World Wide Web that may not have passed editorial scrutiny as other types of publications (periodicals or books) do before printing. The following guidelines can be applied to information gained through research to help the office professional determine its value to a particular writing project.

1. *The Author or Institution:* Each reference should be examined to see how the material originated—who the author is or the institution where the information was gathered. Some of the types of information to look for include the following:

   a. Biographical information about the author

   b. Information about the institution where the research or development took place

   c. Other sources of information or bibliographies that include the author's name or the institution's name

2. *Currency of Information:* Another factor to consider is the recency of the information. Current, up-to-date information will typically have the most relevance to the topic unless the research is for historical purposes. Here are some features of the publication that should be considered:

   a. Date of publication or date on the Web page indicating when the page was created or updated

   b. Date of last update of information and indication of frequency of updates

   c. Outdated information included in the material

3. *The Intended Audience:* The researcher should consider the intended audience when examining an informational reference. The reference may be designed for a specific group of people, such as one of the following:

   a. The general public

   b. Researchers

   c. Business practitioners

   d. Others, such as children or parents

4. *Accurate and Objective Content:* The purpose of the information may be to inform, persuade, or entertain the audience. The content should be examined carefully to determine whether any of the following are present:

   a. Biases present in the content

   b. Brief overview or in-depth analysis

   c. Properly cited facts and statistics

   d. Clearly stated opinions

   e. Purpose of the information

The content of a report or speech will always be strengthened by the inclusion of information gathered from a variety of credible sources. Information is a valuable resource when used carefully to support creative ideas and developments. The office professional often has the important responsibility for collecting information from a variety of sources, ensuring that the originators of that information are properly cited within the writing, and assisting the executive in preparing business documents that enhance the image of the organization.

Review Questions

Directions: Select the best answer from the four alternatives. Write your answer in the blank to the left of the number.

_____ 1. In conducting meaningful research, an administrative assistant must first know

   a. all possible sources of information.
   b. the purpose of the research.
   c. the names of individuals you want to contact for interviews.
   d. the types of records you should access.

_____ 2. Which one of the following represents information that needs to be included on a bibliography card?

   a. The researcher's name
   b. Publisher of the article
   c. Date of first access to the article
   d. Additional references that might be helpful

_____ 3. Copying a published article that is stored on microfiche requires that the researcher

   a. observe copyright laws carefully.
   b. return the microfiche to its jacket as soon as possible.
   c. use a microfiche reader to produce any printed copies needed.
   d. obtain permission before making a copy of the article.

_____ 4. Silverstone, your manager, has asked you to research the ways in which the computer is being used by executives within the company when preparing business materials for speeches and other presentations. You set up an appointment with Symonds, who is the president of the company, to ask about his use of graphics in preparing business presentations. Which one of the following is the most important for you to do prior to your appointment with Symonds?

   a. Confirm the appointment with Symonds' secretary as soon as possible.
   b. Develop a short synopsis of your research results thus far to share with Symonds.
   c. Send Symonds a copy of the questions you wish to ask during the interview.
   d. Check with Silverstone again to be sure that Symonds is one of the people you should contact.

_____ 5. The library classification system that is based on the premise that all knowledge can be classified into ten primary groups is known as the

   a. Library of Congress classification system.
   b. Dewey Decimal system.
   c. interlibrary loan system.
   d. in-house research service.

———————   **6.** Allen's responsibility as a paralegal for Bailey & Swift, a Chicago law firm, is to research past court cases to obtain information relative to present cases for the preparation of briefs and other legal documents. A subscription service that is available for this purpose is referred to as a/an

    a. in-house research service.
    b. computer information bank.
    c. business archive.
    d. records center.

———————   **7.** Businesses, government agencies, and universities have organized business documents that have historical value into

    a. in-house research services.
    b. computer information banks.
    c. active records storage.
    d. archives.

———————   **8.** If you are looking for a new book titled *Business Technology for the Year 2010* and you know the publisher but not the author, which one of the following sources would help you locate the name of the author?

    a. *Ayer's Directory of Publications*
    b. *Webster's Biographical Dictionary*
    c. *Books in Print*
    d. *Reader's Guide to Periodical Literature*

———————   **9.** A listing of the current officers of U.S. corporations would be found in a

    a. periodical directory.
    b. governmental directory.
    c. book directory.
    d. business directory.

———————   **10.** A listing of doctors currently practicing in San Diego, California, would be found in a

    a. business directory.
    b. professional association directory.
    c. biographical directory.
    d. book directory.

———————   **11.** If you were researching companies involved in specific types of manufacturing, you would find the following reference the most helpful:

    a. *The Thomas' Register*
    b. *Ayer's Directory of Publications*
    c. *Moody's Handbook of Widely Held Common Stocks*
    d. *Forbes*

12. Which one of the following would serve as a guide to weekly developments and trends in business and government?

    a. *Reader's Guide to Periodical Literature*
    b. *Roget's International Thesaurus*
    c. *The New York Times*
    d. *Kiplinger Washington Letter*

13. You are looking for an article about media fusion technology that was published in *The New York Times* last spring but do not know the exact date. Which one of the following will help you find the date of publication?

    a. *Kiplinger Washington Letter*
    b. *The New York Times Index*
    c. *John Naisbitt's Trend Letter*
    d. *Standard & Poor's Stock Reports*

14. One of the following references is essential to have on hand so that the use of parliamentary procedure for conducting a meeting can be checked if there are points of order during a meeting:

    a. The U.S. Government Manual
    b. *Robert's Rules of Order*
    c. *Barron's*
    d. *Emily Post's Etiquette*

15. A lexicon of similar words that focuses on synonyms and antonyms is a

    a. directory.
    b. dictionary.
    c. word book.
    d. thesaurus.

16. The content of a source of information found on the World Wide Web and the Internet needs to be evaluated because

    a. the reference may not have faced editorial review as evident with other types of publications.
    b. the general public usually asks for the results of such an evaluation.
    c. the user may be searching for creative references.
    d. originators of the information may be cited in a number of different sources.

Solutions

Answer	Refer to:
1. (b)	[A-1]
2. (b)	[A-5-a]
3. (a)	[A-5-c]
4. (c)	[A-5-d]
5. (b)	[B-1-a(1)]
6. (b)	[B-1-e]
7. (d)	[B-2-c]
8. (c)	[C-3]
9. (d)	[C-4]
10. (b)	[C-4-a]
11. (a)	[C-4-c]
12. (d)	[C-11]
13. (b)	[C-11]
14. (b)	[C-14]
15. (d)	[C-16]
16. (a)	[D]

CHAPTER 11

Conferences and Meetings

OVERVIEW

Many executives are involved in planning, organizing, and/or attending company-sponsored conferences or association-sponsored conventions. Often, executives agree to serve as members of planning committees or as speakers for sessions at such conferences. The administrative professional may become involved in ensuring that appropriate procedures are followed to prepare for the executive's leadership and participation at such conferences or conventions.

Managers tend to spend more than one-third of their time in meetings each week, according to some estimates, and in many organizations as much as 15 percent of personnel budgets are spent directly on meetings. Face-to-face meetings are still seen as the number-one form of communication within the office. Meetings are needed to act on business activities that affect the entire organization. In this chapter, the methods used to organize business meetings are presented: informal (committee and office) meetings and formal (in-house, conferencing, and out-of-town) meetings.

Knowing the correct procedures for setting up meetings is especially important for the administrative professional. Arrangements for meeting rooms, materials, and participants must be taken care of efficiently for the meeting to be a success. The chapter ends with a brief discussion of parliamentary procedure and its importance in conducting effective meetings.

KEY TERMS

Ad hoc committee	Informal meeting	Quorum
Agenda	In-house meeting	Resolution
Audioconference	Main motion	Standing committee
Computer conference	Minutes	Storyboard
Conference	Motion	Subsidiary motion
Data conference	Parliamentary procedure	Teleconference
Electronic blackboard	Petition	Transparency
Electronic slides	Presentation software	Unclassified motion
Formal meeting	Privileged motion	Videoconference
Incidental motion		

A. Conferences

A *conference* is defined as a formal meeting of a group of people with a common purpose. Types of conferences include company-sponsored conferences and association-sponsored conventions. In this context, the two terms *conference* and *convention* are treated as synonymous terms.

1. *Types of Conferences:* Conferences or conventions are sponsored by individual companies or by community, business, or professional associations.

   a. *Company-sponsored conferences:* Conferences are sometimes sponsored by companies for the purpose of discussing timely topics or business events. Such a conference might be sponsored only for company personnel to bring them up to date on new products, services, or research developments within the industry. Companies may also sponsor conferences for customers, stockholders, suppliers, or the community for similar purposes.

      (1) *Location:* The conference may be held on company premises or at a nearby hotel or convention center. Usually, the company prefers to have the conference at or near the corporate headquarters to facilitate the display of new products, the participation of company personnel, and training sessions that might be included.

      (2) *Leadership of the conference:* Depending on the basic purpose of the conference, an executive within the company with responsibilities related to the conference may be appointed as the leader (chairperson). A committee consisting of representatives of the various divisions or departments of the company may be appointed to assist in planning the event. Secretarial support is extremely important to assist with the many arrangements that must be handled before, during, and after the conference.

      (3) *Travel to and from conferences:* Since some of the participants may be coming from other parts of the country or world, travel arrangements will need to be carefully coordinated. If the conference is only for company personnel, the plan may be to obtain all travel reservations through the corporate travel department or through a local travel agency. Travel arrangements for others who have been invited to participate may also be coordinated so that appropriate local reservations can be made to facilitate their participation. If travel expenses are to be paid, procedures for reimbursement should be included.

      (4) *Supportive services:* Consultation will be necessary with the reprographics or in-house printing department to be sure that program booklets, handout materials, and other materials to be printed will be able to be produced in house. In addition, an inquiry service might be established so that callers inquiring about the conference will receive all pertinent information from an administrative assistant or secretary who is assigned this responsibility.

   b. *Association-sponsored conventions:* Numerous annual conventions are sponsored by professional business associations primarily for the benefit of the members of the association.

   EXAMPLES:

   Hixson is the administrative manager for AJAX Company and is a member of the Administrative Management Society. In addition to participating in local chapter events, Hixson attends the national convention each year, which is held in different locations throughout the country.

*Canfield, an executive secretary, is an active member of the International Associ-
ation of Administrative Professionals (IAAP). As the secretary of the local chapter, Canfield will be a delegate to the IAAP International Convention in July.*

(1) *Location:* Conventions are usually held in hotels and civic centers where adequate meeting room space, hotel rooms, and public transportation are available. Trade shows and exhibits are another feature of conventions that help
participants become more up to date in their field.

(2) *Leadership of the convention:* Such a convention is planned by a committee
from the professional association sponsoring the convention. Normally, a vice
president is in charge of programs and serves as the chair of the program planning committee. Many times, a local committee, with association members
from the geographic area where the convention will be held, assists with local arrangements.

  (a) The administrative professional or secretary for an executive who is in
  charge of a professional convention will typically be involved in assisting with the arrangements for the convention.

  (b) Correspondence about the convention and arrangements for attending
  will also be handled by the administrative assistant or secretary if the executive plans to attend the convention.

(3) *Travel to and from conventions:* Executive travel to and from the convention
will need to be handled through the travel department or the travel agency
handling company business. The secretary who coordinates the travel
arrangements with the agency will need to be sure that dates, times, flights, or
other travel information are verified with business travelers before final
arrangements are completed.

(4) *Supportive services:* A file folder should be established for any materials relating to the convention. If the executive is in charge of the convention, a series of folders will need to be prepared to file all the correspondence and related materials (by topic) that will accumulate in the planning stages.

2. *Planning a Convention:* Attending a convention as a participant is relatively easy, but
planning a convention for others to attend is time consuming and requires long hours
of detailed preparation. The success of the convention depends greatly on the way
procedures are handled before, during, and after the convention.

  a. *Before the convention:* Typical activities that need to be accomplished in the pre-
  convention time period include the following:

  (1) Selecting the site for the convention unless this has already been done by the
  association

  (2) Establishing the convention budget

  (3) Reserving adequate meeting-room space in a hotel or convention center and
  making sure that appropriate audiovisual and computer equipment will be
  available

  (4) Meeting with the convention services manager of the hotel or convention
  center to review arrangements for the convention

  (5) Making preliminary meal arrangements with hotel or convention center

(6) Preparing preregistration materials to mail out to participants, including preliminary program, registration information, and fee schedule

(7) Contacting convention speakers by telephone, e-mail, fax, and/or letter confirming speaking arrangements

(8) Contacting exhibitors for the trade show if one is scheduled

(9) Preparing a printed convention program and handbook

(10) Monitoring the publication of the proceedings of the convention if the proceedings are distributed as part of the registration packet at the convention

(11) Preparing publicity for local newspapers, radio, and television coverage

(12) Arranging special tours for convention participants, families, and guests

(13) Reserving a block of hotel rooms for convention participants

(14) Arranging hospitality rooms and other courtesies for the participants

(15) Arranging for audiovisual or video equipment and technicians for recording or taping convention sessions

(16) Arranging for computer equipment and technicians to assist with the installation and monitoring of the equipment

(17) Contacting agents for any special entertainment that will be scheduled during the convention and arranging for performances

(18) Arranging ground transportation (buses, limousines, vans) to transport participants from airport to hotel or convention site

b. *During the convention: Other activities need to be accomplished during the convention, including the following:*

(1) Setting up and supervising the convention registration and information area

(2) Checking in all exhibitors and issuing exhibit spaces assigned

(3) Handing out special packets of convention materials to guest speakers as they arrive

(4) Making arrangements for speakers to be met at the airport and transported to the convention site

(5) Setting up an information desk for distributing information about tours, community, restaurants, and so on

(6) Checking to see that presentation equipment (audiovisual, computer) is in place prior to each convention session

(7) Presenting special folders to hosts, hostesses, chairs, and recorders for the various convention sessions

(8) Finalizing the number of people attending each meal function

c. *After the convention: Once the convention is over, the following types of activities will require administrative professional's time:*

(1) Monitoring the return of all presentation equipment (audiovisual, computer) used for the convention

(2) Preparing checks for honorariums and expenses for guest speakers

(3) Preparing a financial statement for the entire convention

(4) Sending thank-you letters to all speakers, hotel and/or convention personnel, and participants (if the number of participants is rather small)

(5) Sending thank-you letters/memos to all who assisted with the convention: registration workers, hosts, hostesses, chairs for sessions, recorders, members of the planning committee, and so on

(6) Monitoring the publication of the proceedings of the convention if the proceedings are distributed after the convention

(7) Creating a reference file of all procedures used and suggestions for the next convention

The items listed under A-2-a, A-2-b, and A-2-c are not listed in any particular order of priority. Within each category, priorities would need to be established and deadlines set for the activities required when actually planning and carrying through a convention program.

B. Meetings

A recent estimate indicates that managers spend more than one-third of their time in meetings each week and that many organizations spend up to 15 percent of their personnel budgets directly on meetings. With technology and change enveloping the office, it has become even more important in recent years that people communicate with one another in small and large groups to meet the objectives of the organization. The typical business cannot survive without meetings.

1. *Planning and Organizing Meetings:* Meetings tend to be organized either as *informal meetings* or as *formal meetings.*

   a. *Informal meetings:* Usually, an informal meeting involves an informal discussion by a small number of people (two to four) to discuss a particular business matter. Normally, a specific business matter brings these people together for the meeting. The meeting is scheduled in one person's office or in a nearby conference room.

      (1) *Committee meeting:* The people who are meeting may be members of a committee and must meet to further the work of the committee.

      EXAMPLE: The Computer Advisory Committee will meet on Thursday from 9 A.M. to 10:30 A.M. to discuss the utilization of computers for administrative support.

      (a) *Standing committee:* Members of a standing committee are appointed for a definite term (e.g., one or two years). The standing committee has definite objectives assigned for which it is responsible during the term.

      EXAMPLE: Bryson serves on the Program Committee for the Maywood Business Women's Association. As a member of this committee, she is working with three other members to establish a schedule of programs for this year's monthly meetings.

      (b) *Ad hoc committee:* An ad hoc committee is formed to investigate a particular event or problem that has occurred within the organization. The committee has a temporary appointment and will serve until a report is prepared and presented to the standing committee or management.

      EXAMPLE: The ABC Company has a standing committee, the Computer Selection Committee, whose primary goal is to select a new computer network for the company. An ad hoc committee has been formed that will investigate how the major departments in the company plan to use computers and various software programs in their operations. The ad hoc committee will report back to the Computer Selections Committee.

(2) *Office meeting:* Sometimes, problems arise in the day-to-day operation of an office that require two or three people to meet to discuss the problems. A department manager may find it necessary or helpful to ask two or three employees to come into his or her office to discuss some business matter.

b. *Formal meetings:* A more formal meeting would definitely have to be planned in advance so that participants in the meeting would be aware of the meeting and know the agenda items that would be presented and discussed at the meeting. Formal meetings are usually held in conference rooms or special meeting rooms. All types of conferencing (teleconference, videoconference, computer conference, or data conference) can be arranged through a national or an international communications network, depending on the needs of the organization. People who are separated by great distances still can participate in business discussions and decision making.

(1) *In-house meeting:* A formal meeting might be held in-house on company premises. A meeting or conference room would be reserved, and all people who need to attend would be notified in advance. The purpose of the meeting is typically of a more formal nature.

EXAMPLES:

The Board of Directors is planning to hold its next meeting on Wednesday, May 15, from 3 P.M. to 5 P.M. in the Sullivan Room.

The XYZ Corporation is inviting all of the regional marketing representatives to attend a one-day sales meeting at the corporate headquarters on April 4.

The in-house meeting may be for company personnel only, or it may be for outside professionals, depending on the purpose of the meeting.

EXAMPLE: The XYZ Corporation is planning to have a one-day office automation seminar for administrative office professionals from the northern Ohio region. The purpose is to demonstrate the office automation systems that XYZ Corporation is presently marketing.

(2) *Teleconference:* A formal teleconference might be set up so that several business executives from different geographic locations can "meet" through telephone communications. Instead of having to travel to a particular site for the meeting, the conferees can "meet" by speaking with the others directly from their own offices. Teleconferences can be enhanced with group communication software (e.g., e-mail, e-calendar, and electronic blackboard). *Audioconference* is another term for *teleconference.*

EXAMPLE: Stevens made an appointment with Richards (New York office), Whitley and Jackson (Atlanta office), and Clifton (San Francisco office) for a teleconference next Monday morning from 10 A.M. to 11 A.M. She wants to share some marketing strategies that the company is trying to promote. Stevens will be able to communicate through the telephone network and an electronic blackboard so that the statistics and graphs she presents from her location will be transmitted to each of the other three locations. In this way, the other participants will receive all pertinent information and find it easier to view the presentation and participate in the ensuing discussion. The participants (Stevens, Richards, Whitley, Jackson, and Clifton) can participate by using the telephone handset or speaker phone. Whitley and Jackson could meet at one location in Atlanta and participate through the telephone speaker phone.

(3) *Videoconference:* Another type of formal conference is the videoconference, which is really an extension of teleconferencing. Again, an appointment must be set up for the scheduled date and time. Participants are able to view one another on closed-circuit television. Slow scan (freeze frames) as well as full-motion video is possible. The videoconference closely approximates a face-to-face conference. Hard copies of visuals and data are transmitted via intelligent copiers or facsimile equipment.

(4) *Computer conference:* Participants in a computer conference use computer terminals to transmit information to other members of the group. The response may be simultaneous or on a delayed basis, so participants do not have to participate with one another at the same time. Information or messages may be stored for later responses. All records produced, documents transmitted, and written comments are stored in the computer. This type of conference, as a form of electronic mail, may be accomplished on a national or an international network.

(5) *Data conference:* The objective of a data conference is for two or more participants to have access to a document simultaneously for review and editing.

   EXAMPLE: Kelfe (Chicago headquarters) and Donaldson and Smyth (Wisconsin branch) use conferencing software to view a proposed budget spreadsheet. The purpose of the meeting is to modify the proposed budget according to anticipated projections and finalize these changes during the meeting. The results of the modifications can be viewed by all three participants so that discussion and final consensus can be achieved during the meeting.

(6) *Out-of-town meeting:* Business travel to out-of-town meetings is very common for business executives. If the corporation has numerous branch offices, this is one way for the executive to monitor business operations at the different branches. If the scheduling for the meeting has to come from the executive's office, the secretary will need to be sure that all reservations for the travel and the meeting are arranged.

   EXAMPLE: White, vice president for operations, just told Brennan, her executive secretary, that she will be traveling to Montreal on June 3 and 4 to meet with the operations people in the Canadian region. Brennan will need to make whatever travel, lodging, and meeting room reservations will be necessary.

2. *Arranging Meetings:* Informal and formal meetings will run smoothly only if all the necessary arrangements for the meetings are completed ahead of time. The busy executive has no time to worry at the last moment about what room is reserved, where the handouts are, or whether people were notified.

   a. *Selecting convenient date and time:* The first thing to do is to select a date and time that are convenient for those people who must attend. This may mean checking with each person to find alternative times so that, when each person has responded, the best possible time can be chosen. It will be more efficient to access the electronic calendar for each person, determine the best possible time for the meeting, and immediately schedule the meeting.

b. *Notifying participants of meeting date/time:* Of course, no meeting can take place without participants being present, so each one needs to be notified of the meeting date, time, and location.

   (1) *Telephone call:* The secretary should telephone each participant to let him or her know as soon as possible the meeting date, time, and place and to ask them to record this information on their calendars immediately. Through voice mail, the secretary will be able to leave a complete message for each participant.

   (2) *Electronic mail:* If a computer network is available, a memorandum can be transmitted to each participant by e-mail to let him or her know the meeting date, time, and place and to ask them to put this meeting on their calendars immediately.

   (3) *Follow-up letter or memorandum:* Depending on the availability of electronic mail within a firm, a written notice of the meeting and a confirmation of the date, time, and location should follow. It is helpful to the participants if they also know what the agenda is ahead of time.

   (4) *Telephone follow-up:* If a response is required from a participant and none is received, the secretary should follow up by telephone to see whether the person plans to attend the meeting.

c. *Notifying executive of those attending:* Once responses are received from all who should attend the meeting, let the person presiding over the meeting know exactly who will be attending. This is a double check to ensure that you have not forgotten to invite someone.

d. *Preparing materials for meeting:* Copies of materials to be distributed during the meeting should be prepared ahead of time.

e. *Preparing an agenda:* An *agenda* is a list of items of business to be presented and/or discussed during the meeting. Copies of the agenda should be prepared and disseminated to each participant prior to the meeting. Also, the agenda should be available at the beginning of the meeting for anyone who forgot to bring a copy. The usual order of business is as follows:

   • Call to order by presiding officer

   • Attendance

   • Announcement of quorum

   • Reading of minutes of previous meeting

   • Approval of minutes

   • Reports of officers

   • Reports of standing committees

   • Reports of special committees

   • Old (or unfinished) business

- New business

- Appointment of committees

- Nominations and elections (when required)

- Date of next meeting

- Adjournment

See Figure 11-1 for a sample agenda.

f. *Taking notes at meeting:* If requested, the secretary should take notes during the meeting so that a complete set of minutes may be prepared. (If the executive is the secretary for the meeting, the executive's secretary may be called on to take complete notes during the meeting.)

g. *Noting important dates on executive's calendar:* After the meeting is over, the secretary should scan through the notes from the meeting to see whether important dates for future meetings were mentioned. These dates should be recorded on the appropriate office calendars.

h. *Getting room ready for next meeting:* After the meeting has been adjourned, the meeting room should be left in proper order for any other meetings that follow. All extra handout materials should be collected.

Figure 11–1   Sample Agenda

INFORMATION SYSTEMS PROFESSIONALS OF ILLINOIS
Board of Directors Meeting

Parker-Hyatt Hotel
Chicago, Illinois

Peoria Room
Wednesday, November 19, 200X
11:30 A.M.

AGENDA

1. Call to Order: Denise Thomas, President

2. Secretary's Report: Minutes of October Meeting

3. President's Report

4. Treasurer's Report

5. Standing Committee Reports

   a. Program Committee: Eleanor Watson, Vice President

   b. Scholarship Committee: Maurice Thomas

6. Old Business

7. New Business

   a. Theme for Next Year's ISP Trade Show

   b. Representation at the ISP International Convention

8. Adjournment (1:00 P.M.)

i. *Transcribing notes:* The meeting notes should be transcribed as soon as possible so that no important details resulting from the meeting will be forgotten or ignored.

j. *Sending minutes or meeting report:* After the minutes or meeting report has been prepared, the secretary should send one copy to each of the participants for approval. *Minutes* are a record of the proceedings of a meeting (see Section B-2-f).

3. *Conducting Meetings:* Executives participate or preside over many meetings during their working time. In addition to planning and organizing meetings, it is vital that the meetings be conducted in an expeditious manner. The meeting time should be used effectively so that each participant feels that the order of business is handled efficiently. The use of parliamentary procedure establishes a definite routine for conducting a meeting in an efficient and orderly manner.

a. *Using meeting time effectively:* A number of techniques can be applied to permit meeting time to be used as effectively as possible. Here are only a few of the more important ones:

(1) *Time frame for meeting:* A definite time frame should be established for the meeting when scheduled so that participants know the amount of time to plan for. This time frame should be announced to the participants ahead of time so that they know how much time must be devoted to the meeting.

EXAMPLE: *The monthly staff meeting is always scheduled for Wednesday afternoon from 1 P.M. to 2:30 P.M. Having this time already scheduled on calendars means that those who participate will not allow any other conflicts during this time frame.*

(2) *Distribution of agenda and handout material:* If possible, the agenda and supportive handout material should be distributed at least one day prior to the meeting to give people sufficient time to review these materials and prepare for the meeting. Too often, people arrive at a meeting and are given a "stack" of materials that take time to look through, and there is not sufficient time at the meeting to do this expeditiously.

(3) *Promptness in starting meeting:* People appreciate starting meetings on time. A meeting scheduled for 9 A.M. should start at that time. As a general rule, people do not expect a meeting to start on time; but if starting on time becomes the general rule, people will be prompt in getting to the meeting.

(4) *Agenda items:* An agenda helps to organize the order of business for the meeting and to keep the participants on target. If an item is not on the agenda, it should not be discussed at this meeting. If a new item needs to be added to the agenda, the group must decide whether to accept it.

(a) Routine items on the agenda (e.g., reading of secretary's minutes and treasurer's report) should be handled quickly since there usually will be minor revisions in wording and few questions asked.

(b) Taking care of routine items quickly will leave more time to present and discuss other agenda items, which are the primary reasons for the meeting.

(5) *Summary of important points:* During the meeting, the chairperson should act as a facilitator, taking the time to summarize key points that are made so that everyone understands the importance or meaning of particular action taken.

(6) *Closing the meeting:* When the business itemized on the agenda has been acted on, the meeting should be adjourned promptly. The meeting might be scheduled for two hours, but if the business can be taken care of in less time, people will appreciate having those extra minutes to return to other work that needs to be handled.

b. *Using proper parliamentary procedures:* Parliamentary procedure is a necessary part of conducting a formal meeting because its use enables the meeting to be conducted in an efficient and orderly manner. Some have defined parliamentary law as "common sense used in a gracious manner." *Robert's Rules of Order* (first published in 1876) has been revised numerous times over the past 124 years and still is the basis for acceptable parliamentary procedure followed in formal meetings. It is the responsibility of the parliamentarian (someone appointed who is familiar with parliamentary procedure) to ensure that the meeting is conducted according to these rules. A copy should be on hand for reference.

(1) *Basic principles of parliamentary procedure:* For a group of people to arrive at group decisions in an efficient and orderly manner, the basic principles of parliamentary procedure must be followed:

(a) Courtesy and justice must be accorded to all who are participating in the meeting.

(b) Only one topic is considered at one time. (This is the reason that an agenda is so important at a meeting.)

(c) The minority opinion must be heard; every person has an equal opportunity to be heard.

(d) The majority will prevail; a majority vote will result in a motion passed.

(2) *Conducting the meeting with parliamentary procedure:* Each item of business to be presented during the meeting for action by the group must be introduced to the group in the form of a *motion.* This motion must be made by a group member who has secured the floor by being recognized by the presiding officer for the meeting. The motion must receive a *second* by another group member.

(a) *Types of motions:* Items of business are presented, one by one, to the group in the form of *motions.* Once a motion has been made and seconded, the item can be discussed thoroughly. There are five different types of motions: main motions, subsidiary motions, incidental motions, privileged motions, and unclassified motions.

• *Main motions:* A main motion is a motion that states an item of business. The main motion has the lowest precedence in rank among all types of motions. In other words, other motions that impact the main motion must be acted on before the main motion is finalized. The main motion must be seconded and is subject to discussion, debate, and amendment. The motion may be reconsidered or have a subsidiary motion attached to it. A majority vote is necessary to pass the motion.

EXAMPLE:

Watson: *"I move that we accept the report of the Special Committee on Human Resource Development."*

Roth: *"I second the motion."*

- *Subsidiary motions:* A subsidiary motion may assist, modify, or dispose of the main motion. A subsidiary motion supersedes the main motion and must be acted on before the group returns to the main motion. The following subsidiary motions may be applied:

  To table a motion (to lay aside until later)

  To call for the vote

  To refer the motion to committee for further consideration

  To amend a main motion

  To postpone action on a motion indefinitely

- *Incidental motions:* Incidental motions are motions that arise from pending questions. They may be introduced at any time and must be decided before the question to which they are incidental is decided. Here are the incidental motions that may be used:

  To suspend a rule temporarily

  To close nominations

  To reopen nominations

  To withdraw or modify a motion

  To rise to a point of order

  To appeal to a decision of the chair

- *Privileged motions:* Privileged motions are called *convenience motions* since they affect the comfort of the members of the group that is meeting. These motions have precedence over all other motions. The most typical privileged motions include the following:

  To call for orders of the day

  To bring up a question of privilege or an urgent matter, such as noise or discomfort

  To take a recess

  To adjourn

  To set the next meeting time

- *Unclassified motions:* Other motions that are appropriate but cannot be classified in the other four categories include the following:

  To take a motion from table

  To reconsider a motion

  To rescind decision on a motion

(b) *Quorum:* The bylaws of the organization usually specify the number of voting members who must be present in order to transact business at a meeting of the organization. The required number of voting members who must be present to transact business is called a *quorum.*

4. *Preparing and Using Visual Aids:* Presentations of factual information at meetings are greatly enhanced by the use of visuals to complement the verbal or written pre-

sentation. Some typical kinds of visuals representing types of media other than paper are electronic slides, overhead transparencies, and 35-millimeter slides.

a. *Electronic slides:* Presentation software programs are often used to prepare visuals and handouts for a variety of meetings. The following types of materials can be prepared with this type of software: an outline of the content contained in the slides, the electronic slides, handouts with copies of the slides and space for notes, and speaker notes to accompany the slides.

    (1) *Content outline:* An outline of the presentation can be created by using a template provided with the software. The first section is the information that will go on a title slide, with the title of the presentation along with the presenter's name and affiliation. The remaining text on the outline will appear on the slide set. Some people prefer to prepare the slides first, then to see how the content appears on the outline.

    (2) *Templates for creating slides:* Templates are provided in the software program to assist in preparing slides that may vary in design. Here are some of the variations to choose from:

        (a) Bulleted list of items

        (b) Textual material with an illustration

        (c) Two columns of listed items

        (d) Text with chart, graph, and/or animation

    In addition, animation can be added to the slides so that lines of text can come into view from either side or down from the top or illustrations can show movement. Sound can be inserted into the slide from the software library, or short clips from videotaped recordings can be inserted as well. When the slides have been created, they can be sequenced in the order desired for the presentation.

    (3) *Handouts with notes:* When the slide multimedia presentation is ready for use, handouts can be prepared so that the conference participants will be able to follow along with copies of the visuals. One of the options available is to have miniature copies of three slides down the left side of a sheet of paper, with room at the right for notes written during the presentation.

    (4) *Speaker's notes:* Another option available to the presenter is to write a set of speaker's notes for each of the slides in the presentation. These notes can be keyed in for printing out with a copy of the appropriate visual. If the presenter decides to rearrange the order of the slides, the speaker's notes are included with the appropriate slide.

Presentation software provides a unique opportunity to be creative and innovative in designing interesting presentations. Such a multimedia approach requires that the presenter have a computer and projection equipment that is compatible with the software used for preparing the multimedia slides.

b. *Overhead transparencies:* A *transparency* is an acetate sheet that contains an image burned or drawn on it that can be projected on a screen or wall. You can make many different kinds of transparencies: colored background with white or black letters/images, clear background with black/colored images, shaded transparencies, or multiple-part transparencies. Using word processing software and an ink-jet or laser printer, you can produce transparencies at your desktop workstation. Preparing typed or drawn copy for use in making an overhead transparency requires you to use carbon-based materials. You can also make overhead transparencies from printed copy generated from multimedia slides developed with presentation software.

(1) *Using word processing software:* The advantage of using word processing software is that the transparency text, clip art, and charts can be edited before preparing the transparencies. The transparency can be printed on an ink-jet or laser printer. If a color printer is available, the color from the software text is printed onto the transparency. If a printer is not available, a hard copy of the material can be printed and used to make the transparency using a copier.

    (a) Participants who are sitting in the back of the meeting room must be able to see the visual; therefore, a larger font size should be used. Using word processing software, typical font size is either 12 or 14. When using presentation software, typical font size ranges from 18 to 40.

    (b) The word processing font style should also be easy to read. Typical font styles include Courier, Times New Roman, and Arial.

EXAMPLES:

Font size 12	Courier Times New Roman **Arial**
Font size 14	Bernhard Modern Bold **Hobo** Courier New
Font size 16	Courier New **Modern880 BT** Times New Roman

Some of the fonts automatically print out in boldface.

(2) *Preparing typewritten or drawn copy:* Transparencies are prepared from original black-and-white copy that is run through a copier and the images from those copies burned into sheets of transparency acetate.

    (a) If you are typing the copy, be sure to use a typewriter with the lift-off correction feature so that you can correct errors as you go along. Errors must be removed entirely from the page, not covered up, because of the burning process.

    (b) If a typing error is made, it must be corrected either by lifting off, if the typewriter has that feature, or by erasing with a typewriting eraser. The error cannot be covered up with correction fluid or cover-up correction paper. The image would look like a strikeover on the transparency.

    (c) The best element to use in the typing process is an Orator or Orator Presenter element. This is a 10-pitch element that appears very large on the page and is much easier to read from a distance during the presentation. It is very important to have a *readable copy* on the screen in a meeting.

(d) All copy should be prepared on white bond paper in the format desired.

(e) All typed or drawn copy should be proofread very carefully so that any errors will be found *before* the transparency is prepared. The cost of transparency material is high (as much as 40 cents per sheet), and a misspelled word can result in a transparency being discarded.

(f) To include a tracing or drawing as a part of the copy, use a pencil or special transparency marker to do the actual drawing. Remember that everything you want reproduced must be prepared *only* with carbon-based material (film ribbon, pencil, special pen).

(g) If it is necessary to paste up a page with both illustrated material and text, prepare a photocopy of the material (this photocopy is carbon based) and make the transparency from the photocopy.

(3) *Preparing the overhead transparency:* The way the material is burned on the transparency acetate will depend on the type of acetate that is being used. Transparencies may be purchased that have colored background and either white or black letters, and images will be burned into the transparencies.

(a) Shaded transparencies may be prepared by either shading from the software package onto the hard copy to be reproduced or shading in the areas with a felt-tip marker on the transparency itself (permanent or water based, depending on the permanency desired) or with acetate shading material that can be cut to size and attached to the transparency.

(b) Multiple-part transparencies are often called *progressive transparencies.* This means that one transparency will be used to illustrate several steps in a process. Each time the speaker moves to the next step, another portion of the transparency can be flipped over as an "overlay" for the parts already presented.

(c) Cardboard frames are available to use in framing each transparency. These frames make it easier for a speaker to handle the transparencies, and it is possible to mark on each frame an appropriate label describing what is displayed.

Transparencies may be prepared on a number of different types of copiers. Acetate sheets are placed in the paper carrier or in a bypass tray, just as bond paper is, and run through the copier in the same way. The image is burned into the acetate, creating the reproduction of the text or drawing. Permanent or water-based markers may be used to write on the transparency during the presentation. Water-based markers permit the speaker to wipe off any writing on the transparency for another presentation.

c. *35-millimeter slides:* Many speakers prefer to use photographic slides for presentations. Some companies have photographers whose job it is to prepare slides and other photographs for use by professionals in the company. The user's responsibility is to plan the content, order slide preparation, and arrange the slides in sequence when they are ready.

(1) *Preparing copy for slides:* A *storyboard* is a frame-by-frame plan for the preparation of an audiovisual presentation on specially designed sheets that show the description of the picture or illustration plus any narrative that will

accompany the slide. The storyboard is prepared to show exactly what slides are needed before any photography or art work is undertaken. In this way, the correct sequence of the presentation can be planned so that the required slides can be photographed.

    (a) The storyboard gives a brief description of each slide desired—exactly what features/events should be photographed.

    (b) The storyboard contains the written script that will accompany each slide in the presentation. This script is especially helpful when an audiotape or "canned" presentation will be prepared to accompany the slide series.

  (2) *Previewing slides:* Once the slides are processed, the user should preview the slides and compare them with the prepared script to see whether there are any discrepancies.

    EXAMPLE: A particularly useful device in previewing slides is the multiple-slide lighted tray in which a large number of slides can be placed. They can be moved around and the sequence changed until the final order of presentation is agreed on.

  d. *Electronic blackboards:* Another way of displaying business graphics is the electronic blackboard, a device used with teleconferences to transmit visuals to other locations. The electronic blackboard consists of a pressure-sensitive blackboard, microphone, and speaker at one location and a television monitor, microphone, and speaker at a second location (there may be additional locations as well). As someone writes on the blackboard, the coordinates are picked up electronically and transmitted to the monitor at the other location(s) where an image of the blackboard is displayed.

5. *Preparing Resolutions and Petitions:* Formal statements of an organization's appreciation, congratulations, or sympathy may be expressed as a *resolution*. The resolution is a formal expression from an entire group. A *petition* is a formal statement of reasons for introducing and asking for a specific action to be granted. The petition is a formal expression from the people who sign the petition.

  a. *Resolution:* As stated previously, the resolution is a formal statement from an entire group. Preparation of the resolution will require the following steps:

    (1) *Advance preparation:* The resolution must be prepared in advance by a resolutions committee appointed for that purpose. Then the resolution must be reviewed by the presiding officer of the group (chairperson or president) or by the executive board or committee.

    (2) *Presentation of resolution:* The resolution may be presented orally or in writing at the meeting. However, the most effective way of presenting such an expression is in writing.

    (3) *Final form:* After the meeting, the secretary must prepare the resolution in final form and have it signed and included as a part of the official proceedings of the meeting. Since the language used in the resolution is formal, the rationale for the resolution is introduced with the word WHEREAS preceding each reason given. However, the final paragraphs that state the official action to be taken are introduced by the word RESOLVED or, if there is

more than one action taken, RESOLVED FURTHER (typed in all capitals and followed by a comma and a capital letter). See Figure 11–2 for an example of a resolution.

b. *Petition:* A petition is a formal statement, signed by those eligible to sign the petition, asking that some specific action be taken. The petition is a formal expression only from those who sign the petition.

(1) *Advance preparation:* The petition must be prepared in advance with an adequate number of signature lines. Next, the petition needs to be circulated so that the required number of signatures may be obtained.

(2) *Presentation:* Once the required number of signatures has been obtained, the petition may be presented orally and in writing at the meeting. The written petition, with signatures affixed, is the official document. Further action by the group will be discussed at the meeting.

6. *Preparing Minutes of Meetings:* The minutes of a meeting are the official report of the meeting. The purpose of *minutes* is to summarize the business that has been transacted, reports that have been given, and any other significant events occurring at the meeting.

a. *Preliminary writing:* The notes from the meeting need to be transcribed in the format desired by the organization (see Chapter 19, Section E-1, for discussion of the format to be used for preparing minutes). Using the agenda as a guide serves as an outline of the items discussed at the meeting. Complete information—including motions, committee reports, and announcements—must be included in the minutes.

Figure 11–2   Sample Resolution

RESOLUTION
Adopted November 28, 200X

WHEREAS, Georgia L. Stratton, CPS has been a member of Kishwaukee Chapter, International Association of Administrative Professionals, for fifteen years, and

WHEREAS, Ms. Stratton has contributed significantly to the professional activities of the Chapter, having served as Secretary, First Vice President, and President, and

WHEREAS, Ms. Stratton is retiring from her position as Executive Secretary for Dr. Gerald R. Kuhlson, Vice President for Field Operations, Rockville Manufacturing Company, where she has been employed for twenty-five years, therefore be it

RESOLVED FURTHER, That the members of Kishwaukee Chapter, International Association of Administrative Professionals, go on record as expressing their sincere appreciation of Georgia L. Stratton's many services to the Chapter; and be it

RESOLVED FURTHER, That the members of Kishwaukee Chapter sincerely congratulate Georgia L. Stratton on her retirement as an office professional and wish her happiness in her retirement years.

_____   _____
Secretary   President

b. *Approval by presiding officer:* The preliminary draft of the minutes should be approved by the presiding officer before it is finalized and duplicated for distribution to the other members of the executive board or committee.

c. *Distribution of minutes:* The minutes need to be distributed before the next meeting so that members of the group can review them for accuracy. One of the first agenda items for the next meeting will be the approval of the minutes from the previous meeting.

Minutes are the official record of the meeting. Therefore, the secretary must provide accurate minutes so that the official proceedings are correctly filed.

Review Questions

Directions: Select the best answer from the four alternatives. Write your answer in the blank to the left of the number.

——————————

1. A company-sponsored conference provides an opportunity for the organization to

    a. plan a convention for a professional association.
    b. acquaint company personnel with a new product or service.
    c. invite representatives from a number of other companies to participate.
    d. present training seminars for members of a professional association.

——————————

2. Smythe, the administrative manager, tells you that she will be planning next year's convention of the American Office Systems Association to be held in Phoenix. Which one of the following should you proceed to do first to help with the preliminary planning?

    a. Make arrangements for speakers to be met at the airport.
    b. Make arrangements for Smythe's lodging and air reservations.
    c. Reserve a block of rooms at the hotel for attendees.
    d. Develop a checklist of activities that will need to be accomplished before the program is finalized.

——————————

3. One of the planning activities that needs to be accomplished before a convention is

    a. placing audiovisual equipment in rooms where needed for program sessions.
    b. finalizing the number of people who will be attending the meal functions.
    c. monitoring publication of convention proceedings.
    d. creating a reference file for the next convention.

——————————

4. You are the executive secretary for Sullivan, who is the program chair for this year's American Management Association's seminar for administrative professionals. During the conference, you are likely to be responsible for

    a. setting up and supervising the conference registration desk.
    b. preparing checks for honorariums and expenses for guest speakers.
    c. reserving adequate meeting-room space with audiovisual equipment needed.
    d. creating a reference file with suggestions for next year's seminar.

——————————

5. With technology affecting organizational change within business today, there will be

    a. more emphasis on individual participation in meeting organizational objectives.
    b. more emphasis on small- or large-group participation and communication within the firm.
    c. more formal meetings rather than informal meetings within the organization.
    d. less opportunity for small- and large-group communication.

6. Which one of the following committees established by the board of directors of a professional association would be categorized as a standing committee?

  a. Program committee for next year's conference
  b. Computer selection committee
  c. Auditing committee
  d. Chapter liaison for statewide professional certification committee

7. A committee formed to investigate the feasibility of appointing an executive director of the association is known as a/an

  a. standing committee.
  b. status committee.
  c. ad hoc committee.
  d. advisory committee.

8. A meeting of ABC Company's board of directors would be categorized as a/an

  a. formal meeting.
  b. informal meeting.
  c. ad hoc meeting.
  d. stockholders' meeting.

9. A meeting set up so that people located in different parts of the country can use telephone communications to meet and conduct business is called a/an

  a. teleconference.
  b. in-house meeting.
  c. computer conference.
  d. data conference.

10. Your executive has just told you that a special meeting of the executive committee needs to be scheduled for next Monday afternoon at 2 P.M. Which one of the following is the *first* thing you should do?

  a. Send a memorandum to each member of the committee notifying each one of the meeting.
  b. Telephone each member of the committee telling each one of the meeting and the location.
  c. Review materials needed for the meeting with your executive.
  d. Prepare the handout materials for the meeting.

11. An organized list of the order of business to be presented or discussed during a meeting is called a/an

  a. agenda.
  b. proceedings.
  c. minutes.
  d. motion.

12. One of the basic principles of parliamentary procedure is that

    a. more than one topic can be considered at one time.
    b. the majority must be heard.
    c. the minority will prevail.
    d. all participants must be treated courteously.

13. Once a motion has been made and seconded,

    a. a vote may immediately be requested by the person presiding at the meeting.
    b. the motion can be discussed, debated, or amended.
    c. a recess may be called.
    d. only the voting members will be allowed to discuss the motion.

14. Which one of the following is an example of a main motion?

    a. "I move to amend the motion that we hold the conference at the Sea Pines Resort to include the dates July 18 and 19."
    b. "I move that we close nominations for the office of president."
    c. "I move that we postpone action on this motion until our next meeting."
    d. "I move that we accept the report of the ad hoc committee as presented."

15. To table a motion means to

    a. put it aside until a later meeting.
    b. refer the item of business to a committee for further examination.
    c. postpone action on the motion indefinitely.
    d. amend the motion.

16. A motion to close nominations for the position of vice president in charge of programs is a/an

    a. incidental motion.
    b. subsidiary motion.
    c. privileged motion.
    d. main motion.

17. The required number of voting members who must be present in order to transact business at a meeting is called a/an

    a. majority.
    b. agenda.
    c. bylaws.
    d. quorum.

18. Executives are often involved in making presentations before professional groups. Which one of the following represents a method used to prepare visuals and handouts for the audience?

    a. 35-millimeter slides
    b. Presentation software
    c. Electronic blackboard
    d. Computer graphics software

19. When preparing electronic slides, a slide format that includes room for an illustration as well as a short list of bullets can be selected from

    a. a view of templates available in the program.
    b. an outline of the textual content.
    c. clip art available in the program.
    d. animation features of the program.

20. The first step in planning a 35-millimeter slide presentation is to

    a. prepare a script recorded onto a cassette tape.
    b. preview the slides and compare them to the script.
    c. prepare a storyboard of slides needed for the program.
    d. sequence the slides according to the script.

21. An electronic blackboard is most useful in

    a. transmitting statistical information in the form of business graphics to a distant location.
    b. displaying electronic slides during a presentation.
    c. previewing electronic slides prepared at another location.
    d. preparing a storyboard for an electronic presentation.

22. Marshall has served as treasurer for the university alumni association for the past ten years. She will soon be moving to California with her family. At this month's board meeting, a formal statement of appreciation was introduced. This statement is called a/an

    a. petition.
    b. agenda.
    c. resolution.
    d. recognition award.

23. A formal request that a city council consider specific action, such as rezoning a residential area for limited commercial use, would be presented in writing with a required number of signatures of residents of voting age in the form of

    a. a resolution.
    b. minutes.
    c. an agenda.
    d. a petition.

24. An official record of the proceedings of a meeting distributed to the members is called the

    a. quorum.
    b. agenda.
    c. minutes.
    d. petition.

Solutions

Answer	*Refer to:*
1. (b)	[A-1-a]
2. (d)	[A-2-a]
3. (c)	[A-2-a(10)]
4. (a)	[A-2-b(1)]
5. (b)	[B]
6. (a)	[B-1-a(1)(a)]
7. (c)	[B-1-a(1)(b)]
8. (a)	[B-1-b(1)]
9. (a)	[B-1-b(2)]
10. (b)	[B-2-b(1)]
11. (a)	[B-2-e]
12. (d)	[B-3-b(1)(a)]
13. (b)	[B-3-b(2)(a)]
14. (d)	[B-3-b(2)(a)]
15. (a)	[B-3-b(2)(a)]
16. (a)	[B-3-b(2)(a)]
17. (d)	[B-3-b(2)(b)]
18. (b)	[B-4-a]
19. (a)	[B-4-a(2)]
20. (c)	[B-4-c(1)]

21. (a)   [B-4-d]

22. (c)   [B-5-a]

23. (d)   [B-5-b]

24. (c)   [B-6]

CHAPTER 12

Reprographics Management

OVERVIEW

Reprographics is the office system with primary responsibility for preparing copies of documents needed during the operation of the organization. Some reprographics processes, such as copying, enable the operator to make only one copy as needed, while other processes, such as printing, are more complex. Reprographics processes that are more complex permit the rapid reproduction of hundreds or thousands of recorded images.

Reprographics processes may be divided into copying, duplicating, phototypesetting and composition, desktop publishing, imaging, and finishing processes (see Chapter 5). The management of reprographics processes requires an analysis of the reprographics needs of the organization to determine the feasibility of specific procedures within the organization. Many reprographics processes are centralized within firms because of the high cost involved—personnel costs as well as equipment and technology costs. Copying technology, for example, may be decentralized, available within departments, or centralized, available through a reprographics center. Although many production jobs are handled through in-house reprographics services, some custom work may be handled by commercial printing firms.

Above all, analyzing the costs involved in reprographics processes is very important and crucial to increasing the effectiveness of the services offered. Attention needs to be given to the selection of appropriate equipment and technology, matching the production needs with the process, and establishing operations procedures and control.

KEY TERMS

Auditron
Authorization
Centralized control

Commercial printing firm
Copy quality
Copyright controls
Decentralized control

In-house reprographics
services
Procedures
Reprographics

A. Determining Reprographic Needs

Before decisions are made as to the type of reprographics services needed for an in-house operation, the copying, duplicating, and printing requirements of the organization must be examined carefully. The nature and quantity of the materials to be reproduced will be the basis of this needs assessment. The following factors must be considered in determining reprographic needs.

1. *Original Documents:* The types of business forms, reports, correspondence, or other documents that will need to be copied or reproduced are a primary concern. Specific characteristics of these documents that require special attention include text, drawings and illustrations, photographs, halftones, and boxes.

2. *Production Requirements:* Special production requirements will also influence decisions relating to reprographics services. Such requirements as the use of color, reduction and enlargement of images, paper stock required, and other specifications are important considerations when reprographics services are examined.

3. *Copies Needed:* The number of copies of each document used within the business, on a monthly or annual basis, must be determined as well as to whom the copies will be distributed; how copies will be prepared, stored, and retrieved; and the length of time copies of each document will be retained.

4. *Quality Required for Copies:* Image sharpness, uniformity of reproducing, resistance to smudging, and frequency of reproducing specific documents help determine the quality needed during particular processes.

5. *Turnaround Time:* Users need to estimate the turnaround time that affects them on their jobs, while people performing reprographic functions need to estimate the time required for them to handle routine and custom jobs assigned to them.

B. Organizing Reprographics Systems

Reprographics systems are managed differently in small and large firms, depending on the organization of centralized or decentralized office support services within the organization. The size of the firm and its specific reprographic needs have a strong effect on the human resources needed to operate and manage reprographics systems. Monitoring controls are needed to move toward a cost-effective, efficient operation. A basic concern is whether the actual production can be handled efficiently through an in-house reprographics center as opposed to a commercial printing establishment.

1. *Decentralized versus Centralized Control:* Operations that are decentralized are located wherever the work needs to be done in various departments throughout the organization. When a decentralized approach is used, each major department within the organization has its own reprographics equipment and services. With centralization, one person is usually assigned the overall responsibility for managing the reprographics operations for the organization. When centralized, the reprographics area is typically located in a center with all departments having easy physical access to the services provided.

   a. *Advantages of decentralized control:* Organizing reprographics services with decentralized control means that each department would supervise and manage its own reproducing functions. Some of the advantages of decentralized control include the following:

      (1) *Self-service:* Support staff within the department are able to perform copying and duplicating functions as needed. Basic equipment would be available within the department.

      (2) *Flexibility:* Each department could establish its own policies and procedures in regard to what is copied or duplicated, when the equipment is to be used (during work hours), and how many copies may be produced.

(3) *Quick access:* Access to the reprographics equipment would be quick and easy since it is located within the department. The amount of travel time to and from the copier, for example, would be reduced.

(4) *Turnaround time:* Individual office employees performing reprographics functions will be able to control turnaround time as needed since fewer people will be involved in the operation. Priorities can more easily be established within the department. In some decentralized environments, the person needing the copies is responsible for making his or her own copies.

Of course, there are disadvantages of permitting decentralized control of copiers. Once certain types of office support services are departmentalized, it becomes more difficult to maintain organization-wide control over the use and maintenance of equipment. Administrative assistants and secretaries will need to know how to handle basic maintenance, such as replacement of toner. More supervision is generally necessary to be sure that *everyone* using reprographics equipment knows and understands basic operation.

b. *Advantages of centralized control:* If the reprographics operation is centralized, an administrative manager is typically assigned to oversee the operations. In addition, there may be a reprographics supervisor who manages the specific functions within the reprographics center. Here are some of the advantages of centralized control:

(1) *Specialized personnel:* High-quality copying, duplicating, and printing will be accomplished through the use of specialized personnel for typesetting, composition, desktop publishing, layout and design, equipment operation, and photographic work required.

(2) *Equipment variety:* Because the work is centralized, duplicate equipment for departmental use will not be necessary. Therefore, the availability of a greater variety of reprographics equipment is possible. Perhaps the only reprographics equipment needed within the departments will be low-volume copiers.

(3) *Flexibility:* With a centralized operation, there can be more flexibility in the kinds of production jobs accepted. Specialists are available to assist, and a large variety of reprographics work can be done in-house.

(4) *Work scheduling:* Production jobs are scheduled in a centralized operation. Lead time is required to ensure that the work is completed on time and meets quality standards.

(5) *Productivity:* The objective for centralizing reprographics operations is to increase productivity. The technology available, as well as specialized personnel to help, leads to increased productivity on the part of other office professionals.

Perhaps the most significant disadvantage is that more people are involved in the production process and the work may take longer than anticipated. Some people do not allow enough lead time to permit a high-quality job to be done.

2. *In-House Reprographics Services versus Commercial Printing:* Many organizations have initiated in-house reprographics services because of the need to control the copying, duplicating, and printing requirements of the organization. Based on a cost/benefit analysis, firms may decide that an in-house service is necessary because of volume and need. For specialized custom work, commercial printing firms may offer the best solution because of the design and printing expertise required.

a. *In-house services:* The types of duplicating needs vary from small organizations to large organizations. In small firms, one copier and one duplicator may meet the particular needs of the firm. In large firms, however, a centralized reprographics center may be needed to service the needs of all departments within the organization. Some of the specific applications for in-house services include the following:

(1) *Forms:* All the forms used within the business may be printed in quantity to maintain a sufficient inventory.

> EXAMPLES: *Letterhead stationery, envelopes, memorandum forms, order forms, estimates, sales slips, insurance policies, contracts, agreements, and other legal forms.*

(2) *Public relations materials:* Posters, company newsletters, brochures, and annual reports are typical kinds of public relations materials that the organization may need to have printed.

(3) *Desktop publishing services:* The reprographics center can now convert word processing files created by administrative professionals into published materials through the use of desktop publishing. Such items as newsletters, brochures, and financial information may be redesigned from word processing formats into desktop publishing formats, which can include illustrations, drawings, and columnar text.

(4) *Miscellaneous items:* Other items that may be duplicated or printed in an in-house facility include business cards, internal record-keeping forms (log forms, job request forms, and production sheets), and special packaging needed for products.

b. *Use of commercial services:* Some documents demand special attention because of artwork, graphic design, or printing requirements. It is sometimes to the company's advantage to contract with an outside commercial printing firm for design and printing services.

> EXAMPLES: *Production work might include brochures to advertise the company's products, photographic posters to highlight new products, booklets containing the annual fiscal reports of the company to be distributed to stockholders, magazines, and newsletters for which the in-house reprographics equipment is not well suited.*

Some factors to consider in deciding whether to use a commercial service include the following:

(1) Costs for producing certain quantities (e.g., a single copy, 100 copies, 10,000 copies)

(2) Quality of the prepared copy (e.g., black-and-white images, use of color, print quality)

(3) Additional costs for finishing processes (e.g., collating, binding, and folding)

(4) Total time required for completion of a specific production job

C. Controlling Reprographics Systems

Of all the office support services available within a firm, reprographics processes tend to be among the most expensive. The cost of specialized labor, equipment and technology, paper inventories, composition, and other miscellaneous costs must be analyzed in terms of the reprographics services being provided. Adequate attention must be given to selecting of appropriate equipment, matching the production job to the appropriate reprographics process, and establishing operation controls for handling routine as well as custom production work.

1. *Selecting Reprographics Equipment:* Initial investment in reprographics equipment will be relatively high. In a small- to medium-size firm, the investment may be as much as $75,000 to $150,000, while in a large firm the investment can be anywhere from $150,000 to $400,000 or more. Selection of appropriate equipment and technology to handle the reprographics needs of the organization requires attention to the following factors:

    a. *Specific applications:* Determining the specific applications for which the equipment and technology is intended is essential. Consideration should be given to those special features of the equipment that are applied to specific production tasks.

    EXAMPLE: A high-speed copier is needed to handle the high-volume needs of the ABC Company. In addition to its copying capability, the copier's collating and stapling features will enable these operations to be performed quickly with only minimal manual labor.

    b. *Basic equipment operation:* The ease of operating the new equipment will permit new procedures to be implemented more smoothly into the operations of the reprographics center. Speed of operation is also an important consideration.

    c. *Training needed by operators:* The training ease of a new system is important in determining the amount or kind of training needed by operators of the system. Most estimates indicate that it takes anywhere from three to six months for an operator to become productive with a new equipment system. Therefore, the initial cost of training to the organization is high—from the time "lost" through retraining to time spent in special seminars sponsored by various professional associations and vendors.

    d. *Equipment cost:* Of course, the initial cost of the equipment and technology is an especially important consideration. This includes the cost of maintenance and service contracts for the particular systems selected.

    e. *Estimated delivery time:* Most orders for reprographics equipment, other than copiers, will take a few weeks to a few months for delivery. Most vendors of copy equipment have models ready for immediate purchase and delivery. An important factor in selecting equipment will be the estimated delivery time from manufacturer to vendor to purchaser.

    EXAMPLE: Within three months, the X & Z Company plans to start printing a special report for one of its clients. A new equipment system is on order and is scheduled to be delivered within the next three weeks. That should leave adequate time for the operator to be trained on the new system. A delay in receiving the new equipment as scheduled will mean a delay in being able to serve the client.

2. *Matching Production with the Process:* With more than one reprographics process available for producing copies, the production job must be matched with the reprographics

process that will give the desired appearance and quality. Factors that may be applied in determining which process would be the most appropriate for the specific production job include the following:

a. *Copy quality desired:* When various copying, duplicating, and printing processes are compared, there may be considerable differences among these processes. The quality of the paper used for the run as well as the care taken in preparing the original copy or the master also affect the appearance of the copies that are reproduced. Here are some specific questions that need to be answered.

- How important is the appearance of the copy?

- How will the copy be used within the office?

- Will the copy be transmitted externally to other organizations? And how will the copy be used within those organizations?

- Who will see the copy? Someone within the organization? Someone outside the organization?

b. *Number of copies needed:* Depending on the process used, the number of usable copies will vary. Figure 12–1 notes the economical quantity that can be produced with different kinds of reprographics processes (see Chapter 5).

c. *Copy costs:* You will want to choose the reprographics process that produces the quality you need at the lowest possible cost. Refer again to Figure 12–1 and note the average cost per copy for each process.

d. *Preparation time:* When selecting a reprographics process, the amount of time needed to make copies is an important consideration. The total time required for keying text into the computer, word processing and/or desktop publishing, and equipment setup as well as production run time equals the turnaround time needed to ready the document and produce the required number of copies.

3. *Establishing Operations Procedures and Controls:* Often, policies and procedures are established for operations and controls within a specific departmental area. This is important especially when the department or service area is performing tasks for the entire organization. *Procedures* are steps used to complete a specific office task. Naturally, these procedures need to be governed by some controls so that the people performing the various operations will understand what is expected of them.

a. *Operations procedures:* Rather than trying to remember all the intricate procedures involved in certain types of production work or with certain types of reprographics equipment, office professionals have been involved in developing procedures manuals that explain what should actually be done in given office situations. These sets of procedures help standardize the methods used in performing certain work functions.

(1) *Human resource procedures:* Specific procedures must be established for personnel to follow in reprographics operations.

(a) *Training:* One or more people need to be trained in machine operation, depending on their expertise. In addition, equipment maintenance and service are of vital importance to reprographics operations. The training should include a basic understanding of ways to keep costs down in reprographics operations.

Figure 12–1 Comparison of Reprographics Processes

Reprographics Process	Equipment Base Cost	Average Cost per Copy	Copy Quality Produced	Economical Quantity	Average Monthly Volume
Offset duplicating	Medium to expensive ($3,500–$20,000)	Low to medium (0.005–0.015)	Good to excellent	25 to 10,000	—
Low-volume copying	Medium to expensive ($800–$25,000)	Medium to expensive (0.03–0.055)	Good to excellent	1 to 25	Up to 20,000
Medium-volume copying	Expensive ($25,000+)	Medium (0.025–0.045)	Excellent	Over 25	20,000 to 125,000
High-volume copying	Expensive ($30,000+)	Medium (0.015–0.03)	Excellent	Over 25	200,000 to 750,000

(b) *Authorization:* Only authorized personnel should be permitted to use the reprographics equipment. This is due primarily to the specialized nature of the equipment itself. The technical nature of the work plus computerized applications require reprographics personnel to handle very sensitive operations.

(c) *Equipment misuse:* Delays in the completion of production work can be caused by employee misuse of equipment. Once the equipment is "down," valuable time is lost and, of course, productivity suffers. Also, it becomes difficult to meet copying and printing deadlines.

(2) *Records procedures:* In any business procedure, certain records are needed to monitor the work being done or the equipment usage.

(a) *Request forms:* Whenever a user wishes to request work to be done by the reprographics center, a job request form (similar to one used for word processing or document preparation) should be completed describing the reproducing required.

(b) *Equipment usage forms:* In reprographics, it is important to keep track of the amount of equipment usage per job. A charge-back procedure may be used to charge individual departments for costs associated with specific jobs. These costs may include costs associated with equipment, repairs, depreciation, or supplies.

(c) *Equipment repair records:* Detailed records of equipment repair per machine are extremely important in monitoring the effectiveness of the equipment in specific procedures.

EXAMPLE: A digital duplicator that requires continuous repair, almost on a daily basis, will not be very effective in preparing needed copies of documents.

b. *Operations controls:* The administrative manager in charge of the reprographics operations must impose certain operations controls so that reprographics services will function effectively. Here are some controls that might be used:

(1) *Copy monitoring:* An *auditron* is one way of controlling use of a low-volume, convenience copier. This is a plastic card, key, or other insert device that activates the copier for use and keeps a record of the number of copies produced.

(2) *Copyright controls:* Any organization today must be concerned about the handling of copyrighted materials and appropriate procedures to use for making copies, with or without the written permission of the publisher.

Copyright laws do permit materials to be copied in certain circumstances. A single copy is usually permitted when a person needs to use the information for personal research. However, multiple copies are permitted only when permission has been received from the author or publisher. Sometimes a fee is attached for authorization to print copyrighted material.

EXAMPLE: Professor May wanted to use a section of a classic text that was out of print. The publisher was contacted, and written permission was received to copy that portion of the text and reproduce it for classes. This was a standing permission for any semester Professor May taught the course.

(3) *Time controls:* Some copiers are in use only during the business day, from 8 A.M. to 5 P.M.

(4) *Trained operator:* Sometimes, it is more efficient to have an operator available either to run the copies needed or to be available in case a problem develops with the equipment or the supplies.

(5) *Restricting the number of copies prepared:* Since large numbers of copies can be reproduced more economically using other methods, the use of some low-volume convenience copiers may be restricted to 20 copies or less.

4. *Controlling Reprographics Costs:* The primary cost factors in reprographics operations include human resources, equipment and technology, space, and supply costs. Each of these cost factors (and other types of "hidden" costs) must be considered in the per-copy costs when using reprographics services. "Hidden costs" include costs for ordering reprographics supplies and equipment, storing supplies (especially large quantities of paper), keeping accurate stock inventories, and mailing. Procedures need to be implemented and enforced to reduce excess costs. Here are some specific ways that organizations can reduce and control reprographic costs:

a. *Selecting the most appropriate reprographics process:* The fastest method of preparing copies may also be the most expensive. A detailed cost analysis will provide data for comparing the various reprographics processes and selecting the most appropriate one.

EXAMPLE: Ellman has to reproduce 30 copies of a one-page report. If she decides to copy the page on a low-volume convenience copier, the cost will be 3.5 cents per copy, or a total of $1.05. If she uses an offset process to produce the 30 copies, she will probably be able to produce them at approximately 1 cent per copy after the master has been produced. Time may be an important factor for her in deciding which process to use.

b. *Standardizing equipment and supply usage:* If compatible equipment is used in various locations throughout the company, supplies can be ordered for all equipment at the same time, thus taking advantage of quantity ordering. From a maintenance point of view, obtaining service on the same equipment brands will reduce the costs since more than one piece of equipment could be serviced during a single visit from a repair technician. Quantity rates or service contracts may also be available that may reduce repair and maintenance costs. Production usage needs to be monitored to ensure that the brand selected services the quantity needs for all locations.

EXAMPLE: Some companies have established satellite centers within various departments of the company, each with the same type of equipment system. Therefore, the same supplies can be used in each location. The only drawback occurs when a particular brand seems to require constant repair or one center starts reporting excessive repair requests. The administrative manager needs to examine the copy volume and determine whether this particular brand can withstand the usage required.

c. *Conducting departmental surveys:* Departments should be made aware of usage and cost figures for reprographics services incurred at least on a monthly basis. Cumulative figures for annual operations are also helpful when planning annual budgets. Sometimes, department personnel are never shown the figures that would substantiate exactly how much the equipment is actually used. These figures can be helpful in determining future equipment needs or in establishing guidelines for the usage of the different reproduction methods available within the firm.

One of the primary responsibilities of the administrative manager is to reduce office costs in order to make office support a more productive yet cost-effective function within the firm. Controlling the reprographics costs incurred is one way of reducing possible waste of valuable resources within the firm.

D. Innovations and Trends in Reprographics Systems

The "paperless office" has not materialized, as predicted for a number of years. If anything, more records and more paper have been generated as a result of using computers and office automation technology to speed up various processes. The importance of the production of high-quality paper documents cannot be underestimated. Technology is permitting the creation of high-quality paper documents in much less time for the promotion of new products and services.

1. *Integration of Reprographics with Other Systems:* The interface of reprographics with computer systems and computer software has produced some miraculous results. Text created through word processing, spreadsheet, and graphics software is recorded on disk and converted easily to publishing systems. Much time is saved when the office professional can key in the original text with word processing software and convert it to an appropriate systems file that can be applied to a specific reprographics process.

2. *Increased Use of In-House Facilities:* Copying, duplicating, and printing can often be handled more easily in-house than by sending work outside the firm. The computer is enabling more sophisticated composition and desktop publishing work to be handled with much more ease and speed by office support personnel.

3. *Laser Printing:* One of the most profound innovations in reprographics is the laser used for high-speed printing. Copies may be reproduced in different colors, or business forms may be produced with very intricate designs. Laser printers, used with microcomputer systems, enable the use of a wide variety of typefaces and type styles in producing original copy.

4. *Facsimile Transmission (Fax):* A revolution in the costs of using fax has taken place within the past few years. Although facsimile transmission has been available for years, it was always considered an expensive process. Now the costs are low enough that for $1 to $2 per page, you can fax information anywhere in the world by telephone in just a matter of minutes.

5. *Voice Recognition Technology:* Research is still being conducted with communication devices that permit reproduction in print from the human voice. Voice messages are being used in all types of computer networks. Direct lines are available to the computer for information storage, thus integrating voice processing with records management. Some experts predict that once voice recognition technology is perfected and more readily available, keyboarding may no longer be necessary as an input device. The most common voice input products on the market are navigation products, development of voice input products, and dictation products.

   a. Navigation products help the user control the software operations by launching and operating programs through a set of spoken commands.

   b. Programmers develop voice input products that are used in developing customized computer programs.

c. Dictation products involve creating documents using word processing applications through the use of speech commands. Numbers can be placed on a spreadsheet, or words can be placed within textual material.

Voice recognition technology is being used in a growing number of firms, including banking, engineering, medicine, insurance, and transportation. However, its use is still in the pioneer stages.

6. *Visual Information Display:* Information is retrieved from computer storage through the use of a visual display or terminal. By keying in the right codes, copies of information may be ordered. Choices are available for hard copy as well as soft copy.

7. *Optical Character Recognition (OCR):* With OCR equipment, hard copy, either typewritten or handwritten, can be read by the system. The information can be transferred to a magnetic storage medium for later viewing or conversion to printed copies. OCR will continue to play an important role in office systems of the future.

Keeping up to date with the latest reprographics processes will require specialized personnel who read professional journals and participate in professional seminars, trade shows, and training to become familiar with the latest equipment and technical processes being used within the industry.

Review Questions

Directions: Select the best answer from the four alternatives. Write your answer in the blank to the left of the number.

_____
1. A business organization plans to examine the reprographic needs of the organization. One factor to consider when conducting such a needs assessment is

   a. the specific characteristics of business documents that need to be reproduced in a given period of time.
   b. specialized personnel who will perform specific reprographics functions.
   c. the equipment that will be used for the process.
   d. quick access to centralized service.

_____
2. One of the production requirements that may influence a decision about the availability of reprographics services is

   a. the development of a detailed procedures manual.
   b. the decentralization of reprographics services.
   c. the specification of image reductions or enlargements needed.
   d. the appointment of an administrative professional to supervise reprographics services for the firm.

_____
3. Which one of the following is an example of decentralized control?

   a. Specialized personnel are available to assist with custom work requiring layout and design or desktop publishing.
   b. Organization-wide regulations are established for equipment maintenance.
   c. A large variety of production jobs can be scheduled during the same period of time.
   d. More supervision may be needed to be sure that basic operations are understood.

_____
4. If reprographics functions are decentralized within the firm,

   a. layout and design work can be handled by any administrative professional.
   b. workers within a given department are able to perform copying and duplicating functions as needed.
   c. more lead time must be allowed to get the job done.
   d. there will be less duplication of reprographics equipment, even copiers, within the firm.

_____
5. One of the primary advantages of decentralized reprographics services is that

   a. priorities are more difficult to determine within the department.
   b. departmental policies and procedures govern reprographics operations within the department.
   c. turnaround time to get a document produced will be increased.
   d. the use and maintenance of the equipment must be controlled.

6. Which one of the following is a disadvantage of centralized control over reprographics operations?

   a. Production may take longer because of the specialized personnel and equipment involved.
   b. A large variety of reprographics work can be done in-house.
   c. Office productivity is decreased because of the time involved to complete production jobs.
   d. Scheduling production jobs is more difficult.

7. Sometimes, centralized reprographics centers are established within the organization to provide

   a. departmental regulation of reprographics policies and procedures.
   b. production work completed within the shortest possible time.
   c. specialized personnel for desktop publishing.
   d. self-service opportunities to increase production time.

8. Miller, the marketing manager, has initiated a work order for a sales brochure for a new toy robot to Adams, the reprographics manager. In considering the requirements of the job, Adams would most likely

   a. recommend that Miller seek the assistance of a commercial printing firm in the production of the sales brochure.
   b. accept the work order and then talk with his design staff about the feasibility of preparing the brochure.
   c. ask Miller to discuss the plans for the brochure with the design staff to see whether it is a job that can be done in-house.
   d. accept the work order and tell Miller that there should be no difficulty in meeting the deadline.

9. Which one of the following would best be produced in an in-house reprographics service?

   a. Advertising brochure for a new product
   b. Annual report of the company
   c. Company newsletter
   d. Periodical published by the company

10. Contracting with a commercial printing firm would be most cost-effective in creating

    a. business forms for the company.
    b. photographic posters illustrating a new product.
    c. company newsletter.
    d. a Web site for the company.

_____ **11.** Reprographic processes tend to be

   a. more expensive in terms of equipment investment than other office support services.
   b. the least expensive office support services provided.
   c. approximately the same cost as word processing or desktop publishing services.
   d. more expensive because of the use of commercial services.

_____ **12.** When comparing reprographics processes, _copy quality_ refers to the

   a. costs involved in producing the document.
   b. appearance of the document copies.
   c. preparation time involved in producing the document.
   d. number of copies required.

_____ **13.** When more than one reprographics process may be considered for producing copies of documents, selecting the appropriate process depends on the

   a. procedures for submitting the work to be done.
   b. basic operation of the equipment.
   c. training needed by operators.
   d. amount of time needed to prepare the copies.

_____ **14.** Developing a procedures manual helps to

   a. determine the best method to use in preparing copies of a document.
   b. standardize the methods used for performing specific business functions.
   c. decide on the reprographics process for specific copy preparation.
   d. determine whether the technology is being appropriately applied to a specific task.

_____ **15.** One of the devices used to monitor the number of copies that are produced on a copier is to

   a. limit the number of supplies available for use with the copier.
   b. reduce the number of people who have access to the equipment.
   c. require that an auditron be used to activate the copier.
   d. conduct a departmental survey to see how much the copier needs to be used.

_____ **16.** Randall saw a particularly interesting newsletter design in the latest issue of a popular information systems magazine and decided to make a copy of the article for her sample newsletter file. She refers to these samples when people in the organization ask for her help in creating department or division newsletters. Which one of the following statements about copying the article is true?

   a. No copies can legally be made of the article.
   b. Randall must contact the publisher for permission to make a copy of the article.
   c. Anyone can make one copy of a copyrighted article for personal use.
   d. Randall may make as many copies of the article as she wishes.

17. Which one of the following statements illustrates an operations control?

    a. Only authorized personnel should have access to reprographics systems.
    b. People need to be trained depending on their skill and expertise.
    c. Individual departments are charged for costs related to specific work orders.
    d. The number of copies to be prepared at one time is restricted to 25.

18. One of the ways to control the reprographics costs involved in producing documents is to

    a. purchase compatible equipment to be used in various locations around the company.
    b. pay close attention to copyright laws.
    c. provide access to facsimile transmission for more efficient message communication.
    d. establish specific procedures for users who wish to submit production work.

19. Keeping up with the changing technology is one of the most important aspects of Jefferson's job as the manager of reprographic services. Which one of the following demonstrates that Jefferson is making a concerted effort to keep his staff involved in technological change?

    a. Jefferson recommends to the vice president that three employees in the reprographics department be approved to attend the annual seminar of the American Graphics Design Association.
    b. Jefferson subscribes to a number of technical magazines and has them on display within the department.
    c. Jefferson is a member of the state professional graphics design association and attends the trade shows held each year.
    d. Jefferson is active in several community organizations where he is in contact with managers from other nearby companies.

20. Reprographics management within an organization will be affected *most* by which one of the following developments?

    a. The use of word processing to create document text
    b. Laser technology in high-speed printing
    c. The per-copy cost of producing documents
    d. General management of reprographics services provided by an administrative manager

Solutions

Answer	Refer to:
1. (a)	[A-1]
2. (c)	[A-2]
3. (d)	[B-1-a]
4. (b)	[B-1-a(1)]
5. (b)	[B-1-a(2)]
6. (a)	[B-1-b]
7. (c)	[B-1-b(1)]
8. (c)	[B-2-a]
9. (c)	[B-2-a(3)]
10. (b)	[B-2-b]
11. (a)	[C]
12. (b)	[C-2-a]
13. (d)	[C-2-d]
14. (b)	[C-3-a]
15. (c)	[C-3-b(1)]
16. (c)	[C-3-b(2)]
17. (d)	[C-3-b(5)]
18. (a)	[C-4-b]
19. (a)	[D]
20. (b)	[D-3]

CHAPTER 13

Information Distribution

OVERVIEW

Information is a critical asset in today's organization, and the procedures involved in the internal and external distribution of information is of prime importance to organizations. Organizations today are even able to put a value (a price tag) on having usable information at the right time, in the right form, and at an affordable cost.

Although previous chapters have focused on communication technology applied in the distribution of information, this chapter emphasizes some of the methods and procedures that the administrative professional needs to be aware of and use in making decisions about information distribution. The technology involved will be mentioned, but detail is available in other chapters, as specific references will indicate.

KEY TERMS

Bulk business mail
Electronic mail
Express mail
Facsimile (fax)
    transmission
First-class mail
Fourth-class mail
Home page
Information
Information distribution

Internet
Intranet
Mail services
Mailgram
Memorandum
Netiquette
Parcel post
Priority mail
Second-class mail

Telecommunications
Telegram
Telex
Third-class mail
Voice messaging system
Web site
Webmaster
World Wide Web
ZIP code

A. Basic Principles of Information Distribution

Information is a valuable asset in all types of organizations today, and successful management and distribution of information is a critical issue. Office administrators must deal with a multitude of different types of information received from sources through numerous paths and routes. A large quantity of information is stored on paper, but information transmitted electronically is becoming even more popular as business executives, managers, and other office support professionals become more versatile with technology.

1. *Guidelines for Information Distribution:* Specific guidelines for establishing appropriate means of information distribution include the following:

a. *Condition of the information:* The receiver of the information being distributed must be able to use or apply the information to tasks at hand. If the information is not in a usable condition or format, the information is of no value until it can be converted.

EXAMPLES:

If a summary report is required and a detailed report is received, the report is of limited value.

If an unexpected situation requires immediate information (ad hoc [demand] report) and the information system supports only scheduled (periodic) reports for this output, the information system is not meeting the needs of the organization.

b. *Internal and external distribution:* Procedures need to be established for both internal and external information distribution to occur without undue difficulty.

c. *Speed of transmission:* The information being transmitted must be distributed rapidly enough that the contents are still current and applicable to the needs of the receiver. Information that is out of date or too late to be useful is of little value to the receiver.

EXAMPLE: If the information needed for tomorrow morning's meeting was mailed through regular mail service (not express mail), the information will be received too late to be useful.

d. *Accuracy of information:* Another essential element in the distribution of information is the importance of accuracy in information as well as the transmission of that information (verifying that all pages of the document were received).

e. *Distribution cost:* The volume of information to be transmitted, the urgency with which that information is needed, and the means by which the information is transmitted will be important factors in determining the distribution cost of information.

2. *Criteria for Selecting Information Distribution Means:* To select the appropriate method or means to use in distributing information, office professionals must keep in mind these criteria:

a. *Type of information to be distributed:* The amount of information to be distributed and the type of information are important considerations in deciding which means to use in transmitting the information. If the type of information is statistical in nature, it may best be presented in a written form. If the information is more informal in nature, a brief message in the form of a telephone call or an e-mail may suffice.

b. *Speed of transmission desired:* How important is it that the information be transmitted quickly? If transmission must take place within the next few minutes, e-mail, telephone, or fax might be the answer. If the information is in written form, a large quantity, and needed in at least one day, express mail service may be the answer.

c. *Format of the information:* In what format is the information: written or oral? The format of the information will help in determining how to transmit the information where it is needed.

d. *Effect of peak work periods:* "Busy seasons" impact an organization's ability to handle the creation and transmission of information requests and information reporting. During peak seasons, most organizations increase the staff hours to handle information processing.

EXAMPLE: An accounting firm has certain times of the year that are busier than others. A firm involved with taxes has an increased workload from January through April 15 and typically increases the number of staff during those months.

e. *Cost of information distribution:* Information that is to be distributed immediately will tend to be more expensive to send. The use of Internet e-mail capabilities provides efficient distribution service at a lower cost between organizations networked into the World Wide Web environment.

EXAMPLE: A legal document required immediately can be sent via express mail delivery. A 1-ounce envelope costs approximately $11.75 to send (rather than the modest cost of first-class postage). However, the information may be worth the extra expense.

B. Internal Information Distribution

Decisions need to be made on the means used to distribute information within the organization. The types of information services available for internal distribution of information involve an intranet, telephone system, or an interoffice communication system for hard-copy mail. The hard-copy internal distribution is typically handled through a mail distribution center or personnel assigned the responsibility of handling the mail. Specific types of internal distribution include e-mail, intranet bulletins, telephone and voice messaging, and interoffice correspondence.

1. *Intranet:* The intranet is the organization's internal network for making company policies, procedures, news items, and data/information available to the employees electronically. E-mail communication is also available through the organization's network. A simple intranet includes a computer with Web server software; each user's computer is linked with a Web browser to the server. Firewall software protects the intranet information from being accessed by the external public.

a. *Electronic mail:* Many organizations have installed wide area networks (WANs) and local area networks (LANs) to facilitate the type of electronic communication that is expected to occur. When a person wants to access information stored on the network or to transmit an e-mail message, the LAN is put to use. A decision must be made as to whom the message should go: one person or a number of people within the organization. The basic premise of electronic mail and LANs is to make information available to people on the network quickly and effectively, thus reducing the amount of paper that flows through the office. Some individuals abuse the ease of transmitting information by not discriminating who should receive the document. Company procedures regarding e-mail use should establish appropriate guidelines.

EXAMPLE: Edwards has a communication to send by e-mail to department managers regarding a new product. She accesses the directory and finds the mailing list of all department managers. Edwards decides that the department managers can determine whether their assistants should receive the information about the product. She makes a conscious decision to notify only the department managers, sending the e-mail to 20 people rather than 50. This decision helps others with their management of information.

b. *Intranet notices:* The intranet can become an effective way to post general notices regarding company events and news. Also, having policies and procedures available to employees electronically reduces paper costs and maintains more reliable and accurate information. When a policy is changed, it only needs to be corrected on the electronic (soft) copy. An e-mail notice to appropriate personnel informs employees of the change; they can reference the document through the intranet.

2. *Telephone System:* The telephone continues to be a very important way of communicating with other people within the organization. Needed information is often obtained from a quick phone call to the right destination. The primary difficulty in using the telephone is to be able to reach the desired receiver of the information (see Section C-3-d in this chapter as well as Chapter 3, Section A, for more information on telephone procedures and systems).

EXAMPLE: "Telephone tag" is a frequent occurrence, with one person phoning another only to find that the person called is not in. Leaving a message helps, but when that person calls back, perhaps the original caller is not in. Therefore, handling voice messages properly impacts effective distribution of information.

    a. *Voice messages:* When the person is unavailable to answer a call, a message can be left through a voice message system. The effectiveness of this system depends on the quality of the information left in the message. Messages must be left with the idea that the individual will be able to respond directly to the information contained in the message. Voice mail is especially effective for short messages. Many voice messaging systems have only a short period of time (30 seconds) allotted for recording the message. Some of the latest voice messaging systems permit a longer total recording time, for example, 15 minutes, no matter the number of calls received. Most systems incorporate a closing command that indicates the end of the message.

    b. *Telephone messages:* An important part of appropriate interoffice communication is leaving messages that are meaningful to the recipient. Information such as the date, the time of the call, the name of the person who should receive the message, the name and number of the person who is calling, and a brief message should be included. Telephone messages need to be complete so that the receiver can respond appropriately. So that pertinent information is left on the message, the caller should plan in advance and be prepared as to what information needs to be left on the message. When the call is returned, the previous message should be referenced so that the answers provided make sense to the receiver. This saves time for both parties and enables information to be disseminated effectively and efficiently.

3. *Interoffice Communication:* Communication also takes place between offices or departments with hard-copy documents and through face-to-face communication.

    a. *Interoffice correspondence:* Even within an organization, one important decision is to put specific information in writing, depending on business needs or inquiries being made. The format generally used is a memorandum that tends to be written about one topic, short and to the point, and quickly transmitted through internal mail (see Chapter 19, Section C, for an example of a memorandum).

    b. *Face-to-face communication:* Many times, transmitting information in person is best. This is particularly helpful if the information is critical to a particular business function or if the sender (distributor) of the information is not exactly sure how the information will be received. Face-to-face communication is beneficial if there needs to be some discussion about the matter. Written interoffice correspondence, telephone calls, or electronic correspondence cannot replace the interpersonal enhancements of face-to-face conversation.

**C. External
Information
Distribution**

Mail services, delivery services, and telecommunications are the primary means of distributing information externally.

1. *Mail Services:* Postal or mail services are designed to facilitate incoming communication and outgoing communication from the organization. Within the organization, there needs to be a mail distribution center, with appropriately assigned personnel who have the responsibility of handling incoming and outgoing mail services.

   a. *Use of ZIP codes and bar codes:* To expedite mail deliveries throughout the United States, the U.S. Postal Service initiated the nine-digit ZIP code to enable mail to be sorted and delivered faster and more accurately. Bar codes imprinted on envelopes also contain ZIP code information and enable mail to be processed more quickly.

   b. *Procedures for incoming mail:* Once the day's mail has been received, several procedures must be followed so that the mail is delivered to the correct locations within the firm.

      (1) The mail must be sorted and delivered to the correct department or person. This can be accomplished in different ways: a messenger delivering the mail to each department, conveyor systems, pneumatic tubes, or electronic mail carts (see Chapter 3, Section B-1).

      (2) Once the mail is received within the department, the secretary or other office support professionals have the responsibility of opening the mail, date and time stamping the mail, sorting it by priority, and delivering it to the manager or executive for action.

      (3) The contents of the envelopes should be examined by the administrative assistant or secretary to see what additional information might be needed when the manager or executive needs to respond to the correspondence.

         (a) Mail containing checks or money must be recorded and logged. A paper trail must be created for this type of mail.

         (b) Files or specific records may be necessary in order to respond to the correspondence received.

         (c) Stamping the time and date on each piece of correspondence is very important. Even though a date appears on the correspondence, the date of receipt is equally important in the case of incoming mail.

   c. *Procedures for outgoing mail:* Mail that is being sent from the organization must be classified and grouped according to the type and destination.

      (1) *Categories of outgoing mail:* The U.S. Postal Service classifies mail into the following categories:

         (a) *First-class mail:* Personal and business correspondence, handwritten and typewritten messages, bills, statements of account, postcards, printed forms filled out in writing, and business reply mail not requiring the highest priority. First-class mail is transported by air on a space-available basis. There is a minimum charge for up to 1 ounce of first-class mail, with an additional charge for each additional ounce or fraction of an ounce.

         (b) *Priority mail:* First-class mail that weighs over 11 ounces up to a maximum of 70 pounds, usually delivered within two to three days.

(c) *Airmail:* Mail service that is advantageous for distances greater than 250 miles. Airmail is no longer vital for domestic delivery within the United States.

(d) *Second-class mail:* Publications such as newspapers and periodicals. A special fee is required to mail material second class, and the mailing must be sent in bulk lots or volume mailings.

(e) *Third-class mail:* Mail such as advertising brochures and catalogs that is not classified as first- or second-class mail, weighing less than 16 ounces.

(f) *Bulk business mail (BBM):* Domestic third-class mail, bound printed matter, and small parcels weighing less than 16 ounces. Each third-class bulk mailing must consist of a minimum of 200 pieces or 50 pounds. All pieces in the mailing must belong to the same processing category. For example, the mailing must be all letters, all flats, or all machinable parcels. Each bulk rate mailing requires payment of postage: precanceled stamps, permit imprint, or postage meter. Mail has to be sorted and parceled according to ZIP codes for ease of sorting by the post office.

(g) *Fourth-class mail:* Packages, printed matter (books), and all other mailable matter that weighs 16 ounces or more and is not included in first-, second-, or third-class mail; also known as *parcel post.* A library rate may be used by mailers who send books, printed music, academic papers, or similar items.

(h) *Express mail:* The fastest mail delivery service, which guarantees delivery the next day, sometimes even the same day. All express mail travels by regularly scheduled airline flights. Any mailable item weighing up to 70 pounds may be sent. Express mail rates, based on the weight of the item and the distance it must travel, include insurance coverage, record of delivery, and a receipt.

(2) *Other postal services:* Some of the additional mailing services available through the U.S. Postal Service include the following:

(a) *Special delivery/special handling:* Immediate delivery within prescribed hours and distances may be necessary. Special delivery includes regular postage plus an extra fee for the special delivery. Special handling is for third- or fourth-class mail that can travel with first-class mail and that can be delivered on regularly scheduled delivery trips.

(b) *Registered mail:* Protection is given to valuable items, money, checks, jewelry, bonds, stock certificates, and important papers. All classes of mail may be registered, but first-class rates must be paid. The U.S. Postal Service will pay claims up to $25,000 regardless of the amount for which the package was registered.

(c) *Insured mail:* Third- or fourth-class mail may be insured for up to $500 against loss or damage. A receipt is issued to the sender.

(d) *Certificate of mailing:* When proof is needed that an item was taken to the post office for mailing, a certificate of mailing may be purchased, not as proof of delivery but rather as proof of mailing.

(e) *Certified mail:* First-class mail with no dollar value of its own may be certified, thus providing proof of mailing and delivery.

(f) *Collect-on-delivery (COD) mail:* The seller may obtain COD service by paying a fee in addition to the regular postage. Fees and postage must be prepaid by the seller; the seller specifies the total COD charges to be collected from the buyer in cash, including postage and the COD fee. The maximum amount collectible on one package is $500.

(g) *International mail:* Postage for letters and postal cards mailed to Mexico is the same as that for letters and cards mailed within the United States. Rates for mail going to all other countries are higher, and the weights are limited. Customs declaration forms may be necessary for specific contents within parcels.

2. *Private Messenger or Delivery Services:* Many organizations use a private messenger, delivery, or courier service when a guaranteed delivery time is required. Services available and fees charged by different services vary. The office professional should investigate these services to identify the messenger, delivery, or courier service that best meets the needs of the organization.

3. *Telecommunication Systems:* Information distribution services available through telecommunications systems are popular alternatives to postal or delivery services, depending on the type of information to be distributed and the form in which it is required. Telecommunication systems have expanded from telegrams and mailgrams to the new frontier—the Internet.

a. *Telegrams and mailgrams:* A message transmitted over telephone lines by Western Union is a telegram. Two commonly used types of telegrams include the full-rate telegram and the overnight telegram. Full-rate telegrams are transmitted by telephone within two hours or by messenger within five hours. Overnight telegrams are transmitted during the night, with delivery guaranteed by 2 P.M. the following day. A mailgram is a message transmitted by Western Union to the post office that serves the ZIP code of the addressee. At the post office, the mailgram is printed, inserted into an envelope, and included with the next regularly scheduled mail delivery. A mailgram is less expensive than the telegram.

b. *Telex:* Telex is another Western Union service that is used to transmit messages to foreign countries via telephone lines, fiber optic cables, microwave dishes, and space satellites.

c. *Telephone technology:* Procedures for using telephone technology between and among organizations are very important to an office.

(1) *Telephone communication:* Using telephone communication at the workstation is an extremely important aspect of office life. Personal traits such as politeness, courtesy, and tact are vital in placing and responding to telephone communication.

(2) *Procedures for telephone usage:* Here are some of the specific procedures the office professional needs to keep in mind:

(a) Answer the telephone promptly when it rings, preferably after the first or second ring.

(b) If you are going to be away from your desk for an extended period of time, forward your calls to another person or have your calls covered by a voice mail network that will save your messages.

(c) Take accurate messages so that correct information will be transmitted to other people in your office. When people leave messages, they expect the information to be transmitted correctly.

EXAMPLE: A telephone message with numbers transposed or an area code missing is of no value. The call cannot easily be returned. Names of callers should be verified for correct spelling as well.

(d) Place telephone calls with a specific purpose in mind. Know the name of the person you are calling and be ready to give message information if that person is not available to take the call.

(e) Read or listen to telephone messages as soon after arrival at the office as possible. Doing so helps you prioritize the return of telephone calls along with other informational tasks.

(3) *Voice mail:* A telephone system is greatly enhanced through the addition of a voice mail network as a means of recording telephone messages received at a particular workstation. Most voice mail networks are set up so that if the telephone is not answered by the third or fourth ring, the caller will automatically hear a prompt from the person being called requesting that a message be recorded. This type of system enables each person to receive messages directly instead of receiving these messages through an intermediary who may or may not record an accurate message.

d. *Facsimile (fax) transmission:* The way that information is distributed or communicated to or through the office sometimes necessitates quick responses in the form of documents or copies of documents.

(1) Inquiries may require the immediate transmittal of copies of written documents. Fax machines can transmit copies of documents over telephone lines from one fax machine to another in a matter of minutes. Only a few seconds are usually required to transmit one page.

(2) Separate telephone numbers may be assigned to fax machines so that once the connection is made to the other machine, the transmission should take only a few minutes, typically no more than a minute per page. The cost of fax transmission has been reduced greatly within the past few years.

Domestic as well as international transmission is available, with the cost similar to that of a telephone call.

e. *Internet:* The Internet is the largest implementation of internetworking linking millions of individual networks around the world. Web sites and external electronic communication are the most prevalent uses of the Internet.

(1) *Electronic mail:* Most secretaries and busy executives find themselves part of the global network, the Internet, as well as their internal local area network (LAN), providing electronic mail capability for both external and internal communications. The primary reasons for electronic communication are speed in transmitting information, saving time, and reducing the amount of paper involved in communications.

(a) *Electronic mail technology:* An explanation of the technology involved in electronic mail networks is included in Chapter 3, Section E.

(b) *Electronic mail procedures:* Most electronic messages are stored on the individual's electronic mailbox. The secretary or executive assistant can assist the busy executive in accessing electronic mail communications and sorting those that require immediate attention from others that can be delayed. Here are some of the decisions that need to be made about each message:

- Is this an item of information, or does it require a response? If it is an item of information, electronic file folders can be created and titled *Reading Material.* All correspondence received can be moved from the electronic box to the "read" folder. As the executive reads this correspondence, he or she can decide whether it should be deleted or moved to an appropriate electronic folder for future reference. Management of electronic information is very important.

- Does this item require a response? Can you respond to it, or do you need additional information before responding? Should the executive or someone else respond to it? Disseminate the information accordingly.

- Once the item is read and you or the executive no longer needs the information contained in the message, delete it from the electronic mail listing. Keep the e-mail network "clean" from a cluttered and sometimes outdated collection of information items.

- Can you send an immediate response? This will enable you to handle the item only once. Refer to the directory listing to get the appropriate e-mail designation for the individual to whom you are sending the response. Word your response simply and concisely. The system will send the message on command.

- When necessary, make sure that the response was received. Most electronic mail networks identify the date/time when a communication was sent as well as a return receipt showing the date/time that communication was received and read.

(c) *Netiquette:* As more and more office communication is distributed internally and externally, etiquette guidelines should be followed. Etiquette practices for the electronic environment are often referred to as *netiquette.* The following are some of the basic practices which businesses should follow.

- Use a subject line so the recipient knows the topic of the e-mail before opening the message.

   EXAMPLE:

   IAAP INTERNATIONAL CONFERENCE *is a more descriptive subject line than just the word* CONFERENCE.

- Remember to follow the guidelines for well-written communication when composing e-mail messages (see Chapter 16).

- Avoid all caps when keying e-mail communications. A message or a portion of a message in all caps gives the impression that you are shouting. Other means of emphasis include bold, underline, or bullets. Many e-mail systems today also have the option for different-colored fonts. If you cannot bold or underscore, the following e-mail substitutes may be used:

   Underscoring: Key in an underscore (_) at the beginning and end of words needing to be underscored.

Bolding: Key in an asterisk (*) at the beginning and end of the words to be in bold.

Note: When an e-mail message is sent using a different e-mail program than the sender uses, the receiver needs to be able to access the desired type fonts that produce underlining, bold, or other features as needed.

- Abbreviations and emotion icons (faces) are for very informal communication. Even though e-mail is an informal communication, abbreviations and emotion icons should be avoided or used at a minimum in business e-mail.

- When using the reply option and the original message is being returned, your response should be at the beginning of the e-mail message, not at the end of the original message. Sometimes responses are interleaved within the original message. When this option is used, color code your response or use the bold or underscore to highlight your response. At the beginning, make it clear to the receiver that your responses are interleaved in **bold** (note your response method).

EXAMPLE: The following e-mail response is interleaved in bold.

Looking forward to your arrival on Monday. Hoping to have time to meet before the Executive Session at 6 P.M. When do you arrive? **Monday 10 A.M. Limo to hotel (Harrington) by approximately noon.** *Can we meet before the meeting?* **Let's have lunch at the Harrington at 12:30 P.M. . . .**

- At the end, sign your e-mail messages with name, title, company name, e-mail address, and telephone number. Many systems provide a signature option. Once your signature is saved in the system, you can easily affix your signature by selecting that option.

- Do not clog the Internet by forwarding chain letters and other nonbusiness material from the office. Uncontrolled use of the Internet is like sending and receiving "junk" mail through the regular postal service.

Electronic mail can be extremely helpful, especially in terms of speed in communication and ease in getting a quick reply (see Chapter 16 for a review of composing e-mail messages).

(2) *Web site:* Many organizations globally provide information about their firm through Web pages. This new way of communication combines text, hypermedia, graphics, and sound when formatting documents for the Web. The person in charge of an organization's Web site needs to be skilled in communication and artistic design as well as Web site management strategies. The person responsible for these activities is called a *Webmaster.* A *Web site* consists of all the pages collectively for the company. The *home page* is the first page for the Web site and is registered on the World Wide Web through a Web address—a Uniform Resource Locator (URL) (see Chapter 3, Section F, for more information on Web technology).

The distribution of information, both internally and externally, depends on the nature of the information being communicated as well as the means that are available for such communication. The administrative assistant or secretary must take the responsibility for making numerous important decisions about the communication and distribution of information.

Review Questions

Directions: Select the best answer from the four alternatives. Write your answer in the blank to the left of the number.

_____ **1.** Computer technology facilitates many business applications today in creating a relatively new asset known as

      a. capital.
      b. management.
      c. information.
      d. investment.

_____ **2.** The receiver of information being distributed must be able to

      a. file the information for future use.
      b. apply the information to business tasks to be performed.
      c. critique the information to determine its present value.
      d. convert the information to a useful form.

_____ **3.** The cost of distributing information depends most on the

      a. accuracy of the information being transmitted.
      b. application of the information to a specific task.
      c. nature of the information.
      d. means by which the information is transmitted.

_____ **4.** An informal message that needs to be transmitted within the next few minutes might best be sent by

      a. express mail.
      b. memorandum.
      c. fax.
      d. business letter.

_____ **5.** The electronic network within an organization that is used to distribute news items as well as policies and procedures to employees is referred to as

      a. the Internet.
      b. voice messaging.
      c. a browser.
      d. an intranet.

6. The basic premise of a local area network is to

   a. make information available to people on the network quickly.
   b. increase the amount of hard-copy information flowing through the office.
   c. send identical messages to every employee throughout the company at the same time.
   d. establish guidelines for the use of e-mail throughout the organization.

7. Which one of the following types of information should be posted on the intranet?

   a. An e-mail message directed to the ten members of the technology advisory committee
   b. A general notice to employees about working hours during the upcoming holiday season
   c. The agenda for the next board of directors meeting
   d. News release about the company's newest product sent to local and area news media

8. Which one of the following would be the most helpful practice to use in curbing "telephone tag"?

   a. Leaving recorded messages with date, time, name of caller, and nature of the call
   b. Sending information requests through interoffice correspondence
   c. Implementing a voice mail system
   d. Installing a local area network to facilitate interoffice communication

9. One of the primary purposes of electronic mail is to

   a. restrict the information available to individual workstations on the network.
   b. increase the number of messages communicated through the network.
   c. increase the hard-copy correspondence flowing from desk to desk.
   d. make information available to people on the network in an effective manner.

10. Interoffice correspondence is typically written in the form of a

    a. business letter.
    b. telephone reply.
    c. memorandum.
    d. voice message.

11. The sender who is transmitting information of a critical nature regarding a particular business function may prefer to use which one of the following channels?

    a. Electronic mail
    b. Express mail service
    c. Voice mail message
    d. Face-to-face communication

12. Postcards, filled-in business forms, bills, and handwritten messages are considered

    a. priority mail.
    b. first-class mail.
    c. third-class mail.
    d. express mail.

13. A mailing of advertising matter, each piece weighing 1 3/4 ounces, to 275 businesses could most economically be sent as

    a. bulk business mail.
    b. second-class mail.
    c. priority mail.
    d. registered mail.

14. COD mail requires that when the mail or merchandise is delivered,

    a. the buyer must prepay postage for the mailing.
    b. the seller can send goods valued up to $300.
    c. the total charges (price of goods, postage, and COD fee) must be collected in cash from the buyer.
    d. the buyer can charge the total amount, including postage and COD fee, to a credit-card account.

15. The means of distribution that necessitates the immediate transmission of information over telephone lines and arrives at the destination in the form of copies of documents is

    a. electronic mail.
    b. fax.
    c. voice mail.
    d. telecommunications.

16. One of the primary reasons for applying electronic communication to both external and internal business communication is to

    a. transmit information as quickly as possible.
    b. increase the quantity of hard-copy documentation created.
    c. set priorities for information distribution.
    d. concentrate on domestic services available for the transmission of information.

17. Which one of the following statements supports a decision to select electronic mail as the channel for an immediate reply?

    a. Additional information from a customer file needs to be accessed.
    b. The marketing manager is the right person to respond to the message.
    c. The receiver of the message needs to be notified of a time change in her 2 P.M. appointment tomorrow.
    d. The issue is included on the agenda for next week's board of directors meeting.

_____   **18.** Which one of the following business practices illustrates the application of netiquette?

      a. The most important points in an e-mail message should be typed in all caps.
      b. Emotion icons should be used only in informal communication.
      c. A response to an original message should be keyed after the original message.
      d. Chain letters may be forwarded as long as they do not interfere with business communication.

_____   **19.** The first page of a site registered on the World Wide Web is called the

      a. URL.
      b. Web site.
      c. Webmaster.
      d. home page.

_____   **20.** The person who is in charge of an organization's Web site, usually called the Webmaster, needs to be skilled in

      a. business communication strategies.
      b. international business policies.
      c. administrative management theories.
      d. teleconferencing networks.

Solutions

Answer	Refer to:
1. (c)	[A]
2. (b)	[A-1-a]
3. (d)	[A-1-e]
4. (c)	[A-2-b]
5. (d)	[B-1]
6. (a)	[B-1-a]
7. (b)	[B-1-b]
8. (a)	[B-2-b]
9. (d)	[B-1-a]
10. (c)	[B-3-a]
11. (d)	[B-3-b]
12. (b)	[C-1-c(1)(a)]
13. (a)	[C-1-c(1)(f)]
14. (c)	[C-1-c(2)(f)]
15. (b)	[C-3-d]
16. (a)	[C-3-e(1)]
17. (c)	[C-3-e(b)]
18. (b)	[C-3-e(1)(c)]
19. (d)	[C-3-e(2)]
20. (a)	[C-3-e(2)]

CHAPTER 14

Document Production

OVERVIEW

Secretaries are particularly skilled in the preparation of business documents. Skill with word processing and other application software programs is very observable as experienced secretaries perform their job tasks.

Typically, classified advertisements for administrative assistant and secretarial positions identify specific competencies employers require to produce the types of documents needed (e.g., English skills, word processing software skills, and experience with other software application programs). Often, during the application process, employers administer performance tests to evaluate the applicant's abilities in document production.

The process of document production requires the secretary to make many important decisions from planning to producing to perfecting the final document. Chapters 2 and 19 highlight features of the technology and format decisions to be made by the secretary. This chapter focuses on procedures and decisions that the secretary must make during the process of document production.

KEY TERMS

Compatibility	File	Software manuals
Conversion	File management	Tutorials
Dictation	File name	Work measurement
Disk label	Input	Work standards
Document format	Priorities	
External label	Production	

A. Receiving Input for Document Production

Initially, the administrative assistant or secretary must receive information in the form of text or data for a document to be produced, and numerous decisions will need to be made about the way that particular document will be produced. Factors affecting these decisions begin to evolve from the way input is received.

1. *Receiving Input in Different Forms:* Secretaries receive input from a variety of sources and users. Today's secretary may work for several people rather than a single person (the traditional one-to-one ratio). Therefore, input for document production comes from a variety of users and may be received in the form of dictation, handwriting, or

even rough drafts on disks. The way input is provided probably is not standard throughout the organization.

a. *Dictation input:* Dictating messages in the automated office is very important. The secretary or administrative assistant may be required to interpret the dictated message or may have to actually dictate input for transcription by other office support staff.

(1) *Interpreting dictation from others:* When interpreting the dictated message, the secretary must verify that all information and data are accurate.

    (a) *Numeric data:* Addresses, dollar amounts, percentages, and any important fact or figure must be accurate. Often, the secretary will be given a hard copy containing the correct information, perhaps some previous correspondence, or the original data may be found in the organization files. If the information cannot be verified and appears to be inaccurate, the matter should be brought to the attention of the originator of the dictation.

    (b) *Grammar and punctuation:* The use of dictionaries, office manuals, and electronic information processing tools should minimize spelling, grammar, and punctuation errors. Careful proofreading of the document should eliminate any other errors. All documents should be free of spelling, grammar, or punctuation errors.

(2) *Dictating messages:* In an automated office, recording messages on a dictation system is very common. The feedback from face-to-face dictation is missing in the automated environment. The dictator needs to provide complete instructions and speak clearly when using a dictation system.

    (a) *Predictation planning:* It is important that the secretary plan what needs to be covered in the dictation. All information necessary to prepare the dictation needs to be gathered first. Any other documents or files being referred to during the dictation should be numbered so that the person doing the transcription can easily locate and use these materials for reference.

    (b) *Beginning the dictation:* Identification of the person doing the dictating, the type of correspondence or document, and special format instructions should appear at the very beginning of the recorded dictation. When the transcription is being handled through an information processing center, it is particularly important for the transcriber to be given the general instructions for document production and the name of the person who is dictating. General instructions should include the following:

- The type of correspondence that follows (e.g., memorandum, letter, short report, rough draft).

- Letter format, unless the organization has a standard format that is always followed.

- Punctuation style, unless a standard style is followed within the organization. Open punctuation, with no punctuation after salutation or complimentary closing, is recognized as the most efficient style.

    (c) *Dictating:* The person doing the dictating should do so at a moderate pace in thought groups and enunciate clearly. Phrases and clauses help when dictating long sentences in thought groups. Also, a pause before and after instructions separates directions from dictation.

Adhering to the following dictation guidelines will make the transcription easier:

- Do not dictate the inside address and ZIP code when they are available to the transcriber from a document provided. At the time the address and ZIP code are dictated, say "The address and ZIP code are on the letter [or appropriate document reference] in the folder." All materials provided to the transcriber should be enclosed in a folder or similar carrier to be returned to the dictator with the finished transcribed document. By following this practice, all materials are kept together for efficient follow-through on the next phase.

- Spell out unusual names.

  EXAMPLE: "Mrs. Smyth (that's spelled S-m-y-t-h) will be able to . . ."

- Overemphasize the dictation of initials. Many times it is helpful to follow the initial with a word reference.

  EXAMPLE: "B as in boy."

- When a word typically spelled in lowercase should be capitalized, indicate that it should be capitalized. The same is true when a word should appear in all capitals.

  EXAMPLE: The statement "The new Marble top on the credenza . . ." would be dictated as follows:

  "The new (PAUSE) (typist, capital M) Marble (PAUSE) top on the credenza . . ."

  or

  "The new (PAUSE) (typist, all capital letters) MARBLE (PAUSE) top on the credenza . . ."

- To indicate the beginning and ending of quoted material, say "quote" and "unquote." For material to be in bold print, say, "boldface" and "unbold."

  EXAMPLE: "In an ex post facto design, (PAUSE) (boldface) (PAUSE) inferences about relations among variables (PAUSE) (unbold) (PAUSE) are made without direct intervention . . ." would be transcribed like this:

  *In an ex post facto design, **inferences about relations among variables** are made without direct intervention . . .*

- When a word is to be underlined, pause, then say "underline" followed by the word, then pause. If a phrase is underlined, pause, then say, "underline the phrase" before the phrase.

- When you prefer that a character be keyed a particular way, indicate your preference just prior to the character.

  EXAMPLE: For instructions on making a dash, say, "Secretary, make the dash by typing one hyphen preceded and followed by a blank space."

Once the dictator has indicated a preference, the transcriber should be consistent throughout that document. When the dictation is transcribed in a word/information processing center, the dictator should not assume that the same transcriber will key succeeding documents even though they were dictated at the same time on the same recording. A special instruction should be given at the beginning of the dictation or the first time it is needed in a new document.

b. *Handwritten input:* The most common form of input is provided in handwriting by managers and executives. Handwriting is also the slowest form of input, taking much longer to prepare than dictation or even keying in rough drafts of the text on disks. The difficulty in handwriting input is the problem one has sometimes with reading someone else's writing.

c. *Soft-copy input:* In today's electronic environment, executives and managers may prefer to key in drafts of the input text, in no particular format, and then have the secretary make corrections in the text of the document as well as put the document in correct format. Care should be taken in proofreading and editing the document content, using spelling- and grammar-check features. Valuable time is saved in keying in the text, but much time will be spent by the secretary in making editing changes and formatting the document.

2. *Receiving Unambiguous Directions:* One thing that secretaries appreciate most is receiving clear directions. In addition, secretaries pride themselves on their ability to give clear directions when they assign tasks to other office support staff: what the document is, what the content of that document should be, when it is needed and by whom, and where it should be sent. The supervisor or manager who can give clear, unambiguous directions will stand the best chance of receiving an accurate, complete document by the due date.

3. *Obtaining Supplies:* Letterheads, envelopes, computer paper, high-quality bond paper for specific applications, and any other office supplies needed for document production should be readily available. Some business forms are stored as templates on the intranet or company disks, ready for completion by the secretary.

4. *Possessing the Know-How:* Of prime importance is the knowledge or ability to produce the document according to the directions given. The executive assistant or secretary must have the skills and knowledges necessary to carry out the directive. If the person does not have the specific skill needed, training or retraining must be provided or someone else with those skills must be assigned the task.

5. *Determining Document Priorities:* Especially important is the ability to determine the priority of the documents to be produced. The highest-priority items should be completed immediately, while those of lesser priority can wait until later in the day or week, or possibly even later, to be completed. Too many people work "from the top down" in their in-basket of work tasks rather than sorting and categorizing the items into priorities. This type of sorting enables the secretary to "batch process" items that are similar.

EXAMPLE: Processing all documents that require word processing during the same time period is an excellent time management strategy. The person's train of thought is on word processing—the commands and the techniques. A switch to another software package will require a switch in perspective, skills needed, and thought processes.

B. Initiating Document Production

Once the input for the document has been received, decisions must be made about the actual document to be produced—who will do the task and how the document will be prepared.

1. *Making Assignment for Task Completion:* The initial decision of the secretary is whether to do the task or to assign it to someone else in the office. If the task is assigned to someone else, the secretary's responsibility is to give clear directions and to convey exactly the same message as that conveyed by the originator of the document. Basic directions should be very clear so that there is no misinterpretation of information.

2. *Deciding on the Production Method:* Next, an examination of the document will help in deciding exactly how the document will be produced, what hardware and software to use, what operations or instructional manuals will be helpful, and whether complete information is available to produce the document.

   a. *Using technology:* The decision must be made as to the technology to use. At times, it may be more efficient to use an electronic typewriter (with no storage capability) if a form to be filled out is easier handled with that equipment. At other times, a computer with word processing (or other productivity software) should be used. Here are some of the questions an administrative professional needs to respond to before actual document production can begin:

      (1) What is the actual document to be produced: a letter to only one person, a letter sent to a few people or a mailing list, a business form with copies, or a report with copies?

      (2) What software is available for use? What is the preferred software for this particular document?

      (3) Is the information contained in this document going to be used again, or is it being used only once?

      (4) What features of the software will need to be used? Do I know how to use them well enough?

      (5) What other hardware or peripheral equipment is available for me to use?

   b. *Understanding software manuals:* The efficient administrative professional must be able to read, review, and understand instructional and operations manuals for the various software packages that might be used. This is essential for those functions to be used for this particular application.

      (1) *Reviewing software features:* Software has become so sophisticated today that it is difficult, and perhaps impossible, to know and be able to apply all possible features. Therefore, the administrative assistant or secretary must learn to apply new features as needed in a specific document.

      EXAMPLE: A database of names and addresses in one file (a secondary file) and the text for the letter in another file (a primary file) can be merged quite easily once these files have been stored on disk. If the secretary needs a refresher on the merge function, an examination of the procedures contained in the software manual can be extremely helpful.

      The more frequently the secretary does a text merge, the fewer times he or she will need to refer to a manual. Just reading about something does not guarantee that the secretary understands the function or operation.

(2) *Locating features within manuals:* Software application manuals are written in an encyclopedic fashion so that the user can easily locate features through alphabetized indices or sections of the manual. Examples are usually included to illustrate the procedures to be used with a particular feature. Software manuals are generally not read cover to cover, but rather used as a general reference.

(3) *Learning through tutorials:* Software programs also include tutorial (or help) programs that operators can access to learn more about specific functions. Typically, the tutorial can be accessed at any time the secretary needs assistance in using a particular function. When the steps in a procedure have been learned or reviewed, the secretary can return to the document.

c. *Software conversions:* Software programs are available to convert text created with one software program into text for another software program. This is possible if both programs run on compatible disk operating systems.

EXAMPLE: A letter recorded with Corel WordPerfect® word processing software can be converted to Microsoft Word® through a specially designed conversion program that is now available for those systems. The system will request the operator to indicate the version of the software preferred.

A conversion like this would be helpful if the original text was created using a different software program than the secretary now uses in the office or if the secretary has to create a copy to send to someone who is using different software.

C. Document Production

In preparing documents, information is stored on a magnetic medium in a file. Files may be stored on a disk, hard disk, or tape (more common in a minicomputer or mainframe computer environment). When documents contain many graphics and enhanced features and need to be transportable, a Zip drive or Jaz cartridge is typically used for document storage.

1. *Creating Document Files:* A *file* is a collection of related information treated as one unit of storage. When stored, files must be named so that the computer software can retrieve or restore the file. File names are very important to the computer user and should provide an easy reference to the contents of the file. The storage medium can also be named to assist the user in recognizing its contents.

a. *Naming files:* The type and number of characters that can be used in a file name are specified in the computer software. The file name should be descriptive of the document.

(1) *Number of characters in name:* In some cases, a file name can have an extension. In DOS environments, the file name can be up to eight characters followed by an extension (a period plus up to three characters). In Windows environments (Windows 95 or higher), file names can be as long as needed (up to 255 characters) and can contain blank spaces as well as most symbols. The extension is automatically added by the software (spreadsheets, graphics, databases) and thus is not available for the user to add to the file name in those instances.

EXAMPLE—WINDOWS ENVIRONMENT:

FILE NAME: Annual Report-Mkt 2000

(2) *Guidelines for naming files:* The exact guidelines for naming files can vary according to the software being used. However, general guidelines for naming files include the following:

(a) *Characters in file name:* The file name for DOS environments is one word made up of letters, numbers, and/or special characters (no blank spaces). The file name for Windows environments is made up of letters, numbers, and/or special characters and can include blank spaces. Since the use of file names is software specific, the software manual should be consulted to determine which special characters and how many characters can be used.

(b) *File contents:* The file name should reflect the contents of the file. This is important for the computer user in identifying what is stored in the file. The computer reacts to any combination of letters and/or numbers as long as it is referenced in exactly the same way as it originally was stored.

(c) *Unique file names within applications:* Each file name within an application and stored on the same medium must be unique.

EXAMPLE—WINDOWS ENVIRONMENT:

Document 1:   STATUS REPORT MARCH 2000
Document 2:   SMITH, JR RECOGNITION 4-00
Document 3:   SMITH, JR TOAST 4-00
Document 4:   ANDERSON, T EVALUATION 2000

If the user tries to assign the same name to a second file within an application stored on the same medium, the first file may be replaced by the second file. The second file will be stored in place of the first file if the user responds to the query and indicates that the new file should replace the old one.

EXAMPLES:

You compose a sales letter to a customer about a new product, a trim saw for detail carpentry work. You also compose a memorandum to the marketing department about the same new product. You are using a word processing package for both documents. When you save the letter, you decide to reference it by the new product name TRIM SAW. If the memorandum would also be saved under the file name TRIM SAW, the letter document would be erased. This can be avoided by creating file names that are more detailed (including dates) in reflecting the file contents:

Letter file name   TRIM SAW SALES
(indicating to customer; no date as it is a form sales letter)
Memo file name   TRIM SAW MKT 2-00
(to marketing department)

RPT is a typical file name extension for report, LTR for letter, and MEM for memorandum. Here are examples of two different files about the new rent increase as of October, 2000:

RENT RPT 9-00 (report on new rent)
RENT INCREASE LTR 10-00 (letter on new rent)

Notice that the main reference for the document is Rent and was placed first. Managing files is easier if naming conventions for alphabetic filing are applied to electronic files.

Expanding on the new product example, a bar graph was developed on the sales of the new product in the various selling regions. A graphics computer package was used to produce the bar graph. The file name is TRIM SAW SALES. Since the automatic graphics extension is added in the Windows (or DOS) environment, the same file name TRIM SAW SALES can be used for both documents. The file name TRIM SAW SALES is unique for both the letter and memo documents; the automatic extension for the software packages makes the file name unique.

Note: When making revisions to a file, it is usually not important to save the old information. Using the same file name for the new information will erase the old information. This helps you manage your disk files better and purge the old ones.

b. *Naming storage medium:* When working with several diskettes (or when using several tapes or disk packs), it is helpful to identify the contents of the entire storage medium. Since disks are most common in a computer environment when a hard disk is not used, disks will be used as the storage medium reference. There are two ways to label the disk: *external label* and *disk label*. Also, disk organization plays an important role in file management.

(1) *External label:* Write the information about the contents of a disk on a disk label and attach it to the disk in the appropriate area.

(2) *Disk label:* In the Windows environment, when the hard drive is backed up to a disk, the user is prompted for a backup disk label. A pass code to the disk can also be set. When formatting a disk in the DOS environment, the disk can be named. By naming the disk, the disk name can be read on the computer screen.

The computer disk operating system can identify disks by the internal disk label. This is useful in a minicomputer or mainframe computer environment.

(3) *Disk organization:* File management is as important in a computer environment as it is for conventional paper files. Think of a disk like a file drawer. Is it for a person, company, or subject? This becomes the disk label. Only files pertaining to that person, company, or subject are stored on that disk. Unique names for the files on that disk are then easier to manage.

EXAMPLES:

Using the TRIM SAW and RENT examples, two disks would be labeled, one for TRIMSAW and one for RENT. Whenever any document was created pertaining to the new product, it would be saved on the TRIMSAW disk. Whenever a document was created about the rental property, the RENT disk would be used.

EXTERNAL LABEL:	*TRIMSAW*
FILES:	*SALES FORM LETTER 2-00*
	MKT MEMO 2-00
	SALES (graphic)

```
EXTERNAL LABEL:        RENT
FILES:                 REPORT 9-00
                       REPORT 10-02
                       RENT INCREASE LTR 10-02
                       LAWN SERVICE LTR 5-01
                       RENT INCREASE 9-01 (graph)
                       LAWN SERVICE COSTS (graph in Oct 04)
```

Note: Since there is an external label and all files on the disk are only for that one subject (TRIM SAW or RENT), the file names have been changed from the previous example to more clearly reflect what is in the file. TRIM SAW files are a sales form letter, a memo to marketing department written February 2000, and a bar graph. RENT files are a report written in September 2000 and another in October 2002, a letter written in May 2001 and another in October 2002, and a line graph from September 2001 and another from October 2004.

(4) *Hard disk file management:* The organization of documents when stored on a hard disk enables the administrative professional to quickly locate documents that have already been created. By designating a specific location for a set of files, the operator can go directly to that location to find that set of files. In the Windows environment, folders are created; all files pertaining to the folder topic are stored in that folder. In a DOS environment, directory paths are established, and documents are saved under the correct path extension. Folders and directories serve a similar function—storing documents and files by subject or topic.

EXAMPLE: As the president of the Kishwaukee Chapter of the International Association of Administrative Professionals®, Burch has accumulated over 100 pieces of correspondence within the past few weeks. On the hard disk of her Windows environment computer, she established a folder for IAAP so that she can easily store any document related to IAAP within the appropriate folder. By doing so, she finds it much easier and quicker to access a particular document.

2. *Using Compatible Software for Applications:* Compatibility in software has made it possible for a document to be created with one software program (e.g., word processing) and import information that has been keyed in using another compatible software program. Here are some examples of utilizing text input stored with different programs.

EXAMPLES:

Stevenson developed a short report using word processing. In the middle of the report, she includes a spreadsheet of financial information for the current year. Instead of rekeying the financial information, all she has to do is import (bring in) the financial information from the spreadsheet into the word processed document.

Another integrated software application is a letter that needs to be sent to 100 different people. The names and addresses of these people are stored using a dBase® program. The letter was keyed in using a Corel WordPerfect® program. An integrated process makes it possible to merge the data in the database program with the text of the letter.

Similarly, graphic illustrations can be added to text that has been created with word processing, desktop publishing, or digitized images from photographs or off the World Wide Web.

3. *Speed and Accuracy in Keying Text:* Secretarial skills include the ability to key in text with speed and accuracy. The touch-typewriting skill developed in earlier business training is an essential skill in being successful with word processing and other computer applications. Agility in using the alphanumeric keyboard as well as the function keys is an important factor in producing documents. There really are two schools of thought in regard to speed and accuracy.

   a. *Speed first, then accuracy:* When producing documents using software application programs, some persons function with the philosophy that speed in keying in the text is the first and foremost consideration; accuracy will be attained either with more practice or during the editing process when all errors can be quickly corrected.

   b. *Accuracy first, speed will take care of itself:* The second school of thought focuses on the importance of accuracy in the initial keying in of text. Accuracy should decrease the amount of editing time that is necessary so that the secretary will be able to produce an error-free document much faster. The basic premise is that a person who keys in text accurately will spend much less time on editing.

   No matter which approach is used, proofreading, checking, and editing are very important functions during document production. The use of spelling and grammar checks does not guarantee that *all* errors will be detected. The text of the document still needs to be read very carefully to locate any errors that need to be corrected and to ensure that facts (numbers) are accurate.

4. *Establishing the Document Format:* For the most efficient document production, some document format features, such as margins and line spacing, should be set prior to keying in the text for the document. As the text is being keyed, the document begins to take on its final appearance. If the default format (or parts of it) are accepted for the document, only those format characteristics that will be different need to be changed.

   EXAMPLE: Meyer is setting the format for a report to be transcribed for one of the executives. She knows that her left margin must be 1 1/2 inches and the right margin 1 inch because the report will be left-bound. Since the default is a left margin of 1 inch, she will have to change that setting. She also wants to change the widow/orphan protection so that a single line at the bottom or the top of a page will not be left alone. By accessing the correct format command, Meyer will be able to activate the widow/orphan protection. All other default settings are needed for the report.

5. *Using Software Features:* During the document production phase, decisions will need to be made concerning the special features of the software to use. With word processing, some of the features identified in Chapter 2 may be utilized (merge, boldface, changed type styles). Other software programs enable different features to be available. As a new feature is considered, the secretary needs to access operations and instructional manuals or tutorials for the software to see exactly how to activate that feature.

6. *Printing Out Sample Copy:* An excellent procedure to use is to print out one copy of the document after running a spell check or grammar check so that the general appearance of the document can be checked. "Eyeballing" the pages of the document may help detect any glaring errors in judgment with regard to headings, paragraphs, or use of specific features, such as italics, bold, or underlining. This sample copy of the report should also be reviewed by the document originator to see whether any additional suggestions should be considered for final editing.

7. *Preparing Final Copies:* Once the document has been proofed and edited, it is ready for final preparation and duplication of the required number of copies.

    a. *Printing or copying:* Some organizations support the printing of one final copy on the printer, then making additional copies on a convenience copier. Others support the printing of all final copies on the printer. The decision is impacted by available equipment, final copy quality requirements, and costs when one process is used rather than the other.

    b. *Choice of paper stock:* Final copies need to be prepared on the desired bond paper, letterhead, or other paper stock.

    c. *Finishing the final copies:* The final decision to make about the document is the finishing process to complete the document production. Binding, stapling or stitching, or placing the document in a loose-leaf notebook or folder are some of the alternatives. Keeping the businesslike appearance of the document is of prime concern (see Chapter 5, Section D, for review of finishing processes).

D. Evaluation of Document Production

No document production process can function effectively without continual evaluation of the procedures used for document preparation, system operation, and specific operations performed by administrative support personnel.

1. *Work Measurement:* Individual production can be measured in terms of words, lines, pages, or documents produced within a particular time frame (a day, a week, or a month). The amount of work produced correlates with the effective use of established procedures. Attention needs to be given, however, to an analysis of the time spent using word processing, desktop publishing, or other software programs.

   EXAMPLE: Time can be divided into two categories: productive time *and* unproductive time. *This does not mean that the administrative professional is idle during unproductive time. In one organization, productive time is defined as time actually spent keying in the text for the document. Unproductive time is defined as time spent in preplanning and organizing before the keying begins or in proofreading and checking after keying has been finished. Amounts for both categories of time are recorded for each job assigned to an individual.*

2. *Predetermined Work Standards:* Many organizations have developed work standards for information processing. Individual performance may vary from the standards established; this will then give the information processing supervisor an estimate of the work level to expect from each employee. These predetermined standards also give the employee a level of expectation and an aspiration level. Adjustments need to be made, however, for individual differences. A very productive worker may not be the fastest at keying in text for documents but may be so accurate that little revision is ever needed.

In business, a document is either usable or not usable; it is mailable or unmailable. A document that falls between is inaccurate and typically contains errors in facts, spelling, grammar, format, or content. With the application of technology, the need for accurate information has increased, not decreased. Businesses today cannot afford to transmit inaccurate information around the globe. Therefore, an even stronger emphasis must be placed on the production quality of documents.

Review Questions

Directions: Select the best answer from the four alternatives. Write your answer in the blank to the left of the number.

_____

1. A secretary who begins to dictate text for a document should first

    a. refer to a specific file for address and ZIP code to put on the document.
    b. identify any special format instructions.
    c. indicate words to be capitalized.
    d. dictate directions for underlining certain words in the text of the document.

_____

2. Secretaries may receive input for document production in the form of

    a. recorded transcription.
    b. an application software program.
    c. a software conversion program.
    d. soft copy from a manager.

_____

3. If the administrative assistant does not possess the specific skill necessary to perform a document production task,

    a. priorities need to be established for the task.
    b. the task can be delayed until the skill has been learned.
    c. participation in a skill training program is necessary.
    d. hardware and software will be selected for ease of learning.

_____

4. Which one of the following is an example of a time management strategy to implement in document production?

    a. Concentrate on producing all documents that require word processing during the same time period.
    b. Assign another office support professional to complete the task.
    c. Select hardware and software that are essential for producing a quality document.
    d. Use a software manual to learn a "new" word processing feature.

_____

5. The sophistication of software application programs

    a. enables the secretary to be familiar with all features of that particular program.
    b. determines the hardware that needs to be available.
    c. permits the secretary to apply complete knowledge of the program immediately.
    d. makes it difficult to learn and apply all possible features of the software program.

_____ **6.** A software applications manual should be

  a. read in its entirety before working with the software.
  b. consulted about specific procedures pertaining to a particular software feature.
  c. used to determine ease of operation during an initial tryout of the software.
  d. reviewed after the text for the document has been keyed and stored.

_____ **7.** The process that is applied when text created with one software program such as Corel WordPerfect® is stored as a Microsoft Word® file is called

  a. formatting.
  b. document storage.
  c. importing.
  d. conversion.

_____ **8.** A collection of related information, such as pages of a chapter, treated as one unit of storage is called a/an

  a. document.
  b. file.
  c. file name.
  d. extension.

_____ **9.** When using a Windows environment, a document name

  a. can be a combination of any eight letters and/or numbers.
  b. may contain no more than one blank space.
  c. includes a three-letter extension added by the software program.
  d. includes no symbols.

_____ **10.** Each document stored on the same disk

  a. must have a similar name.
  b. can be stored only once on the disk.
  c. cannot be replaced by another document.
  d. must have a unique name.

_____ **11.** Which one of the following represents an example of file management?

  a. Each disk contains an external label.
  b. Only files pertaining to a particular subject are stored on a single disk.
  c. "Old" documents are saved as well as edited versions.
  d. A disk operating system enables the operator to retrieve a document.

_____ **12.** A document that has been created with one software program may be imported (partially or entirely) into a document created with another software program because of the

  a. compatibility of the two software programs.
  b. conversion program that is available.
  c. storing capabilities of the programs.
  d. way the text was keyed in for both documents.

13. The basic document format, such as margins and line spacing, should be established in the system

    a. after the document has been keyed in.
    b. prior to printing out the document.
    c. after the document has been keyed in and saved.
    d. prior to keying in the text.

14. Which one of the following evaluation procedures pertains most to document production?

    a. Number of lines of text keyed in during an eight-hour time period
    b. Number of minutes of unproductive time in an eight-hour time period
    c. Employee adherence to established organizational procedures
    d. Amount of time spent in preplanning a given task

Solutions

Answer	*Refer to:*
1. (b)	[A-1-a(2)(b)]
2. (d)	[A-1-c]
3. (c)	[A-4]
4. (a)	[A-5]
5. (d)	[B-2-b(1)]
6. (b)	[B-2-b(2)]
7. (d)	[B-2-c]
8. (b)	[C-1]
9. (c)	[C-1-a(1)]
10. (d)	[C-1-a(2)(c)]
11. (b)	[C-1-b(3)]
12. (a)	[C-2]
13. (d)	[C-4]
14. (a)	[D-1]

CHAPTER 15

General Office Procedures

OVERVIEW

The application of general office procedures includes those functions that provide support to people throughout the organization through the use of specialized office systems. A recent trend is toward networking information processing (data processing, word processing, communications), reprographics, and records administration. Much attention is being given to the establishment of local area networks (LANs) throughout the organization. Another trend is toward the increased use of automation wherever possible so that more production can be realized in the day-to-day operations of the organization.

Specific office responsibilities require administrative professionals to make appropriate application of the functions of management: to *plan* aspects of their work assignments very carefully; to *organize* materials, supplies, and work areas for specific office tasks; and to *supervise* other office personnel effectively. The process of planning and organizing office tasks efficiently, completing tasks on time, and supervising office personnel who are performing these functions is called *managing*.

In this chapter, administrative professionals will become more familiar with tools and techniques used for developing office procedures that will result in work simplification and the improvement of work patterns.

KEY TERMS

Author	Horizontal communication	Organizational manual
Calendaring	Human resource planning	Organizing
Centralization	Job sharing	Performance standards
Controlling	Logging form	Strategic planning
Cross training	Management-by-	Tactical planning
Decentralization	objectives (MBO)	Tickler system
Editing	appraisal	Turnaround time
Employee manual	Matrix plan	

A. Planning

Planning is the visualization and formulation of proposed activities designed to achieve certain results. In office administration, planning is essential in setting initial objectives, analyzing present situations, determining various alternatives to meet the objectives, analyzing the cost-benefit of each alternative solution, and finally selecting the most appropriate alternative and putting it into action. The secretary is always involved in planning;

but three aspects of planning are perhaps the most crucial: establishing priorities, managing time, and coordinating office activities with other office personnel.

1. *Types of Planning:* Activities that involve planning focus primarily on three types of planning: strategic planning, tactical planning, and operational planning.

    a. *Strategic planning:* The long-term goals and major targets of an organization are the primary focus of strategic planning. This type of planning affects all major divisions within the organization as well as the external environment (e.g., attention to international or global developments). *Strategy* is defined as a pattern of actions and investment of resources to attain organizational goals. Top-level executives are typically involved in developing strategic plans.

    EXAMPLES: Organization's contribution to society, return to shareholders, quantity of outputs, quality of outputs.

    b. *Tactical planning:* Specific goals and plans are developed that are relevant to a definite unit within the organization, such as human resource development or marketing. Tactical plans outline the actions required of that work unit to achieve its part of the total strategic plan. These plans are developed by managers of those particular work units or divisions within the company.

    c. *Operational planning:* Operational managers develop short-term plans for routine tasks within their work units (delivery schedules, production schedules, personnel requirements for specific tasks). Operational planning identifies procedures required at lower levels within the organization.

Strategic, tactical, and operational planning within an organization must network to show consistent and supportive sets of objectives for the entire organization.

2. *Establishing Priorities:* One of the most critical office duties is the organizing of tasks for efficient completion. Deadlines for the work and coordination of employee work schedules need to be considered as decisions are made concerning the work to be done, when it will be done, and by whom.

    a. *Guidelines for prioritizing work:* One of the best ways to manage the work process, in terms of both specific tasks and the time required, is to learn how to set work priorities. Many individuals complete tasks in the order in which these tasks are presented for completion, without consideration for those items that are of the highest priority. Priority of work should not be based on "likes" and "dislikes" but rather on factors such as the following:

        (1) *The due date for the job:* Deadlines established for specific jobs must be considered in establishing a work priority.

        EXAMPLE: A letter that must be in the mail today obviously will take priority over one requesting information for a meeting that will take place a month from now.

        (2) *Consultation with supervisor(s):* Appropriate amounts of time are needed to discuss and review work orders with the supervisor and sometimes the user. It is important that all questions concerning production be answered *before* an office worker begins work on that task.

        (3) *Involvement of other people:* Other people's schedules must be considered. Any deadline for the job must be coordinated with the time schedules of others so last-minute crisis work can be avoided.

(4) *Delegation of work:* Often an executive, manager, or executive secretary will be in a position to delegate work to other office workers. If there is a rush for the work, then a higher priority should be assigned to it. However, if there is no particular rush or there is more lead time for the work to be done, then a lower priority could be assigned. Having the assistance of other office workers relieves some of the secretary's workload but still requires a degree of supervision so that the work is completed on time.

(5) *Length of the task:* Completion time for a given work assignment is often difficult to judge. With experience, however, the secretary should be able to determine approximately how long a particular task should take. *Turnaround time* is defined as the elapsed time between the receiving of a task and its completion.

EXAMPLES:

Carlson had a special report that required a query routine to be designed by the Information Systems Department. On Tuesday morning, Brown and Meyers in IS finalized the output criteria. The IS department had the report query ready for Carlson to test-approve on Friday afternoon. Turnaround time was three days.

Snyder sends a request to the Staff Services Center for the creation of a standard letter to be mailed to 350 clients. His request reached the center on Monday at 9:30 A.M. The 350 letters and envelopes were ready for pickup at 3:30 P.M. the same day. Turnaround time was six hours.

b. *Identifying office tasks:* Each day, those tasks or jobs left in the in-tray or in-basket or on the electronic mail network must be examined to see what work needs to be done. In addition, every secretary receives additional tasks at various times during the day in the form of directives and/or dictation. It is essential to identify *all* tasks that superiors need to have completed.

EXAMPLE: Benson's early-morning routine includes scanning any items deposited in her in-basket to see what is required to complete these tasks. In addition, she must access voice mail (telephone system) as well as electronic mail (computer network) to obtain all *telephone and e-mail messages left for her.*

c. *Analyzing the tasks:* Each task must be examined carefully to determine whether there are specific directions or requirements. Additional information, such as "needed by 8/31" or "special meeting at 4 P.M. today," are clues that are helpful in setting priorities.

(1) *Making priority decisions:* The efficient administrative professional must decide exactly how to categorize (or group) tasks for completion. One of the easiest ways to categorize tasks is, first, to group the tasks into three primary categories:

Priority 1: Those tasks that need to be done immediately
Priority 2: Those tasks that need to be completed within the next one to two working days
Priority 3: Those tasks that can be delayed until time permits or can be scheduled within the week

(2) *Arranging the tasks:* Within each priority category, the tasks need to be arranged in such a way that they can be completed in an appropriate order.

(a) *Importance of task:* One way to arrange tasks is to sequence them from the most important to the least important. It is critical that tasks be completed in the order of priority so that documents needed for an important meeting, a telephone call confirming a speaking engagement, or transcription of a letter going out in the day's mail will be completed on time.

(b) *Use of the computer:* Another way that tasks need to be arranged relates to those items that require use of the computer and those that do not. Perhaps those tasks that require use of the computer can be grouped together for more efficient operation of the computer and software. People lose valuable work time when switching from one software package to another, unless these packages are integrated. Sometimes, the secretary will have to gauge how much time to spend on the computer at any one time. Some experts estimate that the secretary needs a break from computer work every hour; others say every two hours.

d. *Adjusting priorities when interruptions occur:* Receiving another item to handle in the middle of the day or an urgent fax message requesting information on an order received last week will cause the administrative professional to adjust priority categories to include these new items.

EXAMPLE: You are transcribing a letter for Schumacher, your supervisor, that she needs to sign before she leaves at 4 P.M. (This is a Priority 1 item.) Johnson, a marketing representative, enters the office and asks to see Schumacher immediately. The telephone rings just as you begin to respond to Johnson's request. How should your priorities be instantly adjusted? The telephone call will take first priority now, then Johnson's request to see your supervisor will be the next priority item, and finally you return to your transcription.

3. *Managing Time and Work Completion Effectively:* Every administrative professional should be concerned about efficient use of time, especially since the 7½- or 8-hour day provides a limited time frame in which to handle all types of tasks. In managing time for the completion of tasks, the secretary needs to utilize the assistance of other office personnel, including office managers or supervisors, in the process of completing required job assignments.

a. *Scheduling of time:* The development of personal techniques for appropriate scheduling of time should be a high priority in the office. Here are some of the more common scheduling techniques frequently used.

(1) *Identifying daily office tasks:* An excellent scheduling technique is to develop a *daily* list of office tasks that must be taken care of that day. Specially printed memos or electronic task lists like the one in Figure 15–1 may be used to prepare such a list.

(2) *Designing reminder systems:* So that enough time can be set aside for upcoming tasks, create reminder systems that will prompt you as you work toward project/task deadlines on a daily, weekly, and monthly basis.

(a) *Tickler system:* Usually, a manual reminder system consists of a set of folders or cards for each day of the month (1–31), folders or cards for each month in the calendar year, or an expandable file folder with compartments for each day of the month. These special folders are used to file materials or notes about specific work assignments to be done by particular

Figure 15–1   Daily List of Office Tasks

deadlines and prompt the secretary to begin working on these tasks by certain dates. See Figure 15–2 for an example of a tickler system.

(b) *Automated reminder system:* An electronic calendar can be generated easily with an automated calendaring system installed on either a personal computer or a networked system. This system reminds the user of

Figure 15–2   Tickler System

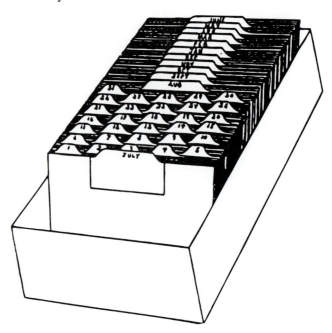

appointments or project due dates for today, tomorrow, this month, on up to a year from now. A daily schedule can be printed out each morning to serve as a reminder list for the day.

(3) *Planning daily/weekly routine tasks:* Such tasks as handling routine reports, correspondence, and filing need to be planned for, too. Time should be set aside each day, week, or month (depending on the need) to perform such routine tasks.

(4) *Batch processing of tasks:* To save valuable time, similar tasks need to be grouped together in "batches" so that related items can be completed during a specific time period. This is particularly helpful with tasks that involve the use of the computer and various software packages.

EXAMPLE: Mansfield's responsibilities include transcription of dictation (which comes from both recorded machine dictation and shorthand dictation), filing copies of correspondence appropriately in the files, answering the telephone (especially to take sales orders over the phone), and preparing a daily report each morning showing all company sales for the previous day. She finds that "batching" helps her to manage her time more efficiently. Correspondence can be handled more easily early in the day, between 8:30 and 11:00 A.M. Preparation of the daily sales report is usually scheduled for 11:00 A.M. each day after the input has been received. The time from 1:00 to 3:00 P.M. seems best for preparing the sales orders received during the day. She usually catches up on the filing late in the day to be ready for the next day's tasks.

Another way that Mansfield uses batch processing is to group all tasks that involve word processing together so that she will complete word processing tasks that require the use of the same software. She also uses a spreadsheet package, primarily for the daily sales report. If she can perform word pro-

cessing functions at one time and spreadsheet functions at another time, she finds that she saves significant time in making smooth transitions between these two types of work.

(5) *Calendaring:* Keeping an up-to-date calendar proves to be one of the secretary's most important time-savers. By keeping accurate notations for upcoming appointments, meetings, or other events, time will be saved in locating needed information. The secretary also needs to coordinate calendar entries with those on the executive's calendar so that both will have complete records of appointments and other events.

Electronic calendaring is a helpful tool in maintaining a complete schedule of appointments and meetings, along with any special notes, on the computer. Copies of daily schedules can be printed out as needed.

EXAMPLE: Networked use of a calendaring system helps the secretary to schedule internal meetings and appointments more easily. Quick access to others' appointment schedules can be made available. Once meeting dates and times are confirmed, entries need to be inserted into each calendar by approved personnel.

All appointments should be entered on the executive's calendar as well as conferences, meetings, or reminders. The schedule may be accessed at any time (with the appropriate password) to see what commitments have already been made. A printout of the daily calendar may take the place of the traditional appointment book on the desk. The electronic calendar can be printed to fit executive portfolios for easy reference throughout the day.

(6) *Simplifying tasks by utilizing office tools:* Electric letter openers, collating racks and/or small electric collators, electric pencil sharpeners, electric staplers, shredders, and other types of automated office equipment simplify work assignments and speed production processes.

b. *Simplifying office assignments:* An analysis of work assignments is necessary to determine ways in which procedures can be simplified to save personal time and energy.

(1) *Analyzing routine office tasks:* One basic goal should be to eliminate unnecessary tasks, steps, or motions in performing office work. Routine tasks should be examined to see how procedures can be modified to save valuable office time.

EXAMPLE: Struthers is an executive assistant for three vice presidents in the firm with a workload that includes many routine functions (running errands, making copies, updating mailing lists) as well as specialized tasks only she can handle (making travel arrangements, assisting in the writing of research reports). She delegates many of the routine tasks to Noonan, a part-time employee, to free her own time for working on more specialized work tasks.

(2) *Analyzing time requirements for specific tasks:* How much time is being spent on specific tasks? Keeping a log of the tasks performed for what is considered to be a fairly typical week and the amount of time required results in a listing of tasks as well as basic time requirements. A two-week log is best. Procedures used in completing the tasks should be scrutinized carefully to see how time can be saved during the entire process.

(3) *Planning schedules:* Daily, weekly or monthly, and long-range planning schedules can be extremely helpful in office work. Planning, a function that is often overlooked, is the real key to more efficient office schedules.

c. *Completing tasks:* What really gives an administrative assistant or secretary a high degree of satisfaction is the ability to complete both routine tasks as well as more difficult, complex tasks on time. Too often, one task gets started, only to be left unfinished while responding to another urgent request. With the multitude of demands placed on the typical secretary, it is essential that the secretary's primary focus in the workplace be: What tasks *can* be completed today? Focusing on the completion of needed tasks may give the secretary a greater sense of accomplishment at the end of the workday, with the feeling of a fresh start the following day.

4. *Coordinating with Other Office Personnel:* Most office tasks require interaction with supervisors and/or co-workers. Communication (both vertical and horizontal) is very important in maintaining productive working relationships among office professionals. Communication from supervisor to employee or from employee to supervisor is referred to as *vertical communication. Horizontal communication* refers to communication on the same level—from one secretary to another secretary or from one employee to another employee.

a. *Coordinating with superiors:* Two-way communication with superiors is essential to coordinate office tasks to be completed.

(1) *Understanding preferences:* Executives and managers have personal preferences as to how the telephone should be answered, messages will be handled, or appointments will be made. The secretary has an obligation to find out preferences for handling these routine office procedures and then to manage office functions accordingly.

(2) *Following directions carefully:* Basic and special instructions for doing a particular task must be considered carefully. With administrative professionals assisting several managers or executives at a time, directions need to be written. Another reason for recording clear instructions is the increased use of technology in the office.

   EXAMPLE: A special meeting of the Board of Directors is scheduled for Friday at 10 A.M. Young, the chairman of the board, has asked Mueller, his executive assistant, to notify each member by telephone and letter. Mueller knows from experience that she will need to set aside time to review with Young what materials will be needed for the meeting. She enters a note on her calendar to ask about the meeting during their next planning session.

(3) *Questioning directives:* When a problem arises relating to the completion of a particular task, the alert secretary should analyze the problem or question first to determine possible solutions. Very often, problems arise because the directives for completing the task are unclear and ambiguous. By asking the right questions early in the process, errors in judgment or performance may be eliminated. (Personal problems should be kept out of the office except when they affect particular work assignments.)

b. *Coordinating with co-workers:* Establishing a spirit of teamwork in the office is important for building rapport among the members of the office staff. Secretaries and other office professionals need to feel that they play vital roles in the success of the business.

(1) *Sharing the workload:* When there is a larger-than-normal project to be completed, is there a way to share the workload?

EXAMPLE: If you offer to help Bingham with that annual report that he must complete by next Tuesday, he should be willing to help you when you need an extra hand with one of your projects.

(a) *Job sharing:* The formal arrangement whereby office personnel are actually collaborating in sharing job responsibilities is called *job sharing.* This means that one full-time job is shared part time by two people on a permanent basis.

EXAMPLE: Smythe and Lockwood are information systems specialists, each employed part time and sharing one full-time position. Because she has school-age children, it is easier for Smythe to work the morning hours; and Lockwood, who is attending college in the mornings, prefers to work the afternoon hours.

(b) *Cross training:* Another means of sharing the work load occurs through cross training. Co-workers are trained to perform the job functions of more than one position so that workloads can be shared when vacations or other emergencies occur. *Cross training* is the process of being trained to handle the responsibilities for more than one job in the office.

(2) *Using others' suggestions:* Encouraging office professionals to make suggestions fosters more cooperation among workers in the office. A secretary must be an attentive listener to ideas posed by others; the result could be improvements in current office procedures.

(3) *Taking responsibility for personal actions:* The administrative professional who makes decisions about work priorities, delegates work assignments to other office personnel, or evaluates work performance must take individual responsibility for these types of decisions. Consequences of specific action taken must be an initial consideration in deciding which action to take.

EXAMPLES:

Lawrence forgot to schedule an appointment for Clark, his supervisor, with the president at 10:00 A.M. this morning. When Clark returns from the president's office stating that the president was not available, Lawrence must be ready to account for his action (or nonaction in this case).

Gates fired Stenburg, a new part-time clerical worker, for insubordination. Gates will need to be ready to present her supervisor with documentation that will present the situation clearly and objectively, especially since Stenburg has approached the Equal Employment Opportunity Commission about the incident.

B. Organizing

The second managerial function, *organizing,* involves the office administrator in establishing specific goals that are to be accomplished through office support services. All resources needed for the successful completion of a project, such as people, supplies, equipment, and space, need to be organized for efficient utilization during the performance of office duties. The application of organizational principles (i.e., span of control and delegation, among others) provides the basis for the organization of personnel and the work itself for the particular assignment.

1. *Organizing Support Personnel:* To the busy executive or manager, adequate office support is a "must" in order to complete the myriad of communication necessary in the day-to-day routine of the office. Such support responsibilities range from receptionist duties to general office duties (e.g., as light typing, filing records, copying, or keying information into the computer system), depending on the specific needs of the office staff. Support personnel may be organized according to a centralized plan, a decentralized plan, or a matrix plan of operation.

   a. *Centralization:* Centers are established for specific purposes such as word/information processing, information systems, records management, or reprographics in locations that provide easy access to and from all departments within the company. Each center requires a supervisor who reports to the administrative manager. Management of centralized office support services usually rests with one administrator whose primary responsibility may include the supervision of all office personnel throughout the organization.

   EXAMPLE: The XYZ Corporation has centralized office support services under the management of Olson, the administrative systems director. Olson has responsibility for several centralized operations: (a) the Staff Services Center, with 15 word processing specialists who perform word processing functions, one desktop publishing specialist, two proofreaders/editors, and one supervisor; (b) the Information Systems Center, with 12 system operators, programmers, and analysts, and one supervisor; (c) the Printing Center, with 11 press operators, design personnel, and one supervisor; and (d) the Records Center, with eight records specialists and one supervisor. Each of the supervisors reports directly to Olson.

   (1) *Physical location:* Related office operations for an entire organization are concentrated at one location.

   (2) *Functions:* Similar office activities are located within one work group or department.

   (3) *Authority:* A few people at the top managerial and executive levels have the authority to make all major decisions.

   b. *Decentralization:* Office support personnel are housed within individual departments (e.g., sales department, finance department, human resources department). Responsibilities generally include office functions needed only by that department. Each department has its own administration—for example, the sales department is managed by the sales manager.

   (1) *Physical location:* Related office operations for an organization are concentrated at several locations throughout the organization, typically within specific departments or divisions of the organization.

   (2) *Functions:* The supervisor of each work group or the department manager is responsible for seeing that office activities are performed at a high level of quality and supervises the office employees within that department.

   (3) *Authority:* Managers at middle-management levels (department or division) are delegated the authority to make decisions for executives at the top-management levels.

   c. *Matrix:* Sometimes, a combination plan that involves both centralization and decentralization occurs that permits some office operations to be centralized and others to be decentralized, depending on the needs of the firm. This combination plan is known as a *matrix plan.* Those activities that are centralized are typically managed by one person within the firm, and those activities that are decentralized are usually managed within specific departments or divisions of the organization.

EXAMPLES:

The ABC Company established a centralized staff services center to prepare documents for various departments in the firm. This center accepts work orders from any department and currently has a turnaround time of eight hours. The legal department has such a profound quantity of document preparation that a satellite center with identical equipment has been established within the legal department to handle only the documents produced for that department. Not only does this alleviate the strain on the centralized staff services center, but it enables the legal department to supervise the intricate detail that is required in law.

The XYZ Corporation utilizes the satellite concept to enhance the operation of the sales department. Within the firm, each department is organized with its own administrative support and secretarial support personnel. The sales department has an executive secretary whose primary responsibility is to serve as the secretary for Adkins, the sales manager, and supervise the other five office support people. The department now produces many Web documents for marketing and advertising. Consequently, it became necessary to update the computer system to handle multimedia and Web page productivity tools. Two additional operators with Web development skills were hired.

2. *Organizing Work:* Work assignments need to be organized, too, so that they may be effectively handled within the timelines established by principals (users) throughout the organization. It is important that the work be analyzed to determine the difficulty level, the priority, and any special instructions needed to complete the assignment.

   a. *Leffingwell's principles of effective work:* Known as the father of office management, William H. Leffingwell applied the principles of scientific management to office work in his book *Scientific Office Management,* published in 1917. These principles are still important today for secretaries and other office personnel to apply in daily office routines, even though procedures and technology have changed over the years.

      (1) *Planning the work:* The work to be done must be identified and how, when, and where it will be done must be determined. Knowing the deadline for its completion is also important in the planning stages.

      (2) *Scheduling the work:* A definite schedule needs to be established for the completion of work even though the work may appear to be difficult to accomplish. Schedules should be established with the intention that they will be kept.

      (3) *Execution of the work:* The work must be performed with skill, accuracy, and speed, without unnecessary effort or delay.

      (4) *Measurement of the work:* Work must be measured according to quantity produced, quality of the work produced, and individual performance.

      (5) *Rewards:* The office worker should be commended for the completion of quality work. Opportunities for self-development and good working conditions are intrinsic ways to show office personnel appreciation for quality performance.

    b. *Analysis of work:* A preliminary analysis of the work to be done will indicate how difficult the work is, what the priority should be, and the sequence in which the work should be done.

        (1) *Difficulty level of work:* Whether to work from the simple to the complex or the complex to the simple depends on the person and how important the work is perceived to be. Some secretaries like to handle a difficult task early in the day and then proceed to less complex tasks. Others work better from simple, relatively easy tasks to more complex ones as the day progresses. Regardless of the method employed, the difficulty level of the work should be determined and compared with the human resources available to work on that particular assignment.

        (2) *Priority of work:* Work needs to be prioritized from the most important to the least important. If the task is very important and the deadline is approaching, it should be handled soon (possibly today or tomorrow). If the task is less important, it may serve as a "filler item" and can be done at any time within the next few days.

        (3) *Sequence of work:* Completion of a work assignment often depends on the sequencing of the steps in the process. Before a task is begun, the steps in the process need to be identified so that the individual worker can proceed without further direction. Especially in working with office technology, the employee who forgets one of the steps will probably have difficulty completing the task.

           EXAMPLE: Sanders uses word processing in her position as a legal secretary for the Porter law firm. Legal forms, with only a few exceptions, are stored on the network file server so that when a new document must be prepared, Sanders can retrieve the form and fill in the new variable information. If she does not follow the sequence of the process carefully, she may fill in variable information in the wrong locations within the document or may not have the variable information needed to complete the form.

  3. *Establishing Work Procedures:* In any office environment, appropriate procedures need to be established for accepting work orders from executives, supervisors, and others who originate work (authors) and for completing it according to company policies and procedures. *Procedures manuals* assist administrative professionals in following the steps required for certain processes (e.g., receiving telephone orders for merchandise).

    a. *Planning and organizing specific tasks:* Each assigned task must be examined carefully to make certain that all requirements and instructions are understood.

        (1) *Logging in the task:* Especially if the secretary works for more than one person, it is imperative to log in each work assignment. A *logging form* can be completed, indicating the date/time the job is received, the number/name of the job, for whom the work is being done, the deadline, the name of the person to whom the task is assigned, and any special instructions. Logging in each task is especially important in centers where production is being handled for the various departments within the firm (e.g., a reprographics center).

        (2) *Reviewing job requirements:* Before assigning the task to someone else (or deciding to do it yourself), the instructions need to be reviewed carefully. Here are other checkpoints that need to be considered:

(a) Files and other needed reference materials should be gathered and assembled.

(b) Formats to be used in the preparation of documents need to be checked for accuracy.

(c) The decision about work assignment (who will complete this particular task) must be made.

(d) If the work is assigned to another person, *all* the details and special instructions need to be reviewed with that person.

(3) *Accepting responsibility for meeting deadlines:* Meeting deadlines is crucial in document preparation. The secretary's ability to meet these deadlines will be enhanced if the following occur:

(a) Production logs are set up so that office personnel who are assigned specific tasks will be more accountable for meeting the given deadlines.

(b) Proofreading, editing, and revision procedures are established.

(4) *Proofreading and editing:* Just as important as keying in input for documents are the proofreading and editing necessary in perfecting the document. Checking the accuracy of format and content of a document is equally important.

(a) *Proofreading:* Reading through the material that has been keyed to detect corrections needed is known as the process of *proofreading.*

EXAMPLE: As part of the proofreading process, Graham runs an initial spelling check of the text as it has been keyed in and saved. With this procedure, she finds most of the obvious errors that have been made when keying in the text. Then Graham reads a hard copy (printout) of the material so that she can review the format and the content carefully.

Proofreading facilitates the detection of errors in keying in the written text as well as errors in word processing commands (bold, underline, indent) that may be needed within the text. Grammar checks may be used to detect flaws in sentence structure, grammar, and word usage.

(b) *Editing:* Editing is the procedure used by an author to make content revisions in the original document.

EXAMPLE: Larson has just delivered a draft copy of a report to Stone, the author, for approval. Stone edits the document, making final revisions for Larson to input. At that time, Larson will also check the final format carefully.

(5) *Completing the job:* Every office requires work assignments to be completed on time and accurately. Accuracy should be a crucial element in every secretary's work.

EXAMPLE: Culver is a legal secretary in a law firm that specializes in probate. When she prepares a will, she must be extremely careful that absolutely no errors in the text go unnoticed or uncorrected. Typing $100,000 instead of $10,000 in a specific bequest would be a very costly (and embarrassing) error to make.

(6) *Logging the job out:* When the job has been completed to the satisfaction of the author, the job should be logged out; in other words, the completion of the job is recorded on a log sheet. The amount of time to do the job, the number of revisions needed, and the production count (lines, pages, or documents) are other important information processing facts to record.

b. *Developing office manuals:* Basic office procedures used in offices organized with a traditional principal-secretary structure tend to be "carried around in people's heads." Perhaps this once-common practice served as a security measure, protecting the knowledge base of the organization. However, with the entry of word processing, information processing, and other office automation systems into the office, more emphasis has been placed in recent years on the use and development of functional office manuals that include written documentation of company policies and procedures.

(1) *Features of office manuals:* Typically, office manuals may include the following types of information:

(a) Job descriptions for specific office positions (or clusters of positions)

(b) Standardized formats used in preparing documents

(c) Individual positions and tasks to be performed

(d) The time schedule for completing specific jobs

(e) Policies related to specific office operations

(f) General goals and objectives of the organization relating to specific procedures or functions

(g) Measurement standards, if applicable

(2) *Specific types of office manuals:* Not everyone within a particular organization needs the same kind of operational information. Therefore, different types of manuals may be needed for people at different levels and in different departments within the organization—and for different purposes.

(a) *Organizational manual:* The formal relationship of divisions or departments within the organization is shown in an organizational manual. This manual also includes a statement of objectives, basic philosophy, organizational structure, change strategies, and other pertinent historical facts and futuristic plans.

(b) *Policy manual:* Courses of action relating to company objectives, day-to-day operations, and departmental conduct of business in effect for the organization are included in a policy manual.

(c) *Employee manual or handbook:* Specific information needed to be a functional worker within the company is summarized in an employee manual or handbook. Included is such information as work schedules and hours, salaries, schedule for salary reviews, dress codes, vacations, benefits, profit-sharing plans available, and retirement plans.

(d) *Procedures or operations manual:* The procedures manual outlines detailed instructions for processing specific tasks or jobs: what is to be done, formats to use, who will do it, when it is to be done, and why it must be done in this way.

EXAMPLE: Word processing supervisors have found procedures manuals extremely useful in ensuring that different word processing operators prepare documents using approved formats and procedures.

(e) *Specialty guide or handbook:* Specialized handbooks are sometimes prepared to give assistance to specific employee groups.

EXAMPLES: Secretarial manuals or handbooks, guides for marketing representatives, established guides for records retention within the company, forms manuals.

(3) *Standardizing procedures for developing office manuals:* Office professionals need to follow the same or similar procedures in performing office tasks. Standardizing the procedures for writing and developing manuals helps to coordinate the efforts of different departments or divisions within the company. Here are a few suggestions that could make manuals easier for employees to use:

(a) The use of action words will communicate more clearly to employees.

(b) A general pattern of "who does what-why-how-when-where" should be followed so that definite procedures and steps result.

(c) Procedures should be written briefly and concisely. The important thing is for the employee to be able to use the manual for quick reference and get to the task at hand.

(d) Any manual should be written to the employee. The "you" approach often used will necessitate the application of language, sentence structure, and illustrations to enable the employee to understand and follow the policy or procedure.

C. Supervising

People whose primary responsibility is to supervise and manage other people in the work environment must be able to understand human behavior to assist in motivating and leading office personnel to be more productive. The typical office supervisor or manager is responsible for a major unit or department within the organization or is a lead coordinator within a major unit with responsibility for both operations and supervision. Although all the major functions of management (planning, organizing, staffing, directing, and controlling) are important to the supervisor, the two functions of *staffing* and *controlling* are especially unique to the supervision of office personnel.

1. *Staffing:* Building a staff of office employees who can work cooperatively with one another and with the supervisor is a major supervisory responsibility. From initial human resource planning to the point at which employees become productive workers, the office supervisor or manager is responsible for working with people through orientation, staff development and training, and special guidance and assistance programs. Here are some of the major staffing responsibilities of the office supervisor:

   a. *Human resource planning:* Determining human resource needs for the future and developing strategies for meeting these needs is what human resource planning is all about. Severe shortages of qualified secretaries have been observed in many organizations throughout the country. Human resource planning is critical in addressing this basic office staffing requirement. These plans should include both short-term (one to three years) and long-term (five years or more) goals.

b. *Recruiting office employees:* Job specifications developed for vacant positions in the organization serve as the basis for the development of appropriate recruitment strategies. These job specifications include the skill and knowledge requirements that an applicant must possess to meet the requirements of the job. Applicants may be recruited from either internal or external sources.

EXAMPLES OF INTERNAL SOURCES: Employee referrals, employee promotions.

EXAMPLES OF EXTERNAL SOURCES: Public and private employment agencies, professional associations, placement services within educational institutions, advertising in local or regional newspapers, temporary employment agencies.

c. *Selecting office employees:* One of the primary responsibilities of the supervisor/manager is to see that qualified, competent office personnel are hired, from either internal or external sources, to fill job vacancies as they occur. Application and interview processes need to be monitored carefully so that the company follows affirmative action guidelines in conducting hiring procedures.

d. *Orienting new employees to the job:* A planned orientation program for new office employees provides the new person with valuable information on the background of the company, the organization and structure of the business, and policies and procedures in effect. Such a program may be scheduled for the first day or two of full-time employment and is often conducted by either the administrative office manager or a person within the company designated to direct the orientation program for new employees.

e. *Providing special on-the-job training:* The immediate supervisor is usually the person responsible for coordinating the on-the-job training (OJT) needed for an office employee to take on new, changed, or additional responsibility. When new equipment is purchased, however, many times the vendor provides training as part of the sales package.

EXAMPLE: Jennings is an information systems specialist for Smith Corporation, with specific responsibility for maintaining the CT-2000 computer system. She has been employed in this capacity for three years. The system is being replaced this month by the latest model, the CT-3000, which has many new software applications available. Her supervisor, Lundberg, has approved Jennings as a participant in a special three-day training program sponsored by the CT Corporation at its training center.

f. *Employee training for different positions:* Cross training is becoming increasingly important in business. There is a great need for more than one employee to know a particular job or task. When employees go on vacation or sick leave, a person who is trained to perform the duties of the position can serve in a backup capacity.

g. *Providing guidance and counseling through special programs:* Many organizations have initiated programs to help individual employees combat problems with alcohol and drug abuse. In addition, personal problems of employees and how these may affect them on the job have also received attention. Many companies provide staff counselors to work with individuals who are experiencing these types of problems. A rather new development is the initiation of stress management programs, especially with office employees who are working with significant technology changes. Office professionals face more stress, too, because of the necessity to try and balance the pressures of family, home, and workplace responsibilities.

2. *Controlling:* An essential phase of office supervision and management involves comparing actual productivity and results with those that were anticipated. In other words, were the actual goals and objectives of the department and the organization achieved? What was actually accomplished? In addition to monitoring and evaluating work processes, the supervisor/manager has the responsibility of evaluating the performance of individual office employees.

   a. *Delegating office assignments:* Perhaps one of the most difficult tasks is delegating responsibility for completing a specific office assignment to another person. Here are some steps to keep in mind when delegating work to others:

     (1) All input (handwritten copy, cassettes, computer disks) needed for the task must be organized and ready for use.

     (2) The supervisor should discuss all instructions with the person who will be doing the work. These instructions should be in writing.

     (3) The supervisor should encourage the worker to ask questions if any of the instructions need clarification.

     (4) The completed work needs to be reviewed by the supervisor prior to its transmittal to the user (author). In this way, needed changes or revisions may be made effectively before submitting the completed work for final approval or signature.

   b. *Conducting performance appraisals:* Office personnel are evaluated in terms of specific jobs assigned and total performance over a period of time (e.g., six months, one year). The responsibility for performance appraisals is usually delegated to the office manager and/or department manager. A performance appraisal is an evaluation of the performance of an individual office employee for a designated period of time.

     (1) *Procedures for performance appraisal:* For performance appraisal to take place, definite procedures must be established. Here are some of the primary considerations in implementing a performance appraisal system:

       (a) *Performance standards:* Each job is analyzed in terms of behaviors, personal traits, and results required to perform the job. From these requirements, performance standards are specified as criteria for evaluating each employee.

       (b) *Employee performance:* Various appraisal methods are used to observe and measure employee performance. Such performance can then be described in terms of what is observed and measured.

       (c) *Appraisal data:* The supervisor and the employee need to discuss the appraisal and establish performance standards for the next appraisal period. General progress should be discussed as well as the determination of future goals or objectives.

       (d) *Decision making:* The appraisal data can be used as input for other types of decision making related to employee appraisal (selection, training, promotion, salary).

     (2) *Performance appraisal methods:* The office manager needs to be aware of the various performance appraisal methods in use today that may be applied to

performance appraisal in the office. There are three primary groups of methods: comparative, absolute, and objective-setting methods. Here are some examples of each of these three methods:

(a) *Rank comparison:* The supervisor ranks employees from the best to the worst (comparative method). This method does not take into consideration the fact that the job responsibilities of the employees differ.

(b) *Paired comparison:* The supervisor compares each employee to be ranked with every other employee in the group, one at a time (comparative method).

(c) *Checklist:* The supervisor selects from a list those statements judged to be descriptive of the employee's job performance (absolute method).

(d) *Graphic rating scale:* Each person is rated on a scale on the basis of factors identified as essential to job performance (absolute method).

(e) *Management-by-objectives (MBO) appraisal:* With the help of the supervisor/manager, the employee establishes job objectives, both for individual performance and for personal development, against which his or her performance will be measured during the next appraisal period (objective-setting method).

(3) *Performance interview:* Once the written evaluation has been prepared, a performance appraisal interview is typically conducted privately with each employee.

(a) *Purpose of interview:* The primary purpose of the interview is to review positive aspects of the employee's performance. In addition, those areas needing improvement during the next evaluation period must be identified. Such a procedure presents the supervisor with the opportunity to provide feedback to each individual being evaluated.

(b) *Emphasis on personal growth:* The emphasis should be on personal growth and needed improvement related to the job. Positive reinforcement of preferred behaviors that have been observed during the evaluation period should be stressed.

Review Questions

Directions: Select the best answer from the four alternatives. Write your answer in the blank to the left of the number.

_____ 1. Tactical planning focuses on actions required of a work unit to achieve specific goals, whereas strategic planning focuses on

    a. the internal environment of the organization.
    b. the division or department level.
    c. the development of long-term goals for the organization.
    d. the achievement of departmental goals.

_____ 2. Which one of the following demonstrates an example of tactical planning?

    a. The organization's involvement in a recycling effort
    b. Increases in production outputs during a specific period of time
    c. The marketing department's plan for sale of a new product with prizes (e.g., a Caribbean cruise) for sales representatives selling the most each month during the coming year
    d. Long-range planning for the installation of a networked computer system

_____ 3. Regional sales representatives are scheduled for personal visits to major accounts during the next month. This is an example of

    a. strategic planning.
    b. tactical planning.
    c. operational planning.
    d. cross training.

_____ 4. The secretary's ability to set appropriate work priorities is most dependent on

    a. the enjoyment derived from performing the task.
    b. the proofreading necessary to check the completed work.
    c. whether the work process is frequently interrupted.
    d. how long the task will take.

_____ 5. The time required from the moment a work order is received until the completed work is returned to the originator (author) is referred to as

    a. turnaround time.
    b. logging time.
    c. planning time.
    d. work in process.

_____

6. Swain, the administrative manager, hands you a draft of a report to be prepared. He tells you, "I need this report for my meeting with the president at ten o'clock on Thursday." (It is now Tuesday afternoon at 1:50 P.M.) Which priority would you assign this task?

   a. Priority 1
   b. Priority 2
   c. Priority 3
   d. The task does not require you to set a priority.

_____

7. To become more efficient in scheduling time, the administrative assistant should

   a. use a manual or electronic tickler system.
   b. assign another secretary the responsibility of scheduling specific tasks.
   c. complete tasks in the order they are presented by superiors.
   d. ask superiors to keep their own calendars up to date.

_____

8. Batch processing applies to which one of the following?

   a. Getting input ready for data processing
   b. Grouping those tasks requiring the use of word processing software and doing the high-priority items first
   c. Delegating office tasks to other support personnel
   d. Scheduling time for the high-priority items first

_____

9. Keying appointments, meetings, and other commitments directly into the computer for scheduling purposes by secretaries, managers, and executives is known as

   a. batch processing.
   b. coordination of work assignment.
   c. calendaring.
   d. priority scheduling.

_____

10. The type of communication most needed to maintain good rapport between the supervisor and employees in a work unit is

   a. interpersonal communication.
   b. both vertical and horizontal communication.
   c. vertical communication.
   d. horizontal communication.

_____

11. Yesterday you were assigned a rather complex research report to be formatted in final form and ready for the author by this afternoon. It is now 4 P.M., and you are still working on it. You realize that the report cannot be done by the time you leave the office. Which one of the following would be the best thing to do?

   a. Finish the report no matter what time you get through.
   b. Say nothing to the author this afternoon about not completing it but plan to finish it first thing in the morning.
   c. Explain the problem briefly to the author.
   d. Tell your manager the status of the report, explaining the amount of time required to complete it.

12. The arrangement whereby one full-time position is held by two people, each one working part time, is known as

    a. job rotation.
    b. cross training.
    c. participative management.
    d. job sharing.

13. Simmons, the administrative secretary for the marketing department, is responsible for the accuracy of the sales report that is sent to all sales representatives each morning. In yesterday's report, a $100,000 error was made in the total sales for the previous week. Which one of the following responses would be the most satisfactory when Hughes, the vice president of marketing, confronts her with the error?

    a. "I don't know how this error could have been made. I checked the data very carefully."
    b. "McKenzie was the person who prepared the report."
    c. "I'm sorry this happened; a revised report can be faxed to the representatives this afternoon."
    d. "Perhaps the best thing to do is just wait and see if any of the representatives notice the error."

14. When records services are provided in a location with easy access to and from all departments within the firm, the records function is

    a. centralized.
    b. decentralized.
    c. matrix.
    d. departmentalized.

15. When all staff support personnel are housed within individual departments, the organizational plan is

    a. matrix.
    b. centralized.
    c. decentralized.
    d. shared.

16. Bradford Co. established a communications center as support for all departments except the human resource department, which has its own communication satellite center. The company is utilizing which one of the following organizational plans?

    a. Matrix
    b. Decentralized
    c. Centralized
    d. Departmentalized

17. Some companies support a staff services center organized within particular departments that produce a large quantity of documents. In this arrangement, the workload would be handled by

   a. word/information processing specialists.
   b. the information processing center for the organization.
   c. a satellite center established within that department.
   d. administrative support personnel.

18. Information about a specific work order, namely, the name of the job, the department for whom the work will be done, and the date needed should be placed on a/an

   a. procedure form.
   b. assignment form.
   c. priority form.
   d. logging form.

19. The process of reading through text to detect needed corrections is called

   a. editing.
   b. proofreading.
   c. checking for accuracy.
   d. production.

20. Information relating to the mission, objectives, and philosophy of the organization will most likely be included in a/an

   a. operations manual.
   b. employee manual.
   c. policy manual.
   d. organizational manual.

21. Information on dress codes, work schedules, hours, and employee salaries is included in a/an

   a. policy manual.
   b. specialty guide.
   c. procedures manual.
   d. employee handbook.

22. Detailed instructions for performing specific job-related tasks will most likely be included in a/an

   a. procedures manual.
   b. organizational manual.
   c. specialty guide.
   d. employee manual.

23. Samples of all business forms used in the organization will appear in a/an

    a. policy manual.
    b. employee handbook.
    c. procedures manual.
    d. specialty guide.

24. Which one of the following relates to a supervisor's staffing responsibilities?

    a. Evaluating a secretary's performance on the job
    b. Orienting a new office employee to tasks performed on the job
    c. Identifying competencies needed for a new office position
    d. Conducting an analysis of a computer system for possible lease/purchase

25. The management function that permits the administrative manager to monitor the staff services center's progress in meeting objectives for the year is

    a. planning.
    b. organizing.
    c. controlling.
    d. directing.

26. One of the secretary's responsibilities involves the delegation of work assignments to other support personnel. Which one of the following examples indicates effectiveness in delegating a work assignment?

    a. "Johnson needs this report for her meeting with the president tomorrow morning at 10 o'clock. Would you please type this right away?"
    b. "Use any format that will give Johnson time to revise the report before her meeting with the president tomorrow morning."
    c. "This report needs to be prepared this afternoon and delivered before 9 o'clock tomorrow morning to the people I have listed on the attached sheet. I'll be glad to help you proofread the report before you make copies for these people."
    d. "Please put everything else aside and work on this report. It is very important—Johnson needs it right away!"

27. Criteria that are established for evaluating each employee in terms of job behaviors, personal characteristics, and productivity results are known as performance

    a. appraisals.
    b. standards.
    c. assignments.
    d. interviews.

28. The supervisor ranks each employee so that a list of the best to the worst employees is prepared. This method of performance appraisal is called

    a. the paired comparison method.
    b. a graphic rating scale.
    c. the rank comparison method.
    d. management by objectives.

_____

29. The performance appraisal method that requires the employee and the administrator to establish goals from which performance objectives will be derived is known as

    a. the rank comparison method.
    b. management by objectives.
    c. the performance standards method.
    d. the paired comparison method.

_____

30. The administrator conducts a performance interview at scheduled intervals with each employee to

    a. provide feedback related to the employee's performance.
    b. inform him or her of objectives developed for the department.
    c. review performance standards for the specific job.
    d. determine the employee's inability to perform specific tasks.

Solutions

Answer	Refer to:
1. (c)	[A-1-a, A-1-b]
2. (c)	[A-1-b]
3. (c)	[A-1-c]
4. (d)	[A-2-a(5)]
5. (a)	[A-2-a(5)]
6. (b)	[A-2-c(1)
7. (a)	[A-3-a(2)]
8. (b)	[A-3-a(4)]
9. (c)	[A-3-a(5)]
10. (b)	[A-4]
11. (c)	[A-4-a]
12. (d)	[A-4-b(1)(a)]
13. (c)	[A-4-b(3)]
14. (a)	[B-1-a]
15. (c)	[B-1-b]
16. (a)	[B-1-c]
17. (c)	[B-1-c]
18. (d)	[B-3-a(1)]
19. (b)	[B-3-a(4)]
20. (d)	[B-3-b(2)(a)]
21. (d)	[B-3-b(2)(c)]
22. (a)	[B-3-b(2)(d)]

23. (d)   [B-3-b(2)(e)]

24. (b)   [C-1-d]

25. (c)   [C-2]

26. (c)   [C-2-a]

27. (b)   [C-2-b(1)(a)]

28. (c)   [C-2-b(2)(a)]

29. (b)   [C-2-b(2)(e)]

30. (a)   [C-2-b(3)]

CHAPTER 16

Composing Written Communications

OVERVIEW

Business communication, both oral and written, is the lifeblood of any organization. In your position as an administrative professional, communication skills will have a tremendous effect on your relationships with executives, co-workers, organization leaders, and customers. Although oral communication is an hourly activity, the skills involved in composing and recording communication in written form for later reference and review is the main purpose of this chapter. Many of these guidelines, however, are applicable to oral communications as well.

As a professional secretary, you have the responsibility of developing clearly written communication. Many executives rely on their administrative assistant to handle the majority of the office correspondence as well as to critique the executive's writing. Realizing this, the administrative assistant or secretary must understand that communication is more than stating those facts that an executive feels are important.

Saying or writing what you have to communicate is called *encoding* the message. However, that message may be delivered to the receiver through a variety of channels: verbal, telephone, formal report, messenger, electronic mail, or computer, to mention only a few. The choice of channel is important in persuading the receiver to listen to the message and interpret it correctly. Message interpretation requires the receiver to decode the message. As a writer, your responsibility is to strive to have the decoded message be the same as the encoded message. A means for assessing whether this has been accomplished is to seek feedback.

Communicating is more than stating what is important to you. Consideration must be given to all aspects of the communication process (receiver as well as sender), or the communication will be weak and ineffective.

KEY TERMS

Abstract	Combination letter	Emphasis
Abstract language	Complements	Experimental research
Active words	Conciseness	External report
Analytical report	Concrete language	Feasibility study
Appendix	Constant information	Form letter
Bibliography	Database	Glossary
Clarity	Deductive style	Goodwill
Coherence	Empathy	Horizontal report

Imprecise descriptors	Parallelism	Special report
Index	Passive words	Standard deviation
Inductive style	Persuasive letter	Statistical report
Informal report	Positive letter	Survey research
Informational report	Precise descriptors	Technical report
Jargon	Primary research	Tone
Mean	Progress report	Unbiased language
Median	Radial report	Unity
Memorandum	Range	Valid data
Mode	Reliable data	Variable information
Narrative report	Routine letter	Vertical report
Negative letter	Scheduled report	
Observational research	Secondary research	

A. Fundamentals of Writing

Written messages must be coherent and logical so that the reader can understand the messages. The reader has no opportunity to ask questions in case any of the ideas presented are not clear. Improper selection of words will prevent the reader from understanding the ideas being presented. Word choice, sentence and paragraph construction, and parallelism affect the presentation of clear, understandable messages. Language must be used that will evoke clear mental images as the message is being read.

1. *Effective Word Selection:* Words selected for use in the message must be appropriate for the situation. Words with the right denotative meaning (literal meaning) and connotative meaning (feeling or impression conveyed) must be selected. The key to effective word selection is to use specific nouns, action verbs, and descriptive adjectives and adverbs.

   a. *Positive language:* Writing needs to be positive in nature. People react to positivism by wanting to do, to act, and to listen.

      (1) Messages should be written from the reader's viewpoint. Direct the message to the reader. Focus on the use of pronouns such as *you, your* rather than *I, me.*

         (a) What has already been accomplished should be the focus rather than what should have been done or what cannot be done. Express what has been done in a positive manner.

         (b) The reader's interest in the subject of the message should be emphasized.

         (c) If appropriate for the situation, the receiver of the message should be complimented.

      (2) Messages should limit the use of negative expressions. A letter or memo should not be written in a moment of anger.

         (a) Avoid using the word *not* or contractions containing *not.*

         EXAMPLES:

         Positive: Remember to call us the next time you need help with your office decor.

         Avoid: Don't forget to call us for help with your office decor.

(b) Avoid using negative expressions that tend to express doubt or sorrow or accuse the reader unnecessarily. Words like *regret, unfortunately, apologize, neglected,* and *failed* have negative connotations.

EXAMPLE: You failed to enclose a check to pay for the order.

b. *Tone:* Tone is defined as the manner in which a certain attitude is expressed. What you choose to say and how you say it determine the tone of the writing. The business writing tone that is more effective is friendly, conversational, businesslike, objective, and personalized. Tone, together with style, forms the overall impression for the reader.

c. *Familiar words:* In conversation and writing during a typical business day, most people use only 1,000 to 1,500 words out of more than 700,000 words in our language. Most words in the English language are unfamiliar to many of us.

(1) Use commonly known synonyms for unfamiliar words.

(2) Avoid confusing unfamiliar words with technical words. Technical words may be used without an explanation when writing to a member of the same profession. However, the same terms may need to be explained when writing to a person not in the profession.

(3) Use the English equivalent for foreign expressions. Using foreign expressions is not recommended in business writing unless these expressions fit the topic or the receiver's cultural background.

(4) Refrain from using jargon in business writing. *Jargon* is defined as "slang" language. Business jargon is generally understood only by others in the specific field of business.

(5) Spell out acronyms when first used in a document followed by the acronym in parentheses. An *acronym* is a word formed by the initials of words in a set phrase. Thereafter, the acronym can be used.

EXAMPLE: The American Management Association (AMA) is a professional organization for business people. The AMA also offers membership to college and university professors of business.

d. *Concrete language:* Being precise and specific in your writing is very important. The use of words and terms with meanings that people generally agree on helps to make language more concrete. Some words are too general to convey a message effectively. *Concrete* language refers to the use of words and terms that are precise in meaning. *Abstract* language refers to the quality of language where meanings can be interpreted differently by different people, even in the same situation.

(1) A word or phrase may be added to an abstract word to define it more precisely.

EXAMPLE: building

The Sears Tower is the tallest building in Chicago.

(2) The abstract term may be explained within the sentence.

EXAMPLE: application

You may use this software package to prepare a mailable letter.

("Prepare a mailable letter" refers to the specific application.)

(3) The most specific, concrete word possible should be used when it is important to the meaning of the message.

EXAMPLE: building

bank, restaurant, library

(4) Short, simple words convey the meaning much more directly and more clearly than do long, complex words. Of course, choose the word most appropriate to the reader.

EXAMPLES:

Short, simple words	Long, complex words
later	*subsequent*
people	*personnel*
car, truck, bus	*vehicle*
use	*application*

e. *Active words:* Active words denote *action,* whereas passive words denote *inaction* or *waiting for something to happen.* The use of active verbs, descriptive adjectives, and descriptive adverbs will create more action in your writing.

(1) *Active verbs:* Verbs denote the action that is taking place. An *action verb* conveys a precise meaning, which is what is needed in business writing. Such verbs convey the degree of precision in the action being expressed.

EXAMPLES:

Active verbs	Passive verbs
speaks	*is conversing*
writes	*is composing*
participates	*will be meeting*

(2) *Descriptive adjectives:* Adjectives are used to describe nouns or subjects and to support active verbs. Descriptive adjectives are sometimes called *key words* or *descriptors.* As descriptors, adjectives may be precise or imprecise in the way they describe a noun.

EXAMPLES OF IMPRECISE DESCRIPTORS:

good   better   best

fine

real

EXAMPLES OF PRECISE DESCRIPTORS:

The Call Director is a <u>sophisticated</u> <u>telephone</u> system with such <u>automatic</u> functions as call forwarding and call pickup.

(3) *Descriptive adverbs:* Adverbs modify verbs, adjectives, or other adverbs. Adverbs, too, need to be descriptive so that a precise meaning is conveyed to the reader.

EXAMPLES OF IMPRECISE DESCRIPTORS:

nearly   well   fairly   barely   likely

EXAMPLES OF PRECISE DESCRIPTORS:

neatly   courteously   concisely   frequently

Mervin <u>politely</u> asked for a <u>neatly</u> prepared report.

The use of active words will make your communication more meaningful to the receiver. Here are two examples of how exact information can be more helpful:

EXAMPLES:

Imprecise: *Come in <u>early</u> tomorrow morning, and Smith will see you.*

Precise: *Come in <u>at 9:15</u> tomorrow morning, and Smith will see you.*

f. *Contemporary words and expressions:* The selection of contemporary words and expressions makes the writing more relevant.

EXAMPLES:

word processing	*modular workstation*
hard copy	*soft copy*
Windows 98 operating system	

g. *Unbiased language:* If due caution is not used, bias can creep into writing very easily. Equal treatment must be given to everyone (men and women, minority groups, and jobholders). Sometimes, people become stereotyped into particular jobs or positions, even though both men and women can be effective jobholders. Here are some basic guidelines that may be followed so that unbiased language will be used in all business writing.

(1) *Gender-fair language:* Language in business writing must be free of gender bias.

(a) Whenever people are referred to in general, asexual words and phrases should be used instead of masculine or feminine words.

EXAMPLES:

manpower	*peoplepower*
manhours	*working hours*

Here are some ways in which these changes in word usage can be achieved:

• Sentences may be reworded to remove unneeded pronouns.

• The number can be changed from singular to plural.

• Masculine pronouns can be replaced with *s/he, her* or *his, one,* or *you* to decrease the use of sexist language.

A variety of these techniques may be used to avoid monotonous, repetitious writing or difficulty in reading the material.

EXAMPLE:

Each secretary needs a complete report on file by the end of the week.

Instead of:

Each secretary needs to complete her report by the end of the week.

(b) Men and women should be referred to as equals, and references to them should be phrased consistently. You should use the person's full name in the first reference to that person; then you may use the first name, the last name, or proper pronoun in later reference.

EXAMPLE:

Erin Gray was recently appointed the chairperson of the awards committee. Gray has been with the company since 1985.

(c) Avoid unnecessary labels and stereotypes in business writing.

EXAMPLES:

female executive	*executive*
just like a man	*(this phrase should not be used)*

(d) The words *man* or *woman* should not be used as a prefix or suffix in job titles.

EXAMPLES:

chairman	*chairperson*
	chair
	presiding officer
foreman	*supervisor*

(e) When referring to people by gender, parallel language should be used.

EXAMPLES:

the ladies and the men	should be:	*the women and the men*
		or
		the ladies and the gentlemen
man and wife	should be:	*husband and wife*

(f) When referring to people by name, parallel language must be used in expressing their names.

EXAMPLES:

Please telephone one of our marketing representatives, either <u>Bill Gray or Mrs. Brown</u>, with the description of the cabinet.

Instead, say:

Please telephone one of our marketing representatives, either <u>Bill Gray</u> or <u>Muriel Brown</u>, with the description of the cabinet.

(g) General expressions used should refer to both men and women. Use generic titles or descriptions for both women and men.

EXAMPLES:

male secretary	*secretary*
female executive	*executive*
male programmer	*programmer*

(2) *Racially or ethnically unbiased language:* Equal treatment of people within certain racial or ethnic groups is a necessity in business writing so that the audience will not be offended by the writing.

(a) Qualifiers may be used to reinforce racial or ethnic stereotypes. Do not add information that suggests that a person is an exception to a racial or ethnic norm.

EXAMPLE:

Schultz, an employee from Germany, has very good spelling skills.

(Does this sentence imply that Germans, as a general rule, have difficulty with spelling?)

(b) The identification of racial or ethnic origin should not appear in the writing unless it is pertinent to the message being conveyed. In proofreading and editing, watch for bias that is sometimes implied in context.

(3) *Job-related language:* In business writing, the types of jobs held by people should not be stereotyped. In other words, examples should be used of both men and women in positions that might easily be stereotyped.

EXAMPLES:

Shirley Stone, an administrative assistant in the financial department, is responsible for the drafting of all research reports. (Are all administrative assistants female?)

Glenn, an administrative assistant in the loan department, supervises the five part-time employees.

2. *Effective Sentence and Paragraph Construction:* Sentences and paragraphs need to be constructed carefully to be effective in meaning. The following points address sentence and paragraph construction.

a. *Constructing effective sentences:* A sentence is a complete thought expressed in words that are understandable. A sentence must have a subject and a predicate.

(1) *Types of sentences written:* The types of sentences written should be varied. A variety of sentence types adds interest to a message and affects emphasis or tone.

(a) A combination of simple, compound, and complex sentences adds variety to the sentence structure.

(b) Simple sentences must have a subject and a verb and may have modifiers—adjectives, adverbs, or complements. *Complements* are additional words for complete meaning.

EXAMPLE:

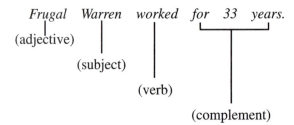

(c) Compound sentences consist of two independent clauses joined by a comma and a conjunction (*and, but, or, nor*) a semicolon, or a conjunctive adverb (*also, however, therefore*). An independent clause conveys a complete thought and can stand alone as a sentence.

EXAMPLE:

Sales increased in June (independent clause*), but* (conjunction*) the vice president of marketing expected a greater increase* (independent clause*).*

(d) Complex sentences consist of an independent clause and one or more dependent clauses. A dependent clause is incomplete; it cannot stand alone as a sentence. Dependent clauses begin with a connecting word showing their subordinate relationship. The connecting word is either a relative pronoun (*who, which, that*) or a subordinate conjunction (*if, because, when, since*).

EXAMPLE:

As far as Harrison determined (dependent clause*), there was no problem with the local area network in the accounting department* (independent clause*).*

(e) A compound-complex sentence consists of two or more independent clauses and one or more dependent clauses. Compound-complex sentences should be used sparingly.

(2) *Length of sentences:* Sentences should normally average from 15 to 20 words. There needs to be a combination of short, medium, and long sentences to keep reading interesting. A sentence that exceeds 40 words, however, should be rewritten into two or more sentences.

(3) *Connectives:* Sentences should be joined when the thought continues. The expression of related ideas needs to be clearly constructed.

EXAMPLE:

The word processing supervisor reviews each document before it leaves the center; this is an important responsibility.

(4) *Sentence formats:* Some ideas are better stated as questions than as statements. A clause or a phrase may begin a sentence, which adds variety to the format. Certain words may be in bold, underlined, or italicized.

b. *Organized paragraphs:* Groups of related sentences are formed into paragraphs, with each paragraph having at least one central idea or theme. When the idea changes, a new paragraph results. A paragraph has one main idea presented, with detailed information to support that idea.

(1) *Deductive style:* This organization is direct. The main idea is stated followed by supporting details.

(2) *Inductive style:* This organization is indirect. Supporting details are presented first; then the main idea is presented.

There must be parallel construction to develop organized paragraphs so that there is equal treatment of ideas that are comparable.

c. *Criteria for effective sentence and paragraph construction:* To be effective, sentences and paragraphs need to be constructed with several qualities in mind: coherence, emphasis, unity, conciseness, variety, clarity, and accuracy.

(1) *Coherence:* Thoughts are coherent if the writing shows consistency in style, word choice, and word usage. Coherence means that the sentences and paragraphs are constructed so each word contributes to the sentence, each sentence contributes to the meaning of the paragraph, and each paragraph contributes to the entire message. The following techniques can help the writer maintain cohesion.

(a) *Stress on words:* Coherence is shown by emphasizing certain aspects of the message, that is, placing special stress on a particular thought, word, or syllable. Repeating a word from the preceding sentence emphasizes that thought. Sometimes specific ideas need to be stressed equally. Comparing or contrasting to show similarities or differences is another way to stress specific points. Sometimes information must be presented in rank order, depending on its importance. Another way to place stress on specific words is to underline words, place words in bold, change the format, or use a different size of type.

(b) *Word choice and usage:* Sentences are directly linked when a pronoun is used to represent a noun from the preceding sentence.

- Begin sentences with connecting words: *however, therefore, also.* Connecting words imply continuation of the same topic.

- Use words that are commonly found together:
  state/federal
  employer/employee
  graduate/undergraduate
  winter/spring/summer/fall

(c) *Parallelism:* Ideas that are equal in thought should be stated in identical grammatical form. Violations of parallel construction lead to misinterpretation and awkward sentence formats.

EXAMPLE:

The purpose of the meeting is <u>to organize</u> our plan for a new networked system and <u>implementing</u> procedures for writing the proposal.

(The words that are underlined are not parallel.)

The purpose of the meeting is <u>to organize</u> our plan for a new networked system and <u>to implement</u> procedures for writing the proposal.

(The underlined words are parallel.)

(2) *Emphasis:* Emphasis is a very important part of developing coherence in writing; the two criteria—coherence and emphasis—are closely related. Emphasis means that greater importance is attached to a particular fact.

  (a) *Word choice and order:* Key information should be placed at the beginning of sentences or messages so that the reader will be sure to see it. Selecting words that relate precisely to the idea being conveyed permits the writer to emphasize the idea correctly.

  (b) *Balance:* Items of equal value should be emphasized equally in the writing.

  (c) *Restatement:* Sometimes, a fact or detail needs to be restated, in different words, so that the reader will be more likely to pay attention to that fact.

  EXAMPLE:

  The importance of setting up appropriate procedures for accepting work will save personnel time. In other words, the procedure for logging in work will enable you to organize the work in less time.

  (d) *Format:* Sometimes the format is changed within a document to add emphasis to specific details. Within the body of a letter, a statistical table might be included to emphasize facts that would otherwise be obscured in the body of the message. Type sizes and styles help to vary the format as well.

(3) *Unity:* The term *unity* suggests that a coherent flow of ideas exists throughout a written work—within sentences, within paragraphs, and between paragraphs.

  (a) *Detailed information:* Factual information to support the main ideas is included within the paragraphs.

  (b) *Connectives:* Conjunctions and other connecting words are used to form relationships between and among words and sentences.

  (c) *Repetition:* Sometimes, key ideas are summarized at the end of the message to emphasize their importance and also as reminders to the reader.

(4) *Conciseness:* Business writing needs to be concise because a busy executive will usually look briefly at the first page of a document to see whether it is worthwhile to read further. *Conciseness* is defined as writing in a brief but comprehensive manner. In preparing communication that is concise, you must first identify the main purpose of the correspondence and plan your approach.

  (a) *Planning:* Planning what you are going to write will result in more concise writing. Determine what needs to be said, keeping in mind that the communication must be clear. What is not required is stating the obvious.

  (b) *Revision:* In the revision stage, when reviewing the communication from the reader's viewpoint, look for short, simple sentences and active voice. Using a conversational style will also lead to more concise writing.

(5) *Variety:* In order to maintain a reader's interest in what you are attempting to say, use a variety of techniques to enhance the message you are conveying. The use of synonyms helps to vary the word usage and the choice of words. Individual sentences may be constructed in different ways. Entire messages may need to be varied in cases where the same letter is being sent to a number of different people—remember to keep the reader's perspective in mind.

(a) *Word usage:* A thesaurus is a reference that is helpful in determining other words that have the same meaning as the one being conveyed in the message. Look for synonyms to add variety to the writing. Thesauri, spelling checks, and grammar checks are writing tools available in most text processing software packages.

EXAMPLES:

action: *performance, movement, working, operation*

record: *account, minutes, diary, journal, proceedings*

(b) *Sentences:* The use of a combination of simple, compound, complex, and occasionally a compound-complex sentence will help to vary the sentence construction. There should also be a combination of short, medium, and long sentences to keep the reader interested in the writing. Sentences should normally average about 15 to 20 words.

(c) *Messages:* To make the writing interesting to both the writer and the reader, messages need to be varied so that they are appropriate for the person receiving them and the purpose for which they are intended. Variable information needs to be inserted so that each message is personalized.

EXAMPLE: In word/information processing, form letters and form paragraphs are used to express the same messages to a number of different people. Even though the basic message can stay the same, paragraphs or other variable information pertinent only to one person can be inserted to personalize the message. The receiver feels that the message was written personally, even though the basic message is standard to all recipients.

(6) *Clarity:* Any message needs to be written in a clear, accurate manner. Knowing the purpose of the message first will help you accomplish clarity in your writing. Combining clarity with the use of the "you" approach will help to direct the message to the reader.

(a) *Purposes:* It is helpful for writers to outline what they wish to accomplish before they begin writing. By identifying the reasons for writing the message, the writer should be able to focus on those points first rather than "going off on tangents."

(b) *Review:* Once the message has been written, it is a good idea to set the material aside for a short time. Rereading it later may help to achieve clarity. Another technique is to have a co-worker read the material to see whether the message is clear.

Administrative assistants, secretaries, and executives need to work together to read and react to one another's writing. Such a critique can be a very helpful strategy in improving the writing transmitted from the office. This is especially important in cases where the writing deals with sensitive issues.

(7) *Accuracy:* Any type of business writing should be accurate in terms of message, format, and language.

   (a) *Message:* The message should contain accurate data and other detailed information. Specific references to data sources are extremely important, especially if the reader needs to know the credibility of the material. The message should present the information in a logical, sequential manner so that the reader can follow the accuracy of the message.

   (b) *Format:* The message should be produced in a document format that is accurate; the margins should "frame" the writing so that the appearance is pleasing to the eye. Also, material can be placed in tables within the document to enhance the presentation of key points. The secretary plays an important role in ensuring that the document format is determined *before* the message is prepared and the writing style fits.

   (c) *Language:* A message must be written using grammatically correct language. Poor English and inaccurate punctuation affect the reader's impression of the message as well as the company. Typical reaction to a poor communication is that the firm probably produces an inferior product as well.

d. *Development of goodwill:* Each message conveyed from one organization to another has the capacity of creating goodwill between the organizations. Goodwill develops when people work together, within the organization or with others outside the organization, and communicate positively, clearly, and courteously.

(1) *Considerateness:* To create goodwill, the communication needs to express consideration for the other person. In other words, the writer must think of the receiver of the message and the effect the message will have on that person. A genuine interest in the reader must be emphasized in the communication.

EXAMPLES:

A message of welcome to the new secretary in the office is a warm, considerate step for office professionals to take.

When an employee has been out of the office because of illness, a "welcome back" message helps bridge the gap for that person—that first day back to the office requires adjustment for all.

(2) *Empathy:* The "you" approach in business writing helps to create empathy in writing. The writer must be able to see the difficulty or problem from the reader's point of view. *Empathy* refers to an understanding of the feelings or emotions of another person. It is important to know the difference between sympathy (feeling sorry for) and empathy (understanding feelings).

EXAMPLE:

Moving to a new location has not been an easy task for you and your family, and I want to be as helpful as I can with the transition.

(3) *Courtesy:* Concern for the reader will help you deliver a courteous message. Words like *please* and *thank you* come naturally when you consider the best interests of others. The best tone your letter can produce is a natural one. A technique that often shows courtesy is the inclusion of the reader's name within the correspondence; it gives the reader the feeling of importance.

EXAMPLE:

Please send us your report as soon as it is convenient for you, Bob. Your writing is always of the highest quality, so I know only minor revisions may be necessary. Thank you for your willingness to help us with this report.

(4) *Sincerity:* Sincerity is a genuine expression of confidence and trust shown in other people. In some business writing, it is important to keep certain facts confidential. Sincere writing eliminates excessive humility, flattery, or overstatement of information.

EXAMPLE:

We know that you will be able to give us the information we need because of your expertise in this area. We want to reassure you, however, that your responses to our questions will be held in confidence and analyzed as part of the aggregate response from the sample.

(5) *Respect:* Effective business communication requires that respect be shown for the company represented, for products or services being provided, and for the reader of the message. The use of tact, consideration, and courtesy is very important in business writing if you want the reader to respond in a given way. Respect needs to be shown not only for the person but for the person's position within the firm as well.

EXAMPLE:

We are very eager to have you try our latest product—SmartLabel—because we think you will find it more adaptable to your needs than other label makers on the market. Some label makers are not compatible with the latest versions of word processing software. Ours is! Your experience as a secretary in an automated office will enable you to give us an honest evaluation of this new product.

Goodwill developed among people is very important in today's business world, and secretaries can do much to further the development of goodwill through attention to considerateness, empathy, courtesy, sincerity, and respect created through effective business communication.

B. Business Letters

The business letter is associated with *external* communication. It is the type of formal written communication used most often for corresponding with others outside the organization. The sender uses the letter as a means to inform the receiver of various kinds of business news and events. Business letters need to be written from the reader's viewpoint by using the "you" approach.

1. *Positive Letters:* Of course, the most pleasant type of letter to write or receive is the *positive* or *favorable* letter—the letter that says "yes" or otherwise presents good news to the reader. The main purpose of the positive letter is to transmit needed information that will please the receiver.

   a. *Types of positive letters:* There are numerous reasons for writing positive or favorable letters. Here are some of the more typical types of positive correspondence:

   (1) *Order for goods or services:* Especially in small companies or in situations where a purchase order is not used in ordering goods or services, a letter will

initiate such an order. Complete information needs to be included, identifying the exact purchase:

- Name of item(s) or service(s)

- Descriptions including sizes, order numbers, or type of service requested

- Prices, if known

- Shipping information

(2) *Letter granting refund or adjustment:* It is important to describe the claim briefly and to explain the exact refund or adjustment made. Such information as purchase order or invoice numbers must be included in the letter.

(3) *Response to inquiry for information:* Frequently, letters are received that request certain types of information. The direct approach enables the writer to provide answers to those questions asked.

   EXAMPLES: Inquiries might include requests for subscription information for a new computer magazine, information needed to obtain a credit account, and information on a new training program available for prospective word processing specialists.

(4) *Goodwill message:* The primary purpose of some correspondence is to generate goodwill (a favorable attitude and feeling) toward you and your organization from others with whom you conduct business. A goodwill message can express sympathy, congratulations, or thanks.

   EXAMPLES:

   Thanks: *A letter thanking Robinson, a business consultant, for presenting a seminar on "Communication Techniques for the Professional Secretary" at the November meeting of the Kishwaukee Chapter of the International Association of Administrative Professionals*™.

   Sympathy: *A letter to Jacoby, one of the company's clients, expressing condolence on the death of her father.*

   Congratulations: *A letter congratulating Moore-Young on being promoted to administrative manager of the Kendall Corporation.*

b. *Writing approach:* The direct or deductive approach is used in writing positive letters. When your correspondence carries good news, get to the point immediately. Why bother with the details when the reader is most interested in hearing the good news first? Then you can follow up with the facts and close the message with a positive, forward-looking comment.

(1) *Direct or deductive approach:* Since goodwill is created in the first paragraph, begin with a general statement of the main point of the message. With the direct approach, you immediately provide the reader with the information he or she wishes to receive.

   EXAMPLE:

   Mr. Randy Dailey, our network manager, will be glad to speak to your trainee group on Tuesday, December 4.

(This first paragraph says "yes" immediately, including a favorable response.)

(2) *Detailed follow-up:* In the next paragraph, the necessary details should be explained. It is important that the recipient understand any conditions or other details relating to the message.

EXAMPLE:

Mr. Dailey will meet with the group in Conference Room B from 1:30 to 3:00 P.M. From your suggestions, he plans to discuss shared resources, watching for viruses, and system demands.

(This paragraph covers the details of the presentation.)

(3) *Closing statement:* The message should close with a general positive statement or a request for action (a courteous request). If you need action by a given date, this deadline should be included as well as any special reasons for needing this information by then.

EXAMPLE:

Please review these areas with the trainees prior to December 4. There should be some interesting discussion following his presentation. It is always exciting to exchange information with interested, young people entering the field.

(This paragraph includes a positive note about a stimulating discussion with the trainee group.)

Figure 16–1 illustrates the complete example of the positive or favorable letter.

2. *Routine or Neutral Letter:* The primary purpose of the routine letter is to exchange day-to-day information. Routine or neutral letters are written more often than any other type of letter. The routine nature of the letters results in a favorable reception to these letters.

Figure 16–1   Example of Positive or Favorable Letter

Dear Ms. Stanley

Mr. Randy Dailey, our network manager, will be glad to speak to your trainee group on Tuesday, December 4.

Mr. Dailey will meet with the group in Conference Room B from 1:30 to 3:00 P.M. From your suggestions, he plans to discuss shared resources, watching for viruses, and system demands.

Please review these areas with the trainees prior to December 4. There should be some interesting discussion following his presentation. It is always exciting to exchange information with interested, young people entering the field.

Sincerely

a. *Types of routine letters:* Primarily, routine correspondence includes either requests for information or responses to information requests received. Following are some typical types of routine or neutral letters:

(1) *Request for information:* A simple request for information can be stated precisely and sometimes briefly.

EXAMPLE: A letter requests a vendor to send pricing information for a new computer just being marketed.

(2) *Response to information request:* Sometimes, inquiries are received that need to be answered within a short period of time.

EXAMPLE: An inquiry is made about appropriate procedures to use in securing an automobile loan from the credit union.

b. *Writing approach:* Again, the direct or deductive approach is used in writing routine or neutral correspondence.

(1) *Direct or deductive writing:* The main point of the message is presented in the first paragraph.

EXAMPLE:

Would you please give me your opinion on a storage problem?

(This opening sentence is a direct request for advice.)

(2) *Detailed follow-up:* Factual information should follow so that the reader understands the need for information.

EXAMPLE:

We have an option to purchase a two-year supply of steel moldings. A decision to expand operations means the factory warehouse is needed for other manufacturing materials. Our production manager suggested that the steel moldings could be stockpiled outdoors.

(This introductory paragraph follows up with factual information.)

My concern with stockpiling outdoors is the effect of rust and pitting. I understand that your company has used this method of storage for a number of years with much success. In your opinion, is there any serious risk in exposing steel moldings to weather conditions for possibly as long as two years?

(This paragraph identifies major concerns and makes the actual inquiry.)

(3) *Closing statement:* A summarizing statement in the closing paragraph reemphasizes the main point of the message or requests some type of action, sometimes according to a specific deadline.

EXAMPLE:

I would appreciate any advice you can offer about outdoor storage. At our June 15 meeting, we will make a final decision on the steel molding purchase. Could I hear from you before that time?

(This closing paragraph asks for action and sets a time line for a reply.)

Figure 16–2 shows the complete example of the routine or neutral letter.

Figure 16–2   Example of Routine Letter

Dear Mr. Boyce

Would you please give me your opinion on a storage problem?

We have an option to purchase a two-year supply of steel moldings. A decision to expand operations means the factory warehouse is needed for other manufacturing materials. Our production manager suggested that the steel moldings could be stockpiled outdoors.

My concern with stockpiling outdoors is the effect of rust and pitting. I understand that your company has used this method of storage for a number of years with much success. In your opinion, is there any serious risk in exposing steel moldings to weather conditions for possibly as long as two years?

I would appreciate any advice you can offer about outdoor storage. At our June 15 meeting, we will make a final decision on the steel molding purchase. Could I hear from you before that time?

Sincerely

3. *Negative Letter:* When correspondence conveys a "no" response or some other form of bad news, you should use the *indirect* approach. This approach may also be referred to as the *inductive* approach. Many times, the reader is more likely to do what you hope she or he will do and is more willing to accept the bad news if the details are presented first. Otherwise, the facts may not be read. Some feel that the bad news should be placed within a paragraph in the middle of the letter. If this approach is used, you must be very careful that the news you are relaying to the reader is clear. And, of course, you will want to close the message with a forward-looking comment that can be positive for both you and the reader. The negative letter is also referred to as an *unfavorable* letter.

   a. *Types of negative letters:* The letter that says "no" or includes a refusal is necessary in many different types of business situations. Here are a few types of negative letters that may be written:

      (1) *Refusal to send information:* You may receive an inquiry for some information that is not readily available or cannot be released. In this case, a refusal letter must be written in a polite, courteous manner so that the reader will not be offended.

      (2) *Refusal to give assistance:* A request asking for help with a particular problem might be received. You may feel that you are not the right person to ask or do not have the time to carry out the request adequately.

      (3) *Problem with order for goods/services:* An order that has been received may not be able to be filled at this time. Perhaps the inventory is low and the order will not be filled until the inventory is replenished. A letter will need to be sent explaining the delay in shipment.

(4) *Refusal to grant particular action:* Perhaps you are unable to grant the particular action requested by the writer. In cases where you will be unable to grant a claim or extension of time, a refusal letter must be written.

b. *Writing approach:* The indirect, or inductive, approach is recommended for writing negative letters.

(1) *Buffer paragraph:* Since the facts need to be read and understood *before* the bad news is communicated, a beginning paragraph setting the stage may be necessary. Such a paragraph is called a *buffer paragraph.* One must be careful not to be too wordy, or the reader will begin to read between the lines, assume the news, and not read the important part of the letter—the facts.

EXAMPLE:

You can count on a large, interested readership for the article you are writing about the importance of sales letters in business.

(This paragraph demonstrates a buffer beginning, yet is not too lengthy.)

(2) *Rationale for refusal:* Next, reasons must be stated for the refusal, followed by a clearly stated refusal. The facts must be put into perspective from two viewpoints:

(a) The philosophy of the business, realizing the goals of the organization

(b) The reader's viewpoint, realizing the wants and concerns of the reader

This is where the balancing act comes into play. By carefully outlining these two viewpoints, the message can be developed in an honest approach, never losing sight of the reader's wants and concerns. The message needs to be delivered in as tactful and understanding a manner as possible.

EXAMPLE:

Our company depends on effective sales letters to interest new clients. Through the years we have tested our letters extensively to find the most effective sales techniques for the written message. Our writers are continually revising, conducting test mailings, and comparing returns. The best letters used by Appleton Enterprises represent a considerable investment in both time and money.

(This paragraph presents reasons. Even though the reasons are based on company policy, company policy is an internal matter and should not be used as a reason in an external communication. Also, reasons given are logical so there is no need for an apology.)

(3) *The "bad news":* Once the rationale has been given, the refusal or other "bad news" should be presented.

EXAMPLE:

Because of this time and research effort, several companies have expressed an interest in using our material. Therefore, it was necessary to copyright all our sales letters and confine them to company use. Should we release them for publication, we would incur the same expense once again because their effectiveness for us would be decreased.

(This paragraph implies "no." Yet this explanation is written clearly enough so that the reader understands that the letters cannot be used in the article.)

(4) *Closing statement:* The ending of the letter will either ask for action on the part of the reader or present a forward look if the news was unfavorable. Since you are hoping to continue correspondence with the reader, you will want a pleasant closing for your message. Avoid being apologetic. If the facts are well thought out, they will be logical and no apology will be necessary.

EXAMPLE:

I am enclosing two bulletins and a bibliography we have found helpful in developing our letters. You may also find the material helpful with your article. I look forward to reading your article in the Writer's Guide *when it is published.*

(This letter closes with a positive note stating interest in reading the article when it is published. In addition, reference materials were sent to the reader in an effort to help.)

In writing a negative or unfavorable letter, you must take the time to write a tactful, courteous letter with the reader's feelings in mind. If the letter discusses a particularly sensitive issue, set it aside for a short time. Then reread it and revise it so that the message is clear and will be interpreted correctly by the reader. Or, have a co-worker read the letter for clarity, empathy, sincerity, and goodwill.

Figure 16–3 shows the complete example of the negative letter.

4. *Combination Letter:* There are times when you can say "yes" to the reader for only part of what is requested. In this case, the message should begin with the positive response,

Figure 16–3   Example of Negative Letter

Dear Ms. Brothers

You can count on a large, interested readership for the article you are writing about the importance of sales letters in business.

Our company depends on effective sales letters to interest new clients. Through the years we have tested our letters extensively to find the most effective sales techniques for the written message. Our writers are continually revising, conducting test mailings, and comparing returns. The best letters used by Appleton Enterprises represent a considerable investment in both time and money.

Because of this time and research effort, several companies have expressed an interest in using our material. Therefore, it was necessary to copyright all our sales letters and confine them to company use. Should we release them for publication, we would incur the same expense once again because their effectiveness for us would be decreased.

I am enclosing two bulletins and a bibliography we have found helpful in developing our letters. You may also find the material helpful with your article. I look forward to reading your article in the *Writer's Guide* when it is published.

Sincerely

followed by facts that support both the positive and the negative responses. The "no" response needs to be clearly stated, with the letter closing on a positive note.

a. *Types of combination letters:* Letters that contain both a positive and a negative response may be written for a variety of reasons. Here are a few examples of how the combination letter might be used:

   (1) *Partial order being filled:* Perhaps only part of a sales order can be filled at this time. The combination letter must identify the part of the order that can be filled, followed by reference to the part of the order that cannot be filled.

   (2) *Partial response to information request:* A request for information may include some questions that can be answered as well as some questions that need replies from other departments or individuals.

b. *Writing approach:* In writing a combination letter, it is best to begin with the positive aspect of the message.

   (1) *Opening paragraph:* Begin the first paragraph with the positive or "yes" response to the original message. Be careful not to lead the reader into thinking the "yes" is for everything.

   EXAMPLE:

   Your four rose bushes should arrive by May 20, just in time for spring planting. They were shipped via AR Express, one of our most reliable shipping companies.

   (The opening paragraph says "yes," making it clear which part of the request is positive.)

   (2) *Detailed follow-up:* Follow the "yes" statement with facts supporting both the positive and the negative aspects of the message.

      (a) The presentation of these facts needs to be logical.

      (b) It should be clear to the reader which facts relate to the positive part of the message and which ones relate to the negative part of the message.

   EXAMPLE:

   You will be more than happy with the blossoms these rose bushes yield. These bushes should be planted in a sunny area, keeping the ground moist with evening waterings. For your climate, it is best to use rose mounds or cones for winter protection.

   (Facts relating to the good news are presented in this paragraph and are separated from the facts in the following paragraph, which carries the bad news.)

   The peach trees you ordered ordinarily bloom in April, a time when the Illinois climate varies between 35 and 50 degrees. These peach trees would almost certainly bloom before the last freeze of the winter season. For trees that bloom after the danger of freezes in your area, we recommend the Ambrosia. This peach tree produces peaches similar to those of the trees you ordered. The Ambrosia blooms in late May; details are presented in the enclosed brochure.

   (This paragraph advises that the item ordered is not the best choice, and facts about the tree ordered are compared with facts of an alternative choice so that

the reader can decide what action to take. A brochure is enclosed with more detailed information.)

(3) *Closing statement:* The letter should close with a positive, forward-looking request for action on the part of the reader. The "no" response to the reader must be clearly stated.

EXAMPLE:

Just indicate your instructions on the enclosed postcard. If we hear from you prior to May 1, we can change your order to the Ambrosia for the same price. Also, you would still be able to plant your trees to take advantage of this season's growth and have them in bloom next year.

Figure 16–4 is the complete example of the combination letter.

5. *Persuasive Letter:* A persuasive letter presents positive information to the reader, but the nature of the information is more complex. The writer requests that the receiver take some action. However, the writer has the task of providing enough justification for the action that the receiver will be motivated to take.

a. *Types of persuasive letters:* Letters that are persuasive in nature may be used for many different reasons. Here are some typical types of persuasive communication that might be used:

Figure 16–4   Example of Combination Letter

Dear Ms. Wieland

Your four rose bushes should arrive by May 20, just in time for spring planting. They were shipped via AR Express, one of our most reliable shipping companies.

You will be more than happy with the blossoms these rose bushes yield. These bushes should be planted in a sunny area, keeping the ground moist with evening waterings. For your climate, it is best to use rose mounds or cones for winter protection.

The peach trees you ordered ordinarily bloom in April, a time when the Illinois climate varies between 35 and 50 degrees. The peach trees would almost certainly bloom before the last freeze of the winter season. For trees that bloom after the danger of freezes in your area, we recommend the Ambrosia. This peach tree produces peaches similar to those of the trees you ordered. The Ambrosia blooms in late May; details are presented in the enclosed brochure.

Just indicate your instructions on the enclosed postcard. If we hear from you prior to May 1, we can change your order to the Ambrosia for the same price. Also, you would still be able to plant your trees to take advantage of this season's growth and have them in bloom next year.

Sincerely yours

(1) *Special requests for assistance:* Community agencies or nonprofit organizations may engage in fund-raising activities. Requests for assistance may be sent to names on mailing lists to encourage contributions.

(2) *Special requests for information:* People who are engaged in research find it necessary to make special requests to persons known in a field to help with certain types of information. Such a request must persuade the receiver to cooperate and assist with the study.

(3) *Marketing goods, services, or ideas:* A frequently used persuasive letter is the sales letter, which attempts to interest the receiver in a new service, product, or idea. Such a letter must be written with the receiver in mind so that the new product or service would appeal to that age-group, a person in that particular position, or a person with specific types of needs.

b. *Writing approach:* The approach used most often in writing the persuasive letter is the *attention-interest-desire-action* approach (also known as the A-I-D-A approach).

(1) *Opening paragraph:* The opening paragraph must get the reader's attention. This may be accomplished by appealing to the reader's interests, problems, or responsibilities. Sometimes, it is helpful to begin with a question for the reader.

EXAMPLE:

May we have your help again this year? Thanks to your very generous donation in the past, we have been able to keep our Oaken Acres Animal Shelter open. This Christmas we need your thoughtfulness and kindness once again.

(This paragraph introduces the reader to the problem and, hopefully, gets the reader's attention.)

(2) *Detailed follow-up:* Next, you need to emphasize the reasons why the reader should respond positively to the request. Describe the details of your request by using words that help the reader identify with the positive benefits of responding favorably to your request. You want the reader to react positively to your message.

EXAMPLE:

The animals we house at the shelter must be kept warm and clean and fed through the winter months. Here are some of the ways in which we use your contributions:

- *Homes are provided for many stray dogs and cats until they are adopted.*
- *Veterinarian care is provided for hurt, sick, or abused animals.*
- *Programs on responsible pet care are made available to the general public.*
- *Visits with the animals at the senior citizens retirement centers are very therapeutic and bring much happiness to the residents.*

(3) *Closing statement:* Explain to the reader courteously what action should be taken. In the closing statement, appeal to the reader's interest in helping solve the problem.

EXAMPLE:

Please use the enclosed reply envelope to send your contribution today. Your Christmas donation will show your continued love and concern for animals and those who benefit from the shelter's service.

Figure 16–5 is the complete example of the persuasive letter.

6. *Form Letters:* Correspondence with some identical parts may be sent to more than one person or company for a specific purpose. Perhaps a person has not paid a bill, and a form letter (always sent to a person who does not pay a bill within the first 60 days) is prepared and sent. Word processing has made it possible for form documents to be created so that the secretary has the time-saving capability of providing only the variable information that must be inserted. Form letters may be of three types: personalized repetitive letters, letters with variable information, and letters created from standard form paragraphs.

a. *Personalized repetitive letters:* Repetitive letters are form letters that are being prepared and sent to a list of different people. One of the benefits of word processing is to help personalize these repetitive letters. Each letter should appear as if it had been individually prepared and typed for the receiver. In addition, the letter may contain personalized messages for the recipients—a postscript on some messages or the use of the person's name in the body of the message. Here is a typical message that is intended for a large group of people.

EXAMPLE:

Every year Royal Travel serves hundreds of Milwaukee area residents who wish to escape from the winter snows and bask in the sunny climate of Florida for the winter.

Figure 16–5   Example of Persuasive Letter

Dear Mrs. Donaldson

May we have your help again this year? Thanks to your very generous donation in the past, we have been able to keep our Oaken Acres Animal Shelter open. This Christmas we need your thoughtfulness and kindness once again.

The animals we house at the shelter must be kept warm and clean and fed through the winter months. Here are some of the ways in which we use your contributions:

- Homes are provided for many stray dogs and cats until they are adopted.
- Veterinarian care is provided for hurt, sick, or abused animals.
- Programs on responsible pet care are made available to the general public.
- Visits with the animals at the senior citizens retirement centers are very therapeutic and bring much happiness to the residents.

Please use the enclosed reply envelope to send your contribution today. Your Christmas donation will show your continued love and concern for animals and those who benefit from the shelter's service.

Sincerely

We have groups leaving Milwaukee during the first week of every month from December through March so they can spend from two to four weeks at their favorite vacation spot. Our service allows you to "leave the flying to us"; let us arrange your flight, ground transportation, and hotel accommodations, if needed.

Our next vacation group leaves from Milwaukee on January 4 for sunny Florida. Won't you let us help you plan your winter vacation in Florida?

(1) *Use of personal names:* Personal names are used mostly in the inside address, the salutation, and perhaps one reference within the body of the message. With repetitive letters, it is important to keep the letter as standard as possible, with very little change from letter to letter.

EXAMPLE:

Mr. and Mrs. Robert Stevens
433 West Wisconsin Avenue
Milwaukee, WI 53215

Dear Mr. and Mrs. Stevens:

Every year Royal Travel serves hundreds of Milwaukee area residents like Robert and Mary Stevens who wish to escape from the winter snows and bask in the sunny climate of Florida for the winter.

(Note: The rest of the message would stay the same.)

(2) *Use of postscripts:* When a number of repetitive letters are being prepared, it may be necessary to add a postscript to some of them to personalize the message. Here is an example of a postscript that might be added to the foregoing example:

EXAMPLE:

P.S. Bob and Mary, we are looking forward to the possibility of having you with us again this year. Didn't we have fun last year? By the way, be sure to ask for the 10 percent discount available to those who have traveled with us before.

b. *Letters with variable information:* A repetitive letter may have variable information as well as constant information. *Constant information* is the wording that will stay exactly the same on every letter produced. *Variable information* is any text that must be inserted to complete the message; this information will change on each letter produced. The letter used in the preceding example may be changed to include variable information.

EXAMPLE:

Variables:

Letter to Mr. and Mrs. Robert Stevens
433 West Wisconsin Avenue
Milwaukee, WI 53215

(1) Milwaukee
(2) Florida
(3) January 4

Letter to Mr. George P. Hendricks
5554 North Michigan Avenue
Chicago, IL 60656

(1) Chicago
(2) Arizona
(3) January 10

Every year Royal Travel serves hundreds of (1) area residents who wish to escape from the winter snows and bask in the sunny climate of (2) for the winter.

We have groups leaving (1) during the first week of every month from December through March so they can spend from two to four weeks at their favorite vacation spot. Our service allows you to "leave the flying to us"; let us arrange your flight, ground transportation, and hotel accommodations if needed.

Our next vacation group leaves from (1) on (3) for sunny (2). Won't you let us help you plan your winter vacation in (2)?

Two methods that are used in word processing for the preparation of letters with variable information include the use of merge codes for keying in variable information or the use of databases to create records of variable information to merge with form letters and other types of forms.

(1) *Use of merge codes:* The form letter is recorded on some form of word processing media (e.g., disks) with appropriate input codes inserted at the "spots" where the variables should be keyed. The insertion of each variable is a manual operation. Once a variable has been keyed and inserted into the document, the secretary can continue the automatic operation until the next point where variable information needs to be inserted.

(2) *Databases of information:* A complete record of variable information may be available in the form of a database. In word processing this is usually referred to as a *mail-merge function,* which requires the preparation of a primary document (the form letter) and a secondary document (the variables). This database of information can include the following types of data:

   (a) Name, address, and telephone number of each person

   (b) Account number

   (c) Employment

   (d) Employer address

   (e) Any other variable information that might be pertinent

When the form letter is prepared, merge commands are inserted at the points where variable information will be inserted into the final letter. These merge commands are prompts that ask for specific information from the database. In the final preparation of the letter, the form letter is merged with appropriate information from the database.

c. *Letters from form paragraphs:* Business organizations use many kinds of form paragraphs to create form letters. Some form paragraphs say "yes," others say "no" or persuade. A series of form paragraphs pertaining to particular situations can be stored so that the secretary can recall only those paragraphs that are appropriate for a given situation. The result is a personalized letter for each recipient.

EXAMPLES OF FORM PARAGRAPHS:

(1) Every year Royal Travel serves hundreds of (1) area residents who wish to escape from the winter snows and bask in the sunny climate of (2) for the winter.

(2) Every year Royal Travel serves hundreds of (1) businesses that wish to schedule conferences in other parts of the country. Getting away from the winter snows and spending time in a sunny climate may appeal to you and your business associates.

(3) We have groups leaving (1) during the first week of every month from December through March so they can spend from two to four weeks at their favorite vacation spot. Our service allows you to "leave the flying to us"; let us arrange your flight, ground transportation, and hotel accommodations if needed.

(4) We can schedule a group tour, if you wish, at any time during the month and at any time of the year. Special rates are available, depending on the length of your conference. Our service allows you to "leave the flying to us"; let us arrange any flight, ground transportation, hotel, or meeting accommodations your organization may require.

(5) Our next vacation group leaves from (1) on (3) for sunny (2). Won't you let us help you plan your winter vacation in (2)?

(6) Please contact our local representative, (4), at (5) to obtain more details on our conference service to business organizations in the area. Try us—you'll like us!

EXAMPLE OF MERGED LETTER:

This example combines form paragraphs (2), (4), and (6).

Note: The underlined information represents the variable information that would be entered from the database or manually.

Robert Jensen & Associates
5430 North Michigan Avenue
Chicago, IL 60656

Dear Mr. Jensen:

Every year Royal Travel serves hundreds of Chicago *businesses that wish to schedule conferences in other parts of the country. Getting away from the winter snows and spending time in a sunny climate may appeal to you and your business associates.*

We can schedule a group tour, if you wish, at any time during the month and at any time of the year. Special rates are available, depending on the length of your conference. Our service allows you to "leave the flying to us"; let us arrange any flight, ground transportation, hotel, or meeting accommodations your organization may require.

Please contact our local representative, C. S. Moore, *at* (312) 555-2300 *to obtain more details on our conference service to business organizations in the area. Try us—you'll like us!*

Sincerely,

Paulette S. Bronson

General Manager

The more routine, repetitive letters are designed as form letters and prepared using word processing software, the more time the secretary will have for customized work. Any time that a letter must be prepared more than once with identical information, this type of procedure should be considered.

C. Memoranda within the Organization

Another common form of communication *within* an organization is the memorandum. Memoranda are correspondence from one office to another within an organization. Some organizations use the memorandum for communication from one organization to another (external to the company). Because memoranda are correspondence between people who know each other and work together, the tendency is to be informal. An electronic mail message is the most informal means of communications. A business letter is a formal means of communication with memoranda falling between e-mail and business letters. Short, informal reports can also be written as memoranda.

1. *Memoranda:* A common medium for corresponding within the firm is the memorandum. The memo (as it is often called) can always be used for communication whenever the writer and the receiver of the message work for the same organization. Just as with business letters, memoranda can be prepared that are favorable, unfavorable, or persuasive in nature.

   a. *Favorable memoranda:* When writing a memorandum that is favorable in nature, the same principles that are used for writing favorable business letters can be applied.

      (1) *Types of favorable memoranda:* Here are some of the more common reasons why favorable memoranda may be written:

         (a) *Request for information:* The memo is written to present an explanatory summary of information.

         (b) *Response to information request:* The memo may be an answer to a previous memo that requested certain information.

         (c) *Request for assistance:* The memo may be a request for help in locating specific information from the files or records.

         (d) *Directives:* The memo may issue a directive from a superior with complete instructions for performance of a particular assignment.

      (2) *Writing approach:* The direct or deductive approach is used in writing favorable memoranda. The style of writing may vary somewhat depending on the purpose of the memo.

         (a) *Direct or deductive approach:* Begin the memo with a statement of the general objective.

            EXAMPLE:

            The attached list of clients who have utilized our services at least once in the last six months will give you the information you requested for your semiannual report.

         (b) *Presentation of details:* Follow the general opening statement with the information supporting the ideas presented in the memo. It is usually a good idea to present information pertaining to only one objective in each memo. Otherwise, it can become difficult to determine under what name or title the memo will be filed for later reference.

(c) *Closing statement:* A closing comment or statement is required if it is necessary to summarize or give an opinion or recommendation. In addition, an offer to help further provides a courteous closing to the message.

b. *Unfavorable memoranda:* Memoranda that are unfavorable in nature and carry a "no" response should be written using the *indirect,* or *inductive,* approach. The position and status of the writer and the receiver of the message should also be considered very carefully so that lines of authority are observed in the tone and style of the memorandum. Techniques similar to those used in writing negative letters should be used.

(1) *Types of unfavorable memoranda:* Here are some of the more common purposes of unfavorable memorandums:

(a) *Refusal of information request:* You may receive a request for information that is confidential in nature and cannot be released or information that is not available to you. Reasons should be given in the memorandum demonstrating why it is impossible for you to supply the information.

(b) *Refusal to give assistance:* You may be asked for your help, but it may be necessary for you to consult with your superior to see whether it would be all right for you to help. When you find it necessary to refuse, you should do it in a courteous way, perhaps suggesting an alternative.

(c) *Performance evaluation:* A memorandum that explains an unfavorable performance evaluation should be handled with care. The contents of the memorandum should be explained in person as well as in written form so that the individual being evaluated has an opportunity to question or discuss aspects of the evaluation with the supervisor.

(2) *Writing approach:* The indirect, or inductive, approach is recommended for unfavorable memoranda. The writing style used will depend on the position of the person who is receiving the memo as well as the nature of the message being presented.

(a) *Buffer paragraph:* A beginning paragraph should set the stage for the explanation to follow. A brief introduction to the nature of the memo should be stated clearly.

(b) *Rationale for refusal:* The basic reasons for having to refuse to assist or give information should be explained briefly and clearly. The details must be presented so that the views of the organization as well as the reader are considered important.

(c) *The bad news:* The refusal or other bad news should be clearly stated so that there will be no misunderstanding on the part of the recipient.

(d) *Options:* Following the refusal, you may present available options: make a referral, offer a substitute, or suggest an alternative procedure. Offering an option is called *refusing with recourse.*

(e) *Closing statement:* The ending of the memo may ask for some further action on the part of the receiver or present an alternative that might be considered.

    c. *Persuasive memoranda:* An approach similar to that used for persuasive letters should be used in writing memoranda that are persuasive in nature. The *attention-interest-desire-action* approach should be used to develop a message that results in some positive action taken by the recipient.

        (1) *Types of persuasive memoranda:* Usually, a persuasive memorandum is designed to get someone else to act or to do something for you. Here are some typical reasons for using persuasive memoranda:

            (a) *Special request for information:* You may find that you need some information for research you are doing. A special request to someone in charge of records for the company may provide you with needed information to complete your research.

            (b) *Special request for assistance:* In office work, there are times when assistance is needed in handling a particularly difficult problem. A special request in the form of a memorandum would be needed in situations where a brief explanation of the problem would help the person decide whether to help.

            (c) *Selling a service or idea:* An offer to help another person within the organization, through a service or an idea, should be put into writing so that the recipient will have time to consider the importance of the offer to particular work being done. A serious offer such as this requires time so that the recipient of the message can consider alternatives.

        (2) *Writing approach:* The writing approach used for persuasive letters will also be used for writing persuasive memoranda. The primary objective of the memorandum is to encourage someone to act positively toward a request that is being made.

            (a) *Opening paragraph:* The opening paragraph of the memorandum must get the reader's attention. Sometimes, an opening question will appeal to the reader's interest.

            (b) *Details:* The rationale for a positive reaction to the request needs to be presented next. You need to emphasize the reasons why the reader should respond favorably to your request, and you need to provide details so that the reader understands your request completely.

            (c) *Closing statement:* End the memo with a courteous request that a certain action be taken. In this paragraph, you need to appeal to the reader's interest in helping to solve the problem or act in a specific way.

            (See Chapter 19 for an explanation of the document format to use in preparing interoffice memoranda.)

2. *Informal or Short Reports:* Another form of interoffice communication is the informal or short report. This type of report is used to transmit meaningful information to other people within the organization or outside the organization. Perhaps the most important aspect of the report, besides its content, is the fact that it is *informal* and *short.* Typically, an informal report is no more than five pages. In fact, the fewer the pages the better; the busy executive will look at the first page of such a report and will need to be persuaded through the message to read further.

a. *Types of informal or short reports:* There are numerous ways in which the informal or short report can present business information. Some of the more common types of short reports include the following:

   (1) *Proposal:* The development of new office procedures or new equipment may necessitate the development of a proposal. The proposal includes information such as *what* the new development is, *why* it is important to the continued efficient operation of the office, *how* it will be used, and *how much* it will cost to implement. A short report should give enough information to management so that the decision can be made whether to continue with the plan.

   (2) *Feasibility study:* An analysis of business systems and procedures obtained through a feasibility study may be reported to management in the format of an informal or short report. An explanation of the procedures used as well as the results will provide management with a summary of the highlights of the research.

   (3) *Progress report:* Sometimes, it is necessary to make a progress report that outlines steps already completed in a project and others that still need to be handled. The format for an informal or short report is very appropriate for this type of progress report, sometimes referred to as a *work-in-process report.*

   Any business report can be written as an informal, short report. In fact, most reports are written in this form.

b. *Acceptable formats:* Basically, three formats are used for informal or short reports: memorandum report (in the form of a memorandum), letter report (in the form of a business letter), and short report in manuscript form (see Chapter 19 for further explanation of memorandum, letter, and report formats).

c. *Writing approach:* The direct, or deductive, approach is often used in writing an informal or short report. Some managers prefer to present results or solutions first and then the detailed information relating to those results. The inductive approach is popular, too, especially for persuasive reports.

   (1) *Personal style:* The writing style may be personal and conversational, with limited self-reference. Writing in the first or second person is acceptable if not overused.

   (2) *Presentation of information and analysis:* Depending on the problem pursued, both basic information and detailed analysis may be included in the report. Attention should be focused on brevity, however, since this is a short report (five pages or less). The data analysis, if any, need not be as detailed as in a more formal report. A limited number of visual aids may be used to support findings.

   (3) *Supplementary information:* The report itself, without supplementary parts like appendices and bibliographies, may be the most important to the reader. Sometimes, the informal or short report includes only the highlights or outline of events that were studied, with a final notation that if the reader wishes access to more detailed information, bibliography, or appendices, a request should be made.

D. Electronic Mail   Electronic mail (e-mail) is becoming a typical way of transmitting informal communications both internally and externally in a very effective manner. Networked organizations are finding that effective use of e-mail has improved the dissemination of information and, consequently, decision making. Here are some of the advantages of e-mail:

- This informal communication is focused, short, and to the point.

- The message is transmitted immediately over the network.

- E-mail is an easy method to use in providing input to and receiving input from all relevant individuals.

- E-mail has lowered the cost of communication.

1. *Fundamentals of Writing E-mail Messages:* As an informal means of communication, it is still important to follow the fundamentals of effective writing. An e-mail message is much like writing a short memorandum dealing with one focused point; this becomes the subject of the e-mail. As a tool in sending short messages, e-mail writing concentrates on the four C's: *c*oncise, *c*orrect, *c*omplete, and *c*ourteous.

   a. *Concise:* E-mail presents only the information pertinent to the subject. If detailed information is required in written format, a memorandum, short report, or appropriate business letter should be sent.

   b. *Correct:* Any facts or information presented in the e-mail message must be accurate. It is the writer's responsibility to not misrepresent the message by being too concise, possibly leaving out important information. Also, e-mail tools for spelling and grammar checks should be used. Sentence structure affects the reader's understanding. Typically, short, simple sentences are used in e-mail communications.

   c. *Complete:* Before invoking the send command, read the e-mail to make sure that it accurately conveys your message and that any important documents are attached. You must be concise, yet complete. Sometimes, there is a very fine line between being concise and being complete.

   d. *Courteous:* With the ease in composing and sending e-mail messages, it becomes easy to be too curt and too much to the point. The reader's perspective, the "you" attitude, is as important in e-mail messages as it is in any other business communications.

2. *E-mail Format:* Although e-mail programs differ slightly, the basic components include the sender of the message (From address), the receiver of the message (To address), the option to send copies or blind copies, the subject of the message, the date and time, the message, and attachments affixed to the e-mail message.

   a. *The sender:* The sender's e-mail address is placed automatically in the From section of the message.

   b. *The receiver(s):* There must be at least one recipient of the e-mail message. With the appropriate punctuation (according to the e-mail package), multiple recipients can be listed. Recipients should only be those individuals involved in the communication; copies should be sent to those who need to be informed of the communication. The recipient is identified through an e-mail address.

      (1) *E-mail address:* An address consists of the person's or organization's name followed by the @ symbol and the domain name.

EXAMPLE:

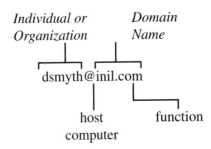

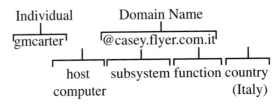

(2) *Domain name:* In order to receive an e-mail message, the person must be connected to a Web server. The Web server will have a unique name that distinguishes it from all other Web servers. This unique name for the Web server is included in the *domain name.*

c. *Copies and blind copies:* Individuals not involved in the e-mail dialogue but who should be kept informed of the communication taking place should receive a copy of the e-mail message. If the original recipient of the message should not know that a copy is sent to others, the e-mail can be copied blind. With a blind copy, only the copy recipient is aware of all participants in the e-mail dialogue.

d. *Subject:* Since the purpose of e-mail is to enhance rapid communication, it is important that the recipient know the topic of the e-mail before opening the message. A descriptive subject line is important for all business e-mails.

EXAMPLE:

<u>*IAAP International Convention*</u> *is a much more descriptive subject line than just* <u>*Convention.*</u>

e. *Message:* The message of the e-mail should be concise, correct, complete, and courteous.

(1) If the From section of the e-mail message does not clearly identify the sender or if the person receiving the e-mail does not know the sender, the sender's name, title, department, and company (if external) should be included in the message section.

(2) If the e-mail does not require the sender identification at the beginning of the e-mail, all business e-mails should end with a signature. Most e-mail programs have a signature option. You can store your signature and automatically affix it to your e-mails where needed. The signature should include your name, title, company name, e-mail address, and telephone number.

EXAMPLE:

Diane Graf
Organization Facilitator
Transformation Dynamics
dmgraf@inil.com
630-879-6213

    f. *Attachments:* Many business e-mails are about sharing other business documents: word processing correspondence, spreadsheets, graphs, or electronic slides. These documents can be attached to the e-mail message. Any documents attached to the e-mail message will automatically be listed in the Attachment line. As with all business correspondence, only send those documents relevant to the message.

E. Business Reports

The purpose of the business report is to transmit meaningful data to one or more persons for either information or decision-making purposes. A business report may be oral or written. (The concentration in this chapter is on the written report.)

1. *Types of Reports:* Reports are classified according to type of text or data material, time interval, informational flow, context, function, and message style.

    a. *Material:* Reports that include primarily text material (words) are referred to as *narrative* reports. Reports that include primarily numerical data are referred to as *statistical* reports.

    b. *Time interval:* Reports known as *scheduled* reports are issued at regular, stated intervals—weekly, monthly, or quarterly. *Progress* reports may be prepared in the middle of projects to report on the status of the project. *Special* reports may be prepared to handle unusual or nonroutine requests for information; these reports are prepared on demand.

    c. *Informational flow:* A *vertical* report may be prepared for someone at a higher level within the organizational structure of the company or for someone at a lower level. A *horizontal* report is communication at the same administrative level and may be distributed from department to department or division to division within the organization. An *external* report is one that will be disseminated outside the organization. Sometimes, these reports are called *radial* reports, which are reports that cut across levels of authority or move both inside and outside an organization.

    d. *Context: Nontechnical* reports convey information to people who do not have backgrounds in a given subject area. In writing such a report, an effort is made to refrain from using technical language. *Technical* reports are designed for conveying information to professionals within the field who will understand the specialized vocabulary and terminology included in the report.

    e. *Function:* Reports may be informational or analytical in nature.

        (1) *Informational report:* Facts are presented in an organized, structured manner within an informational report. Sometimes, the report is prepared using a standardized format, such as in the case of an inspection report or an accident report.

(2) *Analytical report:* In addition to presenting basic information and facts, the analytical report analyzes these facts and provides an interpretation of them. A thorough analysis of the findings will lead to the development of conclusions and recommendations based on the report.

f. *Message style:* The style used in preparing the report may be *chronological* (according to the sequence in which events occurred), *logical* (according to patterns of reasoning), or *psychological* (according to the receiver's needs).

2. *Planning, Designing, and Conducting Research:* Prior to doing the actual research for a report, it is necessary to plan in detail exactly what the research will entail. The report is the *result* of the research. Therefore, if care is exercised in planning the research study, the information required in the final report will be collected in a systematic manner.

a. *Definition of problem:* First, you need to know what problem needs to be solved. It is important that you distinguish the problem from the symptoms of the problem. A clear definition of the problem, as well as any limitations, is necessary.

(1) *Research questions:* The problem may be defined in terms of specific research questions that need to be answered through the study being conducted.

(2) *Subproblems:* The problem might be further defined into subproblem areas that will be undertaken in the study.

(3) *Preliminary research:* To become familiar with the problem, find out how the organization has been involved in this type of problem solving. Research other types of background information that will help you plan the report. Included in this phase is the review of related periodical literature that may give current, practical information from business (see Section D-2-b[1] for more information on secondary research data).

(4) *Limitation of the problem:* Defining the problem requires that the problem be limited. Usually, the general topic of the report must be narrowed so that a particular problem can be pursued. Some typical questions to ask in narrowing the problem include the following:

- *What* do you want to do?

- *Why* is this important?

- *When* will the study take place?

- *Where* will the study take place?

- *Who* are the people (the sample or population) being studied? (This is relevant if people are involved.)

(5) *Scope of the problem:* Another consideration in defining the problem is to determine the breadth of the problem—exactly what will be studied and what will *not* be studied.

(6) *Identification of factors or variables:* Key elements of the research are independent variables, dependent variables, and other factors affecting the design of the study and report. The identification of these elements tends to give structure to the study (and the future report). Such factors as employee attitudes, work flow, and technology help to frame the focus of the study to precise aspects of the problem being studied.

The problem must be defined before the subsequent steps in the process may be pursued effectively. The rest of the report format depends on the data that need to be collected.

b. *Collecting data:* Once the problem has been defined and approved by superiors, the collection of research data may begin. Data collection is the accumulation of data or facts from secondary and primary sources to analyze the problem thoroughly and evaluate possible solutions to the problem.

(1) *Secondary research data:* An examination of secondary research data (research done previously) enables you to gain valuable background information relating to the subject of your study. Secondary research is an investigation to gather information that others have prepared to use as the basis for your primary research.

(a) *Prior research:* A review of prior research will show what research has been done already. This information is valuable to you in determining the direction your research should go, especially in terms of new directions.

(b) *Related areas:* You may find related areas that also need to be considered in your research, some not considered previously.

(c) *Justification for need:* A review of prior research and literature pertaining to the problem should lead to the supportive information needed to justify this particular research study or report.

(d) *Supporting evidence:* Sometimes, you need supportive information for procedures you choose to use or actions you hope to take to solve a problem. If someone has already used a particular procedure, this could support your use of the same procedure in a different research setting.

Secondary research data may be obtained from company publications, general reference books, government documents, periodicals, information banks and databases, and other types of research studies.

(2) *Primary research data:* When you conduct primary research, you are investigating a phenomenon or event to gather original information to use as current data in a report. Three types of primary research are conducted: experimental, observational, and survey research.

(a) *Experimental research:* The purpose of experimental research is to determine whether a change in one factor or variable causes a change in another factor or variable. The research design must ensure that any change that results is due to the factor in question.

(b) *Observational research:* The purpose of observational research is to see or observe the actions or results of individual or group activities. Such research may be conducted in person, actually spending time in the research location observing the behavior of people. An intermediary process, such as videotaping or filming a work process for later review and analysis, is another method of collecting observations.

(c) *Survey research:* In survey research, the primary purpose is to determine opinions, beliefs, or reactions to specific work situations. The types of questions asked could range from questions about the actual work process to questions concerning the environment, technology used, or opinions about the future. A survey can be administered either in written form (a questionnaire) or oral form (an interview).

(3) *Data collection procedures:* Procedures used in collecting valid and reliable data must be planned and monitored carefully. *Valid* research procedures measure what they are intended to measure. *Reliable* data are data that are measured consistently and accurately. Care in using sampling techniques and developing questionnaires will help to increase the validity and reliability of data that are collected.

   (a) *Questionnaire:* Factual data, attitudes, and opinions may be obtained through the use of a questionnaire. A questionnaire is a written form that includes all questions to be answered, with space allowed for providing the answers on the form or on an additional answer form. The use of optical character recognition (OCR) response forms will improve the speed and accuracy of data input for analysis. Specific techniques should be used in developing items for a questionnaire. Here is a sampling of some of these techniques.

   - The items must be worded in a parallel manner so that they will be interpreted accurately.

   - Only one response should be obtained per item; ask only one question per item.

   - Responses to the questions should not be influenced by how the question is written. The statement or question should be stated as objectively and nonjudgmentally as possible.

   - Only items that pertain to the research problem should be included.

   - Write items that will lead to bias-free answers.

   - Include items that can be answered quickly and easily. The format of the question will help in making it relatively easy for someone to respond.

   - The items should be sequenced in a logical, coherent order. Sometimes it is a good idea to place all items pertaining to a particular subproblem in the same section.

   The overall format used for the questionnaire should be designed in such a way that the data will be collected in the order in which you plan to present the results in the report. The tabulation and evaluation of the data will always appear in the same sequence.

   (b) *Mail questionnaire:* Many questionnaires are designed to be administered through the mail. A questionnaire will be mailed, with a letter of explanation, to each person in the sample. Directions will be given for completing the questionnaire, and the deadline for return of the completed questionnaire will be indicated. A self-addressed envelope should be included for ease in responding.

   (c) *Personal interview:* Another technique that is used to obtain responses to a questionnaire is the personal interview. An interview allows you to obtain responses to questions in person. It is important to make an appointment ahead of time for such an interview to be sure that the respondent has set aside adequate time to respond to the questions. If numerous interviews are being conducted, each should be conducted in exactly the same way, with the questions being asked in the same sequence. The personal interview has the advantage of providing the opportunity for a more in-depth response than the mail questionnaire.

(d) *Telephone interview:* The telephone can be an important research tool as well. An interview can be conducted over the telephone, asking the respondents the same questions that would be asked in a mail questionnaire or a personal interview. The telephone interview must be designed to take very little time in administering. Sometimes the data are keyed directly into a computer as the respondent answers the questions. In questions with subquestions (or branches), the computer can be programmed to skip to the next appropriate question.

EXAMPLE:

If the question is this:

Do you believe that the open plan has contributed to better communication in the office?

Yes _____ No _____

If you answer "yes," skip to Questions 15-18.

The interviewer would ask the respondent the question. If the respondent answers "yes," then the computer will immediately branch to Question 15 when the interviewer enters the "yes" answer on the keyboard.

The telephone interview is still not as effective as the personal interview. A relatively small number of questions can be included in the telephone interview compared with the personal interview, but, of course, the personal interview is more expensive.

(4) *Question format:* The format of the question plays an important role in data analysis. Select a format that makes data analysis easy. Question formats can be closed, open, or scaled.

(a) *Closed question:* The closed question provides the respondent with a choice of answers. Choices can be as simple as *Yes, No, Don't know* or *Agree, Disagree, No opinion.* Sometimes the closed question requires a selection from a list.

EXAMPLES:

Current Occupation (please check)

_____ *Student*
_____ *Blue-collar worker*
_____ *White-collar worker*
_____ *Professional*
_____ *Unemployed*
_____ *Retired*
_____ *Other: _____*

Household Income (please check)

(Husband/Wife Combined)

_____ *Below $10,000*
_____ *$10,000–24,999*
_____ *$25,000–39,999*
_____ *$40,000–59,999*
_____ *$60,000–74,999*
_____ *$75,000 and over*

The respondents are to circle or check their responses. Sometimes, it is important to clarify the choice so that the respondent understands what you mean by the category. For current occupation, it may be helpful to provide a definition of blue-collar worker, white-collar worker, and professional. Notice in all cases that a choice for alternative answers (Other, $75,000 and over) is provided.

(b) *Open question:* The open question, sometimes called the *open-ended question,* requires the respondent to provide an answer. No choices are provided. With open questions, data analysis may be more difficult because of the variety of responses. Two respondents may use different terminology but may in fact mean the same answer. Many open questions can be made into closed questions. If open questions are used, provide enough space for the respondent's answer.

EXAMPLE:

What advice would you give a recent high school graduate about entering the secretarial profession? _____

_____

(c) *Scaled question:* Rating scales allow the respondent to rank a list of items or to respond according to a continuum. This question format also makes data analysis easy.

EXAMPLES:

Please rank the job characteristics in order of importance to you. Use 1 for most important, 2 for second most important, and so on, until you have ranked all the items. Two blank lines have been provided for you to write in other important job characteristics.

_____ *Challenge*
_____ *Interaction with people*
_____ *Job responsibility*
_____ *Salary*
_____ *Task variety*

_____ _____

_____ _____

For each job characteristic, please circle the degree to which the characteristic is important to you.

CHALLENGE

1	*2*	*3*	*4*	*5*

Unimportant		*Moderately important*		*Very important*

INTERACTION WITH PEOPLE

1	*2*	*3*	*4*	*5*

Unimportant		*Moderately important*		*Very important*

c. *Analyzing data:* The next step is to analyze, evaluate, and interpret the data that have been collected. Data are really nothing until this phase of the research; this is the step that gives meaning to the data.

(1) *Data organization:* Once the data are collected, they need to be organized for further evaluation and interpretation. Some of the data organization should have occurred during the development of the questionnaire, at least in the grouping of categories of questions on the questionnaire.

   (a) *Data classification:* Data need to be classified into appropriate groups. These groups should be meaningful so that results of the data analysis will have meaning.

   (b) *Data editing:* Data must be examined carefully to see whether there are missing or inaccurate data. It is likely that a respondent did not follow the directions carefully enough in completing the questionnaire. If there are missing data, you can use specific procedures in handling the response, depending on the computer program you are using to assist in the analysis of the data. There may be cases where you will want to eliminate the respondents' answers to the entire questionnaire if there is too much inconsistency in responding.

   (c) *Data coding:* If data are to be entered and analyzed by a computer program, the data coding procedure is very important. Coding means that a number is assigned to each response classification.

   (d) *Data tabulation:* The number of responses in each classification for each statement or question will need to be counted. Frequency distributions are created from the data. The counting can be done manually or by the computer.

   (e) *Statistical analysis:* Statistics can be generated that will result in percentages, measures of central tendency, and measures of dispersion.

   • *Percentages:* Ratios that show relationship between one or more response classifications; a base of 100.

   • *Measures of central tendency:* Statistics that measure the center value of a distribution of data.

   The *mean* is the arithmetic average of a group of responses obtained by computing the sum of all the responses and dividing by the number of responses.

The *median* is the midpoint in a distribution of responses.

The *mode* is the response that occurs the most frequently in a distribution of responses.

- *Measures of dispersion:* Values that show the variation of the data in a distribution.

The *range* is the difference between the value of the highest response and the value of the lowest response in a distribution.

The *standard deviation* is a measure of the degree of scattering of a frequency distribution about its arithmetic mean.

(2) *Evaluation and interpretation of data:* The summary statistics that have been computed can be used to make specific inferences from the data about the problem that was defined earlier. Any inferences are made about the population (even though you might have only used a sample) and are based on the accuracy, significance, and relationships shown in the same data. During this stage, meaning is derived from the data, and you must use logical reasoning in order to develop any conclusions based on the data. The result of the evaluation and interpretation of the data is the development of a set of *findings* (or facts) derived from the study.

d. *Reporting findings and drawing conclusions:* The findings are usually reported immediately following the presentation of the data supporting the findings. In other words, in the data analysis section of the report, the narrative sequence would include the presentation of the data within the paragraphs, followed by the statistical table representing the supportive evidence. Presentation of the complete set of findings and conclusions derived from these findings are presented in a summary chapter or section of the report.

(1) *Findings:* The bulk of a report discusses data in order to derive findings. A summary of the findings is presented immediately following the presentation of the data. This summary provides a capstone to the data analysis section of the report. The findings (or key findings) may also be summarized in the final chapter (or section) of the report if there is a section for such a summary.

(2) *Conclusions:* An informational report merely presents facts to the reader that may be useful in further study or review. However, if your research involves the collection of data that were subsequently analyzed, conclusions should be drawn that are based on the data analysis. The conclusions *must* be based only on the data that were analyzed and nothing else because there would be no proof present for any other inferences. If you find significant differences between two sets of data, reporting the significance is a finding. A conclusion can be drawn from the finding that can present an explanation of what this finding means to the entire population.

(3) *Recommendations:* The conclusions drawn as a result of the findings form the basis for any recommendations that are indicated. There might be recommendations for further research and study, new materials to be developed, or training programs to be initiated. Sometimes, there are implications for organizations that should be considered as well, even though the exact consequences might not be known. There may be implications for organizations in

terms of additional personnel needed, changes in business systems utilized, or developmental plans that should be considered.

e. *Organizing the report:* Developing the final written report will depend most on how well the plan for the report is organized. The sequence of the report must be decided, whether the report will be written inductively or deductively. In addition, the outline for each of the sections of the report needs to be determined.

(1) *Inductive organization:* Inductive writing leads from the specific to the general. This is the most prominent plan used for formal reports. The report begins with an introduction, statement of the problem, and definition of terms, eventually leading to the findings, conclusions, and any recommendations that are included.

(2) *Deductive organization:* Deductive writing begins with a presentation of general information, followed by the more specific information involved in the research. The conclusions and recommendations are presented first, then the statement of the problem, definition of terms, and identification of procedures used. The data analysis and findings follow, and a summary is included as the final section of the report.

(3) *Other types of organization:* Sometimes, a report will be presented chronologically because of the importance of the time frame for the report. Such a report might be divided into phases or sections based on certain periods of time. Reports might also be presented that highlight activities or functions affecting different aspects of the company (e.g., sales according to geographic regions).

The report should be planned in such a way that an outline of the major headings that will be used throughout the report can be developed. This outline serves as a guideline for the writer and eventually will become the table of contents (with the addition of subheadings inserted as the writing goes along). The writer needs to be consistent in outlining, using appropriate outline symbols and sequences (see Chapter 19 for information on how an outline should be developed).

f. *Writing the report:* The final step in the research process is the writing of the report itself. Whether formal or informal style is used to write the report depends on the situation and the needs of people for whom the report is being prepared. A formal, impersonal style may be used for longer reports written primarily for people outside your organization or on the executive level. A more impersonal, less formal style may be used when memorandum reports or letter reports are prepared. In this section, we have emphasized the long, formal report. A formal report may be subdivided into three primary sections: preliminary parts, body of the report, and supplementary parts. The features of each of these three divisions are defined briefly here:

(1) *Preliminary parts:* These parts are included prior to the main body of the report and help to provide the kind of organization needed in the report.

(a) *Letter or memorandum of transmittal:* Sometimes, a letter or memorandum must accompany a report as a brief introduction to the report. The transmittal correspondence begins with a general introduction to the report and may present a brief summary of findings and conclusions. Its purpose is to motivate the reader to read the enclosed report.

(b) *Title page:* The information to be included on the title page includes the title of the report; the name, title, and department or division of the writer; the company name and address, if the report is external; and the date.

(c) *Authorization form:* The person authorizing the research must sign an authorization form prior to the start of the research. This form immediately follows the title page.

(d) *Table of contents:* Every report should have a table of contents that indicates the major subdivisions of the report along with page references.

(e) *Table of illustrations:* All figures and illustrations included in the body of the report should be itemized in a table of illustrations along with the specific page references.

(f) *Abstract:* Sometimes, an abstract is requested to precede the report itself. This abstract is usually 300 to 500 words in length and provides a brief summary of the conduct of the study and the reporting of the data, findings, and conclusions of the study.

(2) *Body of the report:* The body of the report is usually subdivided into the introduction, data analysis and findings, and summary of conclusions and recommendations.

(a) *Introduction:* The main purpose of the introductory section is to present the reader with the problem of the study, research questions, hypotheses, limitations of the problem, rationale for the study or report (with supporting information), definitions of terms used, and procedures used in the study.

(b) *Data analysis and findings:* In this section the complete data analysis must be presented. Each finding must be explained in terms of the statistical analysis that was conducted. These statistical analyses are normally presented in tables accompanied by appropriate narrative.

(c) *Conclusions and recommendations:* The summary provides an overview of the study and a look at the complete set of findings or selected findings if appropriate. In addition, conclusions derived from the findings are included in this section, as are recommendations that can be drawn directly from the conclusions.

(3) *Supplementary parts:* The last section of the report includes the bibliography or works cited, glossary, appendix (or appendices), and index.

(a) *Bibliography:* An alphabetical list of all information sources used for the report, including sources for citations included in the report

(b) *Works cited:* An alphabetical list of all references that were directly cited within the body of the report

(c) *Glossary:* An alphabetical list of terms defined for the reader

(d) *Appendix (or appendices):* Supplementary research material, such as sample questionnaire, sample letters written to respondents, and detailed data analysis not included in the report

(e) *Index:* A list of names and subjects, with page references to find quickly specific information contained in the report

The business report is a very important business document and must be prepared with care so that it will be functional in assisting in the decision-making process. (For more information on business report formats, see Chapter 19.)

F. Cross-Cultural Communication

Today, most businesses are involved in international meetings, trade, or some means of communication. With the proliferation of communications technologies, businesses around the world find themselves in cross-cultural experiences whether over the telephone, in conferences, or through the use of the Internet and electronic mail. No matter how one communicates (voice only, face-to-face, or in writing), the added dimension of cultural differences must be taken into consideration.

Since it is nearly impossible to highlight all the cultural differences one may encounter, and since differences also encompass gender, age, position, and any other human conditions one may live under, strategies oriented toward addressing differences provide a broader basis for better business communication. Five strategies for dealing with differences include awareness, sensitivity, openness, respect, and collaboration.

1. *Awareness:* Cultural differences are embedded in language. All other human differences are embedded in experiences. Dealing with diversity is enhanced as one becomes aware of linguistic and experiential differences. Attempt to understand the backgrounds of the people you are communicating with. Using the "you" attitude in communication demonstrates awareness of the importance of the other person.

2. *Sensitivity:* To enhance understanding, one needs to listen empathically and use feedback to reinforce accurate understanding. In other words, you need to be sensitive to other people—who they are and where they are coming from (see Chapter 20).

3. *Openness:* No matter how different one is, it is the ideas and knowledge that he or she brings to the communication process that is important. By being open to different ideas, new opportunities become possible.

4. *Respect:* As we treat those who are like us with respect and understanding, we must extend that same respect to those who are different. Understanding comes from our openness and sensitivity to others.

5. *Collaboration:* As we respect and understand one another, a collaborative working relationship develops. Through collaboration, the communication process produces information and knowledge, resulting in good decisions for all.

Review Questions

Directions: Select the best answer from the four alternatives. Write your answer in the blank to the left of the number.

_____ 1. Which statement best reflects a positive message?

    a. I apologize for not contacting you sooner.
    b. I have mailed the material by air express.
    c. If further information is needed, do not hesitate to fax your request.
    d. Please contact us if you decide to pursue this alternative.

_____ 2. Which one of the following techniques would demonstrate that concrete language is being used?

    a. Avoid short, simple words.
    b. Industry-specific language should dominate the writing.
    c. Specific words with precise meanings should dominate the writing.
    d. Use acronyms to eliminate unnecessary wording.

_____ 3. Which one of the following uses unbiased language in expressing an idea?

    a. As a result of the new policy, every secretary must use her comp time before July 1.
    b. C. R. Adams, our top salesman, reported that sales for May had increased 7 percent.
    c. Everyone in the audience gave the speaker a standing ovation.
    d. The young male attorney prepared a brief that was highly regarded by his peers.

_____ 4. "After completing the chart, it is important to save the graph so it can be imported into the WordPerfect® document." This sentence is a

    a. simple sentence.
    b. compound sentence.
    c. complex sentence.
    d. compound-complex sentence.

_____ 5. To be effective, sentences in business writing should

    a. average about 25 words.
    b. be joined to another when the thought continues and clarity is enhanced.
    c. be simple sentences.
    d. have a main clause and a dependent clause.

_____ 6. Which group of words is parallel?

    a. administrative assistant / vice president / president
    b. graduate / junior
    c. Mr. Smythe / Betty
    d. plan / organize / staff / directing / controlling

_____   **7.** Placing key information at the beginning of a sentence so the reader will be sure to see it is an example of

     a. balance.
     b. clarity.
     c. emphasis.
     d. variety.

_____   **8.** A reference book for identifying synonyms is a/an

     a. dictionary
     b. office reference manual.
     c. thesaurus.
     d. word-division manual.

_____   **9.** Understanding a situation from the reader's point of view shows

     a. courtesy toward the reader.
     b. empathy toward the reader.
     c. respect toward the reader.
     d. sincerity toward the reader.

_____   **10.** As a type of formal written communication, the business letter is used most often for

     a. external communication.
     b. horizontal communication.
     c. internal communication.
     d. vertical communication.

_____   **11.** Which one of the following examples would be considered a favorable letter?

     a. A letter of explanation with an anticipated ship date
     b. A letter marketing a new product
     c. A request for information
     d. A response to an inquiry for information

_____   **12.** When the direct writing approach is used for a business letter, the first paragraph

     a. is a buffer paragraph that sets the stage for what follows.
     b. is written to get the reader's attention.
     c. begins with a general statement of the main point of the message.
     d. begins with the facts so that the reader immediately knows the reasons for the answer.

_____   **13.** The most commonly written business letter is a

     a. letter that says "no" or includes a refusal.
     b. neutral or routine letter.
     c. persuasive letter.
     d. response to an inquiry for information.

14. Chandler noted the following points for a letter:

- Need pricing sheet for office copiers.
- Importance of quality copying with collating feature (approximately 800 copies daily).
- Model suggestions; need by February 15.

The letter will be a
a. combination letter.
b. persuasive letter.
c. positive letter.
d. routine or neutral letter.

15. When a negative letter needs to be written,

a. company policy should be used as rationale for the refusal.
b. reasons for the refusal should be clearly presented in the first paragraph followed by a goodwill paragraph.
c. the first paragraph should set the stage so that the rationale for the refusal (presented in the second paragraph) is read.
d. the refusal should be clearly stated in the first paragraph and immediately followed by rationale.

16. Mathew noted the following points for a letter:

- Importance of topic
- Constraints in participating
- Identify another possible participant

The letter will be a
a. negative letter.
b. persuasive letter.
c. positive letter.
d. routine or negative letter.

17. Asteck's marketing consultants advised them to contact prospective customers about a new product. Asteck would send a

a. combination letter.
b. persuasive letter.
c. positive letter.
d. routine letter.

18. Marcus is employed for a not-for-profit service organization and has been asked to write a letter for contributions. The opening paragraph needs to

a. appeal to the reader's interests and social responsibilities.
b. create goodwill with a general statement about the main point of the message.
c. emphasize the reasons why the reader should contribute.
d. start with a positive, forward-looking request for action on the part of the reader.

19. The primary purpose of a form letter is to

   a. compose a letter of precomposed paragraphs and eliminate variable data.
   b. personalize a letter consisting of precomposed paragraphs by including the addressee's name and address.
   c. send letters with some precomposed standard data to more than one person or organization.
   d. take advantage of word processing capabilities.

20. Text that stays the same on every form letter is called

   a. constant information.
   b. merged information.
   c. personal information.
   d. variable information.

21. In word processing, a text-merge function requires the preparation of

   a. a primary document and a form letter.
   b. a primary document and a secondary document.
   c. a secondary document and a database.
   d. a secondary document and a variable document.

22. A text-merge database includes the

   a. constant data.
   b. form letter.
   c. primary document.
   d. variable data.

23. A common form of communicating detailed financial information within the firm is the

   a. business letter.
   b. business report.
   c. e-mail.
   d. memorandum.

24. Kim, the vice president of operations, needs to communicate a new company directive with complete instructions for completing a project. Which form of communication is best?

   a. Combination letter
   b. E-mail
   c. Favorable memorandum
   d. Formal report

_____

25. Which type of communication is best for a performance evaluation that stipulates skill improvement?

    a. E-mail
    b. Negative letter
    c. Unfavorable memorandum
    d. Informal/short report

_____

26. Correspondence that is unfavorable and carries a *no* response should be written using the

    a. A-I-D-A approach.
    b. deductive approach.
    c. direct approach.
    d. indirect approach.

_____

27. A three-page informal report recommending a new office system needs to be communicated to several administrators within the organization. This specific type of informal report is called a

    a. feasibility study.
    b. progress report.
    c. proposal.
    d. technical report.

_____

28. Electronic mail is best used for

    a. external communication to a keynote speaker confirming the details of the program.
    b. external and internal communication regarding the new automated teller bank location.
    c. internal communication regarding several new company procedures.
    d. internal and external communication that is focused, short, and to the point.

_____

29. Individuals not involved in the e-mail dialogue but who need to be informed of the communication should

    a. be included in the To address section of the e-mail message along with the e-mail recipients.
    b. be listed in the Copy section of the e-mail message separate from the e-mail recipients.
    c. receive a hard copy of the e-mail message through regular mail services.
    d. be personally informed of the dialogue (face-to-face) in case they have questions.

30. A report summarizing a staff services center work-measurement study was completed by the center manager. The report was distributed to the administrative vice president. This is considered a/an

    a. external report.
    b. nontechnical report.
    c. periodic report.
    d. vertical report.

31. In planning a report that will require both primary and secondary research, the first thing that needs to be done is to

    a. conduct primary research in order to become familiar with the problem.
    b. define the problem that needs to be solved.
    c. develop a questionnaire to gather factual data.
    d. identify the variables of the study.

32. Harris was asked to study the behavior of secretaries on the job and recommend to the office manager how individual assignments could be changed. Which research method would be the *best* to use?

    a. Experimental research
    b. Observational research
    c. Secondary research
    d. Survey research

33. In gathering in-depth data for a report, the best data collection method would be

    a. observation.
    b. personal interview.
    c. questionnaire.
    d. telephone interview.

34. An alphabetical list of all references directly cited within the body of the report is called a/an

    a. appendix.
    b. glossary.
    c. index.
    d. works cited.

35. In dealing with diverse populations, which one of the following strategies enhances our understanding by listening empathically and using feedback to reinforce accurate understanding?

    a. Awareness
    b. Collaboration
    c. Respect
    d. Sensitivity

Solutions

Answer	*Refer to:*
1. (d)	[A-1-a]
2. (c)	[A-1-d]
3. (c)	[A-1-g(1)(b)]
4. (c)	[A-2-a(1)(d)]
5. (b)	[A-2-a(3)]
6. (a)	[A-2-c(1)(c)]
7. (c)	[A-2-c(2)]
8. (c)	[A-2-c(5)(a)]
9. (b)	[A-2-d(2)]
10. (a)	[B]
11. (d)	[B-1-a(3)]
12. (c)	[B-1-b(1)]
13. (b)	[B-2]
14. (c)	[B-2]
15. (c)	[B-3]
16. (a)	[B-3]
17. (b)	[B-5-a(3)]
18. (a)	[B-5-b(1)]
19. (c)	[B-6]
20. (a)	[B-6-b]
21. (b)	[B-6-b(2)]
22. (d)	[B-6-b(2)]

23. (d)   [D-1-a]

24. (c)   [C-1-a(1)(d)]

25. (c)   [C-1-b(1)(d)]

26. (d)   [C-1-b(2)]

27. (c)   [C-2-a(1)]

28. (d)   [D-1-a]

29. (b)   [D-2-c]

30. (d)   [E-1-c]

31. (b)   [E-2-a]

32. (b)   [E-2-b(2)(b)]

33. (b)   [E-2-b(3)(c)]

34. (d)   [E-2-f(3)(b)]

35. (d)   [F-2]

CHAPTER 17
Editing Written Communications

OVERVIEW

One important responsibility for most administrative professionals is providing the final approval to a written document prior to sending it to the receiver. This talent requires English skills: grammatical construction, punctuation, spelling, format knowledge, and an ability to produce a document with visual appeal. The evaluation of these characteristics requires proofreading and editing skills.

Tying these skills together results in a document that has a clear, concise, and courteous tone. The purpose of this finishing touch is to produce a document that will appeal to the receiver. Possessing the ability to communicate with a "smile" in as few words as possible and still be understood is an asset for both the secretary and the executive.

KEY TERMS

Copyediting	Proofreading	Soft copy
Hard copy	Proofreading marks	

A. Proofreading

Proofreading is the process of checking final copy for spelling, punctuation, and formatting. The procedure for proofreading soft copy (text stored on disk) depends on the proofreader's responsibility and authority. If the proofreader is to flag only necessary corrections, then the proofreader will use proofreading marks within the hard copy document using a colored pen or use word processing codes to mark changes or make editorial comments.

If the proofreader has the authority and responsibility of making the changes, then the proofreader can read while making corrections with the soft copy. The procedure used will be an agreement between the secretary and the executive. Once the necessary corrections are made in the soft copy, the document is saved on disk. This eliminates the need for proofreading marks.

When the final copy is prepared on a typewriter, proofreading marks are made with light pencil markings within the margins of the document. Any error can then be corrected and the light pencil marks erased without the entire page being retyped.

1. *Proofreading Methods:* Whether proofreading is done alone or with someone else, the material must be proofread both for typographical errors and for content.

a. *Proofreading for typographical errors:* Proofreading for typographical errors should be done with a spell check when using word processing software or by reading backward with hard-copy material. Reading backward allows the proof-reader to concentrate on each word separately and to check spelling. Neither method can be used for content. For example, if the word *to* were typed as *so,* the spelling error would go undetected.

b. *Proofreading for content:* All material should be read slowly, concentrating on the grammatical accuracy of the message. Many proofreaders find that reading aloud helps them to concentrate on the content of the message. Grammar checks are included with most word processing software; this is a good place to start for checking grammatical structure. The secretary needs to be aware of corporate writing expectations or cross-cultural writing that may not be incorporated in the word processing grammar tool.

c. *Proofreading by other personnel:* Because proofreading is so important, many firms have proofreading departments. Before a document is released, it is sent to the proofreading department, where it is read by someone other than the originator, copy editor, or typist. In many cases, the proofreading is done by two people, one reading the material aloud from the writer's copy and another checking the final document. This technique can also be adopted by secretaries working together within a firm. The original document should be proofread by someone who was not involved in preparing the document. The one who reads from the writer's copy could be someone who was involved in preparing the document.

2. *Proofreading Techniques:* Whether proofreading is done alone or others are assigned to do the proofreading, the following techniques should be used.

a. *Reading the copy:* When proofreading, read the copy slowly and concentrate on the material.

b. *Aligning copy:* Use a ruler to follow the line of print on hard copy. This is particularly helpful with statistical copy. The ruler is also helpful in making sure that a line of text is not skipped in reading. Scrolling one line at a time when proofreading soft copy ensures that a line is not skipped.

c. *Proofreading vertically:* If the material is similar to a table and was keyed horizontally, proofread the copy vertically. This is particularly helpful when proofreading alone.

d. *Counting entries:* If there are lines of entries that can be counted, count the number of entries in the original and compare that with the number of entries typed in the final document.

e. *Delaying final proofreading:* If time permits, do not do the final proofreading immediately after keying the material. If you wait for an hour or more, errors are more likely to be found. The longer the wait, the better—the proofreader will be more objective in making judgments about errors.

3. *Proofreading Symbols:* When proofreading hard-copy text, the proofreading symbols illustrated in Figure 17–1 should be used. If the copy has not been saved as soft copy, the marks on a final document should be made lightly with pencil within the margins of the document to possibly avoid the need to retype the entire page.

Meaning	Symbol	Example	Final edited copy
Transpose	∿	change the letters around	change the letters around
Delete	ℓ	to take ~~something~~ out	to take out
Close up	⌒	to bring to gether	to bring together
Insert	∧	the insert symbol a caret	the insert symbol is a caret
Space	#	insert a space	insert a space
Paragraph	¶	Using the symbol means to begin a new paragraph. ¶A new thought means a new paragraph.	Using the symbol means to begin a new paragraph.

A new thought means a new paragraph. |
Move left	⊏	Align the material to the left.	Align the material to the left.
Move right	⊐	Align the material to the right.	Align the material to the right.
Spelling or spell out	ⓈⓅ or ⌣	When a word is spelled incorrectly, write sp in a circle above the misspelled word. When an (abbrev) is to be spelled out, circle the word.	When a word is spelled incorrectly, write sp in a circle above the misspelled word. When an abbreviation is to be spelled out, circle the word.
Capital letters	≡ or CAPS	underline all letters that are to be capital letters or write the letters CAPS in the margin.	Underline ALL letters that are to be capital letters OR write the letters CAPS in the margin.
Lower case	/ or ℓc	Draw a line through letters that should be Lower Case Letters OR write the letters lc in the margin.	Draw a line through letters that should be lower case letters OR write the letters lc in the margin.
Let stand	- - - or Stet	Keep it the ~~original~~ way. Writing stet in the margin also means "let it stand."	Keep it the original way. Writing stet in the margin also means " let it stand."
Insertion of punctuation	⌃ ⌄ ⌄⌄	When a comma needs to be inserted use the caret symbol but don't use it for an apostrophe or quotation marks. Use the inverse caret ⊙	When a comma needs to be inserted, use the caret symbol but don't use it for an apostrophe or quotation marks. Use the inverse caret.

Figure 17–1
Proofreading and Copyediting Symbols

4. *Proofreading Software:* Most word processing software includes a spell-check feature. The purpose of the spelling feature is to check the document for *spelling* errors.

    a. *Activating the spell-check feature:* When the spell check is activated, the software scans the soft-copy document for words it does not recognize—words that are *not* in the spell-check dictionary.

        (1) The unrecognized word is highlighted on the screen so that the proofreader can verify the spelling of the word.

        (2) If the word is correct, the proofreader activates the continue command.

        (3) If the word is incorrect, the proofreader can correct the word immediately before continuing the spell-check function. A spell check also gives the proofreader possible spellings to choose from. Variations on spell-check features are explained in the word processing operations manual.

    b. *Adding unrecognized words to dictionary:* Some spell-check programs allow the proofreader the option of adding a new word to the spell-check dictionary before continuing.

    c. *Highlighting words appearing twice:* Some spell-check programs highlight words that appear twice (e.g., the last word in a sentence and the first word in the next sentence). This helps the proofreader to check to see whether the sentence structure is correct.

    d. *Checking grammar:* Many spell-check tools now include grammar checks. If the sentence structure is considered grammatically incorrect, the grammar tool highlights that portion of the sentence in question. Also, grammar tools may correct improper word usage.

    EXAMPLE:

    As Madison typed the following sentence

        Their should be a meeting on . . .

    the grammar tool in the word processing software automatically changed their to there (see Section B-9).

B. Editing for Technical Correctness

Command of the English language develops in two ways. First, it develops from everyday usage—speaking, reading, and writing the language. Second, it develops through English reviews that reinforce and expand on rules learned in primary and secondary education. Like any skill, English needs to be reviewed and practiced to maintain accuracy and proficiency.

Command of the English language entails using correct grammar, punctuation, capitalization, spelling, and numbering. The language is further enhanced by appropriate formatting and consistent language style.

1. *Grammar and Word Usage:* The English language is easy as well as difficult to study. It is easy to study because the language has been used since early childhood and developed over the years. It is difficult because many adults feel that they already know and understand the language and are not interested in restudying what they already know. However, the English language is varied and changing. Most adults use what would be classified as informal English—language characterized by short sentences, "chatty" construction, and use of local jargon. Many call this *conversational* English.

In business writing, many of the documents are expected to have a "conversational" tone and yet be formal. Formal English is characterized by adherence to language rules and specialized vocabulary. The purpose of the language guide that follows is to review the structure of the English language, the rules that govern the English language, and the format and language style that packages the business document.

a. *Elements of a sentence:* For a sentence to be complete, it must contain a subject and a verb (predicate). Most sentences also contain an object or a complement. The four components of a sentence are subject, verb, object, and complement.

Secondary sentence elements encompass the use of modifiers, phrases, and clauses.

(1) *Subject:* Each sentence requires one or more subjects. The subject of a sentence is a noun or noun equivalent that is the topic of the sentence. A simple subject consists of a single word, such as *secretary.* A complete subject consists of the simple subject as well as any other words that modify that subject, such as *knowledgeable secretary.*

EXAMPLES:

A knowledgeable <u>secretary</u> aspires to become a CPS. (noun)

<u>He</u> aspires to become a CPS. (noun equivalent—pronoun)

<u>What you study</u> is important to passing the CPS exam. (noun equivalent—noun clause)

<u>Studying</u> is important to passing the CPS exam. (noun equivalent—gerund)

<u>To study</u> requires self-discipline. (noun equivalent—infinitive)

(2) *Verb:* The verb of a sentence tells what the subject has done, is doing, or will be doing, or the verb can express a condition about the subject. When the verb expresses a condition, it is a linking verb; otherwise, it is an action verb.

The verb must agree with the subject. If the subject is singular, the verb must be singular. If the subject is plural, the verb must be plural. Agreement between subject and verb is important. This is where writers sometimes have problems. Questions about agreement usually arise when verbs have compound subjects or when the subject is separated from the verb by many other words.

Typically, the verb follows the subject.

EXAMPLES:

I always <u>ask</u> questions to ensure complete understanding.
(present tense, singular, action)

We <u>ask</u> questions of each other while studying.
(present tense, plural, action)

I <u>asked</u> for a raise.
(past tense, singular, action)

We <u>asked</u> for a new photocopier.
(past tense, plural, action)

I will ask for a computer for this office.
I am going to ask for a computer.
(future tense, singular, action)

We will ask for help during the tax season.
We are going to ask for help during the tax season.
(future tense, plural, action)

I am happy with the computer.
(present tense, singular, linking verb)

We are happy with the new computer system.
(present tense, plural, linking verb)

I was happy when the computer arrived.
(past tense, singular, linking verb)

We were happy when the computer arrived.
(past tense, plural, linking verb)

I will be happy when the computer arrives.
(future tense, singular, linking verb)

We will be happy when the computers arrive.
(future tense, plural, linking verb)

(3) *Object:* Action verbs are usually followed by a *direct object.* The direct object of the verb completes the sentence by answering the question *what* or *whom* after the verb. The direct object is either a noun or a noun equivalent.

Verbs such as *buying, giving, asking, telling,* and the like are followed by an *indirect object.* The indirect object names the receiver of the direct object and precedes the direct object and answers the questions "to whom," "to what," "for whom," or "for what."

EXAMPLES OF A DIRECT OBJECT:

Secretaries who are rushed usually make mistakes.
Make "what"? mistakes (noun)

Morrison likes him for a manager.
Likes "whom"? him (noun equivalent—pronoun)

Clare knows what skills are required.
Knows "what"? what skills are required (noun equivalent—noun clause)

Radkowski enjoys hunting every fall.
Enjoys "what"? hunting (noun equivalent—gerund)

The committee voted to adjourn.
Voted "what"? to adjourn (noun equivalent—infinitive)

EXAMPLES OF AN INDIRECT OBJECT:

Many employees gave United Way a fair-share contribution.
Gave "what"? contribution
  "to whom"? United Way

Dr. Jones should give the <u>tree</u> a pruning.
Should give "what"? pruning
   "to what"? tree

Douglas bought <u>Mother</u> 50 stock certificates yesterday.
Bought "what"? certificates
   "for whom"? Mother

(4) *Complement:* When the verb expresses a condition about the subject (linking verb), it usually is *followed* by a complement. A complement is a noun that refers to the subject or an adjective that describes the subject. Because the linking verb expresses a condition rather than action, *a complement is related to the subject* by that linking verb.

A noun or noun equivalent is called a *predicate noun;* an adjective is called a *predicate adjective.*

The most common linking verbs are the various forms of *be: is, am, are, was, were, has been, might be.*

EXAMPLES:

Johanson is a dynamic <u>speaker.</u>
Is "what"? speaker (predicate noun)

My manager might be <u>unhappy</u> with the committee's decision.
Might be "what"? unhappy (predicate adjective)

b. *Secondary elements of a sentence:* Most sentences have modifiers, clauses, or phrases. These are considered secondary elements of a sentence.

(1) *Modifiers:* Single words used as modifiers usually relate to the element of the sentence they modify. The most common modifiers are adjectives and adverbs. Adjectives relate to nouns, whereas adverbs can relate to the sentence as a whole or modify a particular word (verb, adjective, or adverb).

Adjectives and adverbs assist the writer in being more specific. These modifiers usually add descriptive details or specific definition to key words. The adjective or adverb is usually near the word it modifies, and most adverbs are made by adding *ly* to an adjective.

EXAMPLES:

Our <u>home</u> office is located in Memphis.
Subject: office
Adjective: home (describes which office)

Jennings speaks <u>quite clearly</u> over the telephone.
Verb: speaks
Adverb: clearly (describes how Jennings speaks)
Adverb: quite (describes how clearly)

Mack's <u>extremely</u> small frame makes it difficult to find a comfortable working desk.
Noun: frame
Adjective: small (describes frame)
Adverb: extremely (describes small)

(2) *Clauses:* Clauses can be either independent or dependent. An independent clause contains a subject and verb (predicate) and can stand by itself as a sentence. Usually, a comma separates two independent clauses when the sentences are connected with a conjunction (*and, but, or*) or a conjunctive adverb (*however, consequently, then*). If there is no conjunction or conjunctive adverb between two independent clauses, then the sentences are separated by a semicolon.

A dependent clause also contains a subject and verb (predicate); however, it is part of the sentence and cannot stand by itself as a complete sentence. It is connected to the main sentence by a connecting word that shows its subordinate relationship: either a conjunction (*since, when, because, if, after*) or a relative pronoun (*who, which, that*). When a dependent clause begins a sentence, a comma follows. When a dependent clause appears within a sentence, commas are included before and after the clause.

EXAMPLES:

The new computer arrived this morning, and *Micro-Systems will be out tomorrow to review the operations*.
(two independent clauses connected by the conjunction and)

Muhler is at the board meeting; she should be back at 4 P.M.
(two independent clauses, no conjunction)

If you are serious about taking the CPS exam, *you should register for the review course that begins next month.*
(dependent clause beginning the sentence)

Let me know when the coffee is ready.
(dependent clause ending the sentence)

Mrs. Johnson, who is our new director, *will meet with the board of directors tomorrow.*
(dependent clause within the sentence)

(3) *Phrases:* A phrase is a group of related words connected to a sentence by a preposition or a verb. Such a phrase cannot stand by itself because it has no subject or verb (predicate). Such phrases are modifiers and may or may not require punctuation marks.

A prepositional phrase functions like an adjective or adverb, depending on what it modifies. The phrase begins with a preposition (*from, at, by, of*) and is followed by a noun or noun equivalent.

A verbal phrase does not function as a verb. A participle phrase functions as an adjective; a gerund phrase functions as a noun; and an infinitive phrase functions as either a noun, an adjective, or an adverb. The phrase consists of the verbal element plus the object or complement and modifiers of the phrase.

EXAMPLES:

The cabinet by his desk contains our department manuals.
(prepositional phrase—adjective)

Mr. Klein spoke in a loud voice.
(prepositional phrase—adverb)

Ashley, <u>having passed the CPS exam on the first try</u>, feels very good about herself.
(verbal phrase—participle phrase)

<u>Passing the CPS exam</u> opened new directions for Mason.
(verbal phrase—gerund phrase as the subject)

Dot gave me plenty of work <u>to do</u> before she left.
(verbal phrase—infinitive phrase as an adjective modifying the noun <u>work</u>)

The students in the CPS course want <u>to review</u> their grammar.
(verbal phrase—infinitive phrase as an adverb modifying the verb <u>want</u>)

2. *Punctuation:* The use of correct punctuation is extremely important for the secretary. What is said or written can easily be changed by the misuse of a punctuation mark. This section of the language guide provides a quick summary of the ways in which major forms of punctuation are used correctly in transcripts.

   a. *Apostrophe:* The apostrophe is used to show possession and to form plurals. Its use as a symbol and in contractions is very important in business writing.

   (1) *To show possession:* The apostrophe may be used to show possession.

      (a) *Singular nouns:* Add the apostrophe and an *s* to all singular nouns (unless the singular noun ends in *s*). For singular nouns that end in *s*, only the apostrophe is necessary. However, it is also correct to add an apostrophe and an *s*, particularly if the extra syllable is pronounced.

      EXAMPLES:

      author's manuscript
      (singular noun)

      boss' standards*
      (singular noun ending in <u>s</u>)
      (boss's is also correct)

      James' invention*
      (one-syllable proper name ending in <u>s</u>)
      (James's is also correct)

      Marlys' family*
      (two-syllable proper name ending in <u>s</u>)
      (Marlys's is also correct)

      *Once you decide how you prefer to show possession, be consistent throughout the document.

      (b) *Plural nouns:* Add the apostrophe and an *s* to plural nouns that do not end in an *s*. For plural nouns that end in an *s*, add only the apostrophe.

      EXAMPLES:

      women's organization
      (plural noun not ending in <u>s</u>)

      accountants' pins
      (plural noun ending in <u>s</u>)

   (2) *For plurals:* For the sake of clarity with small letters, the plural is formed by adding *'s.* An apostrophe is generally used to form the plurals of capital let-

ters and numbers; however, just the capital letter and an *s* is sufficient. The only capital letters which should always have an apostrophe before the *s* are *A, I,* and *U,* primarily for clarity. Again, once you choose a style, be consistent throughout the document.

EXAMPLES:

a's	A's	Bs or B's	1s or 1's
b's	I's	Cs or C's	2s or 2's
c's	U's	Ds or D's	3s or 3's

(3) *With symbols:* The apostrophe is used as the symbol for *feet* on business forms and in tables. As part of a sentence within a paragraph of a letter or a report, the word *feet* is spelled out in full.

EXAMPLE:

2′ × 4′ (meaning 2 feet by 4 feet)

A sentence within a letter would read:
The board must be 2 feet by 4 feet.

(4) *Contractions:* The apostrophe is used to indicate the omission of a letter or letters.

EXAMPLES:

it's	(it is)
wouldn't	(would not)
can't	(cannot)

b. *Colon:* When the colon is used in typewritten material, it is followed by two spaces. The only exception is when the colon is used in indicating time (see Section B-2-b[2]).

(1) *After an introduction:* A colon is used after a statement that introduces a long direct quotation, enumerated items, or a series introduced with the expressions *these, as follows,* or *the following.*

EXAMPLES:

The motion was: "The regular meetings will be held on the second Wednesday of each month at 7 P.M. at the Winchester Library Conference Room."

My presentation is divided into three areas:

1. The CPS® Examination

2. Preparation for the Examination

3. Taking the Examination

(For enumeration format, see Sections B-2-i[5] and B-2-h[1].)

The 10 o'clock workshop sessions are as follows: word processing, communication, or integration of data processing and word processing.

(2) *Time:* The colon is used to separate the hours from the minutes when time is expressed in figures. There is no space after the colon. The time is always fol-

lowed by a correct form of *A.M.* or *P.M.* When the time is an even hour, only the hour is used. However, if both even hours and hours with minutes are used within the same sentence, all time is expressed with hours and minutes for consistency.

Variations for typing *A.M.* and *P.M.* are *a.m., A.M., am,* and *AM; p.m., P.M., pm,* and *PM.* For clarity, the more frequent use is with periods. Otherwise, *am* and *AM* could be mistaken for the word *am.* Be consistent with your format; type *A.M.* and *P.M.* notations in the same way (see Section B-7).

EXAMPLES:

The meeting begins at 2 p.m.

Since the meeting begins at 2:00 pm, meet me at 1:30 pm to review the agenda.

c. *Comma:* A comma is used after an introduction to a sentence, in a series, before the conjunction in a compound sentence, before a direct quote, in a parenthetical phrase, before and after an appositive, with a nonrestrictive clause, and when the word *and* is omitted.

   (1) *After an introduction to a sentence:* An introduction can be a word (*However, Therefore*), a phrase (*By hurrying, In case you didn't know*), or an adverbial clause (*As soon as the package arrives, When this meeting is called to order*). A comma is used to separate this introduction from the main sentence.

   EXAMPLES:

   Finally, the meeting began at 3 PM.
   (word)

   Because of the weather, it looks like the company picnic will have to be postponed.
   (phrase)

   As soon as the package arrives, alert the accounting department.
   (adverbial clause)

   (2) *Series:* When there are more than two items in a series of words or phrases, a comma is used to separate the items. If a conjunction (*and, or, nor*) precedes the last word in a series, a comma is not necessary before the conjunction. The comma itself represents the conjunction. However, the comma is often used before the conjunction for clarity. Sometimes, the items within the series contain conjunctions. Again, for clarity, a comma should precede the conjunction before the last item in the series. If *et cetera* (*etc.*) is part of the series, use a comma before and after *et cetera.* If the series contains a series, semicolons are used to separate the main series while commas are used for the inner series (see Section B-2-l[2]).

   EXAMPLES:

   Matthews ordered the paper, folders and gummed labels.

   The shipment contained regular paper and legal paper, pencils and pens, and rulers.

   The order for spring slacks, skirts, blouses, etc., from the Marks Department Store was shipped yesterday.

The Harris shipment on Friday included two pink, green, and gold chairs; one green sofa; and one glass end table.

(3) *Compound sentences:* When two complete sentences are connected with a conjunction (*and, but, or*) or a conjunctive adverb (*also, however*), a comma precedes the conjunction or conjunctive adverb. Sometimes the conjunction is used because of a compound verb; then the comma is not used.

EXAMPLES:

Our secretary was out sick for one week, but we obtained an excellent re-placement from Temporaries, Inc.

You should reconsider your decision to cancel the order and instruct us to reinstate it.
(compound verb: <u>should reconsider</u> and <u>instruct</u>)

(4) *Direct quotes:* A comma is used to set off a direct quotation (the exact words of the speaker), and quotation marks ("") are placed around the exact words (see Section B-2-b[1] for the exception and example). Periods and commas go inside the quotation marks. (For rules pertaining to punctuation marks used with quotations, see the Note following Section B-2-k[3].)

EXAMPLES:

Mr. Jackson said, "Pay the bill immediately."

"Pay the bill immediately," were Mr. Jackson's exact words.

Mr. Jackson said, "Pay the bill immediately," in a very emphatic tone.

(5) *Parenthetical:* When a word, phrase, or clause is used that is not necessary to the grammatical completeness of the sentence, it is considered a *parenthetical expression*. A parenthetical expression within the sentence is set off by commas, but only one comma is needed if the expression comes at the end of the sentence.

EXAMPLES:

Klein, <u>however</u>, is not applying for the position.
(word)

Mr. Smith, <u>I am sure</u>, will be able to handle the matter.
(phrase)

I have prepared a cover letter, <u>a copy of which should be inserted in each booklet</u>.
(clause)

(6) *Apposition:* An appositive is a word, phrase, or clause that identifies or explains a noun, pronoun, or other term. An appositive is set off by commas unless it is at the end of the sentence; then, only one comma is necessary.

EXAMPLES:

The meeting will be on Wednesday, April 15, in the main conference room.
(<u>April 15</u> is the appositive. It is easy to recognize by saying, "Which Wednesday?"

Sally Francis, our IAAP president, will attend the International IAAP Conference.

(<u>Our IAAP president</u> is the appositive. You can identify the appositive by saying, "Which Sally Francis?"

(7) *Nonrestrictive clauses:* Nonrestrictive clauses begin with *which, who,* or *whose.* These clauses may be omitted without changing the meaning of the sentence. A clause beginning with *that* usually is restrictive (essential to the sentence). Only nonrestrictive clauses are set off with commas.

EXAMPLES:

The formula, <u>which was tested at the Medical Laboratories Institute</u>, has really been an advancement for the medical profession.

Emerson, <u>who can type 98 words per minute with 97 percent accuracy</u>, is being considered for the new position.

(8) *And omitted:* When two adjectives modify the same noun and the *and* is missing, a comma is used to replace the missing *and.* However, if the first adjective modifies the combination of the second adjective plus the noun, the comma is not used.

EXAMPLES:

The train is a quiet, smooth way to travel. (The words <u>quiet</u> and <u>smooth</u> modify <u>way.</u>)

This is just a short, friendly reminder that your payment is now due. (The words <u>short</u> and <u>friendly</u> modify <u>reminder.</u>)

The beautiful spring bouquet added a nice touch to the head banquet table. (The word <u>beautiful</u> modifies the combination <u>spring bouquet.</u>)

d. *Dash:* Typically, a dash is used for greater emphasis. For the dash to have any impact, however, you must be selective in substituting the dash for other punctuation marks. The forcefulness of the dash is greatly diminished if overused.

EXAMPLES:

O'Miria—an excellent physician—has been honored by her colleagues.
(The dash is used here instead of parentheses or commas.)

Our favorite place to vacation — Alaska!
(The dash is used here instead of a colon.)

I like the new computer - the new ergonomic keyboard makes typing so much easier.
(The dash [a hyphen with one space before and after] is used here instead of a semicolon.)

Note: The dash is typed with two hyphens and no spaces (preferred style), with two hyphens together and one space before and after the hyphens, or with one hyphen and one space before and after the hyphen. Once a style is selected, use the same format throughout a document; consistency is important. Never type a dash as one hyphen with no space before and after the hyphen. A single hyphen with no spaces is used within a compound word (see Section B-2-g).

e. *Ellipsis:* Ellipsis marks are used to show the omission of words within a sentence. An ellipsis is typed with three periods, with a space before and after each period.

If the ellipsis comes at the end of the sentence, the end-of-sentence punctuation is typed as normal (next to the word); then leave a space before typing the ellipsis. If the end-of-sentence punctuation is never typed, only the ellipsis is used.

EXAMPLES

The president said, "With the rising cost of energy . . . we will keep our thermostat at 72 degrees year round. . . ." She was very emphatic with this statement.

The president said, "With the rising cost of energy . . . we will keep our thermostat at 72 degrees . . ."

f. *Exclamation point:* After a word, phrase, or sentence, an exclamation point is used for emphasis. The exclamation point is followed by two spaces.

EXAMPLES:

The exam is in two days!

Yes! I am impressed with that community project.

g. *Hyphen:* The hyphen is typically used for word division or as a part of a compound word.

    (1) *Compound adjective:* If two adjectives (descriptive words) precede a noun, a hyphen is used to make these two adjectives into a compound word.

        Note: Do not confuse this rule with the *and*-omitted rule (see Section B-2-c[8]).

        EXAMPLE:

        The first-class mail is delivered to all departments by 10 a.m.

    (2) *Replace "to" or "through":* In statistical writing, tables, or charts, the hyphen can be used to replace the words *to* or *through.*

        EXAMPLE:

        The report covers Tables 19-35.

    (3) *Prefixes:* When a prefix is added to a word, the word may be written as a single word or as a hyphenated word. Preferred usage calls for words with prefixes to be spelled as single words without hyphens whenever possible. Typically, if a prefix is a word (e.g., *self*), a word with that prefix will be hyphenated.

        EXAMPLES:

        preemployment
        (The prefix <u>pre</u> is not a word; therefore, <u>preemployment</u> is not hyphenated.)

        self-imposed
        (The prefix <u>self</u> is a word; therefore, <u>self-imposing</u> is hyphenated.)

    (4) *Word division:* The hyphen is used to indicate the division of a word at the end of a typed line. Correct hyphenation rules must be followed (see Sections B-8-a and B-8-b).

EXAMPLE:

When you are typing a lengthy manu-
script, correct hyphenation rules must be followed.

 (5) *Suspended hyphen:* In a series of hyphenated words having the same ending, the hyphen is retained with all the hyphenated words. One space follows each suspended hyphen.

 EXAMPLE:

 Either the blue- or black-colored chairs will match the decor of the new office.

 Note: A hyphen is typed with no spaces before or after it except as used in word division (see Section B-2-g[4]) or as a suspended hyphen (see Section B-2-g[5]).

h. *Parentheses:* Parentheses ( ) are used to enclose words or phrases that are needed for clarification but can be deemphasized.

 (1) *Enumerated items:* Enclose the number or letter in parentheses when the enumerations are continued on the same line.

 EXAMPLE:

 The CPS® Examination has three parts: (1) Finance and Business Law, (2) Office Systems and Administration, and (3) Management.

 (2) *Instead of comma or dash:* If you wish to deemphasize an expression that is not necessary to the meaning or completeness of a sentence, you may use parentheses instead of a comma or dash to set it off from the rest of the sentence.

 EXAMPLE:

 The office picnic (scheduled for August 15) will be held at Tinley Park.

 (3) *References:* When references to tables, pages, diagrams, or other similar references are made for further clarification, these references are placed in parentheses.

 EXAMPLE:

 The section on buying stocks (pages 35-42) is very helpful.

 (4) *Around a complete sentence:* If a complete sentence is placed in parentheses, the sentence begins with a capital letter and the ending punctuation mark would fall inside the parentheses.

 EXAMPLE:

 Dr. Carmichael's automated office presentation lasted over an hour. (However, the time was well spent!) After the presentation, there was a question-and-answer session (requested by the audience).

 Note: Punctuation following a parenthesis within a sentence goes outside the parenthesis, and the first word within the parenthesis is not capitalized. (See Section B-3-b for the punctuation rule when a complete sentence is placed within the parentheses.)

i. *Period:* A period is used at the end of a sentence, after a polite request, with abbreviations, with numbers, following an enumeration, within an outline, and with paragraph headings.

(1) *After sentences:* Use a period to mark the end of a complete declarative sentence. The period is followed by two spaces.

EXAMPLE:

I plan to attend the IAAP seminar on the office of the future. Reservations are needed by October 15.

(2) *After a polite request:* Use a period to mark the end of a question that is a polite request. This type of question implies that the reader will be able to fulfill the request by performing some specific action.

EXAMPLE:

Will you attend the meeting for me next week.

(3) *With abbreviations:* Periods are to be used with personal and professional abbreviations, academic abbreviations, and seniority abbreviations. The ending period is followed by one space unless it ends a sentence; then there are two spaces. There is no space after a period within an abbreviation.

EXAMPLES:

Ms. Lee   Dr. Ross

Ph.D.   B.A.

Frank Johnson, Jr. was here.

(4) *With numbers:* Use a period to denote the decimal point when designating amounts of money or fractions. Omit the decimal and two ciphers after even-money amounts unless the figure is included in a sentence with dollars-and-cents amounts (see Section B-7-d.) In a decimal fraction, the figures are considered as one number. Therefore, no space follows the period.

EXAMPLES:

We still owe $1,537.75 on our microcomputer, which amounts to 3.5 percent of the total bill.

You gave a $50 donation last year.

(5) *Following an enumeration:* A period follows each number or letter of an enumeration that is listed. The periods are to be aligned, and two spaces follow the period.

EXAMPLE:

Please include the following administrators on the invitation list:

1. Mr. George White, Board of Directors

2. Ms. Martha Phiffel, Second Vice President

3. Mrs. Kathy McDoughel, Director of Human Resources

(6) *Within an outline:* A period follows each letter or number used to introduce each item in an outline. The periods are to be aligned, and two spaces follow the period.

EXAMPLE:

    I. Business Letters
      A. Styles
        1. Block
        2. Modified Block
      B. Format

    II. Tables

(7) *With paragraph headings:* When you use a paragraph heading, it is followed by a period and a dash or two spaces. The heading is always underlined (see Chapter 19, Section D-2).

EXAMPLE:

<u>February usage</u>. *The executive dining room was used eight times during the month of February for luncheon meetings.*

<u>February usage</u>. *—The executive dining room was used eight times during the month of February for luncheon meetings.*

j. *Question mark:* A question mark is used at the end of a sentence that asks a direct question. The question mark is followed by two spaces.

EXAMPLE:

Will Julie be sitting for the CPS exam in May? If so, which testing site does she prefer?

k. *Quotation mark:* The quotation mark (") is used with direct quotes, titles, and single letters.

(1) *With direct quotes:* Quotation marks are placed around the exact words that were spoken or written (see Sections B-2-c[4] and B-2-b[1]).

EXAMPLE:

Did Carlson really say, "Since I did not get the promotion, I am going to resign."

(See Note following Section B-2-b[3] for end-of-quotation punctuation.)

Your advertisement must include the following: "Warning! Use of this product may be hazardous to your health."

(2) *With titles:* Quotation marks are used to enclose chapters of books and titles of articles, lectures, or reports.

EXAMPLE:

My lecture, "Office Automation," is going to be published in <u>OfficePro</u> as "The Office of the Future Is Here Today."

(3) *Single letters:* When reference is made to a single letter within the alphabet, that letter may be placed in quotation marks for ease of reading (for alternative format, see Section B-2-m[4]).

EXAMPLE:

You only need to add an "s" to form the plural of all numbers.

Note: Periods and commas are the only punctuation marks that always go inside the closing quotation mark. The question mark, exclamation point, and closing parenthesis go inside the closing quotation mark only when they are part of the quotation. Semicolons and colons always go outside the closing quotation mark. If quoted material comes at the end of a sentence, the punctuation mark that ends the quotation is also used to end the sentence. This is true even when the punctuation mark for the end-of-quotation sentence and the end of the sentence are not the same.

l. *Semicolon:* The semicolon is used to separate compound sentences or a series within a series.

(1) *Compound sentences:* When a sentence consists of two complete sentences with no conjunction, a semicolon is used to separate the sentences. (See Section B-2-c[3] for use of a comma with a conjunction or a conjunctive adverb.)

EXAMPLE:

Our secretary also had the flu; however, she was out for only two days.

Note: When punctuation is required within either of the sentences, follow correct punctuation rules. "However" is an introduction to the second sentence; therefore, it is followed by a comma (see Section B-2-c[2] in this chapter).

(2) *Series:* When a series contains a series, semicolons are used to separate the main series and commas are used for the inner series.

EXAMPLE:

The fall order includes women's slacks, skirts, blouses, and sweaters; men's slacks, shirts, and sweaters; and children's pants, T-shirts, and sweaters.

m. *Underscore:* The underscore is used for underlining titles, specific words, paragraph headings, or single letters. (An alternate method is to use italics in place of the underscore.)

(1) *Titles:* All titles (books, magazines, newspapers, movies, plans, and so on) are underscored.

EXAMPLE:

The president is an avid reader of the Wall Street Journal, Money, and the two local newspapers.

(2) *Specific words:* An underscore may be used to emphasize a word, phrase, clause, or sentence. However, for the underscore to have any effect, be selective with its use.

EXAMPLE:

The main reason for wanting an upgrade on the word processing software in our office is because we exchange many of our documents with consultants who are using a more current version.

(3) *Paragraph headings:* All paragraph headings are to be underscored so they stand out from the balance of the material in the paragraph. Other headings (centered and side) may or may not be underscored (see Chapter 19, Section D-2).

Note: The alternative use of italics is not used for paragraph headings.

(4) *Single letters:* When reference is made to a single letter within the alphabet, that letter may be underscored for ease in reading. (For an alternative format, see Section B-2-k[3].)

EXAMPLE:

You only need to add an s to form the plural of all numbers.

3. *Capitalization:* Proper capitalization is like having good manners. Improper capitalization makes a written document appear sloppy and difficult to read.

Note: An explanation of all capitalization possibilities is impossible in a review manual such as this. Therefore, only the most frequent use of capital letters will be covered in this section.

   a. *Beginning a sentence:* Capitalize the beginning of every sentence or expression that ends with a punctuation mark (period, question mark, or exclamation point).

   EXAMPLE:

   When is the meeting? Originally, it was scheduled for 9 a.m. tomorrow.

   b. *A sentence within parentheses:* When a complete sentence within parentheses stands by itself, the first word is capitalized. If, however, a sentence within parentheses is part of another sentence, it usually does not begin with a capital letter.

   EXAMPLES:

   A good synonym and antonym reference book is important to writers. (A popular reference book is Roget's International Thesaurus.)

   The teacher requires several reference books (we need them for the next session).

   c. *Beginning a quotation:* The first word of a complete sentence from a direct quotation is to be capitalized.

   EXAMPLE:

   In the letter, Johanson wrote, "The stock will double within the year."

   d. *Pronoun* I: The pronoun *I* is always capitalized to distinguish it as a word by itself.

   EXAMPLE:

   Judge Rand and I will take care of the banquet arrangements.

   e. *Titles of people:* When a title is used as part of a person's name, it should be capitalized. This is also true for names of family relationships unless preceded by a possessive or used as a common noun. When any title is a descriptive word, it is not capitalized.

   EXAMPLES:

Part of the Name	*Descriptive Word*
Judge Matthews	*She is the new judge.*
Dr. Andrews	*Your doctor called.*
The President vetoed the bill. (U.S. president)	*The president resigned. (a company president)*
I called Mother.	*She is a grandmother.*

f. *Books and articles:* The first word, nouns, pronouns, verbs, adjectives, adverbs, and prepositions of more than five letters are capitalized in titles of books and magazine or newspaper articles.

EXAMPLES:

<u>*Molloy's Live for Success*</u>

<u>*The World Is Made of Glass*</u>

"Communication—An Important Link Between Secretary and Executive"

g. *Academic courses:* Specific high school or college course titles are capitalized; general subjects are not capitalized unless they are languages.

EXAMPLES:

Business Letter Writing	*English*
Administrative Office Management	*management*
Human Relations 101	*psychology*
Conversational Spanish	*language*

h. *Geographic locations:* Specific geographic locations and directions used to identify geographic areas are capitalized. When used to indicate direction, the word is not capitalized.

EXAMPLES:

Minnesota	*the Midwest*	*west of the Mississippi*
Savannah	*a Southerner*	*a southern custom*
Indonesia	*the Far East*	*in east China*

i. *Organizations:* Names (and abbreviations) of social organizations, business organizations, and clubs are capitalized. When the words *senior, junior, sophomore,* and *freshman* refer to organized groups or functions, they are capitalized.

EXAMPLES:

International Association for Administrative Professionals™ (IAAP)

League of Women Voters

American Management Association (AMA)

Junior Prom

Sophomore Bleacher Bums

j. *Institutions:* Specific public and private institutions are capitalized. When the name applies to a whole class of institutions, it is not capitalized.

EXAMPLES:

Gifford High School	*our high school*
Green Public Library	*the public library*
Daily Medical Clinic	*the medical clinic*

    k. *Groups:* Names of national, political, religious, or ethnic groups are capitalized. Names of social and economic groups are not capitalized.

       EXAMPLES:

English	*Finnish*
Democrat	*Republican*
Lutheran	*Jew*
Negroid	*Caucasian*
upper class	*senior citizens*

    l. *Objects:* Specific objects (brand names, structures, documents, artifacts) are capitalized.

       EXAMPLES: •

       Kodak film
       (Only the brand name is capitalized.)

       Jefferson Memorial

       Declaration of Independence

    m. *Elements of time:* Capitalize words designating specific months, days, holidays, events, and periods. Names of seasons are not capitalized.

       EXAMPLES:

June	*Monday*
Memorial Day	*World War II*
the Renaissance	*summer*

4. *Format and Appearance:* When a written document is seen for the first time, the reader will be more eager to read the document if the format and appearance are familiar and attractively displayed. People are more comfortable when a document looks familiar and has a neat, attractive appearance.

    a. *Format:* Because the visual impact of a document has an impact on the reader even before the material is read, it is important to be familiar with formatting guidelines.

       (1) *Format of an envelope:* The two envelope styles are the OCR style and the conventional style. The position of the address in relation to bar codes on the envelope is another important consideration.

       (2) *Format of a letter:* The three most common letter styles are blocked letter style, modified blocked letter style, and simplified letter style. The style used depends on individual preference. When the reader encounters a style that is familiar and is used properly, the reader develops confidence in the writer. Also, one must decide on either open or mixed punctuation style.

       (3) *Other business documents:* All business documents have guidelines to follow. This is true of preprinted forms as well as original material such as memorandums. Even rough draft copy has guidelines to be followed which make it easy for the writer to edit the material.

Refer to Chapter 19 for details on formatting documents.

b. *Appearance:* A neat, attractive appearance means proper spacing of the document; few and neat corrections; clear, dark print; and a nonglossy paper that is easy to read.

Besides the picture-frame appearance, neat corrections are extremely important. With modern technology, many office professionals have the advantage of word processing systems and correcting typewriters. However, there may be times when possessing skillful correction techniques is advantageous. A secretary who can produce usable copy that is neat, clean, and "looks perfect" is much appreciated. That perfect look can be accomplished by making use of the following correction tips:

(1) *Preparing the original document:* The first step toward that perfect look is preparing the original document. The ink from the ribbon is absorbed into the typing paper; therefore, the sooner a correction is made, the better. A neater correction will be obtained if some of the surface ink is lifted from the original paper before making a correction by using a soft drafting eraser or gummed typewriter cleaner. The drafting eraser is rolled or gently stroked over the error. The typewriter cleaner is like Silly Putty and picks up the excess ink when pressed over the error.

(2) *Choosing the proper correction device:* Once the document is prepared by lifting the surface ink, the proper correction device must be selected: correction fluid, correction tape, correction paper, or an eraser.

(a) *Correction fluid:* On the original copy, correction fluid may be used in areas where the correction is small and correct words will be typed over the correction.

- Shake the container (bottle or pen) to mix the ingredients. Make sure that the correction fluid is thin; if necessary, add some thinner.

- With a small amount of fluid on the brush or tip of the pen, paint over the error like an artist drawing that letter; the liquid will drop into the crevice made by the letter.

- Permit the corrected area to dry thoroughly before typing over the correction (10 to 30 seconds).

Note: With extensive use of copiers, many office employees use the original as a file copy and send a photocopy to the recipient. In such a situation, larger corrections are made with correction materials (fluid or tape), even in areas where nothing is typed over the correction. It is important to realize, however, that if a file copy is kept for many years, the correction material may become dry and brittle and flake off the paper, exposing the error.

(b) *Correction tape:* Errors on the original can be corrected by using correction tape in a dispenser.

- Position the correction tape dispenser over the error.

- Roll the dispenser so the tape adheres to the paper (the takeup wheel pulls the tape backing into the dispenser).

(c) *Correction paper:* On the original copy, correction paper may be used for areas where the correction is small and correct words will be typed over the correction.

- Position the typed document so you can strike over the error.
- Slip a fresh piece of correction paper on top of the paper with the chalky side toward the paper.
- Type out the incorrect letter(s).
- Make sure you always use a clean section of the correction paper while typing the incorrect letter(s).
- Remove the correction paper, and key in the correction.

(d) *Eraser:* Making a correction with an eraser is the most permanent form of correction as well as being the best choice when nothing is to be typed in the area where the incorrect letter(s) is being removed. However, skill is needed when correcting an error with an eraser. The grit from the eraser acts like sandpaper. If the eraser is pressed firmly against the paper and moved with rapid motion, a hole is likely to appear in the paper. The key to a neat correction with an eraser is

- Use the white typing eraser (coarse) for original copies and the pink carbon eraser (soft) for carbon copies.
- Press lightly against the paper.
- Move in a circular motion for oval letters (o, c, e, O) as well as for circular portions of letters (p, b, d, q).
- Move in an up-and-down motion for straight letters (t, i, l, w) as well as for straight portions of letters (p, b, d, q).
- As the grit accumulates, brush or blow it away from the paper and the typewriter.
- Before erasing, be sure the eraser is clean; a dirty eraser leaves smudges. An eraser can easily be cleaned by rubbing it on an emery board. An emery board in the desk drawer specifically for that purpose is helpful.
- When using a typewriter with a movable platen, it is a good idea to move the platen so that the paper with the error extends to the left or to the right of the typewriter before beginning to erase. It is also advisable to move the typing font or daisy wheel away from the error when using a typewriter that does not have a movable platen.

(e) *Other correction techniques:* You may want to consider two other correction techniques—a strikeover and camouflaging with chalk.

- *Strikeovers:* On a few typewriters one letter can be typed over another and the strikeover is invisible. Some possibilities are an *o* or an *e* over a *c;* a *p, q, d, g,* and *b* over an *o;* or an *f* over an *i.* Test your typewriter with various letter combinations, but use this technique *only* if there is no visible sign of the incorrect letter underneath. One must be very careful with this technique because what will cover up on one type-writer may not work on another. This technique must always be checked with different typewriters, and the typist must be very particular that the strikeover is absolutely invisible.

You may combine the strikeover with correction fluid or chalk to camouflage that portion of the letter not covered properly by the strikeover.

- *Camouflaging with white chalk:* After erasing with an eraser, the paper sometimes has worn thin and white paper looks grayish in color. By using white chalk and rubbing over the back of the area, much of the original color will come back to the paper. (Use yellow chalk for buff paper.)

(3) *Reinserting paper for correction:* Even though all highly conscientious secretaries proofread the material before removing the paper from the typewriter, there are times when an error is detected later. Reinserting the paper and aligning the print takes practice and familiarity with the typewriter. Using the typewriter scale as a special realignment tool or utilizing the tissue-paper technique are two easy methods for paper alignment.

(a) *Realignment with the typewriter scale:* The scale on the typewriter is designed to assist in realignment of the paper. Scales vary from machine to machine; therefore, the secretary must be familiar with the office typewriter.

- Insert a piece of practice paper.

- Type some material.

- Examine the position of the typewriter scale to the letters typed. (Make sure to examine the left scale over the print as well as the right scale. Many times the scales on a typewriter are just slightly different from one another.)

- Remove the typing paper.

- Reinsert the paper using the typewriter scale to "judge" exact position visually.

- Use the ratchet release to move your typing paper freely to the left or right (horizontally) if it is out of alignment in that direction.

- Use the variable line-space regulator to move the paper up or down (vertically) if it is out of alignment in that direction.

(b) *Tissue-paper technique for originals:* The tissue-paper technique can be used to reposition originals as well as carbon copies.

- First, eliminate the incorrect letter with correction fluid or an eraser. (The only time you may try to erase an error once the paper has been reinserted is if correction paper or self-correcting ribbon is being used. However, it is very difficult to align the paper exactly so that the incorrect letter is covered adequately by the correction paper or lifted off by the self-correcting ribbon.)

- Reinsert the paper using the typewriter scale, ratchet release, and variable line-space regulator to "judge" exact position visually.

- Insert a piece of tissue paper over a letter next to the incorrect letter that was eliminated when the paper was out of the typewriter.

- Type the aligned letter on the tissue paper. If it is aligned exactly over the original, only one letter will be visible. If not, adjust the original using the typewriter scale, ratchet release, and variable line-space regulator. Test it again to see if only one letter is visible.

- Once the original is aligned properly, remove the tissue paper and type the correct letter on the original.

(c) *Tissue-paper technique for carbon copies:* The tissue-paper technique can also be used with carbon copies.

- First, erase the error with a pink carbon-copy eraser (soft) before realigning the paper in the typewriter.

- Use the typewriter scale, ratchet release, variable line-space regulator, and tissue paper to realign the carbon copy. Follow the steps explained with originals.

- Once the carbon copy is aligned, insert a piece of carbon paper on top of the copy being corrected, insert a piece of scrap paper on the top of the carbon paper, and then type the correct letter. This gives the corrected letter the same appearance as when first typed.

5. *Consistent Style:* The word *consistent* means compatible or uniform. Style in business writing is the manner in which we express ourselves. Each person has a unique writing style, like no one else's. However, business writing requires that the style not draw attention from the reader, who should be concentrating on the content of the writing. Therefore, the writing style needs to be examined in the editing phase to be sure that there is a consistent, uniform pattern to the writing—but not one that will detract from the attention the reader will pay to the content of the message.

a. *Format patterns:* The format used in business writing will help to create a consistent style. Rules of setting margins and tabs according to acceptable formats should be followed so that within a given document the *same* margins and tabs will be used. Here are some of the format features that need to be consistent throughout the report:

(1) Top, bottom, and side margins for first page of document

(2) Top, bottom, and side margins for succeeding pages of document

(3) Indentions of paragraphed material

(4) Placement of footnotes or endnotes

(5) Placement of headings and subheadings throughout the document

b. *Word usage:* Any word that can be written in more than one way should be written only one way throughout a document. When the word is combined with a number, be sure to check the number rules to see how the term should be typed.

c. *Tone:* In editing a document that has already been prepared, evaluate the tone. Tone, as defined in Chapter 16, is the manner in which a certain attitude is expressed. Again, the tone needs to be consistently informal or consistently formal, depending on the purpose of the document.

d. *Punctuation:* Some rules for punctuating sentences are more flexible than others and provide the writer with choices. The comma is a good example.

EXAMPLE:

The comma is used in a series of three or more items. If a conjunction precedes the last word in a series, a comma is optional before that conjunction. However, many times it is still used before the conjunction for clarity. If you decide in your writing to include the comma before the conjunction in a series, be consistent in the entire document so that a comma always *appears before the conjunction in the series. (Thomas, Stevens, and Bryson attended the management seminar.)*

The editing process is the final opportunity to make any changes in business writing before it is distributed to the receiver. It is crucial that editing be considered a necessary step to the final approval of the document before it is sent outside the organization. Every document that leaves the firm creates an image, either favorable or unfavorable.

6. *Spelling and Keyboarding Accuracy:* There has been a cry raised in public education for a return to the basics of education. Much of this is due to entry-level office employees who cannot read, write, or spell.

There is a similar concern with administrative professionals. While seeking better office systems and taking advantage of improved office technologies, many are neglecting the basics. Executives still expect good-quality basic skills. The question here is, "Are you an expert speller?"

English spelling would be easier if each sound were represented by a single letter or a combination of letters. A secretary with good spelling skills is more efficient. However, absolute correctness in spelling is not easy to achieve. Most errors can be avoided, however, if time and effort are spent in the following areas:

- Memorizing the spelling of difficult words

- Using the software spell-check tool or a standard dictionary when in doubt

- Proofreading what has been written

- Reviewing the following spelling rules

a. *ie* and *ei:* The grammar school rhyme is most helpful with this rule: "*I* before *e* except after *c,* or when sounded like *a,* as in *neighbor* and *weigh.*"

EXAMPLES:

freight	*receive*	*achieve*	*lien*

Exceptions to be memorized:

counterfeit	*either*	*foreign*	*leisure*
neither	*weird*		

b. ie *ending:* When a word ends in *ie,* it is changed to *y* before the suffix *ing.*

EXAMPLES:

die	*dying*	*lie*	*lying*

c. *Silent* e *ending:* Words ending in a silent *e* drop the *e* before a suffix beginning with a vowel. The *e* is retained before a suffix beginning with a consonant except when the *e* is immediately preceded by another vowel other than an *e*.

EXAMPLES:

conceive	*conceivable*	*achieve*	*achievement*
true	*truly*	*imagine*	*imaginary*
definite	*definitely*	*nine*	*ninth*

Exceptions (retention of e before a vowel because of pronunciation):

changeable	*noticeable*	*outrageous*	*vengeance*

d. *Silent* e *with compounds:* Silent *e* is retained with compounds whether or not the second word begins with a vowel or a consonant.

EXAMPLES:

hereafter	*household*

e. ee *ending:* When a word ends in *ee,* both *e's* are retained with adding a suffix except when the suffix begins with an *e.* To form the plural of the word, add only an *s.*

EXAMPLES:

agree	*agreeable*	*free*	*freed*
lessee	*lessees*		

f. cle *and* cal: Words ending in *cle* are nouns; words ending in *cal* are adjectives derived from other words ending in *ic.*

EXAMPLES:

article	*icicle*	*logical*	*comical*

Exceptions (words that are both nouns and adjectives):

chemical	*periodical*	*radical*

g. ph, gh, ch, i: In many words, the *gh* and *ph* sound like *f;* the *ch* sounds like *k;* the *i* sounds like *y.*

EXAMPLES:

enough	*physician*	*architect*	*companion*
laugh	*multigraph*	*scheme*	*familiar*

h. cede, ceed, sede: There is no rule for verbs with any of these endings; the words just need to be memorized.

EXAMPLES:

accede	*precede*	*exceed*	*supersede*
concede	*recede*	*proceed*	*secede*
succeed	*intercede*		

i. y *ending preceded by a vowel:* When a word ends in *y* and is preceded by a vowel, the *y* is generally retained when adding a suffix. To form the plural of the word, add only an *s*.

EXAMPLES:

convey	*conveyance*
display	*displayed*
turkey	*turkeys*
pulley	*pulleys*

j. y *ending preceded by a consonant:* When a word ends in *y* and is preceded by a consonant, the *y* is generally changed to *i* when adding a suffix except when the suffix begins with *i*. To form the plural of the word, change the *y* to *i* and add *es*.

EXAMPLES:

rely	*relied*	*relying*	*relies*
liquefy	*liquefied*	*liquefying*	*liquefies*
remedy	*remedied*	*remedies*	
dictionary	*dictionaries*		

k. ful: The suffix *ful* is spelled with only one *l*. The *l* does not double when adding another suffix except for the suffix *ly*. To form the plural of the word, add only an *s*.

EXAMPLES:

powerful	*helpfulness*	*cheerfully*	*handfuls*

l. *Doubling the ending consonant:* The ending consonant is doubled before adding a suffix when

(1) the suffix begins with a vowel.

(2) the final consonant is preceded by a single vowel.

(3) the word is accented on the last syllable.

EXAMPLES:

gripping	*pinned*	*controllable*	*occurrence*

m. *Compounds:* A compound word consists of two or more words that are written as one word, written as separate words, or hyphenated. There is no rule for the use of the hyphen; the decision is based on common usage. However, typically phrases used as adjectives are hyphenated before a noun.

EXAMPLES:

Closed (one word):	*toastmaster*	*workbench*	
Open (separate words):	*attorney general*		
Hyphenated:	*public-spirited*	*one-half*	*hard-hat*

7. *Guidelines for Proper Use of Numbers:* Typing of numbers within documents requires your concentration to maintain consistency throughout the document. The following guidelines for typing numbers should be helpful in deciding exactly how numbers should appear.

    a. *Numbers from one through ten:* The numbers from one through ten are usually spelled out; numbers above ten should be in figures.

    EXAMPLES:

    We ordered ten cases of yarn; however, they shipped only four.

    Please send us 35 copies of your latest bulletin.

    b. *Specific numbers ten or under:* Even though the number is ten or under, the following specific types of numbers should be written in figures: measurements, temperature readings, dimensions, election returns, market quotations, chemical terms, and scores.

    EXAMPLES:

    The temperature today is only 5 degrees.

    The Rebels won the soccer game with a score of 5 to 2.

    The room was 8 feet by 12 feet.

    c. *Sets of numbers within a sentence:* Be consistent when several sets of numbers are within the same sentence. Use figures for all numbers.

    EXAMPLE:

    In our firm there are 9 exempt employees and 18 nonexempt employees.

    d. *Money:* Sums of money are expressed as figures.

    EXAMPLES:

Correct	*Incorrect*
$5.41	*$5.41¢*
92 cents	*92¢ (unless used in material that contains many price quotations)*
	$0.92 (unless in a table with other dollar-and-cents figures)
$25	*25$*
	25 dollars
	$25.00 (unless other amounts within sentence have dollars and cents)

    e. *Percentages:* Express percentages in figures followed by the word *percent.* The word is correctly spelled as *percent* or *per cent.* Once you choose a spelling, be consistent throughout the document. If the percentage is used in technical material, the percent symbol (%) can be used.

    EXAMPLE:

    There will be a 35 percent markup on this group of merchandise.

EXAMPLE OF TECHNICAL MATERIAL:

The federal government requires that this food product contain 95% natural ingredients; our product is 96.3% natural.

f. *Mixed numbers:* Express mixed numbers (whole numbers and fractions) in figures with a space between the whole number and the fraction. Type the fraction with a number, a slash, and another number (no spaces). If the only fractions within the document are fractions on your typewriter keyboard or in the word processing software, these fractions may be used. In other words, be consistent with the format.

EXAMPLES:

The board should be 28 1/4 inches by 35 5/8 inches by 1 1/2 inches.

The frame measures 5 ½ by 3 ¼ inches. (This sentence is not in the same document as the first sentence; therefore, the fraction key on the keyboard or the software-generated fraction could be used.)

Note: Creating fractions with word processing software programs may require you to override an automatic feature that changes a fraction keyed in as 5 1/4 into 5 ¼ automatically. If all the fractions you are using are available in the software-generated characters included in the software, you will not need to override the feature. Be consistent with the style you are using for all fractions.

g. *Beginning sentence with number:* When a sentence begins with a number, write the number as a word or rearrange the sentence.

EXAMPLES:

Seventy of our secretaries are going to the convention.

The convention will be attended by 70 of our secretaries.

h. *Hyphens in numbers:* Use hyphens in numbers between 21 and 99 when the numbers are written as words.

EXAMPLES:

twenty-one

three hundred seventy-eight

i. *Two numbers for one item:* If two numbers describe one item, express the smaller number as a word. Where this is impractical, separate the two numbers with a comma.

EXAMPLES:

There are 30 fifteen-cent stamps.

In 1999, 5,654,098 packages were delivered by our company.

j. *Dates:* Dates are expressed as figures unless used in rigidly formal writing such as an invitation or announcement. The day is written without the suffix (*st, nd, th,* . . .) unless the day is typed before the month.

EXAMPLES:

The open house is Wednesday, June 19.

The 19th of June would be a good date for the open house.

k. *Time:* Time is written in figures unless used with the word *o'clock*. Variations for typing A.M. and P.M. are a.m., A.M., am, and AM; p.m., P.M., pm, and PM. For clarity, the more frequent use is with periods. Otherwise, am and AM could be mistaken for the word "*am*." Be consistent with your format, and type A.M. and P.M. in the same way. Do not use the two ciphers with the even hour unless it appears with another figure containing minutes.

EXAMPLES:

The meeting will begin at two o'clock.

The meeting will begin at 2 P.M.

The time set aside for the meeting is 2:00 to 2:30 P.M.

l. *Grouping of numbers:* No commas should be used in large serial numbers, policy numbers, page numbers, or telephone numbers. It is permissible, and often desirable for clear reading, to insert spaces within large serial numbers or policy numbers. The number is usually clustered in groups of three or four digits. However, when copying a number, type the number exactly as the originator typed it. Area codes for telephone numbers are placed within parentheses, and the phone number is typed with a hyphen.

EXAMPLES:

Our insurance policy is No. 378 9605 789.

Our telephone number is (815) 399-5678.

Assign the new job number 38976.

m. *Expressing large numbers:* A number in the millions or billions is typed as a combination of the word and figure. If a number in the thousands must be written, write it in hundreds rather than thousands (a shorter form).

EXAMPLES:

Our goal is 10 million orders for this fiscal year.

Sixteen hundred orders have already been placed.

n. *Spelling out other forms of numbers:* Spell out numbers when they appear as *first, second, third,* and so on.

EXAMPLE:

This is our third notice. Please call if there is a problem.

o. *Numbers in legal copy:* In legal copy, money is expressed in both figures and words.

EXAMPLE:

The defendant agrees to pay the sum of four hundred fifty dollars ($450) for services rendered.

p. *Descriptive numbers:* Express numbers that follow such words as *chapter, volume no., page, floor,* or *apartment* in figures. The word *number* is not used.

EXAMPLES:

Chapter 2 begins on page 56.

I moved to apartment 8.

q. *Age:* Age is expressed as a word unless days and months are given.

EXAMPLES:

He is two years old.

He is 2 years, 3 months, and 15 days old.

She will be eighty-five on her next birthday.

r. *Street names:* A street name should be typed in the same form as it is typed by the city or on company letterheads.

EXAMPLES:

Harrison Interiors in Rockford, Illinois, is located on Sixth Street.

Ada International is located on 5th Avenue in Des Moines, Iowa.

s. *Plurals:* Express the plural of figures by adding an apostrophe and an *s*, or just adding an *s* is sufficient. Generally, the apostrophe is used. Once you choose a style, be consistent throughout the document.

EXAMPLES:

7's or 7s   35's or 35s

8. *Guidelines for Word Division and Hyphenation:* In some cases, it is necessary that words be divided in order for the right margin to be somewhat even. The most desirable point for dividing a word is really a matter of opinion. By basing word division on the principles of pronunciation and spelling, much time and effort are saved.

You can develop a "feeling" for correct syllabication through careful observation and study of word pronunciation and spelling and through reference to the dictionary. The following general suggestions developed from typewriting and business protocol.

a. *General suggestions for word division:*

   (1) Divide a word only when it is absolutely necessary.

   (2) When a word division must be made, it is best to have enough of the word on the first line to be able to conceptualize the entire word and to carry enough of the word to the next line to balance the division somewhat equally.

   (3) Avoid dividing a word at the end of the first line of a paragraph. The last word in the paragraph should *never* be divided.

   (4) The last word on a page should *never* be divided. Type the complete word on the page where you achieve the best balance between the two lines of print.

   (5) Avoid dividing words at the end of more than two consecutive lines.

   (6) If you can possibly avoid it, do not divide a proper name. The pronunciation of a proper name is not always revealed by the spelling; there may be some doubt as to the correct syllable division (see Section B-8-b[15]).

b. *Rules for word division:* Specific rules for word division are helpful in making appropriate decisions in hyphenating words. In the following examples, the period (.) identifies syllables where it is not advised to divide a word, and the hyphen (-) identifies syllables where it is acceptable to have a word division.

(1) Only divide words between syllables. Therefore, one-syllable words cannot be divided.

EXAMPLES:

One-syllable words:

cream   sound

Correct word division:

for-ward   mo.ti-va-tion

(2) Words of four or five letters should never be divided, and the division of six-letter words should be avoided. A divided syllable should have three or more characters in the division.

EXAMPLES:

a.lone   a.part-ment   co.her-ence

vouch.er   caf.e-te.ri.a

(3) Hyphenated words are to be divided only at the hyphen.

EXAMPLE:

self-ad.dressed

(4) Compound words should be divided between the elements of the compound.

EXAMPLES:

busi.ness-men   grand-fa.ther

(5) The addition of the past tense to a word does not necessarily add an extra syllable.

EXAMPLES:

guessed   missed   laughed

(6) When a word containing three or more syllables is to be divided next to a one-letter syllable, the division should come after the one-letter syllable.

EXAMPLES:

crit.i-cism   sep.a-rate   af.fil.i-ate

(7) When there is a double consonant within a word, the word *may* be divided between the consonants. The pronunciation of the word will help you determine whether it is proper to divide the word at this point; that is, you *could* divide a word with a double consonant sound (see also Examples [8] and [9]).

EXAMPLES:

bel.lig-er-ent   strug-gling

vac-ci-nate

(8) When a final consonant is doubled before a suffix, the additional consonant goes with the suffix (see also Examples [7] and [9]).

EXAMPLES:

be.gin-ning   de.fer-ring

(9) When the double consonant is the ending of a root word, separate the suffix from the root word (see also Examples [7] and [8]).

EXAMPLES:

ad.dress-ing   *a.gree-ing*

(10) Words ending in *able, ible, ical, cian, cion, sion, gion,* and *tion* should be divided between the stem of the word and the terminating syllable.

EXAMPLES:

a.gree-able   *con-ta-gion*   *sus-pi-cion*

cler-i.cal   *mu.si-cian*   *am.bi-tion*

de.duct-i.ble   *ap.pre-hen-sion*

(11) Some word endings are *ble* and *cal* instead of *able, ible,* or *ical.* In these cases, the *a* or *i* is part of the preceding syllable.

EXAMPLES:

chari-ta-ble   *au.di-ble*   *fan-tas-ti-cal*

(12) When a word is to be divided at a point where two one-letter syllables (vowels) occur together, the division should be made between the vowels.

EXAMPLES:

e.vac.u-a.tion   *grad.u-a.tion*

(13) A syllable that does not contain a vowel must not be separated from the remainder of the word.

EXAMPLES:

did.n't   *would.n't*

(14) A date can be divided only between the day and the year, not between the month and the day. In this case, no hyphen is needed; the date (year) is just continued on the next line.

EXAMPLE:

September 18,   *NOT: September*

200X   *18, 200X*

(15) Do not divide a proper name if you can possibly avoid it (see Section B-8-a(6)]. If, however, a complete name cannot be typed on one line, separation of the parts of the name must be made at a logical reading point. A title should not be by itself on a line. A middle name should be typed with the first name. When a name is separated between two lines, no hyphen is used.

EXAMPLES:

Ms. Carla M.
Johanson

not

Ms.   *or*   *Ms. Carla*
Carla M. Johanson   *M. Johanson*

(16) If it is not possible to type a street address on one line, the address should be separated at a logical reading point. There are many variations of a logical reading point; you must use your best judgment. The city, state, and ZIP code can be separated between the city and the state but not between the state and the ZIP code. No hyphen is needed for this type of separation.

EXAMPLE:

Harrisonburg,	*or*	*Harrisonburg,*
Virginia		*VA 22801*

(17) Do not divide figures, amounts of money, figures from an identifying term, or abbreviations. Avoid dividing Web addresses.

EXAMPLES:

Correct	*Incorrect*	
34576539	*3456-6539*	
$50,000	*$50,-000*	*$-50,000*
page 45	*page 45*	
11 inches	*11 inches*	
AT&T	*AT-&T*	
www.amazon.com	*www.amazon-com*	

c. *Hyphenation with word processing software:* Word processing software uses word wrap to move an entire word to the next line whenever a word extends beyond the right margin. If the hyphenation feature in the word processing software is used, words can be divided between two lines. The hyphenation feature commands are explained in the word processing operations manual. Most hyphenation features, however, are programmed with an automatic or manual function.

(1) *Automatic hyphenation feature:* The automatic hyphenation feature hyphenates the word according to the rules established within the word processing software. The word processing hyphenations may or may not be consistent with the rules for word division as accepted by most businesses.

(2) *Manual hyphenation feature:* The manual hyphenation feature permits the secretary (user) to decide where a hyphen should be inserted in a word. The manual function provides the user with the flexibility to follow the rules for word division as accepted by most businesses. However, this process can take more of the secretary's time, particularly with lengthy documents.

Familiarity with the hyphenation feature within the word processing software program will guide the user to select hyphenation when any words in the text need to be hyphenated.

9. *Use of Editing Software:* Word processing software can be enhanced by the addition of software that checks grammatical construction. The purpose of grammar software is to check the document for correct word usage and complete sentences. The grammatical construction programmed into the word processing software may be different than accepted practice at the firm. The secretary needs to be cognizant of the organization's writing expectations and override the software changes where appropriate.

C. Copyediting for Application of Writing Fundamentals

Editing has been in existence for many years, but the term has traditionally been associated with the publishing industry. Secretaries in all types of offices have been performing copyediting, but the task has often been referred to incorrectly as *proofreading,* another important secretarial skill (see Section A). It is important to recognize the difference between these two skills.

A daily phenomenon is the busy executive hurriedly writing down ideas or dictating thoughts to the secretary. After the draft has been written or dictated, the next step—copyediting—is often the primary responsibility of the administrative assistant. *Copyediting* is the revision of a draft or a document for consistency, conciseness, and grammatical accuracy. Revisions are marked within the body of the document using proofreading and copyediting symbols (Figure 17–1). The edited copy is returned to the author for verification. After all revisions have been made and the document is typed in final form, the secretary will *proofread* the document for typing accuracy.

1. *Guidelines for Preparing Copy for Editing:* Copy to be edited can be prepared in rough-draft format. Four guidelines for keying rough-draft copy should be followed.

    a. *Side margins:* Side margins should be wide. Side margins should be 1 inch at a minimum.

    b. *Spacing:* Triple spacing should be used so corrections can be inserted easily. Never single-space rough-draft copy.

    c. *Paragraphs:* Indent paragraphs so that a new paragraph can easily be identified. An alternative is to quadruple-space between paragraphs if triple spacing is used for the document and to triple-space between paragraphs if double spacing is used for the document.

    d. *Readability of copy:* Even though this is a rough-draft copy, neatness should be maintained. When using a word processor, format codes (hyphenation, page rough draft break) are *not* included. These codes are included before printing the final copy. When using a correcting typewriter, corrections do not need to be as neat and camouflaged as with the final copy. Occasionally, putting an *x* over incorrect word(s) is acceptable, and strikeovers (even though noticeable) are also used when it is a clear cover-up (e.g., *l* over an *i, t* over an *l*).

    Readability is the key factor. Rough-draft copy will be read for revisions, and reading is easier if the copy is neat.

2. *Basic Skills for Editing:* An administrative professional needs to develop a strong background in English skills, especially grammatical construction and punctuation. Copyediting requires grammar, punctuation, spelling, and composition skills as well as the ability to maintain consistency in both format and language usage throughout the document. These skills are the underpinnings of the editing process when reading a document for completeness and accuracy.

    a. *Grammar skills:* Because of the complexity of the English language as well as changes made to update grammar rules, a current English handbook should be available and used by every secretary. An executive secretary maintains and updates office skills through review and practice.

b. *Punctuation skills:* A periodic brushup on punctuation skills is also vitally important.

c. *Spelling skills:* Spelling can be improved by using the dictionary, a word book, or a software spelling/grammar tool and concentrating on vocabulary building. There is always the *jargon* of the field to learn. When entering a new field, learn new terminology by adding one word to a vocabulary list every day. This technique can also be used for regular vocabulary expansion. The words should be used in daily communication; periodically, give yourself a spelling test on the words.

d. *Composition skills:* Composition is the ability to accurately tie grammar, punctuation, and spelling together into a written communique. A well-written document is one that is understood (clear), is stated in as few words as necessary (concise), and appeals to the reader (empathy). To develop effective communication skills, much practice is required and a "receiver" needs to evaluate the writing.

(1) *Reading for content:* When reading the copy for content, put yourself in the receiver's position. The aim of all communication is to produce a document that will appeal and communicate to the receiver while maintaining the company's objective. Sometimes, reading for content can best be accomplished by reading aloud. Also, when someone else (a co-worker) reads the document for content, that person should evaluate the document from the receiver's perspective.

(2) *Checking accuracy of content:* Someone other than the author of the document should be reading for accuracy. Usually, an author reads what he or she wants to say, not what has been written.

3. *Effective Word Selection:* When editing copy, it is very important to edit for content; in other words, examine the copy to determine that what was intended by the author is the same as what is written. Content editing is accomplished by reading and concentrating on word selection, sentence structure, sentence completeness, train of thought, and tone.

Effective word selection comes with practice. A few English words are used incorrectly, and their proper usage should be reviewed.

a. Accept *and* except: *Accept* means to receive or approve of; *except* means not to include.

EXAMPLES:

I accept your apology.

I have everyone's time card except yours.

b. Advise *and* advice: *Advise* is a verb meaning to make a recommendation; *advice* is a noun meaning counsel.

EXAMPLES:

My manager advised me to sit for the CPS exam.

I think that is good advice.

c. All ready *and* already: *All ready* is an adjective phrase meaning everyone or everything is prepared; *already* is an adverb meaning before.

EXAMPLES:

The executives are all ready for the communications workshop.

Dr. Pascal already responded.

d. Among *and* between: *Among* refers to more than two; *between* refers to only two. The word *and* should always be used between the choices.

EXAMPLES:

Poor communication causes dissatisfaction among employees.

Between you and me, I did receive my raise.

I cannot choose between green and yellow and red and yellow.
(green and yellow is one item; red and yellow is a second item)

e. Awhile *and* a while: *Awhile* is an adverb meaning a period of time; *a while* is a noun with an article.

EXAMPLES:

Can you stay awhile?
(adverb modifying <u>stay</u>)

Can you stay for a while?
(noun—object of the preposition <u>for</u>)

f. Bad *and* badly: *Bad* is the adjective; *badly* is the adverb. *Badly* is used after linking verbs when emphasis is on the verb. However, *bad* is the *preferred* adjective form after linking verbs.

EXAMPLES:

The stock maneuver looks bad.
(adjective modifying the subject <u>maneuver</u>)

Since the accident, Sutherland limps badly.
(adverb describing <u>limps</u>)

Thompson feels badly about the sale.
Thompson feels bad about the sale.
(Many people object to the use of <u>badly</u> as the adjective after a linking verb; therefore, it is best to use <u>bad</u>.)

g. Complement *and* compliment: Both can be used as a noun or a verb. *Complement* means finished or fitting together. *Compliment* is used when referring to praise.

EXAMPLES:

The new wall hangings complement the furniture.
(meaning fit together)

I must compliment Douglas for his choice in wall hangings.
(meaning praise)

h. Effect *and* affect: *Effect* is a noun meaning result; *affect* is a verb meaning influence.

EXAMPLES:

The effects of telecommunications have had a great impact in the last several years.
(effects = subject of the sentence)

The weather affected our plans.
(affected=verb)

i. Good *and* well: *Good* is an adjective; *well* is either an adjective or an adverb. The most common error is using the adjective *good* in place of the adverb *well*. *Good* and *well* are both used as predicate adjectives with the verb *feel;* however, the connotation is different.

EXAMPLES:

Everyone had a <u>good</u> time at the department party.
(adjective modifying the noun <u>time</u>)

All is <u>well</u> with the new couple.
(adjective modifying the subject <u>all</u>)

After the hurricane, the cleanup went <u>well</u>.
(adverb modifying the verb <u>went</u>)

Johnson doesn't feel <u>well</u>.
(referring to Johnson's health)

Eckels felt <u>good</u> about building the addition.
(referring to Eckels' mental feeling—happiness)

j. Lay *and* lie: *Lay* is a verb meaning to put or place; it takes an object. *Lie* is a verb meaning to recline; it does not take an object.

The principal parts of *lay* are *lay, laid, laid.*
The principal parts of *lie* are *lie, lay, lain.*

EXAMPLES:

I do not know where I laid my folder.
(folder is the object of the verb <u>laid</u>)

Grandpa should lie down for a rest.

k. Lose *and* loose: *Lose* is a verb meaning misplace; *loose* is an adjective meaning not tight or a verb meaning let go.

EXAMPLES:

Don't lose my place.

The dress is too loose.

Martin loosened the dog's collar.

l. Most *and* almost: *Most* is an adjective meaning large in number; *almost* is an adverb meaning nearly.

EXAMPLES:

Most secretaries sitting for the CPS exam take a review course. (adjective modifying the subject <u>secretaries</u>—meaning the majority referring to large in number)

Her writing almost meets specifications.
(adverb modifying <u>meets</u>)

m. Proceed *and* precede: *Proceed* means to continue; *precede* means to go before.

EXAMPLES:

We must proceed with our plans.

Learning the concepts precedes lab application.

n. Principal *and* principle: *Principal* is a noun or adjective meaning first in importance; *principle* is a noun meaning rule or basis for conduct.

EXAMPLES:

The new principal is planning major revisions.

To adhere to one's principles is important.

o. Real *and* really: *Real* is an adjective meaning actual or true; *really* is an adverb meaning indeed.

EXAMPLES:

The real way to make progress is to work hard.

Everyone is really working hard at the office.

p. Set *and* sit: Both *set* and *sit* are verbs. *Set* means to place and takes an object; *sit* refers to remaining in position and does not take an object.

EXAMPLES:

Please set my papers in the red in-basket.
(Set "what?" my papers
*　"where?" in the red in-basket)*

Please sit down on the couch.

q. Site, cite, *and* sight: *Site* is a noun meaning location. *Cite* is a verb meaning quote or recognize. *Sight* is a noun meaning vision.

EXAMPLES:

The new office site has a beautiful view.

Wells cited many abuses of the policy.

James' sight was impaired because of the injury.

r. Their, there, *and* they're: *Their* is the possessive form of *they*. *There* is an adverb. *They're* is a contraction for *they are*.

EXAMPLES:

Their car was totaled. (possessive pronoun)

Put the plant over there. (adverb)

They're going to the theater for the performance. (contraction for they are)

s. Then *and* than: *Then* means at that time and is an adverb; *than* is a conjunction usually used in comparisons.

EXAMPLES:

Call me this afternoon. We can then set a time.

I like the 1850 model better than the new one.

t. To, too, *and* two: *To* is a preposition. *Too* is an adverb meaning also or very. *Two* is the number.

EXAMPLES:

Please bring the car to the garage for repair.

The steak was too rare.

We have two external drives with our computer.

u. Who, which, *and* that: *Who* is used when referring to a person and *which* when referring to things. *That* can be used to refer to either a person or a thing; it is usually used with restrictive clauses. A restrictive clause is one that is necessary to the completeness of the sentence.

EXAMPLES:

Secretaries who have word processing software encounter less frustration with editing.
(who have word processing software refers to secretaries)

This manual, which was written by the information systems manager, is very easy to follow.
(which was written by the information systems manager refers to "manual"; it is a nonrestrictive clause that is not required)

This is software that can be learned quickly. (that can be learned quickly is a restrictive clause referring to software)

4. *Effective Sentence and Paragraph Construction:* Common sentence errors are incomplete sentences, run-on sentences, and improper division for train of thought.

a. *Incomplete sentence:* An incomplete sentence is one that is missing a subject or a verb (predicate). Incomplete sentences occur frequently in speech; therefore, these sentences often appear in written documents. An incomplete sentence can be corrected in one of these ways:

(1) *Supplying the missing subject or verb (predicate):* Many times, incomplete sentences follow complete sentences to which the sentence thoughts are connected. It is important to watch for incomplete sentences and supply the missing subject or verb.

EXAMPLE:

The new chair for the word processing unit was delivered today. Believe it's adjustable.
(The subject in the second sentence is missing. Corrected: I believe it's adjustable.)

(2) *Connecting the incomplete sentence to another sentence:* Sometimes, it is more convenient to connect the incomplete sentence to another sentence that has related thoughts.

EXAMPLE:

The report was sent to the finance department yesterday. The report on building expansion.
(The verb in the second sentence is missing. Corrected: The report on building expansion was sent to the finance department yesterday.)

(3) *Dropping the sentence:* Many times incomplete sentences are explanatory phrases or clauses that can be dropped from the written material.

b. *Run-on sentences:* Just the opposite of an incomplete sentence is running two or more complete sentences together. These sentences can be either made into two separate sentences or connected with correct punctuation.

(1) *Two separate sentences:* Because of the length of a run-on sentence, it is sometimes best to separate it into two separate sentences. Also, it is important that a written document have some variety in the length of sentences.

EXAMPLE:

A four-year degree in office administration is required for the new position because it is a supervisory position in the administrative services department that is the department responsible for information processing.
(Corrected: . . . position. It is a supervisory position in the administrative services department responsible for information processing.)

(2) *Correct punctuation for run-on sentences:* When two complete sentences are connected with punctuation, this is called a *compound* sentence. If the run-on sentence does not have a conjunction, a semicolon is to be used between the two sentences (see Section B-2-l[1]). If the run-on sentence has a conjunction, a comma is used between the two sentences (see Section B-2-c[3]).

c. *Paragraph construction:* A paragraph represents the writer's thoughts on a portion of a specific subject. The entire document represents the writer's thoughts on the whole subject. Therefore, all skilled writers will organize their separate thoughts pertaining to the whole subject in a logical manner before they attempt to write. Writing manuals always advise an outline prior to writing. When writing skills are being developed or improved, the outline is usually written on paper. As writers become more skillful with their writing, some choose to organize their thoughts mentally. However, many writers consistently produce a paper sketch of the topic before writing. It is important to recognize when this step is required to produce logical and clearly written material.

Even though paragraphs will vary in length and purpose, most paragraphs are composed of three types of statements.

(1) *Overview statement:* Many paragraphs contain a statement at the beginning which is general in nature and provides an overview of what is to follow. Such a statement can be a restatement of previous material when the paragraph is an expansion on a previous point. Sometimes, an overview statement comes at the end of a paragraph summarizing what was presented in the paragraph.

(2) *Supporting statement:* Supporting statements are sentences within the paragraph presenting the ideas the writer has on this particular point of the topic.

(3) *Detail statement:* Good writing consists mainly of detail statements, which are statements that present facts about the topic. Generalizations and opinions are best supported by accurate facts.

5. *Tone, Goodwill, Considerateness, and Writing Style:* Tone is determined by what needs to be said and the point that needs to be made. Tone is the manner in which the attitude is expressed. Even with negative newsletters, goodwill is desired. Therefore, the majority of writing has the tone of goodwill, considerateness, friendliness, and being objective and personal.

6. *Editing for Organization:* Before checking to see whether a written document is organized, the copy editor must be organized. The topic should be well understood, the purpose of the document should be well understood, the approach used should be identified, and an outline should be followed while reading the material. All written documents should be clearly written and logical.

   a. *Communication between writer and copy editor:* Open communication between the writer and copy editor is very important. The communication needs to be explained clearly. This requires that either the writer or the copy editor be a listener while the other one is speaking. This dialogue will help in making sure that the topic and purpose of the document is well understood.

   b. *Approach used:* The copy editor needs to know whether the document was written in the direct approach (sometimes referred to as the *deductive approach*) or the indirect approach (sometimes referred to as the *inductive approach*). Letters, memoranda, and short reports can use either approach, depending on the content of the document and the anticipated reaction by the reader.

      (1) *Direct approach:* This approach explains the main point immediately and then presents the facts to support the main point.

         (a) *Good news:* The direct approach is used when the material conveys good news.

         (b) *Analytical reports:* Analytical reports follow the direct approach. With an analytical report, it is important to establish goals. These goals include a statement of the problem and the purpose of the report, which are included at the beginning of the report under the subheadings, *Statement of the Problem* and *Purpose.*

      (2) *Indirect approach:* This approach gives the facts before the whole picture is presented. This approach is followed when it is believed that the reader needs supporting evidence so the main point will be viewed with an open mind.

         (a) *Negative news:* Material that conveys negative news should follow the indirect approach.

         (b) *Persuasive writing:* When the material in the document needs to overcome feelings by the reader, the indirect approach should be used.

   c. *Outline:* The outline used by the writer for organizing his or her thoughts can also be used by the copy editor. However, some writers prefer that the communication between the writer and the copy editor be used by the copy editor to develop an outline to follow for editing. This method allows for a possible different approach to the subject. Utilizing this method typically requires more time. If the copy editor approaches the topic differently, the writer and editor will need time to work out these differences.

7. *Editing for Completeness and Content Accuracy:* There are four basic rules of copyediting that an administrative assistant or secretary must keep in mind when editing for completeness and content accuracy: look it up, check and double-check, be consistent, and maintain the author's writing style.

   a. *Looking it up:* When in doubt, look up the punctuation rule, the correct spelling, or the grammar rule. Reference manuals are the secretary's "right hand" and should be used without hesitation while copyediting.

    b. *Checking and double-checking:* Checking and double-checking means being inquisitive as well as discriminating. The secretary editing the material can never assume that the facts and/or structure are correct. The copy editor's job is to check everything for accuracy. An executive secretary will not remain in that position for long if the excuse "Well, that's exactly what you wrote" is used.

    EXAMPLES:

    When a document indicates facts and figures, check that these figures are correct.

    If a word seems to be incorrectly used, question its use.

    When a specific reference does not seem accurate, check the original source.

    c. *Being consistent:* It is obvious that excellent grammar and punctuation skills will be important for copyediting. However, these skills must be matched with the skill of being observant. A copy editor must be observant of inconsistencies such as the following:

        (1) Transposition of letters and/or words

        (2) Information that is left out of the copy

        (3) Incomplete sentences in the document

        (4) Repetitive use of information

    EXAMPLE:

    When reference is made to a conference in Dallas on the first page of a report and later Houston is mentioned as the conference site, this discrepancy must be detected by the copy editor.

    d. *Maintaining the author's writing style:* The document is the writer's, and the writing style of the writer must be maintained. This skill develops as the writer and copy editor work together over a period of time. However, it can be developed more quickly if an effort is made to identify the writing characteristics peculiar to the writer. Of course, this does not mean that a copy editor should allow incorrect writing habits to continue. A tactful conference between the writer and copy editor can help identify those writing characteristics that the writer will want unhesitatingly changed. There may be certain characteristics that the author may not allow to be changed; these writing characteristics are to remain in the material as the author's style.

8. *Copyediting Style Sheet:* The saying "practice makes perfect" is apropos the development of copyediting skills. When a long document must be edited, a style sheet is a very helpful tool. The function of the style sheet is to assist the copy editor in remembering all the formatting points the author expects to be followed as well as all the editing decisions made while reading the material. The style sheet helps the copy editor maintain consistency throughout the document. The headings of a style sheet will vary to meet individual needs. The style sheet illustrated in Figure 17–2 was developed by an executive secretary to meet the needs of the human resources department within a manufacturing organization. Figure 17–3 illustrates how the style sheet is used.

9. *Copyediting Symbols:* To make copyediting easier, the symbols illustrated in Figure 17–1 are used. When copyediting, these symbols are made within the body of the document. It is helpful when these editing symbols are written with a colored pencil so

SPELLING	PUNCTUATION	REFERENCES	FORMAT NOTATIONS		OTHER NOTATIONS
NUMBERS	CAPITALIZATION	FACTS			

Figure 17–2
Editing Style Sheet

SPELLING	PUNCTUATION	REFERENCES	FORMAT NOTATIONS		OTHER NOTATIONS
			Enumerations		Magazines
① *percent*	① *Comma before and in series*	① *Robert W. Bly* <u>*101 Ways to Make Every Second Count*</u> *(Career Press, 1999)*	*Bold*		*Italics*
② *time-consuming search*	② *Style for dash:* *...resource— your time— conflict is...*	② *Excerpt in* <u>*OfficePro,*</u> *January 2000, pp.10–15.* *"Time on Your Side"*	*Example:* *1. Carry a pocket to-do list...*		*Business Marketing Intercom*
③ *boilerplate*					
NUMBERS	CAPITALIZATION	FACTS			Books
① *16 hours*	① *Web sites*	*Internet survey: disorganized executives waste an hour a day. (Business Marketing March 1997)*			*Italics*
② *April 14*	② *PC*				*How I Raised Myself from Failure to Succeed in Selling*
③ *90 percent*					

Figure 17–3
Editing Style Sheet Used by an Executive Secretary

that they stand out from the black type. Also, the symbol must be written clearly. This aids the author when the material is reread for verification as well as the executive secretary when the material is being typed in final form.

10. *Word Processing and Copyediting:* With current advancements in office technology, word processing software has become a time-saving editing tool. When the executive makes revisions on the first draft, neither the executive nor the secretary need hesitate in making revisions. With the text stored on magnetic media, it is a simple matter to

change the order of the material, reword sentences, insert new text, or delete text not needed.

a. *Using a word processing package:* Many documents dictated by the executive will be typed in document form the first time. If word processing is used, the secretary can proceed with the keying and editing of the document directly on the computer screen, storing of the document on disk, and then printing the document. When editing, deleted or added words sometimes need to be highlighted so that the executive recognizes the major changes that were made by an administrative assistant. This method is often used when legal documents or minutes of meetings have been corrected. Two ways of highlighting deleted or added words are *strike-through* and *shading.*

(1) *Strike-through:* The strike-through is used to highlight words that have been deleted from a document. By invoking the command in word processing, a line is drawn through each letter typed. If the word has already been keyed, the strike-through can be added by highlighting the word(s) and then invoking the strike-through command.

EXAMPLE: ~~Strike-through~~

(2) *Shading:* Through shading, any new words or sections that have been added to the document are easily highlighted. If the section has already been keyed, shading can be added to highlighting the section and invoking the shading command.

EXAMPLE: SHADING

Later revisions will be an easy matter because the text can be stored on disk. Final document format codes should be inserted after all editing is complete and the document is ready for printing.

b. *Using a typewriter:* If a standard typewriter (with or without correction devices) is used, the secretary should read the dictated notes completely prior to typing to be sure that all necessary changes will be made while typing. Reading through the author's input (whether in handwriting, in shorthand from oral dictation, or recorded on a dictation unit) should guarantee a more accurate copy, thus saving time in the long run.

Review Questions

Directions: Select the best answer from the four alternatives. Write your answer in the blank to the left of the number.

_____
1. When proofreading a soft-copy document by reading a hard copy, proofreading marks should be

   a. made with colored pen within the text so that the changes are easily distinguishable.
   b. made with light pencil marks within the body of the document.
   c. made with light pencil marks within the margins of the document.
   d. recorded on a separate sheet of paper.

_____
2. When proofreading,

   a. check tables by reading vertically if the material was typed horizontally or vice versa.
   b. do so immediately while the content is fresh in the typist's mind.
   c. page a screen at a time on soft copy to make sure material is not skipped.
   d. read slowly for content while checking for typographical errors.

_____
3. Proofreading software for computer systems

   a. is not reliable although the software has been refined over the past several years.
   b. corrects all misspelled words, relieving the proofreader of this responsibility.
   c. highlights all words that do not match the spell-check dictionary; the user (proofreader) verifies and corrects spelling.
   d. will not prompt the user (proofreader) when the word is spelled _here_ and it should have been _hear._

_____
4. Secretaries who are rushed <u>make mistakes.</u> The underlined words are the sentence's

   a. action verb (make) and direct object (mistakes).
   b. indirect object of <u>who are rushed</u>.
   c. modifiers of <u>who are rushed</u>.
   d. verb.

_____
5. _Maxwell is in executive session; she should be available at 4 P.M._ This sentence consists of

   a. one dependent clause and one independent clause.
   b. two dependent clauses, no conjunction.
   c. two independent clauses, no conjunction.
   d. two independent clauses, connected with a conjunction.

6. Which sentence is written and punctuated correctly?

    a. Harris' order only included hanging folders, labels and paper.
    b. Since the meeting begins at two, meet me at 1:30 pm to review the agenda.
    c. The desk should be at least 2 ½′ by 5′.
    d. This local womens' organization meets the first Thursday evening of every month at 7:30 pm.

7. Which sentence is punctuated correctly?

    a. Dr. Jones is pleased with the conference. (She called from Boston.)
    b. Mr. Paris article *Management for the 21st Century* covers the importance of the administrative secretary.
    c. We need to finish these projects today; minutes of yesterdays board meeting, monthly stock report, the presentation for Mark's retirement dinner, and the Jagger Yancy report.
    d. The next conference is in California, I need plane reservations because its a fast convenient way for me to travel.

8. Which of the following correctly illustrates a paragraph heading?

    a. Multiple selection criteria Logical operators know that . . .
    b. *Multiple selection criteria*. Logical operators know that . . .
    c. Multiple selection criteria. Logical operators know that . . .
    d. *Multiple selection criteria*.—Logical operators know that . . .

9. Which one of the following sentences shows correct capitalization of words?

    a. Charlotte is taking a course in management information systems from a University in West Texas.
    b. The League of Women Voters is holding an open forum at the Newburg Public Library to discuss the state mandates with Senator Lewis.
    c. The Mayor has an editorial about last week's article "City services will be cut."
    d. One hundred fifty Senior Citizens attended the first meeting on Wednesday, the 6th of June.

10. A neat, attractive appearance of a document

    a. deals with selecting one of the more common letter styles: block, modified block, or simplified.
    b. means proper spacing and formatting; having few and neat corrections; having clear, dark print; and using nonglossy paper.
    c. is important for all documents except rough-draft copies.
    d. is important for external documents but requires minimum attention for internal documents.

11. Which correction procedure is most appropriate in today's automated office?

    a. correct the soft copy and save both versions for future reference.
    b. produce an accurate original by rekeying the document if necessary.

    c. use correction fluid or tape, correct the original, send a copy to the recipient, and keep the original as a file copy.

    d. use a combination of drafting eraser, gummed cleaner, and typing eraser.

12. Which correction technique is *not* acceptable?

    a. Apple, Inc.'s letterhead is on buff paper. In proofreading the letter, Peterson used yellow chalk to camouflage a correction.

    b. In using the electronic typewriter, Meyers realized that an *f* camouflages an *i*. Meyers corrected the word *iig* (correct spelling *fig*) with a strikeover—*f* over the first *i*.

    c. Mayfield had to use the electric typewriter and needed to erase the word *by.* He gently used horizontal and vertical strokes with the eraser.

    d. Stevens is preparing a document for photocopying. She deleted a statement with correction fluid.

13. When preparing documents, consistency is important to

    a. format and word usage.

    b. format, punctuation, and word usage.

    c. punctuation, word usage, and tone.

    d. punctuation, word usage, tone, and format.

14. Proofread the following sentences. Which one has no misspelled words?

    a. The lessees were upset with the change in their agreement.

    b. To acheive her goal, Maxwell definitely had to take the CPS® examination.

    c. To procede, we need to have the document displayed on the extranet.

    d. Yesterday's artical reported that 500 turkeys were ordered for the holiday charity!

15. When typing numbers,

    a. always use the fraction key when available; type other fractions by using the slash.

    b. be consistent; figures should be used for all numbers when several sets of numbers are within the same sentence.

    c. express a percentage as: 23%.

    d. numbers under 10 should be in figures.

16. Proofread the following sentences. Which one is correct?

    a. Twenty-five members attended the 4th of July picnic.

    b. We were surprised when the part cost only 75¢.

    c. When Grandpa was 69, he started writing chapter one of his book.

    d. 1,500 patients received the vaccination today!

17. Proofread the following sentences. Which one is correct?

    a. The meeting is scheduled for June 5th at 2:00 p.m.

    b. The 1st letter referred to policy number 378,469,201.

    c. Their new address is Suite 3, East Sixth Avenue, EauClaire, WI 54701-1732.

    d. There should be 30 5-pound boxes of candy.

_____ **18.** When dividing a word,

   a. it is best to have enough of the word on the first line to be able to conceptualize the entire word.
   b. make sure the pronunciation of a proper name is followed.
   c. the last word on a page should contain most of the letters so the word is easily conceptualized without having to turn the page.
   d. the previous line cannot also end with a divided word.

_____ **19.** Which word is divided correctly?

   a. beginn- ing
   b. grandfa- ther
   c. self-ad- dressed
   d. sepa- rate

_____ **20.** Which word or phrase is divided correctly?

   a. Mr. John R.   David
   b. page   105
   c. should-   n't
   d. $132,   000

_____ **21.** Which statement is correct with regard to hyphenation with word processing?

   a. The automatic hyphenation feature prompts the user to determine whether the word should be hyphenated.
   b. The automatic hyphenation feature hyphenates the word according to hyphenation rules established within the word processing software.
   c. The manual hyphenation feature provides the least amount of flexibility in following hyphenation rules as accepted by most businesses.
   d. The word processing feature relieves the office professional from having to know business word division rules.

_____ **22.** Editing is

   a. checking the final copy for spelling and punctuation accuracy.
   b. checking the document for keying accuracy.
   c. correcting the format of the document.
   d. revising a draft for consistency, conciseness, and grammatical accuracy.

_____ **23.** Guidelines for preparing a document in draft format to be copyedited include

   a. wide margins, single spacing with double-spacing between paragraphs, and readable copy including format codes.
   b. wide margins, double spacing with triple-spacing between paragraphs or indented paragraphs, and readable copy including format codes.
   c. wide margins, double spacing with triple-spacing between paragraphs or indented paragraphs, and readable copy.
   d. wide margins, triple spacing, and readable copy.

_____ **24.** When editing, the purpose is a well-written document that

    a. adheres to correct document format.
    b. adheres to correct grammar and punctuation rules.
    c. adjusts the writing style from an editor's perspective.
    d. is clear, concise, and appeals to the reader while maintaining the writer's objective.

_____ **25.** Proofread the following sentences. Which sentence is correct?

    a. Did you complement Adamski on her new proposal?
    b. The president excepts your recommendation; he wants you to review details with him on Monday.
    c. It's really a matter of principle; I cannot support the recommendation.
    d. Poor communication causes problems between the 5 major divisions.

_____ **26.** Proofread the following sentences. Which example is correct?

    a. A very complete report.
    b. The fiscal year ends next week. Therefore, can we meet the following week?
    c. The meeting is Wednesday. The meeting on reorganizing.
    d. The new assistant starts next month and with Sam gone we need your assistance in welcoming her to our Department.

_____ **27.** A copyediting style sheet

    a. is helpful in maintaining the editor's writing style.
    b. is a useful tool and should be used when any document is edited.
    c. is a useful tool for maintaining consistency when editing long documents.
    d. should have only three areas of concentration for comments.

_____ **28.** When using word processing software, words added to the document during editing should be highlighted by

    a. bolding the word.
    b. shading the word.
    c. underlining the word.
    d. using the strike-through command.

Solutions

Answer   *Refer to:*

1. (a)   [A]

2. (a)   [A-2-c]

3. (c)   [A-4-a]

4. (a)   [B-1-a(3)]

5. (c)   [B-1-b(2)]

6. (a)   [B-2-a(1)(a), B-2-c(2)]

7. (a)   [B-2-h(4)]

8. (b)   [B-2-i(7), B-2-m(3)]

9. (b)   [B-3-e, B-3-i, B-3-j]

10. (b)   [B-4-b]

11. (c)   [B-4-b(2)(a)]

12. (c)   [B-4-b(2)(d)]

13. (d)   [B-5]

14. (a)   [B-6-e]

15. (b)   [B-7-c]

16. (a)   [B-7-g, B-7-h, B-7-j]

17. (c)   [B-7-p, B-7-r]

18. (a)   [B-8-a(2)]

19. (d)   [B-8-b(6)]

20. (a)   [B-8-b(15)]

21. (b)   [B-8-c]

22. (d)   [C]

23. (a)   [C-1]

24. (d)   [C-2-d]

25. (c)   [C-3-n]

26. (b)   [C-4-a, C-4-b]

27. (c)   [C-8]

28. (b)   [C-10-a]

CHAPTER 18

Abstracting Written Communications

OVERVIEW

The ability to summarize articles, reports, books, or letters accurately and concisely is an invaluable skill. Most executives receive volumes of material that must be read. As an executive and secretary team moves up within an organization, more and more material must be absorbed. Yet there are still only 24 hours in a day. Therefore, an administrative assistant who is able to summarize material for executives and managers possesses a special skill. Like all skills, summarizing material requires practice. In this chapter, a distinction is made between preparing an abstract or précis and annotating.

KEY TERMS

Abstract   Précis

A. Techniques for Abstracting

Material can be summarized in several different ways. Many times, all that is necessary is photocopying sections of material or highlighting key points. However, an executive secretary must also be able to prepare an abstract or précis of key points or be able to use computerized searches.

1. *Photocopying:* With the sophisticated copying equipment in offices, sections of material can easily be copied for reference and later use. Often, it will be the secretary's responsibility to identify material important for the executive and to take the initiative for copying the material. Also, the executive will identify material that needs to be photocopied.

   a. *Efficient use of the copier:* The copier can be housed in the reprographics department, where it is operated by the reprographics staff, or it can be located where it is available for all office staff to use. Some cases may require the use of copying services from external organizations.

      (1) *Use by all staff:* Often, a copier is made available for all office personnel, even though there is an in-house reprographics department. When a decentralized copier is available to be used at one's discretion, it is important to schedule the time. Scheduling eliminates unnecessary trips to the copier and saves time. Efficient use of a decentralized copier involves organizing material and scheduling times for copying.

         (a) *Organizing material:* Accumulate the material that needs to be copied in one place.

(b) *Scheduling photocopying:* Schedule one or two times during the day to use the copier. The amount of times scheduled will depend on your photocopying work load. One situation a secretary will want to avoid is scheduling only one or two times during the day and spending 15 minutes or more at the machine because of the volume that needs to be copied. With massive volumes, twice in the morning and twice in the afternoon may be necessary. A typical schedule would include one time in the morning and one time in the afternoon.

(2) *Centralized or external use:* If material to be copied must be sent to a centralized department or out of house, turnaround time must be taken into consideration. Usually, a copy request form must be completed that will allow you to indicate the date needed as well as any special instructions. Figure 18–1 shows an example of a service/copy request form. The secretary must make sure that all material sent is returned and that the copy request was completed accurately.

(a) *Logging requests:* To make sure that all materials sent to be copied are returned, requests should be logged. When the material is returned, a notation should be made on the log. Illustrated in Figure 18–2 is a photocopying request log.

(b) *Completing the request form:* It is important that all information required to do the photocopying is stated on the request form.

- Date of request

- Page numbers to be copied

- Collating and stapling requirements

- Date needed

- Special requirements

(c) *Turnaround time:* Because the material needs to be sent to a department or out of the organization, the turnaround time needs to be considered, along with the volume of photocopying normally done by the reprographics service. A secretary must plan ahead to make sure that the material is returned by the time it is needed. If it is a rush item, many departments can handle these requests if they are infrequent. Sometimes, a rush item may have to be delivered to the photocopying service area in order for it to be completed on time.

b. *Legal use of the copier:* The author of any document has spent time researching, composing, and editing the written word. For this reason, copyright laws have been established for the protection of authors and publishers. *Fair uses* of copyrighted work provide exceptions to the copyright holder's exclusive right to the work. Fair uses include the following:

(1) Making one copy for the purpose of studying and highlighting the material.

(2) Using the copyright material for one-time use in a classroom training situation. This is permissible if the work is short and it would be impractical to obtain the consent of the author or publisher prior to the training session.

Figure 18–1   Service/Copy Request Form

INFORMATION SYSTEMS & COMMUNICATION SERVICES
SERVICE/COPY REQUEST FORM

Name of Staff Member _____   Phone No. _____

Contact Person (if different) _____   Phone No. _____

Department _____   Date Received _____   Date Needed _____

Job Type:

_____ Database (<500) (7 work days)   _____ Manuscript (5 work days)

_____ Database (>500) (14 work days)   _____ Scanning (3 work days)

_____ Digital Camera (7 work days)   _____ Web Development (1 month)

_____ Mail-Merge/<500 (7 work days)   _____ Web Revisions (3–5 work days)

_____ Mail-Merge/>500 (14 work days)   _____ Other (with approval)* _____

_____ Graphics (5–7 work days)   _____

Special Instructions: (Please be specific) _____

No. of copies _____   No. of forms _____   Pages _____

Color of paper _____   Collating _____   Stapling _____

TO BE COMPLETED BY INFORMATION SYSTEMS & COMMUNICATION STAFF:

Completed by: _____   on _____

Assistance from: _____

_____   Job # _____

Notified _____ of completion of job on _____

Picked up by: _____ on _____

Figure 18–2   A Photocopying Request Log

DESCRIPTION OF ITEM	NUMBER OF COPIES	DATE SENT	EXPECTED RETURN	RETURNED

The companion volume, *Finance and Business Law,* contains more complete coverage of copyrights in Chapter 26, Section E.

2. *Highlighting Key Points:* Highlighting key points is an effective and efficient means of emphasizing important information within a document. Sometimes, the secretary can do this on the original, but usually highlighting is done on a copy so that the original is unaltered. Highlighting should be done by underlining or overmarking with a bright-colored marker, pen, or pencil.

   a. *Underlining:* Some executives prefer a thin line underneath the key information. This can easily be accomplished with a fine-pointed marker, a pen, or a pencil. Whichever is used should be in a color other than blue or black. A ruler should be used so the underline is straight.

   EXAMPLE:

   The <u>most common source</u> of information for business reports is information obtained from <u>observations.</u>

   b. *Overmarking:* Some executives prefer a wide mark drawn over the key points. A wide-end, light-colored marker and a ruler are the best tools for this method.

   EXAMPLE:

   The first source for help in library research is the research librarian.

   c. *Colored marker, pen, or pencil:* With highlighting, it is important to use a colored writing instrument other than the typical colors of blue and black.

      (1) *Underlining:* When underlining, a bright, dark color should be used. Good underlining colors are red or green.

      (2) *Overmarking:* When overmarking, a bright, pale color should be used. Good overmarking colors are light blue, pink, yellow, or orange.

      (3) *Color coding:* Through the use of several colors, the material highlighted can also be organized by color code.

3. *Summarizing Key Points:* The task of summarizing is referred to as an abstract or a précis. An abstract or a précis is a concise summary of all key points. Some executives will only require that abstracts be prepared, others will require only précis, and others will require both.

   a. *Abstract:* Many summaries are condensations of the original material so that the executive does not have so much to read. Such a summary is referred to as an *abstract.* An abstract contains key points of the original, usually in the exact wording of the original.

      (1) *Length:* Depending on the depth of the information contained in the original, an abstract can be from one-fourth to one-half the length of the original.

      (2) *Format:* Two formats can be used for presenting an abstract: paragraph format or outline format.

   b. *Précis:* The summary is often used to develop lectures or reports. In this case, it is important that the material paraphrase the original. A précis is a summary of material in your own words.

      (1) *Length:* A précis is usually one-third the length of the original.

      (2) *Format:* A précis is typed in paragraph format.

4. *Computerized Searches:* Computerized searches provide information on many topics. Some services are totally dedicated to one topic (e.g., law, medicine, political data). The advent of the Internet and World Wide Web connectivity has brought locating information globally to the office desktop.

    a. *Commercial database services:* Commercial database services are collections of articles, abstracts, and bibliographic citations from books, periodicals, reports, and theses. Several popular commercial database services are Bibliographic Retrieval System (BRS), News Net, and Dialog.

        (1) *Subscription:* To search the database information electronically, one must subscribe to the computerized service. Subscribers are then provided with database access codes. Database search commands (words or phrases) are used for the information retrieval process. The subscriber is charged for database search time as well as the electronic transmission of the information. Charges are usually higher for daytime access than evening or weekend access.

        (2) *Database search:* A good way to begin a search is with general terms or topics. Using the search commands, the topic is narrowed to more specific, pertinent information. Moving from the general to the specific provides a broader search of the database. Usually, topics are previewed and narrowed to eliminate those not needed before sending the information.

    b. *Internet searches:* With more than one billion Web pages currently on the World Wide Web, business professionals use search engines or Web directories to assist with their searches. The first step in the process, however, is to have a clear understanding of the topic to be searched. One way to approach an Internet search is to classify it as either specific or open ended.

        (1) *Specific topic:* When you can use a word or phrase to identify your output, you will conduct a specific search. This type of search requires you to narrow the search to the answer you seek.

            (a) *Broad category:* Start with the broad word or phrase of your topic.

            (b) *Focused questions:* Sequentially, narrow your questions based on information received until the specific answer appears.

        (2) *Open-ended topic:* Another type of search is more exploratory in nature; you are not sure where the search will lead you since you are just beginning to gather information on the topic and have little base knowledge. With an open-ended search, you begin with general questions in order to determine which direction to proceed.

            (a) *General question:* To start an open-ended search, you know the big picture but are not sure what specific subcategory you should concentrate on.

            (b) *Specific topic:* The open-ended search should help you narrow your topic to a specific subarea. Once you have a more specific topic, you then continue your search following the suggestions for a specific topic.

        (3) *Web search tools:* To conduct a Web search, Internet users typically use either a search engine or a Web directory.

            (a) *Search engine:* A search engine is a Web tool for locating other Web sites or information on the Internet. You enter the query (word or phrase you wish to search) on the search engine Web page. On the computer screen, the search engine displays the results that match your query. These results provide further search directions or the specific answer you are seeking. Typical search engines are AltaVista, HotBot, and InfoSeek.

A meta-search engine combines the power of multiple search engines. Dogpile is a popular meta-search engine.

(b) *Web directory:* Experts have developed Web sites that list Web pages that they determine to be appropriate for specific categories. Yahoo is a Web directory site. When you are sure of the category you wish to search, a Web directory may be the place to start. Typical categories include the following:

Arts and Humanities

Business and Economy

Computers and Internet

Education

Entertainment

Government

Health

News and Media

Recreation and Sports

Reference

Religion

Science

Society and Culture

B. Effective Abstracts and Précis

An abstract or a précis is a concise summary of all key points. Whether an abstract or a précis is needed, all relevant information must be included, major conclusions must be mentioned, the original must be documented, the language must be consistent with the original, and the format must be easy to read.

1. *Concise Summary of Key Points:* The length of the summary will depend on the depth of the material in the original. It must be kept in mind, however, that the purpose of an abstract or précis is to summarize the key points of the original so that time is saved for the executive when reading the material.

    a. *Abstract:* An abstract can be from one-fourth to one-half the length of the original material.

    b. *Précis:* A précis is usually one-third the length of the original. In writing a précis, the original material is recomposed, omitting illustrations, amplifications, or flowery language.

2. *Relevant Information:* Since the purpose of the abstract is to condense the original so that more material can be read in the same amount of time, it is not necessary for the secretary to spend time rewording the material. With a précis, time will be spent on recomposing the original while maintaining the author's point of view, writing style, and tone without using the author's exact words or phrases.

Both an abstract and a précis must include the key points of the original. There are four writing characteristics that can be used as flags to identify key points:

   a. *Facts:* The easiest to identify are facts. Facts are usually represented in figure format. This information clearly stands out from the written word. The secretary must make sure that only relevant facts are contained in the abstract or précis and that the summary includes other key points from the original.

   b. *Listings:* Many authors list important points as 1, 2, 3, and so on. Another listing technique is to make a point without any listing notation and follow up with the word *second* when the author is making a succeeding point. The word *second* would be a flag that a point has previously been made and that there may be more to follow. The word *last* is often used to indicate a concluding point.

   c. *Headings:* Headings throughout the material should be followed for the summary. Headings are usually flags for key points to be discussed. At the end of the material within the heading, there usually will be summary statements.

   d. *Topic sentences:* Sometimes, a new paragraph is a continuation of the previous paragraph, including new thoughts. When a completely new idea or concept is introduced, the paragraph normally begins with a topic sentence. This sentence can be used to identify a key point. Many paragraphs end with a summary statement, or the paragraph itself is a summary of a section.

3. *Reporting Major Conclusions:* Many authors conclude their writing with a summary statement, paragraph, or section. To understand the gist of the material, read the concluding summary material first. For a book, the preface should be read first.

Understanding the concluding remarks will help the secretary locate key points within the document. Also, these concluding points should be part of the abstract or précis.

4. *Complete Documentation:* Credit must be given to the original author; therefore, it is important to include all bibliographical information on the photocopy, abstract, or précis.

   a. *Bibliographical information:* The bibliographical information includes the following:

   (1) Title of the publication (report, book, magazine, or journal)

   (2) Name(s) of author(s)

   (3) Volume number, issue number, and page number(s)

   (4) Title of article in magazine, journal, or periodical

   (5) Date of publication

   (6) Name of publisher and location

   (7) Type of on-line source (electronic reference)

   (8) Web address (electronic reference)

   (9) Retrieval or access date (electronic reference)

   b. *Placement of bibliographical information:* Exactly where to include the bibliographical information can vary. The executive and secretary should identify the format preferred and follow that format for all documentation.

   (1) *Photocopies:* On photocopies, the information can be included on either the front of the first page or the back of the last page. Sometimes, the information is included on the back of the first page or the bottom (at the end) of the last page.

(2) *Abstract and précis:* The abstract and précis will contain source title, author, and title of the article in the main heading of the summary. Page numbers will be included within the abstract as needed. Other bibliographical information may be included in the main heading or at the end of the summary in footnote format.

5. *Level of Language Consistent with Original:* When summarizing the material, it is important to maintain the tone and thought of the author. Even when preparing an abstract, the thought can be altered completely by leaving out a word, punctuation mark, or key point. Also, even though a précis is recomposing the original material, it is important to maintain the author's point of view.

Following guidelines for writing an abstract or précis will help maintain consistent language with the original.

a. *Summaries within original:* Read any summary sections or paragraphs first. This helps establish the general idea of the document.

b. *First reading:* Quickly read the entire material; do not take notes. If the material is lengthy, quickly read the first major division. This also helps establish the general idea.

c. *Second reading:* With the second reading, look up unfamiliar words or references to unfamiliar material. With the unfamiliar clarified, you are better able to understand the material and will more accurately note only the important ideas. Following this procedure will help distinguish amplifications from key points.

d. *Taking notes:* With the third reading, you are ready to take notes. Record only the important ideas and facts using the guidelines presented in Section B-2. If you are writing a précis, use your notes to summarize the material in your own words.

e. *Rough copy:* Type the summarized notes in rough-draft format. Remember, the purpose of an abstract or précis is to be concise yet clear!

f. *Edit:* Compare the abstract or précis with the original for accuracy. Edit the summary by eliminating unnecessary words and making sure that the wording is clear.

g. *Final copy:* Type the abstract or précis in an easy-to-read format.

6. *Easy-to-Read Format:* An abstract is prepared in either an outline format or a paragraph format. Précis are typically prepared only in a paragraph format.

a. *Abstract format:* An abstract can be prepared in outline format or in paragraph format. The decision as to whether the format should be in paragraph or outline form will depend on the executive's preference. If there is no preference, then the format is left to the secretary's discretion. Choose the format that you consider easiest to follow and most appropriate for the material.

b. *Précis format:* A précis should be typed in paragraph form.

An example of an abstract in outline form is illustrated in Figure 18–3. Figure 18–4 illustrates a précis of the same article.

7. *Distinguishing Abstracts from Précis:* For the secretary who needs to prepare both abstracts and précis, it will be important to indicate when the summary is an abstract and when it is a précis. This is necessary for the executive in order to determine how the information might be used in a letter, a speech, or a report. Also, it is important

when the secretary retrieves the summary from the file several months later; the code will help both the secretary and the executive remember whether the material is a direct quote or a paraphrase.

Usually a capital *P* in parentheses or circled identifies the material as a précis; a capital *A* is used for an abstract. This code can be recorded on the front of the first page, top, right corner or on the back of the last page, top, right corner. Or possibly the executive and secretary will identify a different location or code. Whatever is decided on, however, should be consistently followed for all abstracts and précis.

8. *Using the Abstract or Précis:* In using the material for speeches, training sessions, or other writing, the executive would be plagiarizing if credit was not given to the original author. Bibliographical information can be provided in a footnote, or reference to the author and source can be incorporated in the body of the material.

When the material is a direct quote (verbatim) in an abstract, quotation marks are required around the material. When the material is paraphrased in a précis, quotation marks are not required around the material. In both cases, the original author must receive credit for the material.

Figure 18–3   Abstract in Outline Form

AUTHOR: Norma Carr-Ruffino
TITLE: "New Millennium Career Armor"
SOURCE: *OfficePro,* January 2000, Volume 60, Number 1, pp. 16–21

I.   INTRODUCTION—GOALS FOR THE NEW MILLENNIUM
   A. Personal and Leadership Skills
   B. Successful Careers
   C. Balanced Life

II. DEVELOPING HIGH-TECH AND HIGH-TOUCH SKILLS
   A. People Skills (High-Touch)
      1. Demonstrating empathy and sensitivity
      2. Empowering others
      3. Sharing and participating
      4. Enabling and assisting
   B. Traits/Skills Matched to Corporate Culture
   C. High-Tech Skills
      1. Recognizing paradigm patterns
      2. Surviving technological shifts
         a. Digital and microprocessor technology
         b. Internet and Web technology
         c. Smart information appliances and multimedia applications
         d. Object-oriented software
         e. Virtual cyberspace environments

III. GAINING CREDIBILITY AND POWER
   A. Self-Limiting Beliefs and Gender Stereotypes
      1. Becoming aware of self-limiting beliefs
      2. Developing self-empowering alternatives
         a. Understanding corporate cultures
         b. Identifying power lines
         c. Finding potential career paths
         d. Expanding job responsibilities
         e. Identifying fast-track jobs and qualifications
   B. Sexuality Issues
   C. Lines of Power in Organizations
   D. Comfort in Using Power

IV. BUILDING A POWER BASE
   A. Networking in Organization, Industry, or Field
   B. GapS Between Male-Female Views and Communication Styles
      1. Being aware of differing views in workplace
         a. Motivations, behaviors, and communication
      b. Advantages of women's ways of leading

V.   CREATING OWN SUCCESS
   A. Passion and Life Purpose
      1. Identifying skills and interests
      2. Recognizing patterns in personal preferences, skills, motives, and behaviors
      3. Developing clearly stated goals
      4. Balancing career and personal goals
      5. Planning activities for reaching goals
   B. Inner Leadership Tools
      1. Entering state of relaxed focus
      2. Envisioning what you want to create
      3. Letting go of need to control situations and people

VI. NEGOTIATING WIN-WIN RESULTS
   A. Preparing for Negotiation
      1. Taking broad view of situation
      2. Determining what you want and what you think others want
      3. Assessing chances of reaching a win-win agreement
      4. Identifying best alternative for yourself

   B. Negotiating Creatively with Tradeoffs
      1. Building trust
      2. Sharing information
      3. Asking questions to fill information gaps
      4. Getting issues on the table to consider tradeoffs

Figure 18–3 Abstract in Outline Form (*continued*)

      5. Framing options
      6. Moving toward closure
    C. Considering Other Skills
      1. Thinking in terms of win-win outcomes
      2. Letting both sides air views
      3. Helping people find root cause of problems
      4. Identifying resolution strategies
      5. Reaching resolution

  VII. MANAGING MULTIPLE PRIORITIES
    A. Time Management
      1. Activities
      2. Attitudes
    B. Evolving Ways of Doing Business
      1. Coordinating and organizing communication
      2. Upgrading office tasks
      3. Handling administrative, managerial, technical, or professional work
      4. Conferencing through computer networks

 VIII. MANAGING STRESS
    A. Support Networks for Assistance
    B. Prevention of Stress Buildup
      1. Identifying typical stressors
      2. Taking responsibility for own health
        a. Managing diet and exercise regimen
        b. Managing work and home environments
      3. Commanding inner resources to release stress

  IX. CHANNELING EMOTIONAL POWER
    A. Potential Blocks to Career Progress
    B. Differences Between Male and Female Emotional Patterns
      1. Uncovering root fears that underlie feelings
      2. Experiencing range of feelings
      3. Recognizing thinking patterns
      4. Creating new responses to recurring stressful situations

   X. EMPOWERING WITH ASSERTIVE COMMUNICATION
    A. Developmet of Your Set of Rights
      1. Standing up for own rights
      2. Respecting others' rights
      3. Negotiating outcomes when conflict arises
    B. Mastering Range of Assertive Techniques
    C. Selection of Best Techniques for Situation

  XI. MANAGING DIFFICULT PEOPLE SITUATIONS
    A. People's Inability or Unwillingness to Act Assertively
      1. Aggressive actions that violate other people's rights
        a. Maintaining your own self-respect
        b. Maintaining respect for other person's rights
        c. Getting at root of the problem
        d. Working toward joint resolution
      2. Passive-aggressive actions that involve hidden agendas
        a. Discovering underlying problem(s)
        b. Leading other person toward discovery
        c. Discussing the problem
        d. Working toward joint resolution
      3. Passive actions of others
        a. Discovering what others are thinking
        b. Reaching resolution others can agree with
    B. Development of Powerful People Skills
      1. Learning more about yourself
      2. Leading others to deeper levels of self-awareness
    C. Techniques for Managing Difficult People Situations
      1. Being alert and perceptive to political games
      2. Looking for causes for people's actions
      3. Focusing on win-win solutions
      4. Focusing on asserting own rights while respecting others' rights
      5. Staying goal-oriented
      6. Using support networks

Figure 18–4   Précis in Paragraph Form

NEW MILLENNIUM CAREER ARMOUR[1]

The new millennium will offer new opportunities for secretaries and other administrative professionals to develop personal and leadership skills that will help them be successful in their careers. Office professionals today are very concerned about balancing their work with their family lives.

Carr-Ruffino identifies ten essential skills for the new millennium:

1. *Developing high-tech and high-touch skills:* People skills (high-touch skills) enable office professionals to demonstrate empathy and sensitivity toward others and to empower, share, participate, and assist other people in the workplace. Office professionals must learn to recognize paradigm shifts in order to survive changes being caused or affected by technology, such as the Internet and Web technology and multimedia applications.

2. *Gaining credibility and power:* Women especially need to become more aware of self-limiting beliefs and, instead, develop self-empowering alternatives. An understanding of corporate cultures and power lines within an organization will help office professionals be more aware of potential fast-track career paths.

3. *Building power base:* Networking within the organization, industry, or field is a necessity. The office professional needs to become more aware of differing male and female views within the workplace. Women can become leaders, too, through their innate abilities to nurture and communicate.

4. *Creating own success:* People must experience passion in their work as well as their family lives. Identifying skills and interests as well as developing personal and business goals will help determine life's purposes. The application of inner resources enables a broader vision of what is possible.

5. *Negotiating win-win results:* A broad view of the situation will lead toward alternatives that might best be considered. Sometimes, tradeoffs must be made in order to move toward closure. Other skills are sometimes extremely helpful: letting both sides air views, helping individuals find the root cause of problems, or identifying resolution strategies.

6. *Managing multiple priorities:* Time management also concerns activities and attitudes. New and creative ways of doing business are evolving. Office tasks are being upgraded, and techniques for handling other administrative or professional work are being devised.

7. *Managing stress:* Support networks are being established within business to assist with stress management. To prevent stress buildup, individuals must take responsibility for their own health by managing diet, exercise, or work/home environments.

8. *Channeling emotional power:* Expression of emotions can sometimes block career progress. Differences do exist between male and female emotional patterns. Men and women need to develop new responses to recurring stressful situations.

9. *Communicating assertively.* Not only is it important to stand up for your own rights; you need to respect others' rights as well. When conflict arises, outcomes sometimes need to be negotiated so that win-win situations occur.

10. *Managing difficult people situations:* A person's inability to act assertively is affected greatly by the aggressive, passive-aggressive, and passive actions of others. To develop powerful people skills, you need to learn more about yourself and others need to be led to their own deeper levels of self-awareness. Techniques for managing difficult people must be applied in all kinds of business situations.

Possession of these ten essential skills will enable office professionals to prepare for greater career success and promotion in the new millennium.

[1]Norma Carr-Ruffino, "New Millennium Career Armor," *OfficePro,* January 2000, Volume 60, Number 1, pp. 16–21.

Review Questions

Directions: Select the best answer from the four alternatives. Write your answer in the blank to the left of the number.

_____

1. When material needs to be sent to the reprographics department or out of house to be copied, it is important to keep a copy request log so that

    a. copy requests not returned can be tracked down.
    b. sufficient turnaround time is scheduled.
    c. the material sent for copying will be returned quickly.
    d. the reprographics department will know what to copy and how many copies to make.

_____

2. Fair use of copyrighted work

    a. allows a single copy to be made for the purpose of studying and highlighting material.
    b. allows continued copying as long as it is for classroom training situations.
    c. means that material cannot be copied.
    d. protects the author's exclusive right to the work.

_____

3. Using a wide-point marker to shade with a light color is

    a. annotating.
    b. color coding.
    c. overmarking.
    d. underlining.

_____

4. Underlining should be done with a

    a. bright, dark red or green thin marker.
    b. bright, pale pink or yellow wide marker.
    c. dark blue or black thin marker.
    d. dark red or purple wide marker.

_____

5. A paraphrased summary is a/an

    a. abstract.
    b. annotation.
    c. copy.
    d. précis.

_____   **6.** In conducting a computer search for summaries on a legal issue, begin the search

     a. by providing a list of generic key legal words and reviewing the material for similar cases.
     b. using one term that references the issue.
     c. with general terms pertaining to the issue, then narrow it down to specific information.
     d. with a specific case pertaining to the legal issue in order to cross-reference related cases.

_____   **7.** When conducting an Internet search by starting with a broad word or phrase related to the topic and sequentially narrowing and focusing questions, you are using the

     a. exploratory approach.
     b. general question approach.
     c. open-ended approach.
     d. specific-topic approach.

_____   **8.** In conducting an Internet search, a meta-search engine combines the power of multiple search engines. An example of a meta-search engine is

     a. AltaVista.
     b. Dogpile.
     c. InfoSeek.
     d. Yahoo.

_____   **9.** For conducting Internet searches, experts have developed sites that list Web pages that are appropriate to specific categories (arts, business, government, and so on). These Internet search sites are called

     a. meta-search engines.
     b. search engines.
     c. service providers.
     d. Web directories.

_____   **10.** When reading a document for the first time, key points can be identified by

     a. lists.
     b. statements written in the form of a question.
     c. subheadings.
     d. transition sentences.

_____   **11.** Bibliographical information for a précis should include

     a. title of the material, author, and publisher.
     b. title of the material, author, publication date, and publisher.
     c. title of the material, author, publication date, publisher, and page numbers.
     d. title of the material, author, publication date, publisher, page numbers, and editor.

_____ **12.** When typing a précis, the biographical information should

    a. be in footnote format at the end of the summary.
    b. be typed at the beginning just after the main heading.
    c. be in a consistent location as agreed on by the executive and the administrative assistant.
    d. include the source and article title/author in a main heading with all other information either in the main heading or at the end of the summary in footnote format.

_____ **13.** The level of the language of the summary

    a. can vary from the original when writing an abstract.
    b. will vary from the original when writing a précis because a précis is a paraphrased summary.
    c. needs to be consistent with the original on verbatim material only.
    d. should be consistent with the original.

_____ **14.** When using material from a précis for other writing,

    a. a bibliography is sufficient for credit to the original author.
    b. the executive should reword the précis material to avoid plagiarism.
    c. the original author does not have to be referenced since a précis is paraphrased.
    d. quotation marks should enclose the précis wording.

Solutions

Answer	Refer to:
1. (a)	[A-1-a(2)(a)]
2. (a)	[A-1-b]
3. (c)	[A-2-b]
4. (a)	[A-2-c(1)]
5. (d)	[A-3-b]
6. (c)	[A-4-b]
7. (d)	[A-4-b(1)]
8. (b)	[A-4-b(3)(a)]
9. (d)	[A-4-b(3)(b)]
10. (a)	[B-2-b]
11. (c)	[B-4-a]
12. (d)	[B-4-b(2)]
13. (d)	[B-5]
14. (a)	[B-8]

CHAPTER 19

Preparing Written Communications in Final Format

OVERVIEW

Document format is the key to the creation of an attractive, accurately prepared business paper. Such factors as vertical and horizontal placement; use of acceptable style; correct punctuation, capitalization, word usage, and word division; and acceptable correction techniques determine the usability of a particular document. Without proper application of all these factors, a typed document is unmailable or unusable. Therefore, attention to document formatting must receive high priority in preparing all printed business papers.

The first impression any document makes on the reader depends on the visual quality of the document. In the discussion of various document formats, appropriate horizontal and vertical placement for each format will be emphasized and examples shown to demonstrate how each format is used.

Office professionals must make many judgments with regard to document format in the course of the workday. The more the fundamental knowledges and skills of document format are applied, the more effective the document.

KEY TERMS

Annotated bibliography	Loc. cit.	Pie graph or chart
Bar graph or chart	Memorandum	Reading position
Bibliography	Minutes	Reference initials
Blocked letter style	Mixed punctuation	Reference notes
Copy notation	Modified blocked letter	Report
Documentation	style	Salutation
Endnote	News release	Sentence outline
Figure	Op. cit.	Simplified letter style
Footnote	Open punctuation	Speech
Graphics	Optical character	Table
Ibid.	recognition (OCR)	Topical outline
Inside address	Pagination	Widow line
Itinerary	Parenthetical citation	Works cited
Line graph or chart	Phrase outline	

A. Business Letter Format

One important business paper created in the office today is the business letter. The format used for preparing the letter will help to create attractive, well-placed copy.

1. *Format of Business Letter:* Proper placement of a letter on an 8½- by 11-inch sheet of letterhead or bond paper can be determined by using the Letter Placement Table (Figure 19–1). Once the total number of words in the body of the letter has been determined, the table can be used to decide the length of line, the line on which the date will be typed, and the blank lines between the date and the inside address.

   Note: When using a word processing package, the software defaults may differ from the recommended guidelines presented in this section. The secretary and executive need to determine acceptable formats for business use. Software defaults can be changed to other settings, turned off, or overrode.

   a. *Date:* The current date, with the month spelled in full followed by the day and the year, should be used.

   EXAMPLE:

   September 19, 200X

Figure 19–1   Letter Placement Table (Using Letterhead)

Number of Words in Body of Letter	Fixed Date Line		Variable Date Line	
	Date on Line	Blank Lines between the Date and Inside Address[a]	Date on Line[b]	Blank Lines between the Date and Inside Address[c]
Up to 100 words (short)	2 lines below letterhead (usually around line 12 or 2 inches from top of paper)	6–10	15–18	3
100–200 words (average)		4–7	14–16	3
Over 200 words (long)		3–5	13	3
Over 300 words (2-page)		3–5	13	3

[a]Blank lines mean that you would need one more return to begin your keying. The space varies because of font size in word processing software (10-point equivalent to elite [12-pitch]; 12 point equivalent to pica [10-pitch]) and word length in the body of the letter. In a word processing package, a 12-point font size would have fewer blank lines between the date and the inside address than 10 point. Special notations would be placed within the blank space. There should be a minimum of three blank lines between a special notation and the inside address.

[b]The position of the date line depends on the font size (10 to 12 point) used and word length in the body of the letter. A 12-point font (or pica type) requires fewer blank lines. More words in the letter require fewer blank lines. A special notation after the date line requires fewer blank lines.

[c]Blank lines mean that you would need one more return to begin your typing. When a special notation is typed after the date, use three blank lines between the special notation and the inside address.

b. *Inside address:* The address to whom the letter will be mailed is called the *inside address.* Use the Letter Placement Table (Figure 19–1) for correct spacing between the date line and inside address.

   (1) *Titles:* A title should precede all individual names. Titles include *Mr., Ms., Honorable, Dr.,* and so on.

   (2) *State:* In the inside address, the state can be abbreviated with the two-letter state abbreviation, or it can be spelled in full. On the envelope, it should be the two-letter state abbreviation in order to be optically scanned at the post office.

All addresses should be addressed to an individual or an organization; should have a mailing address (a post office box or a street); and should have a city, state, and ZIP code as the last line. The post office *prefers* that envelope addresses be no longer than four lines.

EXAMPLES—INSIDE ADDRESS:

```
Mr. Terry Addams          Mrs. Martha Boes
567 Wills Drive           Personnel Department
Rockford, IL 61108-1917   Colonial Brothers, Inc.
                          1111 Railway Blvd.
                          Clifton, NJ 00186-0500


Harrington Bank           Honorable T. M. Carr
PO Box 345                Carr & Carr Ltd.
Butternut, WI 54514-9504  Newberry, MI 49868-1222
```

EXAMPLES—ENVELOPE ADDRESS:

```
MR TERRY ADDAMS           MRS MARTHA BOES
567 WILLS DRIVE           COLONIAL BROTHERS INC
ROCKFORD IL 61108-1917    1111 RAILWAY BLVD
                          CLIFTON NJ 00186-0500


HARRINGTON BANK           HONORABLE T M CARR
PO BOX 345                CARR & CARR LTD
BUTTERNUT WI 54514-9504   NEWBERRY MI 49868-1222
```

c. *Attention line (optional):* The attention line is typed a double space after the inside address. The word *attention* may or may not be followed by a colon, may be in all capital letters or initial cap, and may or may not be underlined. If both an attention line and a subject line are in the letter, use the same style for each.

EXAMPLES:

ATTENTION: Mrs. Amy Miles

Attention Mrs. Amy Miles
        Accounting Department

Attention Mrs. Amy Miles

d. *Salutation:* The greeting to whom the letter is being sent is called the *salutation* and is typed a double space after the previous notation (either inside address or attention line). The salutation begins with *Dear* when addressed to a person and is followed by either the person's title and last name only (formal) or just the person's first name (informal). If the letter is sent to a company, proper salutations are *Gentlemen, Ladies and Gentlemen,* and *Dear* followed by use of a title within a department.

EXAMPLES:

Dear Mrs. Miles   *Dear Amy*

Ladies and Gentlemen   *Dear Sales Manager*

e. *Subject line (optional):* The subject line, if used, is typed a double space after the salutation. The word *subject* may or may not be followed by a colon, may be all capital letters or initial caps, and may or may not be underlined. If both a subject line and an attention line are in the letter, use the same style for each.

EXAMPLES:

SUBJECT: Invoice No. 9874

Subject Invoice No. 9874

<u>Subject</u> *Invoice No. 9874*

f. *Body of the letter:* The first paragraph begins a double space after the previous notation (either salutation or subject line). Paragraphs are single spaced with double spacing between the paragraphs. A letter should have at least two paragraphs; three is the most common number of paragraphs. Paragraphs may begin at the left margin or may be indented five or more spaces.

g. *Complimentary closing:* The closing of the letter is typed a double space after the last line in the body of the letter. Only the first word of the complimentary closing is capitalized. The complimentary closing should be in agreement with the salutation (formal or informal). The most common complimentary closings are as follows:

Formal	
Yours very truly	Very truly yours
Cordially	Cordially yours
Informal	
Truly yours	Yours truly
Formal/Informal	
Sincerely	Sincerely yours

The complimentary closings *Respectfully* and *Respectfully yours* are usually used when the letter has been addressed to individuals holding important positions in government (president, governor, or legislative members), military (captain), and religious organizations (pope, pastor, or board members).

h. *Typed signature line:* The name of the person sending the letter is typed four returns (leaving three blank lines) after the complimentary closing. Only the writer's name need be used in the signature line. If it is difficult to identify the individual as male or female by the typed signature, a title (Mr., Mrs., Miss) should be included with the name. If a woman wishes to be addressed by her title (Mrs. or Miss), this title should be included with the name. The title can be typed before the name or after the name. Any other title that the person holds may be included with the typed signature. A visual balance should always be maintained when titles are included with the typed signature.

EXAMPLES:

Mr. T. M. Johnson	*T. M. Johnson, Miss*
Miss Terry M. Johnson, CPS	*Theresa M. Johnson* *Personnel Director*

T. M. Johnson (Mrs.)

i. *Reference initials:* Reference initials include the initials of the typist of the letter and may also include the writer's initials. They are typed a double space after the signature line. The most common style today is the use of the typist's initials only. If the writer's initials are used, they are typed first followed by a slash or colon and the typist's initials.

EXAMPLES:

> *ri (typist's initials only)*
>
> *TJ/ri (writer's initials with typist's initials)*
>
> *TMJ:ri (writer's initials with typist's initials)*

j. *Enclosure notation:* If material is enclosed with the letter, an enclosure notation should be typed a double space after the reference initials. (See Section A-1-k for proper order when both copy notation and enclosure notation are included in the letter.) The word *enclosure* may be abbreviated or typed in full.

(1) If there is only one enclosure in the letter, the notation is typed in singular form.

(2) If there are two or more enclosures in the letter, the notation is typed in plural form.

(3) The enclosure notation may be typed by itself, or it may be followed by the number of enclosures contained within the letter or a listing of the enclosures.

(4) If additional information follows the enclosure, a space, a colon, a slash, or a dash should be typed between the word *enclosure* and the additional information.

EXAMPLES:

Enc.	*Encs.: 2*
Enclosure/Brochure	*Encs.—Prints* *Order Blank*

k. *Copy notation:* This special notation is used only when a copy of the letter is sent to another person or persons. In today's automated office, the copy is usually a photocopy of the original. The notation is typed a double space after the reference initials. However, if there is also an enclosure notation, the copy notation comes before the enclosure notation if these additional people are *not* receiving the enclosure. If these additional people are also receiving a copy of the enclosure, the notation is typed a double space after the enclosure notation. The word *copy* is abbreviated to *c* in the notation and followed by a blank space, a colon, or a slash and then the person's name and title and/or company name.

(1) The notation can be in lowercase or capital letters, but there are never any periods.

(2) If several people are receiving copies, the names are listed under one another, but the first name is the only one preceded by the notation.

(3) The copy notation appears on all copies: the original, the copies, and the file copy.

(4) When the copy is a carbon copy, the notation is typed with two *c*'s, that is, *cc*.

Before the letters are presented for signature, the copies are identified with a marking next to the name of the person who is to receive that copy. Copy markings are as follows:

• Placing a check mark next to the name

• Underlining the name

• Highlighting the name with a marker

EXAMPLES (Copy Notation for Photocopies):

c Betty Appleton, Apex Corporation

C: B. Appleton, Apex Corporation
*   Martha Thornton, Martin Engineering*

EXAMPLE:

Check Mark Notation on Copy sent to Martha Thornton:

c/B. Appleton, Apex Corporation
✓ Martha Thornton, Martin Engineering

l. *Spacing summary:* The paragraphs of the letter are single spaced with double spacing between. There should be a double-space between all other parts of the letter *except* between the date line and inside address (see Figure 19–1) and between the complimentary closing and signature line, where the *minimum number of returns is four* (three blank lines).

m. *Special notations:* All special notations (*CONFIDENTIAL, PERSONAL, AIRMAIL, CERTIFIED, REGISTERED,* and *SPECIAL DELIVERY*) are typed a double-space below the date line, at the left margin, and in all capital letters. The spacing between the special notation and the inside address will vary according to the length of the letter. Follow the Letter Placement Table (Figure 19–1).

EXAMPLES:

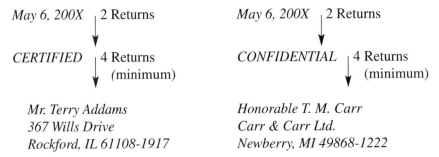

2. *Letter Styles:* There are several letter styles commonly seen in business. Acceptable formats for business letters typed in different styles are outlined in the following section. In addition, each format is discussed in detail within the paragraphs of the illustration for each business letter style. Punctuation styles are also explained, and the punctuation style used for the letter illustrated is discussed within the paragraphs of the illustration. Three letter styles are used in business today: *blocked* (considered to be very efficient), *modified blocked,* and *simplified* (most efficient).

a. *Blocked letter style:* Figure 19–2 shows an example of a business letter prepared in blocked letter style. All lines of the blocked letter begin at the left margin.

b. *Modified blocked letter style:* Figure 19–3 shows an example of a business letter prepared in modified blocked letter style with blocked paragraphs and mixed punctuation. Figure 19–4 shows an example of a business letter also prepared in modified blocked letter style but with indented paragraphs and open punctuation.

(1) The date line begins at the center point of the paper or may end at the right margin.

(2) The complimentary closing and signature line begin at the center point of the paper.

(3) Paragraphs may be blocked (beginning at the left margin) or indented (five or more spaces). When indented paragraphs are used, the letter style is referred to as *modified blocked style with indented paragraphs.*

(4) All other parts of the letter begin at the left margin.

c. *Simplified letter style:* Figure 19–5 shows an example of a business letter prepared in simplified letter style.

(1) All lines of the letter begin at the left margin.

(2) There is no salutation.

(3) There is *always* a subject line typed in all capital letters that begins a triple space (two blank lines) after the inside address. After the subject line, there is a triple space (two blank lines) to the body of the letter.

(4) There is no complimentary closing.

(5) The signature line is typed in all capital letters four lines after the body of the letter.

3. *Punctuation Styles:* There are two punctuation styles used in business today: open punctuation (considered to be the most efficient) and mixed punctuation.

a. *Open punctuation:* No punctuation is typed after the salutation or the complimentary closing. These two notations are OPEN at the end of the line (see Figures 19–2 and 19–4).

b. *Mixed punctuation:* There is a colon (:) after the salutation. The colon is used in both the formal and the informal salutation style. In business writing, there is never a comma after the salutation. Even the informal salutation (Dear Ted) follows with a colon. There is a comma (,) after the complimentary closing. These are the only two punctuation marks used in this style (notice that they are different—MIXED) (see Figure 19–3).

In Figures 19–2, 19–3, 19–4, and 19–5, some of the letters have open punctuation and some have mixed. Any letter style can have any punctuation style except the simplified letter style. Since there is no salutation or complimentary closing in the simplified letter style, no punctuation style is used.

Figure 19–2   Blocked Letter Style with Open Punctuation

Transformation Dynamics
125 Broadway, P.O. Box 2001
Batavia, IL 60510-2001

Telephone 631-878-2700
Fax 631-878-2702

April 14, 200X ↓5 returns   Date Line
       (4 blank lines)

Mrs. Marline Walsh   Inside
Administrative Manager   Address
Lewis Medical Clinic
3619 Parkview Lane
Montclair, NJ 07915-0913 ↓2 returns

Dear Mrs. Walsh ↓2   Salutation

Over the past years, many firms have adopted the Blocked Letter Style with the Open Punctuation Style.
The reason is efficiency. Once the margins are set, the administrative professional can quickly key in the   Body
letter because all lines of the letter begin at the left margin. Also, there is no worry about making sure   of
you have the correct punctuation after the salutation and complimentary closing. There is no punctua-   Letter
tion mark following either the salutation or complimentary closing when using the Open Punctuation
Style. ↓2 returns

With regard to spacing: ↓2

1. The paragraphs are always single spaced with double spacing between. ↓2

2. There is double spacing between all parts of the letter except between the date line and inside address and the complimentary closing and signature line. ↓2

3. The spacing between the date line and inside address is a minimum of three blank lines (four returns). However, the spacing could be as many as ten blank lines for a short letter using the fixed
   date line. ↓2

4. The spacing between the complimentary closing and signature line is three blank lines (four returns).
   ↓2

This letter is an illustration of Blocked Letter Style with open punctuation. Remember, a letter prepared
in Block Letter Style can also be prepared with Mixed Punctuation Style. ↓2

Sincerely yours ↓4 returns   Complimentary
       (3 blank lines)   Closing

Dr. Diane M. Graf, CPS   Typed Signature Line
Transformation Facilitator ↓2   Title

bls   Reference Initials

Figure 19–3   Modified Blocked Letter Style with Blocked Paragraphs and Mixed Punctuation

Transformation Dynamics
    125 Broadway, P.O. Box 2001   *Telephone 631-878-2700*
    Batavia, IL 60510-2001   *Fax 631-878-2702*

                          September 10, 200X ↓5 returns   Date Line
                                (4 blank lines)

Mrs. Marline Walsh   Inside
Administrative Manager   Address
Lewis Medical Clinic
3619 Parkview Lane
Montclair, NJ 07915-0913 ↓2 returns

Dear Marline: ↓2   Salutation

Subject: Modified Blocked Letter Style with Mixed Punctuation ↓2   Subject Line

Many businesses still prefer the appearance of a Modified Blocked Letter Style. Some choose to use   Body
mixed puntuation with this letter style, and some prefer to use open punctuation. Either punctuation   of
style is appropriate. This is an illustration of Modified Blocked Letter Style with mixed punctuation.↓2 Letter

With the Modified Blocked Letter Style, the secretary may key in the current date either beginning at
the center point of the paper or so the current date ends at the right margin. In this illustration, the date
begins at the center point of the paper. All other letter parts begin at the left margin unless paragraphs
are indented (see Figure 19–4).↓2

With mixed punctuation style, there must be a colon (:) after the salutation and a comma (,) after the
complimentary closing. In business writing, a comma is never used after the salutation. With mixed
punctuation, the colon is used after the salutation whether you are using a formal or an informal salutation. In this letter, the salutation and complimentary closing are informal. ↓2

The spacing of the Modified Blocked Letter Style follows the same guidelines as the Blocked Letter
Style. Because of your current needs, Marline, I am sending you a copy of our Office Style Manual
which has just been published. ↓2

                          Yours truly, ↓4 returns   Complimentary
                                (3 blank lines)   Closing

                          Dr. Diane M. Graf, CPS   Typed Signature Line
                          Transformation Facilitator ↓2   Title

DMG:bls ↓2   Reference Initials

Enclosure: Office Style Manual   Enclosure Notation

4. *Second Page of a Letter:* The heading for the second page of a letter should include the name of the person receiving the letter, the date, and the page number. A department name may be included along with the person's name. If the letter is addressed to a company, the company name is used instead of the person's name. For the page number, also use the word *Page* for clarity.

   a. *Blocked style:* If the letter is typed in blocked style, each line of the heading begins at the left margin. The first line can begin either 0.5 inch (line 4) or 1 inch (line 7) from the top of the page. The heading is single spaced. Triple-space after the last line of the heading to continue the letter. Blocked style is also used for the

Figure 19–4   Modified Blocked Letter Style with Indented Paragraphs and Open Punctuation

Transformation Dynamics   *125 Broadway, P.O. Box 2001*
      Telephone 631-878-2700   *Batavia, IL 60510-2001*
         Fax 631-878-2702

                                           September 10, 200X ↓4 returns   **Date Line**
                                                         (3 blank lines)

Mrs. Marline Walsh   Inside
Administrative Manager   Address
Lewis Medical Clinic
3619 Parkview Lane
Montclair, NJ 07915-0913 ↓2 returns

Dear Marline: ↓2   Salutation

          Again, I am using a Modified Blocked Letter Style, but
this time the paragraphs are indented. Paragraphs typically are indented
one standard tab ($\frac{1}{2}$ inch), but I have chosen to indent the paragraphs   Body
to the end of the salutation, which is also appropriate. Some feel this   of
allows enough space to refer to the salutation at the beginning of each   Letter
paragraph. The maximum paragraph indentation usually does not exceed
$1\frac{1}{2}$ inches (three standard tabs). ↓2

          Also with this letter style, the current date ends at the
right margin. The right margin is justified in this example, since I am
using a proportional font. A ragged right margin is more appropriate
when you use a font with standard spacing. The complimentary closing
and typed signature line will begin at the center point of the paper.
↓2

          Because this letter is average length and I have chosen
to use the variable date line format, the date for this letter was typed
three lines below the letterhead ($2\frac{1}{4}$ inches from the top edge of the
paper). Four returns (three blank lines) were keyed in between the date
and the inside address. ↓2

          After you peruse the material I sent you last week, Mar-
line, please do not hesitate to call me if you have any questions. Otherwise, I look forward to seeing you at the regional conference in Chicago
in November. ↓2

                              Sincerely, ↓4 returns   Complimentary
                                         (3 blank lines)   Closing

                              Dr. Diane M. Graf, CPS   Typed Signature Line
                              Transformation Facilitor ↓2   Title

DMG/bls   Reference Initials

Figure 19–5   Simplified Letter Style

Transformation Dynamics
125 Broadway, P.O. Box 2001   *Telephone 631-878-2700*
Batavia, IL 60510-2001   *Fax 631-878-2702*

February 15, 200X ↓4 returns   Date Line
                        (3 blank lines)

Mrs. Marline Walsh   Inside
Administrative Manager   Address
Lewis Medical Clinic
3619 Parkview Lane
Montclair, NJ 07915-0913 ↓3 returns
                        (2 blank lines)

SIMPLIFIED LETTER STYLE FORMAT ↓3   Subject Line

The Simplified Letter Style was introduced in the 1950s by the Administrative Management Society,   Body
then known as the National Office Management Association. The purpose of adopting a new letter style   of
was for efficiency with a crisp, neat appearance. Here are the primary features of the Simplified Letter   Letter
Style: ↓2

➤ To maintain typing efficiency, the Blocked Letter Style Format of typing everything at the left margin was adopted.↓2

➤ The variable date line format is used; therefore, there are always four returns (three blank lines) between the date and the inside address. ↓2

➤ To be more efficient, the salutation and complimentary closing are omitted. ↓2

➤ Immediately after the inside address, a subject line is always typed in all capital letters. The spacing
   before and after the subject line is a triple space (three returns). ↓2

➤ After the last paragraph, the secretary keys in four returns (three blank lines) and types the signature
   line in all capital letters. ↓2

➤ If there are any enumerations or bulleted items within the letter, each point begins at the left margin
   and is treated as a new paragraph. ↓2

➤ If there is a copy notation, it begins with c/ followed by the names of people who are to receive
   copies.↓2

Over the years, many businesses have adopted this letter style. The features of the Simplified Letter Style
should be studied and considered as a possible style for future use. ↓4 returns
                                                  (3 blank lines)

DR DIANE M. GRAF, CPS ↓2   Typed Signature Line

bls ↓2   Reference Initials

c/Melissa Thompson, CPS   Copy Notation

Figure 19–6   Second-Page Heading—Blocked Style

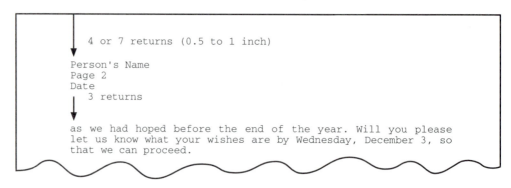

Figure 19–7   Second-Page Heading—Modified Blocked Style

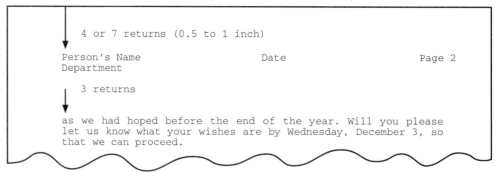

second page of a simplified letter format. An example of the second-page heading using blocked letter style is shown in Figure 19–6.

b. *Modified blocked style:* If the letter is typed in modified blocked style, the addressee's name is typed at the left margin, the date in the center, and the page number at the right margin. The heading may be typed either 0.5 inch (line 4) or 1 inch (line 7). Triple-space after the heading to continue the letter. An example of the second-page heading using modified blocked letter style is shown in Figure 19–7.

c. *Word processing headings:* Most word processing software provides a header feature. The header allows the user to key the information once for automatic placement at the top of the second and succeeding pages. The page number automatically increments when the appropriate page number code is used on the header line. To follow the recommended inches from the top of the page, the top margin will need to be changed for second and succeeding pages.

B. Envelopes

The two standard envelope sizes are No. 10 (9½ by 4⅛ inches) and No. 6¾ (6½ by 3⅝ inches). There are three styles used in addressing envelopes: conventional style, addressing for optical character recognition, and labels. Envelope and label addresses may also be computer generated.

1. *Conventional Style:* When typing an address on either a No. 10 or a No. 6¾ envelope, follow these procedures:

a. Always use blocked style and single spacing.

Figure 19–8 Business Envelope With Special Notations (No. 10 Envelope)

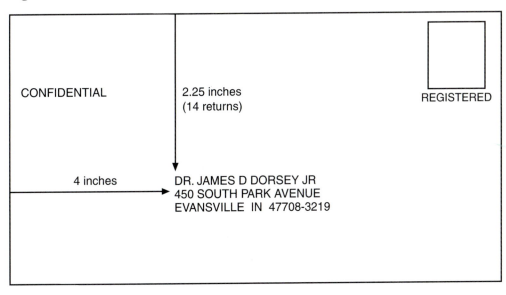

CONFIDENTIAL

2.25 inches
(14 returns)

REGISTERED

4 inches

DR. JAMES D DORSEY JR
450 SOUTH PARK AVENUE
EVANSVILLE IN 47708-3219

Note: On a No. 6¾ business envelope, the address would be typed 2 inches from the left dedge of the envelope and down 2 inches (12 returns) from the top edge. Otherwise, the positioning of the special notations would be identical.

    b. All words are to be typed in all capital letters for postal efficiency. When proportional spacing is used, such as a Times Roman font, use two spaces between words for ease in reading.

    c. Do not use punctuation marks.

    d. Type the city, state, and nine-digit ZIP code on the last line. Leave one to five spaces between the state and the ZIP code.

    e. Use the two-letter abbreviation for optical character recognition.

    f. Use the nine-digit ZIP code.

    g. Notations such as *Personal, Confidential,* or *Please forward* should be typed below the return address on the third line.

    h. Special mailing notations such as *Registered, Special Delivery,* or *Certified* should be typed in all capital letters in the upper right corner of the envelope, just under the postage block.

Figure 19–8 shows a properly typed address on a No. 10 envelope with special mailing notations. The address begins 4 inches from the left edge of the envelope and 2.25 inches (14 returns) from the top edge. On a No. 6¾ business envelope, the address would be typed 2 inches from the left edge of the envelope and 2 inches (12 returns) from the top edge.

2. *OCR Requirements:* The U.S. Postal Service uses optical character recognition (OCR) equipment to process volumes of mail. The following guidelines have been developed so that mail can be OCR-readable.

    a. The entire address should be located *within* an imaginary rectangle, which is the OCR-read area, formed by the following boundaries:

        (1) One inch from the left edge

        (2) One inch from the right edge

(3) Bottom margin of ⅝ inch

(4) Three inches from the bottom edge

See Figure 19–9 to see how these boundaries are formed.

b. Within the OCR-read area, the entire space below the top line of the address block should be clear of printing other than the address itself. This includes information such as boxes, advertising, computer punch holes, or other similar types of information. No printing should appear in the bar code read area.

c. The address should have a uniform left margin and be legible.

d. No punctuation is typed in the address.

e. The address format includes the following:

(1) The name of the recipient (top line)

(2) Information/attention line (second line)

(3) Delivery address (third line)

(4) City, state, ZIP code (fourth line)

The address should not exceed four lines.

f. Unit, apartment, office, or suite numbers should be used in the address. This information should be placed at the end of the delivery address line.

g. The standard two-letter state abbreviations and the nine-digit ZIP code should be used. The preferred location for the ZIP code is on the city, state, and ZIP code line. If this is not possible, the ZIP code may be placed at the left margin on the line immediately below the city and state.

h. The entire address must always be visible. If a window envelope is used, the entire address must have at least a ¼-inch clearance between the edge of the window and all sides of the address.

i. Mail addressed to a foreign country must have the full name of the city and country of the destination written in capital letters.

Figure 19–9 Business Envelope Typed for OCR Requirements (No. 10 Envelope)

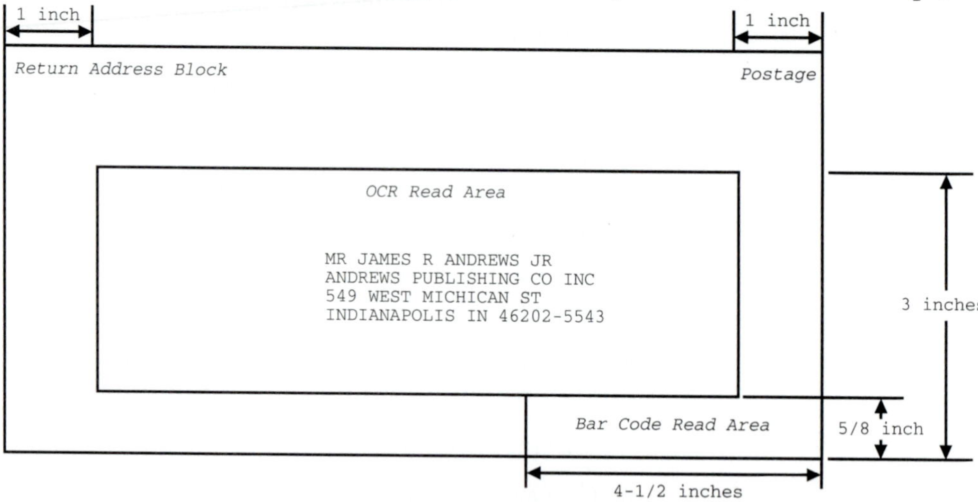

j. Italic, artistic, Cyrillic, and scriptlike fonts cannot be read by OCR equipment. Characters or numbers should not touch or overlap within a word or ZIP code.

k. The use of uppercase characters is preferred but required only when the line spacing is 8 lines per inch. Preferred spacing is 6 lines per inch.

l. The character pitch should be in the range of 7 to 12 characters per inch.

m. The space between words should be one to two character spaces; however, the space between the last character of the two-letter state abbreviation and the first digit of the ZIP code can be one to five character spaces.

Additional information about OCR requirements may be obtained from the U.S. Postal Service.

3. *Label:* Addresses are sometimes prepared on labels. The amount of space for the address is confined to the label.

    a. The maximum number of key strokes you can get in one line is only 26 to 28. Therefore, some words will need to be abbreviated.

    b. The two-letter state abbreviations help keep the address within the confined space.

    c. All lines should be typed in all capital letters, single-spaced, and blocked at the left, with no punctuation. This adheres to postal OCR requirements.

    EXAMPLE:

```
MS BETTY RUSSELL-WADE
DEACON RAYMOND & BROOK ATTYS
4 OAK WOOD TR SUITE 214
SAN DIEGO CA 92103-9632
```

    d. The address block should be imprinted or placed (if on label) with at least a ⅝-inch bottom margin and a left margin of at least 1 inch. Nothing should be written, typed, or printed below the address block or to the right of it.

    e. Sometimes, special information is imprinted above the address block, typically one or two lines above the name, to indicate account number, expiration date of subscription, or other descriptive words. Here is an example:

    EXAMPLE:

1STK5 11622 PIN91 FEB01

B L STOCKTON
1622 PINE ST APT 3
SYCAMORE IL 60178-2136

4. *Computer-Generated Addresses:* Envelope addresses or labels are often generated using computer software. The address style used could be conventional, OCR, or label (see Sections B-1, B-2, and B-3). The most common software used for this purpose is database management or word processing. Label-making equipment compatible with the word processing software is also common in today's automated office.

When many addresses are printed, it is faster to print labels. Printers with platens use labels on strips fed by a tractor feeder. Laser printers use labels on sheets fed through the sheet feeder.

a. *Database management software:* The creation of files and printing addresses on labels or envelopes are possible with database management software.

(1) A file must be created for all addresses. A file consists of a record for each addressee. Each addressee record will contain the necessary variable address data. Each address variable is referred to as a *field*. A field should reference only one variable; this provides the most flexible use of the address variables. Here is an example of addressee data (fields) for one record:

EXAMPLE:

Variable Name	*Addressee Data*
Title	MRS
FirstName	MARLENE
LastName	KITTLESON
Position	ADMINISTRATIVE MANAGER
Department	WORD PROCESSING DIVISION
Company	ABBOTT REGAL INC
Address	325 LINCOLN HIGHWAY
City	SYCAMORE
State	IL
ZIPCode	60178-2235
AreaCode	815
WorkPhone	895-2366
PhoneExtension	23

(2) Most database management software includes a label command to print labels from the address file. Reference only those fields that you want to print in the address.

b. *Word processing software with text merge:* Most word processing software provides a text-merge facility. The options available will depend on the word processing software. A text-merge option will do the following:

(1) A primary file is created. This file contains the actual document that will be merged with data from the addressee files, in this case, a label or envelope form.

(2) Next, a secondary file is created with data recorded for all addresses. Like database management, the file will consist of a record for each addressee that will contain the necessary variable address data (fields).

(3) Labels or envelopes can be printed using the mail-merge function, merging only selected address variables from the secondary file.

c. *Word processing software with no text-merge function:* If text-merge is not available, an address code file can be created in any word processing software.

(1) An address code file is created that contains all the paper-size, top/bottom margins, and left/right margin codes for proper address location on the envelope or label. *Save this file for future use.*

(2) The address file can then be used for printing. Immediately following the codes, type the address data. Insert a page-break code between multiple addresses. If form-fed envelopes or labels are used, do not insert a page-advance code.

(3) An envelope (or labels) must be inserted into the printer. Print one page at a time unless form-fed envelopes (labels) are used.

An address-code file may be used for printing envelopes or labels whenever an individual document is mailed. It may also be used to maintain a mailing list. To maintain data integrity (accuracy), however, one should not create multiple address files. When multiple files are created, address maintenance becomes burdensome and data become vulnerable to inaccuracies.

C. Memoranda Format

Memoranda are used for correspondence between individuals, departments, and branch offices of the same company. Usually, a heading is printed on the memorandum form, and the side margins are determined by this heading. When you do not have a memorandum form, the top and side margins must be set to produce visual appeal.

1. *Format of a Memorandum:* The general appearance of a memorandum depends on the format that is used for the entire message.

   a. *Top margin and heading:* The top margin for a memorandum varies from 1 to 2 inches. The most common is 1½ inches. The words *MEMORANDUM* or *MEMO* are usually centered horizontally in all capital letters. Another variation is to type the heading in initial caps and underlined.

   b. *Side margins:* The left and right margins of the memorandum will vary depending on the length of the memorandum. The longest line of print would be 1-inch left and right margins (narrowest margin). This would be used for a long memorandum. The smallest line of print would be 2-inch left and right margins (widest margin). This would be used for a short memorandum. However, the left margin may be aligned with the preprinted headings on memorandum forms normally used in an office.

   c. *Notation lines:* A memorandum begins with the notation lines:

      TO:

      FROM:

      SUBJECT:

      DATE:

   These lines are typed a triple space after the heading or may be preprinted on the memorandum form. A skilled secretary would then align the variable information with the printed notation. There should be at least two spaces after a colon. Various styles for the notation lines are as follows:

   (1) Align notations at the left and variable data after the longest notation (subject).

   (2) Align notations with the colon and key all variable data two spaces after the colon.

   (3) Type in all capital letters
   or
   Type with initial caps only.

   (4) Include titles or departments.

   (5) Place the date as the fourth notation line
   or
   Place the date on the same line as the notation *TO*.

After the notation lines, triple-space (two blank lines) to the body of the memorandum. Paragraphs are single spaced with double-spacing between and typed in blocked style.

EXAMPLE (with left side aligned and in all capital letters):

TO:	*Leon Dresser*
FROM:	*Mary Louise Westcott*
SUBJECT:	*Request for Professional Leave*
DATE:	*February 4, 200X*

EXAMPLE (with colon aligned and with initial caps):

To:	*Leon Dresser*
From:	*Mary Louise Westcott*
Subject:	*Request for Professional Leave*
Date:	*February 4, 200X*

EXAMPLE (with left side aligned, with initial caps, including titles; date aligned at right):

To:	*Leon Dresser*	*Date:*	*February 4, 200X*
	Personnel Director		
From:	*Mary Louise Westcott*		
	Information Systems		
Subject:	*Request for Professional Leave*		

EXAMPLE (with colon aligned, in all capital letters, including titles; subject line and date to the right):

TO:	*Leon Dresser*	*SUBJECT:*	*Request for*
	Personnel Director		*Professional Leave*
FROM:	*Mary Westcott*	*DATE:*	*February 4, 200X*
	IS Supervisor		

   d. *Reference initials:* Reference initials are also included on a memorandum. They are typed a double space after the last paragraph at the left margin. Formats for reference initials are included in Section A-1-i.

   Figure 19–10 illustrates a memorandum using these basic style guidelines.

2. *Using Word Processing Forms:* Several word processing packages include memorandum forms where only the variable notation data and the message need to be inserted. Even the date is automatically inserted from the computer system. If the memorandum is saved to be printed again at a later time, be sure to hard code the date so it remains fixed to the date keyed and sent.

D. Business Report Format

A business report is a common means of communication *within* business firms as well as *between* business firms. Figure 19–11 highlights the parts of a report. Format guidelines for reports vary in office reference manuals. However, the following guidelines are acceptable in any office.

1. *Physical Layout:* The physical layout of the format includes decisions on margins (top, bottom, right, left), how the title of the report should be typed, and the general spacing of paragraph material.

Figure 19–10   Memorandum Style

```
                        MEMORANDUM
        TO:      Jerry Rankowski
                 Vice President, Operations

        FROM:    Darla Johnson
                 President

    SUBJECT:     PREPARATION FOR AUGUST BOARD MEETING

        DATE:    August 2, 200X


                 Sang Lee, Asian Operations, will be attending our August 19 board meeting. He arrives
                 on August 17 and plans to spend the day with you and me in going over details.

                 Our meeting begins at 7 a.m. in the Executive Conference Room. Breakfast will be
                 served.

                 ri
```

a. *Margins:* Specific guidelines need to be followed for the top, bottom, left, and right margins of a report written in manuscript format.

    (1) *Top margins:*

        (a) The top margin on the first page of the report should be 2 inches when there is a title included on the page.

        (b) The top margin on the first page of the report without a title is 1½ inches.

        (c) On the second page and succeeding pages, there should be a ½-inch margin (four returns) and then a typed page number, followed by three returns; then continue typing text. Most word processing programs provide a header notation for including the page number at the top of the second and succeeding pages with appropriate returns to the text which follows. An alternative technique is to type the page number 1 inch (seventh line) from the top followed by three returns to the continuation of the report.

    (2) *Left margin:* The left margin will vary, depending on whether the report is bound or unbound.

        (a) The left margin on an unbound report is 1 inch.

        (b) The left margin on a left-bound report is 1½ inches.

    (3) *Right margin:* There should be a 1-inch right margin on all reports.

    (4) *Bottom margin:* There should be at least a 1-inch bottom margin on all pages of a report.

b. *Title of report:* The title of the report is the first item typed on the first page, centered and typed in all capital letters. If the title is excessively long, it can be typed on more than one line. If the title is more than one line, single-space the title. Each successive line of the title must be shorter than the previous line.

    (1) *Spacing:* Triple-space between the title and the text unless there is a subtitle.

Figure 19–11   Example of Business Report

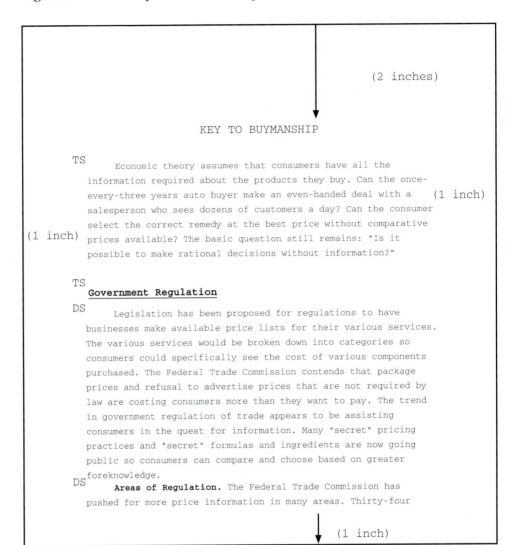

KEY TO BUYMANSHIP

TS
      Economic theory assumes that consumers have all the
   information required about the products they buy. Can the once-
   every-three years auto buyer make an even-handed deal with a
   salesperson who sees dozens of customers a day? Can the consumer
   select the correct remedy at the best price without comparative
   prices available? The basic question still remains: "Is it
   possible to make rational decisions without information?"

TS
   Government Regulation
DS
      Legislation has been proposed for regulations to have
   businesses make available price lists for their various services.
   The various services would be broken down into categories so
   consumers could specifically see the cost of various components
   purchased. The Federal Trade Commission contends that package
   prices and refusal to advertise prices that are not required by
   law are costing consumers more than they want to pay. The trend
   in government regulation of trade appears to be assisting
   consumers in the quest for information. Many "secret" pricing
   practices and "secret" formulas and ingredients are now going
   public so consumers can compare and choose based on greater
   foreknowledge.
DS
      Areas of Regulation. The Federal Trade Commission has
   pushed for more price information in many areas. Thirty-four

(2 inches)

(1 inch)

(1 inch)

(1 inch)

BUYMANSHIP   2(Line 4)
states have passed some form of law permitting pharmacists to
substitute less expensive generic drugs which are chemically
equivalent to the expensive brand name prescription drugs. In
1977 alone, more than 60 bills were introduced to Congress to
bring more information to consumers via the food label. In the
1990s many more bills are expected to be introduced. Proposed
regulations would force funeral directors to have available price
lists for their various services.

TS
Critics of the Information Boom
      Critics of the information, however, have voiced strong
   concerns about the ways in which information is being handled.

(2) *Subtitle:* If there is a subtitle, double-space after the title, type the subtitle (centered and with initial caps), and then triple-space to the text.

c. *Line spacing and paragraphing:* The following guidelines can be followed for determining the spacing of the text of the report as well as space needed for paragraph indentions.

    (1) *Spacing within text:* The text of the report is double-spaced for ease in reading. Some short reports (one page) are single-spaced, and periodically a business may decide to single-space a report to conserve on paper. However, it is advisable to double-space all reports unless otherwise instructed.

    (2) *Paragraph indentions:* Because reports are double-spaced, the paragraphs must be indented *five spaces* (½ inch) to identify the beginning of each paragraph. If a report is single-spaced, the paragraphs may or may not be indented, but there must always be double-spacing between the paragraphs.

d. *Headings:* There can be as many as seven divisions of headings. When using headings, the number of divisions used is determined by the number of breakdowns needed under a main division.

    (1) *Hierarchy of divisions:* The hierarchy of divisions, moving from the most important to the least important, is as follows:

        (a) Centered heading in all capital letters

        (b) Centered heading in initial caps and underlined

        (c) Centered heading in initial caps and not underlined

        (d) Side heading in all capital letters

        (e) Side heading in initial caps and underlined

        (f) Side heading in initial caps and not underlined

        (g) Paragraph headings always underlined and ending in a period or a period and a dash

    Headings should begin with (1), (2), or (3). Then, you may move down the hierarchy by skipping to the next level of heading you desire. Let's say you had three divisions and began with Hierarchy (2). The next division could be Hierarchy (5), and the last division could be Hierarchy (7). Heading divisions must be consistent throughout a document.

    EXAMPLE:

Progress Report on Bradford-Brown Sale

Preliminary Investigation of Property

    Abstract of Title.—The title to the property is in the name of Arthur J. Bradford, Jr., as shown in the deed from Thomas J. Cochran to Arthur J. Bradford, Jr., dated September 23, 1984.

    (2) *Spacing for headings:* When headings are inserted into the text for a report, consistent spacing is required for each level of heading.

        (a) *Centered headings:* Triple-space before a centered heading and double-space after. If a centered heading is immediately followed by a side heading, triple-space *before* the side heading.

    (b) *Side headings:* Triple-space before a side heading and double-space after.

    (c) *Paragraph headings:* A paragraph heading begins a paragraph. Therefore, there is always double-spacing before a paragraph heading. Paragraph headings are always underlined and followed by a period and two spaces or a period and a dash.

e. *Pagination:* The appropriate numbering of pages helps to keep the report organized and the pages in order.

    (1) *Numbering the first page:* When the first page has a title, there usually is no page number on that page. If a page number is used for this first page, it is typed at the bottom of the page a triple-space after the last line of text and at the center of the line of writing. This number can be typed in the 1-inch margin at the bottom of the page.

    When the first page does not have a title, a page number is typed in the same position as on succeeding pages.

    (2) *Numbering succeeding pages:* The page number is usually typed at the top of the page on the fourth line (½ inch), or it can be typed on the seventh line (1 inch). It can be typed either in the center of the page or at the right margin. The number is usually typed by itself without the word *page* or any notations. After the page number, there is a triple-space to the continuation of the report.

f. *Automatic generation of supplements:* When reports or other long documents are prepared, a table of contents; list of tables, figures, or maps (when included in the document); and bibliography (when references are used) must be included.

Most word processing software includes a feature to create the table of contents, lists, or bibliography from the document being prepared. This automatic feature eliminates the retyping of headings for the table of contents; table, figure, or map titles; or bibliographic references. Also, as changes are made within the document, the information contained in these document supplements changes automatically. The word processing operations manual explains the steps to follow to utilize this automatic feature.

g. *Word processing format for printing reports:* When word processing software is used, the placement of codes is very important. Once a code is read by the computer system, all text following the code is formatted according to the word processing code. For this reason, final printing codes should be inserted after all editing has been completed. The life cycle of a document is plan, create, edit, format, and save/print. The function of each phase of the cycle is as follows:

    (1) *Plan:* Know the purpose of the document; outline.

    (2) *Create:* Compose the document according to the plan, including all tab, centering, bold, and underscore codes. For documents where extensive editing is anticipated, use double- or triple-spacing so that a rough-draft hard copy can be printed. Save often so that the information being keyed in will not be lost.

    (3) *Edit:* Make changes; at the same time, make grammatical corrections. Editing should be done on soft copy (reading the text on the computer screen). Hard-copy editing is usually required for long documents or when editing is done by someone else. Save and print when necessary. This step can be repeated. From an efficiency perspective, editing should not be done more than twice.

(4) *Format:* Insert final-copy printing codes for spacing, margins, widow/orphan lines, and hyphenation. Editing is easier when format codes (final printing codes) are not in the document. When sentences, paragraphs, or pages are moved or deleted, one does not have to be so careful about moving the appropriate codes or responding to code prompts (e.g., manual hyphenation).

Figure 19–12 shows an example of final printing codes inserted at the beginning of the document so that all text that follows adheres to the format code. Consult the word processing operations manual for format procedures specific to a particular software package.

(5) *Save/print:* When corrections are made, they are made only to the document that is in primary memory. If corrections are to be kept, it is important to save the document to a secondary storage medium. Diskette, hard disk, or network server are common for permanent storage. Often, a hard copy is required.

h. *Margin guide:* When the print cannot appear in the top and bottom margin or left and right margin area, a margin guide becomes a helpful tool. For some legal, government, or research documents or documents prepared for publication, it is important to keep print out of these margin areas.

(1) *Preparing the margin guide:* With a ruler, draw a straight *dark* line where the margins are set. Be careful to be accurate with the measurement of the margin

Figure 19–12   Example of Placement of Word Processing Codes in Business Report

Placement of Codes without Header and Page Numbering

```
[T/B Mar:2:,1:][W/O On] [Hyph On][L/R Mar:1",1"][Center]KEY TO
BUYMANSHIP[HRt]
[HRt]
[HRt]
[Ln spacing:2][Tab]Economic theory assumes that consumers have
all the information required about the products they buy. Can the
once[-]every[-]three[-]years auto buyer make an even[-]handed
deal with a salesperson who sees dozens of customers a day? Can
the consumer select the correct remedy at the best price without
comparative prices available? The basic question still remains:
"Is it possible to make rational decisions without information?"
[HRt]
[Ln Spacing:1][HRt]
[UND] Government Regulation[und][Ln Spacing:2][HRt]
[Tab] Legislation has been proposed for regulations to have
businesses make available price lists for their various services.
```

Placement of Codes with Header and Page Numbering

```
[T/B Mar:2:,1:][W/O On] [Hyph On][L/R Mar:1",1"][Header A: Every
page; BUYMANSHIP][Pg Numbering:Top Right]
[Suppress:HA][Center]KEY TO BUYMANSHIP[HRt]
[HRt]
[HRt]
[Ln spacing:2][Tab]Economic theory assumes that consumers have
all the information required about the products they buy. Can the
once[-]every[-]three[-]years auto buyer make an even[-]handed
deal ...
```

area. With horizontal and vertical line drawing features in word processing packages, margin guides can easily be created. The guide should then be measured with a ruler.

(2) *Using the margin guide:* Place the final hard copy on top of the margin guide. The dark ruler lines will show through the top final-copy sheet. No print on the final copy should extend beyond the ruler lines from the margin guide.

Figure 19–13 illustrates a margin guide for 1- and 2-inch top margins, 1- and 1½-inch left margins, and 1-inch right and bottom margins. Measurements can be set from the outside edge of the paper.

i. *Widow line:* To avoid a widow line at the bottom of any page or at the top of any page, you may have more than a 1-inch bottom margin. A *widow line* is one line of a paragraph by itself on a page. You must always have two or more lines of a paragraph on a page. If you are using word processing software, check the manual to see whether there is a widow-line function. If so, activate the widow protection function with the appropriate code at the beginning of the document.

2. *Documentation:* Preparing appropriate documentation of information contained in a report is very important when the report contains the results of both primary and secondary research. *Documentation* is defined as the creating, collecting, organizing, storing, citing, and disseminating of descriptive information. Depending on the documentation format selected, documentation typically refers to the form of reference notes (footnotes, endnotes, or parenthetical citations) and the bibliographic information in the reference list at the end of the report. A bibliography or works cited reference list at the end of the report identifies complete information about the sources of information used in the preparation of the report.

a. *Types of citations:* Reference notes, or *reference citations* as they are sometimes called, are used to cite specific information that is quoted or paraphrased from other sources. These citations are used to acknowledge published and unpublished sources of information and give proper credit to the authors of the passages referred to in the text.

EXAMPLES:

<u>*Published sources*</u>*: Books, periodical articles, or research reports*

<u>*Unpublished sources*</u>*: Television programs, lectures, letters, personal interviews, or World Wide Web references*

The style selected for the reference citations must be a commonly used documentation style. The *Chicago Manual of Style* (CMS) requires a choice of footnotes or endnotes as documentation of sources used in the writing of the material. The Modern Language Association (MLA) and the American Psychological Association (APA) have included the use of parenthetical citations within the text in their style manuals. When preparing a report with citations, one documentation style must be selected, and that style must be applied throughout the report.

(1) *Source footnote or endnote:* The CMS style requires the use of footnotes or endnotes. A footnote or endnote gives credit to a source of information included in a report. Footnotes are included on the page where the reference is made, whereas endnotes appear on a separate page at the end of the report. The first time the reference is referred to, the citation must have complete information about the source; later reference to the same work can be

Figure 19–13 Margin Guide

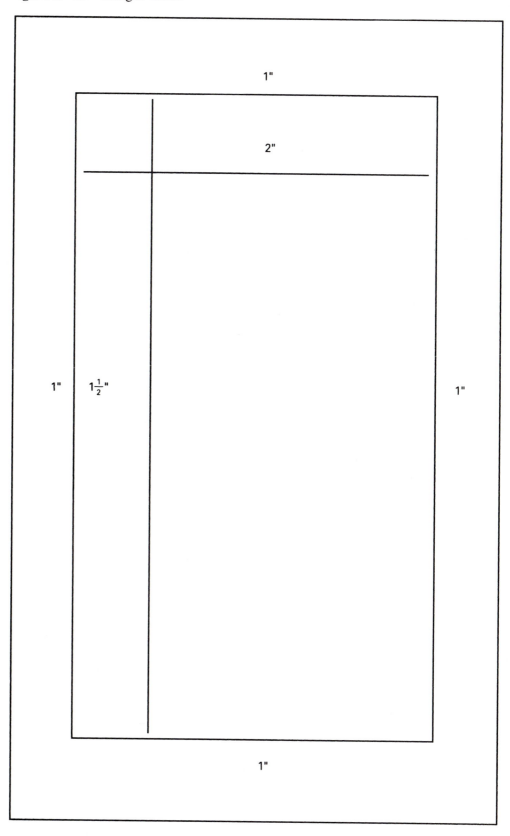

abbreviated. The source information in the footnote or endnote includes the following:

- Name(s) of author(s)
- Name(s) of editor(s)
- Publication title
- Publication information (name of publishing company, city, and publication date; or Web site name and URL)
- Type of online source
- Page number(s) referenced
- Retrieval or access date for electronic reference

(a) *Formats for footnote or endnote citations:* The format is the way the reference actually appears on the typewritten or printed page. Numbering, indentation, and spacing are very important considerations.

- *Numbering:* Each reference must be numbered consecutively with arabic numerals. All footnotes within a report may be numbered consecutively; or, if the report is particularly lengthy, all footnotes within a particular chapter may be numbered consecutively. Each number is a superscript, raised slightly above the writing line, within the body of the report. This number must correspond to the arabic numeral in the footnote or endnote.

- *Indentation:* The first line of the footnote must be indented five spaces (½ inch). All other lines begin flush left.

- *Spacing:* References should be single-spaced with a double space between if there are two or more citations on the same page.

EXAMPLES:

Book with one author:

[1]Jeffrey Pfeffer, <u>The Human Equation</u> (Boston: Harvard Business School Press, 1998), 93.

Book with two authors:

[2]Bill Capodagli and Lynn Jackson, <u>The Disney Way: Harnessing the Management Secrets of Disney in Your Company</u> (New York: McGraw Hill, 1999), 131-148.

Book with editor only:

[3]Dennis LaBonty, ed., <u>Integrating the Internet Into the Business Curriculum,</u> National Business Education Yearbook No. 36 (Reston: National Business Education Association, 1998), 55.

Magazine or journal article with author given:

[4]Neil Gross, "E-mail That Won't Come Back to Haunt You," <u>Business Week,</u> 15 November 1999, 136.

Magazine or journal article with no author given:

[5]"E-postage Gets Stamp of Approval," OfficePro 59, no. 9 (November/December 1999): 7.

Newspaper Article:

[6]Leslie Kaufman, "Web Retailers Empty Wallets on Advertising," The New York Times, 2 November 1999, A1.

Interview:

[7]Mary Ann Jirak, president, Career Performance, Inc., 29 May 1999. Interview by author, Glen Ellyn, IL.

Electronic Reference:

[8]"Searching the Web," Michael Lerner Productions, Learn the Net. [Online] 10 August 1999 *<http://www.learnthenet.com>* (Retrieved 19 November 1999).

For additional examples of reference citations (footnotes, endnotes, or parenthetical citations), refer to the following:

Guffey, Mary Ellen, Business Communication: Process and Product, Third Edition (Cincinnati: South-Western College Publishing, 2000), A-40 to A-47.

Campbell, William Giles, Stephen Vaughan Ballou, and Carole Slade, Form and Style: Theses, Reports, Term Papers, (Boston: Houghton Mifflin Company), latest edition.

(b) *Discussion footnote or endnote:* This type of citation gives additional information that might be related indirectly to the topic.

EXAMPLE:

[9]*The verbs used by office systems researchers in submitting critical incidents were modified to conform to the original taxonomy developed by Huffman et al.*

(c) *Reference footnote or endnote:* This type of citation refers to related sources or serves as a cross-reference to other parts of the report.

EXAMPLE:

[10]*See Figure 19–10, "Memorandum Style," 395.*

(d) *Later references to same citation:* Sometimes, you need to footnote a particular source more than once in a report. You may shorten these references either by using traditional Latin abbreviations or by using the author's name and page number.

- *Ibid.:* The word *ibidem* means "in the same place." This term may be used when reference is made to the immediately preceding footnote or endnote.

EXAMPLES:

^{10}*Ibid. (Reference for same page as preceding footnote)*

^{11}*Ibid., 334–345. (Citation for same reference as preceding footnote, but different page reference)*

- *Op. cit.:* The words *opere citato* mean "in the work cited." This term is used when reference is made to a previous source but there are intervening references.

EXAMPLE:

^{12}*Pfeffer, op. cit., 44.*

- *Loc. cit.:* The words *loco citato* mean "in the place cited." This term refers to the same page reference as the previous footnote for that source.

EXAMPLE:

^{13}*Pfeffer, loc. cit.*

- *Author's name and page number:* Another way of writing subsequent references to a previous source is to use the author's name and the page number.

EXAMPLE:

^{14}*Kaufman, C5.*

(2) *Parenthetical citations:* The American Psychological Association (APA) and Modern Language Association (MLA) documentation styles use in-text citations rather than footnotes or endnotes. Each reference citation is shown in parentheses in the appropriate location within the body of the text. APA style consists of the author's last name, year of publication, and page number(s).

EXAMPLE:

An abbreviated citation appears in the text and a complete citation appears in the bibliography at the end of the report (Guffey, 2000, p. 350).

(a) *Author's name included in text:* If the author's name appears within the sentence, only the year and page number are necessary in the citation.

EXAMPLE:

Guffey states that an abbreviated citation appears in the text and a complete citation appears in the bibliography at the end of the report (2000, p. 350).

(b) *Format for MLA style:* MLA style includes only the author's last name and the page reference in the parenthetical citation. If the author's name is included in the sentence, only the page reference is required.

EXAMPLES:

An abbreviated citation appears in the text and a complete citation appears in the bibliography at the end of the report (Guffey 350).

Guffey (350) states that an abbreviated citation appears in the text, with a complete bibliographic entry at the end of the report.

(c) *No author name in source:* If the source has no author, the first major word of the title of the article should be used, along with the date and page number (if there is one).

EXAMPLE:

From a marketing perspective, the combination gives the two corporations the potential to do things that neither could do alone (What 37).

Note: In this example the parenthetical citation using APA style would be *(What, 1999, October 18, 37).*

b. *Placement of citations:* Footnote references are placed at the bottom of each report page (the "foot"); endnotes are placed at the end of the report on a separate page (the "end"). Parenthetical citations are placed within the text of the report.

(1) *Placement at foot of report page:* When footnotes are placed at the foot of the same page where the reference is made, the superscript numbers must appear in the text of the report as well as in the footnote.

(a) *Separation line:* A 1½-inch horizontal line should separate the body of the text from the footnotes. There should be one blank space above and below this typed line. A blank line above the underscore comes from typing the underscore; a blank line below requires a return for the blank line (double-space).

(b) *Indentation:* The first line of each footnote should be indented five spaces (½ inch or the number of spaces each paragraph in the report is indented). The remaining lines should be flush left.

(c) *Spacing:* The footnotes should be single-spaced with one blank line between footnotes if there is more than one.

(2) *Placement at end of report:* If the reference notes are typed at the end of the report as endnotes, they should be typed in the same order as they appear in the report. When the reference is made, the superscript numbers must appear in the text of the report as well as in the endnote.

(a) *Title:* The title *Endnotes* should be typed at least 1½ inches from the top edge of the paper and centered.

(b) *Indentation:* The first line of each endnote should be indented five spaces (½ inch or the number of spaces each paragraph in the report is indented). The remaining lines in the endnote are to be flush left.

(c) *Spacing:* The endnotes should be single-spaced with one blank line between endnotes.

Most word processing software programs have a footnote/endnote feature for referencing within the text and setting up the footnote/endnote format at the same time. Using this feature can save the secretary a great deal of formatting time, particularly if changes are made since the changes are then automatically corrected throughout the document. The author of the report and the secretary should review the software format to see whether it adheres to guidelines required for the final copy.

(3) *Placement of citations within text:* When APA or MLA style is used, parenthetical citations are placed appropriately within the text. The citation either contains words that are directly quoted (verbatim) or that have been paraphrased (written in the writer's own words). In either case, a citation is required so that proper credit is given to the source and author of the ideas.

EXAMPLES:

"The U.S. economy is so robust that its impact is reaching right into the heart of America's long-suffering cities" (Bernstein, 1999, October 18, 157). (This is a direct quote; therefore, it must be verbatim and placed within quotation marks.)

America's cities are experiencing the impact of the strength of the economy (Bernstein, 1999, October 18, 157). (The author's words are paraphrased here; a citation is still required to give the author appropriate credit.)

Note: When quoting directly, notice that the final quotation mark is keyed in after the last word of the quote, immediately before the parenthetical citation. The ending punctuation appears after the citation.

The Copyright Act of 1976, which became effective January 1, 1978, influences the way in which copyrighted works are used for reference and cited within documents.

c. *Bibliography:* A bibliography is a list of all references consulted by the author that contributed to the content of the report. The bibliography is placed at the end of the report on a separate page.

(1) *Types of bibliographies:* The basic types of bibliographies that are used with reports include a general bibliography, a works cited bibliography, and an annotated bibliography.

(a) *General bibliography:* This type of bibliography, sometimes referred to as a *working bibliography,* includes all references used in researching the content of the report. A general bibliography includes references that were directly cited in the text as well as others that were helpful but not the basis for any of the citations (see Figure 19–14).

(b) *Works cited bibliography:* Only those references pertaining to the topic that have been cited within the report will be included in the works cited bibliography (see Figure 19–15).

(c) *Annotated bibliography:* After each bibliographic entry, a brief paragraph comments on the content and value of the reference. The annotated bibliography gives basic information about each reference used in preparing the content of the report.

EXAMPLE:

[3]*Dennis LaBonty, ed., Integrating the Internet into the Business Curriculum, National Business Education Yearbook No. 36 (Reston: National Business Education Association, 1998).*

The Internet and its influence on the business education curriculum. Three parts (history and policies, Internet applications related to National Standards for Business Education, and Internet-related visions and topics). Chapter authors from business education profession.

Figure 19–14   Bibliography

BIBLIOGRAPHY

Capodagli, Bill and Lynn Jackson. *The Disney Way: Harnessing the Management Secrets of Disney in Your Company.* New York: McGraw-Hill, 1999.

"E-postage Gets Stamp of Approval." *OfficePro* 59, no. 9 (November/December 1999): 7.

Gross, Neil. "E-mail That Won't Come Back to Haunt You." *Business Week.* 15 November 1999, 136.

Jirak, Mary Ann. Interview by author. Glen Ellyn, IL, 29 May 1999.

Kaufman, Leslie. "Web Retailers Empty Wallets on Advertising." *The New York Times,* 2 November 1999, A1–C5.

LaBonty, Dennis, ed. *Integrating the Internet into the Business Curriculum,"* National Business Education Yearbook No. 36. Reston, Va.: National Business Education Association, 1998.

Pfeffer, Jeffrey. *The Human Equation.* Boston: Harvard Business School Press, 1998.

"Searching the Web." *Michael Lerner Productions, Learn the Net.* <http://www.learnthenet.com> (Last Update 10 August 1999; retrieved 19 November 1999).

Note: Entries are formatted according to the *Chicago Manual of Style.*

Figure 19–15   Works Cited Bibliography

WORKS CITED

Capodagli, Bill, and Lynn Jackson. *The Disney Way: Harnessing the Management Secrets of Disney in Your Company.* New York: McGraw-Hill, 1999.

Gross, Neil. "E-mail That Won't Come Back to Haunt You." *Business Week.* 15 Nov. 1999: 136.

Kaufman, Leslie. "Web Retailers Empty Wallets on Advertising." *The New York Times* 2 Nov. 1999: A1–C5.

Pfeffer, Jeffrey. *The Human Equation.* Boston: Harvard Business School Press, 1998.

"Searching the Web." *Michael Lerner Productions, Learn the Net.* <http://www.learnthenet.com> (Last Update 10 Aug. 1999; retrieved 19 Nov. 1999).

Note: Entries are formatted according to Modern Language Association (MLA) style.

---

(2) *Format for bibliography:* The format dictates the appearance of the bibliography. The placement of the bibliography on the page, the way the entries are typed, and the spacing required are important to an attractively prepared bibliography.

  (a) *Placement on page:* The placement of the bibliography depends on the documentation style being used. These directions pertain to a bibliography formatted according to the *Chicago Manual of Style.*

   • The word *BIBLIOGRAPHY* should be centered 2 inches from the top edge of the page (line 13).

- There should be a triple space after the title.

- The first line of each entry must be flush left. The second and succeeding lines are indented at least five spaces (one standard tab).

- Each entry is single-spaced with a double space (one blank space) between entries.

- The second and succeeding pages of the bibliography continue the entries beginning 1 inch (line 7) from the top edge.

(b) *Arrangement of entries:* The bibliographic entries may be listed in two different ways—in an alphabetic list or in categories of references.

- *Alphabetic list:* The entire bibliography is alphabetized and typed as a single list of references.

- *Reference categories:* Each reference is included in the appropriate category (books, articles, research reports, electronic references, interviews, miscellaneous). Within each category, the entries are alphabetized according to the documentation style selected. Side headings highlight the different categories.

(c) *Preparation of entries:* The following procedures help to standardize the way in which the bibliographic entries are typed:

- If the author is known, the author's last name is listed first.

- If the author is unknown, the title is listed first.

- Within the alphabetic sequences, if an author is listed for more than one reference, a 1-inch line is typed instead of the author's name in the second and succeeding entries.

- Periods, rather than commas, separate the various sections of each entry.

- The title of the work should be shown exactly as it appeared in the citation; that is, the name of a periodical article is typed in initial caps, lowercase, and enclosed in quotation marks; the name of a book is typed in italics or underlined.

  EXAMPLES:

  Article: "Hold Technology in Your Palm"

  Book: *The Electronic Cottage*

- In entries for periodical articles, the exact page numbers should be included.

- In entries for books or works that are used in total, the entire reference is cited rather than individual pages.

Figure 19–14 illustrates a sample bibliography using the citations included in the preceding section and following the *Chicago Manual of Style.* Figure 19–15 is an example of a works cited bibliography, following MLA style, using only the citations that were cited within a report.

3. *Graphics:* The term *graphics* refers to any form of illustration (chart, picture, or map) that is a visual representation of successive changes in the value (quantity) of one or

more variables. A *graphic aid* is an illustration that is used to clarify data presented within a report.

a. *Purposes of business graphics:* Business graphics are used for a variety of purposes. Exactly what type of graphics is desired depends on the particular use to which it will be put.

  (1) *Presentation of ideas:* Ideas that are presented either in a written report or an oral presentation will be enhanced through the use of supplementary graphic aids. Illustrations may be used to present ideas in printed matter (company manuals or reports) or at meetings and conferences (speeches or research papers).

  (2) *Explanation of business events:* Graphics are used to explain business events that are affecting the company (the economy, sales for the month, or decreasing inventories).

  (3) *Presentation of company image:* Graphics are used to project a professional image of the company to the public. Graphics included on business cards, letterheads, and company forms, such as company logos, can help to create a company image. Pamphlets and brochures describing the company, its products and services, and its community efforts are usually available, too.

b. *Placement of graphic illustrations within text:* Graphic illustrations included in a written report must meet five requirements: each graphic illustration must be identified, documented, introduced within the narrative, interpreted within the narrative, and placed appropriately within the text.[1]

  (1) *Identifying graphic illustrations:* Graphic aids must be labeled, numbered, and titled within a report.

    (a) *Labeling:* All graphic illustrations in a report must be numbered. A common way to label these visual aids is to call them "Figure" or "Table" and assign arabic numbers to each one consecutively (e.g., Figure 1). Graphics may include different categories of information such as tables, charts, maps, and other types of illustrations.

    (b) *Title:* The title should be descriptive and clearly identify the information presented in the illustration.

  Once the identification is complete, the label, number, and title may be placed either above or below the illustration. Typically, these lines appear above a table and below a figure.

  (2) *Documenting the illustration:* Proper credit must be given in the report to the source of the illustration. Three types of sources are commonly used.

    (a) *Primary source:* Data obtained through primary research may be documented by placing the words *Source: Primary* directly below the illustration; or the source note may be omitted, implying that the illustration was constructed from primary data collected during research.

---

[1]C. Glenn Pearce et al., *Principles of Business Communication: Theory, Application, and Technology* (New York: John Wiley & Sons, 1984), 248–252; Raymond V. Lesikar et al., *Lesikar's Basic Business Communication,* 8th ed. (Boston: Irwin/McGraw-Hill, 1999), 398–417.

(b) *Secondary source illustration constructed from narrative:* Sometimes, data contained in a secondary source, like a newspaper or a journal article, is converted into an illustration by the writer. The specific citation of the secondary reference should be included in the documentation as a source acknowledgement or source note.

EXAMPLE:

Source: Chicago Tribune, 9 December 1999, D-3.

(c) *Secondary source illustration presented verbatim:* When an illustration that appeared in a secondary source is presented verbatim with no change, the entire reference should be acknowledged, along with the table or figure number if there is one. The page number should be included.

EXAMPLE:

Source: Anna Bernasek, "First: Decoding Greenspan What's He Thinking," Fortune 140, No. 10, 22 November 1999, 50.

Note: In this article, the table appears on page 50 but is not numbered.

Footnotes may be used to explain information contained in the illustration. Use a superscript letter or an asterisk rather than a number.

(3) *Introducing graphic illustrations:* Before presenting the illustration in the text, reference to the illustration must be made within the text to make its presence clear.

(a) The reference should refer to the illustration by label, number, content, and possibly the title.

EXAMPLE: Table 19–1 shows the vertical placement of business letters when using a letterhead.

(b) The same procedure should be used to refer to an illustration in an appendix. The reference should indicate the label, number, and content.

EXAMPLE: A copy of the final draft of the survey instrument is included in Appendix C.

(c) The page number(s) of the table, figure, or appendix is also appropriate since this enhances the reader's ability to locate the illustration quickly.

EXAMPLE: For further information on the blocked letter style, refer to Figure 19–2 (page 356).

(4) *Interpreting graphic illustrations:* Without an accurate interpretation, a graphic illustration will have little meaning in context. The purpose of the text material is to present and explain the data in the illustration. Specific data in the table or figure should be emphasized in the text. The graphic illustration is used to enhance the text material. The importance of the data to the overall presentation of the topic should be stressed.

(5) *Placing graphic illustrations within text:* The placement of the graphic illustration where it can best complement the text requires careful planning. Here are a few guidelines that will help in determining where the illustration might best be placed:

(a) If possible, the illustration needs to be placed immediately after its introduction in the text but near its interpretation.

(b) The size of a graphic illustration should be at least one-quarter of an 8½-by 11-inch page for ease of reading.

(c) If the size of the illustration is less than a half page, it may be placed directly after its introduction and interpretation, as long as it fits on the same page. Thus, the illustration and introduction may often be on the same page.

(d) When text appears on the same page as the illustration, leave about three line spaces above and below the illustration to separate the illustration clearly from the text. Some writers prefer to place the illustration between the introduction and the interpretation. Ruled lines around the text or lines separating the text from the visual can be very effective.

(e) If the size of the illustration is a half page or more, it should be placed on the first full page that comes after the introduction. A full-page illustration can be placed either vertically or horizontally (landscape) on the page, depending on the margins of the text. An illustration may be longer than one page. If this occurs, the second page of the illustration is treated as a continuation page.

(f) The label, number, and title of the illustration should be centered at the top of the illustration.

These five requirements for preparing graphic illustrations that will enhance the text can be applied to the selection of appropriate types of illustrations to be included in the report.

c. *Types of graphic illustrations:* The basic types of graphic illustrations used to display detailed data are tables and figures. The relationships between factors being measured are shown in graphic illustrations to support and clarify the content of the report.

(1) *Table:* A *table* is used to communicate by means of textual graphics and shows text material in the form of words and numbers presented in a columnar format. An orderly arrangement of the data is achieved through the use of stubs, heads, rows, and columns to structure the data. Usually, a table is preferable to a chart if exact numbers are to be shown (see Section D-9). Tables may be general purpose or special purpose.

(a) *General-purpose table:* A general-purpose table presents a broad area of information.

EXAMPLE: *Table 5 shows the responses to Questions 1 through 25 on the office systems survey.*

(b) *Special-purpose table:* More particularly, a table can be designed to display only the data for one specific type of information.

EXAMPLE: *Table 10 summarizes the responses to Question 10 concerning the application of word processing software to specific office tasks.*

(2) *Figure:* The communication of some form of chart or picture is called *visual graphics.* Some specific types of visual graphic illustrations include bar graphs, line graphs, pie graphs, pictograms, and drawings.

(a) *Bar graph or chart:* Typically, a bar graph or chart shows a comparison from one time period to another, for example, sales for the year 1999 as compared with sales for the year 1998. The bar graph uses bars of equal width to show quantities (values) on one axis and the factor to be measured on the other axis (see Figure 19–16).

(b) *Line graph or chart:* The line graph consists of a series of connected lines showing a particular trend in business data for a period of time, for example, sales for each month during a particular year. The vertical axis (Y) identifies the factor and quantity being measured, and the horizontal axis (X) identifies the time period under observation. These axes form the grid on which the data are recorded (see Figure 19–17).

(c) *Pie graph or chart:* The pie graph or chart represents the parts that make up a whole. The circle equals 100 percent; the sections represent parts of the whole (smaller percentages of the whole). When totaled, the smaller percentages always equal 100 percent (see Figure 19–18).

(d) *Pictogram:* Symbols represent the factor being measured and a specific number of units. An interpretation of the symbol is included so that the reader knows what the symbol represents and the exact quantities represented by the symbol.

(e) *Drawings:* In business, drawings are required to illustrate products or services of the firm. Sketches of proposed new products, engineering drawings, and product designs are a few of the types of drawings that are needed. These types of drawings are all examples of business graphics.

These are only a few examples of the types of graphic illustrations that are used in the preparation of business reports. The saying that "a picture is worth a thousand words" has much bearing on the type of graphic illustrations that will best depict business events.

d. *Preparation of graphic illustrations:* Today, many graphic illustrations can be developed using computer software. In some cases, a design staff either from an

Figure 19–16   Example of Bar Graph

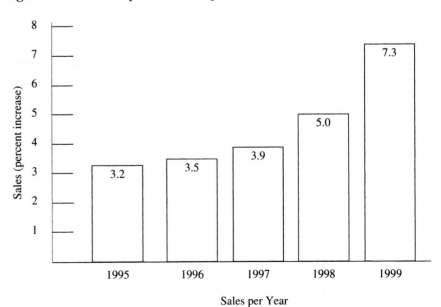

Sales per Year

Figure 19–17   Example of Line Graph

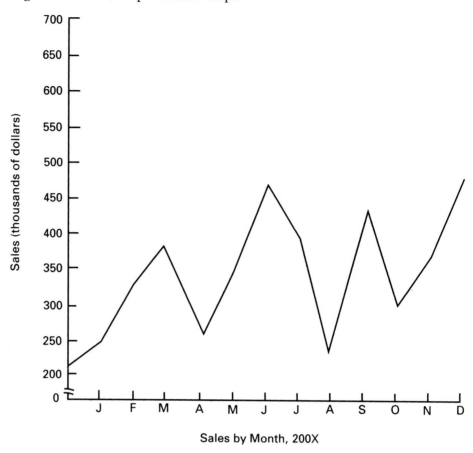

Sales by Month, 200X

Figure 19–18   Example of Pie Graph

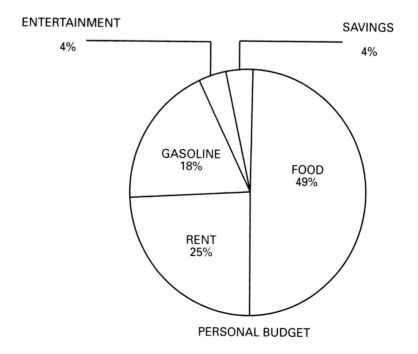

PERSONAL BUDGET

in-house operation or a commercial agency is involved. In both cases, it is important to develop appropriate illustrations that will be able to be reproduced by reprographics services. The following steps are important in the design process for preparing graphic illustrations:

(1) *Computer software for generation of graphics:* Various software packages are available that are capable of generating graphic illustrations. If an appropriate software program is available, much developmental time will be saved in making appropriate use of such a program.

(2) *Original illustrations:* Drawings and sketches may need to be developed by designers. Designers need to work closely with the user department, keeping the primary purpose of the project in mind. This step would include special qualities such as lettering that might be needed as well.

(3) *Composition of typeset text:* In addition to illustrations, text may need to be written that will be converted by typesetting, composition, or desktop publishing processes to the text material needed to complement the drawings, lettering, or other illustrations being produced.

(4) *Transfer designs available:* Books with sketches and designs may be purchased to use for cutting out the designs and using them in creating copy. This is especially helpful when a commercial artist or designer is not available within the company. Symbols, letters, and lines of various sizes and styles are also available on transfer sheets and can be transferred easily from these plastic sheets to the original copy.

(5) *Original draft of design:* Once the illustrations have been prepared in black-and-white copy and the typeset text material is ready for pasteup, the initial layout is prepared. The copy is prepared and pasted up so that the user will get a better idea of what the final copy will look like. At this point, the user must critique the design and approve it before final layout and printing can be done.

(6) *Final layout of design:* A final layout of the design is prepared in consultation with the user; any modifications suggested by the user are considered. The text should be carefully proofread. The designer will be able to judge whether certain changes are feasible at this point, but the final approval lies with the user.

(7) *Finalizing the design:* Once any modifications suggested by the user are incorporated in the design, the completed work is ready for a final proofing. It is important at this point to read every word and look at each illustration carefully to be sure the total message is accurate.

(8) *Preparation of design for printing:* If copies are to be printed of the design copy, a negative of the copy will need to be prepared. If the copy is more than one page, as in the case of a booklet, a negative of each page will need to be prepared. If the original design is to be reduced, it is at this point that a photographic reduction is made. The negatives for each page are used to make plates for the printing process.

(9) *Printing of copies:* The final stage in the preparation of a graphic design is the printing of copies that are required. Most printing processes can handle almost any number of copies from 50 to 5,000, depending on the specific requirements of the job.

4. *Statistical Data Format:* The primary technique used to present statistical data within reports is through the use of tables that present text material in columnar formats. A table may be placed within the text closely following its introduction in the text, or it may be placed on a separate page if it is larger than a half page.

a. *Word processing table feature:* The purpose of the table feature in word processing software is to create and edit rows and columns of tabular data, without entering tabs or tab settings. This feature is useful for creating forms that are formatted in tabular form. Input includes the number of columns and rows you want in the table. There is a text-editing mode for editing the text you enter in the table, and there is a table-editing mode that allows you to change the structure of the table. The math feature is used to perform any computations that are necessary within the table. Lines can be added by drawing vertical and horizontal lines where desired to separate column heads from text.

b. *Importing a spreadsheet into a text document:* Using compatible software packages, importing a spreadsheet document into a word processing text document is easy and eliminates the rekeying of data.

c. *Placement of table:* When we refer to placement of the table, we are referring to centering the table (horizontally and vertically) on the page.

(1) *Horizontal placement:* The horizontal placement of a table will be the same whether it is typed within the paragraphs of a document or on a page by itself. When the table function in word processing is not used, there are two methods for determining horizontal placement: the mathematical method and the backspace method.

(a) *The mathematical method:* This method requires careful arithmetic but is useful for determining the left margin and tab stops when using either a word processor or a typewriter.

- Count the number of characters and spaces in the longest line. (*Note:* The longest line consists of the characters and spaces in the longest line in each column.) Remember, when you are counting the number of spaces, that also means the number of spaces between the columns.

EXAMPLE:

In this table, the longest line is underlined. Include five spaces between the columns in planning the placement of the table.

Mary Jones	*1718 Jefferson Drive*	*Rockford, IL 61107-1867*
Thomas Smith	*321 West Avenue*	*DeKalb, IL 60115-1321*

- Divide this total number of characters and spaces in half.

- Subtract the answer from the center point for the left margin. You need to know the center of the *paper* if the table is typed on a page by itself and the center of the *line of print* if the table is typed within a document.

- The tab stops are determined by adding the column spaces plus the spaces between the column to the previous position.

EXAMPLE:

Using the preceding example, there are 65 total characters and spaces in the longest line. Divide 65 by 2, then subtract 32 from the center point for the left margin. From the left margin, add 17 for the first tab stop. From the first tab stop, add 25 for the second tab stop.

(b) *The backspace method:* This method is most convenient when using a conventional typewriter.

- Determine the center of the page or line of print.

- Bring your typing point to the center.

- Backspace once for every two characters and/or spaces in the longest line. (*Note:* Longest line in each column plus spaces between columns.)

  When you begin backspacing from the center point, you will backspace once for every combination of two characters or spaces. Using the example from the mathematical method, the longest line is the following:

  Thomas Smith   1718 Jefferson Drive   Rockford, IL 61107-1867

  Backspace as follows:

  Th om as space/S mi th space/space space/space space/1 71 8/space Je ff er so n/space Dr iv e/space space/space space/space Ro ck fo rd ,/space IL space/6 11 07 -1 86 7

  This totals 32 backspaces and the point where your left margin would be set for the table or the point to begin a table if it is typed within text material.

- The one letter left at the very end of the longest line is dropped in determining the left margin.

(2) *Vertical placement:* The vertical placement of a table depends on whether the table is being placed within text or on a separate page.

(a) *Placement of table within text:* When centering a table vertically within a document, follow these guidelines:

- Make sure that there is sufficient room for the entire table on the same page.

- Triple-space from the last line of text to the title of the table.

- Once you have typed the title, single-space and type a double underscore. When using word processing, use the double-underscore code or superscript the second underscore. On a conventional typewriter, use the variable line spacer to adjust the line of print so the underscores are close together.

- After the double underscore, double-space to the column headings. (Column headings are optional. If they are omitted, double-space to the body of the table.)

- Type the column headings.

- Single-space and type a single underscore.

- After the single underscore, double-space to the body of the table.

- The body of the table may be single-spaced or double-spaced.

- After you have completed the table, single-space and type a single underscore.

- Triple-space after the table to continue the document.

See Figure 19–19 for an example of correct placement of a table within the body of the report text.

Figure 19–19   Placement of Table Within Text

During this period there were four main classes of auxiliary storage devices: tape, disk, drum, and mass storage. Of the four, magnetic tape and magnetic disk were the two most widely used in business during the 1980s. Typical media storage capacity and typical input/output rates for that decade are summarized in Table 6.

Table 6
AUXILIARY STORAGE: HISTORICAL SUMMARY

Device	Storage Media	Input/Output Rates (k per second)	Media Storage Capacity (m per unit)
Magnetic tape drive	Cassette	0.03 to 106	0.3 to 0.7
	Reel	100 to 1250	15 to 60
Magnetic disk drive	Floppy disk	30 to 60	0.25 to 1.0
	Disk pack	00 to 1000	30 to 300

The input/output rate describes the speed at which characters were moved from the . . .

(b) *Placement of table alone on page:* Use a word processing page format command to center a table *vertically* by itself on a sheet of paper. Type the table after the command. The table will be positioned vertically. When centering a table vertically with a conventional typewriter, follow these steps for accurate placement:

- Determine the number of lines available on the page:

    8½ by 11-inch paper:
        Full sheet = 66 lines
        Half sheet = 33 lines

- If you place an odd-sized sheet of paper in the typewriter, there are *six lines to an inch.*

- Count the number of lines in the table. Remember that each blank line equals *one.* Therefore, if you are single-spacing, there are no blank lines. If you are double-spacing, there is one blank line between the lines. With triple-spacing, there are two blank lines between the lines.

- Subtract the number of lines in the table from the number of lines on the sheet of paper you are using. This lets you know how many blank lines are left on the sheet of paper.

- Divide the blank lines that are left by *two* (half for the top of the paper and half for the bottom of the paper).

- If you want your table to be exact, add one. This will let the typing begin on the line immediately below the exact number of blank lines required at the top of the paper.

- If you want your table in *reading position,* subtract 3 from your answer in the previous step. This places the table three lines above exact vertical placement.

When using the format command in word processing for page center, add six hard returns after the last line of the table. This places the table three lines above exact vertical center when printed.

EXAMPLE 1:

Let's add some more names to the horizontal placement example and figure the vertical and horizontal placement if this material is centered on a half sheet of paper, single-spaced. The longest line is underlined for horizontal centering.

Mary Jones	*1718 Jefferson Drive*	*Rockford, IL 61107-1867*
Thomas Smith	*321 West Avenue*	*DeKalb, IL 60115-1321*
Sara Car	*55 Pheasant Avenue*	*Wilmington, IL 60481-2196*
Betty Dryden	*333 Chase Avenue*	*Wenona, IL 61377-0112*
Richard Fremont	*987 Campbell Drive*	*Grafton, IL 62037-1918*

VERTICAL PLACEMENT:

Half sheet of paper = 33 lines

Lines in table = 5 lines

33 − 5 = 28 blank lines available for margins

28 blank lines divided by 2 = 14 lines for the top margin and 14 lines for the bottom margin. To print the material so that it will be centered vertically on the half sheet, add one to 14 and return 15 times to begin typing the first line.

To print the table in reading position, subtract 3 from 14 and begin typing the first line on line 11.

HORIZONTAL PLACEMENT:

Centering the longest line horizontally with five spaces between the columns calculates to 35 backspaces from the center.

Ri ch ar d/space Fr em on t/space space/space space/space 17 18 space/J ef fe rs on space/D ri ve space/space space/space space/W il mi ng to n, space/I L/space 60 48 1- 21 96

EXAMPLE 2:

If you were to type the same five lines on a full sheet of paper, you would end up with a remainder of ½ when you divide by 2. The remainder is dropped. Calculate the vertical placement in this way:

66   lines on a full sheet of paper
_–5_   typed lines in table
61   blank lines available for top and bottom margins

61 divided by 2 = 30 with a remainder of 1 (to be dropped)

To have exactly 30 blank lines at the top of the paper, add 1 to 30 and begin typing the table on line 31.

To print the table in reading position, subtract 3 from 30 and begin typing the table on line 27.

The horizontal centering remains the same.

EXAMPLE 3:

If the material is to be double-spaced, there would be nine lines in the problem:

5   typed lines

1   blank line between first and second line

1   blank line between second and third line

1   blank line between third and fourth line

1   blank line between fourth and fifth line

9   total lines

If the material is to be triple-spaced, there would be 13 lines to the problem (two blank lines between each of the typed lines).

The horizontal centering remains the same.

E. Other Forms of Business Communications

Communication is so important in the office, and there are many forms in which written communication is transmitted. Only some of the most common are presented here along with highlights of the formats used for minutes, news releases, itineraries, outlines, and speeches.

1. *Minutes:* The purpose of *minutes* is to summarize the events of a meeting. The minutes become the official report of the meeting. Figure 19–20 shows an example of minutes prepared by the secretary of an organization. Sometimes, detailed minutes are preferred; at other times, only brief coverage of topics is required. All minutes, however, should be prepared in the following way:

   a. *Heading:* The heading must contain the following types of information:

      (1) Name of the organization (or department) holding the meeting

      (2) Date of the meeting

      (3) Time of the meeting

      (4) Place of the meeting

      (5) Type of meeting (regular or special)

   The heading begins 1½ to 2 inches from the top edge of the page, is either centered or arranged across the line of print, and is either typed in initial caps or in all capital letters. After the heading, triple-space to the next section.

Figure 19–20   Minutes of Meeting

VALLEYVIEW, INC.
Homeowners' Association ↓2 returns

DATE: March 10, 200X   LOCATION: ValleyView Conference Room ↓3

PRESENT: (10) C. Albergetti, T. Brock, J. Carpenter, M. Dollman, F. Hardanger, L. James,
A. Longsman, M. Planters, M. Rintamaki, S. Tillman↓2

ABSENT: (2)↓2

The ValleyView Homeowners' Association monthly meeting was held on Wednesday, March 10,
200X, in the ValleyView Conference Room. President Brock called the meeting to order at 7:30 p.m.
The secretary circulated minutes from the February 8 meeting. It was moved, seconded, and passed
that February minutes be approved. ↓3

Grounds Committee ↓2

The planning and maintenance contract was granted to BBW Lawn and Garden Care. The contract
is for April 1, 200X, through October 21, 200X. The 200X schedule is as follows: ↓2

April 1	Spring flower beds
	Lawn grooming/mowing
April 30	Tree planting ↓3

Recreation Committee ↓2

Thus far, the spring schedule of events is as follows: ↓2

April 4	Spring Showers Picnic	Recreation Hall
May 10	Eagle River Cruise	Pier 3
May 30	Memorial Weekend Picnic	Hopkins Park ↓2

A. Longsman moved and J. Carpenter seconded that "Detailed information regarding the social
events be included in the ValleyView Bulletin." The motion passed unanimously. ↓2

No additional business was brought before the Association. It was moved and seconded that the
meeting be adjourned. The President announced that the next regular meeting is scheduled for
Wednesday, April 11, at 7:30 p.m. in the ValleyView Conference Room. ↓2

Respectfully submitted, ↓4 returns
(3 blank lines)

Lois R. James, Secretary

Note: No reference initials are shown here because these minutes were prepared by the secretary of the
organization. Notations for desired spacing are inserted ↓2 = 2 returns (1 blank line); ↓3 = 3 returns
(2 blank lines).

b. *Attendance:* An alphabetical list of the names of the people (members) who attended the meeting are included in the first paragraph at the beginning of the minutes. Including an alphabetical list of people (members) who are absent (or the number of people absent) is desirable but optional. Special guests at the meeting may also be identified.

c. *Body:* Minutes are a summary of the topics discussed at the meeting. It is helpful to follow the agenda while taking minutes at a meeting. The presentation of this summary information is usually in paragraph form. The marginal format for typing reports is followed for typing minutes. If headings are used, follow the same format as for reports. Minutes are usually single-spaced, with double-spacing between paragraphs. However, double-spacing is also appropriate.

d. *Motions:* For routine motions, the secretary can record, *It was moved and seconded that . . .* When a motion is made where the exact wording is required, the names of those making and seconding the motion are also recorded. The recording of any motion is included in the topic paragraph pertaining to the motion. Some correctly stated motions are as follows:

EXAMPLES:

Caldwell moved and Heartland seconded the motion that . . .

The motion was made by M. Caldwell and seconded by R. Heartland that . . .

It was moved and seconded that . . .
(This example is for routine motions only.)

Note: Last names may be used when identifying people who made or seconded motions or entered into the discussion of motions. However, when two participants have the same last name, initials or first names must be used to properly identify the persons involved in the motions or discussion. In the latter case, all participants should be identified in the same way throughout the minutes.

e. *Closing:* The complimentary closing for minutes is *Respectfully submitted.* There are three blank lines (four returns) between the complimentary closing and the typed signature of the secretary. If you are typing the minutes for the secretary, your reference initials should follow a double space after the typed signature.

EXAMPLE:

Respectfully submitted, ↓4 returns
                                        (3 blank lines)

Melvin E. Schneider
Secretary ↓2 returns

gmd

2. *News Release:* The *news release* is an item that usually needs to be typed immediately by the secretary. The urgency of the item will depend on the date of the news. From the reader's viewpoint, news is news only if it is announcing something before the fact or immediately after it happens. If you are responsible for making sure news releases get to the press in time (whether the press is in-house or the local newspapers), you should be aware of the lead time required. This is particularly true for announcement news. Typical lead time required for a news release is 10 days. To find out specifically for your local paper, contact the newspaper's City Desk. A news release should include these parts: heading, body, and closing symbols.

a. *Heading:* The heading should include the fact that it is a news release, when it should be released, the company name and address, the name of a person to contact in case there are questions, and a telephone number. The heading may also include the date of the release. After the heading, there should be a break by either underscoring or typing asterisks across the line of print. (See Section F-2-d[5]: single-space to an underscore break; double-space to an asterisk break.)

b. *Body:* The body of the news release should have a title that is indicative of what is in the news. A news release is written in the direct approach: The news is presented in the first sentence. Important facts to remember for the beginning are *who, what, where, when,* and *why.* The balance of the release follows up with pertinent facts. A good news release is written clearly and concisely.

c. *Closing symbols:* To indicate the conclusion of the release, printer's closing symbols are centered at the end. The symbol can be either three number symbols or a number 30 with a hyphen before and after.

EXAMPLES:

or   # #

–30–   *or*   *– 30 –*

d. *Spacing the news release:*

(1) *Top margin:* The top margin can vary from ½ to 2 inches, depending on the length of the news release. If the news release is lengthy (although remember, good news is clear and concise), the top margin should be narrower to keep the release to one page.

(2) *Side margin:* Side margins can also be adjusted to make sure that the release is one page in length. Side margins should never be narrower than 1 inch, however. You must be able to judge the length of the news release and strive to have it set up attractively on one page.

(3) *Bottom margin:* A minimum of 1 inch is necessary at the bottom. However, with shorter news releases, the bottom margin could be more than 1 inch.

(4) *Heading:* Single-space lines in the heading that belong together and double-space between groups of lines. Information that should stand out should be typed in all capital letters. Using spread-typing for some of the heading information is also appropriate.

(5) *Break line:* There should appear to be a blank line between the heading and the break line. If you use the underscore, single-space to the underscore. If you use asterisks for the break line, double-space to the asterisks.

EXAMPLE 1:

N E W S R E L E A S E	*ALFO INDUSTRIES*
	1321 Manchester Court
	Silver Spring, MD 20901-1221
RELEASE IMMEDIATELY	*For Further Information*
	Contact Sally Mitchell
	(301-754-3214)

EXAMPLE 2:

NEWS RELEASE
RELEASE IMMEDIATELY

ALFO INDUSTRIES   *For Further Information*
1321 Manchester Court   *Contact Sally Mitchell*
Silver Spring, MD 20901-1221   *(301) 754-3214*

* *

(6) *Body:* Triple-space from the break line to the title of the news release. The title should be centered and typed in all capital letters. If the title consists of more than one line, it is to be single-spaced. Triple-space to the paragraphs. Double-space the paragraphs with standard (½ inch) paragraph indentations. If block paragraphs are used, triple-space between the paragraphs.

(7) *Closing symbols:* Triple-space after the last paragraph to the closing symbols. The closing symbols are to be typed in the center of the page.

3. *Itinerary:* An *itinerary* is an executive's travel plan that specifies all details concerning a business trip. Copies should be available prior to the trip so that the office, the secretary, the executive, and the executive's family know the details of the trip.

  a. *Types of information:* The itinerary typically includes the following details:

  (1) Departure date, time, and place

  (2) Type of confirmed transportation

  (3) Arrival data, time, and place

  (4) Lodging reservation(s) for each date or segment of the trip

  (5) Scheduled appointments and meetings

  (6) Complete travel information for return trip

  b. *Parts of the itinerary:* The following guidelines will help in preparing an itinerary for the executive to share with the office, the secretary, and family (see Figure 8–1 for a sample itinerary).

  (1) *Headings:* The itinerary should be titled "Itinerary for (name of business traveler)" with the dates of the trip as a subheading. These lines should be centered.

  (2) *Columns of information:* Two groups of information are included on the itinerary: the dates and times of business commitments during the trip on the left and the travel and meeting information on the right.

    (a) *Dates/times:* On the left side of the itinerary, the dates and specific times of flights, meetings, appointments, and any other events must be typed. A special notation of the time in effect for each location (e.g., CST for Central Standard Time) should be included so that there will be no misunderstandings in regard to appointment times.

    (b) *Travel and meeting information:* To the right, entries give detailed information regarding reservations (transportation and/or lodging), meetings, luncheons, conferences, or other commitments. Complete information for companies (names, addresses, telephone numbers, contact people) and any other special details should be included.

    c. *Format of itinerary:* The itinerary is prepared in printed form so that it can serve as an easy-to-understand reference for the executive and others to use.

        (1) *Margins:* Side margins should be at least 1 inch, with the top margin on the first page 2 inches and the bottom margin on the first page 1 inch. (These are minimum space allocations.)

        (2) *Spacing:* Headings should be double-spaced, with a triple-space before the body of the itinerary begins. The text material should be single-spaced with a double-space between each entry.

        (3) *Headings:* Headings should be double-spaced and centered. The main heading should be typed in all capital letters, while the subheading should be typed in initial caps and may be underlined.

        (4) *Second-page continuation:* If the itinerary is more than one page, the second-page continuation and succeeding pages should have a page heading like this:

ITINERARY FOR MARLENE T. BAILEY
Page 2
January 10-12, 200X

This continuation-page heading should begin ½ inch (line 4) from the top edge, with the text continuing three returns from the last line of the heading.

    4. *Outline:* There are times when a document must be in outline format. An *outline* consists of key words coded in descending order, using roman numerals, numbers, and letters of the alphabet.

    a. *Coding the outline:* The roman numeral is considered the highest in coding sequence. In descending order, the outline adheres to the following sequence:

        (1) Roman numeral, beginning with I

        (2) Capital letters of the alphabet, A–Z

        (3) Numbers, beginning with 1

        (4) Lowercase letters of the alphabet, a–z

        (5) Numbers in parentheses, beginning with (1)

        (6) Lowercase letters of the alphabet in parentheses, (a)–(z)

Each section starts the sequence from the beginning code, and each section should have at least two codes within the sequence. Also, when setting up the side margins for an outline, you should determine the code that will require the most space. Indent from that point so the decimal points for all codes within the sequence are aligned. All codes end with a period or parenthesis. Space twice after the period or parenthesis.

In a word processing environment, indent (or tab) once after the period or parenthesis. If the text that follows the enumeration is longer than one line, the use of the indent or tab feature that allows succeeding lines to indent and align with the text until there is a return should be used. See Figure 19–21 (II-A in the illustration).

Figure 19–21 is an example of an outline format with two major divisions (identified by roman numerals). Division II includes the lowest sequencing. Notice that all sequencing consists of at least two codes within that sequence.

Figure 19–21   Example of Outline Format

BUSINESS TECHNOLOGY EXPOSITION

I. Sponsored by IAAP Chapter, Rockford, Illinois
   A. Date: April 25, 200X
   B. Location: Charleston Hotel
II. Reasons Why Abby Corporation Should Participate
   A. Participation last year by 45 local and area businesses who displayed technology, office
       equipment, and supplies
      1. Ten of these businesses are direct competitors
         a. Eight are networking
           (1) Client-server model
              (a) Ongoing demonstration
              (b) Presentation (10 to 11 a.m.) *The Internet and the Client/Server Model*
           (2) Value-added networks
         b. Two are on-line services
      2. Five of the businesses are those considering location in Rockford
   B. Goodwill established with participating businesses
   C. Goodwill established with clients
      1. Attendance last year was 10,595
      2. Projected attendance for 200X is 15,000

---

    b. *Spacing an outline:* The first consideration must be given to readability from the reader's viewpoint. Therefore, judgment on your part as to single-spacing or double-spacing the outline is important. Once spacing format has been determined, be consistent throughout the document. When the text for an enumeration consists of more than one line, single-space for that section.

        (1) If the outline consists mainly of phrases that are two or more lines in length, the outline is usually double-spaced between all points.

        (2) If the key words are short in nature, you may decide to single-space within that outline.

    Spacing before the main sections (those coded with roman numerals) is always double-spacing. Spacing after the main sections may or may not be double-spaced. In Figure 19–21, double-spacing was used for readability because of the length of the typed lines. The outline still fits on one page.

5. *Speech:* When a speech must be prepared, some of the same techniques that are used to prepare a written report are used, especially in the planning stages. The basic steps in preparing a speech include the selection of a topic, background research, organization of the material, and the actual presentation of the information. The administrative assistant or secretary may play a very important role in assisting with the background research and organization of the material for the speech. In addition, printed copies of the outline of the speech, the actual speech (if a complete text is required), and any related handout materials will be needed.

    a. *Printed outline of speech:* Many speakers use outlines to remind them of important points to make. The outline also has these points in sequential order so that the speaker can instantly refer to the next point without turning pages. The majority of speeches do not require a complete typed text; typed or printed outlines (and sometimes notes) are sufficient for most presenters.

(1) *Topical outline:* This type of outline directs the speaker from point to point with a brief listing of nouns rather than lengthy phrases. The speaker must rely heavily on memory.

(2) *Phrase outline:* This type of outline is more extensive than a topical outline, with more information related to each point. Only essential words are included, however.

(3) *Sentence outline:* Key sentences are included to prompt the speaker to expand on these ideas. This type of outline includes the most complete information.

No matter which type of outline is employed, details or facts that might be forgotten easily by the speaker should be noted on the outline, too.

EXAMPLE:

If the speaker highlights population trends in the United States and compares these trends with the number of employed persons in the country, perhaps it is a good idea to include these numbers on the outline as well—near the topic, phrase, or sentence used.

b. *The actual speech:* If the entire text of the speech needs to be typed, as is the case of a paper to be read by the speaker, the secretary will need to type the text for easy reading at the podium. Here are some techniques that are often used to prepare a typed or printed speech.

(1) *Spacing:* The speech should be double-spaced with a triple-space between paragraphs. One-inch side margins should be sufficient as well as 1-inch top and bottom margins.

(2) *Type font and size:* At least a 12- or 14-point font when using word processing software or a pica (10-pitch) type size when using a typewriter should be used for ease of reading. A larger type face will create images that will appear large and much easier to read from a distance. The speaker who has trouble with bifocals or lighting conditions will have an easier time reading larger type.

(3) *Accuracy of typing:* Be sure that there are no noticeable corrections that will distract the speaker while he or she is speaking. The speech should be arranged neatly on the page and prepared accurately.

c. *Handout materials:* The speaker may want to share some sample handout materials with the audience. In this case, the secretary should make sure that these are prepared ahead of time and arranged so that the speaker can integrate these with the presentation. With speeches that are being read, the handout material may be a copy of the speech; this is the case for research presentations. These copies should be available in quantity for the speaker to distribute either at the beginning or at the close of the presentation.

d. *Visual aids:* Some speakers will require visual aids (transparencies, 35-millimeter slides, or electronic slides) to be prepared ahead of time to accompany the speech. The secretary should work in cooperation with the executive to determine exactly what types of visual aids to prepare. These should be ready ahead of time so that the executive can use them in practicing for the presentation (see Chapter 11 for directions on the preparation of audiovisual aids).

Review Questions

Directions: Select the best answer from the four alternatives. Write your answer in the blank to the left of the number.

_____ 1. The address to whom a business letter will be mailed is called the

    a. inside address.
    b. salutation.
    c. return address.
    d. letterhead.

_____ 2. If the letter contains both an attention line and a subject line, the attention line

    a. is typed a double-space after the inside address, with the subject line immediately following.
    b. may be underlined while the subject line is typed in all capitals.
    c. should follow the same style as the subject line: both all caps, initial caps, and/or underscored.
    d. immediately follows the subject line, which is typed a double-space after the inside address.

_____ 3. Which one of the following salutations is most appropriate for a congratulatory letter being addressed to the Norbort Corp., Sales Division, Attention R. N. Johnson?

    a. Dear Mr. Johnson
    b. Dear Sales Division Manager
    c. Dear Norbort Corp.
    d. With an attention line, the salutation is omitted.

_____ 4. The best complimentary closing for a formal letter from the president of Morris Inc. to new members of the board of directors is

    a. Cordially
    b. Sincerely
    c. Yours truly
    d. Respectfully yours

_____ 5. If material is enclosed with the letter, an enclosure notation is typed

    a. a double-space after the complimentary closing as either a full word or abbreviated.
    b. a double-space after the reference initials and typed as a full word; do not abbreviate.
    c. in all capital letters, spelled as a full word or abbreviated, a double-space after the reference initials.
    d. in initial caps, spelled as a full word or abbreviated, a double-space after the reference initials.

6. Copies of a business letter are being sent to two other people, but the enclosure sent
with the original letter is not being sent with the copies. The copy notation is typed
immediately after the

a. typed signature line and title.
b. enclosure notation.
c. reference initials.
d. body of the letter.

7. A letter is being sent by certified mail to each member of the board of directors. The
special mailing notation CERTIFIED will appear in all capitals

a. a double-space below the date line at the left margin.
b. a double-space below the inside address at the left margin.
c. on the envelope only just below the postage.
d. a double-space below the enclosure notation.

8. A letter with all lines beginning at the left margin, including the salutation and complimentary closing, is prepared in

a. modified blocked letter style.
b. blocked letter style.
c. simplified letter style.
d. indented letter style.

9. Which one of the following letter styles includes a subject line instead of a salutation?

a. Blocked letter style
b. Modified blocked letter style
c. Indented letter style
d. Simplified letter style

10. The use of open punctuation style in a business letter requires

a. a comma after the complimentary closing.
b. a colon after the salutation.
c. no punctuation after the complimentary closing or salutation.
d. a comma after the salutation.

11. Which one of the following is a correctly typed second-page heading for a two-page
letter addressed to Mr. James P. Smith, Jr., prepared in blocked style?

a. Mr. James P. Smith, Jr.—Finance Department—Page 2
b. Mr. James P. Smith, Jr.
   January 21, 200X
   Page 2
c. Mr. James P. Smith, Jr.
   Page 2
   January 21, 200X
d. Smith—Finance—January

————————

12. When typing an address on a standard business envelope,

    a. the five-digit ZIP code is sufficient.
    b. punctuation marks should be used after any abbreviated word.
    c. the name of the state should be written in full.
    d. all words are to be typed in capital letters.

————————

13. Where should special mailing notations, such as REGISTERED and CERTIFIED, be typed on a business envelope?

    a. In the lower-left corner
    b. In the upper-left corner, a double-space after the return address
    c. In the upper-right corner, a double-space under the postage block
    d. A double-space above the first line of the mailing address

————————

14. To process large volumes of mail, the U.S. Postal Service uses

    a. magnetic ink character recognition (MICR).
    b. optical character recognition (OCR).
    c. point-of-sale (POS) terminals.
    d. express mail.

————————

15. When addresses are printed using database management software, the variable address data are stored in a

    a. code file.
    b. file.
    c. document.
    d. label.

————————

16. If your word processing software does not have a mail-merge function, the best way to address envelopes would be to

    a. create a code file to be used whenever an address needs to be printed.
    b. upgrade the word processing software to a package with a mail-merge function.
    c. use a conventional typewriter.
    d. write the addresses by hand.

————————

17. A correspondence format specifically designed for internal use between individuals, departments, and branch offices is the

    a. business letter.
    b. memorandum.
    c. news release.
    d. report.

_____   **18.** Which one of the following statements is correct?

a. For an unbound report, the left margin is 1½ inches and the right margin is 1 inch.
b. The right margin on each page of the report needs to be 1½ inches.
c. The second page of the report can have a header ½ inch from the top edge at the left margin.
d. The top margin on the first page of a report should be 2 inches where there is no title on that page.

_____   **19.** A helpful tool for making sure text does not extend into the top or bottom margins or into the left and right margins is a/an

a. automatic supplement function in word processing.
b. page-end guide.
c. margin guide.
d. widow function in word processing.

_____   **20.** Documentation typically refers to the style in which the

a. works cited bibliography is prepared.
b. reference list at the end of a report is prepared.
c. citations appear within the text.
d. reference notes and bibliographic information appear within the report.

_____   **21.** Reference notes that appear at the end of the report on a separate page are referred to as

a. works cited.
b. endnotes.
c. parenthetical citations.
d. footnotes.

_____   **22.** The term *Ibid.* means that reference is made to

a. a previous source, but there are intervening references.
b. more than one reference appearing previously in the report.
c. the immediately preceding reference.
d. the same page reference as a previous reference whether or not there are intervening references.

_____   **23.** Which one of the following is an in-text citation written in APA style?

a. (Parkinson 25)
b. (Stevens 1999 25)
c. (World 225)
d. (Williams & Parke, 1999, 251)

24. If a source has no author name, the in-text citation must include the

    a. date of publication and page number of the reference.
    b. first major word of the title of the reference.
    c. page number being referenced.
    d. name of the publisher and date of publication.

25. An in-text citation or reference note is required when

    a. a passage is a verbatim quote of the original work.
    b. the original author's ideas are paraphrased.
    c. either a passage is directly quoted or is paraphrased from the original work.
    d. the source is correctly identified in the bibliography.

26. A list of all references cited by the writer in the content of the report is called a/an

    a. annotated bibliography.
    b. in-text citation.
    c. works cited bibliography.
    d. general bibliography.

27. When a graphic illustration based on primary data is used within text, the source reference

    a. is included as a part of the subtitle of the illustration.
    b. is typed immediately after the title of the illustration.
    c. may be omitted.
    d. should be included with the other reference citations.

28. Text material in the form of words and numbers presented in a columnar format is called a

    a. table.
    b. figure.
    c. pictogram.
    d. line graph.

29. An illustration consisting of a series of connected lines showing a particular business trend over a period of time is a

    a. bar graph.
    b. line graph.
    c. pictogram.
    d. pie graph.

30. An illustration that depicts the parts of a whole is a

    a. bar graph.
    b. drawing.
    c. pictogram.
    d. pie graph.

31. A table summarizing the results of an employee survey will be prepared using word processing software. Horizontal placement is best determined by

    a. beginning at the center of the line and backspacing once for every two characters or spaces in the longest line.
    b. beginning at the left margin and spacing forward for every character or space in the longest line.
    c. counting the number of characters and spaces in the longest line, dividing by two, and subtracting the answer from the center point for the left margin.
    d. using the table function.

32. A table is being prepared using word processing software. The body of the report is single-spaced. For the vertical placement of the table on a page following text material,

    a. double-space from the last line of text to the title of the table.
    b. triple-space from the last line of text to the title of the table; write *(Continue)* at the bottom of the page and repeat the table title followed by *(Continued)* at the top of the next page.
    c. triple-space from the last line of text to the title of the table.
    d. use the center-page code before typing the title of the table.

33. Statistical data that have been entered onto a spreadsheet

    a. must be reformatted before being imported into a document created with word processing software.
    b. can be imported into a compatible word processing text document.
    c. can only be saved in a spreadsheet format.
    d. must be reentered as text within a word processing text document.

34. The official report of a meeting summarizing the events that occurred during the meeting and distributed to those who attended is known as

    a. an agenda.
    b. minutes.
    c. proceedings.
    d. a summary.

35. A secretary is sometimes called on to assist with the executive's preparation for a speech. Which one of the following tasks would be particularly applicable to this situation?

    a. Gathering background research on possible content for the speech
    b. Reminding the speaker to prepare visual aids
    c. Preparing a rough copy of the speech to assist with the presentation
    d. Acting as a ghostwriter for the speaker and writing the speech

Solutions

Answer	*Refer to:*
1. (a)	[A-1-b]
2. (c)	[A-1-c]
3. (b)	[A-1-d]
4. (a)	[A-1-g]
5. (d)	[A-1-j]
6. (c)	[A-1-k]
7. (a)	[A-1-m]
8. (b)	[A-2-a]
9. (d)	[A-2-c]
10. (c)	[A-3-a]
11. (c)	[A-4-a, Figure 19–6]
12. (d)	[B-1-b]
13. (c)	[B-1-h]
14. (b)	[B-2]
15. (b)	[B-4-a(1)]
16. (a)	[B-4-c]
17. (b)	[C]
18. (c)	[D-1-a(1)(c)]
19. (c)	[D-1-h]
20. (d)	[D-2]
21. (b)	[D-2-a(1)]
22. (c)	[D-2-a(1)(d)]

23. (d)   [D-2-a(2)]

24. (b)   [D-2-a(2)(c)]

25. (c)   [D-2-b(3)]

26. (c)   [D-2-c(1)(b)]

27. (c)   [D-3-b(2)(a)]

28. (a)   [D-3-c(1)]

29. (b)   [D-3-c(2)(b)]

30. (d)   [D-3-c(2)(c)]

31. (d)   [D-4-a]

32. (c)   [D-4-c(2)(a)]

33. (b)   [D-4-b]

34. (b)   [E-1]

35. (a)   [E-5]

CHAPTER
20

Oral Communications

OVERVIEW

Studies show that people spend about 80 percent of their waking hours communicating in one form or another—reading, writing, speaking, or listening. Therefore, effective communication is extremely important for an office to run efficiently. Communication represents the glue that binds the various management functions together and keeps the organization vibrant. Because communication is so important, secretaries must understand the communication process and the reasons for misunderstandings that occur as well as ways to decrease misunderstood communication within the organization.

This chapter involves the major elements of oral communication: interpersonal communication, listening, nonverbal cues, and effective presentation skills. Some of the more widely encountered communication barriers are presented, followed by an explanation of approaches and techniques that can be utilized to improve communication effectiveness in organizational, interpersonal, and personal settings.

Since secretaries are often asked to give presentations to management and colleagues within their professional organizations, this chapter highlights preparation for giving a speech.

Communication affects the daily lives of everyone because of the constant barrage of various types, forms, and sources of messages. An active understanding of communication is thus essential for both organizational and personal success.

KEY TERMS

Ambiguous
Body language
Brainstorm
Channel
Communication
Communication environment
Consistency
Criticism
Culture
Decoding
Encoding

Enunciate
External distractions
Feedback
Hearing
Inherent
Internal distractions
Interpreting
Listening
Long-term memory
Message
Nonverbal communication

Praise
Semantic distractions
Short-term memory
Space and distance
Speaker
Touch
Transactional
Verbal communication
Visual aids
Visualization
Vocal attributes

A. The Enhancement of Understanding

As the lifeblood of any organization, communication represents the uniting force that directs the many activities and efforts toward achieving both organizational and personal goals. The importance of effective communication cannot be overstated. The key to effective communication is understanding. However, so many factors and elements are associated with the communication process that one can easily appreciate how and why misunderstandings arise.

1. *A Working Definition of Communication: Communication* is the process of sharing information and meaning, both knowingly and unknowingly, that requires the response of a receiver.

    a. *Communication as a process:* Communication is an ongoing process that involves an exchange of information between speakers (senders) and listeners (receivers) in which those roles are shared. Thus, speakers and listeners simultaneously send and receive messages. When you are not conversing with someone, you are talking to yourself. Sometimes you speak to yourself while you are listening to and even talking with another person.

        EXAMPLE: Jackson is busy organizing the work on her desk when Struthers stops by to ask how her granddaughter is feeling. While Jackson gives Struthers a report on her granddaughter's condition, she is thinking to herself that she needs to mail the card she bought. During the conversation, Jackson is attentive to Struthers and responds to her questions. When Struthers leaves, Jackson immediately writes herself a note and puts it in her purse so she does not forget to mail the card.

    b. *Sharing of information:* Communication requires sharing messages that you want the receiver to understand. When you have something to say to someone else, you purposely select words and symbols that you think have a shared meaning with the person with whom you are communicating. You would not choose to speak or write in a language unfamiliar to the receiver of the messages; otherwise, you would be wasting your time and energy as well as that of the receiver. In addition, if understanding is not reached, communication does not really exist. Transmission without reciprocal understanding is not communication.

    c. *Meaning of the message:* Communication requires the attachment of some meaning to the message that has been sent or received. One of the biggest problems associated with communication is that the meanings that the sender intended may not be the receiver's perceived meanings. Cultural backgrounds and previous experiences help to shape the meaning attached to words. In the communication process, a preconceived notion of what a person is going to say often exists. When this happens, you tend not to hear the words that come out. Instead, you fulfill your own expectations of the conversation. Participants in a conversation must always attempt to understand what the others are saying and hearing. This active participation in communication will improve the full understanding of the message.

    d. *Transmission of information:* When you communicate, you transmit information both knowingly and unknowingly. Although just the right words are usually carefully selected when speaking, people seldom think about the way they are speaking. People often fail to realize that how something is said is often more important than what is said. Therefore, not only should you concentrate on the words (the verbal aspect of communication), you must also think about that part of the communication consisting of nonverbal cues that is beyond words (e.g., tone of voice, posture, and facial expressions). (For a better understanding of the role non-verbal communication plays in sending messages, read Section D). Because intentional and unintentional messages are often sent, the receiver can easily get confused as to the "real" meaning. When this happens, the listener often jumps to conclusions that might be far from the truth.

EXAMPLE: Wilson is running a little late for work this morning and not as careful in selecting her outfit. In her rush, she selects a dress that is not the most flattering. Consequently, she feels self-conscious the entire morning. After lunch, another administrative assistant in the office asks Wilson whether she has lost some weight. Sure that Cooper is just rubbing in the fact that the dress makes Wilson look heavier, she gives him a nasty glance, comments that he looks like he's the one who has gained weight, and then turns back to her work. Cooper goes back to his desk wondering why Wilson did not like the report submitted that morning. Pulling on his belt, he makes plans to start a diet that evening.

    e. *Response of the receiver:* For effective communication to take place, the receiver needs to respond to the message that is sent. This response, often referred to as *feedback,* helps the sender determine whether the message sent was truly received and understood. The listener's response can take any form, including words, action, thinking to oneself, and even silence. If you have ever telephoned someone for information, you know the frustration of not receiving a response to comments and questions. When communicating face to face, you can often tell whether someone is confused about what is being said. Sometimes, however, the receivers of messages pretend to understand. Although many reasons might exist for this, some people are too self-conscious to ask questions or make comments. Depending on cultural upbringing, others believe that asking questions of a superior is a sign of disrespect.

  2. *The Importance of Communication:* Communication is vital to any organization's successful existence. When communication within an organization becomes ineffective, the organization will encounter many problems and will experience a decline in effectiveness. Communication is very important in all interpersonal relationships. The following highlights are important communication outcomes for the workplace.

    a. *Method of influencing task performance:* Communication is the method through which leaders and managers attempt to influence others to perform tasks required for achieving organizational goals.

    b. *Link between plans and actions:* Communications activate an organization by serving as a linking pin between plans and actions. An organization can have a clear and understandable mission, general objectives for implementation, and specific work plans explaining the roles of each person in goal achievement. However, if the mission and plans are not shared and understood in basically the same way, chaos and inaction result. Employers cannot act effectively if they do not know what to do and what performance standards are expected.

    c. *Integral device for effective decision making:* Communication ensures that relevant information necessary for effective decision making is shared and that the decisions are then passed along to the appropriate office personnel.

    d. *Means for enhancing effective working relationships:* Most jobs require work with others, often in a team. Without effective communication skills, a person cannot relate appropriately with other people. Effective communication enables people to resolve office conflicts in a more productive way. Positive communication skills can make the office a less stressful and more enjoyable place to work.

e. *Way to share emotions:* Through communication, workers can share their feelings of excitement and frustration with their peers and with management.

f. *Social need for belonging:* Communication permits people to share mutual experiences, preferences, likes, and dislikes and to become part of informal groups, satisfying the basic need for belonging and relatedness.

g. *Aids for instruction:* Teaching new or temporary office workers what they must do in their positions requires clear communication.

h. *Assistance in problem solving:* Work groups are becoming more prevalent, especially in today's office. Managers and subordinates are expected to engage in give-and-take discussion sessions to help solve problems. This task can be accomplished more efficiently through effective group communications.

3. *The Communication Process:* Communication is conducted through a complex process. This transactional process consists of many distinct factors interacting together, often simultaneously. Problems can occur as a result of breakdowns during the interactions between any of the elements, although many communication misunderstandings are the result of failures occurring within several factors of the process at the same time. The worst assumption anyone can make about a message just sent or received is that it was received as intended. Since so many things can go wrong, you should always assume that something will! Recognizing the presence of communication obstacles is by far the biggest battle in achieving understanding. For you to be a successful speaker and listener, you must first recognize the barriers that create misunderstandings and that must be overcome within each element of the communication process. The major factors in the communication process, shown in Figure 20–1, are the speaker, the message, the channel, the listener(s), feedback, distractions, and the communication environment.

a. *The speaker:* Communication involves a speaker who is the source of a message. The speaker can be anyone. Secretaries may communicate with top-level managers, maintenance personnel, administrative assistants, clients, suppliers, public officials, and lay citizens. The speaker has an idea or information that needs to be shared with others.

(1) *Encoding:* Before any communication occurs, the idea, feeling, information, or action the speaker is purposely trying to transmit needs to be formed into symbols that the other person understands. The process of assigning and organizing symbols (e.g., words or gestures) to formulate the message you want to send is called *encoding.*

(2) *Speaker's communication problems:* Many communication problems are associated with the speaker. Here are some typical problems speakers encounter and some recommended solutions.

(a) *Planning:* The speaker needs to plan what message to convey. Without planning, messages can be vague and/or inconsistent, thus confusing to the listener(s). Think about the intent of the message from the point of view of the speaker as well as the receiver before speaking. Select words that are as specific as possible. To ensure understanding, ask the listeners

Figure 20–1   The Communication Process

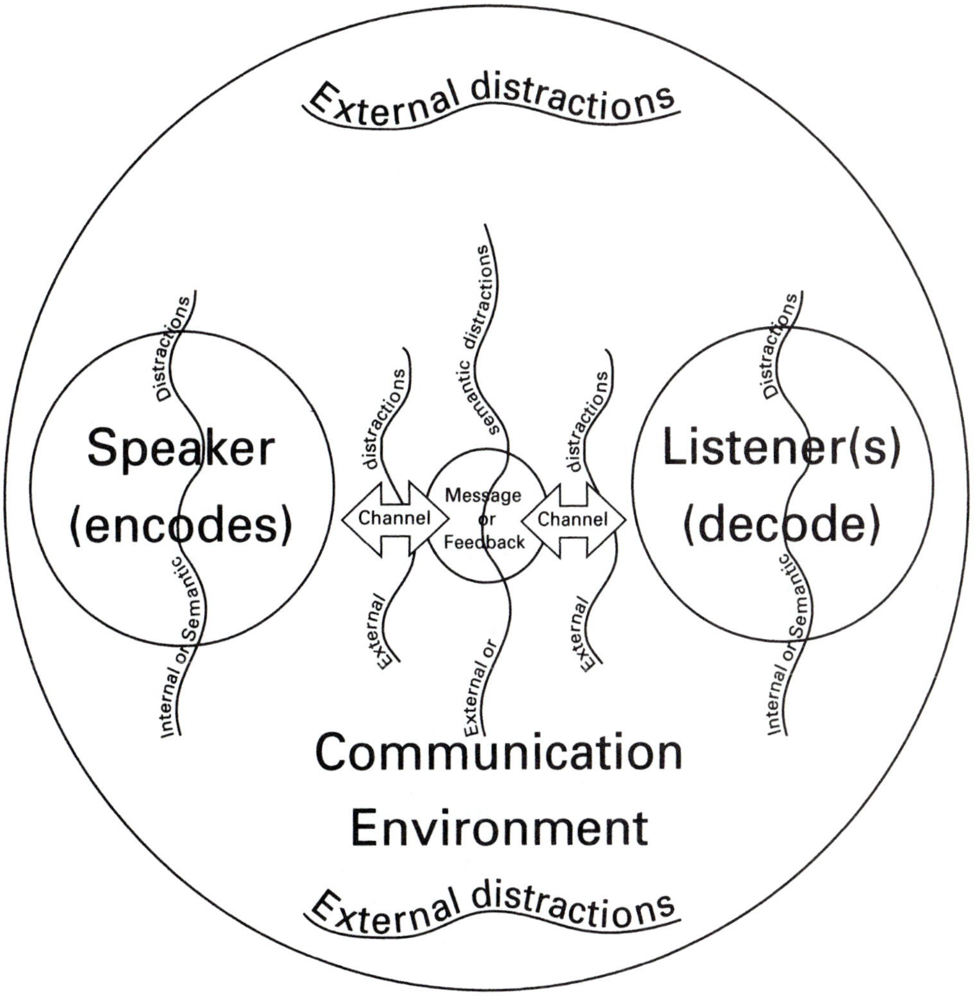

to verify what they heard (understood) by having them paraphrase or repeat your directions. In turn, when the speaker becomes the listener, verification of understanding is very important.

(b) *Distinct speaking:* Speaking too quickly or too softly or not enunciating clearly affects the listener's ability to understand. Obviously, the key is to speak distinctly. Again, verify understanding. Often, facial expressions and posture can help determine whether the message is being understood by the listener.

Note: Understanding does not mean agreement.

(c) *Paying attention:* Concentrate on the nonverbal messages being sent. If participants do not pay attention to nonverbal messages, interference and conflict with verbal messages may occur that will confuse the listener. Nonverbal cues are an important part of all communication encounters and should enhance the communication process. Paying attention to all aspects of the message is vital for communication to take place.

b. *The message:* The result of the encoding process is the development of the message to be sent.

   (1) *Selection of symbols:* The symbols you select to convey the message can be verbal (words), nonverbal (facial expressions, gestures, and movements), or a verbal-nonverbal combination.

   (2) *Source of misinterpretation:* The message can be the source of misinterpretations.

   (a) Many people believe words have an innate meaning that is understood and agreed upon by all who use them. Words, however, have different meanings for each person. This dilemma is especially true for people from diverse backgrounds. Can you think of a word that means different things depending on what region of the United States you grew up in or what country you are from?

   EXAMPLE: Harrington, a Minnesotan, is visiting out west. While shopping in a mall, he suddenly gets thirsty. Harrington asks a clerk where the nearest "bubbler" is. Where Harrington lives, a water fountain is a "bubbler."

   (b) Sometimes, the problem may simply be semantics. When the words are not chosen carefully or the listener does not have the vocabulary to understand them, a problem of semantics is encountered. The words you select may also be technical terms. People outside the discipline may not understand these words. Remember, the goal is communication; simple words that enhance understanding affect the listener more than a string of words that illustrate an extensive vocabulary in a certain discipline.

   (c) Difficulty may stem from the use of nonspecific phrases or vague terms.

   EXAMPLE: Castle sends her secretary to the office supply store to buy a large envelope to mail a special project to a client. Assuming that Johnson will remember the project she showed him two days ago, Castle does not bother to give specific measurements. When Johnson returns, Castle is irritated because he bought the wrong size. By not being more specific in describing the size of the project to be mailed, an extra trip to the supply store was necessary. Extra activities cost extra time and money.

c. *The channel:* The connecting device between the speaker and the listener(s) through which the message is sent is the *channel.*

   (1) *Types of communication channels:* Many different types of communication channels are available to the speaker (e.g., telephone, memorandum, bulletin board, face-to-face conversation, electronic mail, and fax messages). One of the major considerations during the communication process is to ensure that the proper channel has been selected.

   (a) *Impersonal channels:* Impersonal channels such as written reports and notices on bulletin boards or in the electronic mailbox are best for clear, simple, and routine messages. Such channels are considered to be useful when a small amount of information needs to be communicated and the message is simple and straightforward.

   (b) *Direct personal channels:* These channels consist of face-to-face conversations, telephone calls, and meetings/conferences and are best for sharing lengthy, complex, ambiguous, and nonroutine messages.

(2) *Number of channels used:* Another consideration is the number of channels a message may have to go through to reach all the people involved. The amount of time allocated to get the information out is also important.

    (a) *Retention of basic meaning:* You cannot expect to communicate information, especially through a multiplicity of channels or to a large number of people, and still retain the basic meaning. Remember the game of "telephone"? The philosophy is the same in real life. Every time you pass the message on to others, the message is filtered through the receivers' own perceptions; some pieces are added while others are left out. Eventually, the message can get so changed, the sender may not even recognize it. A message that must go through a number of people is best put in writing or video- or audiotaped.

    (b) *Interactive channels:* The shorter the time allowed, the more important face-to-face conversations, telephone calls, and meetings become. These interactive channels allow for questions and concerns to be immediately addressed.

d. *The listener:* The person(s) to whom the message is directed is the listener(s). The speaker must take the listener(s) into account when encoding the message and selecting the channel for transmission (see Section C for more detailed information on listening).

(1) *Receiving the message:* Often, the listener may not receive the message, persons other than the intended receiver may receive it, or the receiver and unintended people accept the message simultaneously. The speaker must be cautious to ensure that proprietary (confidential) messages designed for particular people are received only by the intended parties. The medium and symbols used can play an important role in this respect.

EXAMPLES:

During the Persian Gulf War, the NATO troops led by the American military used sophisticated systems for sending messages so that the Iraqis would not be able to determine what they were planning. At the same time, the communication systems of the Iraqis were destroyed so that their efforts would be hindered.

Stories about corporate "spies" abound, especially during negotiations between management and labor.

(2) *Decoding the message:* The process by which the listener(s) interprets the meaning(s) of the message is known as *decoding.* If the speaker (or source) has used symbols, words, or gestures unfamiliar to the receiver, interpretation mistakes can easily occur.

Effective listening is a skill that can be practiced and enhanced. As people learn how to increase their listening effectiveness, the communication process improves.

e. *Feedback: Feedback* is the listener's response to the message. Feedback is valuable when the receiver indicates how the message was interpreted.

(1) *Indication of feedback:* Feedback may be as simple as a nod, a return call, or an initial next to someone's name on a memorandum sent in response.

(2) *Sources of misunderstanding:* Since feedback is in essence a message itself, the same sources of misunderstanding previously attributed to messages apply equally in this area. However, two additional issues may arise with feedback.

(a) *Feedback delays:* Feedback usually does not follow the original message quickly enough. Thus, the feedback is not received in a timely or sufficient manner to aid the speaker. The speaker needs to ask the listener to promptly respond. Also, the listener should make every effort to respond as soon as possible after the message is received. To reinforce understanding, ask questions or have the speaker repeat ideas and information for clarification.

(b) *Need for specific feedback:* The feedback needs to be specific enough to help the speaker know how to adapt the message to increase understanding and its total impact. When providing feedback, respond in detail and give specific examples. The speaker should ask for precise comments.

EXAMPLE: Roth has to give an important presentation to a prospective client. He asked the office staff to listen and critique his sales "pitch." After Roth was done, everyone complimented him on his presentation. Only after watching a videotape did he realize the little distractions he could have corrected if he had only been aware of them. When he asked the staff whether they had noticed these problem areas, they reluctantly said "yes." They explained their concern about affecting his enthusiasm if they pointed out things he should correct (details concerning presentation skills can be found in Section E).

f. *Distractions:* Barriers, blocks, noises, problems, and interferences are some of the names attributed to distractions that interfere with effective communication and affect understanding.

(1) *Time as a distraction:* Time is a common problem, especially when the time allotted to decode a message might not be comparable to the proper amount of time required. Also, the time of day or the timeliness of the transactions might interfere with understanding.

(2) *Types of distractions:* Although distractions can occur at virtually any point in the communication process, the different types fit within three categories: external, internal, or semantic.

(a) *External distractions:* External distractions happen within the channel or the environment and context within which the communication is taking place.

EXAMPLES:

Radio static, television "ghosts," and blurred facsimile (fax) reproductions are common examples of channel "noises."

Some people are better able to concentrate in the morning, whereas others don't even begin to function properly until the afternoon.

After a disaster, listeners, especially in the immediate area, are not able to focus their attention on other matters.

Disturbances (background signs, people moving around, extraneous sounds, bright lights or colors, obnoxious smells) can impair the speaker's and the listener's abilities to concentrate on the communication exchange that is taking place between them.

(b) *Internal distractions:* Internal distractions are often difficult to identify because they take place within the minds of the speaker and/or listener(s). Even when you have a close relationship with the person, you cannot always tell whether he or she is suffering from depression or low self-esteem. In addition, people do not always tell you when they are experiencing physical discomfort or illness. Also, prejudices, biases, and preoccupation with another issue are often hidden. Occasionally, a person's attitude reflects the true inner feelings of the communicator. It is important to work at understanding and addressing your internal distractions.

(c) *Semantic distractions:* The word *semantic* refers to the meanings assigned to the words that we use when we communicate with others. Words and gestures mean different things around the world as well as within subcultures of a society. Many books have been written to help travelers learn the perspectives of the language of other cultures. A person only needs to travel across the United States to see that different geographic regions within the same country may interpret the same words in different ways. Also, words can mean unique things depending on the professional environment in which they are used. Since meanings differ between individuals, the words used can create misunderstandings (Section A-4-b[2] also illustrates this point).

EXAMPLES:

At some transportation companies, semi-tractor trailer trucks are called "feeders." Yet, in a manufacturing environment, a "feeder" could be a belt that feeds materials into a particular piece of machinery.

A study of a major dictionary showed that an average of 28 separate meanings were listed for the 500 most widely used words in the English language.

g. *Communication environment:* The environment is the context in which the communication encounter is taking place. The place may be relaxing, as in an office with low background music, or stressful, as in an uncontrolled meeting.

(1) *Context:* Context refers to the reasons for the discussion in the first place. A friendly chat during break creates a different communication event than a disagreement in the manager's office.

(2) *Personal moods:* In addition, environment encompasses the moods of the people involved in the conversation. Messages may be interpreted differently, depending on where, when, and to whom communicated.

B. Giving and Receiving Praise and Criticism

Two diametrical opposites in interpersonal communication are praise and criticism. Studies have found that both areas have potential as positive motivators.

1. *Communicating Praise: Praise* is acknowledging the effective work of others. Most people like to work in an environment where their hard work is complimented. Studies on motivation have found that numerous people place more value on recognition

than money. Yet for many people, the only thing that seems to be harder than giving praise is graciously accepting it.

    a. *Giving praise:* Although criticism should be a private matter, praise should be a public event. Many companies have incorporated recognition as reward for excellence. When you give compliments, be specific. Tell the person what she or he did to deserve your commendations. Also, you must be sincere. People quickly learn that praise is basically worthless if compliments are given to everyone for just about anything.

    b. *Receiving praise:* When someone gives you a compliment for a job well done or an extraordinary effort, say "thank you." People who are being complimented should not be embarrassed or make demeaning remarks about themselves or their efforts, such as "That was nothing" or "I was lucky, I guess." The most gracious response is a simple appreciation for their recognition.

2. *Communicating Criticism:* Criticism unfortunately conjures up a negative image in most people's minds. Yet when done correctly, criticism helps to enhance a person's knowledge and skills. Constructive criticism is what we want to achieve. As people strive for excellence, they need to know what areas of their performance require improvement.

    a. *Giving constructive criticism:* Constructive criticism starts with respect. First, we need to recognize the positive contributions the person makes to the organization. Using the "sandwich" theory, constructive criticism is balanced between positive remarks about the person's overall efforts. The goal is to "sincerely" assist the employee to improve in certain aspects of performance. Maintaining self-esteem and motivation is important. Make giving criticism a "learning" event allowing everyone to speak and listen. If the participants attempt to understand an agreed-on outcome and discuss the circumstances with respect and sincerity, criticism can be a positive influence.

    b. *Receiving criticism:* For many people, the natural tendency when criticized is to become defensive. Their reaction is self-defense; they are protecting their self-esteem. To truly learn from a critique, the following guidelines need to be applied. By adhering to these suggestions, people will seek open and honest input from others.

        (1) *Responding to criticism:* Whenever someone gives you criticism, first attempt to understand that person's perspective. Let the person know that you appreciate their taking the time and caring enough to approach you with the issue. If you have ever critiqued someone else's performance, you know how important it is to put the criticism into context. Also, recognize how much they must care about you by being honest. Let them know how much you want to know where your problem areas are so that you can improve. By being open to accepting criticism and by putting it into a positive context, you are assisting them in helping you to become a better contributor to the organization.

        (2) *Seeking other opinions:* Just because someone has given you advice, however, does not mean that he or she is correct. The next thing to do, after thanking the person, is to go to other people whose confidence you trust and ask for their opinions on the matter. Remember, others like you will think like you and agree with you. Now is the time to obtain diverse opinions and to weigh

and balance the input you receive. Through the process of verification by others, you can decide what is right for you.

(3) *Modifying personal behavior:* As you evaluate the opinions and contributions from others, the changes you may or may not make are personal and collective. If you realize that you have been criticized fairly, you will decide what needs to be changed. Let the person who brought the criticism to your attention, as well as others who provided input, know how you addressed the issue. Make sure to offer thanks for their concern.

C. Becoming a More Effective Listener

Research indicates that most office personnel spend approximately 40 percent of their workday listening. Yet very few people have studied the listening process. Although many people judge themselves to be good listeners, studies have found that without formal training in listening, the average person listens at a 25 percent efficiency level. Operating a business requires more than a 25 percent effort from employees.

Listening goes beyond *hearing* what someone has said. *Listening* is a mental process that involves hearing, seeing, and interpreting what was said and seen. *Interpreting* is determining what the speaker meant by assigning meaning to verbal and nonverbal symbols received. Effective listening is an active, energetic process, not a passive one. To really listen requires concentration and hard work. This process demands that a high degree of energy be expended to maintain an appropriate attention level.

Poor listening habits result in communication problems that can be costly to the organization—missed meetings, errors in shipments, or inaccurate correspondence. A good listener recognizes these problems and works at developing techniques to help improve personal listening effectiveness.

1. *Problems Inherent in the Listening Process:* The first step in correcting any problem areas is to recognize the issues. In listening, the way that people's minds function creates a dilemma in and of itself. Three problems are inherent in the listening process. The word *inherent* means that these obstacles are established as a part of the auditory system, "built in," so to speak.

   a. *Paying attention:* The first problem inherent in the listening process involves paying attention. No matter how excited you are about the subject, by nature, paying attention for an extended period of time is difficult.

   (1) *Attention span:* Studies have determined the attention span for adults to be approximately 20 minutes. With the development of modern technology to test brain functions, scientists have found that the brain takes a "break" from whatever it is the person is concentrating on every two to three *seconds*!

   (2) *Attention wandering:* When the brain is taking a respite from the duties at hand, attention automatically wanders to other things on your mind, such as the other tasks you need to complete that day, an upcoming meeting, or a parent who is hospitalized.

   (3) *Concentrating on the speaker's message:* Sometimes, you become more interested in the "side trips" your mind is taking than concentrating on what the speaker has to say, especially if the presenter has not taken the audience into consideration. At that point, the internal message you are listening to becomes more appealing, which makes it harder to refocus on the message coming

from the outside. (For more information about presentation skills, refer to Section E.)

b. *Understanding the meaning:* Understanding is the key to effective communication. Without understanding, effective communication cannot really take place.

   (1) *Comprehending the message:* Obviously, if the participant's mind is not focused on what is being said, problems will arise in comprehending the entire message. The real dilemma comes when directions from your superior are misunderstood.

   EXAMPLE: A divergent train of thought distracts Edwards when her manager said, "Do not order the extra part." Edwards heard only ". . . order the extra part." This can become a costly and time-consuming problem.

   (2) *Speaking and listening:* Another issue related to both attention and understanding has to do with the rate of speech versus the rate of listening. The average person speaks at a rate of 125 words per minute. Yet the average listener can follow and understand information at a rate of 350 words per minute! The gap time between these two speeds is usually filled with "daydreaming" of some sort. Often, the listener's attention is not completely on what is being said. Part of the message is missed, thus affecting complete understanding.

c. *Remembering information:* At the end of most conversations, only a portion of what was said is remembered. Even as participants leave staff meetings, they forget what was talked about the moment they walk out the door. This situation, as frustrating as it is, is not uncommon. Research shows that the average person remembers only 50 percent of what he or she heard in the listening process.

   (1) *Attention:* Part of the difficulty is related to attention and understanding as previously mentioned.

   (2) *Short-term memory:* Another factor has to do with how short-term memory works.

      (a) When you hear information and then decode the meaning, you place the idea into your short-term memory. Short-term memory is limited in its storage capacity.

      (b) If the listener or the speaker relates new information to knowledge previously acquired or uses some other memory aid, the information is transferred to long-term memory, where later recall is greater.

2. *Behaviors That Inhibit Listening:* In addition to the problems inherent in the listening process, people engage in poor listening behaviors that compound listening ineffectiveness. Because most people have not been trained to be better listeners, they are not even aware that their actions are detracting from the communication process. Studies have concluded that the average American has several listening habits that may need to be changed.

a. *Calling the subject uninteresting:* When topics are not interesting to the listener, it is nearly impossible to pay close attention. Concentrating on a message is hard enough. Therefore, when something is not interesting, the listener needs to make an extra effort to listen to the entire presentation. During time gaps, ask yourself questions such as "What is this person saying that I can use?" Identify information you already know that can make the topic more interesting. In this way, every listening encounter becomes a learning experience.

b. *Judging delivery instead of content:* Many people excuse themselves from listening to what is being said because of the way the presenter looks, sounds, or moves. The good listener looks beyond the "cover" and seeks to "read" the message. (For more information about appearance, refer to Section D.)

c. *Jumping to conclusions:* Although this suggestion may seem extremely difficult to follow at times, you must learn to withhold judgment until the message is complete. The natural tendency for most people is to start planning a rebuttal as soon as a speaker gives an opposing viewpoint. Key points can be missed when someone concentrates on the response instead of listening to the opposing view. Also, if you believe the presenter is mistaken, the best approach is to respond to the opponent's reasoning. If you are not listening, you will not know what points were brought up and discussed. Keep an open mind during the presentation. After the conclusion, ask questions in an attempt to better understand the issue. The issues need to be discussed openly and with respect for diverse perspectives.

d. *Listening for details instead of the "big" picture:* Poor listeners try to commit too many facts to memory too rapidly. A good listener, on the other hand, works at understanding the central ideas. Once the principles are recognized, it is easier to remember the details that support them.

e. *Taking excessive notes:* Although you can listen at a much faster rate than anyone can talk, you cannot take notes at a quick enough pace to keep up with even a relatively slow speaker unless you have excellent note-taking skills. Jotting down the key points, interesting phrases, and memorable quotes, however, helps to keep a focus on the presentation and improves the opportunity to learn and to remember.

f. *Attentive listening:* Listening needs to be active, not a passive act.

    (1) *Physiological changes while listening:* When actively listening, your body goes through the same physiological changes as when you are engaged in physical activity. Your heart rate increases, your blood circulates faster, and your body temperature rises slightly.

    (2) *Listening and concentrating:* Sometimes, we listen to unwind. After a busy day at the office, propping our feet up and listening to soft, soothing music can help us relax. In the work setting, however, we typically listen to gain information. In these cases, we need to actively listen. Various studies support the fact that when you *look* like you are listening, people believe you are paying attention. Demonstrating your concentration not only helps to keep you focused; this behavior is courteous and encouraging to the speaker. When we listen to other people, we show them that we respect them, value their opinions, and really care about them. Here are some ways you can show that you are listening:

        (a) Establish and maintain eye contact with the person who is talking.

        (b) Jot down a few notes.

        (c) Face the speaker and lean forward slightly.

        (d) Nod occasionally to demonstrate your understanding of the message.

(e) Show by facial expressions that you are interested in gaining as much as you can from the talk.

(f) Express attention by occasionally uttering expressions such as "um," "oh," and "uh huh."

(g) When appropriate, ask relevant questions.

(h) Where appropriate, switch roles; while you speak, others should actively listen.

g. *Creating or tolerating distractions:* Not only are poor listeners easily distracted, many times they are the cause of distractions. A good listener works at overcoming interference by closing a door; shutting off television, radio, or other equipment; and, if necessary, moving closer to the person who is talking or asking her or him to speak louder. Sometimes, however, the disruption cannot be eliminated. In that case, concentration is the key.

h. *Failing to listen to difficult material:* A good listener gains invaluable experience by taking the time to listen to a variety of material no matter how difficult or unfamiliar. New material challenges mental capacities, thus strengthening the mind for other difficult listening endeavors.

3. *Techniques for Improving Listening:* Effective listening is a skill that, through practice, can be improved. In addition to the aforementioned suggestions, listening effectively can be increased by following these recommendations:

a. *Deciding to listen:* Before meeting with the person with whom you will be communicating, set listening as your goal. Decide ahead of time to focus your attention on the message. As best you can, clear your mind of extraneous thoughts (things to do, people to see, places to visit).

b. *Getting rest and food:* It is easier to concentrate on listening when you are well rested. Also, eating properly contributes to a healthy life both mentally and physically. Too much to eat can make you sleepy; however, not eating can affect you physically, and hunger pangs become distracting.

c. *Finding comfortable seating close to speaker:* When seated in the back of the room, the tendency is for the mind to wander. It is easier to focus more attention on the presentation when you sit closer to the speaker. Also, other people in the audience are less likely to disturb your concentration when you are seated closer to the front. A firm but comfortable chair allows you to sit for a longer period of time before becoming fatigued.

d. *Learning from every encounter:* Look at every communication encounter as a learning experience. If you are having trouble concentrating, try and analyze why. Change anything you can that will help your attention level: What can be done differently next time? Look for the precious gems of knowledge hidden under all the rough spots. With learning, every listening activity will be a positive experience.

D. Nonverbal Communication: Listening between the Words

Almost everyone agrees that effective communication skills are important for success in business. However, one area that is most often overlooked is the important role the various elements of nonverbal communication play in this success.

Many senders of communication believe that if they carefully choose the right *words,* their messages will be understood. Moreover, receivers often believe that if they carefully listen to the *words* spoken or read a document thoroughly, they do all that is necessary for communication. However, nonverbal factors also affect the message.

According to research in nonverbal communication, as much as 90 percent of the impact of messages is based on nonverbal aspects. Thus, those who want success in business and in their personal lives should seek guidance in improving their nonverbal awareness.

The American workplace will continue to take on both an international emphasis with global trade and a cross-cultural flavor with the diverse domestic population. Therefore, learning the effective use of nonverbal communication with an awareness of diversity is very important. Those in business need to realize that their messages are being received by people from different backgrounds. Although many members of a society react similarly to communication stimuli, business people need to learn to avoid stereotyping individuals.

1. *Defining Nonverbal Communication:* That part of communication that is beyond the words is referred to as *nonverbal communication.* The old axiom—*It's not what you say, but how you say it and what you are doing when you say it!*—is true. Although many different nonverbal cues are present in any encounter, you especially need to be aware of the major ones to increase your communication effectiveness and clarity of messages.

   a. *Body language:* The most prominent element in nonverbal communication, *body language,* refers to posture, facial expressions, eye contact, gestures, and movements. By watching others, you can determine a great deal about their attitude toward you and the situation.

      EXAMPLE: Before movies had sound, body language was how actors and actresses "talked."

   b. *Vocal attributes:* When talking, the voice adds a new dimension to the words. Hopefully, vocal quality adds variety and excitement. Speed, intensity, volume, accent, and even silence are characteristics of voice that communicate a message to another person. Even the nonverbal utterances muttered ("oh," "ah," and "um") and deep sighs send a message.

   c. *Space and distance:* The distance you stand away from someone communicates your degree of like or dislike. Also, the way you arrange your work and living spaces demonstrates personality attributes.

      (1) *Close proximity:* Usually, only those considered to be close friends are comfortable within the one-foot communication circle. Sometimes, however, circumstances require us to include (or to enter others') personal space. When you are in a small area with strangers, most people stiffen, stand up straight, and stare ahead or at the floor. Americans, especially, are uncomfortable standing close together but are tolerant of the situation for short periods of time.

         EXAMPLES: An elevator, a crowded bus or train.

      (2) *Effect of culture:* In some cultures, people expect to stand close to those with whom they are talking. Being unaware of such a background, you may think that he or she is trying to be intimidating or too friendly.

         EXAMPLE: Maxim was involved in a conversation with Azdiz who always stood very close to her. When Maxim stepped back to give herself some room to breathe, Azdiz took the movement as rudeness and became insulted.

    d. *Touch:* With the increased concern over sexual harassment in the workplace, touch has become taboo in most offices. Still, communication can occur through a pat on the back or a "high five." The most common form of touch in the business environment is the handshake. If you want to give a favorable impression, a firm, brief handshake is best, regardless if the other person is a man or a woman.

    e. *Clothing and accessories:* Several books address "dressing for success." Appropriate business attire is affected by the change in styles, but the conservative classic styles have remained constant over the years. The "latest rage," when extreme, should be reserved for your personal life outside the office. Accessories also communicate a message.

        (1) *Making character judgments:* Studies show that many people make character judgments of others based on their clothes, shoes, or jewelry. The influence your clothing and accessories have on others as they make these judgments is something over which you have control. Being aware of the impact that clothing and accessories have on others is important. In today's diverse environment, firms expect employees to work together collaboratively—with respect and overcoming stereotyping. However, first impressions do have an impact on communication. Therefore, by being aware of the tendency for people to judge you based on appearance, assess your current style, and adapt it to communicate the message you want to send.

        (2) *Social status:* In some cultures, clothing and accessories help to identify the social status of the wearer. Bright colors, expensive cloth, and an abundance of jewelry may look gaudy to some; yet others find that these items represent a creative, happy nature. They look at traditional American business attire as "stuffy" and might even consider the person wearing this outfit as uncreative or boring.

    f. *Time:* The way you spend time and treat time communicates a message about responsibility.

    EXAMPLE: Are you always on time for an appointment?

        (1) *Paying attention to time:* Time management is important to an efficient office operation. Having the office open during office hours tells co-workers and clients that you assume the responsibility of accessibility. Completing projects on time demonstrates your ability to assume responsibility, prioritize tasks, and meet deadlines.

        (2) *Relating to time in other geographic regions:* Some foreign countries have a more lax view of time and time limits. These cultural differences need to be respected, particularly if international communication commences with business in these countries. Some regions of the United States also have a more relaxed attitude about time. An agreed-on working style is important when doing business with companies in these areas; all need to be open and respectful of one another and adapt for an effective working relationship.

        EXAMPLE: People who get transferred from a slow-paced community may complain if their relocation work ethic is different. Similarly, those who have spent most of their lives in a fast-paced environment find themselves frustrated when they are transferred to a region where life is slower and they have to wait for their "sluggish" co-workers. These new opportunities require peo-

ple to be open, flexible, and adaptable for their own happiness as well as that of their co-workers.

2. *Interpreting Nonverbal Cues:* Looking at one or two nonverbal cues does not necessarily give an accurate picture of what is happening. Picture someone standing in the corner of the office, away from everyone else, arms crossed and head lowered. Is the person angry? Sad? Before interpreting what we see (the nonverbal), remember that a complete picture is necessary. To more accurately interpret nonverbal cues exhibited by others, both consciously and unconsciously, you need to consider the four Cs of nonverbal behavior (clusters, consistency, culture, and communication). Also, remember that nonverbal cues are clues, not facts.

   a. *Clusters:* Nonverbal signs do not happen in isolation. You need to look at and receive as many cues as possible. When looked at together, as one big picture, the nonverbal message can be read more accurately.

   b. *Consistency:* This deals with two areas: how consistent nonverbal signals are and how consistent the signals are with the person's personality.

      (1) *Consistency of signals:* The first area has to do with how consistent the nonverbal cues are with other signals. To obtain a more accurate picture, determine whether the signals point to the same conclusion.

      EXAMPLE: If you see a person with arms crossed and an intense facial expression, you might infer anger. But when you talk with the person, you discover a pleasant tone of voice. The two signals are not consistent. Understanding what the nonverbal message means will require more information about the person, situation, and setting.

      (2) *Consistency with personality:* The second area has to do with how consistent the cues are with the personality of the person. If you already know the person, you should have an idea as to what constitutes that person's normal behavior.

      EXAMPLE: When Jensen walks into a room and he is sad-faced, you might get concerned since he is normally smiling and happy. On the other hand, when Bertrand walks in with a sad face, you know Bertrand's facial expression looks sad, but she really is a pleasant, positive person.

   c. *Culture:* A person's cultural upbringing influences the way she or he communicates. The workplace in the United States is diverse. Even people who are born in the same country can assign different meanings to nonverbal cues. Many books address various methods of communicating nonverbally within regions of the United States.

      EXAMPLE: Kragan enjoys working with Ching-seh; however, she notices that Ching-seh never looks at her when they talk. Kragan has always believed that failure to establish eye contact meant you were lying or trying to hide something. She cannot figure out what Ching-seh could be hiding. One day, Kragan asked Ching-seh why she never looked at her when they talked. Ching-seh said that, in her culture, staring at someone or looking them directly in the eyes is a sign of disrespect. Now that Kragan understands Ching-seh's motives, she is no longer uncomfortable carrying on a conversation with Ching-seh. Kragan attempts to modify her eye contact, while Ching-seh knows she can look at Kragan when they are talking and Kragan will not be insulted. Both women learned something new through their friendship by being respectful and open with one another.

    d. *Communication:* The only way to find out what message someone is intending to send with nonverbal cues is to ask. Often, questioning is not necessary. But before you judge someone on an incomplete message or when conflicting messages are detected between and among nonverbal and verbal elements, obtain more information from the sender. When in doubt, the best thing to do is be respectful and seek additional information.

E. Giving a Professional Presentation

At some point in your career, you will be asked to prepare and present a report either at work or at some organizational meeting. Knowing how to prepare and present a professional report not only builds your confidence but adds to your credibility in the audience's eyes.

The concepts necessary for an excellent presentation are easily mastered. Knowing how to anticipate difficult situations and planning for all possible courses of action may help maintain control.

The oral presentation is nearly identical to a good sales call. The objective is to sell the audience (the customer) on the value and validity of the research performed and to satisfy the customers' need for goods, services, or information.

1. *Speech Writing:* To deliver a speech, it needs to be written. Keep in mind these steps as you begin preparing the speech.

    a. *Know your audience:* The more familiar you are with the audience, the more comfortable you will be when you stand up in front of them to speak. To get more information on the audience, ask the following questions:

- How many people will be listening to the presentation?
- Does this group meet regularly (as a committee), or are they meeting just to hear ideas?
- Will the listeners be predominantly men or women?
- Will this be a diverse audience?
- What positions do the attendees hold?
- Who are my allies?
- Who are the skeptics in the audience?
- What types of hobbies or other interests do the listeners have?
- What other characteristics typify this audience?

    b. *Know the occasion:* When you are asked to speak to a group, an occasion is drawing these people together. Learn as much as you can about the situation surrounding the speech. By learning more about the audience, you will feel more in control of the situation. Ask the following questions as you contemplate your speaking engagement:

- Is the occasion solemn, formal, or casual?
- Are these people coming together to hear a presentation, or is another event the draw?
- Does the audience hope to be persuaded or just informed?
- Will other speakers be present as well? If so, what order is established for speaking?

- How important is my role? Keynote speaker? Main session speaker? Subsession speaker?

- How long must the presentation be?

- Should there be time for discussion or a question-and-answer session after the presentation?

   c. *Prepare a rough draft of the speech:* Now that you know more about the audience, why you are being asked to speak, and the arrangement of the facilities, you are ready to start jotting down the first draft of the speech.

   (1) *Brainstorm for a topic:* Begin by brainstorming, a process whereby you write down as many ideas as you can within a set amount of time. One crucial rule of brainstorming is to avoid any evaluation of ideas until the process is completed. After brainstorming, build on your thoughts. Brainstorming is an excellent creative technique to use in starting to write. Contemplate the following questions during this critical thinking stage.

- What information do I have that provides the most benefit to the group members (the audience)?

- What information am I the most enthusiastic about sharing with the audience?

- Have I assembled the necessary facts and statistics to make my case convincing?

   (2) *Write the introduction:* The first words the audience hears will set the stage for the rest of the presentation. Therefore, you want the introduction to be exciting. Ask these questions in preparing this important part of the speech:

- Does the introduction capture the audience's attention?

- Does the introduction make the topic clear?

   (3) *Plan the body:* The body encompasses the main points of the speech. No matter how interesting the introduction, if the body of the speech is not well organized and relevant, you will lose the audience. The following questions will help plan this section of the presentation:

- Is the language clear and vivid enough to assure the audience that the speech is well organized?

- Does the presentation concentrate on developing a few points clearly and precisely?

- Have I used charts and graphs to help the audience visualize the meaning of the facts and statistics present (refer to Section E-3)?

   (4) *Write concluding remarks:* Some studies suggest that the audience will remember your last remarks more clearly and vividly than anything else said during the speech. This step is often neglected, however. A presenter who quits rather abruptly at the end of the speech can leave the audience feeling unsatisfied. Address the following questions when writing the conclusion:

- Have I cued the audience that a conclusion is forthcoming?

- Are the important points clearly summarized?

- Are recommendations included?

End with a statement of finality by using a quotation, a short story, or other device.

d. *Transfer the speech to notes:* After completing the rough draft, redraft the speech until you are comfortable with the words and the flow. To deliver a speech so the audience does not feel like they are being read to, use speech notes.

(1) *Using speech notes:* Relying on memory tends to make a speaker more anxious about the presentation. Using notes instead of reading or memorizing the speech keeps the presentation fresh and spontaneous. A set script tends to restrict you from maintaining eye contact with the audience.

(2) *Organizing notes:* Organize notes clearly using an outline form. An example of a speech outline is shown in Figure 20-2.

(3) *Preparing notes:* Prepare your numbered notes using large lettering and open space. Make sure to write out all numbers or quotations that need to be cited exactly.

e. *Practice the speech:* Practice makes perfect. Practice is a very important step in speech writing. Practicing helps to smooth out the rough edges: to find out where wording is awkward and where pauses and pacing can be adjusted. *How* the speech is delivered can be even more important than *what* is said (refer to Section D). Videotaping practice is an excellent way to prepare. If a videotape recorder is not available, another alternative is audiotape. In order to see gestures and facial

Figure 20–2   Speech Outline Form

I. Introduction
  A. Attention-Getting Device
    1. Quotation
    2. Short Story
    3. Visual Aid
    4. Questions
  B. Preview of Subject to Be Covered
II. Body
  A. Main Point #1
    1. Discussion and Elaboration
    2. Support and Illustrations
  B. Main Point #2

Note: Continue in the body of the speech until all points have been included. Be careful not to have too many issues. Simplicity is important.

III. Concluding Remarks
  A. Review Subject, Main Points Covered, and Recommendations
  B. Finality Step
    1. Quotation
    2. Short Story
    3. Visual Aid
    4. Questions
    5. Motivational Appeal

expressions, practice in front of a mirror. Practice at least once in front of a "live" audience. Colleagues and friends are a good mock audience. Detailed feedback from a mock audience can be very valuable and useful. When practicing delivery, consider the following important questions:

- Have I created conditions as similar as possible to the actual speaking environment?
- Have I practiced varying my eye contact?
- Have I practiced varying vocal pitch, rate, and volume?
- Does my voice sound conversational?
- Did I use natural movements and gestures?

f. *Build confidence:* Most speakers become apprehensive before the presentation. Studies show that the fear of speaking in public is high. This fact should make you feel more confident. Audiences admire a speaker's courage for giving presentations. Remember, an audience is typically on the speaker's side. Ideas for building up enthusiasm instead of nervousness include the speaking environment, visualization, visuals, anticipation, and focus.

(1) *The speaking environment:* When entering a room to deliver a speech, it is comforting to know that the place looks familiar and holds no surprises. Ask the following questions about the place where you will be presenting:

- How large is the room?
- Will the audience be sitting in rows (chairs or chairs and tables)? Or will they be standing?
- Will there be a lectern or a head table with a podium?
- Is a microphone needed? If so, will it be portable or fixed?
- Is the audiovisual equipment I need readily available? Where will it be placed?
- Exactly where will I be? Where will the audience be? Where will any important guests be?

(2) *Practice visualization:* Imagine your audience responding exactly how you want them to, with eager faces and positive reactions.

EXAMPLE: Professional athletes practice visualization as they prepare for a game.

(3) *Use bright, bold visuals:* Visuals give the audience something other than the speaker to focus their attention on. Visuals also serve as guides for the speaker and help minimize speech anxiety.

(4) *Plan for all situations:* Anticipate all situations that might occur during the speech and plan for them.

EXAMPLES:

Have notes to refer to if you lose your train of thought.

Open the floor for discussion.

If the computer system for the electronic slide presentation does not work, have a set of transparencies available.

Take a break, if appropriate.

If the overhead projector's light bulb burns out, have a spare bulb available.

(5) *Anticipate possible questions:* Think about all possible questions listeners might ask, and design responses ahead of time. No one expects you to know everything about the topic. Do not be afraid to say that you do not have an answer. The following tactful suggestions may be used to tell the audience you do not have the information.

(a) Offer to get back to them with a response. If this offer is extended, make sure to contact them within a week.

(b) Open the floor for discussion about a difficult question. Someone in the audience might have experience in that area and have a response to share with the group.

(6) *Focus on the topic:* Accept the fact that you may have some nervous symptoms on the day of your speech and focus instead on being excited about what you have to share.

Remember, you have prepared your speech thoughtfully and carefully. Giving the presentation more than once will help, too, as each time you gain more confidence and skill. Before very long, you will probably start to enjoy the experience!

2. *Tips for Better Oral Presentations:* Studies show that most professional speakers are not trained in giving presentations; they are content experts. The main thing to remember is to be yourself and practice. The following tips will help polish your presentation skills as you strive for excellence.

- Establish a clear objective in the beginning.
- Eliminate all physical barriers. Do not stand behind a lectern; try to keep open space between you and the audience.
- Strive for simplicity. Do not try to cover too much material in a short amount of time.
- Use language your audience understands.
- Present a varied program.
- Support your statements with facts.
- End on a positive note.
- Smile!

3. *Incorporate Visual Aids:* Research has proven that presentations using visual aids (charts, graphs, pictures, maps, objects, and models) are 43 percent more effective than those without visual aids when considering attention span, understanding, and remembering (see Sections C-1-a, C-1-b, and C-1-c). Anything the speaker can do to help increase the audience's efficiency in these areas is important.

a. *When to use visual aids:* Even though visuals add to a presentation, the potential for them to become major distractions is great. You need to know when visuals are appropriate. The best time to plan the visuals is after developing the total presentation strategy. The preparation of a script, outlining the ideas, facilitates this development. After ideas are identified, the points at which visuals are needed become apparent. Here are some situations in which the use of visual aids would be appropriate.

(1) *Clarifying a point:* A visual aid can show a process, procedure, relationship, cross-section, or quantitative view of topics.

(2) *Emphasizing a point:* Visual aids call attention to key ideas much more vividly than words do.

(3) *Simplifying a point:* Relationships among ideas, facts, and statistics can be shown simply in graphic form.

(4) *Unifying points:* Several ideas can be brought together in one visual aid.

(5) *Impressing the viewer:* Viewers are persuaded by an imaginative approach to the communication of ideas.

b. *Designing and using a good visual:* Visual aids are carriers for ideas. Since the idea is the most important element, visual aids supplement the presentation of that idea and help to explain and clarify it. The speaker should concentrate on developing the idea first and then find the appropriate visuals that will assist in the presentation of that idea.

EXAMPLE: Each day between 15 and 30 million presentations are made in the United States. In a year's time, over 1.5 billion transparencies will be produced in the United States.

(1) *Number of visuals:* Do not plan for too many visuals. Keep a visual on the screen long enough for it to be read and appreciated by the audience.

(2) *Content outline for each visual:* Know in advance what you want to say about each graphic before you present it. Visuals help keep you on target and guide your presentation.

(3) *Illustrations:* When illustrations are used, use no more than one illustration per visual.

(4) *Simple language to get point across:* Use language that is clear and focused. The shortest word may do the job. Avoid technical jargon and "corporatese." Verbalizing the words as you write them on the graphic helps in this area.

(5) *Focus on one idea at a time:* A good visual is simple, accurate, and emphasizes one clear idea. Highlight *key* information only. Use key words or phrases rather than lengthy blocks of verbiage. The message on the visual should be read with little more than a glance.

(6) *Color for emphasis:* Color has impact and emotional appeal. Use color when possible even in type-only visuals, but use no more than four colors on any graphic.

(7) *Graphic features:* Use a border around the chart if feasible. This technique focuses attention on the words and makes for a neat, attractive briefing chart. However, be consistent in the presentation format of your charts.

EXAMPLE: If one chart has a border, all should have the same border. If the heading on one chart is all caps, follow that format on all other charts.

(8) *Allowing for text lines:* Use a maximum of six to seven words per line and a maximum of six to seven lines per visual.

(9) *Keeping visuals readable:* Ensure that handwriting, printing, and graphics are large and clear enough to be read by the audience from any point in the room.

(10) *Keeping visuals easy to see and read:* Use no more than three sizes of letters per visual and do not randomly mix upper- and lowercase letters. Uniformity makes the visual easier to read.

(11) *Planning the sequence:* Sequence the visuals in order of usage so that you will not have to fumble when looking for the one you want.

Oral presentations will be enhanced greatly through the use of visual aids. Illustrations, charts, graphs, and other visuals will help you explain simple as well as complex concepts related to the topic. The time spent in planning the presentation will make the time spent in presenting much easier and more enjoyable—for both the speaker and the listeners.

Review Questions

Directions: Select the best answer from the four alternatives. Write your answer in the blank to the left of the number.

_____ 1. The key to effective communication is

       a. creating a relaxed atmosphere.
       b. solving conflicts.
       c. understanding of a shared meaning.
       d. watching for nonverbal cues.

_____ 2. The human resources manager pauses during an office meeting because she notices several quizzical expressions on the faces of the staff. She is illustrating that communication

       a. is irreversible.
       b. is a process.
       c. is not always positive.
       d. requires the attention of the listeners.

_____ 3. Feedback occurs when

       a. an outside noise interferes with communication.
       b. the channel chosen is appropriate for the message.
       c. the listener responds to the message sent.
       d. the speaker selects the appropriate words to communicate a message.

_____ 4. Feedback is valuable when the

       a. receiver indicates how the message was understood.
       b. receiver writes down what the speaker said.
       c. speaker repeats the key points.
       d. verbal message also includes nonverbal cues.

_____ 5. Effective communication impacts the workplace in many ways. Which one of the following is _not_ a communication outcome?

       a. Communication ensures that information is shared for effective decision making.
       b. Communication improves as employees work on making sure they are understood.
       c. Communication is a linking pin between plans and action.
       d. Communication provides a means for enhancing positive working relationships.

_____ 6. Communication is a complex process that is

       a. only verbal in form.
       b. transactional in nature.
       c. effective when interacting one-on-one.
       d. incorporates speech preparation with visual aids.

7. The process by which the speaker determines which symbols to include in the message is called

   a. decoding.
   b. encoding.
   c. interpreting.
   d. translating.

8. Properly pronouncing words when speaking is an application of

   a. decoding.
   b. encoding.
   c. enunciation.
   d. pitch.

9. You understand that the cause of a misunderstanding was semantics. This means that

   a. the communication was too fast for the receiver's level of attention.
   b. the meanings of the words used were difficult to comprehend.
   c. the words used were too vague.
   d. too much noise was occurring in the communication environment.

10. When communicating, the shorter the time allowed for the message to be received and understood by a large number of people, the more apt you are to use which one of the following channels?

   a. Direct personal channels
   b. Electronic channels
   c. Impersonal channels
   d. Multiple channels

11. The decoding process is

   a. identifying feelings and emotions.
   b. interpreting the meaning of symbols, words, and gestures.
   c. organizing thoughts into ideas.
   d. receiving acknowledgment that a message has been received.

12. Since feedback is a very important part of the communication process, it is important that

   a. specific detail does not clutter the message.
   b. the response is delayed long enough to consult colleagues as to the proper wording.
   c. the speaker feels the message is understood even though there is some ambiguity.
   d. questions are asked to clarify the meaning of the message.

_____

13. Ling did not get enough sleep the night before an important division meeting. As a result, she is extremely tired and has trouble concentrating on the agenda. This is an example of a/an

    a. external distraction.
    b. internal distraction.
    c. feedback.
    d. speech-thought rate differential problem.

_____

14. Studies show that praise and criticism can be

    a. a source of misunderstandings.
    b. easy-to-use techniques for encouraging work teams.
    c. effective when used often and equally with all employees.
    d. positive motivators in the workplace.

_____

15. Constructive criticism starts with

    a. discussing the issues with colleagues who are most like you.
    b. realizing that the advice (critique) cannot be modified.
    c. respect between the parties involved.
    d. self-confidence in realizing you do not need to change.

_____

16. Which statement below best describes the relationship between listening and hearing?

    a. Listening and hearing are the same thing.
    b. Listening and hearing always occur simultaneously.
    c. You can hear and not listen.
    d. You can listen and not hear.

_____

17. What is the relationship between the rate that people speak and the speed at which people listen?

    a. No predictable relationship exists between speech rate and rate of understanding.
    b. People speak and listen at approximately the same rate.
    c. People can speak faster than others can listen.
    d. People can understand speech at rates much faster than people can speak.

_____

18. What percentage of a message do most people remember immediately after hearing it?

    a. 25 percent
    b. 35 percent
    c. 50 percent
    d. 75 percent

19. Listening is a skill that can be learned; therefore, which one of the following should be practiced to improve listening skills?

   a. Allow emotions to influence your response.
   b. Note unusual speaking patterns so that you can inform the speaker of these distractions.
   c. Pay close attention and do not take notes because people speak faster than you can listen.
   d. Use both verbal and nonverbal actions to demonstrate attention.

20. An effective listener is one who

   a. learns from all listening situations.
   b. seeks opportunities to respond to the message.
   c. uses all communication for personal gain.
   d. uses the rate difference between speaking and listening to sort out extraneous thoughts from your mind.

21. Nonverbal communication refers to

   a. a combination of words and body movement.
   b. body language.
   c. messages expressed by ways other than words.
   d. vocal cues.

22. The study of body movements, gestures, and posture is called

   a. body language.
   b. communication distractors.
   c. the language of space and distance.
   d. vocal enhancements.

23. When you are in a face-to-face conversation, the distance you stand from someone communicates your

   a. ability to handle diverse groups.
   b. body language.
   c. degree of liking or disliking that person.
   d. interest in the topic.

24. The reason you should consider nonverbal messages as clues rather than facts is

   a. nonverbal clues are similar from one culture to another.
   b. nonverbal signs do not happen in isolation.
   c. the context of the communication encounter does not always have to be considered.
   d. communication is a process.

25. Wang, who is normally very cheerful, sat through the budget review with a concerned look on her face. During the break, you found out from her that her assistant was called home for an emergency just before the meeting. Which *C* regarding nonverbal behavior was applied?

    a. Cluster
    b. Communication
    c. Consistency
    d. Culture

26. Which one of the following is a major concern when analyzing your audience?

    a. How culturally diverse is the audience?
    b. Is this the keynote session, a main session, or a roundtable discussion?
    c. Should there be time for a question-and-answer session?
    d. What time of day is the presentation?

27. The conclusion of the speech is a good time to

    a. clarify the topic by opening the session up to questions.
    b. confirm the speaker's credibility by reviewing credentials.
    c. reinforce the main points.
    d. use visuals that emphasize the speaker's interest in the subject.

28. Reed was one of the main speakers for the annual IAAP International Convention. Just before the speech, he became anxious about the presentation. What is the best advice for Reed to follow?

    a. Ask a colleague to give his speech in his place.
    b. Be prepared for the worst on the day of the speech.
    c. Call the program chair and explain that you are not well and cannot attend the convention.
    d. Sit in a comfortable environment visualizing himself giving a successful speech.

29. When the speaker is asked a question and the answer is not known, the speaker should

    a. avoid the question by calling on someone else to ask a different question.
    b. open the floor for discussion on the question.
    c. provide a break so that he or she can review notes and formulate a logical response.
    d. rephrase the question so that the speaker can respond with an answer that he or she knows.

30. Which one of the following is a good suggestion for using visual aids?

    a. Make them simple and easy to understand so that little has to be said about the visuals.
    b. To avoid overuse of visuals, incorporate several illustrations on one visual.
    c. Visuals are best during the conclusion so that they do not detract from the presentation.
    d. Use visuals as a guide for keeping the presentation on target.

Solutions

Answer	Refer to:
1. (c)	[A]
2. (b)	[A-1-a]
3. (c)	[A-1-e, A-3-e]
4. (a)	[A-1-e, A-3-e]
5. (b)	[A-2-d]
6. (b)	[A-3]
7. (b)	[A-3-a(1)]
8. (c)	[A-3-a(2)(b)]
9. (b)	[A-3-b(2)(b), A-3-f(1)(c)]
10. (a)	[A-3-c(1)(b), A-3-c(2)(b)]
11. (b)	[A-3-d(2)]
12. (d)	[A-3-e(2)]
13. (b)	[A-3-f(2)(b)]
14. (d)	[B]
15. (c)	[B-2-a]
16. (c)	[C]
17. (d)	[C-1-b(2)]
18. (c)	[C-1-c(1)]
19. (d)	[C-2-f(2), C-3]
20. (a)	[C-3-d]
21. (c)	[D]
22. (a)	[D-1-a]

23. (c)   [D-1-c]

24. (b)   [D-2-a]

25. (c)   [D-2-b]

26. (a)   [E-1-a]

27. (c)   [E-1-c(4)]

28. (d)   [E-1-f(2)]

29. (b)   [E-1-f(5)(b)]

30. (d)   [E-3-b(2)]

Glossary

*69   Telephone number of the last incoming call; set charge per use. (3)

911   Emergency service that connects a caller with an operator who can give emergency help and can pinpoint the type of emergency and the geographic location. (3)

Absorption   Engulfing of sound waves by environmental materials. (7)

Abstract   Brief summary of the conduct of the study and the reporting of the data, findings, and conclusions of the study. (16) Concise summary of all key points expressed in a document, using keywords from the document. (18)

Abstract language   Quality of language where meanings can be interpreted differently by different people, even in the same situation; the opposite of concrete language. (16)

Access time   Measurement of the time to find the data location in secondary storage and the time required to transfer the data (*see* Transfer rate). (1)

Active records   Those records that are accessed and utilized in the current administration of business functions. (9)

Active words   Words that denote action on the part of the individual. (16)

Ad hoc committee   Small group formed to investigate a particular event or problem that has occurred within the organization; has a temporary appointment to serve until a report is presented to a standing committee or management. (11)

Administrative support   Office functions that typically include those not requiring keyboarding or typewriting, such as telephoning, receiving visitors, and managing records. (2)

Administrative value   Importance of records that are needed for a business to conduct current operations. (9)

Agenda   List of items of business to be presented and/or discussed during a formal meeting. (11)

Almanac   Book or publication, usually published on an annual basis, that includes factual information about international and national events of the year. (10)

*The number in parentheses after each entry indicates the chapter location in the text.

Alphabetic classification system   Set of filing procedures that is based on the use of the alphabet as a means of organizing the records. (9)

Alphanumeric classification system   Set of filing procedures that is based on a combination of alphabetic and numeric codes as a means of organizing the records; requires the use of a relative index. (9)

Ambient lighting   Indirect lighting that illuminates the area surrounding the work surface. (7)

Ambiguous   Vague and unclear, with more than one meaning; leaving the listener unsure of the speaker's intention in the message. (20)

Analog technology   Equipment systems that permit voice storage on dictation media for later transcription. (2)

Analytical report   Document that presents basic information and facts obtained through primary research, analyzes these facts, and provides an interpretation of them; report culminates in the development of conclusions and recommendations. (16)

Annotated bibliography   Listing of all references used in the report, in alphabetical order, with a brief paragraph following each entry commenting on the content and value of the reference. (19)

Aperture card   Punched card that contains a slot into which at least one microimage can be inserted and space on the face of the card for any explanation or interpretation of the data. (4)

Appendix   Supplementary research material (sample questionnaire or detailed data analysis) not included in the report. (16)

Applications programs   Programs (software) that include the logical steps (instructions) to perform specific processing tasks to solve business information needs (*see* System programs). (1)

Applications software   Sets of programs that direct the computer to solve specific business problems or perform particular applications. (6)

Appraisal of records   Evaluation of records to determine their administrative, legal, fiscal, or research value. (9)

Archive(s)   Facility that houses collections of records and business documents that are being retained for research or historical value by businesses, government agencies, or educational institutions. (9, 10)

Audioconference   Type of teleconference in which only voice or sound communication takes place. (11)

Audioconferencing   Telephone linkage of three or more people at two or more separate locations for voice communications. (3)

Auditron   Device that controls use of a convenience copier through the use of a plastic card, key, or other insert device to activate the copier. (12)

Author   Executive, manager, supervisor, or other person who originates work to be completed by office professionals or word processing support specialists; may also be called a *user*. (15)

Authorization   Procedure implemented that permits only certain personnel to use the reprographics equipment. (12)

Automated indexing   Naming, coding, numbering, or classifying the file so that it will later be retrievable through electronic means. (4)

Automated record system   System that permits the user to store records in various locations on electronic storage media in image, digital, or voice form for accurate and efficient retrieval at a later time. (4)

Background printing   Keying in the text for one document while another document is printing out. (1)

Bar graph or chart   Illustration that shows a comparison from one time period to another; uses bars of equal width to show quantities (values) on one axis and the factor to be measured on the other axis. (19)

Batch processing   Procedure for processing data for similar transactions by holding them for a predetermined period of time so that they can be processed as a group in a single computer run. (1)

Bibliography   Alphabetical list of all information sources (references) consulted by the author that contributed to the content of the report; placed at the end of the report on a separate page. (10, 16, 19)

Biographical directory   Publication that highlights the achievements of noted individuals who contributed to their professions, government, or country. (10)

Biomechanics   Study of the musculoskeletal effort of human beings. (7)

Bit   Two-state (binary) condition of digital representation in a digital computer; off (0) or on (1). (1)

Block codes   Groups of numbers reserved for records that have a common feature or characteristic. (9)

Blocked letter style   Standard letter style that begins all lines of the letter, including the opening and closing lines, at the left margin. (19)

Body language   Use of posture, facial expressions, eye contact, gestures, and movements as methods of communicating. (20)

Brainstorm   Thinking technique used to create ideas, alone or as a group, preferably within a set time frame, while avoiding any evaluation of ideas until the process is completed. (20)

Bulk business mail   Domestic third-class mail, bound printed matter, and small parcels weighing less than 16 ounces, consisting of a minimum of 200 pieces (or 50 pounds) belonging to the same processing category. (13)

Business form   Record that contains constant information appearing on it (printed or electronically imaged on a computer screen) and space provided for variable information to be inserted. (9)

Business report   Final outcome of a specific information-gathering activity within the organization, summarizing the problem, background, procedures, and results of a business project or research, that conveys information to top-level management. (9)

Byte   Unit of storage that equals one character; 8 bits equal 1 byte—required for each character. (1)

Calendaring   Making appropriate notations of upcoming appointments, meetings, or other events on office calendars or on the computer so that a printout of appointments and meetings can be obtained on a daily basis. (15)

Call director   Desktop unit that can handle as many as 100 lines at one location and can be connected to a switchboard or an intercom system. (3)

Call forwarding   Telephone feature that sends any incoming calls automatically to a different telephone location. (3)

Call waiting   Telephone feature that notifies the person being called (who is already using the phone) that a second call is on the line. (3)

Caller ID   Display of information about who is calling (e.g., telephone number) before the receiver is picked up. (3)

Career path   Sequencing of employment positions toward advancement and promotion along professional lines for which one prepares in terms of education, training, and work experience. (2)

Cellular call   Telephone call that can be placed or received at any time and in any place with a cellular telephone. (3)

Central processing unit (CPU)   Heart of a computer system that consists of the control unit and the arithmetic/logic unit (*see* Processor unit); the part of a computer system that processes and manipulates the raw data by performing informational and arithmetic operations. (1)

Centralization Operational plan that organizes support personnel in work centers with easy access to and from all departments of the organization. (15)

Centralized control Organizational pattern used to locate reprographics operations in one physical location in the organization under the direction of one manager. (12)

Centralized dictation system Input equipment that allows users to dial into a telephone access number and record dictation into the system, which will be transcribed later by word/information processing personnel. (2)

CENTREX system Telephone switching system leased from the regional telephone company that allows direct inward dialing; each extension is assigned a seven-digit number. (3)

Channel Connecting device between the speaker and the listener(s) through which the message is sent. (20)

Chat room(s) Internet facility that permits two or more people to have an interactive discussion, in writing, over the Internet. (3, 6)

Chip Piece of silicon ⅒ of an inch square that contains miniaturized integrated circuits that enable computers to store millions of units of information. (1)

Chronological system Set of filing procedures used when records are filed according to date, either most recent date first or oldest date first. (9)

Clarity Construction of an effective message so that sentences and paragraphs are written in an accurate, nonconfusing manner. (16)

Classification system Set of procedures used in a filing system based on standard rules for alphabetic, numeric, or alphanumeric filing. (9)

Closed system Storage/retrieval system consisting of banks of metal file containers for holding paper documents of any acceptable size that is controlled from a keyboard either at an operator workstation or near the files. (4)

Coded numeric system Filing system in which records are assigned numeric codes that really tell something about the person or item. (9)

Coding Making notations on the record itself as to exactly how the record will be stored (under what names or numbers). (9)

Coherence Construction of sentences and paragraphs so that there is consistency in style, word choice, and word usage, resulting in sentence, paragraph, and message unity. (16)

Collating Process of gathering a series of different pages into a combined set of ordered pages. (5)

Collect call Operator-assisted call that will be paid by the person or company receiving the call. (3)

Color coding Identification system that uses colored tabs or strips on the side of file folders to represent numeric or alphanumeric codes for topic areas pertaining to the organization and/or division. (9)

Combination letter Message in which there is both a positive and a negative response. (16)

Commercial printing firm Outside business organization that provides services such as artwork, graphic design, or special printing requirements through contracts with the organization. (12)

Commercial travel agency Business firm specializing in making travel arrangements for individuals, companies, and other organizations requesting travel services. (8)

Communication Process of sharing information and meaning, both knowingly and unknowingly, that requires the response of a receiver. (20)

Communication environment Context in which a communication encounter takes place, including both the physical setting and personal moods or perspectives of individuals involved. (20)

Compatibility Integration of information that has been keyed in using one software program within a document that has been created using another software program without the necessity of converting either program. (14)

Complements Words in addition to subjects, verbs, and adjectives that are used in a sentence to help complete the meaning, such as a prepositional phrase. (16)

Composition process Formatting of text for publications into appropriate page and document layout, resulting in camera-ready copy. (5)

Computer-aided transcription Automated system for converting machine shorthand symbols into stored digital codes, resulting in hard copies (printouts). (2)

Computer-assisted retrieval system (CARS) Automated system in which documents that are stored on microforms are accessed through the computer system; integrated records management and computer technologies. (4)

Computer-based records management system (CBRM)   Automated system that consists of data files and records tracking systems within an information processing system. (4)

Computer conference   Electronic meeting for people in different locations who need to communicate with each other in writing through computers and exchanging information using such devices as special-topic bulletin boards; may be simultaneous or on a delayed basis. (3, 11)

Computer data bank   Information bank to which an individual, a company, or a library may subscribe in order to have access through the computer to a data bank available within a particular profession or field. (10)

Computer input microfilm (CIM)   Relatively recent development in which paper documents, usually in large quantity, are converted to microfilm first, without rekeying the information, with the microfilm serving as input for reading the files of information into the computer for storage. (4)

Computer output microfilm (COM)   Means by which data that are electronically stored are converted to microfilm (output) so that hard copies (paper copies) of only the data needed are obtained in printout form. (4)

Computerized branch exchange (CBX)   Computer-based telephone communication system designed to provide a computerized management system. (3)

Conciseness   Writing in a brief but comprehensive manner. (16)

Concrete language   Use of words and terms that are precise in meaning; the opposite of *abstract language.* (16)

Conference   Formal meeting of a group of people with a common purpose; may be company-sponsored or association-sponsored meetings. (11)

Conference call   Telephone call that links several people into one conversation. (3)

Confirmed reservation   Notification from a transportation carrier or a lodging company that a reservation is being held for a given individual. (8)

Consistency   Normal way a person tends to behave in a similar situation, expressing the same attitude through nonverbal cues within a cluster. (20)

Constant information   Descriptors, keywords, or phrases preprinted on a business form or electronically imaged on a computer screen that remain the same on all forms of a particular kind. (9) Wording that will stay exactly the same on every message produced. (16)

Controlling   One of the functions of supervising that involves comparing actual productivity and results with those that were anticipated during a specific period of time. (15)

Convenience copier   Copier used for low-volume output typically located near the users and operated by any administrative assistant or secretary. (5)

Conventional format   Layout and design for correspondence, business forms, or business reports that results in paper copies (hard copies) or disk copies (soft copies). (9)

Conversion   Process of changing text created with one software program into text for a compatible software program. (14)

Copy notation   Special notation used only when a copy of the letter is sent to another person or persons; typed a double space after the reference initials. (19)

Copy quality   Examination of the appearance of the copy produced to be sure that it has been prepared accurately and according to instructions. (12)

Copyediting   Revising a draft of a document for consistency, conciseness, and grammatical accuracy by making revisions within the body of the document; edited copy is returned to the author for verification. (17)

Copying process   Creation of exact images directly from original documents through xerographic, fiber optic, or laser technologies. (5)

Copyright controls   Appropriate procedures to follow in using copyrighted materials, especially when making copies, with or without the permission of the copyright holder (publisher or author). (12)

Correspondence   Written messages prepared through word processing that are in the form of business letters created primarily as external communication and memoranda created as internal communication. (2, 9)

Courier services   Privately operated companies that handle shipments of correspondence and parcels for the general public on a regularly scheduled basis. (3)

Credit-card call   Long-distance call that allows the caller to charge the service to a specific account number. (3)

Criticism   Act of respecting a person's positive job performance but offering constructive remarks about areas of performance that need improvement and helping that person make suggested corrections. (20)

Cross-referencing   Notation in the file that indicates where the original document or complete file can be located; used whenever a record could be filed in more than one place in the files. (9)

Cross training Process of being trained to perform the job functions of more than one position in the office. (15)

Culture Particular form of civilization; a society of people from either a different region within a country or from a diverse nation. (20)

Cybernetics Information flow resulting from the communications systems being used. (7)

Data Input needed for processing to produce meaningful information (*see* Information). (1) Information items that describe a person, place, event, or object. (9)

Data conference Electronic access to a document by two or more participants for purposes of simultaneous review and editing. (11)

Data element Descriptive characteristic of a person, place, or thing; another common term for *data field*. (1)

Data field Descriptive characteristic of a person, place, or thing; also referred to as a *data element*. (1)

Data integrity Assurance that reliable and accurate data are available to the users. (6)

Database Set or collection of two or more interrelated files (records), with at least one common element, arranged so that information contained in the records can be manipulated by the user in organizing needed information into document form; a complete record of variable information. (1, 2, 3, 4, 9, 16)

Debit card Card issued by a bank, similar to a credit card, which allows the cardholder to receive cash or pay for purchases of merchandise or services and have that amount deducted immediately from the cardholder's bank account. (8)

Decentralization Operational plan in which office support personnel are housed within individual departments and perform office functions needed only by that department. (15)

Decentralized control Organizational pattern used to locate reprographics operations within the various departments where they are utilized; usually under the direction and supervision of the department manager. (12)

Decibel Unit measure of the intensity of sound. (7)

Decimal-numeric system Numeric filing system that divides subjects (topics) into major divisions with assigned numbers, followed by a decimal point and additional numbers representing subdivisions of the topics (e.g., Dewey decimal system for cataloging library books). (9)

Decoding Process by which the listener interprets the symbols, words, and gestures encoded in the message sent by the speaker and understands the intended meaning(s) of the message. (20)

Deductive style Direct approach to business writing in which the main idea is stated first, followed by supporting details. (16)

Default format Format that is in effect when the system has been initialized with a software program. (2)

Demand reports Documents that are made available on an ad hoc basis to display or print desired information in an acceptable format. (3)

Density Amount of information that can be stored in a certain area of the storage media. (2)

Department (work-group) strategy Implementation of office automation so that users will be able to share information with other users within that particular department (work group) or throughout the organization. (6)

Descriptor Keyword used to enable users to access specific information on a particular topic to be retrieved from stored documents. (4)

Desktop publishing Combination of computer technology with word processing, graphics, page layout, and laser printing to create high-quality documents that incorporate both text and graphics. (2, 5)

Dewey decimal classification system Library cataloging system that is based on the premise that all knowledge can be classified into 10 primary groupings. (10)

Diazo Copying process used for engineering and architectural drawings that requires the original document to be in a translucent state; only documents with printing on one side of the page can be reproduced with this process. (5)

Dictation Input for document production that may come from a variety of users in the form of recorded information to be listened to, interpreted, and keyed into document format. (14)

Digital duplicating Process that interfaces personal computing with convenience copying and offset printing to meet medium- to high-volume printing requirements. (5)

Digital electronic system Equipment system that is designed to receive dictated business information and to create digitally recorded electronic files. (2)

Digital storage Recording of information within a digital computer by using a binary code (a special two-number code representing 0 and 1 in different combinations); computer capability of locating any record that has been stored; also referred to as *document management*. (4)

Digital technology Conversion of oral information (analog) into digital pulses for storage on disks rather than cassette tapes. (2)

Direct access Method whereby the system is capable of going directly to the data needed, bypassing the data preceding it. (1)

Direct-access procedures Filing system that permits a person to go directly to the storage system and locate the file or document. (9)

Direct-distance dialing (DDD) Procedure used to place a long-distance call to another telephone number without the intervention of the operator. (3)

Direct entry Inputting data directly into the computer through a terminal, without intervention from an input medium. (1)

Discrete media Recording media used in dictating units that can be physically removed from the unit as soon as dictation is complete. (2)

Disk label Name assigned to a computer disk that will appear on the screen and enable the disk operating system to identify and locate the disk. (14)

Disk operating system Set of programs written for a computer system to help the computer manage its various functions and to communicate with application software programs. (2)

Dispersal Duplication of hard copies of documents and their storage in other locations. (9)

Document format Decisions made about the final appearance of the document, recorded at the beginning of the text or within the document at the point where such settings must take effect. (14)

Document management Computer-based methodology for storage and retrieval of documents that have been stored in a digital format; also referred to as *digital storage*. (4)

Document retrieval Obtaining an image, a copy of an entire document, or the original document from the automated record system. (4)

Documentation Creating, collecting, organizing, storing, citing, and disseminating descriptive information in the form of reference notes and bibliographic information within the body of a report. (19)

Domestic travel Transportation services provided for travel within the boundaries of a country. (8)

Duplex-numeric system Arrangement of files according to two or more sets of code numbers separated by a dash, comma, period, or space; requires use of a relative index. (9)

Duplexing Copying text material on both sides of a sheet of paper at the same time. (5)

Duplicating Creation of multiple copies of originals as required for business meetings, internal distribution, or other routine functions. (5)

Early adapter Person who is quick to change, to study a new system, and to implement it; a pioneer. (7)

Editing Procedure used by an author to make content revisions in the original document. (15)

Electronic blackboard Device used with teleconferences to display business graphics on a pressure-sensitive blackboard and transmit these visuals to other meeting locations. (11)

Electronic calendaring Procedure that enables an office professional to keep a stored record of appointments, meetings, and other commitments. (6)

Electronic filing Process whereby documents are stored electronically in active and inactive digital document storage for future access by users within the department or throughout the organization. (4, 6)

Electronic mail (e-mail) Computer-based message system whereby written communication is transmitted electronically over cable, telephone lines, or a satellite network to locations within the organization or to external organizations; may be managed as part of the electronic files of the organization; also referred to as *electronic messaging*. (3, 4, 6, 13)

Electronic master Master produced on an electronic scanner, with the original being scanned and the image electronically reproduced onto a stencil or offset master. (5)

Electronic slides Visuals that are prepared to accompany an oral presentation of factual information at a meeting. (11)

Electrostatic imaging Producing an offset master by inserting a sensitized master and the original document into a copier. (5)

Emotional disturbance Mood disturbance (anger, frustration, irritability, anxiety, and depression) or psychosomatic disorder (gastrointestinal disturbance, muscle tension, and psychic tension) affecting an employee's ability to perform work functions. (7)

Empathy Understanding the feelings or emotions of another person. (16)

Emphasis Attachment of greater importance to particular words or ideas within a message; placing special stress on specific syllables or words. (16)

Employee manual Handbook that provides specific information needed to be a functional worker within the company; includes work schedules, hours, salaries, schedules for salary reviews, dress codes, vacations, benefits, and other types of employee information. (15)

Encoding Process used by the speaker to assign and organize symbols (e.g., words or gestures) to formulate messages to be sent. (20)

Encryption   Coding of messages before transmission to prevent unauthorized users from accessing the information. (1)

Endnote   Reference note that appears on a separate page at the end of a report; citation that gives credit to a source of information indicated by a superscript in the body of the report. (19)

Enunciate   Pronounce all necessary parts of a word clearly. (20)

Ergonomics   Scientific study of the relationship of workers to their physical environment, including the work space and the technology being used. (7)

Euthenics   Science of bettering employee conditions by improving the work environment. (7)

Evidence value   Importance of records that trace the development of an organization from its beginning to the present. (9)

Experimental research   Conducting a study to determine whether a change in one factor or variable causes a change in another factor or variable. (16)

Express mail   Fastest mail delivery service that guarantees delivery of mailable items weighing up to 70 pounds the next day, sometimes even the same day. (13)

External distractions   Those barriers to understanding that happen within the channel or the environment and context within which the communication is taking place; often referred to as *noise.* (20)

External label   An adhesive label that may be attached to a disk with identification of the disk's contents. (14)

External report   Document that will be disseminated outside the organization; sometimes referred to as a *radial report.* (16)

Facsimile transmission (fax)   Sending an image (copy) of an original document electronically between two points over telephone lines, private transmission lines, or microwave relay systems; imaging an original document to a duplicating master or stencil (electronic scanning). (3, 5, 13)

Feasibility study   Analysis of present and future business systems needs of the organization used as a basis for the selection of alternative solutions to best meet those needs. (7, 16)

Feedback   Listener's (receiver's) response to the message, which helps to assure the sender that the message was received and understood. (20)

Fiber optics   Use of fine glass wires to transmit light beams that are faster, lighter, and more durable than wire media. (3)

Fiber optic process   Imaging process in which tiny glass strands transmit information in the form of pulsating laser light from the original document to a drum; each fiber carries a portion of the image. Toner is fused to the paper instead of the drums, providing a copy of the original document. (5)

Fiche   Sheet of film, usually 6 by 4 inches, containing microimages arranged in rows and columns. (4)

Field   Type of descriptive information or data (characteristic of a person, place, or thing) entered in a specific location. (1, 9)

Figure   Visual graphic illustration that is used to communicate some form of chart or picture (e.g., bar graph or line graph). (19)

File   Set of related records that contain a unified collection of data (e.g., a personnel file) stored together or under the same file name. (1, 9, 14)

File folder   Individual container used to store the documents pertaining to one correspondent, case, or account. (9)

File management   System for storing records or information pertaining to a person, company, or subject on specific disks. (14)

File name   One or more words or character strings assigned to a file so that the computer software can retrieve or restore the file; different guidelines are followed in DOS and Windows environments. (14)

Filing segment   One or more filing units (the total name, a number, a subject) used in determining filing order. (9)

Filing unit   Number, letter, word, or any combination of these used in determining filing order. (9)

Finishing processes   Collating, stapling or stitching, binding, and folding used to complete a document production job and give it a "professional look." (5)

First-class mail   Personal and business correspondence, handwritten and typewritten messages, bills, statements of account, postcards, printed forms filled out in writing, and business reply mail not requiring the highest priority. (13)

Fiscal value   Importance of documents that relate to the financial transactions of the organization. (9)

Floppy disk   Magnetic medium encased in a square plastic protective jacket and coated with a magnetic recording medium on which 70 to over 1,000 pages (or 250,000 to 2,800,000 characters) of text can be stored. (2)

Flow diagram   Chart of the movement of a document, showing the actual floor plan of the office to develop the resulting work-flow pattern; also referred to as an *office layout chart.* (7)

Flowchart Illustration of existing office procedures, in chart form, showing the distances and delays involved in the entire process or procedure from start to finish. (7)

Foot-candle Amount of light produced by a standard candle at a distance of 1 foot. (7)

Foot-lambert Unit of measurement of the amount of brightness; approximates 1 foot-candle of light transmitted or reflected. (7)

Footnote Reference note that appears on the bottom of the page where the reference is indicated with a superscript; citation that gives credit to a source of information included in the body of a report. (19)

Form letter Correspondence with some identical parts that may be sent to more than one person or company for a specific purpose. (16)

Formal meeting Meeting with a prepared agenda that is planned in advance and is usually held in a conference room or special meeting room. (11)

Forms management Important element of a total records management program; program designed to provide an organization with forms that are both necessary and efficient and that can be produced at the lowest printing and processing costs. (9)

Fourth-class mail Packages, printed matter (books), and all other mailable matter that weighs 16 ounces or more and is not included in first-, second-, or third-class mail; also known as *parcel post.* (13)

Freeze-frame video Process in which a single frame of a moving object (program) is frozen and then transmitted. (3)

Geographic filing System in which records are arranged alphabetically according to geographic locations. (9)

Global strategy Implementation of office automation on a worldwide basis so that internationally based organizations and individuals will be able to communicate and share information through interorganizational networks. (6)

Glossary Alphabetical list of terms defined for the reader. (16)

Goodwill Positive feeling that develops between organizations or between people working within organizations that results in positive, clear, and courteous communication. (16)

Graphic aid Illustration that is used to clarify data presented within a report. (19)

Graphical user interface (GUI) Combination of hardware and software that uses icons (pictures) to rep-

resent system options available to the user in communicating with the computer. (1)

Graphics Any form of illustration (chart, picture, or map) that is a visual representation of successive changes in the value (quantity) of one or more variables. (19)

Guide Divider for a group of records that indicates a particular section of the file. (9)

Hard copy Information printed in document form; tangible copy. (1) Document produced from a computer or word/information processing system and printed out on paper. (2, 17)

Hardware Equipment used in processing data, including input, output, and storage devices; technology along with software programs and functions hardwired into the system. (1, 7)

Hearing Process of recognizing sounds created when sound waves strike the eardrum and cause vibrations that are transmitted to the brain. (20)

Home page First page for a Web site that is registered on the World Wide Web through a Web address or a Uniform Resource Locator (URL). (13)

Horizontal communication Communication on the same level within the organization, from one supervisor to another supervisor, from one secretary to another secretary. (15)

Horizontal report Document prepared for written communication at the same administrative level and distributed from department to department or division to division within the organization. (16)

Hot-desking Desk or work area that is still warm from being used by a previous worker. (7)

Hotelling Application of the open-office arrangement that features an open office with unassigned desks; office professionals reserve desk space for specific time periods. (7)

Human resource planning Process of determining short- and long-term human resource (personnel) needs for the future and developing strategies for meeting these needs. (15)

Ibid. Term used in a footnote or endnote when referring to the immediately preceding footnote or endnote. (19)

Identifier Keyword that somewhat describes the information contained in a stored document; also referred to as a *descriptor.* (4)

Image storage Storage of documents or other data that include text, graphics, tables, and pictures; includes optical disk and micrographics technologies. (4)

Imaging process Method of electronically preparing copies, masters, or stencils of original text material through xerographic, fiber optic, or laser technologies. (5)

Impact printer Output device that forces the type character from a font or print wheel against the ribbon and paper, creating images of characters directly on the paper. (1, 2)

Important records Records that contribute to the continued smooth operation of an organization and can be replaced or duplicated (with considerable expenditure of time and money) if lost or destroyed in a disaster. (9)

Imprecise descriptors Adjectives that describe nouns or pronouns in general terms. (16)

In-house meeting Formal meeting that is planned in advance and held on company premises. (11)

In-house reprographics services Those copying, duplicating, and printing services that are provided within the organization by specialized personnel trained to perform these functions. (12)

In-house transportation department Department within a firm organized to provide travel services only to personnel and departments within the company; sometimes organized as an in-house travel agency. (8)

Inactive records Those records no longer referred to on a regular basis but still of limited importance. (9)

Incidental motion Motion that arises from pending question; may be introduced at any time and must be decided before the question to which it is incidental is decided. (11)

Index Directory that contains a list of all documents stored on media (magnetic tape, disk, or microform) in alphabetical order, in numeric order, or in the order of creation. (4) List of names and subjects, with page references to find quickly specific information contained in the report; appears at the end of the report. (16)

Index record Record containing only reference information that may be part of a relative index for files based on either a numeric or an alphanumeric classification system. (9)

Indexing Decision making that is necessary in deciding what names or numbers to use in filing. (9)

Indirect-access procedures Filing system that requires a person to consult a relative index in order to locate the name, subject, or number under which the file is stored. (9)

Inductive style Organizational approach to business writing that implies that the writing will lead the reader to the main idea; the details and supporting information are presented first, with the main idea following; also referred to as the *indirect approach*. (16)

Informal meeting Discussion involving a small number of people (two to four) in regard to a specific business matter. (11)

Informal report Business writing used to transmit meaningful information to other people within the organization or outside the organization; usually no more than five pages. (16)

Information Processed data that are meaningful and useful to the user and considered a valuable asset in all types of organizations today. (1, 13)

Information distribution Means whereby organizational information is communicated internally to the different divisions or departments within the organization or externally to other organizations. (13)

Information retrieval Selection of only certain portions of the information or data contained in a record. (4)

Information value Importance of records that have accumulated over a period of time and contain information relating to people, places, events, and other phenomena. (9)

Informational report Document that presents background information and facts obtained through secondary sources and secondary research in an organized, structured manner. (16)

Inherent Essential or "built in" as part of a process. (20)

Input Source information in the form of text or data for a document to be produced. (14)

Inside address Address to which a business letter will be mailed. (19)

Inspecting Examining a record to be sure that it has been released for filing by an appropriate authority within the firm. (9)

Integrated software Programs that provide a variety of software applications to the user at any one time rather than separately. (6)

Integrated system Communication linkage (interface) that provides the exchange of data among different application programs, such as word processing, spreadsheet, graphics, database, and electronic mail. (6)

Integration Linkage (interface) of two or more office information technologies to communicate and share information in order to achieve a new set of goals. (2, 6)

Intelligent copier Copy equipment with microprocessor technology that allows the copier to accept input from one or more machines and to provide hardcopy output at local or distant sites. (5)

Intelligent printer High-speed printer that combines computer, laser, and copying technology. (1)

Intelligent retrieval Use of content words in creating an index so that searching for data or information within documents can take place more efficiently. (4)

Interactive operations Operations in which there is frequent interchange between the user and the processor unit during execution of a program. (1)

Interface Connection (linkage) between two parts of a larger system to integrate equipment and technologies throughout an organization. (6)

Interlibrary loan Networking system that has been established between libraries for references located in one library to be loaned to a person through another library for a specific period of time. (10)

Internal distractions Barriers, both physiological and psychological, taking place within the minds of the speaker and/or the listener(s) that interfere with the communication process and hamper understanding; often referred to as *noise*. (20)

International travel Transportation services provided for travel in, to, and from other countries. (8)

Internet Global network of thousands of computers linked together around the world that includes sites to access electronic mail, discussion lists, newsgroups, Web browsing, and electronic commerce. (3, 13)

Internet travel site On-line site available for researching airline schedules, fares, and other types of travel information and for placing on-line orders. (8)

Interpreting Act of assigning meaning to a set of verbal and/or nonverbal symbols received from a speaker. (20)

Intranet Organization's internal network for making company policies, procedures, news items, and data/information available to the employees electronically. (13)

Inward wide area telephone service (INWATS) Telephone service that is provided to an organization through subscription so that clients or customers may telephone the organization without having to pay for the long-distance calls; the call is charged to the organization's account. (3)

Isolation Prevention of sound waves from passing through environmental materials. (7)

Itinerary Business traveler's plan that includes all details concerning a business trip: departure and arrival information, confirmed transportation and lodging reservations, and scheduled appointments and meetings. (8, 19)

Jacket Plastic unitized record the same size as a microfiche in which strips of film can be inserted in single or multiple channels; standard size (6 by 4 inches) can hold as many as 60 images. (4)

Jargon Words used in business writing that are generally understood only by others in the profession; often referred to as *slang language* in business writing. (16)

Job analysis Accumulation of all tasks required within a particular office position, examined within the framework of entire office functions. (7)

Job recovery After an interruption, the copier will "remember" the stop point of the original job and continue from that point. (5)

Job sharing Formal arrangement whereby two office employees collaborate in sharing the job responsibilities of one full-time job on either a temporary or permanent basis. (15)

Keyword One of the descriptors or identifiers of a record. (4)

Laser process Imaging technology that utilizes a beam of light that reflects off a series of mirrors. The final mirror diverts the image to a drum, which transfers the image to paper. (5)

Late adapter Person who waits for others to implement a new system and then tries to "catch up" with the technology. (7)

Lateral career path Sequence that permits people to advance to positions comparable to the one presently held but located in different areas or departments, as opposed to promotion or demotion. (2)

Lease Contract permitting a user (the lessee) to use equipment by making payments to the vendor (the lessor) over a specified period of time. A lessee may accumulate equity in the equipment that can be applied toward its purchase. (7)

Legal value Importance of documents that contain provisions or agreements that relate to the legal rights and obligations of the business. (9)

Letter of credit Letter from a bank or other financial institution stating the maximum amount of money available through that bank or institution to the person carrying the letter. (8)

Library of Congress classification system Library cataloging system with a larger number of major classifications (21 major areas of knowledge) than the Dewey decimal system. (10)

Line graph or chart Illustration consisting of a series of connected lines showing a particular trend in business data for a period of time. (19)

Listening Mental process that involves hearing, seeing, and interpreting what was said and seen. (20)

Loc. cit. Term used in a footnote or endnote that refers to the same page reference as that of the preceding footnote or endnote. (19)

Local area network (LAN) Physical communication linkage designed to connect workstations with each other and with other office systems to support communication within an office, building, or firm; usually part of the department or work-group strategy. (2, 3, 6)

Logging form Record that indicates the date/time the job is received, the number/name of the job, for whom the work is being done, the deadline, the name of the person to whom the task is assigned, and any special instructions. (15)

Long-term memory That part of the brain where information is stored after it has been processed and then repeated or associated with previously acquired information. (20)

Mail services Postal services designed to facilitate incoming written communication and outgoing written communication from the organization. (13)

Mailgram Message transmitted by Western Union to the post office that serves the ZIP code of the addressee where the mailgram is printed, inserted into an envelope, and included with the next regularly scheduled mail delivery. (13)

Main motion Motion that states an item of business; has the lowest precedence in rank among all types of motions; must be seconded and is subject to discussion, debate, and amendment. (11)

Mainframe computer system Full-scale computer that offers greater operating speed and storage capacity than minicomputers or microcomputers and is able to support hundreds of terminals and on-line secondary storage devices. (1)

Management-by-objectives (MBO) appraisal With the help of the supervisor/manager, the employee establishes job objectives, both for individual performance and for personal development, against which his or her performance is measured during the next appraisal period. (15)

Management information system (MIS) Result of implementation of the organizational strategy that permits users throughout the organization to communicate and share information through electronic means; wide area networking (linkage of local area networks) of information throughout the entire organization. (6)

Marine call Call made to or from a ship at sea. (3)

Marketing support Company representatives who are directly involved with the sale of hardware or software systems and training for word/information processing specialists. (2)

Masking Use of a low-level, nondisturbing background noise to blend with regular office noise, eliminating the "silent" sound or covering distracting noise; also referred to as *white noise* or *white sound*. (7)

Matrix plan Operational plan that permits some office operations to be centralized and others to be decentralized, depending on the needs of the organization. (15)

Mean Arithmetic average of a group of responses obtained by computing the sum of all the responses and dividing by the number of responses; a measure of central tendency. (16)

Median Midpoint in a distribution of responses; a measure of central tendency. (16)

Memorandum Interoffice correspondence between individuals, departments, and branch offices of the same company that tends to be written about one topic, short and to the point, and quickly transmitted through internal mail. (13, 16, 19)

Message Speaker's (sender's) intentional and unintentional words and nonverbal behaviors sent along a channel to a listener (receiver). (20)

Message unit Standard base rate used to determine the cost of a call; measurement used for distance points within the local telephoning area so that charges can be determined for telephone calls made within that area. (3)

Microcomputer Desktop workstation (stand-alone or networked) with software programs available for a variety of business applications. (2)

Microcomputer system Digital computer, about the size of a typewriter, that uses a microprocessor, an internal storage chip, an input/output chip, and any additional chips required by the system; used for specific business operations. (1)

Microfiche Standard 6- by 4-inch sheet of film that can hold up to 98 page images in 7 rows, with 14 images in each row, when the standard 24× reduction ratio is applied. (4)

Microfiche reader Equipment that is designed to help the operator locate particular images on a microfiche and display the selected images on a viewing screen. (4)

Microfilm Oldest form of microform that stores images of document pages side by side on 16-, 35-, 70-, or 105-millimeter film. (4)

Microfilm reader Equipment that displays the images stored on microfilm on a viewing screen. (4)

Microform Any record that contains reduced images on film. (4, 9)

Microform reader-printer Equipment that allows the operator to view a microform (microfilm, microfiche) as well as print a hard copy of a microimage. (4)

Micrographics Process whereby documents (or pages of documents) are reduced through photographic processes and stored on microforms. (4)

Micrographics center Centralized service within a library where research studies, dissertations, newspapers, periodicals, and other references are stored on micro-forms (microfiche and microfilm); technology for access to these materials is typically available only within the center. (10)

Microprocessor   Single chip on which the circuitry of the control unit, the arithmetic/logic unit, and internal storage is etched. (1)

Middle-digit system   Numeric filing system that uses the middle digits of a number as the primary indexing units. (9)

Minicomputer system   Computer system best utilized for on-site processing, small business processing, and/or front-end processing to a mainframe computer. (1)

Minutes   Official record of the proceedings of a meeting that summarizes the business that has been transacted, reports that have been presented, and any other significant events occurring at the meeting. (11, 19)

Mixed punctuation   Style in which a colon is keyed in after the salutation and a comma after the complimentary closing in a business letter. (19)

Mnemonic code   Numeric code that takes on additional meaning about the item (e.g., ZIP codes or catalog numbers). (9)

Mode   Response that occurs the most frequently in a distribution of responses; a measure of central tendency. (16)

Modem   Digital device at the sending location that MOdulates (converts) data into sound waves for transmission over telephone lines (analog communication channels) and at the receiving location DEModulates the sound waves back to the binary code for processing by the computer. (1, 3)

Modified blocked letter style   Standard letter style in which the date line begins at the center point or ends at the right margin, the complimentary closing and signature line begin at the center point, and paragraphs may be blocked or indented. (19)

Modular approach   Type of open-office arrangement in which individual work areas are designed to allow for a variety of interchangeable combinations to meet individual needs and to serve as a basis for expandable office systems. (7)

Motion   Presentation of an item of business to the group. (11)

Multiprocessing   Two or more program instructions executed *simultaneously* in a single computer system; requires two or more processor units. (1)

Multiprogramming   *Concurrent* execution of two or more programs, switching back and forth between several application programs that are being processed. (1)

Musculoskeletal problems   Pain or discomfort occurring in various body parts (neck, back, shoulders, arms, fingers) experienced during the work process. (7)

Narrative report   Report that includes primarily text material (words). (16)

Negative letter   Correspondence written with an inductive (indirect) approach that conveys a "no" response or some other form of "bad news"; also referred to as an *unfavorable letter*. (16)

Netiquette   Etiquette practices for the electronic environment that businesses should follow. (13)

Networked system   Cable connection of computers within an office or an organization to enable users to access business information and software programs stored on the system. (2)

News release   Message to be disseminated to newspapers or magazines with business news about the organization. (19)

Nonconventional format   Microforms, audiovisual media, videotapes, and information or image processing media that are becoming more versatile than paper documents for storing records. (9)

Nonessential records   Records that are not necessary for the restoration of the business, have no predictable value, and probably should be destroyed once their usefulness is over. (9)

Nonimpact printer   Printer that creates images on the paper through the use of ink jets, electrothermal imaging, xerographic processes, and laser processes. (1)

Nonrecords   Documents prepared for the organization's convenience or temporary use in an operation but normally disposed of after use. (9)

Nonverbal communication   Aspect of communication that involves all the symbols of communication—body language, vocal attributes, space and distance, touch, clothing and accessories, and time—but not words. (20)

Nonvolatile storage   Storage that is not affected by interruptions of electrical power to the unit. (1)

Numeric classification system   Indirect-access filing system that consists of numeric codes assigned to names of individuals, businesses, or subjects. (9)

Object program   Saved machine-language program translated (compiled) from a source program that is read into the main memory for execution by the central processing unit. (1)

Observational research   Conducting a study that permits the researcher to actually see the actions or results of individual or group activities. (16)

Office automation   Process of integrating separate technologies (text, data, voice, and image processing) into a single system that is capable of managing the information flow for a variety of office applications. (6)

Office information system Utilization of technology, personnel, and organization/procedures combined to perform needed office functions; the result of implementation of the department or work-group strategy. (6)

Office landscaping Type of open-office arrangement that places primary emphasis on analyzing office procedures and controlling work flow; use of partitions, modular furniture, planters, and well-designed workstations to complement work functions. (7)

Office layout Effective arrangement of furniture, equipment, and other physical components to accommodate assigned work tasks and to facilitate efficient work flow within available floor space. (7)

Official Airline Guide (OAG®) Published guide available through a variety of media that contains detailed information on airline schedules and fares for both domestic and international flights. (8)

Offset duplicating Duplicating process based on the principle that oil and water do not mix; utilizes original documents that are prepared on offset paper masters, electrostatic masters, or metal plates; can produce large quantities of copies economically with relatively good quality. (5)

On-line device Equipment that is physically connected to the central processing unit. (1)

On-line reservation system Computer network or Internet site that provides access to up-to-date travel information and opportunity to make travel reservations. (8)

Op. cit. Term used in a footnote or an endnote when reference is made to a previous source but there are intervening reference notes. (19)

Open-office arrangement Planning of office space without permanent walls and with modular furniture and aisle space to accommodate the communication flow through the office; also referred to as the *modern approach*. (7)

Open punctuation Style in which no punctuation is keyed in after the salutation or the complimentary closing in a business letter. (19)

Operating system Set of programs that supervise and manage the work of the computer system as well as communicate with peripheral devices. (1, 2)

Optical character recognition (OCR) Process used to scan typewritten, printed, or handwritten information for machine identification using light-sensitive devices and the data converted to digital form for pro-

cessing by the computer; used by the U.S. Postal Service to scan addresses in the processing of volumes of mail. (4, 19)

Optical disk technology Image-based form of electronic storage in which text, graphics, tables, and pictures are stored on optical disks or recordlike devices used to write and read data through the use of laser beams. (4)

Organizational manual Handbook that shows the formal relationship of divisions or departments, including duties and responsibilities, within the organization; includes statement of objectives, basic philosophy, organizational structure, change strategies, and futuristic plans. (15)

Organizational strategy Implementation of office automation on an organization-wide basis so that users will be able to communicate and share information with other users throughout the organization; total management information systems effort of the organization. (6)

Organizing Managerial function that permits the office administrator to establish specific goals that are to be accomplished through office support services. (15)

Original Actual typewritten, printed, typeset, or graphic copy from which copies or masters can be prepared. (5)

Out folder Special folder that is substituted for a file folder that has been temporarily borrowed from the file. (9)

Out guide Special guide substituted for an individual record that has been temporarily removed from a file. (9)

Outline Key words coded in descending order, using roman numerals, numbers, and letters of the alphabet to show the basic topics of a report or speech. (19)

Overseas call Telephone call placed to a company or individual in another country either by dialing direct or through operator assistance. (3)

Pager Device consisting of a cellular radio that can be carried by a person who needs to be signaled, usually with a tone or buzz, when a call to the home office needs to be returned. (3)

Pagination Appropriate numbering of document pages from the first page through the last page to keep the document organized. (19)

Paging system In-house communication system that signals people who are away from their desks that they need to contact their office. (3)

Paper storage Closed record system consisting of banks of metal file containers for holding paper documents of any acceptable size; traditional form in which documents have been stored. (4)

Parallelism Statement of ideas that are equal in thought in identical grammatical form. (16)

Parcel post Packages, printed matter (books), and all other mailable matter not included in first-, second-, or third-class mail that weighs 16 ounces or more. (13)

Parenthetical citation Abbreviated in-text documentation giving credit to a source of information that is shown in parentheses in the appropriate location within the body of a report; complete information about the source is included in the bibliography at the end of the report. (19)

Parliamentary procedure Set of rules established for the appropriate conduct of formal meetings in an efficient and orderly manner (e.g., *Robert's Rules of Order*). (10, 11)

Partial-page display Visual display screen that shows only part of a page of text at a time, typically up to 24 lines. (2)

Passive words Words that denote inaction or waiting for something to happen. (16)

Passport Formal document issued by the citizen's government, certifying citizenship and protection for the traveler and granting permission to the citizen to travel in certain foreign countries. (8)

Performance standards Criteria for evaluating the behavior, personal traits, and results of office production. (15)

Periodic transfer Physical movement of records from active status within a particular department or office to a centralized records center or remote storage as of a specific date each year. (9)

Peripheral equipment Office equipment used occasionally (copiers, postage meters, folding machines, collators, filing equipment, and data processing equipment, other than the central processing unit) placed in an area where they may be shared among office workers. (7)

Perpetual transfer Physical movement of records from active to inactive status at any time that the event has been completed or the case closed and future referral to the records will be infrequent and limited. (9)

Person-to-person call Operator-assisted telephone call charged to the caller only if the person being called is able to receive the call. (3)

Persuasive letter Correspondence that tends to be positive but complex in nature, requesting the receiver to take some action after justification for such action is presented in the message. (16)

Petition Formal statement, signed by those eligible to sign such a statement, asking that some specific action be taken. (11)

Photocomposition Process whereby the composer automatically sets the type as the text is being keyed from the keyboard. (5)

Phototypesetter Typesetting equipment that produces typeset copy by electronically converting typewritten words into professional-looking type. (5)

Phrase outline Groups of key (essential) words included in an enumerated listing of the content of a speech to prompt the speaker to provide details or facts. (19)

Pica Measurement used for width and length of a line in typesetting and composition; 6 picas to an inch. (5)

Pie graph or chart Illustration that represents the parts that make up a whole; the circle equals 100 percent, and the sections represent smaller percentages of the entire circle. (19)

Plain-paper copier Copy equipment that produces copies on plain bond paper through an electrostatic, fiber optic, laser, or digital process. (5)

Plotter Special-purpose printer that outlines drawings and graphics; drum plotters or table plotters. (1)

Point Measurement of character size; common sizes for text are 10 or 12 points; 72 points to an inch. (5)

Positive letter Favorable correspondence that transmits needed information that will please the receiver; often referred to as a *good news letter*. (16)

Posted record Card record that may be used to update, change, delete, or add to information contained in the record. (9)

Praise Act of acknowledging the effective work of others through compliments and approvals. (20)

Précis Paraphrased summary of the content of a document. (18)

Precise descriptors Adjectives that describe a noun or pronoun in specific terms. (16)

Presentation software Programs that enable a user to prepare an outline, a set of electronic slides, handouts, and other supportive materials for an oral presentation or speech. (11)

Primary guide Guide that highlights a major division or subdivision of records stored in a file drawer or on a shelf. (9)

Primary research Investigation of a phenomenon or event to gather original information to use as current data in a report. (16)

Primary storage Main memory or internal storage of the processor unit. (1)

Printer Computer hardware that transfers stored images of recorded keystrokes onto a sheet of paper. (2)

Priorities Importance of the documents (tasks) to be produced, with the highest-priority items completed immediately and lower-priority items completed according to specific deadlines. (14)

Priority mail First-class mail that weighs over 11 ounces up to a maximum of 70 pounds, usually delivered within two to three days. (13)

Private automatic branch exchange (PABX) Switching system that allows telephone calls to be distributed automatically to extensions, in the order in which they are received, without the intervention of an attendant. (3)

Private branch exchange (PBX) Switching system that requires that all incoming calls be answered by an attendant and then transferred to appropriate extensions within the firm. (3)

Private-office arrangement Office plan with executives housed in offices separated from general office areas of support personnel; also referred to as the *traditional approach, conventional approach, closed plan,* or *bull-pen approach.* (7)

Privileged motion Convenience motion that affects the comfort of the members of the group that is meeting; has precedence over all other motions. (11)

Procedures Way that word/information processing is organized and made available for application within the organization; organization of word/information processing operations into step-by-step instructions. (2) Steps used to complete a specific office task. (12)

Procedures analysis Study of specific office processes used to determine the number of steps, the time for each step, the distance in each step (if applicable), and the departments involved in the procedure. (7)

Processor unit Central processing unit (CPU) plus primary storage (main memory/internal storage). (1)

Production Processing of a document or task into final format. (14)

Programming Process of logically translating the steps in a problem solution into sequential instructions for execution by the computer. (1)

Progress report Business writing that identifies work in process, the steps already completed, and the current status of a project; also referred to as a *work-in-process report.* (16)

Proofreading Process of checking final copy for adherence to spelling, punctuation, and formatting guidelines. (17)

Proofreading marks Symbols written within the margins or within the text of a document to indicate an error that needs to be corrected. (17)

Protocol Rules and guidelines to be followed during a meeting or conference. (3)

Psychosocial disturbance Specific problem related to the work environment, such as job-related stress, the workload, the pace of work in the office, and poor or inadequate supervision. (7)

Purging Process of automatically deleting the contents of a record that have been electronically stored on a magnetic medium. (9)

Quorum Required number of voting members who must be present to transact business at a meeting of the organization. (11)

Radial report Documents that cut across levels of authority or move both inside and outside an organization. (16)

Random access Method of storage through which information is stored in no particular order on a disk but provides for immediate retrieval of any particular document without first having to access the documents preceding it on the disk. (2)

Random access memory (RAM) Main memory (primary or internal storage) available to the user. (1)

Range Difference between the value of the highest response and the value of the lowest response in a distribution. (16)

Read-only memory (ROM) Internal storage that permits data to be read only by the computer or the user through the CPU but not revised or changed in any way. (1)

Reading position Placement of a table (or other business document) three lines above exact vertical placement. (19)

Real-time processing Procedure for processing each transaction (input data) immediately. (1)

Record Collection of *related* data fields pertaining to a single unit. A collection of *related* records makes up a *file.* (1) Official document of the company or organization valuable enough to be retained, using a format for storing information to be used and distributed later. (9)

Records cycle Series of steps from the moment a record is created until its final disposition. (9)

Records management Systematic control of information from the moment of creation through the use, storage, transfer, and disposal phases of the records cycle. (9)

Records transfer Physical movement of records from active status within a particular department or office to a centralized records center or remote storage in a computer facility or an off-site records facility. (9)

Reference initials Initials of the typist of the letter; may also include the writer's initials. (19)

Reference notes   Documentation within the body of the report that is used to cite specific information that is quoted or paraphrased from other sources; also referred to as *reference citations, footnotes, endnotes,* or *parenthetical citations.* (19)

Reflection   Bouncing of sound waves off a material and back into space. (7)

Relative index   File (on cards or computer) that identifies the numeric or alphanumeric codes that have been assigned to individual files. (9)

Reliable data   Data that are measured consistently and accurately. (16)

Report   Document that transmits meaningful data within business firms as well as between business firms for either information or decision-making purposes. (16, 19)

Reprographics   Preparation of multiple copies of images through copying, duplicating, printing, or imaging processes. (5, 12)

Research value   Importance of records consisting of technical information that results from primary or secondary research. (9)

Resolution   Formal statement of an organization's appreciation, congratulations, or sympathy. (11)

Retention schedule   Agreement between the department creating the record, the user (if not the department of creation), and the records manager specifying the period of time each type of record is to be held in active, semiactive, or inactive storage and when the record may be purged or destroyed, if ever. (9)

Reverberation   Echo (rain-barrel) effect that characterizes the sounds picked up by a microphone within a meeting room. (3)

Routine letter   Correspondence that is used to exchange day-to-day information; often called a *neutral letter.* (16)

Salutation   Formal greeting to the recipient (person or organization) of a business letter. (19)

Scheduled report(s)   Documents that are issued at regular, stated intervals—weekly, monthly, quarterly—in either detailed or summary form as needed (e.g., income statements, sales summaries). (3, 16)

Second-class mail   Publications such as newspapers and periodicals mailable in bulk or volume mailings requiring a special fee. (13)

Secondary file   Data file where variable information is stored until needed for a text-merge with constant information. (2)

Secondary guide   Special guide that is used to highlight frequently referenced sections of the records. (9)

Secondary research   Investigation to gather information that others have prepared to use as the basis for primary research or to prepare an informational or analytical report. (16)

Secondary storage   Peripheral storage devices (e.g., magnetic tape, magnetic disks, optical disks, Zip disks) where data, programs, and information are kept for future use; also called *auxiliary storage.* (1)

Semantic distractions   Misunderstandings in communication that occur when people assign meanings to words in different ways; often referred to as *barriers* or *noise.* (20)

Sentence outline   Key sentences to prompt the speaker to expand on these ideas during the presentation. (19)

Sequential access   Method of retrieving records from a file, in order, from the beginning of the file to the end of the file. (1)

Shared-resource system   Computer system with independently functioning workstations that share equipment, storage, or processing power. (2)

Short-term memory   That part of the brain with a limited storage capacity where information is stored immediately on listening to it and decoding the meaning. (20)

Simplified letter style   Standard letter style in which all lines begin at the left margin, there is no salutation or complimentary closing, and a subject line is typed in all capital letters a triple space after the inside address followed by a triple space to the body of the letter. (19)

Soft copy   Electronically stored copy; information viewed on a visual display screen or heard over a recorder. (1, 2, 17)

Software   Programs and programming support (procedures) developed to direct computer hardware to perform specific information processing functions; systems software and application programs. (1, 7)

Software manuals   Instructional and operational manuals for the specific software programs being utilized for document production. (14)

Sound control   Monitoring and regulation of the noise level in an office. (7)

Source book   Guide or index containing specific travel information useful in making appropriate transportation and lodging reservations. (8)

Source data automation   Applications where data input are captured electronically in machine-readable form at the time the transaction originates. (1)

Source document   Original record showing the business transaction to be recorded. (1)

Source program   Program written in a high-level computer language. (1)

Space and distance   Communication factors as evidenced by the way people handle physical space around them, physical closeness to other persons, and the arrangement of items within living and working spaces; often referred to as *proxemics*. (20)

Speaker   Creator of a message who is involved in the process of encoding the message before transmitting it to a listener(s). (20)

Special report   Document that is prepared on demand to handle unusual or nonroutine requests for information. (16)

Speech   Planned oral presentation made before a business, professional, or community group; preparation includes selection of topic, background research, organizing the material, and actual presentation. (19)

Speed calling   Telephone feature that permits the user to assign special number codes to frequently dialed numbers; keying in the number code will activate a call. (3)

Spirit duplicating   Preparation of copies from a spirit master that has been typed with carbon images on the back of the master. (5)

Standard deviation   Measure of the degree of scattering of a frequency distribution about its arithmetic mean. (16)

Standing committee   Small group of individuals appointed for a definite term with specific objectives assigned for which the group is responsible during the term. (11)

Statistical report   Document that includes primarily numerical data. (16)

Stencil duplicating   Preparation of multiple copies from one master or stencil; copies are duplicated using a mimeograph. (5)

Stored program   List of instructions stored in the computer's main memory to control computer operations. (1)

Storyboard   Frame-by-frame plan for the preparation of an audiovisual presentation that shows a description of each picture or illustration and any narrative that will accompany the slide. (11)

Straight-numeric system   Arrangement of files in consecutive order, from the lowest number to the highest number; also referred to as *sequential files* or *serial files*. (9)

Strategic planning   Actions taken to determine the long-term goals and major targets of an organization. (15)

Subject filing   Classification system that uses the alphabetic system as a base to arrange records by topics or categories. (9)

Subsidiary motion   Motion that assists, modifies, or disposes of the main motion and supersedes the main motion. (1)

Survey research   Study to determine opinions, beliefs, or reactions to specific work situations; may be administered in written (a questionnaire) or oral form (an interview). (16)

System programs   Programs (software) that supervise the work of the computer system as well as communicate with peripheral devices; the operating system is part of the system program. (1)

System software   Set of programs that controls and supervises the operations of the various hardware components of the system and the software elements in the performance of specific tasks. (6)

Tab   Projection on a file folder that contains a label with a typed caption. (9)

Table   Text material in the form of words and numbers presented in a columnar format within a document. (19)

Tactical planning   Outlining the actions required of a specific work unit to achieve its part of the total strategic plan of the organization. (15)

Task analysis   Study of the skills, knowledge, and behaviors that are required for specific tasks performed by an office worker, in a specific assignment, over a specified period of time. (7)

Task lighting   Direct lighting that illuminates the work surface. (7)

Technical report   Business writing that is designed to convey information to professionals within the field who will understand the specialized vocabulary and terminology included in the report. (16)

Technical support   Customer support usually provided for a fee to assist word/information processing specialists with more advanced applications or problem solving after the system implementation. (2)

Technology   Specialized computer systems (hardware) available for input, processing, and output and such software programs as communications, word/information processing, spreadsheet, or database applications, with detailed instructions for applying hardware and software to specific office applications. (2, 6)

Telecommunication systems   Electronic networks for transmission of oral and written communications in the form of text, voice, data, and image (or combinations). (3)

Telecommunications   Information distribution services often referred to as electronic mail networks (telegrams, mailgrams, Telex, telephone technology, facsimile transmission, and the Internet). (13)

Teleconference Meeting of several people, who may be in different geographic locations, that is held through telephone communications so that the people can speak with each other about specific business matters. (11)

Telegram Message transmitted over telephone lines by Western Union as a full-rate telegram or an overnight telegram. (13)

Telex Western Union service that is used to transmit messages to foreign countries via telephone lines, fiber optic cables, microwave dishes, and space satellites. (13)

Terminal-digit system Numeric system that uses the last digits of a number as the primary indexing units. (9)

Thesaurus Lexicon (dictionary) or similar book of works or information that focuses on synonyms and antonyms. (10)

Third-class mail Advertising brochures and catalogs that are not classified as first- or second-class mail and weigh less than 16 ounces. (13)

Tickler system Reminder system that includes deadlines and prompts for beginning work on projects or tasks on a daily, weekly, and monthly basis. (15)

Time plan Charting of the progress of a given project over time. (7)

Tone Manner in which a certain attitude is expressed in writing. (16)

Topical outline Brief listing of nouns that directs the speaker from point to point during a speech and prompts the speaker to provide additional details and facts. (19)

Touch Nonverbal cue, such as a handshake, that communicates a message to the listener. (20)

Transactional Simultaneous sending and receiving of messages in an ongoing, irreversible communication process. (20)

Transcription Process that occurs when the word processing operator listens to recorded dictation and keys in the text of the material so that the text can be stored and printed transcript produced. (2)

Transfer rate Speed with which data can be transferred from secondary storage to main memory (primary storage). (1)

Transparency Acetate sheet that contains images burned or drawn on it that can be projected on a screen or wall; also referred to as *overhead transparency*. (11)

Transparent Noninterference of the technical aspects of the system with the operator's attention to a particular application. (2)

Travel advance Funds received from the organization to be used for payment of out-of-pocket expenses incurred while on business travel. (8)

Travelers' checks Drafts purchased through local banks, credit unions, savings and loan associations, and the American Automobile Association that can be cashed *only* by the purchaser. (8)

Trip file Folder (or series of folders) tracking all information and procedures involved in business travel, either in making arrangements for business travel or in preparing business materials the traveler needs to carry on a business trip. (8)

Turnaround time Time it takes between submission of the data and receipt of the output. (1, 15)

Tutorials Software programs available on the computer system that operators can access at any time to learn more about one or more specific functions. (14)

Ultrafiche Standard 6- by 4-inch sheet of film (fiche) that can store the largest number of microimages of any microform because images are normally reduced more than 90 times. (4)

Unbiased language Expression of thoughts and ideas so that equal treatment is given to everyone (men and women, minority groups, and jobholders); refers to gender-fair language, racially or ethnically unbiased language, and job-related language. (16)

Unclassified motion Motion that is appropriate but cannot be classified as a main motion, a subsidiary motion, an incidental motion, or a privileged motion. (11)

Unity Existence of a coherent flow of ideas throughout a written work—within sentences, within paragraphs, and between paragraphs. (16)

Useful records Records used in the operation of the organization that can be easily replaced. (9)

User Author of a document; person for whom a document is prepared. (2)

Utilities Generalized routines for performing specific data processing functions in an efficient way. (1)

Valid data Information that measures what it is intended to measure. (16)

Variable information Data inserted on the original document that change each time the document is prepared. (9) Any text that must be inserted into each document produced to complete the message. (16)

Verbal communication Aspect of communication that involves the words used, either in written or spoken form. (20)

Vertical career path   Sequence that leads from the present position to other positions at supervisory or managerial levels within the same department or division. (2)

Vertical file service   Pamphlets, booklets, leaflets, and other loose-leaf materials stored in a file cabinet for easy access. (10)

Vertical report   Document prepared for someone at a higher level within the organizational structure of the company or for someone at a lower level. (16)

Videoconference   Formal meeting that is an extension of teleconferencing where participants who are located in different geographic locations are able to view one another on closed-circuit television and discuss specific business matters during the same time period. (11)

Videoconferencing   Electronic meeting where both visual and audio contact is possible for the participants; audio contact is one- or two-way, but visual contact is one-way. (3)

Virtual memory   Use of secondary storage along with primary storage for the execution of information processing applications. (1)

Visa Endorsement stamped or written on a passport, showing examination by the proper officials of a country and granting the bearer entry into that country for a specific period of time. In many foreign countries, a visa is not required. (8)

Visual aids   Guides such as charts, graphs, pictures, maps, objects, and models that can be viewed by the audience as the speaker is presenting; used to gain attention, enhance understanding, and increase memory. (20)

Visual display   Screen that shows the text of the document as it is being keyed in or retrieved from storage. (2)

Visual dysfunction   Pain and discomfort resulting from computer vision syndrome or temporary visual distress (eye irritation, visual fatigue, blurred vision, headaches, and chronic disorders). (7)

Visualization   Technique applied by an athlete or a performer before an event to imagine the audience responding positively. (20)

Vital records   Those records essential for the effective, continuous operation of the firm; irreplaceable records. (9)

Vocal attributes   Those characteristics (cues) of your voice, such as speed, intensity, volume, accent, and silence, in addition to the words spoken, that communicate a message to another person. (20)

Voice messaging system   Telephone system that permits a caller to leave a detailed recorded message for a return call from the receiver. (13)

Voice storage   Recording voice messages as stored documents in a records management system. (4)

Volatile storage   Temporary storage in equipment that will be affected by interruptions in electrical power to the unit. (1)

Web site   All the pages collectively for a company located in one place on the World Wide Web. (13)

Webmaster   Person responsible for an organization's Web site who needs to be skilled in communication, artistic design, and Web site management strategies. (13)

Wide area network (WAN)   Combination of public or private lines, microwave, or satellite transmission for long-distance communication; network for distant communications that may be used for either interorganizational or intraorganizational communication. (3)

Wide area telephone service (WATS)   National, regional, or state service where the company pays a fixed fee for an allotted number of hours for outgoing long-distance calls. (3)

Widow line   One line of a paragraph by itself on a page, either at the top or bottom of a page. (19)

Windows operating system   Set of programs designed to enable more efficient switching back and forth between compatible applications, integrated networking, and interfaces with the World Wide Web. (2)

Word processing   Preparation of business documents in correct format by trained personnel using computer hardware and software technology. (2)

Word processing support   Personnel directly involved in document preparation through the use of technology. (2)

Work flow   Transmission of information from one location to another, as related to a specific process, through either face-to-face or electronic communication. (7)

Work logs   Means of recording actual time spent in performing specific office tasks. (7)

Work measurement   Amount of work produced in terms of words, lines, pages, or documents produced within a particular time frame. (14)

Work standards   Predetermined individual performance, based on past levels of performance, in the production of documents or completion of tasks. (14)

Works cited   Alphabetical list of all references that were directly cited within the body of the report; placed on a separate page at the end of the report. (19)

Workstation   Work area planned and designed for productive and efficient use by an individual office professional (executive, manager, or secretary). (7)

Workstation strategy   Implementation of office automation in the work area of one person who utilizes computer technology to enhance specific work functions; the lowest level of office automation implementation. (6)

World Wide Web (WWW)   On-line global network of information sites available to users, with each site having a unique address called a Uniform Resource Locator (URL) and subject to universally accepted standards for storing, retrieving, formatting, and displaying information. (3, 13)

Xerographic process   Imaging process in which a camera projects an image of the original text onto a positively charged drum, a negatively charged sheet of plain paper passes over the drum, the image adheres to the paper, and toner is used to develop the image on the paper. (5)

ZIP code   Nine-digit code initiated by the U.S. Postal Service that is added to a mailing address to enable mail to be sorted and delivered more efficiently. (13)